THE HUMAN RIGHTS WATCH GLOBAL REPORT ON WOMEN'S HUMAN RIGHTS

Human Rights Watch Women's Rights Project

Human Rights Watch
New York · Washington · Los Angeles · London · Brussels

ISBN 0-300-06546-9
LCCCN 95-79554

ACKNOWLEDGMENTS

This report is a compilation of investigations by Human Rights Watch from 1990 to 1995 on women's human rights violations. It is based on the work of many staff members and consultants of the Women's Rights Project and the regional divisions of Human Rights Watch, who researched and wrote the initial reports from which the case studies in this volume are adapted.

Contributors to this volume include: Aziz Abu-Hamad, Cynthia Brown, Allyson Collins, Patti Gossman, Jeannine Guthrie, LaShawn Jefferson, Robin Kirk, Sarah Lai, Robin Levi, Juan Méndez, Michael McClintock, Ivana Nizich, Binaifer Nowrojee, Regan Ralph, Lenee Simon, and Dorothy Thomas.

This report was edited by Sarah Lai and Regan Ralph of the Women's Rights Project, with invaluable editorial advice from Cynthia Brown, Michael McClintock and Juan Méndez of Human Rights Watch. Sonja Lichtenstein and Evelyn Miah provided production assistance.

We wish to express our deep gratitude to and admiration for the numerous advocates of women's human rights around the world who helped make this report possible, and particularly to the women and girls who spoke out about abuses they have experienced in order to make change.

This report was made possible in part by funds granted to Robin Levi through a fellowship program sponsored by the Charles H. Revson Foundation. The statements and views expressed in the text of this report are solely the responsibility of Human Rights Watch.

CONTENTS

INTRODUCTION

Few movements have made so large an impact in so short a time as the women's human rights movement. Working across national, cultural, religious and class lines, advocates promoting the human rights of women have waged a campaign to ensure respect for women's rights as fundamental human rights. The movement's emergence and growth over the past decade have, to a large extent, also transformed the way human rights issues are understood and investigated, both by intergovernmental bodies and by nongovernmental human rights organizations. The result has been to turn the spotlight on—and to place at the center of the social and political debates at the United Nations and between governments—the role that human rights violations play in maintaining the subordinate status of the world's women. Their impact was powerfully apparent at the World Conference on Human Rights in Vienna in 1993, when governments recognized women's rights as "an inalienable, integral and indivisible part of universal human rights."

Clearly the international women's human rights movement has raised the visibility of abuses against women, and the international community has made welcome statements supporting women's human rights. But the gap between government rhetoric and reality is vast. The challenge now is to ensure that governments that should be combatting violations of women's rights do not get credit for deploring abuse when they do nothing to stop it.

The Range and Severity of Abuse

In 1990 Human Rights Watch began working with colleagues in the human rights and women's movements around the world to apply the fact-finding and advocacy tools of the international human rights movement to documenting violations of women's human rights and seeking remedies for such abuse. We have exposed state-directed and state-approved violence against women; violence against women by private actors that is legally endorsed; violence against women by private actors that is illegal but is tolerated by the state through discriminatory enforcement of the law; and discriminatory laws and practices. We have explored abuses that are gender-specific either in their form—such as forced pregnancy and forced virginity exams—or in that they target primarily women—such as rape and the forced trafficking of women for purposes of sexual servitude.

Rampant abuses against women have traditionally been excused or ignored. Rape in situations of conflict by combatants is prohibited under international humanitarian law but until recently was dismissed as part of the inevitable "spoils of war." Domestic violence was regarded as a "private" matter only, not as a crime that the state must prosecute and punish. To the extent that control of women's sexuality and physical integrity is regarded as a matter of family or community honor rather than personal autonomy and individual rights, women in much of the world still face enormous obstacles in their search for redress when they have suffered abuse committed in the name of custom or tradition. Throughout the world, women are still relegated to second-class status that makes them more vulnerable to abuse and less able to protect themselves from discrimination.

As the country studies in this report show, governments often are directly implicated in abuses of women's human rights. Prison guards in many countries—studies in this report include the United States, Pakistan and Egypt—sexually assault women prisoners and detainees. Rape of women by combatants is frequently tolerated by commanding officers in the course of armed conflict and by abusive security officials in the context of political repression, as the examples of Kashmir, Bosnia-Hercegovina, Peru, Somalia and, Haiti illustrate. And, as our investigations of the trafficking of women and girls into forced prostitution have demonstrated, this ostensibly private commercial trade in human beings would be impossible without the active involvement of government officials, such as corrupt border guards and police who alternate between raiding brothels and profiting from them. Refugee and displaced women, in zones where U.N. or governmental protection is inadequate, are robbed and raped by security forces and camp officials, as described in the case study on Burmese women in this report.

Governments also have imposed, or refused to amend, laws that discriminate against women. In Pakistan, discriminatory evidentiary standards not only deny rape survivors access to justice, but also result in their arbitrary detention and thus expose them to further sexual violence by their jailers. As mothers or potential mothers, women face *de jure* discrimination in many countries. For example, Botswana men who marry foreigners have the right to pass Botswana citizenship on to their children; Botswana women do not.[1] In Russia, women are routinely turned away from public sector jobs because they are considered less productive workers on account of their maternal responsibilities.

---

[1] Human Rights Watch/Africa and Women's Rights Project, "Botswana: Second Class Citizens: Discrimination Against Women Under Botswana's Citizenship Act," *A Human Rights Watch Short Report*, vol. 6, no. 7, (September 1994).

In other situations, governments apply gender-neutral laws in discriminatory ways or fail to enforce constitutional and other guarantees of nondiscrimination. In Thailand, laws that penalize both prostitution and procurement are applied in a discriminatory manner resulting in the arrest of female prostitutes but impunity for their predominately male agents, pimps, brothel owners, and clients. The Brazilian constitution, in another example, guarantees women equality before the law yet courts in Brazil have exonerated men who kill their allegedly adulterous wives in order to protect their honor.

The women's human rights movement has prompted investigation into another important area of human rights abuse: violence against women carried out by private actors that is tolerated or ignored by the state. As intractable as state-perpetrated violence against women is, women's health and lives are equally endangered by abuse at the hands of husbands, employers, parents, or brothel owners. Domestic violence, for example, is a leading cause of female injury in almost every country in the world and is typically ignored by the state or only erratically punished, as the studies of Brazil, Russia, and South Africa in this report reveal. In Kuwait, employers assault Asian women domestic workers, driving hundreds of women to flee to their embassies each year. Yet only a handful of abusive employers are investigated or prosecuted. To fulfill their international obligations, states are required not only to ensure that women, as victims of private violence, obtain equal protection of the law, but also that the conditions that render women easy targets for attack—including sex discrimination in law and practice—are removed.

Women's lack of social and economic security has compounded their vulnerability to violence and sex discrimination. We have found, for example, that numerous Burmese, Nepali, and Bangladeshi women and girls, seeking to escape poverty at home, accept fraudulent job or marriage offers that result in their being trafficked into forced prostitution. In South Africa, women's lack of access to alternative housing is one reason why some of them hesitate to report domestic violence. At the same time, the lack of access to political power and to equal justice—through the right to organize, to express opinions freely, to participate in the political process, and to obtain redress for abuse—is a central obstacle to women seeking to improve their social and economic status within their societies. At the International Conference on Population and Development in Cairo in 1994, governments recognized that "advancing gender equality and equity and the empowerment of women, and the elimination of all kinds of violence against women, and ensuring women's ability to control their own fertility, are cornerstones of population and development-related programs." Similarly, the stated goals of the Fourth

World Conference on Women in Beijing—peace, equality and development—suggest that protection of women's human rights is inextricably connected to the improvement of women's status more generally.

Silence and Impunity

Silence about abuses against women hides the problems that destroy, and sometimes end, women's lives. Governments excuse and fail to take action against soldiers and prison guards who rape, police officers who forcibly traffick women, immigration officials who assault, judges who exonerate wife-murderers, and husbands who batter. They accept and defend domestic laws that discriminate on their face or in practice. Until recently, local and international human rights organizations, the United Nations and regional human rights bodies have approached human rights advocacy by focusing on a narrow interpretation of politically motivated abuse, while often failing to respond to the repression of women even when they challenge existing legal, political or social systems. Also neglected by governments and international organizations have been the range of abuses that women suffer because many of these violations did not conform to standard ideas of what constitutes human rights abuse. Thus, "Nada," a Saudi woman who sought political asylum in Canada in 1992, initially was denied refuge because persecution for her feminist views on the status of women in her country and her activities flowing from those beliefs—attempting to study in the field of her choice, to refuse to wear the veil, and to travel alone—was not deemed political. Similarly, in a notorious case in 1988, a U.S. immigration judge denied political asylum to Catalina Mejia, a Salvadoran woman who was raped by soldiers. In the judge's opinion, Mejia's rape by a Salvadoran soldier, who accused her of being a guerrilla, was not an act of persecution but rather the excess of a soldier acting "only in his own self-interest."[2]

The lack of documentation of violations of women's rights reinforces governments' silence; without concrete data, governments have been able to deny the fact of and their responsibility for gender-based abuse. Where human rights violations against women remain undocumented and unverified, governments pay no political or economic price for refusing to acknowledge the problem and their obligation to prevent and remedy abuse. One of the first challenges faced by the women's human rights movement has been to transform women's experiences of violence and discrimination into fact-based

---

[2] Susan Forbes Martin, *Refugee Women* (London: Zed Books, Ltd., 1991), p. 24.

proof of the scale and nature of such abuse and governments' role in its perpetuation.

Just as human rights groups historically have been the primary force in ensuring accountability for politically motivated human rights abuse, women's rights advocates are the vanguard in the fight for justice for gender-based violations. Thus, for example, they have won recognition that traditional notions of the political actor must be modified to acknowledge the political nature of women's efforts to challenge their subordinate status and the violence and discrimination that reinforce it. Women's rights advocacy has rejected the argument that governments bear no responsibility for the wide range of abuses perpetrated by private actors and argued to the contrary that governments must remedy and prevent such acts.

By building regional and international linkages that extend across cultural religious, ethnic, political, class, and geographic divides, women have developed effective political and legal strategies that strengthen their work domestically. Women's ability to secure their rights domestically is always subject to their countries' laws and willingness to enforce those laws. By calling upon the protections of the international human rights system, women are claiming rights that are not only morally desirable but also legally enforceable. Thus, for example, women's rights groups combating rape in custody in Pakistan cast the abuse not only as a criminal act under domestic law, but also as torture, a gross violation of international human rights norms. This strategy helped them to secure legal reform in Pakistan and to influence the approach of the international human rights community to the problem of custodial rape in their country.

In the past, absent support from their domestic legal systems, human rights organizations, and intergovernmental agencies, women often chose not to seek redress rather than risk reprisal and social ostracism in cultures that often blame the victim. As the international human rights system becomes more responsive to gender-based human rights violations, women who have previously been silent about their experiences of abuse are speaking up. Their testimonies add to the evidence of the scale and prevalence of abuses against women that the international community simply cannot afford to ignore.

The Challenge Ahead

The global women's human rights movement has won important battles in the international arena as well as on the home front. In March 1993 the U.N. Commission on Human Rights adopted for the first time a resolution calling for the integration of the rights of women into the human rights mechanisms of the United Nations. Later that year, governments participating in the World Conference on Human Rights declared:

> the human rights of women and of the girl-child are an inalienable, integral and indivisible part of universal human rights. The full and equal participation of women in political, civil, economic, social and cultural life, at the national, regional and international levels, and the eradication of all forms of discrimination on grounds of sex are priority objectives of the international community.
>
> Gender-based violence and all forms of sexual harassment and exploitation, including those resulting from cultural prejudice and international trafficking, are incompatible with the dignity and worth of the human person, and must be eliminated.[3]

This declaration was a milestone for the women's human rights movement because governments around the world had for a long time refused to acknowledge that women, too, are entitled to enjoy their fundamental human rights. In December 1993 the General Assembly took another key step toward integrating women into the U.N.'s human rights work by adopting the Declaration on Violence Against Women. With this declaration, the U.N. member states recognized explicitly that states are obliged to fight specific forms of violence against women and called on governments to exercise due diligence to prevent, investigate, and punish acts of violence against women.

With the appointment in 1994 of a Special Rapporteur on Violence against Women, its Causes and Consequences, the U.N. recognized the need to address the gender-specific aspects of violence against women.[4] The special rapporteur was given the authority to investigate violence against women, to recommend measures to eliminate this violence, and to work closely with other special rapporteurs, special representatives, working groups, and independent experts of the Commission on Human Rights and the Sub-

---

[3] "The Vienna Declaration and Program of Action," adopted by the World Conference on Human Rights, June 25, 1993, pp. 33-34.

[4] U.N. Commission on Human Rights, Fiftieth Session, Resolution 1994/45, March 4, 1994. Endorsed by Economic and Social Council, decision of 1994/254, July 22, 1994.

Commission on Prevention of Discrimination and Protection of Minorities and treaty bodies to combat violence against women.

Despite such indicators of progress in promoting women's rights, the dismal record on preventing abuse persists. Even those governments that profess a strong commitment to promoting human rights in general have balked at fulfilling their obligation to protect women's rights. On the international level, the Special Rapporteur on Violence against Women lacks sufficient technical and financial support from the U.N. to carry out her work. Similarly, despite the strengths of the Committee on the Elimination of Discrimination Against Women, its effectiveness in promoting women's rights remains severely compromised by inadequate technical and financial resources and its inability to consider individuals' complaints against states. Moreover, the U.N. has failed to integrate women's human rights into its treaty-based and non-treaty-based bodies' system-wide work on human rights. International financial institutions are also in a position to influence the governmental response to abuses against women, yet they generally have refused to address the discriminatory barriers to women's participation in development, or gross violations of women's human rights.

In far too many cases—many of them documented in this report—overwhelming evidence of human rights violations goes unheeded by repressive governments with the tacit acceptance of other governments and international institutions. In very few instances has the international community denounced abuses against women and pressured abusive governments to prevent and remedy them. Thus, in Peru, President Alberto Fujimori has not prosecuted one soldier accused of rape in the context of the counterinsurgency offensive; instead he declared an amnesty for all security forces that makes it legally impossible to investigate the many egregious abuses, including rape by soldiers and police, committed over the past fifteen years. In the United States, the federal government has failed to use its authority to stop torture and other cruel and inhuman treatment of women prisoners in state prisons. In Turkey, the government has yet to investigate police and state doctors for forcing women and girls to undergo virginity exams; indeed the government tried recently to adopt regulations specifically endorsing such exams. And, in the former Yugoslavia, Serbian forces reportedly have renewed their campaign of massive human rights abuse, including rape, to drive non-Serbs out of so-called safe areas.

The challenge for the governments attending the Fourth World Conference on Women in September 1995 is clear. They must act now to make good on past promises, to eliminate discrimination from their laws and their practices, and to stop and punish violence against women wherever it occurs.

Recommendations

In each of the thematic chapters that follow, we present a series of recommendations for responsible governments and the wider international community—including donor countries, the United Nations and other intergovernmental bodies—to end impunity and to prevent future abuse. More generally, the challenge to the women's rights and human rights movements, and to governments that support the goal of gender equality, is to insist that women's human rights be continually integrated into all official programs, legislation, and discourse related to human rights.

Governments should review national legislation and practices in order to eliminate discrimination on the basis of sex and adopt necessary legislation for promoting and protecting women's right to be free from sex discrimination in all spheres. This requires governments to amend criminal, civil, family, and labor laws that discriminate on the basis of sex, including pregnancy and maternity. Governments further should eliminate gender bias in the administration of justice and particularly discriminatory laws and practices that contribute to the wrongful incarceration of women. All victims of discrimination on the basis of sex should be afforded an appropriate forum to challenge the practice and obtain an effective remedy.

As a matter of urgency, governments should protect women's human rights and fundamental freedoms regardless of whether such abuses are attributed to tradition or custom. In countries where customary and/or religious law co-exist with statutory law, governments should ensure that each legal regime is in full compliance with international human rights norms, with particular attention to matters of family and personal status law.

Governments should also implement existing laws and policies that protect women from and guarantee them remedies for gender-based violence. States must guarantee women equal protection of the law through rigorous enforcement of criminal laws prohibiting violence against women, and reform legislation and practices that mischaracterize domestic violence, marital rape and wife-murder as private matters or crimes of honor, and thus allow perpetrators to receive lenient treatment or to go unpunished altogether. Governments should exercise their obligations to investigate and prosecute alleged instances of torture or other forms of cruel, inhuman and degrading treatment, including rape, that occur within their territories and to exercise jurisdiction over torturers who enter their territories.

Governments should promote the universal ratification of the International Covenant on Civil and Political Rights, the International Covenant on Economic, Social and Cultural Rights, the Convention against Torture and Other Cruel, Inhuman or Degrading Treatment or Punishment, and the Convention on the Elimination of All Forms of Discrimination Against Women (CEDAW). Governments should further withdraw all reservations to these treaties that undermine their object and purpose.

Finally, governments should integrate considerations of women's human rights into bilateral and multilateral foreign policy. To this end, governments should systematically use all available leverage to combat violations of women's rights, including bilateral, diplomatic, trade, and military relations; their voice and vote at international and regional financial institutions; and the stigma of public condemnation of abusive governments.

The international community should also do more to promote and protect women's human rights. Member states of the U.N. should adopt and ratify a protocol to CEDAW that would allow women whose domestic legal systems have failed them to submit complaints directly to the Committee on the Elimination of Discrimination Against Women. The committee's current inability to consider individual communications or complaints against states severely limits its effectiveness in promoting the rights embodied in CEDAW. Further, countries that are parties to CEDAW should include information in their periodic reports on efforts to combat all forms of abuse identified in this report.

The international community further should integrate women's human rights into the system-wide activities of the United Nations' treaty-based and non-treaty-based bodies on human rights. Member states should seek to ensure that existing thematic and country-specific special rapporteurs, working groups, and special representatives consistently address violations of women's human rights that fall within their mandates. In this regard, the international community should ensure adequate support for the work of the Special Rapporteur on Violence against Women and renew her mandate beyond the first term of three years.

United Nations agencies, particularly the U.N. Development Program and the U. N. Population Fund, donor governments, and regional and multilateral development banks should seek to ensure that population programs and policies that they support include safeguards for the protection of basic civil and political rights. International financial institutions, such as the World Bank, as well as donor governments should extend the concept of "good governance" to include a firm commitment to the protection of human rights.

1
RAPE AS A WEAPON OF WAR
AND A TOOL OF POLITICAL REPRESSION

Widely committed and seldom denounced, rape and sexual assault of women in situations of conflict have been viewed more as the spoils of war than as illegitimate acts that violate humanitarian law. As a consequence, women, whether combatants or civilians, have been targeted for rape while their attackers go without punishment. Not until the international outcry rose in response to reports of mass rape in the former Yugoslavia did the international community confront rape as a war crime and begin to take steps to punish those responsible for such abuse. Rape, nonetheless, has long been mischaracterized and dismissed by military and political leaders—those in a position to stop it—as a private crime, a sexual act, the ignoble act of the occasional soldier; worse still, it has been accepted precisely because it is so commonplace.

Human Rights Watch investigations in the former Yugoslavia, Peru, Kashmir, and Somalia reveal that rape and sexual assault of women are an integral part of conflicts, whether international or internal in scope.[1] We found that rape of women civilians has been deployed as a tactical weapon to terrorize civilian communities or to achieve "ethnic cleansing," a tool in enforcing hostile occupations, a means of conquering or seeking revenge against the enemy, and a means of payment for mercenary soldiers. Despite rape's prevalence in war, according to the United Nations Special Rapporteur on Violence against Women, "[Rape] remains the least condemned war crime; throughout history, the rape of hundreds of thousands of women and children in all regions of the world has been a bitter reality."[2]

---

[1] Generally speaking, international conflicts are those between two or more recognized nations, whereas an internal conflict is between a recognized government and an armed insurgency. International humanitarian law prohibits rape in both international and internal conflicts but distinguishes between the two. When rape occurs in international conflict, universal jurisdiction exists to prosecute. In internal conflicts, the right and obligation to prosecute rape is placed only in the authorities of the country where it was committed and on the insurgent forces if they have a system of impartial justice.

[2] Preliminary report submitted by the Special Rapporteur on Violence against Women, its Causes and Consequences, Commission on Human Rights, Fiftieth session, November 1994, U.N. Document E/CN.41995/42, p. 64.

Our investigation of rape in Haiti under the former military regime led by Lt. Gen. Raoul Cédras revealed that rape may also serve as a tool of political repression much as it has a weapon of war. Women activists, members of the opposition or, in many instances, the female relatives of opposition members were the focus of such attacks. Individuals were attacked in their homes, on the streets, or in detention. As with rape in conflict, rape as a means of suppressing and rooting out political opposition has long been hidden—both because sexual attacks on women are not viewed as political and because such abuse often is carried out by the only authorities in a position to provide remedies.

Of all the abuses committed in war or by repressive regimes, rape in particular is inflicted predominantly against women. Although men also are raped, efforts to document human rights abuse reveal that women are overwhelmingly the targets. Despite its pervasiveness, rape has often been a hidden element of strife, whether political or military, a fact that is inextricably linked to its largely gender-specific character. That this abuse is committed by men against women has contributed to its being narrowly portrayed as sexual or personal in nature, a characterization that depoliticizes sexual abuse in conflict and results in its being ignored as a crime.

Yet rape in conflict or under repressive regimes is neither incidental nor private. It routinely serves a strategic function and acts as a tool for achieving specific military or political objectives. Like other human rights abuses, rape serves as a means of harming, intimidating and punishing individual women. Further, rape almost always occurs in connection with other forms of violence or abuse against women or their families. Under Haiti's brutal former regime, for example, police or paramilitary troops raided the homes of families accused of supporting then exiled President Jean-Bertrand Aristide, killed or detained some family members, looted families' property, and raped one or more of the women they found. In the conflict in the former Yugoslavia, combatants have raped and beaten women while shooting or taking their family members away to concentration camps. Women who are raped are often murdered or left to die by their attackers; Peruvian soldiers who served in the security forces have recalled gang-raping and then murdering civilian women. Far from being an isolated sexual or private act unrelated to state agents' violent attacks on others, rape often occurs alongside other politically motivated acts of violence.

Human rights investigations demonstrate the different ways in which rape functions as a tactical weapon. In Kashmir, Indian security forces use the threat of rape to intimidate local civilians into carrying out their orders.

Women in Kashmir have also been raped and killed after being abducted by rival militant groups and held as hostages for their male relatives. Similarly, in Somalia, rival clan members force women to choose between betraying their husbands by revealing their hiding places or being raped. Soldiers in Bosnia-Hercegovina rape women of particular ethnic identities as part of their campaigns to drive these women, their families and communities out of the country. Women have also been abducted from their homes and forced by the military into prostitution.

Rape also functions as a way to punish women suspected of being sympathetic to the opposition. Thus, in Peru's emergency zones, where the military has acted as the ultimate authority over civilian officials and where numerous civil and political rights have been suspended, security forces have punished female civilians with rape for their perceived sympathy with armed insurgents of the Shining Path. In Kashmir, when women considered allied with or known to be related to the militants are raped, authorities use the accusation that the women are associated with "terrorist" militants to discredit their testimony and, at least implicitly, to shirk responsibility for the abuse.

Rape may also serve strikingly sex-specific functions, as is the case when rapists attempt to impregnate their victims and compel them to carry the pregnancy to term as an added form of suffering and humiliation. In the former Yugoslavia, non-Serbian women report being taunted by their rapists that they will be forced to carry and give birth to Serbian babies.

Combatants and other state agents rape to subjugate and inflict shame upon their victims, and, by extension, their victims' families and communities. Rape, wherever it occurs, is considered a profound offense against individual and community honor. Soldiers or police can succeed in translating the attack upon individual women into an assault upon their communities because of the emphasis placed in every culture in the world on women's sexual purity. It is the premium placed upon protection and control of women's purity that renders them perfect targets for abuse. In other words, women are raped precisely because the violation of their "protected" status has the effect of shaming them and their communities.

The choice of particular women as targets of rape is almost inevitably determined by their identities, for example, as citizens of a particular country, adherents to a certain faith, or members of an ethnic group, a race or a class. Thus, in Somalia, rapists target women from rival clans, and in the former Yugoslavia, Bosnian Muslim women are raped by Serbian men.

History of Impunity

As common as the fact of rape in war or under repressive regimes is the failure to investigate and punish those accused of this crime. In every instance investigated by Human Rights Watch, officials, whether military or civilian, have been more likely to excuse the actions of rapists or to blame the victims than to denounce the practice as criminal and abusive or to take steps to end it. In Kashmir, for example, where security forces, army and paramilitary troops have engaged in widespread rape, few of the reported incidents have been investigated. There, authorities seek to discredit the victims by casting doubt on their motives in reporting rape, pointing to their relation to or sympathy for the militants challenging the government. In Bosnia, Radovan Karadzic, leader of the Bosnian Serbs, denied reports of widespread rape by his troops, admitting only that "psychopaths" were responsible for less than twenty rapes.[3]

Reports of the widespread use of rape as a tactic of war in the former Yugoslavia have been instrumental in focusing attention on the function of rape in war. The situation has provoked international condemnation and prompted investigations into reports of rape by all parties to that conflict. The stated commitment of the judges and chief prosecutor for the war crimes tribunal, created by the United Nations initially to try crimes committed in the former Yugoslavia, to prosecuting rape as a war crime marks a critical turn away from accepting rape in war. In late 1994, the United Nations expanded the mandate of the tribunal to investigate and prosecute violations of the laws of war that occurred during the 1994 genocide in Rwanda. In carrying out its expanded mandate, the tribunal should ensure that reports of rape during the Rwandan genocide are vigorously investigated and tried. For these rape victims, an international tribunal may be their only opportunity to hear the crimes against them denounced, to see both the perpetrators of such abuse and the commanders who allowed and participated in rape and other abuses prosecuted, and to seek a remedy for the assaults they have suffered.

This attention to rape in war has also increased awareness that repressive governments use rape, among other abuses, to crack down on and undermine perceived threats to their power. In Haiti, politically motivated rape was well-documented by local activists and international observers, including the United Nations/Organization of American States International Civilian Mission. Their work linking reports of rape to the many abuses perpetrated

---

[3] Roy Gutman, "Rape Camps: Evidence in Bosnia Mass Attacks Points to Karadzic's Pals," *New York Newsday*, April 19, 1993, pp. 7, 31.

by the military and police against supporters of President Aristide promoted recognition of the intrinsically political function rape may serve and led to calls to end impunity for this form of abuse. Victims of rape in such situations may not be able to seek redress before international tribunals, but governments should ensure that they too receive justice by trying alleged abuses in national courts.

The Role of Domestic Law

International action against rape also would serve as a critical precedent for domestic responses to politically motivated rape. National laws generally mischaracterize rape as a crime against honor or custom, not as a crime against the physical integrity of the victim, and thus minimize its seriousness. This inaccurate portrayal of rape reduces the likelihood that rape victims targeted by political or military forces will receive justice, for often a woman's honor is more on trial than the alleged rapist's actions.

In India, for example, torture is a crime, and criminal law explicitly prescribes punishments for members of the police or other security forces who commit rape, but there is no evidence that authorities are willing to enforce these laws. Further, in rape cases, the credibility of the victim may be impeached by showing that she was of "generally immoral character." A survey of rape case judgments in the mid- to late 1980s, following legal reform in India, revealed that judges continued to base their decisions in rape cases largely on the character of the victim.[4] And, in Peru, rape until recently was considered a "crime against honor." Thus, as a matter of law, rape was perceived as a harm to the community as represented by women's honor and not as an injury to the physical integrity of the victim herself.

International Protections

Rape is explicitly prohibited under international humanitarian law governing both international and internal conflicts. The Fourth Geneva Convention of 1949 specifies in Article 27 "[W]omen shall be especially protected against any attack on their honor, in particular against rape, enforced prostitution, or any form of indecent assault."[5] Further, Article 147 of the

---

[4] Flavia Agnes, "Fighting Rape—Has Amending the Law Helped?" *The Lawyers*, (Bombay: February 1990), pp. 4-11.

[5] Convention Relative to the Protection of Civilian Persons in Time of War, August 12, 1949, 6 U.S.T. 3516, 75 U.N.T.S. 287 [Fourth Geneva Convention], Article 27.

(continued...)

same convention designates "wilfully causing great suffering or serious injury to body or health," "torture," and "inhuman treatment" as war crimes and as grave breaches of the conventions.[6] As the International Committee of the Red Cross (ICRC) has recognized, rape constitutes "wilfully causing great suffering or serious injury to body or health" and thus should be treated as a grave breach of the convention.[7] The ICRC has also stated that "inhuman treatment" should be interpreted in light of Article 27 and its specific prohibition against rape.[8] The Geneva Conventions specify that governments are obliged to find and punish those responsible for grave breaches and to make those accused available for trial.

As with international conflicts, humanitarian law clearly prohibits rape in internal conflicts. Rape committed or tolerated by any party to a non-international conflict is prohibited by Common Article 3 of the Geneva Conventions insofar as it constitutes "violence to life and person," "cruel treatment," "torture," or "outrages upon personal dignity." Moreover, Protocol II to the Geneva Conventions, which applies to conflicts between a government's and its opposition's armed forces that control territory within the country, prohibits "outrages upon personal dignity, in particular humiliating and degrading treatment, rape, enforced prostitution and any form of indecent assault" committed by any party.[9] The ICRC explains that this provision "reaffirms and supplements Common Article 3 . . . [because] it became clear

---

[5](...continued)
The reference to rape as an attack on women's honor is problematic in that it fails to recognize explicitly rape as an attack on women's physical integrity.

[6] War crimes are violations of the laws of war that "are committed by persons 'belonging' to one party to the conflict against persons or property of the other side." Theodor Meron, "Rape as a Crime Under International Humanitarian Law," 87 *American Journal of International Law* 424 (Washington, D.C.: American Society of International Law, 1993). Certain war crimes are designated by the Geneva Conventions to be grave breaches.

[7] Ibid., p. 426, citing International Committee of the Red Cross, Aide Mémoire, December 3, 1992.

[8] Ibid., pp. 426-27, citing *Commentary on the Geneva Conventions of 12 August 1949: Geneva Convention Relative to the Protection of Civilian Persons in time of War*, Oscar M. Uhler & Henri Coursier, eds. (1958), p. 598.

[9] Protocol Additional to the Geneva Conventions of 12 August 1949, and Relating to the Protection of Victims of Non-International Armed Conflicts, opened for signature Dec. 12, 1977, Article 4(2)(e), 1124 U.N.T.S. 609, 16 I.L.M. 1442 (1977) [Protocol II].

that it was necessary to strengthen . . . the protection of women . . . who may also be the victims of rape, enforced prostitution or indecent assault."[10]

Rape committed not in the course of conflict but as part of political repression is also prohibited under international law as torture or cruel, inhuman or degrading treatment. The Universal Declaration of Human Rights, the International Covenant on Civil and Political Rights, and the Convention Against Torture and Other Cruel, Inhuman or Degrading Treatment or Punishment all promote the dignity and physical integrity of the person and prohibit torture and cruel, inhuman or degrading treatment. Various international authorities have recognized rape to constitute a form of torture, as defined by the Torture Convention, when it is used in order to obtain information or confession, or for any reason based on discrimination, or to punish, coerce or intimidate, and is performed by state agents or with their acquiescence.[11]

Whenever committed by a state agent or an armed insurgent, whether as a matter of policy or an individual incident of torture, rape constitutes an abuse of power and a violation of international humanitarian and/or human rights law. That rape often functions in ways similar to other human rights abuses makes all the more striking the fact that, until recently, it has not been condemned like any other abuse. The differential treatment of rape makes clear that the problem—for the most part—lies not in the absence of adequate legal prohibitions but in the international community's willingness to tolerate sexual abuse against women.

---

[10] *ICRC Commentary on the Additional protocols of 8 June 1977 to the Geneva Conventions of 12 August 1949*, Yves Sandoz, Christophe Swinarski, Bruno Zimmerman, eds. (Geneva: Martinus Nijhoff Publishers, 1987), p. 1375, Paragraph 4539.

[11] See, for example, Meron, "Rape as a Crime Under International Humanitarian Law," p. 425; Report by the Special Rapporteur on Torture, P. Koojimans, appointed pursuant to Commission on Human Rights resolution 1985/33, U.N. Document E/CN.4/1986/15 (February 19, 1986), Paragraph 6.

RAPE IN BOSNIA-HERCEGOVINA

Human Rights Watch has been documenting violations of the rules of war in Croatia and Bosnia since the beginning of the wars there in 1991 and 1992, respectively.[12] The wars in the former Yugoslavia are in fact wars against civilians who have been subjected to violent and abusive practices on the basis of nationality. Crimes have been committed by all sides, but the chief offenders have been Serbian military and paramilitary forces. The aim of their vicious policy of "ethnic cleansing" has been to rid an area of an "enemy ethnic group" through murder, forced displacement, deportation, detention or confinement to ghetto areas, destruction of villages and cultural and religious objects of the "enemy" ethnic group. Mass rape of women has also been used as a tool of "ethnic cleansing," meant to terrorize, torture and demean women and their families and compel them to flee the area.

In Croatia, the Croatian government has been engaged in an armed conflict with rebel Serbian authorities that control approximately 20 percent of Croatia, have established their own "state" and seek secession from Croatia. Similarly in Bosnia, the predominantly Muslim government is battling rebel Bosnian Serb forces that control approximately 70 percent of Bosnia, have established their own "state" and seek secession from Bosnia. Rebel Serb forces in both Croatia and Bosnia seek to join Serbia proper in a single Serbian state. Croats from Bosnia also have established their own quasi-state in Bosnia, but, as of this writing, are ostensibly allied with Bosnian government forces. Bosnian Croat forces are not part of the armed forces of Croatia proper but are armed and otherwise supported by the Croatian government.

The heartland and geographic center of the former Yugoslavia, Bosnia was a microcosm of the country, where two million Muslims, 1.3 million Serbs, and 750,000 Croats lived together in ostensible harmony. The Bosnian Muslims are distinguished as an "ethnic group," which is both a means of national self-definition and religion.

When Bosnia proclaimed its independence in 1992, it was open, vulnerable, and unarmed, susceptible to attacks from its warring and heavily armed neighbors. Just a few months after the shaky truce that ended the first stage of the Serbian-Croatian conflict, Bosnia became the ground on which the Serbs and Croats continued their separate quests for territory. Although the

---

[12] The following material was adapted from Helsinki Watch, *War Crimes in Bosnia-Hercegovina, Volume II* (New York: Human Rights Watch, 1993).

Croats and Muslims were first allies, then enemies, and then ostensibly allies again, their alliance remains fragile, as each side jockeys for control of territory and armaments.

Most of the abuses attributable to the predominantly Muslim forces of the Bosnian government are perpetuated by individuals and do not appear to be part of a pre-meditated plan of the Bosnian authorities. Nevertheless, Bosnian Croat and Muslim forces are guilty of serious abuses of human rights and humanitarian law. Moreover, the destruction of Serbian property and the holding of hostages in many cases appear to be known to local or regional officials who have done little to prevent such abuses. Bosnian Croat officials of at least two detention facilities knew of, or participated in, the commission of abuses in the facilities under their control. The authorities of the self-proclaimed "Croatian Community of Herceg-Bosnia" also are guilty of organizing the arbitrary arrests and internments of non-Croats in the Mostar, Stolac and Capljina areas. Although Croatian and Muslim forces have improved treatment in detention centers under their control, few soldiers have been held accountable for any abuses they may have perpetrated.

Many of the abuses attributed to Serbian forces have followed a recognizable pattern that has come to be known as "ethnic cleansing," first used during the war in Croatia and, more recently, in Bosnia-Hercegovina. The primary aim of Serbian forces is to capture or consolidate control over territory by forcibly displacing or killing non-Serbs in the area. Forced displacement is itself a violation of international humanitarian law (the laws of war). The abuses that constitute "ethnic cleansing" often occur together in various combinations: attacks against civilian targets, the use of siege warfare and the indiscriminate and disproportionate use of force; pillage and the destruction of civilian homes and cultural objects; summary executions; abuses in detention; rape; mutilation; hostage-taking; and the obstruction of humanitarian aid and attacks on relief personnel.

In most Serbian-held areas of Bosnia, abuses against non-Serbs appear to be the result of a premeditated plan by local and regional civilian, military and/or police authorities. In some instances, such abuses are perpetrated by individual soldiers or single military, paramilitary and police units. The public nature of the abuses and the frequency with which they take place indicate that individual soldiers and military units do not anticipate disciplinary action by their superiors. Human Rights Watch is not aware of any case in which Bosnian Serb forces guilty of abuses have been punished by their superiors for their crimes. The failure by civilian, military and police officials of "Republika Srpska," the self-proclaimed Bosnian Serb state, to punish soldiers involved in abuses, despite documentation of and international attention to human rights abuse by Serbian soldiers, indicates that such officials knowingly tolerate and even condone the violations.

In the Bosnian war, unlike other wars, rape has been widely reported and condemned, in part because it represents yet another unchecked horror in an ongoing, brutalizing war. This unprecedented attention to rape may also reflect a change in the public perception of rape, due largely to the efforts of the international women's movement to condemn rape as a weapon of war and ensure accountability for those responsible. Under the 1949 Geneva Conventions, rape, as a form of torture and of cruel and inhuman treatment, is a violation of basic human rights and a war crime. The rapes in Bosnia have heightened public awareness of this crime and may help to ensure that rape in the future will be prosecuted with the same vigor as other war crimes.

Combatants for each of the parties to the conflict in Bosnia-Hercegovina have raped women and girls in their homes, in front of family members and in the village square. Women have been arrested and raped during interrogation. In some villages and towns, women and girls have been gathered together and taken to holding centers—often schools or community sports halls—where they are raped, gang-raped and abused repeatedly, sometimes for days or even weeks at a time. Other women have been taken seemingly at random from their communities or out of a group of refugees with whom they are traveling and raped by soldiers. Whether a woman is raped by soldiers in her home or is held in a house with other women and raped over and over again, she is raped with a political purpose—to intimidate, humiliate and degrade her and others affected by her suffering. The effect of rape is often to ensure that women and their families will flee and never return. Rape by Bosnian Serb soldiers has been particularly systematic and widespread.

Women interviewed by Human Rights Watch described how they were gang-raped, taunted with ethnic slurs and cursed by rapists who stated their intention forcibly to impregnate women as a haunting reminder of the rape and intensification of the trauma it inflicts. In our view, the forcible impregnation of women, or the intention to so impregnate them, constitutes an abuse separate from the rape itself and should be denounced and investigated as such. Moreover, the rape of women in an organized fashion—whether in buildings where they are kept for the purpose of being raped or in camps where they are detained with family members—establishes that local commanders must know that their soldiers are raping women and do nothing to stop these abuses.

Although we have not found hard evidence showing a policy of deploying rape as a means of tactical warfare, we also found no evidence that any soldier or member of a paramilitary group has been punished or held to account for raping women and girls.   To the contrary, soldiers often rape without regard for witnesses, and, on occasion, identify themselves to their victims.   These are not the actions of men who fear retribution.   The failure to punish rapists appears to be as consistent and widespread as the act of rape itself.

Assault by Bosnian Serb Forces

Croat, Muslim and Serb, these rape victims together represent the three major ethnic groups involved in the brutal war that has ravaged Bosnia-Hercegovina.   Women who have been raped in their homes are usually attacked by soldiers who randomly enter to loot from or to terrorize the inhabitants.   For example, K.S. is a housewife from a village in the municipality of Ključ, born in 1939 and illiterate.[13]   She could not recall the day of her assault but did specify that it had taken place approximately four months before Human Rights Watch interviewed her, probably in late September 1992.   She could only identify the approximate month by the farming season at the time of her assault, which she identified as the period during which corn is harvested and potatoes are dug out of the ground.   According to K.S.:

> One evening soldiers pounded on our front door. They had
> already been in our village near Ključ. I do not want to tell
> you the name of the village. Six of us women and my man
> [i.e., husband] were in the house. The women were our
> relatives and neighbors. They had taken refuge in our house
> because the house had two cement and iron-reinforced floors,
> so it provided a good shelter. That night, they pounded on
> the door. I asked: "Who is banging? We are alone, please
> don't bang." My mother-in-law's bed was situated exactly
> below the window. After I'd spoken, they broke the window
> with their rifle butts. The glass shattered all over my
> mother-in-law. I opened the front door, and five armed
> Serbian soldiers came in.

---

[13] Interview, refugee camp in Croatia, January 22, 1993. All names withheld by Human Rights Watch unless otherwise indicated.

K.S. testified that she recognized one of the soldiers, who was dressed in fatigues, but did not know his name. She claims that the soldier used to man Serbian barricades in the vicinity of the police station in Ključ. K.S. continued:

> They lined us up in front of the house. With knives hanging from their belts, they thrust guns in our throats, yelled and threatened us. They pressed a knife up to my husband's neck and said [to me], "If you want the old man alive, give us gold and [German] marks." Then one of my cousins brought out all her gold [jewelry], so that they would spare my man. One of them grabbed me by the chest and pulled me over. "Come here," he said. I was calling for help and begging them to kill me rather than separate me from the rest of my folks. He grabbed me by the shoulders and threw me on the ground. He screamed at me, asking which of the villagers had the most gold and money. I told him that I did not know. Our men have never worked abroad; we were not rich. My man and I have lived on his pension. It took three of my man's pensions [to buy] a sack of flour. He hit me on the shoulder and threw me on the ground again. My shoulder still hurts very much. He started tearing off my clothes. Then the three of them took turns on me.

K.S. claims that her husband and the other women did not witness the rape but heard what was happening. According to K.S.:

> That man took me behind the house—to the side—while the others remained in front of the house. It all took place on the concrete [floor]. I was cold and sore all over. I pleaded with them, "Children, don't. I could be your mother." Then I collapsed and knew nothing more. When I had regained my senses, they were no longer around me, but I heard their voices and the shouts coming from the front of the house.

K.S. then crawled into the house, only to be found and raped again. According to K.S.:

I crawled into the house. [I] went upstairs, found the room, lay down on the bed and slipped a blanket over my head. Then, one of them came in. He pulled the blanket, lit my face with a flashlight and roared: "Did you try to hide again? Out with [the German] marks!" I wept while telling him that we had no marks. He then spread my legs and raped me. He was very strong—you cannot defend yourself. When he was done, he inserted his hand inside me and began pinching me with his fingers, as if he wanted to pull everything out. I screamed and he grabbed my right breast and twisted it so hard that I screamed again; long afterwards my entire breast was blackened. He thrust the knife to my throat and said that, if I screamed one more time, he would slaughter me. He inserted his fingers inside me again—it hurt tremendously—and then he thrust his hand at my face and I had to lick his fingers clean, one by one. He repeated the whole thing once more.

He lowered his knife down and said that he would rip me open, He kept cursing at me and shouting: "Where is your [Bosnian President] Alija [Izetbegović] now?" He called me an Ustaša.[14] I thought it was the end of me. But then, he left. I do not know why he did not kill me. Before they left, they threatened to burn everything if we told anyone what happened. I was covered with blood all over. Once they left, I vomited. I felt very ill. The women helped me; they washed me up. We were afraid that they would come back again.

---

[14]During World War II, with the backing of the Nazi and Italian fascist governments, Croatian fascists (known as Ustaše) established the puppet Independent State of Croatia (Nezavisna Država Hrvatska - NDH). Under the Ustaša regime, thousands of Serbs, Jews, Gypsies and others were killed between 1941 and 1945. Some Muslims were members of the NDH government and some Muslim forces fought on the side of the Ustaša regime during World War II. Serbian military and paramilitary forces commonly refer to Croat and Muslim forces in the current war as "Ustaša." Both Croats and Muslims reject the label and vehemently deny that they are Ustaša sympathizers or fascists.

K.S. claims that her husband reported the incident to the Bosnian Serb police authorities, who sent a car to take K.S. to the hospital. K.S. told the doctor and a police officer that she had been raped. However, K.S. claims that perpetrators of such crimes are never brought to justice. According to K.S.:

> [The doctor] said that something like that should not be allowed to happen and that they were going to locate those who did it. But they say one thing and do another. What happened to me has been happening to other women. During the day, they tell you that that ought not to be happening, that they will find those soldiers [responsible for the rapes], and then, at night, the soldiers come again and they act as they please.

> During the day, the Serbian neighbors greet you and pretend that everything is as usual, but at night, these very same people shoot at windows and raid houses. The policeman who took me to the hospital was writing something down but they put on a big act, you know. They leave it all alone.

K.S. believes she was assaulted because her husband refused to sign over their house to the Bosnian Serb authorities. According to K.S.:

> [My husband] said he did not want to leave, although most of the people had left our village by that time. I was not aware of the fact that somebody would provide for us in this way [i.e., as in the refugee camp]. I thought we would be hungry. That's why they did it, so that we would have to leave. The next morning, after that all had happened, my man signed everything of ours over to them, just so they would let us leave.

In regions where Bosnian Serb forces retain absolute control over territory, rape is used as one of many terror tactics to force the flight of the non-Serbian population from the areas. Serbian soldiers attacking houses in the Banja Luka area have raped women and girls in their homes, and sometimes in the presence of family members. I.T., a married woman with two children, describes how she was raped:[15]

> On the third of May 1993, a group of Serbs came to our house; they all wore uniforms of the Serbian Army. I was on the second floor when they surrounded the house, broke the main entrance and came upstairs. I was in the bedroom with my children and our neighbors—a husband, his wife and their daughter. The Serbs wore black ski masks which covered their faces, but in spite of that, I recognized Mišo Trivić our neighbor who was in the Serbian Army; he used to come into the shop where I worked for many years. They [the soldiers] told us to lie down on the floor, after which they covered us with blankets. Mišo asked me to give him our money. I told him we had 1,400 German marks [approximately US $875] and brought it to him. He cursed me all the time.
>
> Then Trivić and three other soldiers took me into the living room and raped me there. The name of the second man was Siniša Milovčić; the third man I didn't know. The fourth man left the room; he didn't rape me. My neighbor was raped too. My husband and children were in the adjoining room while all this was happening. Before they left, Trivić said that he'd take my son if I didn't pay him another 5,000 German marks [approximately US $3,125], and hit him a few times. They took all our documents—driver's license, passports, everything.
>
> The next morning our neighbor, S.N., went to the ICRC to tell them what had happened. Two police inspectors came the next morning to take our statements. But nothing was done until August, when the same men who attacked and raped us did the same thing to another girl in Vrbanja whose surname was Hodžić; after raping her, they killed her. But after that, they raped and killed a daughter of some Serbian general from Banja Luka; she was thirteen years old. The

---

[15] Interview, Croatia, February 27 and 28, 1994.

mother of the girl who was killed told me that the Serbian
general visited her and said that the men will be caught.

L.D., a sixty-seven-year-old Muslim man from Prjnavor, and his
Serbian wife were evicted from their home in Bosnian Serb-controlled territory
in February 1994.[16] After being evicted, they lived in the house of L.D.'s
sister-in-law. The couple was forced to move into the basement of the sister-
in-law's house because it had been occupied by a Serbian military officer.
According to L.D. the military police officer, N.E., was rarely home, but his
wife A. was there. The entrance to the house was upstairs, and L.D. and his
wife rarely left the basement or said anything in front of them. Three months
prior to our interviewing L.D. and his wife, three male youths claiming to be
"Serbo-Četniks" came to their basement apartment. It is evident that the men
must have entered through the military officer's entrance, because that is the
only door into and out of the house. Two of the men raped L.D.'s wife. L.D.
believes that the men were working in conjunction with the military police
officer who lived upstairs, because the officer came to the door after they had
raped L.D.'s wife and told the rapists to"cut it out." The three youths then
went upstairs and spent about an hour drinking with the military officer.
        L.D. reported the rape to the local Red Cross who then reported the
rape to the police. The police questioned L.D., his wife and the military
officer who lived upstairs. Ten to fifteen days later, L.D.'s brother-in-law
went to see the police inspector, and was told that the three rapists had been
caught and that the case had been sent to municipal court. Three months later,
L.D. and his wife received a notice in the mail from the public prosecutor's
office, stating that the charges against the three men had been dropped because
there was no basis for the indictment. L.D left Prjnavor, but his wife [a Serb]
did not want to leave because of the Serbian media propaganda depictions of
Muslims persecuting Serbs in Bosnian government-controlled territory.
        Other women are interned in makeshift prisons where they are
routinely raped. B., a forty-year-old Muslim woman from Doboj, recounted
to Human Rights Watch that Serbian forces assumed control of Doboj on May
1 or 2, 1992.[17] People were allowed to leave the city of Doboj, so B. fled
with her family to their home in the village of Grabska. Thereafter, Serbian
forces started shelling Grabska and B.'s son, her mother-in-law and sister-in-
law were evacuated. B. and her husband chose to stay because they had

---

[16] Interview, Han Bila, Bosnia-Hercegovina, September 24, 1994.
[17] Interview, Zagreb, Croatia, January 1993.

helped to found the local chapter of the predominantly Muslim Party of Democratic Action (Stranka Demokratske Akcija—SDA) and felt an obligation to remain. On May 10, according to B.:

> They [i.e., ground troops] were coming from two sides, forcing everyone to come out of their houses and burning the houses. They forced some women and children to lie down in the main road; they threatened to drive over them with tanks if those in hiding did not emerge.

After everyone had emerged from their houses, the Serbian soldiers gathered them on the main road and separated the men from the women and children. According to B., the Serbian soldiers had lists from which they called out women's names; they directed these women to board buses. Some children appeared to have boarded the buses with their mothers. B. was among those women who boarded one of the three blue-and-white buses after her name was read from a list. The men were left standing in a group.

The women and children first were taken to a school in Srpska Grabska. They were then transferred to a factory warehouse used by the Bosanska company that produced jams and juices in Doboj. B. then was transferred to a high school in the Usara section of Doboj, where she was held for twenty-eight days. According to B.:

> It began as soon as I arrived. They told us not to look at the soldiers so that we wouldn't remember them. We were not allowed to talk with each other. During the day, we stayed in a big sports hall. The guards were always there. If they caught us talking, they would take a woman out, beat her and more than the usual [number of men] would rape her. They liked to punish us. They would ask women if they had male relatives in the city; I saw them ask this of one woman, and they brought her fourteen-year-old son and forced him to rape her.

> Some of us were selected by name; some would just get chosen. If a man could not rape [i.e., if he was physically unable] he would use a bottle or gun or he would urinate on me.

B. remembers that four different types of soldiers were present at different times in the camp: local Serbian militia; the Yugoslav army (JNA); police forces based in the Serbian-occupied town of Knin in Croatia;[18] and members of the "White Eagles" (Beli Orlovi) paramilitary group, who wore an insignia bearing three eagles and *kokarda*[19] on their hats.

B. claims that local Serbs, including several doctors whom she knew from the hospital where she had worked, also raped women detained at the high school. According to B.:

> Some of the local Serbs wore black stockings on their heads
> to disguise their faces because they didn't want to be
> recognized.   [Nevertheless,] I recognized many of them.
> [They were] colleagues—doctors with whom I worked. The
> first [man] who raped me was a Serbian doctor named Jodić.
> I had known Jodić for ten years. We worked in the same
> hospital. I would see him every day in the employees'
> cafeteria. We spoke generally, "Hi, how are you." He was
> a very polite, nice man.   Another doctor whom I had
> previously known also raped me; [his name was] Obrad
> Filipović. I wasn't allowed to say anything. Before he raped
> me he said, "Now you know who we are. You will
> remember forever." I was so surprised; he was a doctor!

B. claims that women were most frequently raped in classrooms of the high school.

> Once I saw the face of a woman I knew; her daughter was
> with her. Three men were with them inside [the classroom].
> I was brought in by one man, and another four men
> followed. On that occasion, I was raped with a gun by one
> of the three men already in the room. I didn't recognize him.
> Others stood watching. Some spat on us. They were raping

---

[18] B. referred to the police forces from Knin as "Martičevci," because their one-time commander was Milan Martić, now president of the so-called Republic of Serbian Krajina in Serbian-occupied areas of Croatia. B. also claims that the forces from Knin wore high black hats and an insignia on their uniforms.

[19] The kokarda is a Serbian emblem which depicts a double-headed eagle and is worn by some Serbian paramilitary groups.

me, the mother and her daughter at the same time. Sometimes you had to accept ten men, sometimes three. Sometimes when they were away, they wouldn't call me for one or two days. I wanted nothing, not bread, not water, just to be alone. I felt I wanted to die. We had no change of clothes and couldn't wash ourselves.

B. remembers that the school hall where the women were forced to sit during the day with their knees pulled up to their chests was packed full of women of all ages. A woman sitting close to B. tried to speak with her, but B. feared punishment and did not respond. The guards took the women to the bathroom only at designated times. They also placed a pot in the middle of the room and told the women to use it to relieve themselves. However, the pot was punctured and if the women used it, urine and feces would leak in the area where other women were sitting.

The guards also brought a man who they said was a gynecologist to the school and submitted the younger women to gynecological exams. Recalls B.:

A gynecologist would come to the hall, to one of the classrooms. They told us that he was a doctor, but I'm not so sure because he didn't realize that I had an IUD and he examined me internally. Only the younger women would see the doctor. I think they were checking to see if we were pregnant because he would say, "You're not pregnant." The Serbs said to us, "Why aren't you pregnant?" Once they brought girls not older than seventeen into the hall. They were clean and dressed nicely. They said, "See how well we treat them. They are pregnant."

The [pregnant girls] were from outside, and I didn't know them. I didn't pay too much attention. I think they wanted to know who was pregnant in case anyone was hiding it. They wanted women to have children to stigmatize us forever. The child is a reminder of what happened.

Non-Serbian women were raped while interned in concentration camps. J., a thirty-nine-year-old Croatian woman from the town of Prijedor, was raped by a reserve captain of the self-proclaimed "Republika Srpska."[20] According to J., the reserve captain named Grabovac took her into a separate office away from the other prisoners. Other men entered the office but, due to faulty electricity, J. could not see the other assailants. J. was then beaten by these men. The men called J. an Ustaša and said she needed to give birth to a Serb. "Then she would be different," they said. After the other men left the room the reserve captain, Grabovac, raped J.

Selima,[21] a Muslim woman in her forties, was arrested in her home in Prijedor on May 30, 1992, and detained in a former local government building for four days. She was allowed to go home but was arrested again on June 11, 1992, and then detained in the Keraterm, Omarska and Trnopolje camps. While in Keraterm, Selima states she was raped by an unknown assailant and by Zoran Sikirica, whom she claimed was the commander of the camp. Other former Keraterm detainees interviewed by Human Rights Watch identified Sikirica as a soldier at the Keraterm detention facility. Selima was summoned to give a statement at the local police station by policemen she knew. Selima was not apprehensive about giving her statement because she believed herself to be guilty of "nothing." She was not politically active and was not a member of any political party. However, after giving her statement, she and two other women were taken to the Keraterm camp, which had been a factory for bricks and ceramic tile. The women were separated. While locked in one of the halls, Selima was raped by Sikirica. Selima also heard the screams of men who were being tortured in the same building. After Sikirica left, three other young men entered her detention hall. One of the men raped Selima while the other two laughed, insulted Selima and cheered the rapist. Another soldier intervened and stopped the abuse. Later, when asked by soldiers if she had been abused, Selima replied,"no" fearing for her life.[22]

---

[20] Interview, Zabreb, Croatia, October 15, 1992. Human Rights Watch interviewed two other women who had been held in Omarska, and they confirmed that women had been raped in the camp.

[21] Interview, Zagreb, Croatia, February 22, 1993. The woman provided her name to Human Rights Watch but asked that it remain confidential. The name here is a pseudonym, and other identifying features have been deleted to protect the confidentiality of the witness.

[22] Selima believes Zoran Sikirica personally sent a soldier the next day to ask if anyone had molested her, but she did not indicate to Human Rights Watch how she knew that her assailant had personally sent a soldier to question her.

Human Rights Watch interviewed a young married couple, both Muslims, from Čarakovo. A Serbian soldier named Rajko Dragić broke into the house where the couple was staying with their four-year-old daughter. Rajko Dragić, whom Selim identified as part of the Serbian Army because he wore a camouflage uniform with a bullet belt and a red beret, looted their home of a videotape player and a television. Intimidating the family with a machine gun, he raped Senada in front of her husband and their child. He then burned down their house. The young couple fled with their family after the house was set on fire, but did not report what had happened for fear that they would be killed.[23]

Assault by Bosnian Croat, Bosnian Government, and Muslim Forces

Human Rights Watch conducted separate interviews with Serbian women who were raped by Croatian forces in the municipalities of Bosanski Brod and Odžak, when the area was under Bosnian Croat and, to a lesser extent, Muslim control.[24]

Two of the victims had been detained after Muslim and Croatian forces assumed control of their village of Novi Grad. Following a twenty-one-day battle, Serbian forces relinquished their weapons and negotiations began. Both witnesses claim that although the Serbs had been promised safe passage to the predominantly Serbian village of Miloševac, they were detained in the high school in Odžak. According to each of the two women, the men were held in the school gym and the children and some men were released and settled in Odžak, in the homes of Muslims who appeared to have been family friends of the Serbian captives. About two weeks later, the women and children were told that they could return to their homes in Novi Grad. Several Serbian women were then taken from Novi Grad and raped in the village of Posavska Mahala and in the Bulek settlement, near Bosanski Brod.

Human Rights Watch interviewed two women who were raped on two separate occasions by Croatian forces in the village of Posavska Mahala.[25]

---

[23] Interview, Zagreb, Croatia, January 1993.

[24] The two victims were introduced to Human Rights Watch representatives by the Serbian government's Commission for War Crimes and Genocide. They were interviewed in January 1993 in Belgrade, Yugoslavia. Although the women had testified on numerous occasions on behalf of the Serbian government, Human Rights Watch found their testimonies credible.

[25] Interview, Belgrade, Yugoslavia, January 1993. The witnesses were identified by the Yugoslav State Commission on War Crimes and Genocide.

The men responsible for both instances of rape appear not to have been members of the Bosnian Croatian forces (HVO) but of a paramilitary group identified as the "Fiery Horses" (Vatreni Konji). The women reported the rapes to the authorities in the town of Novi Grad, but the offenders were not prosecuted.

Gordana, a forty-three-year-old housewife, was raped by Croatian soldiers in the village of Posavska Mahala. According to Gordana:[26]

> The first few days [in Novi Grad] were not bad. [However,] for reasons of safety, several families lived together in one Serbian house. The violence started on June 20. One day, they took three of us women from the house in which I was living, and four women were taken from another house. They dragged us out of our beds, barefoot, at about 1:00 a.m. There were five of them, men in green uniforms without any insignia.

> We were taken to a Croatian village, Posavska Mahala, where we were met by another thirty of their soldiers. I know that they were soldiers because I saw their green uniforms in the bright moonlight. One of them grabbed my arm and insisted that I tell him that I loved only him and no one else in the world. As he was dragging me around, he said that he was from Županja [Croatia]. He brought me to an abandoned barn, and we both had to jump in through the window. He then ordered me to undress. I had 4,000 German marks tied around my waist, and he took this away from me.

> He raped me, ordered me to get dressed again and handed me back to the others. Another man took me to the house where the other two women were being raped. I told him I had AIDS, so instead of raping me, he forced me to perform fellatio. I was forced to do the same to another soldier. All of this happened on a bed, in one of the rooms in the house where [two other women,] M. and D., were being raped. They were in the other rooms.

------

[26] Interview, Belgrade, Yugoslavia, January 1993.

L.L. is a thirty-seven-year-old Serbian woman originally from Potičanski Lipik, near Odžak.[27] She, too, says that she was raped by Croatian soldiers in the village of Posavska Mahala.

L.L. claims that her village was first shelled from the Croatian side of the Sava River on April 18 or 19, 1992. The attack continued for approximately three weeks. On May 8, L.L., her sister, a neighbor and their four children fled to the village of Hasić, where they were taken in by a Muslim man, I.D. According to L.L., Croatian military police officers told the displaced Serbs in Hasić to return to their homes in Potičanski Lipik, where the Serbian women were sexually abused by Croatian forces. According to L.L.:

> The Croatian military police came [to the village of Hasić]. They said we had to go back home. They wore green army uniforms and white belts. They said they would burn the Muslim houses if they kept the Serbs with them. When we got home, we had to work in the fields. The Croatian soldiers—my neighbors—started mistreating women in their homes.

In the early morning hours of June 5, 1992, soldiers broke into the house of D.N., where L.L. had taken refuge with a group of women and children. L.L. was taken to another house and told to call out the names of three women staying there. According to L.L.:

> There were fifteen of them. They called themselves the Fiery Horses. They took me to a house that belongs to M.B. They hit me and told me to call out of the house three women who were staying there: M.D., M.N., and S.S.

> All four of us were put in the back of a car and taken to their headquarters in Posavaska Mahala, where they took us to two separate houses and started to mistreat us. I know that seven of them raped me two times each. I counted seven and then I fainted.

---

[27] Ibid.. Prior to speaking with us, she talked to numerous journalist and others.

> I was in a large room of the house that belonged to J.B.
> They ripped off my clothes and started raping me. They
> didn't spare my mouth or my anus. When this man Marijan
> came [toward me], I asked him, "What are you doing to us?"
> He [cursed me]. He threatened to kill my sons if I told
> anyone about the rape.

L.L. identified several of her rapists by name. They were Marijan
Brnić, Jozo Barukčić, Jozo's father, Martin Barukčić, another Martin Barukčić,
Ilija Jurić, and Ilija Glavaš. According to L.L.:

> The fifteen men were going from one woman to another.
> They kept me there until 5:30 that morning. They made me
> leave the house naked. Marijan kicked me from behind and
> told me to walk home through the fields. I said I couldn't,
> and he cursed me and said, "You survived fifteen of us and
> you can't walk home?"

L.L. reported the rapes to the Croatian police in Novi Grad. The
police took her to a doctor in Odžak and arrested the rapists. According to
L.L., Croats[28] accused the police of defending "Četniks"[29] and attacked the
police station. The rapists were later released.

Rape has been described as part of the "spoils of war." However, in
Bosnia-Hercegovina, this abuse has been used as a weapon of war against the

---

[28] The witness did not specify if the Croats were members of the armed forces, the
police or civilians.

[29] During the Second World War, Serbian forces loyal to the Serbian king fought
against the Croatian fascists known as Ustaša, Tito's communist Partisans, and at times
with and against the Nazis. The main objective of the Četniks was the restoration of
the Serbian monarchy and the creation of a Greater Serbia. Feared for their brutality,
the Četniks committed atrocities against non-Serbs and Serbs opposed to their policies
in Bosnia-Hercegovina, Croatia and Serbia. Croats and Muslims both in Croatia and
Bosnia-Hercegovina commonly refer to Serbian military and paramilitary forces engaged
in the current wars in Croatia and Bosnia-Hercegovina as "Četniks." The Yugoslav
army and some Serbian paramilitary groups vehemently reject the label "Četniks,"
claiming they are merely defenders of their people and their land and that they are not
extremists. Others, such as paramilitary units loyal to the ultra-right wing former leader
of the Serbian Radical Party, Vojislav Šešelj, commonly refer to themselves as Četniks.

civilian population. In Bosnia, all parties to the conflict have raped civilian women of the "enemy" ethnic group, but the use of rape by Bosnian Serb forces' has been particularly widespread and designed to further the policy of ethnic-cleansing. By attacking and terrorizing individual women, Serb soldiers and paramilitary forces send the message to the entire community that no one is or will be safe from violence. As a result, entire families and villages have fled.

RAPE IN SOMALIA

Since early 1991, when the twenty-one-year dictatorship of former president Mohamed Siad Barre was overthrown by the United Somali Congress (USC), Somalia has been rocked by civil war as rival ethnic factions have attempted to take control.[30] Throughout the Somali conflict, rape has been used as a weapon of war by all the factions to punish rival ethnic factions. The complete breakdown of the government and the ensuing crisis has allowed these factions' combatants to rape women with impunity. The country continues to be in crisis despite the two-year intervention of United States and United Nations peacekeeping operations which unsuccessfully attempted to end the fighting. The withdrawal of the United Nations Operation in Somalia (UNOSOM) in March 1995 has once again opened up the possibility of intensified fighting among the various clan leaders and with that, the likelihood that widespread rape will continue.

Rivalry continues between self-proclaimed "interim president" Mohammed Ali Mahdi Mohammed and Gen. Mohammed Farah Aideed. Ali Mahdi, a politician of the Abgal clan, nominally heads the Somali Salvation Alliance (SSA) and controls the North Mogadishu and Middle Shebelle region. General Aideed, of the Habr Gedir subclan of the Hawiye clan, heads the Somalia National Alliance (SNA) and controls South Mogadishu and other parts of the area between the south's two rivers. The area of Kismayu is controlled by Mohamed Siad Hersi "Morgan" of the Harti subclan who heads the Somali Patriotic Movement. Another faction is headed by Col. Ahmed Omar Jess of the Ogadeni subclan. All the rival groups have forcibly consolidated control over resources and transportation routes through

---

[30] The following material was adapted from Human Rights Watch/Africa, "Somalia Faces the Future: Human Rights in a Fragmented Society," *A Human Rights Watch Short Report,* vol. 7, no. 2 (April 1995).

indiscriminate killings, selective assassinations and executions, forced displacement, and the widespread use of rape as a weapon of terror and intimidation. All of these abuses appear in patterns that reflect discriminatory treatment along clan lines.

A staggering number of rapes, as well as abductions of women and forced marriages, have occurred during the civil war, particularly during the fighting of 1991-1992 but by no means confined to those years. Somali women are targeted with sexual abuse when marauding clan-based militias—or *moryan* raiders—loot or forcibly occupy territories inhabited by members of rival clans. Women who lack the protection of powerful clan structures or who belong to particularly vulnerable groups, such as ethnic minorities, are particularly at risk. The tens of thousands of Somali women who live in displaced persons camps are also susceptible to sexual abuse.

Protection from and remedies for abuses, where available, depend almost exclusively on clan affiliation. The absence of a central government, and the ensuing violence and chaos, has resulted in virtually no recourse for women who have been raped. In some areas, local authorities have agreed to impose either traditional forms of judgment and punishment for crimes, or *shari'a* (Islamic law). However, the ability of women to seek redress depends on whether her subclan is militarily strong enough to petition a rival clan on her behalf. As a result, most perpetrators of sexual violence enjoy total impunity.

The enormous toll of the famine and war that peaked in 1992 had Baidoa, in Bay region, as its virtual epicenter, with women and children predominant among the dead. The women who have survived, many of them displaced by the conflict and living in and around Baidoa, are vulnerable both to a renewal of the conflict and to the everyday threat of sexual abuse. Members of a Somali organization for displaced people in Baidoa described rape as a frequent threat to women in the region. In a Bay region women's association visited by Human Rights Watch in October 1993, the members estimated that about three-quarters of their approximately 500 members had been raped.[31]

In the Benadir region, which includes the capital Mogadishu, "the moryan rape indiscriminately."[32] One woman told Human Rights Watch that

---

[31] Interviews, members of women's group, Baidoa, Somalia, January 24, 1995, and October 1993. All names withheld by Human Rights Watch unless otherwise indicated.

[32] Interview, Somali official, Nairobi, Kenya, January 19, 1995.

she had witnessed a raid in August 1994, when she was in Jowhar, to the north of Mogadishu in Middle Shebelle region, in which "Abgal gunmen crossed the main road and raped numerous Galgaal women." In Kismayu, a health officer stressed that "mothers and children suffer worst in war."[33]

A Baidoa women's organization established a cooperative in April 1993 in order to create employment for the women in town. The program now has sixty-five women participating in training and income-generating activities. It also runs a school. Most of the members have small children, and 40 percent are widows; most survive by collecting firewood or engaging in local trading. The displaced are mostly members of the Hariin subclan of the Rahanweyne and have little protection from rape:

> One woman from the organization—who is now in hospital—was looking for firewood when she was raped by sixteen men. She couldn't walk and was left for two days until she was discovered. This was in November 1994. . . She lives in BP1, one of the displaced camps in Baidoa. She is Hariin, as are most of the women in the displaced camps. Subclan fighting devastated the Hariin, especially at the hands of the Hadamo subclan of the Rahanweyne.[34]

The women's vulnerability to sexual assault is compounded by the long walks in isolated areas required by their struggle to survive. According to the women interviewed, each woman usually requires six trips a day to bring water for their family and to the market to sell. The firewood collection often requires a walk of up to fifteen kilometers out of the center of town. Rape is always a danger: "men wait for them to leave the camp."[35]

In the course of research in Somalia in October 1993, Human Rights Watch received accounts of rape by all the Somali factions. A forty-year-old woman in a camp for displaced persons in the Bay region gave the following account of an attack by Marehan militia:

> The Marehan killed, looted, raped and kidnapped women. As far as I know, about sixty women were taken. I know

---

[33] Interview, U.N. health officer, Kismayu, Somalia, January 24, 1995.

[34] Interview, members of the women's program, Baidoa, Somalia, January 24, 1995.

[35] Ibid.

them personally. They even took one of my daughters...She is nineteen years old. [She] is now in Kenya...She was forcibly married to a Marehan, a gunman.[36]

Testimonies about the activity of Aideed's forces in 1992 were similar. A fifty-two-year-old Rahanweyne woman from Baidoa interviewed in the Bay region during October 1993 said, "The Aideed forces came and took Baidoa from the Marehan by force...Where they found Marehan people were staying, they raped the women and killed many people." A twenty-two-year-old Elai woman from Jawarey, a village between Saco Weyne and Bardera, recalled:

I was in the market early in the morning when people started shooting both in the air and at people. It was the Aideed militia, all Hawiye. They raped many women. They looted the market stalls of money, clothes, and sugar. That is what they came for. Not grain or anything else. Then they moved through the town collecting all the animals they could find. Many more women were raped.[37]

A forty-year-old man from the Darod, interviewed in Gedo region during October 1993, told of an attack by the Ajuran, a Hawiye clan: "They raped many women and then killed some of them. They did not take any captives." An Ajuran woman of about the same age from Middle Juba region, interviewed in October 1993, described an attack by other Hawiye soldiers. She said, "They took about ten women to care for the animals that they stole. I have not seen any of them again. They raped nearly all the women."[38]

Other women of the Rahanweyne described attacks by Ogadeni militia. One, from the Leisan clan, described how women were forced to betray their husbands or face being raped: "Nine of ten women were raped. When they came to the village, they asked the women where the men, the livestock, and the grain were. If the woman didn't answer, she got raped. If she did, she had to escort the soldiers to the food or livestock or the husband."[39]

---

[36] Interview, Baidoa, Somalia, October 1993.
[37] Interview, Gedo region, Somalia, October 1993.
[38] Ibid.
[39] Interview, Baidoa, Somalia, October 1993.

A UNOSOM official gave Human Rights Watch examples of cases in Gedo region, gathered during a UNOSOM visit to the area in October 1993. Early that month, a woman was raped by more than twenty men on the road from Bardera to Baidoa; the previous week, when a group of women was stopped on the same road, the Rahanweyne women were singled out and raped.[40]

The women of vulnerable communities, notably the non-Somali minority known as the Bantu (or Gosha), are particularly vulnerable to sexual abuse, because their communities fall outside the Somali clan structure, fail to field their own militias, and are accorded low social status by ethnic Somalis. A Rahanweyne official told Human Rights Watch the Bantu suffered because "many believe that the Bantu are inferior, and think they shouldn't have rights."[41] One observer described this attitude toward Bantus as placing them largely outside traditional systems of arbitration and compensation:

> There are constant compensation meetings between elders—agreeing blood money—that are very elaborate. The individual receives money after the clan negotiates in an everyday process. But social status dictates level of recompense; it is not a process of equals. The Bantus can't take advantage of these processes.[42]

Members of the Bantu agricultural communities of the Juba river area described rape as routine for raiders who loot, intimidate and sometimes kill the rural population. When militia from clans seeking to take over an area raid Bantu communities, rape is endemic. "The number of rapes is so large, it is uncountable. Rapes happen during attacks, as well as against women in the fields."[43] One case was cited of a person killed in 1994 for having tried to stop the rape of his wife:

> Mohammed Sekondo was killed in Fagan village in Jamaame District. He was killed by Ogadenis. Abdi "Dhere" is the militia man who killed him. Abdi tried to rape Mohammed's wife, and Mohammed said "You will never rape my wife in

---

[40] Interview, UNOSOM official, Gedo region, Somalia, October 1993.
[41] Interview, U.N. aid officer, Baidoa, Somalia, January 22, 1995.
[42] Interview, aid officer, Nairobi, Kenya, January 21, 1995.
[43] Interview, Bantu displaced persons, Kismayu, Somalia, January 29, 1995.

front of me,"' so then Abdi shot him. The leader of the
Ogadeni militia responsible for this is Ahmed Hanshi, a
Mohammed Zubeir [an Ogadeni subclan] commander. They
are trying to move Bantus off their land; they loot and tell
Bantus to leave. This is only happening northwest of Gelib.
The attacks are usually carried out by twenty or more
men.[44]

For Somali women who have suffered rape, there is virtually no
recourse. Protection, compensation and justice are in many areas strictly
applied on the basis of one's clan identity. Traditional means of arbitration
between clan elders has been revived in many areas to provide some means of
redress for both abuse by rival authorities and common crime—but they only
work so long as a victim of abuse has a subclan strong enough to act on her
behalf. A leader of a women's group noted, "No one has dealt with rape: not
UNOSOM, the elders or the police. No one believes the woman's testimony
over the man."[45] In some cases, the woman's clan can seek monetary
restitution from the offending clan. But in most cases, the woman herself does
not receive the damages paid; the money is given to the male relatives of the
family.
    The lack of a state legal system has led many Somali women to
support the imposition of traditional shari'a. They believe that the shari'a
penalties for rape are effective both as a method of holding rapists accountable
and as a deterrent. A leader of a women's group working with Rahanwayne
displaced in Baidoa, for example, told us, "All of the women support shari'a,
because it would mean that rape would be severely punished: if a man rapes
a woman, he will be beaten badly the first time and killed the second."[46] The
same women told us that, in their view, a Somali interpretation of shari'a
would adapt to Somali tradition.:

> Shari'a supports women's rights. Inheritance is fair under
> shari'a—it recognizes women's rights. It allows Muslim
> women to go outside the house and have jobs. The branch
> of Islam in Sudan is different than in Somalia. If women

---

[44] Ibid.
[45] Ibid.
[46] Interview, leader of a women's organization, Baidoa, Somalia, January 24,
1995.

don't want to cover themselves in Somalia, there is no
problem. Women are collecting water, tending livestock;
they can't wear heavy clothes covering themselves up.[47]

Other sources in Baidoa told Human Rights Watch that elders and
religious leaders are presently discussing shari'a, and that "the restrictions on
women wouldn't be compulsory."[48] Bantu community leaders also saw
shari'a as effective in reducing sexual abuse: "When the fundamentalists came
into the area, they reduced the problems; rapists are afraid of the
fundamentalists, who were preaching that it was against Islam."[49]

Now that the international community has withdrawn from Somalia,
Somalis face the task of bringing the war to an end. There has been some
limited progress toward political reconstruction, particularly at the local level.
Subclans have in some cases taken steps to limit or withdraw support for their
warleaders, as measures to promote cross-clan reconciliation. In other areas,
local religious or authority structures have been reestablished. However, these
traditional structures are limited. They frequently carry the potential for abuse
of personal power in the absence of a national system of law, and their
presence is easily destabilized by renewed violence in an area. Ultimately,
protection from rape and the establishment of mechanisms of accountability
for perpetrators of rape can only come with an end to the conflict and the
restoration of civil society in Somalia.

RAPE IN HAITI

The military *coup d'état* against President Jean-Bertrand Aristide on
September 30, 1991, plunged Haiti into a maelstrom of state-inflicted and
state-sanctioned human rights abuses.[50] These abuses included numerous
political assassinations, arbitrary arrests and detentions, and the torture of
prisoners. Following the coup d'état, military authorities suspended virtually
all constitutionally guaranteed rights and procedures. By late 1993

---

[47] Ibid.

[48] Ibid.

[49] Interview, Bantu displaced persons, Kismayu, Somalia, January 29, 1995.

[50] The following material was adapted from Human Rights Watch and National
Coalition for Haitian Refugees, "Rape in Haiti: A Weapon of Terror," *A Human Rights
Watch Short Report*, vol. 6, no. 8 (July 1994).

documented cases of politically motivated rape, massacres, forced disappearance, and violent assaults on entire neighborhoods had increased greatly.

Both women and men suffered abuse at the hands of the military and police forces, their armed civilian auxiliaries—commonly known as *attachés*—and bands of thugs called *zenglendos*.[51] The Front for the Advancement and Progress of Haiti (Front pour l'Avancement et le Progrès d'Haïti, FRAPH) also was implicated in gross abuses of human rights, including assassinations and forced disappearances, arson and a massacre.[52] Like men, women were killed, arrested for their actual or imputed political views, beaten while in detention, forced into internal hiding (called *marronage*), disappeared, and denied the most basic civil and political rights to free expression, humane treatment, and due process.

Reports from women's rights groups in Haiti revealed that women were also targeted for abuse in ways and for reasons that men were not. Uniformed military personnel and their civilian allies threatened and attacked women's organizations for their work in defense of women's rights and subjected women to sex-specific abuse ranging from bludgeoning women's breasts to rape. Rape also was a part of apparently random violence committed by bands of zenglendos. Social unrest, which was both fostered

---

[51] According to the UN/OAS International Civilian Mission, the word zenglendo "denotes criminals who are recruited from groups ranging from the marginal societal strata found in working-class districts to police officers themselves usually acting at night, in civilian clothes and with official weapons." *Interim Report by the International Civilian Mission to Haiti* for the period of 9 February - 31 May 1993, A/47/960, p. 8.

[52] In the second half of 1993, bands of civilian thugs armed by the Haitian military were fashioned into the quasi-political organization known as the Front for the Advancement and Progress of Haiti (FRAPH). FRAPH's membership includes long-time Duvalierists, as well as Tontons Macoutes, attachés, and other army supporters. The organization's co-founders were Jodel Chamblain, a former Tonton Macoute, and Emmanuel Constant, the son of an army commander under François Duvalier (Papa Doc). From early 1992 to early 1994, Emmanuel Constant was a paid CIA informant. FRAPH was nurtured by the military from its emergence in September 1993. For details on FRAPH's involvement in human rights abuses, see Human Rights Watch/Americas and National Coalition for Haitian Refugees, "Terror Prevails in Haiti: Human Rights Violations and Failed Diplomacy," *A Human Rights Watch Short Report*, vol. 6, no. 5 (April 1994).

and exploited by the military authorities in order to repress opposition to their rule, contributed to increased levels of seemingly random violence.

In February 1994 Human Rights Watch conducted a joint fact-finding mission to Haiti with the National Coalition for Haitian Refugees to investigate reports that state agents were using rape as a political weapon against women. We interviewed women's rights activists, human rights monitors, officials of various governments, journalists, doctors and women victims of sexual assault.

The investigative efforts of the United Nations/Organization of American States' International Civilian Mission (MICIVIH) substantiated reports of state agents engaging in the rape of perceived political opponents. The mission's October 1993 report included several instances of rape. Further, between January 1994 and June 1994, MICIVIH collected evidence of another sixty-six rapes "of a political nature."[53] In a separate investigation conducted from May 16 through 20, 1994, the Inter-American Commission on Human Rights documented first-hand twenty instances of rape by the military and its auxiliaries. We documented first-hand nearly a dozen additional rape and attempted rape cases in the period between August 1992 and February 1994, including instances of vaginal and anal rape, one case of a woman who became pregnant as a result of her assault, and one case of a woman who died as a result of vaginal hemorrhaging following rape.

Human Rights Watch and the National Coalition for Haitian Refugees found that military forces and attachés used rape and sexual assault to punish and intimidate women for their actual and imputed political beliefs, or to terrorize them during violent sweeps of pro-Aristide neighborhoods. Rape also functioned as punishment for the political beliefs and activities of the victims' male relatives. In one instance, a woman was raped not only because of her suspected political affiliation and her gender, but also seemingly because of the fact that she was light brown-skinned.

To our knowledge, the military authorities never publicly denounced these practices or fully disciplined state agents known to have engaged in them. The military authorities' use and tolerance of rape made rape victims reluctant to report such abuse; victims feared that lodging a complaint would only further endanger their own and their family's lives, as they did not expect to see their attackers caught or disciplined. According to former President of the Haitian Supreme Court André Cherilus, it was "not worthwhile for the

---

[53] See UN/OAS International Civilian Mission in Haiti, Press Release, Ref. CP/94/28, June 17, 1994; Press Release, Ref. CP/94/20, May 19, 1994; Press Release, Ref. CP/94/8, March 21, 1994.

victim of rape to go to the police to report the crime in the current situation. It would be even worse for the woman, given the extremely high probability of retaliation."[54]

The participation of state agents and their armed civilian auxiliaries in the rape of women violated Haiti's international obligations to refrain from persecuting its citizens for their political beliefs and from subjecting them to torture and other cruel, inhuman or degrading treatment.[55] Further, the military authorities' failure to investigate and prosecute rape and other violence against women, especially where state or state-supported actors were involved, violated domestic and international guarantees of due process and equal protection under law for all citizens.[56]

In the early morning hours of September 18, 1994, U.S. President Bill Clinton deployed U.S. troops to begin an occupation of Haiti, after former President Jimmy Carter, U.S. Senator Sam Nunn and Gen. (Ret.) Colin Powell had flown to the island and secured Lt. Gen. Raoul Cédras's promise to renounce power. On October 15, 1994, Haitian President Jean-Bertrand Aristide returned to Haiti after a three-year exile. American troops had forced all members of the ruling triumvirate—Cédras, Brig. Gen. Philippe Biambi, and Lt. Gen. Michel François—to renounce power and leave the country, and had secured all military installations and disarmed many of the military and paramilitary forces in the country, in preparation for Aristide's return and a peaceful return to democracy. The Haitian triumvirate was allowed to retire from the army with full military honors; economic sanctions against Haiti were lifted; participants in the coup that had deposed Aristide in 1991 were given a general amnesty. In April 1995 U.N. international troops took over responsibility for maintaining security in the country.

Efforts to investigate the human rights violations that took place in Aristide's absence are just beginning. Prior to his return to Haiti, Aristide characterized the rapes against Haitian women during the coup years as ". . .

---

[54] Telephone interview, May 25, 1994.

[55] These rights are protected by the International Covenant on Civil and Political Rights (ICCPR), the Convention against Torture and Other Cruel, Inhuman or Degrading Treatment or Punishment, and the Convention on the Elimination of all Forms of Discrimination against Women (CEDAW).

[56] The 1987 Haitian Constitution, Chapter II, Section A, Article 19 obliges the state to "guarantee the right to life, health, and respect of the human person for all citizens without distinction in conformity with the Universal Declaration of Human Rights."

a crime against humanity as serious as any other."[57]   Nevertheless, nine months after Aristide's return from exile, not one rape committed during the coup has been investigated and tried.[58]   A National Commission for Truth and Justice began its work on April 1, with a six-month mandate, renewable for three additional months. The commission, created by presidential decree, is to investigate violations of human rights committed between September 29, 1991 and October 15, 1994. Article 3 of the commission's charter reiterates its commitment to investigate politically motivated, gender-based crimes against women. Nevertheless, substantive investigations into allegations of human rights abuses have yet to begin because of poor funding and lack of a clear mandate. Ultimately, the commission's effectiveness may be minimal because it has no judicial authority and is limited to making public recommendations.

Upon returning to Haiti, Aristide created a Ministry on the Status and Rights of Women. The ministry is responsible for, among other things, the coordination and implementation of policies aimed at promoting the rights of women; the facilitation of women's access to education, health, economic opportunity, and professional training; and coordinating of policies aimed at preventing violence against women. We hope that the ministry, headed by Dr. Lise Marie Dejean, will be able to address and remedy the concerns we delineate in this report regarding the bias inherent in the criminal code regarding rape and the general inadequacy of the judicial system to respond fairly to rape claims. We urge Minister Dejean to demand accountability for rapes committed during the coup years and to ensure that obstacles to reporting rape are eliminated.

The military officers who ousted Jean-Bertrand Aristide in September 1991 withstood international efforts to unseat them for over three years, skirting a U.N.-mandated oil and arms embargo and reneging on the U.S.-brokered Governors Island Accord of July 3, 1993, which was designed to induce the military high command to step down and to restore Aristide to power by October 30, 1993.[59]

---

[57] Radio speech by exiled President Jean-Bertrand Aristide from the U.S., recorded in Washington, D.C. on July 23, 1994.

[58] Telephone interview, Haitian women's rights activist, May 19, 1995. All names withheld by Human Rights Watch unless otherwise indicated.

[59] The Governors Island Accord called for Aristide to propose a new prime minister; the Haitian Parliament to approve the nominated prime minister; sanctions to be lifted,

(continued...)

After the unraveling of the Governors Island Accord, repression escalated unchecked, most notoriously with the high-profile political assassinations of Aristide's Justice Minister Guy Malary on October 14, 1993, and political supporter Antoine Izméry on September 11, 1993.[60] The military provided Haiti's only police, even though the 1987 Haitian Constitution mandates the separation of civilian police and the military.[61]

The onslaught after the failure of the Governors Island Accord created increasing numbers of internally displaced people, described as "in hiding" or "en marronage." The forced displacement of tens if not hundreds of thousands of Haitians was part of the military's strategy to destroy all forms of social and political organization. Men were the majority of those driven into hiding, and women often were kept from taking this drastic, but often life-saving, measure by their responsibility for their children. Thus women became *de facto* single parents, forced to shoulder the economic burden that marronage created and to live with the uncertainty of not knowing whether their husbands or partners were alive or dead.

In late August 1994 the situation further deteriorated, including the August 28 assassination of the Rev. Jean-Marie Vincent, a close adviser to Aristide. The perpetrators of the attack have not been identified, although the assassination was thought to have been politically motivated. In a last-ditch effort to persuade Haiti's military leaders to leave peacefully, a U.S. delegation led by former President Jimmy Carter flew to Haiti on September 17 to deliver an ultimatum. Finally, on September 18, 1994, after the delegation had secured Cédras's promise to step down, President Clinton authorized the deployment of U.S. troops to occupy Haiti, precipitating the end of the three-year military dictatorship. President Aristide returned to office on October 15,

---

[59](...continued)
after the approval of the new prime minister; foreign aid to be resumed to Haiti; a presidential amnesty to be granted for those military figures involved in the coup d'état against Aristide, within the parameters of the 1987 constitution; the military high command to resign, allowing Aristide to name a replacement who would then go on to restaff the high command; and President Aristide to return to power on October 30, 1993.

[60] See Human Rights Watch/Americas and National Coalition for Haitian Refugees, *Terror Prevails in Haiti*.

[61] The Governors Island Accord also required that a separate civilian police force be trained and operate independent of the military.

1994, to reorganize his cabinet and plan for local and parliamentary elections in June 1995.

Women under the Cédras Regime

During the military crackdown, women often were targeted for sex-specific forms of abuse. Women left behind when men were driven into hiding were terrorized and attacked by local section chiefs, attachés and uniformed soldiers. Women's rights organizations were intimidated or destroyed, and women's rights activists reported being attacked with beatings on the breasts and abdomen. Increasingly, the military's weapon of choice was rape. The UN/OAS civilian mission in Haiti underscored this in a press release:

> The OAS/UN International Civilian Mission continues to be strongly concerned about the emergence of rape as a tool of political repression . . . . the scenario is always substantially the same. Armed men, often military or FRAPH members, burst into the house of a political activist they seek to capture. When he is not there and the family cannot say where he is, the intruders [sexually] attack his wife, sister, daughter or cousin.[62]

Women suffered human rights abuses not only as those left vulnerable by the high level of marronage, but also as those who fought against repression and defended women's human rights through participation in women's organizations. Women's rights groups were targets of political repression after the coup d'état as a part of an overall strategy of the military authorities to uproot and close down all popular organizations. All the women's rights groups with which we spoke reported a sharp decrease in membership following the coup d'état, citing their members' fear of being associated with any popular organization, regardless of its political or social agenda.

Women's rights activists also reported specific attacks. The head of one Haitian women's rights organization reported that her house was ransacked and that, in September 1993, she received a late-night telephone call, in perfect French, from a man identifying himself as being aligned with the military authorities. He threatened to rape her if she continued her work on behalf of

---

[62] UN/OAS International Civilian Mission in Haiti, Press Release, Reference CP/94/20, May 19, 1994.

women.[63]   The headquarters of another Haitian women's rights group was burned down in the early morning hours of December 13, 1993. Although this office was one of several in a building, it was the only office completely destroyed by the fire.[64]

Members of another women's rights group reported that they received numerous accounts of their members being targeted for violence. This was so especially in the countryside, where activists were more easily identified. They believed that "this repression is especially directed at women because in this society women have no right to organize."[65]

Interviews with women's right groups in Port-au-Prince also revealed a startling picture of women activists being attacked in sex-specific ways, including rape and beatings of their breasts and abdomens. One activist told us that her fellow organizers often were "beaten in their female parts—primarily their breasts and abdomen."[66]   On November 21, 1993, Alourdes Metayer was arrested by soldiers in Gonaïves and beaten so badly in the abdomen that she miscarried.[67]   Members of one Haitian women's rights group recounted another assault in which soldiers beating a woman told her, "We'll beat you until you can't have kids, until you can't have kids like yourself [activist]."[68]

Sexual Assault

The greatest number of rapes documented by Human Rights Watch and the National Coalition for Haitian Refugees were committed by attachés, followed by rapes committed by police and soldiers, and then by rapes committed by zenglendos. Although crimes committed by zenglendos are not clearly attributable to the military, rape committed by zenglendos is reported here because these crimes flourished under a cover of impunity assured by the military authorities.

---

[63] Interview, Port-au-Prince, February 16, 1994.

[64] Interview, members of the women's rights group KAY FANM, Port-au-Prince, February 11, 1994.

[65] Interview, Port-au-Prince, February 16, 1994.

[66] Interview, Port-au-Prince, February 11, 1994.

[67] Human Rights Watch/Americas and National Coalition for Haitian Refugees, *Terror Prevails in Haiti*, p. 31.

[68] Interview, Port-au-Prince, February 16, 1994.

Assault by Military Agents

Assaults on women in their homes often were accompanied by the destruction of the house and personal belongings and assaults on other family members. Such search and destroy missions were carried out by the military, often with the assistance of FRAPH and other armed groups.

Previous to Aristide's return, no meaningful distinction existed between the military and the police. Both forces arrested citizens for common offenses as well as offenses against the state. Notes one expert on the Haitian military:

> . . . in Haiti the military forces are the police . . . . Even in major cities such as Port-au-Prince and Cap-Haïtien the police departments function as units of the army. In the vast majority of Haitian cities and villages, the military basically has a police function.[69]

The army thus maintained control of the investigatory and enforcement aspects of the justice system.

An attack on August 14, 1993 demonstrates how the military—whether soldiers or police—and its civilian allies worked together. Two soldiers, one policeman, and two attachés, all armed with pistols and rifles, broke down the front door of M.B.'s home and shot their way through the house as M.B. and her family slept. The men were looking for her father-in-law, who was constantly seen around the neighborhood discussing how much he anticipated Aristide's return. When they were unable to find him, they robbed his family, shot his twenty-three-month-old granddaughter, attempted to rape his daughter-in-law, M.B., and molested her cousin. M.B. told us:

> My mother-in-law was downstairs sleeping with S.M., the baby who died. She got up and tried to warn us that there were intruders in the house. While she did this, the men entered the room where S., my husband's other child, and my cousin were sleeping. My cousin was seventeen and they tried to rape her, but they realized she had her period and left her alone. They were screaming, "Where is the old man?"

---

[69] Michel S. Laguerre, *The Military and Society in Haiti* (Knoxville, TN: The University of Tennessee Press, 1993), p. 125.

One of the armed civilians put a gun across my cousin's legs and molested her. He put his hands under her gown and felt her breasts, and rubbed his hands over her stomach and thighs.[70]

The soldiers and attachés then ransacked M.B.'s house, terrorized her family with threats, called them "*Lavalas*,"[71] slapped and beat her and threatened to shoot her husband. The soldiers and attachés emptied out sacks of flour and sugar from the family's store and filled them with radios and other items from the house. Although only two of the men wore uniforms, M.B. recognized another in civilian dress as a local policeman. M.B. told us:

I recognized the guy who was blocking the door of the bedroom, the one who pointed the gun at my husband. He was a policeman from the neighborhood and would buy goods from our little store. Although that night he was dressed in civilian clothes. They made me accompany them to the gate to let them out. By then it was about 4:00 a.m. or so. Once we arrived at the gate, one of the ones in uniform made me take off my underwear and was going to rape me. Luckily, I had my menstruation.

On the way out, the men warned M.B., "We know your father-in-law likes to talk about JBA. If Aristide comes back, we know you will seek revenge, but we will come back for you first."[72]

On August 15, a day after the baby's murder and the other assaults, M.B. and her family left their home and went into hiding, staying at different times with various family members. M.B. explained her reluctance to report the assaults to the police:

We never went to the police. There would have been no use doing this. It would just have resulted in more hardship and terror for the family, and we were all too shocked by my daughter's death and everything else that happened. We

---

[70] Interview, Port-au-Prince, February 14, 1994.

[71] *Lavalas* is the Creole word meaning "flood" or "landslide"; as used colloquially, it refers to the broad-based popular movement that elected President Aristide.

[72] "JBA" is a popularly-used nickname for President Aristide.

were more concerned with our safety and with preventing further problems.

M.B. declined to pursue an investigation because it would have been an "investigation involving the police basically investigating themselves, and that would only mean more bad news for me and my family."[73]

Given the overt and frequent involvement of law enforcement officials in rape and other forms of abuse, individual Haitians had nowhere to turn for help when they were attacked or when they witnessed attacks upon others. During our investigation, we obtained the following eyewitness testimony:

> As my friend and I were returning to our hotel one night in late January 1994, we heard a woman screaming at the top of her lungs. We stopped and looked over to where the sound was coming from and saw a mixture of about eight to ten armed civilians and police milling near a car and not responding to the screams. We did not approach the car. These were armed men and police. I felt incapable of doing anything. I could not see well into the car, but the screams were piercing, and it looked like there were at least two uniformed policemen inside the car raping a woman. I did not report what happened to the police. What would have been the use? They were the ones responsible. I can't even imagine what eventually happened to that woman.[74]

The October 1993 report on human rights in Haiti by the UN/OAS civilian mission includes several cases of soldiers raping women with impunity:

- • On June 10, a thirteen-year-old girl was raped by a corporal at the military post of Bayeux, Department of the North.
- • On July 24, a group of twenty armed men, some in uniform, surrounded the house of a Cité Soleil grass roots activist who was in hiding. Three went in and raped and threatened his wife.

---

[73] Interview, Port-au-Prince, February 14, 1994.
[74] Interview with foreigner who spoke on the condition of anonymity, Port-au-Prince, February 15, 1994.

- A sixteen-year-old girl was raped by a soldier from the barracks of Fort Liberté at Dérec, Department of the Northeast.[75]

Assault by Army Attachés

Since Haiti's army was disarmed by U.S. troops upon their arrival and later disbanded by Aristide, attachés, as an arm of the military, have ceased to exist. Many fled when U.S. forces invaded. Previous to Aristide's return, however, attachés were civilians employed, armed and directed by the military and police. Attachés were omnipresent and abused their enormous discretionary powers through murder, torture, arrests, beatings, extortion, imprisonment, and rape.

Interviews with Haitian human rights monitors, journalists and activists revealed a disturbing profile of attachés. According to one worker with the UN/OAS civilian mission in Haiti:

Although not a uniform practice, attachés are paid and carry an identification card. Some behavior is very common. They operate with absolute impunity or apparent acquiescence on the part of the military; they commit crimes in the presence of the military and police; they are heavily armed; and they act with an air of authority.[76]

In a country wracked by generalized lawlessness, repression and terror, it was at times difficult to know who was an attaché and who was not. The military authorities benefitted from keeping the identification of attachés as fluid as possible. In this way the military could intimidate the general population while disavowing any responsibility for the abuses committed by ubiquitous armed civilians.

F.F. was stopped and assaulted by two attachés on the evening of January 29, 1994. F.F., a twenty-six-year-old student, was an active supporter of President Aristide. She and her fellow students organized demonstrations in support of Aristide's policies while he was in office. The comments and actions of F.F.'s attackers illustrate the assumption made by the military,

---

[75] UN/OAS International Civilian Mission in Haiti, *Report on the Situation of Democracy and Human Rights in Haiti*, A/48/532, October 25, 1993, p. 18.

[76] Interview, William O'Neill, former legal director of the UN/OAS International Civilian Mission in Haiti, March 29, 1994.

attachés and others that residents of poor neighborhoods necessarily are Aristide supporters. She told us:

> It was about 7:00 p.m., and I was walking home from a visit at a friend's house. I saw two guys ahead of me and it looked like they were talking together. I tried to pass around them, and one of them grabbed my arm. . . . They both had guns and asked me where I was coming from. Then they threatened me, saying if I screamed out they would kill me.
>
> They asked me my name, where I lived, and what my political opinions were. When one asked about my political opinions, I thought to myself, "If he is just going to rob me why is he asking me this?" I said I was not political. They started looking through my purse, but I had no money and that is why I was walking. Then one said, "In the area where you live, I know you do not have any money, and I do not care what you say, I know everyone in your neighborhood supports Aristide."
>
> While we were standing there I heard a gunshot. One of the guys said, "What's that noise?" and the other responded, "It is just the sergeant killing someone who resisted." They proceeded to inquire more about my political beliefs, and they asked if I had a boyfriend, to which I responded, "Yes." Then one said, "I am going to rape you. Tell your boyfriend and your 'Father' [a reference to Aristide] that I am going to rape you."

Both men raped F.F. After the rape, one wanted to kill her to prevent her from identifying him later. The other succeeded in dissuading him. They told her to walk "normal like nothing has happened to you." Once out of their sight, F.F. did not stop running until she reached her home.

F.F., unlike most of the women interviewed, sought medical attention. Her Port-au-Prince gynecologist treated her with antibiotics to prevent infection and tested her for sexually transmitted diseases. She did not, however, report the rape to the police:

I did not file a police report. I would never speak to the
police. I have heard that it is worse when you talk to them.
You really risk your life going to talk to them, because
everyone knows they are part of the crime problem.[77]

Assault by Zenglendos

A UN/OAS civilian mission report described the role and origin of
zenglendos in Haitian society:

The term "zenglendos" is used to refer to members of armed
criminal groups, usually operating at night and particularly in
the slums and working-class districts of Port-au-Prince.
Some of this violence may be assumed to be purely criminal,
without political motivation. However, it is widely believed
in Haiti that even zenglendos operate under the cover, or
with the express tacit consent of the police, and that their
operation, while involving armed robberies, may also be
intended to intimidate the population of localities most
opposed to the post-coup authorities and committed to the
return of President Aristide.[78]

Many Haitians believe that the army encouraged and even participated
in zenglendo violence as a means of further terrorizing the civilian population.
A Haitian human rights attorney described the typical zenglendo as "an armed
thief who works with the complicity of the army."[79]   One Port-au-Prince
women's rights activist told us that she believes:

the military formed the zenglendos as a paramilitary force.
All these people are connected with the military—they just
do not have uniforms.   The police let armed civilians do
these things.   They create an atmosphere in which
lawlessness prevails.   It is to their advantage to have the
population cowed.[80]

---

[77] Interview, Port-au-Prince, February 16, 1994.

[78] UN/OAS International Civilian Mission in Haiti, *Report on the Situation of
Democracy and Human Rights in Haiti*, A/48/532, October 25, 1993, pp. 12-13.

[79] Telephone interview, Pierre Raynand, April 26, 1994.

[80] Interview, Port-au-Prince, February 16, 1994.

While it is difficult to ascertain the precise relationship of zenglendos to the military during the coup regime, there was a clear coincidence of interests and targets: violence attributed to zenglendos often targeted pro-Aristide activists who also were targeted by the army, and their violence was tolerated by the regime.

In one example of zenglendo violence, S.E., twenty-four, and R.A., seventeen, were raped and beaten by four zenglendos on September 21, 1993, in Port-au-Prince. That day, four armed civilians broke into a church during a prayer service, demanded the church's collection plate, kicked and threatened the parishioners, and demanded to know which of them was the pastor. The pastor of the church believes he was the actual target of the assault because he is a known Aristide partisan and keeps a picture of Aristide in his home. The pastor told us:

> They never asked for me by name. They kicked people and
> hit them with the butts of their rifles and with their fists.
> They also hit people in the head with their revolver butts.[81]

Eventually the men grabbed S.E. and R.A., took them outside the church, and assaulted them. According to the pastor, "The girls tried to resist, but two men each forced them. When they left with the girls, they said, 'You women who are watching, we are going to come back to get you to do the same.'"[82] According to S.E.:

> I was the second girl they chose. The other girl had been
> lying near me, and they chose her first. Before selecting her
> they said they were looking for a "grimelle."[83] They tried
> to force the other girl to walk, but she resisted. So they
> started pushing her and slapping her with their hands.
>
> They took us to a clearing not far from the church. They
> tried to rape me but could not succeed. One came upon me
> as if to rape me, but since I am a virgin, I was too tight to
> be entered. Two of the men tried to rape me, while the other
> two raped the other girl. When the second one did not

---

[81] Interview, Port-au-Prince, February 13, 1994.
[82] Ibid.
[83] Someone with a light-brown complexion.

succeed in entering me, he started to beat me. He started
hitting me with the butt of his pistol and with his fist. Then,
the other one joined in, hitting me in the head and breasts.
They also kicked me in the stomach and buttocks. When
they finally stopped beating me, they wanted to know where
the pastor was and if I was a supporter of Aristide like my
pastor. During this time, the other two were raping the other
girl. I could hear her screaming.[84]

After the rape, the men returned S.E. and R.A., both badly beaten and
traumatized by the assaults, to the church. The assailants had threatened to
"shoot up the place" if anyone came after them. Neither victim filed a police
report. They told us they were "putting their faith in God." The next week,
they both left for the provinces to stay with relatives.
    The pastor went into hiding for one month after the incident, taking
it as a warning.   While he was in hiding, armed civilians visited his
neighborhood searching for his house.

Impunity and the Non-Report of Rape
    The pattern of impunity for abuse perpetrated by both state and non-
state actors in Haiti was not unique to sexual assault. The Haitian military was
notoriously corrupt—characterized by one prominent social scientist as
"organized in practice, not in theory, on the basis of corruption . . . .
[C]orruption is found in the process at all levels, from promotions to post
assignments, and in the daily routine of military life."[85]
    The Haitian judicial system was widely regarded as corrupt and
dominated by the army. Following the 1986 flight from Haiti of Jean-Claude
(Baby Doc) Duvalier, each successive army-backed regime, despite lip service
to the need for judicial reform, presided over a system utterly lacking in due
process guarantees as well as dependent on and subservient to the military.[86]

---

[84] Interview, Port-au-Prince, February 15, 1994.

[85] Laguerre, *The Military and Society in Haiti*, p. 155.

[86] Emile Jonassaint, appointed president on May 11, 1994 by a group of
parliamentarians allied with the army, was appointed head of the Supreme Court after
the coup d'état against Aristide. For a detailed discussion of the Haitian legal system
and its historical domination by the executive and the army, see Lawyers' Committee
for Human Rights, *Paper Laws, Steel Bayonets: Breakdown of the Rule of Law in Haiti*
(New York: November 1990).

Judicial redress in ordinary criminal and civil proceedings was difficult to obtain. Few cases were adjudicated each year, and prisoners were commonly held for lengthy periods without a trial or sentence. The resolution of these cases often depended more on money or power than on justice. Since before the coup d'état, the police handicapped investigations by refusing to gather evidence. Moreover, the army interfered with the judicial process at every level, including the harassment and punishment of attorneys and judges for carrying out their duties.

While military authorities ruled Haiti, it was extremely unlikely that a victim of abuse by the military, police or others associated with the military authorities could expect justice. In fact, according to reports by Human Rights Watch and the National Coalition for Haitian Refugees and other human rights groups, despite an appalling record of human rights abuses over the past two and a half years, very few perpetrators have ever been held accountable.[87] Thus for victims of rape:

> A system that already is so rife with intimidation, bribery, corruption, and outside pressures cannot ensure that victims' rights will be respected, and that perpetrators of assaults will be punished in accordance with the law. Even in business disputes and other simple crimes, there is just too much room for something to go wrong.

> There is no reason for anyone, and especially a victim of rape, particularly if her assailants are the military, paramilitary forces, or anyone else even nebulously associated with the military, to believe that there is a chance for judicial redress. It just won't happen. Furthermore, the woman would probably be putting her life in danger. It is no accident that the justice system in Haiti does not work. The government [military authorities] has fostered this and benefits from it.[88]

---

[87] *See* Human Rights Watch/Americas and National Coalition for Haitian Refugees, *Terror Prevails in Haiti*; Americas Watch and the National Coalition for Haitian Refugees, *Silencing a People: The Destruction of Civil Society in Haiti* (New York: Human Rights Watch, 1993).

[88] Telephone interview, William O'Neill, former director of legal services for the UN/OAS civilian mission, April 18, 1994.

In cases documented by the UN/OAS civilian mission, women trying to seek legal redress for rape were met by official indifference and incredulity. One woman, raped by attachés, told us that going to the police would be the equivalent of a "death wish." In general, the women feared that the perpetrators would discover that they were pressing charges and return to do them greater harm.

Not everyone we interviewed shared this point of view. The president of the Port-au-Prince Bar Association, Louis Gary Lissade, told us that he believed strongly that any woman who had been raped by a soldier or attaché could go to the police to report her assault, would be appointed legal representation and could proceed with her trial. However, Mr. Lissade also added that the justice system was "weak" in general and that the investigation of a rape is affected by the wealth of the family:

> If a [raped] woman belongs to a wealthy family, the family
> will finance the investigation. They can put a car and money
> at the disposition of the police. The policemen will have an
> incentive to conduct a thorough investigation. However, if
> the women is from the lower class and does not know the
> author of the rape, the police will have no car, no gas
> [because of the embargo]. It is all so expensive. It will be a
> difficult situation for the girl.[89]

Since Aristide's return, although the Haitian army has been disbanded and the interim police force is civilian-controlled, the justice system is being evaluated in preparation for reform but as yet does not provide meaningful protection of due process or guarantee expeditious trials. In the meantime, to our knowledge, not one case of politically-motivated rape has been investigated, tried, or prosecuted.

Failure to Investigate

Despite the risks of abuse and harassment, as reported by the UN/OAS civilian mission, some women did report rape to the authorities during the coup regime. In theory, these cases should have been investigated by civilian authorities and tried in civilian courts. In practice, however, they were handled by the military, with the result that allegations of rape were seldom investigated formally and rapists were rarely brought to trial or punished for

---

[89] Telephone interview, May 4, 1994.

their crimes according to applicable law. The military's failure to ensure that rape cases were adjudicated by the proper civilian authorities clearly violated the 1987 Haitian Constitution, which specifies that conflicts between civilian and military personnel should be handled by civilian courts.

The UN/OAS civilian mission documented a case of rape committed by soldiers where the victim reported the assaults to military authorities who then conducted their own, informal investigations and never referred the cases to the civilian authorities.[90] In this case, a thirteen-year-old girl was raped in Bayeux, Department of the North, by a corporal at a military post. According to the UN/OAS civilian mission: "The military authorities first tried to dismiss the rape by saying that the girl was not a virgin. The corporal was eventually given a punishment of ten days' detention."[91] In a second case, a sixteen-year-old girl in the Department of the Northeast was raped by a soldier from the barracks of Fort Liberté. Her family took her to see a doctor who verified the rape and gave her a certificate of his diagnosis. The young woman's family presented all the evidence to a regional commander, who promised to order an investigation. According to the UN/OAS civilian mission's report, "The soldier was arrested for a few days and then released. He has been seen since, in uniform, circulating freely in the area."[92]

The results of the military-conducted investigations in these cases differed from the requirements of Haitian criminal law. In the case of the thirteen-year-old who was raped, according to the Haitian penal code, the soldier, if found guilty, would have been sentenced to imprisonment and hard labor.[93] In the case of the sixteen-year-old who was raped, the soldier, if found guilty, would have been sentenced to imprisonment from three to nine years. Moreover, because soldiers and police act as public guardians and hold positions of trust and power over Haitian citizens, they, if convicted of rape, would have been subject to more severe punishment for abusing their positions

---

[90] UN/OAS International Civilian Mission in Haiti, *Report on the Situation of Democracy and Human Rights in Haiti,* A/48/532, October 25, 1993, p.18.

[91] Ibid.

[92] Ibid.

[93] Article 279 of the Haitian penal code provides: "Whosoever commits the crime of rape, or who attempts other indecent assaults, whether consummated or attempted, involving violence against individuals of either sex, will be punished with imprisonment." Article 280 further provides: "If the crime is committed against a minor under the age of fifteen, the guilty will be subjected to punishment of hard labor of limited duration."

of authority or guardianship.[94]   Instead, the assailants in these two cases were detained for less than two weeks.

Practical Obstacles

When seeking redress for crimes committed against them, rape victims in Haiti confront not only the obstacle of a corrupt and ineffective judicial system, but also procedural hurdles which impede them from pursuing their charges of rape.   One such impediment is the difficulty women have in obtaining a certificate verifying sexual intercourse.   Haitian women alleging rape must provide a medical certificate from a doctor certifying that sexual intercourse took place.   However, the dearth of medical facilities and professionals in Haiti has made it extremely unlikely that alleged rape victims can collect the critical forensic evidence[95] and document injuries sustained during rape.   Without these evidentiary requirements, which are critical to the prosecution of rape cases, the survivors are denied due process.

In theory, women can go to local, public hospitals or clinics to obtain certification of intercourse.   In practice, in the rural areas outside of Port-au-Prince and Haiti's other larger cities, public hospitals or clinic facilities are scarce to non-existent.   Even where public hospital or clinic facilities are available, they are frequently undersupplied with materials and overwhelmed by the demand for services.

Given the lack of medical services available in public facilities, the only option for obtaining medical diagnosis and treatment for many women is with private doctors.   But many rape victims are unable to afford private medical attention.   Consequently, these women go untreated and their rape allegations go uninvestigated for lack of evidence.   According to one Haitian family law attorney, "It has always been a problem to prove a rape in Haiti. Material conditions prevent them [the women] from going to a doctor.   A woman who has been raped will probably not be seen at the Port-au-Prince General Hospital, since they tend to treat only grave injuries, and she would be forced to go to a clinic or private hospital."[96]

---

[94] Section IV, Article 279 states that "The punishment shall be a life sentence of forced labor if the guilty one is of the class of those who have authority over the person towards that which they have committed the attack, if they are primary school teachers or wage servants, or if they are civil servants or clergy...."

[95] During these exams, the doctor collects semen, public hair and other such evidence from the woman's vaginal area.

[96] Telephone interview, March 13, 1994.

The Port-au-Prince General Hospital currently is more capable of providing treatment for victims of rape because it is no longer overwhelmed by the injured victims of violence associated with the now replaced coup regime. Nevertheless, since physical evidence is essential to the prosecution of cases in Haiti and public clinics and hospitals are scarce, and many women lack the financial means to pay for such an exam, the Aristide government should make a commitment to ensure that victims of rape have immediate access to free medical attention to document the physical assault.

The Role of Discrimination and Stigma

At least four factors influenced the reporting and adjudication of rape cases which made it particularly difficult to obtain redress under the coup regime. Of these, two affected the general population as well: the fear of reprisal and the ineffectiveness of a military-dominated justice system. The remaining two, longstanding sex discrimination in the criminal justice system and the social stigma associated with rape, affected women victims of sexual assault in particular and may continue to affect women's access to justice for sex crimes.

Rape, under the Haitian penal code, is among those crimes considered to be "assaults on morals." This classification of rape reflects the perception that the harm inflicted by the assault consists of damage to the victim's morals or honor, rather than to her physical integrity and well-being.[97] The investigation and prosecution of rape thus routinely stress not the physical harm done to the woman but rather the status of her honor or morals. Consequently, women who allege rape must endure public scrutiny of their "morality"; the rape of a non-virgin may be considered a less serious offense because her honor is perceived to be already compromised. In the case of the thirteen-year-old raped in Bayeux described above, for example, military authorities tried to dismiss a rape accusation based on the assertion that the victim was not a virgin. In their eyes, her putative status as a non-virgin rendered her story not credible and meant that she could not be raped.

Assessing a woman's credibility in light of her sexual history reinforces the discriminatory standards by which men's and women's behavior are judged. Sexual behavior is considered normal for a man but is viewed as

---

[97] For a discussion of the biases reflected in rape laws, see generally Dorothy Q. Thomas and Regan E. Ralph, "Rape in War: Challenging the Tradition of Impunity," *The [Johns Hopkins University School of Advanced International Studies] SAIS Review*, vol. XIV, no. 1 (Winter-Spring 1994), pp. 81-99.

undermining a woman's honesty and as rendering her automatically sexually available. These different standards for assessing the behavior and credibility of women and men, when accepted by the courts, allow bias and discrimination to compromise the effective investigation and prosecution of women's allegations of rape.

Rape in Haiti, as in most of the world, is considered an extremely shaming act. Women, particularly unmarried women, do not want anyone to know that they have been raped. A Haitian human rights activist told us that when a girl is about to be married, both sides of the family are interested in her virginal status. If she is not a virgin, it is a "dishonor for the girl and especially for her family."[98]

Despite Haiti's return to democratic rule, we remain concerned that legal redress for rape may still be hampered by a biased criminal justice system. To date, there has been no substantive change in the criminal code that lists rape under such a misleading heading as "assaults on morals." Neither judges nor police have extensive training in how to handle rape cases. Absent necessary legal reform and training, women may continue to find themselves inhibited in bringing charges of rape, given the possibility that their character and comportment receive more attention than the crime committed against their physical integrity and personal dignity.

U.S. Policy

For months prior to helping restore Aristide to power, U.S. policy consisted of downplaying the human rights crisis in Haiti and turning back refugees fleeing by sea.[99] On April 12, 1994, for example, a cable from the U.S. Embassy in Port-au-Prince to Secretary of State Warren Christopher cast doubt on rising reports of human rights abuses, particularly reports of rape, and sought to discredit the work of human rights organizations monitoring the situation in Haiti.[100] Then, in response to criticism from human rights

---

[98] Telephone interview, March 18, 1994.

[99] For a comprehensive analysis of U.S. foreign policy in Haiti, see Human Rights Watch/Americas and National Coalition for Haitian Refugees, *Terror Prevails in Haiti*.

[100] Regarding rape, the cable read: "We are, frankly, suspicious of the sudden, high number of reported rapes, particularly in this culture, occurring at the same time that Aristide activists seek to draw a comparison between Haiti and Bosnia." The cablegram, written by human rights officer Ellen Cosgrove, approved by Ambassador William Swing and reviewed by in-country processing Refugee Coordinator Luis Moreno, was leaked to the U.S. press in early May.

groups, members of Congress, and the American civil rights community, President Clinton imposed sanctions against the Cédras regime, began screening refugees to determine their eligibility for political asylum, and acknowledged the severity of the human rights abuses in Haiti.

The Asylum Process

Review of Haitian asylum claims through In-Country Processing (ICP)—closed down since the invasion—was the only procedure available to fleeing Haitians. It was criticized as seriously flawed and incapable of providing consistently fair hearings for asylum applicants. The U.S. mischaracterization of the human rights situation skewed the asylum process at every stage. Human Rights Watch and the National Coalition for Haitian Refugees criticized the program's deficiencies, including its application of a stricter standard than that contemplated in the 1951 Convention Relating to the Status of Refugees and the apparent skepticism by U.S. interviewers regarding the veracity of Haitian claims of political persecution.[101]

Human Rights Watch and the National Coalition for Haitian Refugees were particularly concerned about the review of asylum claims involving rape. Numerous Haitian women sought political asylum on the grounds that they had been targeted and sexually assaulted as Aristide supporters. In February, the U.S. Embassy's refugee coordinator, Luis Moreno, estimated to Human Rights Watch that 25 percent of the principal applicants[102] for asylum were women and that approximately 5 percent of these claimed to have been raped for political reasons.[103]

In our February 1994 interview, Moreno assured us, "Everything possible is done to steer these cases to women case workers . . . and the case workers are quite sensitized to the problem." But, contrary to Moreno's assurances, the U.S. asylum process not only disregarded rape as a human rights abuse but also failed to understand its function as a tool of political persecution and hence its legitimacy as the basis for an asylum claim. Olen (Sam) Martin, who until June 1994 was the INS officer-in-charge in Port-au-Prince,[104] stated:

---

[101] Ibid.

[102] The "principal applicant" is the person whose name is on the asylum application, as opposed to dependent family members who, if the principal applicant were granted asylum, would also gain asylum.

[103] Interview, Port-au-Prince, February 8, 1994.

[104] He was replaced in June 1994 by Jean Christianson.

[The women] mostly blame attachés. I don't know if it is
true or not—it must be true in some cases, but women have
a tendency to blame the worst person they can think of to
justify why it happened. It's hard to sort out imagination and
what really happens. . . . They always say armed civilians,
but again, it's perception versus whether they are really
armed. . . . Attachés live in the same neighborhoods,
everyone knows everyone. There have been some [asylum]
cases approved based on a rape argument. [There can be]
story inconsistencies—if the husband is sitting there you can
figure it out. The way the woman acts when she tells the
story, etc.[105]

Martin apparently believed that rape was a basis for asylum only if it
was both politically motivated and premeditated:

If people really went after someone and did it, then the
victim [of rape] would certainly have a case. But you have
the intentionality question, did they set out to do it? We
look for why they [the alleged perpetrators] went there [to
the house]. If they went with the intent to rape, if it was an
attaché, etc. You see the section chiefs or the military
disputing with people over property, for example. The cases
are very complex.[106]

To our knowledge, no legal requirement exists that a victim of
persecution show that his or her attacker had formulated a premeditated intent
to commit assault of any kind. Rather, to make a successful asylum claim
under U.S. law, an individual must demonstrate a well-founded fear of
persecution based on his or her actual or imputed political opinion, or other
recognized status.[107] Thus an individual targeted by the military or its
civilian allies for actual or perceived support of Aristide should have his/her
asylum claim reviewed on the basis of his/her ability to establish these criteria
without distinction as to the type of abuse suffered—whether rape, beating or

---

[105] Interview, Port-au-Prince, February 11, 1994.
[106] Ibid.
[107] Also eligible for asylum are those who fear persecution on the grounds of race,
religion, nationality or membership in a particular social group.

arbitrary detention. This standard should be applied without discrimination and should not be altered in light of the kind of abuse underlying an asylum claim.

As the ICP program was administered, Human Rights Watch and the National Coalition for Haitian Refugees doubted that women victims of political violence could receive a fair asylum hearing. Misconceptions about how rape functions as a form of political or other persecution and the lack of clear guidelines as to how to assess rape for purposes as the basis of an asylum claim only hampered the process. These problems needed to be remedied for those involved in the new screening procedures outside of Haiti, as well as those who processed claims through ICP, so that female asylum-seekers would receive fair asylum hearings.

Overcoming such barriers to women's ability to receive fair asylum hearings requires acknowledging the nature of rape as a tool of political persecution. In a May 1993 decision, the U.S. Board of Immigration Appeals (BIA) granted asylum to a Haitian woman who alleged that she had been gang-raped by three soldiers after they broke into her family home and identified her as an Aristide supporter. BIA found that she had demonstrated a well-founded fear of persecution on the basis of political opinion because she "suffered grievous harm in direct retaliation for her support of and activities on behalf of Aristide." This is the first BIA decision that explicitly recognized rape as a form of grievous harm that could be imposed in retaliation for political activities.[108] In May 1995 BIA formally designated the case as a binding precedent for future asylum adjudication and thus officially acknowledged that women may suffer persecution in the form of rape.

In order to ensure that women's asylum claims are fairly interpreted and processed, Human Rights Watch and the National Coalition for Haitian Refugees also urged the INS to adopt guidelines to ensure that women's asylum claims received a full and fair hearing.[109] On May 26, 1995, the INS issued revised instructive guidelines for adjudication of asylum cases based wholly or in part on gender. These guidelines are intended to make the

---

[108] Deborah Anker, *Law of Asylum in the United States* (American Immigration Law Foundation, forthcoming winter 1996), p. 117. We are grateful to Ms. Anker for her assistance in locating and analyzing this case.

[109] See Nancy Kelly (Women Refugees Project), Deborah Anker (Women Refugees Project) and Michele Beasley (Women's Commission for Refugee Women and Children), "Proposed Guidelines for Women's Asylum Claims," presented to the Immigration and Naturalization Service on April 19, 1994. Human Rights Watch Women's Rights Project participated in the preparation of the proposed guidelines.

asylum process more responsive to the particular circumstances female claimants have encountered. The guidelines also explain how an asylum applicant's gender may determine the nature of her claim. In other words, the guidelines recognize that certain kinds of harm, such as rape, may be gender-specific and that, in other instances, women may be targeted for persecution because they are women. These guidelines represent an important step toward recognizing that abuses of women's human rights that drive them into flight from their home countries often are political in nature and may constitute a form of persecution.

Haiti's military regime presided over a campaign of human rights violations aimed at destroying all forms of opposition to its rule. As part of this campaign of terror, the military and its auxiliaries targeted women known or perceived to be Aristide supporters with sexual assault. Soldiers, police and attachés also attacked women activists working with women's rights organizations and other social or political groups. The military regime failed both to denounce rape committed by its agents and to punish those responsible. In this environment—where no one was held accountable for gross human rights abuses—women had no protection against rape and no way of seeking redress after they were assaulted.

Haiti's military regime compromised the integrity and autonomy of the entire criminal justice system. The police operated as part of the military, and both lawyers and judges were constantly harassed and intimidated by soldiers and police. Thus all aspects of law enforcement in Haiti—from investigation of reported crimes to trying alleged criminals—were controlled by the military, which was itself responsible for perpetuating and sanctioning abuse. As a consequence, rape victims knew that they could not expect full and fair investigation of crimes committed against them. Moreover, women feared retaliation at the hands of police should they attempt to report rape. These factors, and the fact that women are stigmatized as rape victims, made women extremely reluctant to report rape either to authorities or to those monitoring the human rights crisis in Haiti.

Nonetheless, reports of rape in Haiti under the Cédras regime pushed the international community and U.S. policy makers to recognize the function of rape and sexual assault as weapons of political persecution. We commend the efforts of the UN/OAS civilian mission and the Inter-American Commission on Human Rights to document and denounce rape as an instrument of repression. Their documentation was crucial to establishing the extent of the human rights crisis in Haiti and to identifying those responsible for abuse.

In the end, the U.S. government acknowledged the use of rape as a tool of political repression and apologized for casting doubt on the credibility of the reporting of U.S. human rights organizations. However, it first failed both to denounce rape adequately as a human rights abuse and to create conditions for the fair review of asylum claims based on sexual assault.

We urge that while the Haitian Truth Commission has dedicated itself to documenting and exposing human rights violations that took place in Aristide's absence, and while Aristide has created a Ministry on the Status and Rights of Women to address women's concerns and coordinate women's issues throughout the country, these efforts be supplemented by substantive changes to the criminal code and reform of the judicial system in Haiti to afford women victims of political, other persecution and crimes such as rape and sexual assault, legal redress. What is required is a mandate from Aristide's government reiterating the absolute necessity of implementing such changes.

INDIA: RAPE IN KASHMIR

Since the Indian government crackdown against militants in the disputed territory of Kashmir began in earnest in January 1990, both security forces and armed militants have used rape as a weapon: to punish, intimidate, coerce, humiliate and degrade.[110] Rape by Indian security forces most often occurs during crackdowns, cordon-and-search operations during which men are held for identification in parks or schoolyards while security forces search their homes. In these situations, the security forces frequently engage in collective punishment against the civilian population by assaulting residents and burning their homes. Rape is used as a means of targeting women whom the security forces accuse of being militant sympathizers; in raping them, the security forces are attempting to punish and humiliate the entire community.[111] Rape has also occurred frequently during reprisal attacks on civilians following militant ambushes. In many of these attacks, the selection of victims is seemingly arbitrary and the women, like other civilians assaulted or killed, are

---

[110] The following material was adapted from Asia Watch and Physicians for Human Rights, "Rape in Kashmir: A Crime of War," *A Human Rights Watch Short Report*, vol. 5, no. 9 (May 1993).

[111] Male detainees have been subjected to sexual molestation. For more on this see Asia Watch, *Kashmir Under Siege* (New York: Human Rights Watch, 1991), p. 73.

targeted simply because they happen to be in the wrong place at the wrong time.

Kashmiri militant groups have also committed rape. In some cases, militants have raped women whose family members were believed to be informers or supporters of rival groups. In other cases, women have been raped and killed after being held as hostages for their male relatives. Although some militant leaders have condemned these abuses and vowed to take action against those who have committed rape, few have been able to discipline their own members, and the abuses continue.

The significance of rape as a gender-specific form of abuse in Kashmir must be understood in the context of the subordinate status of women generally in South Asia, as in much of the rest of the world. Women who are the victims of rape are often stigmatized, and their testimony and integrity impugned. Social attitudes which cast the woman, and not her attacker, as the guilty party pervade the judiciary, making rape cases difficult to prosecute and leaving women unwilling to press charges.

Rape by Security Forces: The Pattern of Impunity

Reports of rape by Indian security forces in Kashmir emerged soon after the government's crackdown began in January 1990.[112]   Despite evidence that army and paramilitary forces were engaging in widespread rape, few of the incidents were investigated, and fewer still resulted in criminal prosecutions of the security agents involved.   In 1994, in response to international pressure, the government made public several courts-martial of soldiers accused of rape. In one case, on July 29, 1994, two soldiers were sentenced to twelve years in prison after being court-martialed for raping a village woman in Kashmir. However, the authorities have refused to prosecute many documented cases of rape, including the October 10, 1992, rape of nine women in Shopian.[113]   The findings of investigations ordered into many other incidents made never been made public, leaving the victims to believe that such abuse is committed with impunity.

---

[112] Numerous incidents of rape have been reported by Indian and Kashmiri human rights groups. See, for example, Committee for Initiative on Kashmir, *Kashmir Imprisoned* (Delhi: July 1990).

[113] For more on this case, see Asia Watch and Physicians for Human Rights, *The Human Rights Crisis in Kashmir: A Pattern of Impunity* (New York: Human Rights Watch, 1993), p. 102.

India's own criminal law makes torture a crime and explicitly prescribes punishments for members of the police or other security forces who have committed rape. Under Section 376(1) of the Indian Penal Code (IPC), a minimum term of seven years' imprisonment may be imposed for rape. In addition, the Criminal Law (Amendment) Act of 1983, which for the first time provided for the offense of custodial rape, prescribes a mandatory ten years' imprisonment for police officers who rape a woman in their custody.[114] The sentence may be extended to life, and may also include a fine. Commissioned officers of the paramilitary and military forces are included under Section 376(2)(b) of the IPC and are thus also subject to this mandatory sentence. The Criminal Law (Amendment) Act (1983) also shifts the burden of proof regarding consent to the accused.[115]

Despite the changes in the law, there is no evidence to show that the authorities have been willing to enforce it.[116] Moreover, Section 155 (4) of the Indian Evidence Act remains in effect. It states:

> The credit of a witness may be impeached in the following ways by the adverse party, or, with the consent of the Court, by the party who calls him . . . when a man is prosecuted for rape or an attempt to ravish, it may be shown that the prosecutrix was of generally immoral character.

A survey of rape case judgments in the seven years following the adoption of the Amendment Act reveals that judges continue to base their decisions largely on the "character" of the rape victim, in effect blaming her, rather than her assailant, for the crime.[117]

---

[114] Custody is customarily understood to include situations where the victim is effectively under the control of the police or security forces and is not limited to conditions of detention in a prison or lockup.

[115] Indian Evidence Act, Section 114-A. The inclusion of this provision in the Criminal Law Amendment Act provoked considerable controversy among civil liberties groups, women's organizations, bar associations and others. See Flavia Agnes, "Fighting Rape—Has Amending the Law Helped?" *The Lawyers*, February 1990, p. 6.

[116] See Amnesty International, "India: New Allegations of Rape by Army Personnel in Jammu and Kashmir," AI Index: ASA 20/02/93, January 1993, p. 3; and Agnes, "Fighting Rape...," pp. 4-11.

[117] Agnes, "Fighting Rape... ," pp. 4-11.

India's military laws, notably the Army Act and equivalent legislation governing the federal paramilitary forces, also prescribe courts-martial and punishments for members of these forces responsible for rape. In general, military courts in India have proved incompetent to deal with cases of serious human rights abuses and have functioned instead to cover up evidence and protect the officers involved.

In one well-publicized case, in May 1990 a young bride, Mubina Gani, was detained and raped by Border Security Force (BSF) soldiers in Kashmir while she was traveling from the wedding to her husband's home. Her aunt was also raped. The security forces had fired on the party, killing one man and wounding several others. The government claimed that the party had been caught in "cross-fire." After the incident was publicized in the local and international press, Indian authorities ordered an inquiry. Although the inquiry concluded that the women had been raped, the security forces were never prosecuted.[118] The government of India provided the following information on this case:

> The inquiry was not held by the police but by a Staff Court
> of Inquiry. A criminal case was registered and investigated.
> Seven BSF personnel have been suspended.

The BSF personnel responsible had only been "suspended"—for a crime which carries a minimum ten-year sentence under Indian law.

In July 1990 police in Sopore registered a case against the BSF for the rape of Hasina, a twenty-four-year-old woman from Jamir Qadeem, on June 26 of that year. According to doctors at the Subdistrict Hospital in Sopore, the BSF had entered the neighborhood at about 11:00 p.m. after an exchange of cross-fire between their forces and some militant groups. The BSF had then conducted a search of the neighborhood. The doctors stated that when Hasina was brought to the hospital she had vaginal bleeding. The medical superintendent's report also recorded bite marks on her face, chest and breasts and scratches on her face, chest and legs, and injuries to her genital area. A police report filed on July 5, 1990 charged members of the BSF with rape.[119]

The reported rape on February 23, 1991 of a large number of women from the village of Kunan Poshpora by soldiers of the Fourth Rajputana Rifles

---

[118] Amnesty International, *India: Torture, Rape and Deaths in Custody* (London: March, 1992), p. 21.

[119] Asia Watch, *Kashmir Under Siege*, p. 87.

became the focus of a government campaign to acquit the army of charges of human rights violations. The incident provides a telling example of the government's failure to ensure that such charges are properly investigated and that those responsible are held to account.

The rapes allegedly occurred during a search operation. The village headman and other village leaders claimed that they reported the rapes to army officials on February 27, and that the officials denied the charges and took no further action. Officials countered that no clear complaint was made. A local magistrate who visited the village requested that the divisional commissioner order a more comprehensive investigation, only to be told that officials in Delhi had denied the charges without checking with state authorities. A police investigation that was eventually ordered never commenced because the police officer assigned to conduct it was on leave at the time and was then transferred by his superiors.

In response to criticism of the government investigation, army officials requested the nongovernmental Press Council, a body composed of editors and other media professionals which monitors press laws and other issues concerning the press, to investigate the incident. A committee designated by the Press Council visited the village more than three months after the incident occurred. After interviewing a number of the alleged victims, the committee concluded in its report that contradictions in the women's testimony, and the fact that the number of alleged victims kept changing, rendered the charge of rape "baseless." The committee examined medical reports based on examinations conducted on thirty-two of the women two to three weeks later, on March 15 and 21, 1991, which confirmed that the hymens of three of the unmarried women had been torn. The committee concluded that the medical evidence was "worthless," that "such a delayed medical examination proves nothing," and that such abrasions are "common among the village folk in Kashmir." About the torn hymens, the committee argued that they could be the result of "natural factors, injury or premarital sex."

While the results of the examination do not, by themselves, prove the charge of rape, they do raise serious doubts about the army's version of events in Kunan Poshpora. The alacrity with which Indian military and government authorities in Kashmir discredited the allegations of rape and their failure to follow through with procedures that would provide crucial evidence for any prosecution—in particular prompt independent medical examinations of the alleged rape victims[120]—undermined the integrity of the investigation and indicates that the Indian authorities have been primarily concerned with shielding government forces from charges of abuse. The Press Council report echoes the government's concern about international criticism by arguing that the charges against the army constituted "a massive hoax orchestrated by militant groups and their sympathisers and mentors in Kashmir and abroad . . . for reinscribing Kashmir on the international agenda as a human rights issue."

In response to this report, the Indian government stated that the Kunan Poshpora case was investigated not only by the government but by an independent and highly regarded body, the Press Council of India. The Divisional Commissioner, Wajahat Habibullah, after his inquiry into the allegation stated, "While the veracity of complaint is thus highly doubtful, it still needs to be determined why such a complaint was made at all . . . I am of the opinion that the allegation of mass rape cannot be sustained." Another investigation at the level of Superintendent of Police concluded that the case was not fit to be prosecuted because of contradictions and gaps in the evidence.

It is significant that the government uses only selective comments from D.C. Habibullah's report, omitting the fact that he criticized the authorities in Delhi for dismissing the reports before any investigation had taken place, and recommended a thorough inquiry—which never took place. If the authorities had conducted a proper investigation, including a medical examination, and had taken semen samples from the accused, then it would be possible to determine the truth about what happened in Kunan Poshpora. The Press Council does not constitute a judicial investigative body, and the severe shortcomings of its visit have been noted above. A senior government official familiar with the incident revealed that although the number of women alleged to have been raped may have been inflated, they believed it was likely that several of the women were raped by the soldiers.

Even when investigations are ordered, they rarely result in prosecutions. A magisterial inquiry was ordered in the case of five women reportedly raped near Anantnag on December 5, 1991, but as of July 1995, no report has been made public. According to the *Kashmir Times* of January 14, 1993, the state government has ordered inquiries into eighty-seven incidents of killings, rape and arson. None resulted in criminal prosecutions.

---

[120] For example, the investigation could have availed itself of internationally accepted forensic procedures to substantiate the charges.

In seven courts-martial held between April 1990 and July 1991 involving incidents of rape, deaths in custody, illegal detention and indiscriminate firing on civilians by army soldiers, only one officer was dismissed.   The most severe punishment for the remaining officers was either a postponed promotion or marks of "severe displeasure" in their files.[121]

Those who have attempted to document incidents of rape have also been abused by Indian security forces.   In November 1990 Dr. K., a surgeon at the Anantnag District Hospital, was arrested after he had made arrangements for a gynecologist to examine seven women who had alleged rape by security forces.   The women, who had been brought to the hospital while Dr. K. was on night duty, reported that the security agents had disrupted a wedding and raped all of them, including the bride.   On November 29, Dr. K. was arrested at his home by members of the Central Reserve Police Force (CRPF) who had surrounded his house. The CRPF blindfolded him, along with two friends who were with him at the time, and took them to a military camp.   There, agents asked Dr. K., "Why did you call the gynecologist?"   When he replied, "I treat people irrespective of who they are,"   the police interrogators beat him with *lathis* (canes) and a metal belt. His friends were also beaten in this way.   The three men were detained for four days.

The impunity with which Indian security forces commit rape can also be gauged by the function the threat of rape plays when security forces attempt to intimidate local civilians into carrying out their orders. After killing several reported militants in Sopore on October 18, 1992, BSF troops then ordered five men from the area to bring in the bodies, threatening that if they did not do so, the soldiers would "rape their women."   When the men complied, and towed in the boat carrying the bodies of the dead militants and a boatman injured in the shooting, the BSF took the bodies and slit the throat of the boatman.[122]

Shopian

During an October 1992 mission to Kashmir, Human Rights Watch and Physicians for Human Rights documented fifteen individual cases of reported rape by forces of the Indian army and BSF.[123]   Thirteen occurred

---

[121] South Asia Human Rights Documentation Centre, "Massacre in Sopore," January 31, 1993, p. 12.

[122] For a full discussion of this case see Asia Watch and Physicians for Human Rights, *The Human Rights Crisis in Kashmir*, pp. 40-41.

[123] All names have been withheld by Human Rights Watch unless otherwise noted.

during two incidents which took place in the two weeks prior to the mission; the other two occurred in July 1992.

On the night of October 10, 1992, an army unit of the 22nd Grenadiers[124] entered the village of Chak Saidapora, about four kilometers south of the town of Shopian, district Pulwama, on a search operation for suspected militants. During the operation, at least six and probably nine women, including an eleven-year-old girl and a sixty-year-old woman, were gang-raped by several of the army soldiers.

A gynecologist and assistant surgeon at the Shopian District Hospital examined seven of the women on October 11 and the remaining two on October 12. The doctor stated that seven of the women were brought to the hospital at 1:30 p.m. by the Station House Officer (SHO) of the local Jammu and Kashmir police station in Shopian.[125] She stated:

> All of the women were weeping. They told me that "something bad" had happened at about midnight, that twenty-five army men had come into the village and into their homes. They told me that the soldiers had accused them of feeding and sheltering the militants, and asked them how many militants stay there.

The doctor conducted sperm tests and examined the seven women separately that day. Because the SHO had mentioned nine cases, the next day, October 12, the doctor went to the village where the rapes reportedly occurred to locate the other two, N., twenty, and her sister A., eighteen. She examined both of the young women, but did not conduct a slide test for sperm at that time. On October 14, the assistant subinspector of the Jammu and Kashmir police station in Shopian, Ghulam Nabi, brought A. and N. to the hospital for complete examinations. The doctor described the following findings for all nine women:

> Z., eleven, had abrasions and bruises on her chest and face. Her vaginal area was tender, and she had a ruptured hymen with a one half centimeter vaginal tear. Blood from the tear

---

[124] A military unit that traditionally was armed with grenades.

[125] The local Jammu and Kashmir police are not generally involved in counter-insurgency operations in Kashmir; their functions are limited to collecting bodies of persons killed during such operations and informing the families.

had coagulated. The sperm test was positive. X., sixty, had no marks of injury elsewhere on her body but was very tender around the vagina. The sperm test was positive. H., thirty, had abrasions and bruises on her face and in the genital area. The sperm test was positive. N., twenty, was also tender around the vagina and had a torn hymen. P. had marks on her chest and abdomen. The sperm test was positive. A., eighteen, was very tender around the vagina. Her hymen had been torn. The sperm tests for G., S., and A.B. were negative, the doctor noted, but they exhibited similar tenderness and some marks of injury.

The doctor gave a copy of the medical report to the local police station house officer. On October 12, an army official came to the hospital to ask about the incident, and she told him the findings of the examinations. The nine women narrated the following accounts:

S., about twenty-five, testified that on the night of October 10 she was in the house owned by her father-in-law, who is about seventy, and his wife. Both of her in-laws were in the house at the time. S.'s father-in-law stated that during the night, there was knocking at the door and three soldiers entered and asked, "Where are the womenfolk?" [S. continued] I told them they are sleeping. They went into that room to search it and as they started searching they told me to get out. I was taken away by other soldiers. One soldier kept guard on the door, and two of them raped me. They said, "We have orders from our officers to rape you." I said, "You can shoot me but don't rape me." They were there about half an hour. Two raped me, and two raped [her sister-in-law] H. Then they left.

Their father-in-law was released about half an hour later.

A. and N. stated that they lived nearby and were asleep around midnight when about eight or nine soldiers came to the house. Their brother went to the door and said, "The army has come to search our house." Four soldiers entered the house and ordered the father and brother to be taken out. The soldiers entered a room where the women were sleeping. A. and N. recalled:

> They did not say anything when they came in, but they were
> talking among themselves, but we could not understand.
> They covered my eyes and mouth with cloths and told us to
> lie down.

N. and A. said they had been raped by each of the soldiers. The soldiers struck their ten-year-old sister-in-law with rifle butts and sent her out of the room.

P. stated that there was a knock at the door of her in-laws' house at about midnight.

> When my father-in-law answered, he was sent away. Three
> soldiers came into the room, and told me to put my daughter
> aside. When I refused, he picked her up and put in her in a
> corner. I told him not to touch me, and he said, "We have
> orders, what can we do?" All three of them raped me.

Z. stated that four soldiers came to the house, but only two came inside while two remained outside. She said that when her father opened the door, the soldiers kicked him and sent him away. At that point in our interview, Z. broke down and was not able to continue.

G. stated that three soldiers entered her house and took her husband outside. Only one came into her room.

> He told me, "I have to search you." I told him women are
> not searched, but he said, "I have orders," and he tore off my
> clothes and raped me.

A.B. stated that three soldiers came into her room and told her to take off her clothes. When she protested that she was an old woman, one of them kicked her in the chest and she fell. Then he put one hand over her mouth, pulled off her *salwar* (loose trousers), and raped her.

In response to requests for information, the authorities stated that the army unit, normally stationed in Chak Saidapora, "conducted search operations in the village on specific information that some militants were hiding there." They stated that the search was carried out "from 0010 hours to 0145 hours during which seven houses were searched in the presence of an elderly man." Senior government officials also admitted that the search was carried out in violation of military regulations prohibiting soldiers from entering villages after dark.[126]

In a statement released to Human Rights Watch, Indian authorities claimed that:

> the residents of the seven houses identified and confirmed that the same three army persons had entered and searched each house and hence it is difficult to believe that the same persons could have indulged in acts of rape in different houses within an hour and thirty-five minutes.

The government statement adds that, "Two of the women who have been alleged to have been raped were wives of terrorists viz. Takub Hussain a Platoon Commander of Hizbul Mujahideen and Mohd. Yakub a Group Commander of the same militant group."

To our knowledge, the women did not identify the soldiers as being the same three in each case.[127] As we have noted above, one of the ways security forces in Kashmir use rape is as a weapon against women suspected of being sympathetic to or related to alleged militants. While it is not known whether such suspicions motivated the soldiers responsible for the rapes of these women, it is clear that the authorities intend to use the accusation that the women associated with "terrorists" both to discredit the women's testimony and—implicitly at least—to shirk responsibility for the abuse. Moreover, even if the women were affiliated with any militant group, that in no way justifies the use of rape by security personnel. In response, the government has claimed that "the statement that two of the alleged victims in the Shopian case were wives of terrorists is by no means an attempt to shirk responsibility. The Government's intention in bringing this fact to light was to caution Human Rights Watch about the possible motivations behind the allegations which would be to malign the security forces."[128]

---

[126] Amnesty International, "India: New Allegations..."

[127] Human Rights Watch and Physicians for Human Rights received no further details from the government about how the soldiers were identified by the residents, i.e. by unit, rank or other marking. If any individuals were identified, a semen and blood test could provide corroborating evidence.

[128] Government of India press release, "Comments on Asia Watch-PHR Report 'Rape in Kashmir,'" May 14, 1993, published in Asia Watch and Physicians for Human Rights, *The Human Rights Crisis in Kashmir*, p. 210.

The government also claimed that only four of the women were medically examined and questioned the credibility of their testimony on these grounds. Human Rights Watch and Physicians for Human Rights were provided with specific medical evidence and testimony on all nine cases. Hospital authorities stated, moreover, that the evidence was also provided to army officials and was, presumably, a significant factor in the government's decision to order a police investigation into the case.

The government statement attempted in particular to discredit the testimony of the eleven-year-old Z.: "During the enquiry she was not found to have any visible signs or marks of injury or any physical excesses nor did she display any fear or anger and appeared to be oblivious of the alleged incident." In fact, the doctor who examined Z. the day after the incident confirmed that her hymen was torn, that blood had coagulated around the tear, and that she was very tender around the vaginal area. When Z. described how she was raped, she broke down and was unable to continue speaking.

According to the English-language *Kashmir Times* of October 14, 1992, police in Shopian registered a criminal case of gang-rape against the BSF on October 13. The statement provided by the government stated that the case had been transferred to the Crime Branch—a special investigative branch of the police. However, after Human Rights Watch and Physicians for Human Rights published this case in "Rape in Kashmir: A Crime of War," the government of India provided a statement claiming:

> The case was enquired into by a senior officer of the army as well as by an officer of the level of Senior Superintendent of Police M.M. Rafiqi who concluded that the complaints and the evidence were both unreliable and the allegations could not be sustained. Two independent enquiries thus came to the same conclusion, exposing the efforts of the militants to make false charges and terrorise or otherwise use innocent citizens to discredit the security forces.

This statement provides no explanation for the claim that the evidence—presumably including the medical report—was "unreliable." The way the government inquiry was conducted reveals one of the most serious problems with government investigations into human rights violations in India. An inquiry by the army or the police can in no way be considered "independent." The government should have ensured that the investigation was conducted by a judicial magistrate, as is provided under Indian law.

After the Human Rights Watch and Physicians for Human Rights report was published, a former government official who had interviewed army officials about this and other incidents told Human Rights Watch that the army had confirmed that the women were raped but had not wanted to publicize the fact for fear of hurting morale.

Haran

On July 20, 1992, during an army search operation near the town of Haran, approximately twenty-five kilometers west of Srinagar, at least two women appear to have been raped. J., a resident of Haran, stated that at about 6:30 a.m., five soldiers came into the courtyard and ordered her to give them some water. Two of the soldiers then dragged her into her room and then one of them removed her clothes while the other stood at the door. She stated:

> The first soldier slapped me and then pushed me to the ground where I fell on a wooden stake and hurt my back. Both of the soldiers raped me. At some point I fainted, and when I regained consciousness, I discovered that my husband had placed a blanket over me.

A second woman, H., stated that she was at home at about 9:00 a.m. when two Sikh soldiers entered the house. H. was pregnant at the time. Other soldiers remained outside in the compound. She stated:

> They told me that I had to go to a shop with them to search it. My father said he would come, but they said, "No, she has to come." I refused. Then one of them asked for some milk, but when I gave it to him, he touched my breasts and pushed me into a corner. One covered my mouth with his hand while the other held a gun. They ordered me to lie down. One of them raped me. Then I fainted.

H. did not go to a doctor until three days later.

F., H.'s mother, stated that she was in bed when the soldiers came. She tried to run away when she saw the soldiers enter H.'s room, but other soldiers caught her and took her back to the room. She was not raped or assaulted.

About this incident, the government of India stated, "At the time of the search operations, conducted by the army, no complaint of rape was made."

The statement implies that the women should have complained about the rape to the very soldiers who raped them.   The government has stated that a complaint was filed with the deputy commissioner of the district.

Gurihakhar

The security forces have committed rape as a form of retaliation against civilians, most of whom are believed to be sympathetic to the militants. Such reprisals have occurred frequently after militant attacks on security patrols.   In one such case, on October 1, 1992, a BSF patrol returning from a crackdown in the village of Bakhikar, in Handwara district, came under attack by militant forces.   One member of the BSF patrol was killed. Following the ambush, BSF forces rampaged through the nearby village of Battekut, killing ten people and burning houses and grain stores. After leaving Battekut, the BSF forces entered the village of Gurihakhar.

B., thirty-five, a resident of Gurihakhar, testified that on October 1 at about noon, she was in her home with her sister-in-law and mother-in-law, when security forces came to the house.   One stayed outside while the other came inside the room where she was with her child. She stated:

> He put his gun to the baby and told me to put him aside. I
> refused, and he beat me with the gun butt on my back and
> covered my mouth with his hand.   Then he forced me to the
> floor and took off my clothes and raped me.   Then we heard
> a gunshot outside, and he left.

R., twenty-five, stated that two security men came into her room where she was feeding her child.   She told us:

> One of them forced me to the floor and covered my mouth
> with a cloth, and blindfolded me with a scarf. He threatened
> me, "If you scream, we will shoot your children." Then he
> raped me.

On October 2, 1992, local police took the women to a female doctor in Handwara, who confirmed that the women had been "severely molested" but that, because they were not virgins, it was not possible to confirm whether rape had occurred with the tools at her disposal.

The mother of a thirteen-year-old girl in the same town provided an account of the rape as if she, and not her daughter, were raped, seemingly to protect her daughter from public humiliation. As a rape victim, the daughter would likely be socially ostracized and unable to marry.

About this series of reported rapes, the government of India has stated: "There was an exchange of fire between security forces and militants in which one army personnel was killed, two injured and a number of civilians died in cross fire. There was no report of rape as alleged even when senior district officials visited the site after the incident."[129] In fact, the civilians who were killed were deliberately shot by the soldiers in reprisal for a militant attack which had occurred outside the village.[130]

Rape by Militant Groups

The increase in reports of rape by militant groups in Kashmir has coincided with the rise in other violent crimes against civilians by these groups. Extremist militant groups seeking to enforce an "Islamic" code of behavior have launched other violent attacks on women.

While as early as 1990 there were reported threats to women, most frequently by groups reportedly seeking to enforce their interpretation of "Islamic" culture in Kashmir, reports of rape by militant groups were rare in the conflict's early years. A July 1990 report cited frequent threats to women by one group, "warning the women that severe action will be taken if they do not maintain *purdah* (or wear a *burqa,* clothing which entirely conceals the body)."[131] Such threats have continued, and women who have challenged the militants have been attacked. On May 13, 1993, members of the women's militant organization, Dukhtaran-e-Millat (Daughters of the Nation) issued warnings to women in Srinagar not to come outside without wearing burqas. The militants reportedly sprayed paint on women who defied the order, such that four students were hospitalized with eye injuries from the paint.[132]

---

[129] Government of India press release, "Comments on Asia Watch-PHR Report 'Rape in Kashmir,'" May 14, 1993, published in Asia Watch and Physicians for Human Rights, *The Human Rights Crisis in Kashmir*, p. 206.

[130] The incident is documented in Asia Watch and Physicians for Human Rights, *The Human Rights Crisis in Kashmir*, pp. 76-80.

[131] Committee for Initiative on Kashmir, *Kashmir Imprisoned* (Delhi: July 1990), pp. 46-47.

[132] The incident was reported by the South Asia Human Rights Documentation Centre, a human rights organization based in New Delhi, in a private communication to Human Rights Watch dated April 7, 1993.

In some cases, women have been raped and then killed after being abducted by rival militant groups and held as hostages for their male relatives. In other cases, members of armed militant groups have abducted a woman after threatening to shoot the rest of the family unless she is handed over to a militant leader.   The fact that local people sometimes refer to these abductions and rapes as "forced marriages" gives some indication of the social ostracism suffered by rape victims and the code of silence—combined with fear—that prevents people from openly condemning such abuses by militant groups.

Some incidents of rape by militants appear to have been motivated by the fact that the victims or their families are accused of being informers or of being opposed to the militants or supporters of rival militant groups. One of the earliest such cases involved a staff nurse at the Saura Medical Institute, Sarla Bhat, twenty-seven, who was kidnapped from the institute on April 14, 1990. Her body was found four days later. A note found near the body stated that the Jammu and Kashmir Liberation Front (JKLF) took responsibility for the killing and accused Bhat of informing the security forces about the presence of a number of wounded militants in the hospital.[133]   The post-mortem report concluded that she had been raped before she was shot dead.

The fear of rape has reportedly been a factor in the flight of Muslim families from Kashmir. However, cases of rape by militant groups are difficult to investigate because most Kashmiris are reluctant to discuss abuses by the militants out of fear of reprisal.   According to one report, the increasing number of rapes has led to an increase in abortions in Kashmir, resulting in one case in the murder of a doctor who complained about having to perform them. Militants from the Hezb-ul Mujahidin and Al Jehad reportedly accused the doctor of being an informer.[134]

A 1992 case of rape and murder by militants attracted publicity in part because the incident provoked street protests condemning the militants for the crimes. The incident involved the family of a retired truck driver named Sohanlal, sixty, who lived in Nai Sadak, Kralkhud. At about 8:30 p.m. on March 30, 1992, armed militants entered Sohanlal's home. According to his son, the men demanded food and shelter. The family complied. After about two hours, Sohanlal and his wife, Bimla, heard their daughter, Archana, crying

---

[133] Yusuf Jameel, "Ex-Minister Shot Dead by J&K Militants," *Telegraph* (Calcutta), April 20, 1990.

[134] Harinder Baweja, "People Turning Against Militants," *India Today*, May 31, 1992, p. 42.

for help from a room on the ground floor of the house. When they reached the room, the militants shot Sohanlal, killing him instantly. The bodies of the two women were discovered in the street outside the house. According to the autopsy report, both women had been raped before being shot. According to one report, 5,000 women staged a protest march to condemn the rapes and murders.[135] To our knowledge, no group has claimed responsibility for the incident.

International attention to the human rights situation in India has encouraged the government to take a number of positive steps recently toward improving human rights conditions, but much more needs to be done. On June 22, 1995, the Indian government took an important step in deciding to allow the International Committee of the Red Cross (ICRC) to conduct humanitarian visits to detention facilities in Kashmir. However, the fact that international human rights groups (Human Rights Watch, for example) have not been allowed to conduct investigations in Kashmir underscores the urgent need for continued international pressure. Abuses in Kashmir continue to mount, including deaths in custody, disappearances, torture and rape. In a welcome step, the government has publicized a number of prosecutions of security personnel for rape and other abuses. However, the number of security force members actually sentenced remains very small relative to the number of known abuses. Too often Indian officials, when confronted with the evidence of rape, attempt to impugn the integrity of the victims and witnesses, discredit the testimony of physicians, lawyers and human rights activists, or simply deny the charges without thorough investigation—everything except order an impartial inquiry and prosecute those responsible. We are also unaware of any successful efforts by militant groups to prevent their forces from committing rape. By failing to take action, rigorously and consistently, against those who commit rape, both government and militant forces have ensured only that the use of rape as a weapon of war in Kashmir will continue.

---

[135] Ibid.

VIOLENCE AGAINST WOMEN IN PERU'S ARMED CONFLICT

Throughout Peru's fifteen-year internal war, women have been the targets of sustained and frequently brutal violence committed by both parties to the armed conflict.[136] Both sides often use violence to punish or dominate women believed to be sympathetic to the opposing side. Women have been threatened, raped and murdered by government security forces; and women have been threatened, raped and murdered by the Communist Party of Peru (*Sendero Luminoso* or Shining Path). Many times, the same woman has been the victim of violence by both sides.

During our 1992 investigation, Peruvian human rights monitors agreed that the number of rapes by security forces in any given year was high, although no group maintained aggregate statistics. Reported cases involved the insertion of foreign objects into the vagina and anus combined with other forms of torture including electric shock to the genitals and breasts; rape of pregnant women and of minors; and gang rape by police or security force personnel. Government soldiers have used rape as a weapon: to punish, intimidate, coerce, humiliate and degrade. Often, women were raped while blindfolded, so they could not identify their attackers. Frequently, the women have been told that they or their family members will be killed if they report the rape. In some instances, groups of women reportedly have been raped by the security forces and then killed. In many cases, soldiers have forced family members to witness such abuse. Just living in a certain area can put women at risk for rape because of suspected sympathy with the insurgency or because they happen to be in the wrong place at the wrong time.

Despite the pervasiveness of the abuse, few police officers and even fewer members of the security forces have been prosecuted, even when the

---

[136] The following material was adapted from Americas Watch and the Women's Rights Project, *Untold Terror: Violence Against Women in Peru's Armed Conflict*, (New York: Human Rights Watch, 1992). The information on government security forces was gathered for this case study during a three-week mission to Peru in July 1992. Interviews were held with victims and their families, the military, judicial and Public Ministry officials, journalists, human rights monitors, social workers and women's rights groups. Information on Shining Path threats and attacks was gathered during the same mission and from the same sources mentioned above, as well as from interviews with women who belonged to the Shining Path.

cases were reported to the appropriate authorities.[137] To the contrary, evidence demonstrates that the police and army actively protect rapists from their ranks and continue to promote them, thus implicitly condoning their crimes.

As far as the military is concerned, rape is an occasional, regrettable excess. General E. P. Petronio Fernandez Dávila, under-secretary of human rights and pacification in the Defense Ministry, told Human Rights Watch in July 1992, "Those boys are far from their families and suffer a great deal of tension because of the nature of combat." He went on to claim that many of the women who report rape are subversives who seek to damage the image of the armed forces.

Rape of women by the Shining Path has been much less common, perhaps because the organization explicitly prohibits it and because of the high number of woman militants. Shining Path attacks against women have been more a result of women's role in founding and participating in survival organizations, like community soup kitchens, than because they were women. Moreover, the type of violence used against women has been used against male non-combatants as well.

To some extent, women activists also have been targeted by the Shining Path because of their efforts on behalf of women's rights. Some women community activists killed by the Shining Path also have been leading feminists. From 1985 until 1992, ten female grassroots leaders were killed by the Shining Path.

On September 12, 1992, government forces captured the Shining Path's leader, Abimael Guzmán, leading to a reduction in the fighting between government forces and the guerrillas. Since the arrest of Guzmán and more than fifty of his top followers, who remain incarcerated, attacks on women and other civilians by the Shining Path have declined. Nonetheless, although much weakened and diminished in geographical scope, the Shining Path continues to violate international humanitarian law.

Violence against women, including rape, by government security forces also has decreased as a result of the overall decline of the internal

---

[137] From 1985 to 1990, only ten police officers were sanctioned formally and dismissed from the force for rape. Local human rights groups suspect that most of the cases involved officers who committed rape while off-duty and in circumstances unrelated to detention or counterinsurgency operations. Statistics from the Department of Statistics, National Police, and elaborated on by the *Instituto de Defensa Legal*. To our knowledge, no police officers have been punished for rape since 1990.

conflict. But little has been done to end the impunity for security forces who commit rape. Moreover, on June 15, 1995, President Alberto Fujimori approved a law providing a blanket amnesty to members of the security forces who have committed human rights violations in the counterinsurgency hostilities since 1980. Among the crimes that are excused are extrajudicial executions, "disappearances," torture, and rape.

A Pattern of Impunity

Rape prosecutions are among the most difficult cases to win in Peru, even when the alleged rape is committed by common criminals, not members of the security forces. General attitudes, social relations and their reflections in the law often work to stigmatize the victim, not her attacker, and reduce the likelihood of a fair trial. Moreover, inadequate medical facilities, cumbersome and sometimes negligent police procedures, and popular mistrust of the judicial system further complicate women's search for justice.

The above factors frequently inhibit women from reporting rape. In 1992 Peruvian legal experts and police estimated that reported cases represent less than 10 percent of the rapes that actually occur. Once rape was reported, there is no guarantee that such abuse would be prosecuted or the accused rapist punished. Of the 1,180 formal charges of rape filed with the Peruvian police in 1988, only 257, or about 14 percent, resulted in convictions.

A Question of Honor

Until April 1991, rape was treated as a crime against honor under Peru's civilian penal code. Although women's rights activists successfully advocated to modify the definition of the crime of rape to reduce the importance of "honor," attorneys maintain that biased attitudes about women's honor continue to influence the prosecution of rape and are revealed in the inadequate penalties and low conviction rate for this crime.

Lawyers who defend rape victims say the enduring emphasis on honor places a female victim at a legal disadvantage in pursuing a rape case. Her age and sexual past can be as important as the details of the attack. Irrelevant information about the victim's sexual past often is introduced into rape trials and can fuel a highly prejudicial presumption of consent.

To have a chance of convicting her assailant, an adult woman must be able to demonstrate visible and serious physical injuries, according to Dr. César San Martín, a former justice with the Lima Superior Court. A threat with a weapon, like a gun, is not sufficient. Psychological trauma, even a threat against a family member, is not admissible evidence. "The [rape] cases that have the best chances involve minors under fourteen, women who were seriously injured or killed or women who were gang raped. Otherwise, the possibility of conviction is nearly zero."[138]

Moreover, according to Dr. Sylvia Loli, a defender of rape and domestic violence victims for the Lima-based Flora Tristán Women's Center, a great deal of ignorance exists among the general population about the value of preserving the direct, physical evidence of violence. Many women, horrified by the rape, bathe and throw away their torn clothing. Using current techniques, sperm samples must be taken within eight days of a rape or are useless. Adult women especially must have such evidence taken promptly, or they risk being accused of having sex with someone else in the interim.

During our 1992 investigation, we found that few medical or police professionals were trained or equipped to collect such evidence. For instance, in Lima, as of 1992, only five doctors in the Judicial Palace examined all victims of violent crime, Dr. Loli told us. Women who were raped on the weekend or holidays—the most common time according to police—had to wait until a working day for attention. By then, much evidence can disappear. Some women were assigned doctors attached to police clinics. In Huamanga, the capital of Ayacucho, all exams of rape victims were performed by police doctors, although the police often were implicated in rape. In rural areas, building a case could be especially difficult. The nearest police station could be days of hard walking away, and most department capitals lacked the tools or trained professionals to collect admissible evidence.

If a suspect is identified, the rape victim must make a second formal accusation, called the *ratificación* or reaffirmation. This time, the accusation is made in public and while facing the accused. Occasionally, rape cases are dismissed at this point, because the victim decides not to go public with the charge.

"If this is the picture when the perpetrator is a civilian," Dr. Loli told us, "what about a police officer or soldier on active duty? Forget it." Emergency legislation mandates that offenses committed in the line of duty be placed under military jurisdiction, subject to the Code of Military Justice. Despite the fact that rape and murder are common crimes, and thus should be subject to the civilian penal code, we are aware of no case in over fifteen years of internal conflict in which civilian courts have exercised jurisdiction. Instead, human rights-related cases are tried in military court and soldiers

---

[138] Interview, Dr. César San Martín, Lima, Peru, July 7, 1992.

accused of rape are never made available to civilian courts for prosecution. To our knowledge, no officer has ever been punished for rape.

A Weapon of War

Rape by the security forces threatens all women, but four elements characterize women who face greater risk of actual attack: race, social class, occupation and the explosive mix of gender and armed insurgency particular to the Shining Path and its female cadre. These elements combine to put certain women—poor, brown-skinned (*chola* in the Peruvian racial argot), young and belonging to certain suspect groups like students or teachers' unions—at greater risk.

During our investigation, we discovered no situation in which wealthy or white women reported such sexual assaults. Almost all the women who told us they had been raped by security forces were lower middle class to poor *mestizas* (mixed white and Indian) and cholas. For example, Ruth[139] was detained by the police during a routine document check of city bus passengers in Lima in 1991. Ruth, a mestiza, believes she was detained for two reasons: her lower middle class appearance and her student identification card from National University of San Marcos, Peru's largest university. The government frequently accuses universities of being centers for guerrilla activity, although the great majority of students have no connection with the insurgents. Ruth says she was blindfolded, beaten and threatened with death shortly after exiting the city bus. In the police station, where the beating continued, the police said, "These are the *senderistas* that give us the *coup de grace*."

The police comment to Ruth about the coup de grace (death blow) indicates the explosive gender twist to Peru's internal conflict. The Shining Path is unique among armed insurgencies for the high number of women in its ranks, particularly in leadership positions. Often, women take part in the assassination squads that the guerrillas send to kill local authorities, government officials and police and military officers, and give the coup de grace during public executions.

For Peruvian society, this violation of gender stereotypes—not peace-loving girls, but women who kill—provokes an intense fear of and anger against women suspected of participating in armed actions. In the press, female senderistas are frequently described as monsters, killing machines and crazed automatons. These fears also are incorporated into special police training courses, which claim that women are more dangerous, fierce and

---

[139] All names withheld by Human Rights Watch unless otherwise indicated.

bloodthirsty than men. One 1990 National Police training manual describes "female subversives" as more determined and dangerous than men, [they have] extreme conduct . . . [and are] very severe."[140]

The rape of female militants detained by police and soldiers has been so common that the Shining Path incorporated the risk into its training for young women recruits. Women militants are told to expect to be raped and exhorted to consider it a political test that transforms them into more perfect cadres.[141]

Rape also tends to be perpetuated down Peru's race and class ladder or within a racial group. In other words, whites rape cholas, not the other way around, or mestizos rape mestizas. In most cases, women identified as chola or Indian receive the most brutal treatment. Mestizo or *criollo* (white) police officers tend to rape mestiza or chola detainees. We have documented several cases where a light-skinned officer demanded to rape first, and was followed by his darker-skinned subordinates in order of rank.

Emergency Legislation and the Military Code of Justice
Special provisions included in the "state of emergency" legislation protect rapists in uniform and create conditions under which rape occurs with impunity. The legislation, which was first invoked in December 1982, lasts for a renewable period of three months for each defined region. Therefore, the amount of the country covered by the legislation fluctuates. As of the end of 1994, about one-quarter of the country and just under 50 percent of the population lived under emergency legislation.

Although the legislation allegedly was designed to facilitate the government's fight against guerrillas, in practice many of its provision institutionalize impunity for human rights abuses. Independent human rights groups like Amnesty International have estimated that up to 85 percent of the human rights violations that occur in the areas declared emergency zones are the work of the armed forces, particularly the army.[142]

Under the emergency legislation, the military is given control of a defined region, and is the ultimate authority over the civilian elected and

[140] *VI Curso Superior de Guerra Política y Seguridad del Estado: Participación de la Mujer en la Subversión y en las Fuerzas Antisubversivas,* (Surquillo: National Police Criminalistic Institute, 1990), p. 15.

[141] Interview, Miguel, Castro Castro prison, February 1991.

[142] Amnesty International, *Peru: Human Rights During the Government of President Alberto Fujimori* (London: May 1992).

appointed officials. Certain rights, like freedom of assembly and movement, the inviolability of the home, freedom from arrest without a judicial warrant and bans on incommunicado detention, have been suspended. Anyone living in an emergency zone can be arrested without warrant and kept fifteen days in incommunicado detention; typically this is when torture, including rape, disappearances and extrajudicial executions occur. Although any detention must be reported to civilian authorities, formal charges made and the detainees notified of them within twenty-four hours, in practice the military routinely ignores these fundamental protections.

Our 1992 investigation found that while in the "emergency zone," police and soldiers were ordered to assume war names to hide their identities. On patrol, officers purposefully avoided using uniforms that displayed rank. Frequently, arrests or patrols are carried out while personnel are masked. Thus, women who had been raped often said they could not identify their attackers by name or rank, a legally required first step to prosecution.

Finally, emergency legislation also mandates that offenses committed in the line of duty be placed under military jurisdiction, subject to the Code of Military Justice. Thus, in the few cases where an accused rapist has been identified, he has not been put at the disposition of civilian courts for investigation and trial. The impartiality of military courts is highly suspect. Military judges are not legal professionals but officers drawn from the ranks to serve set terms. According to Peru's military code, they are responsible for hearing only cases involving soldiers accused of military-specific crimes. Prior to 1991, military courts judged those accused of human rights-related offenses on only two grounds: negligence and abuse of authority. Sessions of the military court are held in secret. Even the victims or surviving family members are not allowed to participate and are not informed of the verdicts.

Human Rights Watch is aware of only two cases in which an officer has been found guilty of human rights abuse. One involved a massacre of sixty-nine peasants in Accomarca, Ayacucho, on August 14, 1985, by members of four army patrols. It remains the largest single massacre of civilians in Peru's emergency zone. Witnesses asserted that soldiers raped numerous women before killing them. Despite the evidence and eyewitness testimony linking five officers to murder, torture and rape, a military court in 1987 sentenced only one man, Second Lt. Telmo Hurtado, to four years in prison and immediate dismissal on the charge of "abuse of authority with disobedience."

But Hurtado was never confined. Indeed, he was never even dismissed from active duty and was promoted during his supposed sentence.

In a rare move, the general prosecutor of the Military Supreme Court, Gen. Luis Carnero Deernardi, questioned the leniency and irregularities involved in the case and filed an appeal. A subsequent army investigation, later leaked to the Lima daily *La República*, found that all five officers and their men engaged in rape, the burning alive of captured peasants, on-the-spot executions, the murder of witnesses and the wanton destruction of houses.

Again, in 1988, only the most junior officer involved, Hurtado, was found guilty on the same charges—abuse of authority—as in 1987. The others were absolved for only following higher orders. Although the sentence against Hurtado was confirmed and increased to six years in March 1992, he has yet to be dismissed and holds the rank of captain.

The military court made a significant change in the adjudication of human rights cases in 1991, when it adopted part of the civilian penal code to try officers accused of theft, rape and murder in the department of Huancavelica. According to witnesses, on July 4 a combined civil defense-army patrol from the Pampas, Huancavelica military base beat and detained villagers in Rodeopampa, Pallccapamba, Huaraccapta and Miguelpata. About fifteen villagers were taken to the Farallón mine near Rodeopampa and killed, their bodies blown up with grenades. The case, which is known as the Santa Barbara massacre, resulted in formal charges against six officers. For the first time, the military adopted sections from the penal code to convict military men. According to the army, Second Sgt. Carlos Prado Chinchay was charged with aggravated murder, theft and the rape of two women in his custody. Second Sgt. Dennis Pacheco Zambrano was charged with cattle theft and rape. This case was one of nine that were monitored by the U.S. Congress in fiscal year 1991 as a condition for the release of military aid to Peru.

Unfortunately, only one woman, Isabel Quispe Hilario, was willing to testify to a public prosecutor about her rape. Other witnesses who originally agreed to testify, relatives of the victims, and government officials attempting to investigate were subsequently harassed by the security forces and some government officials. Although civil authorities attempted to wrest the case from the military courts, their efforts were unsuccessful.

A dramatic blow against human rights was struck on April 5, 1992, when President Alberto Fujimori violated Peru's constitution by dissolving Congress, suspending the judiciary, jailing members of the opposition and assuming dictatorial powers. These conditions have continued to the present. President Fujimori defended his actions as being necessary to pursue government reforms, combat widespread corruption and bolster the war against the Shining Path. The combined effect of these laws is that anyone can be arrested at any time, on charges that no one has a responsibility to make public, and held indefinitely. Women accused of terrorism or treason and who say they have been raped are now held in circumstances that violate their rights and severely handicap any attempt to obtain justice.

President Fujimori was reelected in April 1995. This vote represented a show of support for Fujimori's economic policies and his government's success in reducing violence, especially from the Shining Path. President Fujimori has retained his emergency powers since his reelection.

Rape by the Security Forces

Some common denominators emerge from the testimonies about rape by the security forces. Women did not see the men who raped them because they were blindfolded or the men wore masks. Women were kept naked, blindfolded and bound. They were raped during interrogation, as punishment, coercion or just because they were around when the officers were drunk and wanted sex they did not have to pay for. The women were raped, then threatened with more rape. Physical evidence of rape, such as semen or injuries, often was eliminated before the woman was presented to judicial authorities.

This section examines Peru's failure to punish rape by the security forces. We divide the examinations of rape by the security forces into two categories: rape during interrogation and rape in the emergency zones in the midst of armed conflict. Rape during interrogation is committed in order to get information or to frighten a detainee into complying with the wishes of her captors. Frequently, it is combined with other forms of torture: beatings, the "submarine" (near-drowning), electric shocks, and the "little bird" (hanging from ceiling hooks by her elbows with the detainee's arms bound behind her back). Rape in the emergency zones is committed in the course of armed conflict, usually to punish the civilian population for perceived sympathies with armed insurgents and to demonstrate domination.

Rape during Interrogation

Rape during interrogation appeared to occur most frequently when women were in police detention. In these cases, the victims were generally mestiza, Spanish-speaking women from urban areas. Arrested as suspected subversives, they were incarcerated alone or in small groups and systematically denied access to the public prosecutors whose job it is to ensure their well-being. Often, the women were raped until shortly before their appearance before civil judicial authorities, when they were forced to wash away evidence and threatened against disclosing torture and ill-treatment. The cases documented here are presented in chronological order and span the country. Some of these rapes were formally reported; most were not.[143]

One of the first rape cases to provoke national outrage was that of Georgina Gamboa, who says she was raped by the *Sinchis,* members of a police anti-terrorist unit, in January 1981. According to her testimony, she was raped first in her house, then in a police station in Vilcashuamán, Ayacucho. Gamboa was sixteen years old at the time.

The rape left Gamboa with a severe infection and an unwanted pregnancy, which she carried to term. She spent five years and three months in prison before being found not guilty of terrorism. During that time her father disappeared after detention by the security forces. Her mother was detained and raped and later gave birth to a girl. Despite the fact that Gamboa identified the eleven officers and one civilian who raped her and filed formal charges, they were found not guilty. In the decision, Judge Guillermo Hermoza Moya echoed the common perception that women lie about being raped: "The allegations against the police officers, in this case rape and mistreatment, are nothing more than the already familiar reaction of violence against order, crime against law, in order to in this way to invalidate the evidence found in the area."[144]

Many women have reported being raped after pressing for the release of family members or pursuing legal action against members of the security forces on relatives' behalf. For instance, Balbina traveled to the city of Cuzco to vote in 1986. There she discovered that her brother recently had been detained for not having his identity papers in order.

A few days after pressing for her brother's release, Balbina was approached by three Civil Guard (GC) officers who promised to take her to see her brother. In Peru the GC are responsible for maintaining order at the local level. Once she joined them in a taxi, they blindfolded and handcuffed her and beat her when she protested. Later, she learned that nine other people, including two women, had also been arrested by the GC and were accused of forming a Shining Path assassination squad with her.

> As I insisted that I had done no one any harm, much less of
> this type, they proceeded with more force, tearing my clothes

---

[143] For other cases, see Human Rights Watch, *Untold Terror,* pp. 27-34.

[144] Mabel Barreto, "Hijas de la Violencia," *Sí* (Lima), September 21, 1987, pp. 77-83.

until I was completely nude. Not content with this, they
lifted me up by the handcuffs and threw me against
something hard, and then several of them grabbed me and
began to beat me with some sort of stick, which they also put
inside of me.

The torture continued for several hours, punctuated by the application
of electric shocks to her breasts and labia, the submarine, hanging her from
ceiling, and threats to her family. Several times, metal objects, which Balbina
says she cannot identify, were used to rape her. Her physical state was so
poor that when the GC officers tried to transfer her to the local investigative
police (PIP) station for further questioning, PIP officers refused to accept her,
for fear that they would be later held accountable for the torture.

A day before they wanted to transfer us to the PIP, they
concentrated on curing us, giving us pills and massages with
special ointments, cleaning us and changing our clothes, but
it didn't matter, the PIP still wouldn't receive us. So the PIP
called a doctor [to do a report] so that they wouldn't be
found responsible. Later, the PIP did its own investigation
and found us innocent.

When family members reported the torture in December, the case
provoked outrage and mass protests in Cuzco and Lima. Two separate
investigations—by the Ministry of the Interior and the Senate Human Rights
Committee—confirmed the torture and identified the three officers responsible:
GC Col. Antonio Ruiz Caycho, GC Lt. Col. Edgard Sánchez Bedoya and GC
Capt. Oscar Collantes. Examining the women later, a medical examiner
reported that both women had perforations in the vagina, uterus and rectum.
Some of the men detained in the same group also had wounds in their rectums
from rape with metal objects.

Despite an arrest order issued soon after the incident, none of the
officers was arrested. While the eight detainees who remained in custody were
formally charged with terrorism in a civil court, the accusation of torture,
including rape, was sent to a military court. To our knowledge, the police
officers ultimately were tried in civil court, but were given light sentences,
including brief suspensions from their duties. They were not dismissed from
the force. In contrast, the female lawyer who represented some of the victims,

Dr. Martha Luza, was attacked for conducting the prosecution and was forced to leave the country for her safety.[145]

Iris Yolanda Quiñones Colchado, twenty-seven years old, was detained on November 3, 1989, while she was on her way to buy fish at a Lima market. Members of the police blindfolded her with her sweater and took her to a police station that she never saw. There Quiñones says she was forced to take off her clothes. The following is testimony that she gave to a public prosecutor six days later, after being transferred to the anti-terrorism police (DINCOTE).

> They forced me against my will to take off my clothes and then pushed my head down, and then every officer who passed stuck his hand inside my vagina, then they took one of my earrings and punctured my bottom with it, and then placed the barrel of a machine gun in my anus, then pulled me up and just like that, naked with my face blindfolded took me to a desk in the same room where they wanted to force me to sign a declaration where I said that they had found on me an explosive, a notebook and a fuse; I refused.[146]

Pilar Coqchi was arrested on January 23, 1990, in Huamanga, Ayacucho. A nursing student, she was accused of leading Shining Path actions in the Belén neighborhood. Coqchi says the police raped her first in the station. The rape was accompanied by other forms of torture, such as beatings, the little bird and the submarine.[147]

Despite threats made against her, Coqchi reported the torture to the public prosecutor, who ordered a medical examination. But police waited five days before complying, enough time for the worst bruises to fade and the evidence of rape to disappear. Coqchi was later sentenced to fifteen years in prison. No formal charges were made against the police because of insufficient evidence.

---

[145] Interview, Asociación Pro Derechos Humanos (APRODEH), Lima, December 1992.

[146] Testimony, Iris Yolanda Quiñones Colchado, taken in DINCOTE, November 9, 1989.

[147] Interview, Pilar Coqchi, Huamanga, Ayacucho, July 5, 1992.

On September 21, 1990, soldiers from the Julcamarca base in Huancavelica detained María Flores Valenzuela and her seventeen-year-old daughter, Zunilda Pineda Flores, peasants from the village of Carcosi.[148] The soldiers accused Flores of being a guerrilla because they found military-style boots and a blanket in her house. According to the family, the items belonged to Flores's uncle, an army veteran. The two women were taken to the Julcamarca base and tied to stakes in the central plaza, where they were left in the sun for several hours. The next day, they were again tied to the stakes.

When María fainted, she was dragged to a room. There she says three soldiers who appeared to be drunk raped her. Then they raped her daughter. That night the two women were released. Almost two weeks after the rapes, the family contacted Lima human rights groups. But filing a formal charge was impossible, because no physical evidence of rape remained. In addition, the pair believed they were under army surveillance and could not leave Carcosi.

Paulina Choquehuanca, a twenty-three-year-old from the village of Uchupata, was the secretary of communication and culture of the Huanacabamba Association of Women Peasant Workers.[149] On December 23, 1993, while returning from a workshop and training session, the army detained Choquehuanca and accused her of terrorism. She was raped and tortured. Her tormentors accused her of supporting the release of Antero Peña, the detained president of the peasant community to which Choquehuanca belongs. Although the investigative judge concluded she was not guilty and signed an order giving her unconditional liberty while the trial progressed, the faceless court charged with processing such orders revoked it. Later, even this court found Choquehuanca not guilty, and she was released on March 20, 1995. There is no current investigation of the abuses committed against her.[150]

María de la Cruz Pari was raped by DINCOTE agents in January 1993. De la Cruz had gone voluntarily to DINCOTE headquarters in Lima on January 6 to testify on behalf of a relative accused of membership in the

---

[148] APRODEH testimony.
[149] Information from Instituto de Defensa Legal (Peruvian human rights organization).
[150] Letter from Instituto de Defensa Legal to Human Rights Watch/Americas, June 12, 1995.

Shining Path.[151]   Instead, she was arrested and held incommunicado. Between January 7 and 10, de la Cruz, along with five other female prisoners, was blindfolded and taken to a beach south of Lima, at which time she was repeatedly raped and tortured with near-drowning.   De la Cruz claims that she was impregnated during the rapes and singled out an official named "Zárate" as one of the rapists.   Although the governor's investigation into this accusation concluded that de la Cruz was pregnant when she was detained, an independent examination conducted by two doctors from the Lima Maternity hospital concluded that de la Cruz conceived while in custody.   The Democratic Constituent Congress, which is the legislative body in place since the April 1992 coup, investigated the rapes, but its findings were never published. The district prosecutor closed the investigation of the officer named "Zárate" on the grounds that no officer of that name worked for DINCOTE, without taking into account that police frequently use nicknames or "war names" to hide their identities. De la Cruz was acquitted of treason, but her case was referred to a civilian faceless court, and in November 1994 the court sentenced her to twenty years. The case currently is being appealed before the Supreme Court.[152]

Rape in the Emergency Zones

Women who are victims of rape in the emergency zones have tended to be brown-skinned, poor, Quechua speakers, often monolingual. They have been forced to provide soldiers at local bases with meals, cleaning services and their bodies; or they have been raped during military incursions into their villages.

One local authority from Huancavelica described how soldiers threatened local women after a base was established in Acobamba in 1983:

> To save their lives, the women put themselves at the service
> of the soldiers, even if they are good girls, and also the
> soldiers are leaving the women pregnant and when the
> children are born, no one accepts paternity. Even if the
> woman has principles and is married, the soldiers ignore it,
> they have their list, "No, you must join us tonight, let's see,
> we're going to take your statement." So there are 300 or 400

---

[151]   Telephone   interview,   Committee   of   Family   Members   of   the Detained/Disappeared (COFADER), December 16, 1994.

[152] Interview, COFADER, Lima, June 12, 1995.

fatherless children. . . [then] the soldiers go to another base, who can you complain to, they are the only ones because they are the highest authorities.[153]

On the rare occasion women press for justice, they are met with silence or open ridicule. In 1991 María went with her father to ask an army commander to gather his troops so that she could identify the soldiers who raped her near Pampa Cangallo, Ayacucho. He complied but began to make fun of her in front of the troops. His scorn was so intense—including suggesting that she call her gestating baby "Navyman" if the rapist was a sailor, or "Little Soldier" if it was an army recruit—that María gave up in tears.[154]

Unlike rape in interrogation, rape in emergency zones has had a regional character, concentrated in the southern highlands of Ayacucho and Huancavelica. Only rarely has it occurred in urban centers or very populated areas. Often large numbers of soldiers participated; many women have been gang-raped by twenty or more men. Frequently, the rape has occurred in the context of a running confrontation between the security forces and armed insurgents, when troops were moving from village to village in search of a guerrilla column. Finally, these rapes often have transpired in front of women's families, including children.

"Probably less than 10 percent of the women who are raped in the emergency zones, especially in Ayacucho and Huancavelica, ever make a formal report," Sabina Villarroel, a social worker who helps internally displaced women, many of whom are rape victims, told us. "The main reasons are fear and shame, as if talking would advertise the terrible thing that happened to them."[155]

Lorenza Quispe, thirty-eight years old, is originally from Tinquoy, Ayacucho. In 1983 she says soldiers came to her and husband's house and forced her husband to accompany them, ostensibly to learn how to use a weapon. Later, Quispe learned her husband was being held in the Tambo military base.

Quispe made unsuccessful efforts to find her husband. Nevertheless, she kept pressuring soldiers at the base for information. In 1986 Quispe says

---

[153] COFADER testimony from Acobamba, Huancavelica.
[154] Interview, Huamanga, Ayacucho, July 5, 1992.
[155] Interview, Sabina Villarroel, Lima, July 6, 1992.

that, after she left some papers at the base related to her husband's disappearance, two soldiers began following her:

> They said to me, "Your husband's body was put there, in the gorge." Innocently, I thought it could be true. I followed them. And there they caught me, saying, "Why are you always bothering us? I don't know where your husband is. Do you want to live or will you die?" There is where they raped me. One stood watch, it was just him. . . [Afterwards] people have asked me why I went with them, but I reply that it was a rape.[156]

Quispe told us that she never reported the rape, however. She says they told her that if she talked they would kill her or "disappear" her like her husband. "Who would care for my children?" Quispe asks, "I am their father and mother."[157]

On June 5, 1988, Nilda, fourteen years old, says she left her Huamanga home early to visit the market. A truckload of soldiers picked her up, demanding identity documents. The soldiers forcibly dragged her into the truck, gagged her, then held her down as four of them raped her. The soldiers left Nilda lying in the street. According to the doctor interviewed by the reporter who collected Nilda's testimony, in less than a month he had treated four women raped by soldiers.[158]

Florencia, thirty-nine years old, says she not only lost her husband to a Shining Path execution squad on March 12, 1992, but also was raped by the guerrillas and then, a week later, raped by the army. She says the guerrillas killed her husband and six others because they were local authorities in San José de Ticlias, Ayacucho. When the army arrived a week later, they accused the villagers of having collaborated with guerrillas. The soldiers arrived by helicopter and immediately separated the men and women. Florencia told Human Rights Watch the men were made to lie face down in the dirt while soldiers marched over them, beating them with rifles. Other soldiers began

---

[156] Interview, Lorenza Quispe, Huamanga, Ayacucho, July 3, 1992.

[157] For other cases, see Human Rights Watch, *Untold Terror*, pp. 35-41.

[158] Mariella Balbi, "Ayacuchanos viven entre dos fuegos," *La República* (Lima), June 27, 1988.

pulling at her skirt. Her children, watching, screamed and cried. She did not remember how many raped her. *Bastante*, many, is all she could remember.[159]

On June 7, 1992, fourteen-year-old Froyli Mori Veal reported to the public prosecutor that she was raped after soldiers searched her family's home in the hamlet of La Unión, Nueva Lima district, San Martín. They said a Lieutenant "Juan" and six soldiers entered the house around midnight.

> After searching the house, they insisted that I accompany them, because they needed to talk to me. When both my parents and I refused this request, they threatened my parents with their weapons and made a soldier guard them so they couldn't leave the house while they dragged me outside. They took me to the back of the garden behind the house and there they raped me one after the other, beginning with the lieutenant. All seven raped me.[160]

A medical exam requested by the local priest was performed three days later. The doctor found that Mori had a serious vaginal infection, inflamed labia and a broken hymen. However, the doctor's inexperience with rape cases was evident. He took no note of any presence of sperm, focusing primarily on the infection.

The Case of Raquel Martín Castillo de Mejía

This history of impunity and the shame and guilt associated with rape were what initially convinced Raquel Martín Castillo de Mejía to hide the rape she suffered in 1989, when her husband was abducted by members of the army from their home in Oxapampa, in the department of Pasco. Her experience forcefully illustrates many of the obstacles to prosecuting cases of rape by the security forces. At the same time, it is the only rape case from Peru to have been presented to an international legal body, in this instance the Inter-American Commission on Human Rights.

Martín's husband, Dr. Fernando Mejía Egochaega, forty-one years old, was a journalist, lawyer and chair of the Oxapampa Provincial Committee of the United Left, a coalition of leftist political parties. Mejía was also a legal advisor to several peasant communities in Pasco and a well-known

---

[159] Interview, Lima, July 6, 1992.
[160] Sworn testimony of Froyli Mori Vela.

defender of the rights of the poor.   Martín, forty-three years old, was a school teacher, and the couple has a daughter, then three years old.[161]

On the night of June 15, 1989, at about 11:00 p.m., hooded men carrying machine guns and wearing military uniforms pounded on the door of the couples' home. When Mejía answered, he was beaten and forced from the house.   One of the abductors, stocky and over six feet tall, seemed to be directing the operation.   In the bright moonlight, Martín saw her husband blindfolded, forced into one of the waiting vehicles, and driven away. About fifteen minutes later, the tall man who had given the orders again pounded on the door. Martín remembers seeing six to ten men behind him. According to Martín, the man smelled of liquor.   He demanded her husband's identity documents and followed her into the bedroom as she searched for them. Then he showed Martín a list of names of supposed members of the armed guerrilla group the Movimiento Revolucionario "Tupac Amaru" (MRTA), including her husband and professor Aladino Melgarejo, president of the local branch of the National Teachers Union. Unbeknownst to her, Professor Melgarejo had been detained under similar circumstances the same night.

The man told Martín that she too was on the list as a suspected subversive. But he asked her no questions. Instead, he talked about "having a good time." He sprayed himself with her perfume and told her she was pretty. Then he removed his munitions belt, tore off her pants and raped her.

> [Afterwards] I was in a state of shock and sat in my bedroom. I had no telephone and no family nearby, and I didn't want to leave in case they brought back my husband. Around 11:45 p.m., I heard another blow on the door. When I opened it, the man who had raped me entered. . .He said my husband would be taken to Lima by helicopter the next day. Then he raped me again and left. I washed myself and sat speechless in my room.

Despite Martín's efforts over the next three days to locate her husband, she was unsuccessful.   On June 18, two bodies were found on the

---

[161] The following information is taken from sworn statements by Ms. Martín and witnesses to the events described, personal interviews with her by Human Rights Watch and the petition for relief filed on her behalf by the Washington, D.C. law firm Arnold and Porter before the Inter-American Commission for Human Rights on October 17, 1991.

banks of the Santa Clara river. Both her husband, still blindfolded, and Professor Melgarejo had been brutally tortured and summarily executed.

Martín reported her husband's murder but not her own rape. "What the military did to me they do wherever they go," Martín told Human Rights Watch. Soon after her husband's murder, Martín received three threatening phone calls and was forced to leave for exile in Sweden. Only then did she feel safe enough to talk about the rape.

Little action has been taken to investigate Mejía's murder. Independent of Martín's efforts, a petition was filed on her husband's behalf before the Inter-American Commission on Human Rights on September 25, 1989. The government of Peru did not respond; in January 1990, the commission declared that it presumed the allegations of human rights violations against Mejía to be true.

Following that decision, Martín formally filed a new petition for relief before the commission on October 17, 1991, asking that it be incorporated into the previous one. Her petition details the rape and asks for a full consideration of the case. Her lawyers argued that special consideration must be made for rape, on the grounds that local legal action constitutes a remedy that is "totally inadequate and ineffective." As of this writing, the petition was still before the commission.

Rape by the Shining Path

Although this chapter focuses on rape of women in conflict situations, women have experienced other forms of violence during conflict situations. In our original 1992 report we also documented murders of women leaders. Since the arrest of its leader, Abimael Guzmán, in September 1992, the Shining Path has operated at a greatly decreased level but it remains active.[162] Within the framework of Shining Path ideology, sex discrimination is prohibited. Men and women are considered equal, the only distinction being class and whether or not an individual has accepted a role in the so-called people's wars.   In addition, an informal Shining Path code of conduct explicitly forbids "men to sexually molest women and women should also avoid sexually molesting men."[163]

---

[162] On May 23, 1995, the Shining Path exploded a car bomb in Miraflores, a wealthy suburb of Lima. The apparent target was a tourist hotel.

[163] These rules are not necessarily distributed to all militants nor equally enforced. Juan Lázaro, "Women and Political Violence in Peru," *Dialectical Anthropology*, vol. 15 (1990), pp. 233-47.

Nevertheless, rape by male cadres of female civilians has been documented. Generally, it has occurred in areas contested by guerrillas and the security forces, where women believe they have to submit because of threats or overwhelming armed strength. To refuse would risk being labelled uncooperative and potentially hostile to the guerrillas' political goals. Few have sought to report rape afterwards, fearing retaliation or that their neighbors or the security forces would assume they are senderistas.

That was the case of Marcelina, who lives near Huamanga, Ayacucho and speaks only Quechua. One night in 1989, a man forced his way into her home and threatened her with a knife. He claimed that he was a member of the Shining Path and that his fellow cadres, waiting outside, would kill her if she screamed. He told her that their commander wanted her to climb to the *puna*, the high-altitude desert, and cook for the unit, which was preparing to celebrate his birthday. Then he raped her.[164]

> That morning, I went and told my father what had happened.
> I was afraid too that they would find my twelve-year-old
> daughter [and rape her]. I reported this to the local
> authorities, but they said to me, "What can we do?". . .I did
> not tell the police this because I was afraid they would arrest
> me. One judge said to me, "Why pick a fight with them?
> Just report the things that were stolen."

Marcelina became pregnant as a result of the rape and gave birth to a boy. In 1991 the civil defense patrol in her town captured two senderistas, one of whom was the rapist. The civil defense leader who questioned the man says he admitted the rape and paternity of the boy. He later escaped, however, and to their knowledge has never been punished.

Threats and Murder of Women Leaders

Women also have come under special fire from the Shining Path because they belonged to women's groups or were feminists. The reasoning behind these attacks is rooted in the Shining Path's ideology. As a Maoist insurgency, they believe that anything not related directly to the class struggle is a diversion. Other struggles, for instance, those to abolish racism or sex discrimination, are to be postponed until after a guerrilla victory.

---

[164] Interview, Ayacucho, July 4, 1992.

In fact, Shining Path literature argues that feminist issues like equal work for equal pay and freedom of choice are actually international conspiracies aimed at derailing the revolution. The Shining Path has combined these absolutist beliefs with the systematic use of terror and murder to force women to abandon their activism or join guerrilla ranks. Those who hesitate have been threatened. Those who refuse often have been killed.

Groups like the Flora Tristán Women's Center, the Manuela Ramos Movement, the Women's Center-Arequipa, the Association for the Development and Integration of Women, and Peru-Mujer have been accused of defending the existing order and being government collaborators. On numerous occasions, guerrillas have accused NGOs of "pimping off" the poor.[165] Since many NGOs also receive funds from abroad, guerrillas link them to other alleged international conspiracies against their new society.

As a result, in the late 1980s women's groups were forced to take special security measures and curtail projects in shantytowns where guerrillas have a strong presence.[166] Since 1992, the security measures have been decreased but still exist. The Manuela Ramos Movement instituted new precautions after receiving suspicious visits by men identifying themselves as journalists interested in writing about a Manuela-sponsored event. Neither turned out to be employed by a media outlet. "A street vendor we know who works nearby told us the pair had been talking about *perras feministas* (feminist bitches) before approaching the door, which is typical Shining Path language," Dr. Teresa Hernández, a lawyer who directs a Manuela legal aid service for female victims of violence, told Human Rights Watch.[167]

Disturbingly, the government did not protect women leaders against the Shining Path during this time of increased danger for female leaders. This lack of protection left women vulnerable to harassment and attacks and, consequently, compromised their ability to participate in society by running organizations.

Attacks on Survival Organizations

In urban areas, most grassroots organizations are run by poor women. When Peru's economy floundered in the 1980s, the number of these "survival

---

[165] "Between Political Parties and NGOs: The untold story of Mother Courage," *El Diario Internacional* (newspaper of the Shining Path), April 1992, pp. 10-14.

[166] Interviews, representatives of various social centers, Lima, June 24, 1992.

[167] Interview, Lima, June 24, 1992. For other cases, see Human Rights Watch, *Untold Terror*, pp. 48-49.

organizations," such as soup kitchens, expanded dramatically, keeping hundreds of thousands from starvation. Many feminists work with survival groups to press for legal reforms to benefit women, education and family planning.

The Shining Path criticized these groups as hiding a sinister plan "to maintain an enormous, extremely impoverished mass of people as beggars without a critical spirit, without the will to fight, who think of nothing more than the next plate of food to be given.[168] For senderistas, survival groups were the seeds of what they call battle committees, to be indoctrinated in the "people's war" and used to feed, house and protect armed militants.

Certain areas of Lima were of vital importance to this strategy, shantytowns on the central highway and shantytowns closely allied with the left or with a strong NGO presence. In those areas, survival group leaders had only two options: pledge to the guerrilla cause or become enemies. From 1985 until 1992, at least ten female leaders of survival groups were assassinated. Hundreds more were threatened with death or harm to their families and forced to collaborate or flee. The threats continue, but the reduction in the Shining Path's size and power has significantly diminished the likelihood of harm.

For example, Ceferina was a community activist in Ate-Vitarte in 1992. Like many others, she was forced to flee her Ayacucho home because of threats from the army. Then, in Lima, the Shining Path began giving her nightmares.[169] In her settlement, guerrillas threatened the soup kitchens and community-run pharmacies until they shut down. She told us that out of a total of thirty soup kitchens, only two remained in the summer of 1992. The army, which established a base near her home, only patrolled during the day, leaving guerrillas free to hold mandatory public meetings at night. Once, she says, thirty people, some masked, forced their way into her small house after midnight to intimidate her into taking part.

> It was midnight, just after a municipal meeting had ended.
> If I didn't open the door, they shouted, they promised to kick
> it in. If I didn't agree, they said I would have to leave the
> settlement. None of my neighbors came out to help me, even
> though I used my whistle when they first beat at the door.
> It was as if the whole thing had been planned. They know

---

[168] "Mother Courage," *El Diario Internacional.*
[169] Interview, Lima, July 8, 1992.

perfectly well who organizes things in each settlement, and
these are the people they pressure to join or resign.[170]

Murder of María Elena Moyano

Maria Elena Moyano, thirty-three years old in 1992, founded the
Popular Federation of Women of Villa El Salvador (FEPOMUVES) when she
was twenty-four and was its president for many years. She knew her ties to
the left, her popularity as Villa's vice mayor, and feminist beliefs made her a
prime Shining Path target. In one interview with the Lima daily *La República*,
Moyano admitted that for many years she did not criticize the guerrillas
publicly, even though she disagreed with their methods, because she thought
they were committed to improving society. But, as guerrillas began to train
their sights on her colleagues, she did speak out.

Moyano was the final speaker at a march on September 27, 1991, to
protest Shining Path threats, and she gave a series of interviews to newspapers
and magazines calling on the Shining Path to end its violent attacks.
Convinced by her colleagues that her life was in danger, she left the country
briefly in November. On her return, she asked for and was assigned two
police bodyguards. At year's end, she was honored by *La República* as the
Personality of the Year.

On February 14, 1992, Moyano was one of the few well-known public
figures to protest publicly and energetically against the Shining Path armed
strike called for that day. The next day, at a local barbecue to raise funds for
a local women's committee, an assassination squad trapped her. Guerrillas
seriously wounded one bodyguard, shot Moyano, and then destroyed her body
with dynamite as Moyano's two sons and nephew watched.

The murder caused outrage and anger. Moreover, it marked a critical
turning point in the attitude of independent organizations confronted by the
Shining Path. No longer were women leaders in positions as vulnerable as
Moyano's willing to risk attack. Instead they restricted their work, resigned
or left the country. "[FEPOMUVES hasn't] met since her death, and we
believe some of the newer leaders are not to be trusted," Alicia, a
FEPOMUVES activist told Human Rights Watch in 1992.

Although Peru's internal civil war has cooled down in recent years,
women continue to be targeted for attacks by both sides. President Fujimori
has pledged to "drastically punish" soldiers and police officers who commit

---

[170] For other cases, see Human Rights Watch, *Untold Terror*, pp. 51-54.

rape, but there have been no concrete steps to investigate allegations of rape in detention or punish members of the security forces who have committed rape. Human Rights Watch continues to receive reports of detainees raped by soldiers. To our knowledge, the pattern of impunity for uniformed rapists persists. In addition, the recent amnesty law insulates security officers from future investigations and prosecutions for past abuses.

Violations of women's basic rights by both sides routinely go unpunished, as do human rights abuses in Peru more generally. However, female victims of human rights abuse face an added obstacle, particularly with regard to the prosecution of rape. Courts require significant physical evidence of force and routinely accept evidence of women's alleged sexual history. Because military courts are secret, their conduct is unknown, but police and soldiers accused of rape and tried under the code of military justice are often acquitted. They are never made available to civilian courts for prosecution. The government should repeal the amnesty law and investigate both the previous rapes and the rapes that continue to occur. Moreover, as part of its efforts against the Shining Path, the government should take concrete steps to protect any female activist threatened by the guerrillas. And the Shining Path, which supports members who murder women as furthering its cause, cannot continue to do so. The Shining Path must instruct its members that violence against women is not tolerated by the leadership and punish any members that commit such acts.

GENERAL RECOMMENDATIONS

To Governments:
- All incidents of rape and sexual assault by soldiers or other state agents should be fully and fairly investigated and, where appropriate, prosecuted and punished.
- Military and civilian authorities should publicly condemn the use of rape by any and all parties to conflicts, whether international or internal, and emphasize their intent to investigate and punish those responsible for such abuse.
- Explicit bans on rape should be included in all training for enlisted men and officers to make clear that rape and sexual assault will not be tolerated and are in no way unofficially condoned by the state.
- To ensure the equitable prosecution of rape, governments should review domestic rape laws and their application and undertake reforms to ensure women's equal protection under law. Specifically, we urge

governments (1) to classify in their legal codes rape as a crime against women's physical integrity and not as an offense against individual or community honor; (2) to ensure that discriminatory attitudes about female rape victims neither prevent serious investigation of rape nor undermine rape's equitable prosecution; and (3) to ensure that medical and legal services provided by the state for the purpose of investigating rape are available to all women when and where they are needed.

- Governments should exercise jurisdiction to investigate and prosecute alleged instances of torture or other forms of cruel, inhuman and degrading treatment, including rape, that occur on their soil or that are committed by individuals residing in their territory.
- Governments should support the efforts of international tribunals, such as that established by the U.N. for former Yugoslavia and Rwanda, to investigate reported war crimes, grave breaches of the Geneva Conventions, and crimes against humanity, including rape and other forms of sexual assault. Governments should further make those indicted for such offenses available to stand trial.

To the International Community:
- Rape and sexual assault should be recognized as constituting violations of international human rights standards and humanitarian law. To this end, all international tribunals should fully and fairly investigate and prosecute rape as a war crime under the Geneva Conventions. Further, rape—like murder, deportation and other serious crimes—should be recognized and prosecuted as a constituent crime against humanity, as that term was defined in Article 6(c) of the Nuremberg Charter.
- Investigations of rape and other forms of sexual assault should be conducted by those trained in working with victims of such crimes. Efforts should be made at all times to guard the identity of the victim, to protect her against potential reprisal, and to assist her in receiving the services she requires, such as medical attention.
- The United Nations should ensure that its monitoring of human rights abuse and violations of humanitarian law include reporting on rape and sexual assault against women and that such offenses are properly denounced as torture or cruel, inhuman and degrading treatment.
- All troops deployed by the United Nations, including peacekeeping forces, should receive explicit training that all acts of rape and sexual

assault are prohibited, will not be tolerated, and will be investigated and punished.

2
SEXUAL ASSAULT OF REFUGEE
AND DISPLACED WOMEN

While the conflicts that cause women to flee often make news headlines, the plight of women who become refugees and displaced persons frequently remains unpublicized.[1] In many cases, refugee and displaced women flee conflict after being terrorized with rape and other sexual and physical abuse. Although they seek refuge to escape these dangers, many are subjected to similar abuse as refugees. United Nations High Commissioner for Refugees Sadako Ogata has called this widespread sexual violence against refugee women a "global outrage."[2] Similarly, the U.N. Special Rapporteur on Violence against Women, Radhika Coomaraswamy, has found:

> Sexual violence against refugees is a global problem. Refugees from Bosnia, Rwanda, Somalia and Vietnam have brought harrowing stories of abuse and suffering. It constitutes a violation of basic human rights, instilling fear in the lives of victims already profoundly affected by their displacement.[3]

---

[1] As of February 1995, twenty-three million people had fled across borders becoming refugees, and another twenty-six million had been internally displaced in their own countries. According to the United Nations High Commissioner for Refugees, a staggering figure of one in every 115 people is on the run or in exile. Africa has nearly 7.5 million refugees and as many displaced; Asia has 5.7 million refugees and Europe six million, not including the internally displaced, particularly in Bosnia. Women and children account for roughly 80 percent of all refugees worldwide. "This is No Place Like Home," *The New York Times*, March 5, 1995 and United Nations High Commissioner for Refugees, *The State of the World's Refugees* (Geneva: UNHCR, 1993), p. 87.

[2] United Nations High Commissioner for Refugees, "Sexual Violence Against Refugees: Guidelines on Prevention and Response" (Geneva: UNHCR, March 1995) [hereafter Sexual Violence Guidelines], Preface by Sadako Ogata, U.N. High Commissioner for Refugees.

[3] Ibid., foreword by Radhika Coomaraswamy, Special Rapporteur on Violence Against Women.

100

Refugee and displaced women, uprooted from their homes and countries by war, internal strife, or natural catastrophe are vulnerable to violence both as a result of the surrounding problem and because of their dependency on outsiders for relief provisions. The internally displaced are further at risk because the abuses they seek to escape are often being committed by the very government that should afford them protection.[4] Moreover, because they have not crossed any international border to seek refuge or asylum, displaced persons can claim only minimal protection from international law. While the United Nations High Commissioner for Refugees (UNHCR) is tasked with primary responsibility for ensuring protection and assistance to refugees, no similar organization exists within the United Nations system for internally displaced persons. The programs run by the UNHCR and the U.N. Development Program (UNDP) for the internally displaced operate only on an ad hoc basis.

The wide range of abuses against refugees and displaced persons include, frequently, rape and other sexual assault. Women refugees are raped because they are refugees, because of their actual or perceived political or ethnic affiliations, and because they are women. The use of this gender-specific form of abuse frequently has political or ethnic, as well as gender-specific, components. In some cases, refugee and displaced persons' camps are relatively close to the site of the conflict that caused displacement. As the Kenya section in this chapter illustrates, women in such camps are the object of attacks from factions that enter the camps in order to dominate and punish those refugees perceived to be supporting opposing factions. In other cases, combatants who support or even participate in the different sides of a conflict

---

[4] At present, there is no internationally agreed-upon definition for the internally displaced. The U.N. secretary-general's special representative for issues relating to internally displaced persons has recommended that the following definition be adopted by the international community: "persons who have been forced to flee their homes suddenly or unexpectedly in large numbers, as a result of armed conflict, internal strife, systematic violations of human rights or natural or man-made disasters; and who are within the territory of their own country." The first report of the special representative also recommended that the international community strengthen legal protections for the internally displaced and create U.N. human rights machinery to monitor their treatment and initiate actions on their behalf. *See* U.N. Doc E/CN.4/1993/35 *as quoted in* "The 49th Session of the U.N. Commissioner on Human Rights," *International Journal of Refugee Law*, vol. 5, no. 2 (1993), p. 257; and Roberta Cohen, "International Protection for Internally Displaced Persons—Next Steps," (Refugee Policy Group, Washington D.C.), focus paper no. 2, January 1994, pp. 959-960.

may mingle with civilian populations within camps. The humiliation, pain and terror that the rapist inflicts on an individual woman in this context is intended to degrade the entire ethnic or political group.

Rape and other forms of sexual assault are frequently gender-specific not only in their form but also in their motivation. Thus, refugee and displaced women and girls are raped because of their gender, irrespective of their age, ethnicity, or political beliefs. In host countries, local residents and even police, military and immigration officials, often view refugee women as targets for assault. They subject refugee and displaced women to rape or other forms of sexual extortion in return for the granting of passage to safety, refugee status, personal documentation, or relief supplies.

Fellow refugees may also target displaced and refugee women for sexual abuse. The dislocation and violence experienced by displaced and refugee populations often destroy family and social structures, and with them, the norms and taboos that normally would have proscribed sexual violence against women. Moreover, the anger, uncertainty and helplessness of male refugees unable to assume their traditionally dominant roles are often translated into violent behavior toward women.

The injuries that refugee and displaced women sustain from being violently raped persist long after the incident. Refugee women interviewed by Human Rights Watch have reported ongoing medical problems, including miscarriages by women raped when pregnant; hemorrhaging for long periods; inability to control urination; sleeplessness; nightmares; chest and back pains; and painful menstruation. For women who have undergone the practice of female genital mutilation, the physical injuries caused by rape are compounded.[5] Moreover, refugee and displaced women who become pregnant as a result of rape are often unable to procure safe abortions because abortion is either illegal or too expensive.

---

[5] Female genital mutilation, also known as female circumcision, is the collective name given to several different traditional practices involving the cutting of female genitals. In the most extreme version, infibulation, the clitoris and inner vaginal lips are removed and the outer lips are stitched closed leaving only a small opening (sometimes the size of a match stick) for the flow of urine and menstrual blood. Sexual intercourse for women who have undergone this operation is painful unless the opening is gradually expanded over time or they are re-cut to widen the opening.

Human Rights Watch strongly opposes nonconsensual female genital mutilation or circumcision as a violation of the rights to physical security (ICCPR, Article 9), and to nondiscrimination on the basis of sex (ICCPR, Article 26).

Strong cultural stigma attached to rape further intensifies the rape victims' physical and psychological trauma. Women in refugee and displaced camps who acknowledge being raped may be ostracized, or even punished, by their families. As a result, women survivors of sexual violence often are reluctant to seek medical assistance or to file police reports, because they do not want it known that they were raped. Even when incidents are reported, however, effective responses may not be forthcoming, since international humanitarian organizations as well as countries of asylum often do not recognize and are not properly equipped to handle such gender-related abuse.

The Responsibility of Governments

International law imposes clear obligations on governments to prohibit rape and other forms of sexual violence. At a minimum, such abuses violate the right to security of the person.[6] Rape committed by or acquiesced in by a state agent is torture under international law, which defines torture as any act:

> . . . intentionally inflicted on a person for such purposes as obtaining from him [sic] or a third person information or a confession, punishing him [sic] for an act he [sic] or a third person has committed or is suspected of having committed, or intimidating or coercing him [sic] or a third person, or for any reason based on discrimination of any kind, when such pain or suffering is inflicted by or at the acquiescence of a public official or other person acting in an official capacity.[7]

International human rights norms also require governments to ensure that all individuals within their territories, regardless of citizenship, enjoy the equal protection of the law.[8] The U.N. Human Rights Committee, which

---

[6] International Covenant on Civil and Political Rights (ICCPR), Article 9.

[7] Convention Against Torture and Other Cruel, Inhuman or Degrading Treatment or Punishment, opened for signature by General Assembly resolution 39146 of December 10, 1984, art. 1. In addition, Article 7 of the ICCPR and the U.N. Code of Conduct for Law Enforcement Officials, adopted by the General Assembly by resolution 34/169 on December 17, 1979, also prohibit torture.

[8] Article 2(1) of the ICCPR states: "Each State Party to the Covenant undertakes to respect and to ensure to all individuals within its territory and subject to its jurisdiction
(continued...)

monitors the compliance of all state parties with the International Covenant on Civil and Political Rights, has further held that state parties have a duty to safeguard persons from such violations as well as to investigate violations when they occur and to bring the perpetrators to justice.[9]   In the case of refugees, the responsibility to protect "remains the primary responsibility of the countries where the refugees find themselves."[10]

Notwithstanding human rights standards, host governments often show little concern for the violence experienced by refugees, including rape of refugee women.   Their indifference is demonstrated by ineffective security arrangements in the camps and by inadequate investigation and prosecution of rape and other forms of sexual violence against refugee women, even when the perpetrators are state agents tasked with refugee protection.

Aside from international norms, the domestic laws of virtually all host governments also prohibit rape. However, the ability of refugee and displaced women actually to seek legal redress is undermined for a number of different reasons. They are often destitute, unable to speak the local language, fearful of dealing with authorities, or situated in remote areas miles from the nearest police post or court. Where the local criminal justice system is unresponsive to allegations of rape, many refugee survivors of sexual violence consider legal redress futile. In particular, local police often are unwilling to investigate complaints against fellow police, military or immigration officials. These factors, alone or in combination, effectively deny refugees who have survived rape access to justice.

Recognizing the frequent, and in some situations, rampant occurrence of rape and sexual assault of refugee women, the UNHCR in 1995 promulgated "Sexual Violence Against Refugees: Guidelines on Prevention and Response" [hereafter "Sexual Violence Guidelines"]. These guidelines note that governments have an obligation to investigate, prosecute and punish

---

[8](...continued)
the rights recognized in the present Covenant, without distinction of any kind, such as race, colour, sex, language, religion, political or other opinion, national or social origin, property, birth or other status." Article 26 further provides that all persons are "equal before the law and are entitled without any discrimination to the equal protection of the law."

[9] *See* Report of the Human Rights Committee, 37 U.N. GAOR Supp. (no. 40) Annex V, general comment 7(16), paragraph 1(1982) U.N. Doc. A/37/40(1982).

[10] Report of the U.N. High Commissioner for Refugees, 38 U.N. GAOR Supp. (no. 12) p. 8, U.N. Doc. A/38/12 (1983).

perpetrators of sexual violence. They urge governments to adopt a "firm and highly visible policy against all forms of sexual violence" by (1) enacting and enforcing national legislation; (2) maintaining cooperative contact with national women's organizations; (3) facilitating the investigation of complaints of sexual violence; (4) ensuring protection of the victim and any witnesses from reprisal; (5) taking disciplinary action in cases involving government officials; and (6) providing adequate security at refugee camps and, where appropriate, deploying female security forces or guards. Unfortunately, as discussed below, these and other guidelines to improve refugee protection have been inconsistently implemented.

The Responsibility of the Relief Community

The international relief community has been slow to address the problem of rape in refugee camps. Guidelines have been developed to improve protection, but while these documents reflect enhanced awareness of the urgent plight of refugee women, they have not been consistently implemented by UNHCR, host countries or nongovernmental relief organizations. UNHCR—the lead U.N. agency for refugee relief and protection—has promulgated two sets of guidelines to deal with sexual assault of refugee women. In July 1991, UNHCR promulgated the "Guidelines on the Protection of Refugee Women" to assist the staff of UNHCR to identify and respond to the issues, problems and risks facing refugee women. In March 1995, UNHCR issued the Sexual Violence Guidelines described above to improve or initiate services to address the special needs and concerns of refugees who have been subjected to sexual violence.

The "Guidelines on the Protection of Refugee Women" [hereafter "Protection Guidelines"] prescribe measures that "can" or "may" be taken to counter physical and sexual attacks and abuse of women during flight and in their countries of asylum.[11] They call for, among other things: (1) changing the physical design and location of refugee camps to provide greater physical security; (2) using security patrols; (3) reducing the use of closed facilities or detention centers; (4) training staff regarding the particular problems faced by refugee women and employing female staff to work with women refugees to identify their concerns; (5) establishing mechanisms for law enforcement within the refugee camps; (6) educating refugee women about their rights; (7) giving priority to assessing the protection needs of unaccompanied refugee

---

[11] UNHCR, "Guidelines on the Protection of Refugee Women," (Geneva: UNHCR, July 1991).

women; and (8) ensuring women's direct access to food and other services, including whatever registration process is used to determine eligibility for assistance.

The Sexual Violence Guidelines supplement the Protection Guidelines by suggesting a range of preventive measures that can and should be taken to prevent sexual violence. In particular, these steps include, among others: (1) ensuring that the physical design and location of the refugee camps enhance physical security; (2) providing frequent security patrols by law enforcement authorities and by the refugees themselves; (3) installing fencing around the camps; (4) identifying and promoting alternatives to refugee camps where possible; (5) organizing inter-agency meetings between UNHCR, other relief organizations and relevant government officials, as well as the refugees themselves, to develop a plan of action to prevent sexual violence; and (6) assigning to the camps a greater number of female protection officers, field interpreters, doctors, health workers and counselors.

Despite some progress in implementing both these guidelines in UNHCR-run refugee camps, violence against refugee women is far from ended. In many cases, implementation problems stem from the fact that refugee situations often are crisis-driven, with relief workers overwhelmed by a seemingly endless refugee flow.

Aside from the exigencies of each situation, consistent implementation of the guidelines is also undermined within UNHCR. The UNHCR itself has acknowledged that its staff may avoid confronting or remedying widespread sexual violence in refugee camps because of personal discomfort with addressing the issue or a perception that such acts are a "private matter" or "an inevitable by-product" of the conflict.[12]   Additionally, underreporting of sexual assault allows relief workers to deny the scale of such violence.

Refugee Asylum Law

International refugee law protects the right of persons who have fled a country to seek asylum in another if they have a well-founded fear of persecution should they be returned to the country they have fled. However, refugee women who have suffered sexual violence have faced great difficulty in obtaining asylum elsewhere for three reasons. First, the procedure to determine asylum eligibility is generally insensitive, and even hostile, to refugee women who have suffered sexual abuse or who for other reasons may have difficulty relating their claims. In this procedure, all refugees are

---

[12] UNHCR Sexual Violence Guidelines, p. 7.

required to describe the persecution they have suffered to asylum adjudicators. However, refugee women are often reluctant to disclose experiences of sexual violence, particularly if the asylum adjudicators are men, due to the stigma attached to sexual violence or as a result of trauma.[13]   Other refugee women might refuse to detail the abuses they have experienced for fear of retribution against their family members or rejection by their communities.   Asylum adjudicators who are not aware of such concerns have negatively interpreted women's reluctance to describe the sexual violence inflicted on them and incorrectly judged their testimony not credible.[14]

Second, asylum adjudicators have tended to dismiss gender-specific violations experienced by refugee women as "personal" or "cultural" harms that do not qualify as political persecution.   Often, accounts of rape and other sexual abuse perpetrated against refugee women for political purposes have been treated in a discriminatory manner by asylum adjudicators who have dismissed such persecution as "personal" harm and denied asylum.

Third, asylum adjudicators have presumptively excluded women asylum applicants on the grounds that gender is not specifically listed in the U.N. Convention Regarding the Status of Refugees.   That convention requires states to grant asylum to refugees fleeing a well-founded fear of persecution on the grounds of "race, religion, nationality, membership of a particular social group, or political opinion."

Gradually, however, the international community is recognizing that gender-related persecution is a basis for asylum. The UNHCR has interpreted the refugee definition to consider women asylum seekers with gender-related claims as members of a "particular social group." Two broad categories of gender-related claims have been identified: those in which the persecution

---

[13] Victims of sexual violence may exhibit a pattern of symptoms referred to as Post Traumatic Stress Disorder or Rape Trauma Syndrome that makes it difficult for them to testify. These symptoms may include persistent fear, a loss of self-confidence and self-esteem, difficulty in concentration, an attitude of self-blame, a pervasive feeling of loss of control, and memory loss or distortion. Nancy Kelly, "Guidelines for Women's Asylum Claims," *International Journal of Refugee Law*, (Oxford: Oxford University Press, 1994), vol. 6, pp. 533-534.

[14] This is not to discount the fact that there have been some fabricated claims of rape by refugee women hoping to be resettled. These false cases will diminish in number as the relief community's response to helping rape survivors becomes more immediate and mechanisms are put into place for monitoring, reporting and effectively responding to sex-based abuses as they occur.

constitutes a *type* of harm that is particular to the applicant's gender, such as rape or genital mutilation; and those in which the persecution may be imposed *because of* the applicant's gender, for example, because a woman has violated societal norms regarding women's proper conduct.[15]

Several countries have taken actions that have contributed to the growing acceptance of gender-related persecution as a grounds for asylum. In 1984 the European Parliament determined that women fearing cruel or inhuman treatment as a result of seeming to have transgressed social mores should be considered a "social group" for the purposes of determining their status. Both Canada and the United States have issued guidelines to their immigration officials to help them identify women who should be granted asylum in cases where gender-specific forms of abuse have been used for political persecution in their homelands. Their guidelines educate asylum adjudicators to recognize gender-specific forms of violence and provide them with procedures and methods to better evaluate whether individual claims meet the refugee standard. While these guidelines do not change the standard that women asylum seekers must meet, they do recognize that human rights abuses faced by women because of their gender can rise to the level of persecution.[16]

Refugee situations can ultimately be solved only with an end to the conflict or other catastrophe that caused the refugee flight. In the meantime, governments and the UNHCR have a responsibility to ensure the safety of refugees. This obligation extends to the protection of refugee women from gender-based abuse.

BURMESE REFUGEES IN BANGLADESH

Beginning in late 1991, wide-scale atrocities committed by the Burmese military, including rape, forced labor, and religious persecution, triggered an exodus of ethnic Rohingya Muslims from the northwestern

---

[15] Kelly, "Guidelines for Women's Asylum Claims."

[16] *See also,* "Guidelines for Women's Asylum Claims," Women Refugees Project, Harvard Immigration and Refugee Services. This set of guidelines gives recommendations to asylum adjudicators on dealing with gender-based asylum claims and were developed in collaboration with thirty-six refugee and human rights organizations in the United States, including Human Rights Watch.

Burmese state of Arakan into Bangladesh.[17] The Burmese military had embarked on a policy of ridding the country of ethnic Rohingyas by any possible means, including sexual and physical violence against Rohingya women. Investigations by Human Rights Watch revealed the constancy of such dangers to Rohingya women at home, during flight and as refugees. Since the State Law and Order Restoration Council (SLORC) regime remains in power, Rohingyas who were later repatriated, often involuntarily, by the Bangladeshi government may have been re-exposed to this cycle of abuse.[18]

In many ways, the mistreatment of these Muslims, called Rohingyas, seemed to be integral to the stepped-up military offensive against ethnic minorities and opposition activists by the SLORC, the military junta that has become one of the most abusive governments in Asia. Intensive fighting took place from February to April 1992 along Burma's eastern border against the Karen and Mon people as well; refugees who fled to Thai border camps brought with them accounts of rape and forced labor, similar to those given by Rohingya refugees in Bangladesh.

But several particularities about the Rohingya situation distinguish it from the pattern of human rights violations in the east. The Burmese government claims the Rohingyas are illegal immigrants from across the border in Bangladesh and never belonged in Burma in the first place,[19]

---

[17] At its height in late 1993, the refugee population in Bangladesh numbered nearly 240,000. The following material was adapted from Asia Watch, "Burma: Rape, Forced Labor and Religious Persecution in Northern Arakan," *A Human Rights Watch Short Report*, vol. 4, no. 13 (May 1992); and Asia Watch, "Bangladesh: Abuse of Burmese Refugees from Arakan," *A Human Rights Watch Short Report*, vol. 5, no. 17 (October 1993).

[18] For further background on the Rohingyas and the political situation in Burma, *see* Asia Watch, "Burma: Rape, Forced Labor . . ."

[19] The Burmese government's claim that Rohingyas are illegal immigrants is specious, but the efforts to deny them full citizenship go back to Burma's first citizenship law in 1947. By the terms of that law, anyone who could demonstrate that family members had been living in Burma at the time of the Anglo-Burma War of 1824 qualified for full citizenship. The law clearly favored ethnic Burmese rather than residents of ethnic minority areas where borders had been more clearly defined and where cross-border movement had been frequent. Even the 1947 law, however, was preferable to a new citizenship law passed in 1982. That law gave full citizenship only to Burmese who could trace the families of both parents back to pre-1824 Burma. Some 10 percent of the population who could not meet this criterion were considered

(continued...)

whereas it clearly acknowledges the minorities in the east as Burmese nationals (whether or not they regard themselves as such). The armed insurgency among the Rohingyas is small and not a significant fighting force comparable to the Karen guerrillas or other insurgent armies in the east; SLORC does not even attempt to justify the campaign against the Rohingyas in terms of counterinsurgency. The religious persecution of the Muslims appears to be much stronger than persecution of other religious minorities. And the sheer scale of the human disaster, with hundreds of thousands fleeing to one of the poorest, most flood-ravaged countries in the world, has no parallels on Burma's borders with China or Thailand.

Rohingyas interviewed by Human Rights Watch said that the routine of SLORC oppression became one of concerted brutality following the National Assembly elections of May 27, 1990, in which the military junta was soundly defeated. Like the rest of Burma, the Arakan province voted heavily against the ruling National Union Party and in favor of the opposition. The votes were divided among Aung San Suu Kyi's National League for Democracy; the Arakan League for Democracy; and the National Democratic Party for Human Rights. In fact, the military's increased efforts to tighten control over the country in the wake of the 1988 mass pro-democracy movement had only reached Arakan by late 1989 and the Buthidaung and Mawdaung townships in northwest Arakan, bordering Bangladesh, by late 1990.[20]   At that point, food supplies were suddenly confiscated by the military, and physicians then in Bangladesh said they could measure the onslaught of malnutrition in children by the desperately reduced diet since 1990. Forced labor, population resettlement and land confiscation increased, and so did the flight of Rohingyas to Bangladesh.

In April 1991, Edith Mirante of the nongovernmental organization Project Maje interviewed a number of Rohingya refugees who had left

---

[19](...continued)
non-nationals and were classified as Associates or Naturalized. The aim of the law was to isolate Indian, Chinese and Muslim ethnic groups; any "non-national" was barred from serving in state or party positions, serving in the armed forces or the police, attending higher education or national institutions and owning property or business. No steps have been taken to modify the citizenship law, despite repeated recommendations from the United Nations Special Rapporteur on Burma.
[20] *Far Eastern Economic Review*, Hong Kong, 1991, p. 6.

Buthidaung between one and three months earlier.[21]   They said thousands were fleeing then, long before the international community began to take notice, and reported Rohingya men being seized for forced labor, women being routinely raped, houses, land and farm animals being taken by the soldiers.

Rape by the Burmese Military

By August 1991, there were an estimated 10,000 refugees from Arakan, mostly Rohingyas, in Bangladesh. On December 21, 1991, Burmese troops from the Lon Htein security forces crossed into Bangladesh and attacked a well-marked Bangladesh border post. Four Bangladeshis were killed and twenty-two wounded. In response, Bangladesh massed troops along the border, and SLORC was reported to have sent an additional 50,000 to 70,000 troops to Arakan. These included the Lon Htein forces, who had played a key role in the bloody crackdown in Rangoon in 1988. The increased military presence spelled more suffering for the Rohingyas. Against this backdrop, Human Rights Watch conducted interviews among then newly arrived refugees in several camps outside the Bangladeshi town of Cox's Bazaar in mid-March 1992, documenting, among other atrocities, rape of Rohingya refugee women by members of the Burmese army.

Rape of women after their husbands or fathers had been taken for forced labor was common. Sometimes the rapes occurred in the homes of the victims with children and relatives left to watch; other times the women were taken to a nearby military camp where they were sorted out by beauty. In some cases, the women were killed; in others they were allowed to return home.[22] The following testimonies, taken in March 1992, reveal how sexual and physical violence by the Burmese military against Rohingya women was a direct cause of the exodus to Bangladesh of women, their families and even entire communities.

Eslam Khatun (E.K), thirty-one, mother of six children, was the wife of the village headman of Imuddinpara, Rama Musleroi, Buthidaung. About February 1, 1992, she was at home with her children, brother-in-law and sister-in-law named Layla Begum (L.B), aged sixteen; her husband had been taken by the Burmese military for forced labor and had not returned home. It had been cold, and the family was sitting next to the fire, about to get ready for bed. It was about 9:00 p.m. when they heard the sound of soldiers' boots and

---

[21] Edith Mirante, "Our Journey: Voices from Arakan, Western Burma," May 1990 (unpublished report).

[22] For other testimonies, *see* Asia Watch, "Burma: Rape, Forced Labor . . ."

voices speaking Burmese outside. When the soldiers forced open the door, the fire lit up E.K.'s face, and they saw her. First, they pulled her up by her arms, and her brother tried to stop them. They began beating him, while undressing and violently molesting E.K., though not raping her there. When they dragged her and her brother from the house, the brother was bound and E.K. was naked.

Eslam Halim's (E.H.) husband, Abdul, returned from forced labor duty to learn of his sister's and brother's abductions. He had been regularly forced to work for the military but, since he was a village headman, he was also obliged to provide male laborers to the soldiers. Hoping he had a more privileged position than most villagers, he decided to go to the local army camp to ask about E.K. Eight days later, E.H. found E.K's body in the jungle near their house. She appeared to have bled to death from her vagina. "The soldiers had been satisfied with her," E.H. said.

About twenty-one days later, the bodies of Abdul Halim and his brother were found dumped in the same area. E.H. herself buried her husband. She said his genitals had been cut off, his eyes gouged out, both hands cut off and he was cut down the torso into two pieces. A few days later, E.H. and her six children walked for two days with 250 other villagers to reach the Naaf River. Soldiers opened fire on the boats in her group, but she was uninjured. About two-thirds of her village fled to Dechuapalang 1 Camp in Bangladesh.

Jahura Khatu (J.K), thirty, is the widow of a farmer in Naikaengdam village, Buthidaung. She arrived in Bangladesh on February 1, 1992. Over the last decade, she said, Muslim villagers had been harassed continuously by local SLORC military personnel and told they were not Burmese. J.K's only Burmese identification card indicated she was a Muslim foreigner. Chickens, cows, rice harvest and cash were taken freely by soldiers at any time. If there was no cash in the house when they appeared and demanded it, she said, the women were beaten and raped.

At the start of 1991, a military camp with some 1,200 soldiers was established in Naikaengdam on the site of the local mosque and cemetery, which had been just next to Jahura's house. Men were abducted house-to-house for forced labor; J.K's husband Fazil Alam, forty-five, had been taken many times for road construction, usually for two or three days of service. In December 1991, her husband was taken for labor again. One day soldiers appeared at her house to give her a bundle of bloody clothes she recognized as Alam's. They said he had been unable to carry the assigned load, and they had beaten him to death.

After that, soldiers came back to her home again and again to rape her and to demand money and food. A month after they brought the clothing, several soldiers came late one night and raped her again. Afterward, they took her out of her house and forced her at gunpoint along with three young women, all unmarried, to walk to Naikaengdam Camp, about fifteen minutes away. The women were kept together, given no food or water, and raped by officers throughout that night and the following day. J.K noted that an officer named "Arbanku" was in charge. They were told that if they promised to bring other women to camp, they would be released. After sunset the women were let go, and decided on the walk home they would escape to Bangladesh.

Half the village left at the same time, in broad daylight. One hundred families walked for seven days, most carrying nothing but a little rice. On the eighth day they met soldiers at the river bank; their pillows, bedding and household items were all confiscated, and they crossed the Naaf River to Bangladesh.

Jaharu Begum (J.B.), twenty, from Lapia, Devina in Akyab district arrived in Bangladesh on February 11, 1992. She said that in November 1991, four or five Burmese soldiers came to her house at about 1:00 a.m. They ordered the door to be opened. J.B., knowing they were abducting forced laborers, said her husband, Animullah, was not home.

The soldiers then kicked down the door, spotted her husband in the room, and tied his hands. They dragged him outside the house and beat him badly. After three days J.B. still had no word about her husband. That night the same soldiers came back at 1:00 or 2:00 a.m. This time they took her alone to the small camp, punching and hitting her with rifle butts during the one-hour walk. At the camp various soldiers raped her continuously for about sixteen hours, until they appeared to be "satisfied," as J.B. stated. The village head was at the camp at the time. He happened to recognize her and convinced the soldiers to release her.

After a month at home with no information about her husband, J.B. decided to flee to Bangladesh. She had no children and no remaining relatives other than her mother who had escaped to Bangladesh over a year and a half before and of whose whereabouts J.B. had heard nothing. She joined five or six families in the trip to the river and believed only two or three families remained in her village of Lapia.

Aisha Khatun (A.K.), twenty-five, from Labadogh village, Buthidaung, crossed into Bangladesh with her five children and her father. She explained that about a year and a half previously [toward the end of 1990], the Burmese army had set up camp in the village rice fields. They gave notice to the villagers to leave, announcing the local Muslims were all "Bangladeshi." They forced abducted male laborers to destroy their village mosque and build a Buddhist temple in its place. Unable to cultivate their fields because of the camp, many farmers stayed idle in their homes. Sometimes the soldiers ordered them out. When they refused, their homes were burned. Everyone lived in fear.

One afternoon in early December 1991, Burmese soldiers announced that all Muslims must leave. A.K. and her husband made no preparations to do so because they had no place to go. That night, while her husband and children were sleeping under their blankets, five soldiers kicked down the door of their house. They said they were collecting laborers. A.K. told them her husband was not there. "Then we'll take you," she said they told her. They then carried her outside, tore off her clothes, blindfolded her with a rag and while two or three held her, each of the five took a turn raping her.

At some point during the violence, she was aware of her husband emerging from the house to defend her. There were blows, and her husband briefly appeared to escape the group of soldiers. Two or three of the rapists chased him, he was caught and brought back. Using a long-blade work knife, the soldiers then hacked him to death, leaving his body in front of A.K. She herself lay on the ground injured and bleeding. The soldiers said they would return for her. When she had recovered enough to travel, she gathered her five children and father, and left on foot. They caught a boat to Bangladesh at Parampur Crossing.

Having abandoned their homes to escape rape and other physical violence, Rohingya refugee women continued to be terrorized in other ways during flight.

Mohammad Shah (M.S.), thirty, from Azarbil, Maungdaw, arrived in Bangladesh on February 13, 1992. He recounted what happened to a group of about 200 Muslims from the Azarbil area in Burma who left for Bangladesh about January 3, 1992. The group included M.S.'s best friend, his uncle and many neighbors.

His friend returned to Azarbil in a panic later the same day, describing how the group was stopped by Burmese civilians and soldiers, and how he had fled the scene. A day later, a villager reported to M.S. that his uncle was now in the military post called Napru Camp. He went to the camp but learned nothing. He distinctly recalled the screaming of women from buildings at the camp. On January 5, M.S. himself discovered his uncle's body floating on the river near their village. The following day, M.S. found more bodies, this time four females, floating near the same place. He recognized them as his neighbors, from the group that had departed for the border.

Fatema Khatun (F.K.), thirty, arrived in Bangladesh on March 5, 1992. She left Goalangi village, Buthidaung, on February 26, together with her son, husband, father, father-in-law, mother-in-law, and two brothers-in-law, and a group of 600 to 700 people. F.K. and her son had trouble keeping up, as she suffers from high blood pressure and her son had injured his left foot badly on the trail.

On March 3, as the group of refugees neared the Daijarkhal river, they saw SLORC soldiers for the first time on the trip. There were about forty to fifty armed soldiers on both sides of the stream, and soon the crowd was completely surrounded. F.K. and her son had fallen behind, and separated from the group on the top of a little hill, were not spotted. Suddenly, the soldiers began firing into the crowd. Everyone tried to flee or drop to the ground as the firing continued. F.K. kept her eyes on her family members in the group as best she could. She clearly saw her father shot in the chest and saw her husband take at least one bullet as well.

F.K. and her son hid until the firing stopped and then had no choice but to continue their escape on foot, alone. They walked for two more days; by then they had no food. Over the whole nine-day trek, the two of them ate rice only three times. Eventually they met a small groups of refugees also traveling to the river, but F.K. could find none of her family among them. At Balukhali Crossing, 200 to 250 people had gathered to hire boats to Bangladesh. F.K. could identify just about one hundred from her original group.

Rape by Bangladeshi Military and Paramilitary Forces in Refugee Camps in Bangladesh

For many Rohingya refugees, the ordeal of violence and intimidation did not end with their arrival in refugee camps in Bangladesh. During visits to three Bangladeshi camps of origin (Gundhum I, Dechua Palong and Balukhali II) and one transit camp (Jumma Para) in April 1993, Human Rights Watch compiled evidence of verbal, physical and sexual abuse of refugees at the hands of Bangladeshi military and paramilitary forces in charge of the camps. Many incidents of human rights violations occurred in the context of sustained efforts by the Bangladeshi government to repatriate Rohingya refugees to Burma amidst widespread allegations of force and coercion.[23] Bangladeshi government officials have suggested that much of the violence in the camps was the product of Rohingya "terrorist" or "fundamentalist" organizations' pressure on the refugees to remain in Bangladesh. There is no question that Rohingya militants were responsible for some incidents of violence, which, on at least two occasions, may have included murder. But there is also ample evidence to suggest that security forces engaged in a systematic pattern of abuse and torture as a means of coercion, and that they have not been held accountable for their actions. Other abuses appeared to have been committed with impunity by camp authorities to satisfy greed or for sexual gratification.[24] The following testimonies were taken in April 1993.

J.S.K., a thirty-nine year-old resident of Balukhali II, left Barchara village, Maungdaw, Burma in early 1992.[25] She went to Bangladesh as a widow with two children. Her husband, a porter for the Burmese army, was taken about six months before she left. She later heard that he had died.

On April 20, 1993, between 11:00 a.m. and noon, a Bangladeshi camp official named Iddris entered her shed. The official touched the aluminum roof of her shed and said, "It's not hot, it's cold. If it's not hot, you will not return to Myanmar." Then the official grabbed her breast and said, "You are Urdu but you have a big stomach." J.S.K. used her arm to push the camp official away. He told her he wanted to have intercourse with her. J.S.K. said she had come to Bangladesh to save her honor. The official said if she did not have intercourse with him, he would take action against her. Then he left.

The following morning, April 21, two Bangladeshi policemen came to J.S.K.'s shed. She was standing at the entrance when she saw them approach, and she went inside. One of the policemen came inside after her and shouted at her, "Take your knife and cut down the trellis!" Then, as J.S.K. went to get her knife to comply with that order, the policeman struck

---

[23] In a letter to Bangladeshi Prime Minister Zia on December 22, 1992, U.N. High Commissioner for Refugees Sadako Ogata wrote that there was "strong evidence to suspect refugees are being coerced [by Bangladeshi authorities] to return, in some cases, having been physically assaulted, their ration cards confiscated, with several hundred persons detained in jail."

[24] For further information on treatment of Rohingya refugees, see Asia Watch, "Bangladesh: Abuse of Burmese Refugees . . ."

[25] The following names are withheld by Human Rights Watch unless otherwise indicated.

her with a stick on the back and then pushed the stick hard against her groin area. J.S.K. got her knife and started cutting down the trellis in front of her shed. The policeman then began to take firewood from J.S.K.'s shed. She protested, saying she was a widow. The policeman then asked if she would marry him, and asked how many children she had. She said two. The policeman said he would arrange a man for her. When interviewed two days later J.S.K. still had difficulty walking from the pain in her groin area.

K.K.B., approximately nineteen, is a resident of Balukhali II. She left Tambezar village, Buthidaung, Burma in 1992 with her brother and father and sister-in-law, and arrived in Balukhali II in February 1993. Previously she was in the Ukhia transit camp for one month.

On April 19, 1993, at about midnight, several Bangladeshi policemen and three local villagers (not refugees) went to her shed and called out for her twenty-year-old brother, M.K. He came out, and two policemen took him to a nearby water pump. Then three other policemen came into the shed and forced K.K.B. into the woods near the camp. K.K.B.'s mother and sister-in-law protested. In the woods, the police grabbed a piece of jewelry from K.K.B.'s pierced nose, as well as a watch she was wearing on her wrist. Her nose was bleeding. The three policemen then each raped her. Two of the policemen had a knife, which they showed to her while telling her that, if she attempted to resist, they would use the knife against her. K.K.B. was also told that if she told anyone about the rapes, they would use their knives against her. After raping her, the police left K.K.B. in the woods. She cried out for help, and her brother came for her.

L.N.Z., twenty-eight (mother); S.K., fifteen (daughter); S.K.II, eighteen (neighbor), all originated in Khar Khali village, Maungdaw, Burma, and sought refuge in Balukhali II camp. On April 20, 1993, the Bangladeshi Camp-in-Charge (CIC)[26] accompanied by several camp officials and police, went to L.N.Z.'s shed, and asked to have the family sewing machine. At the time, L.N.Z., S.K. and S.K.II were inside the house. L.N.Z. refused to give them the sewing machine. The officials shouted at her, calling her names, and hit her once. They asked for her ration book. L.N.Z. said she would not give it to them. One official called the CIC over. The CIC then grabbed S.K.'s wrist. Another camp official said that the family ration book was hidden in S.K.'s clothing. The CIC and the other official put their hands inside S.K.'s clothing and touched her all over her body, including her vagina.

---

[26] The Camp-in-Charge is the highest Bangladeshi authority in each refugee camp.

The CIC and the other official then tied L.N.Z.'s arms in front of her, and did the same to S.K. S.K. asked S.K.II for another cloth to cover her head. When S.K.II came to give her some cloth, one policeman fondled S.K.II's breasts and struck S.K. on the back of the neck with a stick. The police then brought L.N.Z. and S.K. to a nearby latrine at the bottom of the hill on which their shed is perched. L.N.Z. and S.K. were told that, if they did not give up the sewing machine, they would be tortured. L.N.Z. then said that the sewing machine was in the house of a local villager (not a refugee) who lived next door to L.N.Z. and S.K. The police then went to the house of the local villager and repeatedly struck the thatched roof with sticks, damaging the roof. The police took the sewing machine from the villager's house.

Z.H., twenty, was a resident of Balukhali II camp in April 1993. She had arrived in Bangladesh in 1992, with two children and her mother and brother from a village in Buthidaung, Burma. Just before crossing the border to Bangladesh, she had previously been arrested in Burma and spent eighteen days in jail. Her husband had been jailed in 1991 in Burma for murdering a village leader who had confiscated the family's property.

In mid-March 1993 a Bangladeshi police inspector went to her shed in the Balukhali II camp and told Z.K. that he wanted to have sex with her. The inspector told her that if she did not have sex with him, he would jail her or deny her food rations. Some time thereafter, Z. was called down to the CIC office by the same police inspector, who repeated his threats. When several other refugees came to the office, Z.K. was let go. The inspector threatened to shoot Z.K. if she repeated his threats.

Response of the Bangladeshi Government and the UNHCR

There has been little new information on the treatment of Rohingya refugee women in the refugee camps in Bangladesh since Human Rights Watch last reported on their situation in October 1993. The overall security situation in the camps improved considerably following the May 1993 agreement between UNHCR and the Government of Bangladesh, which gave UNHCR daytime access to all camps. The conclusion of a Memorandum of Understanding between UNHCR and Burma in November 1993 also allowed for a permanent UNHCR presence in Arakan to monitor the safety of the returnees. As of April 1995, nearly 200,000 refugees had been repatriated to Burma. Despite these developments, there are still reports of abuse in the camps and in Arakan.

In May 1994 a cyclone hit southern Bangladesh, causing severe damage in the refugee camps and an increase in disease among the refugees, mainly due to sanitation problems. Following the cyclone, the Bangladeshi authorities appear to have prevented speedy repairs in the camps; in some camps allegations continued that the already meager food rations were further reduced to "encourage" refugees to leave. In July, the UNHCR altered the repatriation process. The transit camps that housed refugees who had been interviewed by UNHCR officials and had expressed willingness to be repatriated were closed, and refugees were moved directly from the main camps. Registration was no longer conducted by UNHCR officials, but by the Camp-in-Charge.

During this period, nongovernmental relief organizations working in the camps reported an increase in the coercion and alleged forced repatriation of refugees. Bangladeshi authorities allegedly extorted refugees and beat and denied food rations to those who refused to return to Burma. Nongovernmental organizations also claimed that the UNHCR was not providing refugees with sufficient information regarding their right not to be repatriated involuntarily and the situation they might face in Burma. In October 1994, Human Rights Watch applied for permission to visit the refugee camps but received no response from the Government of Bangladesh. We also applied to visit Arakan, but the Burmese government never replied to our request.

Some Rohingya refugees have reportedly returned to Bangladesh after being repatriated. In April 1994 Bangladesh made an official complaint to Burma after nearly 200 Rohingyas returned. The "double-backers" said they had experienced further abuses by Burmese authorities, who would not permit them to return to their own homes. Once back in Bangladesh, however, the refugees were arrested as illegal immigrants.

In April 1995 the UNHCR presence in Arakan increased to a total of eighteen people. The UNHCR has stated that the situation in Arakan is now safe for the refugees to return and that forced labor requirements for Rohingya males, one of the main causes of the exodus in 1991, have been reduced to one day a week from four to five days per week. Throughout this period, the Burmese authorities have continued to deny the allegations of abuse which resulted in the exodus of Muslims from Arakan in 1991 and 1992.

SOMALI REFUGEES IN KENYA

From 1991 to 1993, approximately 300,000 Somalis fled across the 800-mile Kenyan-Somali border.[27]   Most refugees walked miles over Somalia's desolate savanna into Kenya's North Eastern Province; others risked their lives in makeshift boats to reach Kenya's coastline further south. As of this writing, most of the refugees continue to remain in camps in Kenya, and over 80 percent are women and children.[28]   Many were the victims of violence, including rape, as they fled war-torn Somalia. They went to Kenya to escape these dangers, only to face similar abuse upon arrival.

In July 1993 Human Rights Watch visited Kenya to investigate reports of widespread rape of Somali women refugees. While in Kenya, our researcher met with relief workers, Kenyan government officials and others working on refugee protection issues and traveled to Dagahaley, Liboi, Marafa and Hatimy camps, where she interviewed Somali refugee women who were raped.

Human Rights Watch found that hundreds of Somali women in the refugee camps in Kenya's North Eastern Province have been raped in Somalia and in Kenya. In 1993 the United Nations High Commissioner for Refugees (UNHCR) documented close to 300 rape cases. Of these cases, almost one hundred had occurred in Somalia, while the remainder took place in the Kenyan refugee camps. Between January and August 1994, forty-five more cases of rape in the camps were reported. While these figures are profoundly disturbing, they represent only the cases actually reported to UNHCR, which believes the actual incidence of rape in that period could be as much as ten times higher.[29]

In an overwhelming number of cases, Somali refugee women and girls were violently attacked by unknown armed bandits at night or when they went to the outskirts of the refugee camp to herd goats or collect firewood. According to the UNHCR, nearly all the rape cases that occurred in the

---

[27] United Nations High Commissioner for Refugees (UNHCR), *Information Bulletin*, (June 1993) p. 4. The following material was adapted from Africa Watch and Women's Rights Project, "Seeking Refuge, Finding Terror: The Widespread Rape of Somali Women Refugees in North Eastern Kenya," *A Human Rights Watch Short Report*, vol. 5, no. 13 (October 1993).

[28] UNHCR, *Information Bulletin*, p. 10.

[29] Interview with Fauzia Musse, UNHCR consultant on sexual violence, Nairobi, Kenya, July 16, 1993.

Kenyan camps were committed by bandits. Increasingly, these bandits join forces with former Somali military men or fighters from the various warring factions who launch raids across the Kenyan-Somali border. To a lesser extent, refugee women were also vulnerable to attack by Kenyan police officers posted in the area. Between January and August 1993, the Kenyan police were responsible for seven reported rape cases.

Somali women as old as fifty years of age and girls as young as four have been subjected to violence and sexual assault. Most of the women whose cases wc investigated were gang-raped at gunpoint, some by as many as seven men at a time. Frequently, the agony was repeated; some women were raped twice or three times in the camps. In the vast majority of cases, female rape survivors were also robbed, severely beaten, knifed or shot. Those who had been circumcised often had their vaginal openings torn or cut by their attackers. Many we interviewed were suffering ongoing medical problems.

Kenya's North Eastern Province is an arid, barren area sparsely populated by nomadic pastoralist groups such as the Somali, Boran, Rendilles, and Turkana. Because of the artificially constructed colonial border between Kenya and Somalia, the area is inhabited almost exclusively by ethnic Somalis who are classified as Kenyan citizens but retain strong cultural, political and economic ties to Somalia. The rise of a secessionist movement to join Somalia between 1963-1967 resulted in the Kenyan government's committing widespread human rights abuses by the Kenyan authorities against large numbers of Somali-Kenyans. Indiscriminate government killings, arrests and security crackdowns in turn generated widespread suspicion and hatred of the government among the area's inhabitants. Emergency powers in North Eastern Province remained fully operational until 1993, when they were finally repealed.[30]

Throughout this period, the government deliberately invested little or nothing in the infrastructure of the North Eastern Province, with the result that the province experienced barely any economic growth. The area has remained undeveloped and isolated, and its population politically marginalized. Much of the nomadic population has increasingly resorted to cattle-rustling, banditry,

---

[30] Africa Watch, *Kenya: Taking Liberties* (New York: Human Rights Watch, 1991), p. 269.

and poaching. These local bandits, known as *shiftas*, make a living from robbing local inhabitants.[31]

The outbreak of the Somali civil war in 1991 dramatically increased the insecurity in North Eastern Province. After January 1991, when former Somali President Siad Barre was forced from power, the situation in Somalia degenerated, as rival clan factions vied for power. The fighting continues, and as the Somali government collapsed in 1991, there are no recognized authorities to restore order. Meanwhile, the fighting has resulted in the deaths of at least 300,000 of its citizens based on the political manipulation of clan and sub-clan allegiances, and prompted another 300,000 to flee.[32] Over 80 percent of these refugees are women and children.

By 1993 approximately 200,000 Somali refugees were housed in six camps set up by the UNHCR along the Kenya-Somali border.[33] Refugees in these camps were housed in appalling conditions in squalid "igloo"-type hovels made of branches covered with patches of plastic, burlap or cloth.[34] These large refugee camps soon became targets of the often well-armed shiftas in search of money and food and—all too frequently—sex. As a relief official told Human Rights Watch, one reason the refugee camps were constantly attacked was that the local nomadic population was as indigent as the refugee population, but was not receiving relief assistance.[35] Relief workers also speculated that some of the shiftas might even have been refugees who took up arms at night and terrorized their compatriots.[36]

---

[31] The term shifta, meaning bandit in Kiswahili, was deliberately used by the Kenyan government to describe the secessionists in the 1960s and downplay the political significance of the movement. Shifta has since become a catch-all term to describe any ethnic Somali criminal in Kenya and has acquired a derogatory connotation.

[32] U.S. Department of State, Office of Foreign Disaster Assistance, *Somalia - Civil Strife, Situation Report no. 19*, March 12, 1993.

[33] The camps housing Somali refugees in 1993 were: Mandera (pop. 44,841); El-Wak (pop. 8,200); Dagahaley (39,441); Ifo (48,476); Hagadera (43,829); and Liboi (pop. 44,841). UNHCR, *Information Bulletin*, (June 1993) p. 4.

[34] In 1993, another 70,000 Somali refugees were housed in noticeably better conditions in three camps at Kenya's Coast Province. These camps were further from the Somali border and therefore safer. The camps were Marafa (pop. 29,392 Somali and non-Somali refugees); Hatimy (pop. 2,935); and Utange (pop. 42,361 Somali and Ethiopian refugees). Ibid.

[35] Interview with relief worker, Dadaab, Kenya, July 1993.

[36] Interview with UNHCR official, Nairobi, Kenya, July 16, 1993.

The location of these camps, just a few miles from the Kenya-Somali border, also exposed refugees to attacks from Somali fighters. Former Somali government soldiers or combatants with the warring factions routinely staged raids into North Eastern Kenya and then retreated over the border, eluding capture by Kenyan security forces. Often, these shiftas were better armed than the Kenyan security forces. It is difficult to distinguish the Somali shiftas from those of Kenyan origin, and the term shifta is used by the refugees broadly to describe any attacker of Somali ethnicity in that area. As these armed gangs joined forces with local bandits, law and order in the area broke down.[37]

Gradually the area turned into a virtual free-for-all zone because of the mounting insecurity and increasing number of weapons. Shiftas regularly terrorized the relief community, the refugees, and even the Kenyan police force. Relief workers began to travel with an armed escort for protection. In 1992 bandits attacked the compound of an international relief organization, *Médecins Sans Frontières* (MSF), and gang-raped a female doctor.[38] In response, MSF temporarily withdrew its workers, until assured of increased security. Kenyan police themselves did not leave their compounds at night for fear of being shot. In January 1993 the Kenyan government reported fifty-three attacks by shiftas in the refugee camps resulting in the deaths of nine security personnel and thirty-eight refugees.[39] In the following six months, approximately twenty-five other police officers were killed by shiftas in search of the officers' weapons and ammunition.

The refugees were particularly vulnerable to abuses from all sides. They complained of looting, beatings and killings by shiftas and Kenyan police alike. Often, refugees also became the helpless victims of police brutality after attacks by shiftas were carried out against the Kenyan police. In one particularly egregious incident on March 3, 1993, Kenyan police fired without provocation into a crowd of refugees waiting in line at a food distribution center, killing three and wounding several others. This unprovoked assault came the day after four policemen were killed in a shifta attack. The overall

---

[37] "Refugee Criminal Gangs wreak 'Havoc' in Kenya," Reuters Information Services, August 11, 1993.

[38] Interview with relief official, Dagahaley camp, Kenya, July 26, 1993; *see also* "Belgian Charity Withdraws Workers from Refugee Camps," Associated Press, July 7, 1992.

[39] Letter from the Lawyers Committee for Human Rights, New York, to Kenyan authorities, May 11, 1993.

security situation was deplorable, but sexual assault and rape affected almost exclusively women and girls.

Rape in the Refugee Camps in North Eastern Kenya

Overwhelmingly, Somali women refugees who were raped in the camps in North Eastern Kenya were raped by unknown bandits—either Somali-Kenyans or Somalis. A significantly smaller number of women were raped by Kenyan police authorities or other refugees in the camp. In a six-month period beginning February 1993, 192 cases of rape were documented in camps. In August 1993 alone, forty-two rape cases were reported to UNHCR officials, who believed that rape was on the rise in the camps. Because rape victims are often unwilling to report their cases to police or medical authorities, the actual incidence of rape in that period could have been as much as ten times higher.[40]

Since the attackers routinely spoke to the women in Somali it can be inferred that they were either Somali-Kenyan nomads, Somali fighters who had crossed over the border, or perhaps even other refugees. The attackers were usually described by the women as men dressed in black shirts and trousers. Most were armed with guns and knives and often covered their faces to avoid being recognized.

Some sexual assaults have had an ethnic as well as gender dimension. The persecution of civilian noncombatants solely on the basis of clan affiliation by the warring factions has been prevalent throughout the Somali conflict, in violation of the Common Article 3 of the Geneva Conventions.[41] Incidents of sexual assault in Kenya at times manifest these clan tensions, suggesting that Somali fighters from the warring factions do cross the border. Somali refugee women in Kenya reported their rapists asked which clan they belonged to. According to relief workers, women from the same clan as their attackers were often spared the rape and only robbed. Developments in Somalia also affect the numbers of refugee women subjected to rape from certain clans. According to the UNHCR consultant on sexual violence, when the town of Dobley in Somalia was occupied by the Marehan warlord Gen.

---

[40] Interview with Fauzia Musse, UNHCR consultant on sexual violence, Liboi camp, July 19, 1993.

[41] Geneva Conventions of August 12, 1949, Common Article 3; *See also* Africa Watch, "Somalia: Beyond the Warlords: The Need for a Verdict on Human Rights Abuses," *A Human Rights Watch Short Report*, vol. 5, no. 2 (March 1993), p. 5.

Mohamed Said Hersi "Morgan,"[42] rapes of Ogadeni women at Liboi refugee camp in Kenya increased.[43]

There have also been a number of pregnancies resulting from these rapes. In these cases of which we have knowledge, the Somali women have all carried the pregnancy to term, both because abortion is illegal in Kenya and because of the cultural stigma attached to abortion.[44] For Somali women, the physical injuries caused by being raped are compounded, in some cases, by the practice of female genital mutilation. Rape becomes excruciatingly painful for the refugee women who have undergone this procedure. In some cases, shiftas preparing to rape a refugee woman, have slit open her vagina with a knife before raping her.

Rape by Shiftas

Most of the refugee women interviewed were attacked, robbed and raped in the middle of the night in their huts by groups of armed shiftas. Maryam, a thirty-eight-year-old woman of the Marehan clan, arrived at Ifo camp in North Eastern Province in Kenya around July 1992.[45] A month after she arrived at the camp, she was sleeping at the hut of a friend when they were attacked by nine unknown assailants. "They came around 9:00 p.m.," Maryam told us.

> We were in the house sleeping. They came into the house
> with guns and knives and told us to give them our money.
> We didn't know them. They were wearing black jackets,
> trousers and hats. We were so scared, we gave them
> everything. Then they began to beat me. They beat me for
> hours, and then six men raped me. After the rape I was in

---

[42] Siad Barre's son-in-law and the former commander of the Somali army.

[43] Interview with Fauzia Musse, UNHCR consultant on sexual violence, Liboi camp, July 19, 1993.

[44] "Any person who, when a woman is about to be delivered of a child, prevents the child from being born alive by any act or omission of such a nature that, if the child had been born alive and had then died, he would be deemed to have unlawfully killed the child, is guilty of a felony and is liable to imprisonment for life." Section 228, Cap. 63 Penal Code (rev. 1985), Laws of Kenya.

[45] "Maryam" is not the victim's real name. All names withheld by Human Rights Watch unless otherwise indicated.

so much pain I could not walk. The doctor had to come into
the hut to see me.[46]

Maryam continued to suffer from chest pains where the attackers
kicked her with their boots and hit her with gun butts. She reported the case
to the Kenyan police, who took her statement but at the time of our
investigation had not taken any further action. In July 1993, because she was
a rape victim, Maryam was transferred by the UNHCR to a safer refugee camp
located in Kenya's coastal area.

Usha, a twenty-three-year-old Asharaf woman, fled Somalia in
October 1992 from Mogadishu. She found refuge at Ifo camp in North
Eastern Kenya. On June 6, 1993, Usha and another young woman were
sleeping in a hut at the camp. Around 2:00 a.m., her friend went to the
outdoor toilet, leaving Usha alone in the hut. Minutes later, three unknown
men wearing traditional Somali dress entered the hut. Usha explained:

> They started hitting me and telling me to wake up. They
> told me to give them what I had or they would kill me. I
> was so scared I gave them the shs. 1,000 [US$12.50] that I
> had and all my clothes and rations. Then they said "You,
> yourself. . .we want you." I was so scared because I had
> never done this before. They made me lie down, and they
> tore me with a knife. There were three, but only two men
> raped me. I was so scared that I passed out. I don't know
> how long they were there for, maybe half an hour. I'm not
> sure. I was not conscious.[47]

Usha was seen by a doctor the following day. At the time of the rape
she was a virgin and had undergone female genital mutilation. Her vagina was
severely torn during the rape, and she lost a considerable amount of blood.
The police were informed of the rape and visited the hut where the rape
occurred, but had taken no further action as of one month later. In July 1993
Usha was transferred by the UNHCR to a safer refugee camp at the coast
because she was a rape victim.

Conditions at Dagahaley camp, a few miles from Ifo, are no better.
Asali, a twenty-year-old Ogadeni woman, had been recently married and was

---

[46] Interview, Marafa camp, Kenya, July 23, 1993.
[47] Ibid.

expecting her first child. In March 1993 she and her husband were asleep at night when two unknown men entered their house. She described them as being dressed in olive-colored jackets and trousers and both carrying guns. They threatened both Asali and her husband and looted the few belongings in the hut. Asali told us:

> They took me to the bush outside the camp. I was so scared
> that no sound was coming from my mouth. They asked me
> what clan I was and then told me to remove my clothes.
> Both men raped me—each twice.[48]

As a result of the rape, Asali suffered a miscarriage. She saw a doctor and informed the police about the rape. The police visited the site and took a statement. At the time of our investigation, more than three months later, nothing further had happened.

Habiba, a twenty-seven-year-old woman from the Ajuran clan, arrived in Dagahaley around July 1992. On April 15, 1993, she was sleeping in her hut at night when three unknown men wearing trousers and shirts surrounded her hut. They woke her up and ordered her outside. They threatened to kill her if she did not give them any money she had. They then ransacked the house, taking her blanket and few other possessions. Habiba told us:

> They ordered me to show them where they could find some
> girls. I refused to do that so they told me that I would
> satisfy them. They took me into the bush and ordered me to
> take off my clothes. When I refused they beat me up and
> tore off my clothing. Two of the men raped me. After the
> rape, they told me not to say that it was shiftas that had
> raped me or they would return.[49]

Hawa is a twenty-two-year-old woman whose hut was attacked by shiftas at Hagadera camp in January 1993. As she and her family tried to escape, she was shot and superficially injured in her right temple. After she fell, she was caught and blindfolded before being raped in the bush. She never went to the police but finally saw a doctor. Her medical report verified her

---

[48] Interview, Dagahaley camp, Kenya, July 26, 1993.
[49] Ibid.

account, reporting a six inch scar on her right temple and a ruptured hymen. The report also noted genital mutilation (partial infibulation).

Women in the camps were also targets for rape when they went to the outskirts of the camps either to herd goats or collect firewood during the day. The surrounding countryside is desolate and isolated, and once women leave the camp area, they were vulnerable to attack.

In many cases, the younger girls are sent to herd goats during the day, and there have been several cases of girls as young as age eight being raped. Sadia, an eight-year-old Ogadeni girl, was living with her parents, three sisters and brother at the Hagadera refugee camp from mid-1992. On July 2, 1993, she was herding goats with five other children when a Somali-speaking man of about thirty approached them. He greeted them and began asking them questions, including which clan they belonged to. The children became suspicious and started to run away in different directions. As Sadia ran, a thorn got lodged in one of her bare feet, causing her to stop. The man grabbed her by her wrist, pulled out a knife and threatened to kill her if she made any noise. He then raped her. She limped back to the camp an hour later in extreme pain. A doctor who examined her shortly afterwards verified that she had been raped and that her hymen was ruptured.[50]

Another young Ogadeni girl, Fatuma, was fourteen years old when she was raped on June 30, 1993. Fatuma was herding goats on the outskirts of Dagahaley camp when she was approached by a man with a gun. He asked her a number of questions, including what clan she belonged to and whether she was alone. When she tried to run away, he grabbed her, blindfolded her and forced her to lie down before raping her. When she struggled, he beat the sides of her head and body with the gun butt. He raped her three times before finally releasing her. The doctor who examined her recorded that she was bleeding and in severe pain. The medical report verified that the rape had taken place and that her hymen was ruptured.[51]

Multiple and Repeated Rapes

Most of the rapes in the camps in the North Eastern Province are gang-rapes by more than one man. In addition, the chronic insecurity in the area has put refugee women at risk of being raped more than once. At the time of this visit, in July 1993, numerous women in the camps in North

---

[50] Information collected from case documents, Dagahaley camp, Kenya, July 26, 1993.

[51] Ibid.

Eastern Province had been subjected to repeated cases of rape on different occasions. The UNHCR had begun to give priority to rape victims for resettlement to safer camps. Many of these transfers, however, occurred only after a woman had been subjected to violent rape several times. Bishaw, a thirty-two-year-old Marehan woman, was raped three times by shiftas at the Ifo camp before she was transferred to Marafa camp in July 1993. Although she felt safe there, she told us that she still suffered from headaches, sleeplessness and nightmares.[52] She also bore scars from knife wounds inflicted when she was raped, including a large gash on her right buttock that made walking difficult. She had gone originally to Ifo camp with her five children in April 1992, after walking miles from Kismayo, Somalia.

> In July 1992 nine shiftas with guns came into my house at night. They were wearing black trousers, black jackets and hats pulled low. I did not know them. They all had guns and big boots like soldiers. They pulled my arms behind my back and tied my hands. They told me not to scream and pushed knives into my upper arms and head. They kicked me with their boots. They told me to give them all the money I had. I traded at the market during the day, and they must have followed me to know where I stay. After they tied and cut me I gave them the money which I had buried in a safe place. Then three of the men caught me and dragged me into my home and raped me. One man raped me while another held a gun at my head and told me he would kill me if I made a noise. My daughter of ten years woke up and cried, and they beat her on the head with guns. Up to today she has problems. I tried to shout, but the shiftas shot in the air and so people ran away.

As a result of the attack, Bishaw's ten-year-old daughter has had neurological problems and chronic ear infections. Terrified by the attack, Bishaw and her family moved to another location in the hope that the attack would be the last. Bishaw, however, was targeted a second time by shiftas in August 1992. "They came back again in the middle of the night," she told us:

---

[52] Interview, Marafa camp, Kenya, July 23, 1993.

> This time with more men—so many men I couldn't count. Four of them came into the house while the others guarded outside. My friend was sleeping in the house, as well as two of my children. Both of us had been raped before. This time they did not beat me. They came into the tent and told us to give them all our money from the market. I think they knew me from the market. We gave them the money. After that, two of the men raped me, and the other two raped my friend. Then we heard a shout outside and they all ran away.

"The third time I was raped was in March 1993," Bishaw explained with tears in her eyes.

> It was just as I was eating breakfast at Ramadan time [at dawn]. I saw about forty men with guns. Six of them came into the hut and took my money. I didn't know any of them. They were not wearing uniform. Thankfully, they didn't beat me or hurt me—but two of the men raped me.

Bishaw reported each of the rapes and robbery to the police at Ifo. At the time of our investigation, the police had only taken a statement, and done nothing further.

Halima, a twenty-eight-year-old from the Marehan clan, fled to Kenya in early 1992 with her family. During her seventeen months at Ifo camp, she was raped twice by unknown shiftas. The first rape occurred on April 10, 1993, when two men entered the hut where Halima was living with her four children and niece (ages two to twelve). According to Halima, the two men woke her and ordered her out of the house. "I was scared and did not know who they were," she told us.

> I went outside, and they told me that if I valued my life I would give them what they asked for. I begged them to leave me alone and told them I had no money. They beat me until finally I gave them the shs. 1,000 [US $20] which I had made working for MSF [Médecins Sans Frontières]. Then they took off my clothes. The one with the gun raped me first. When he finished, they changed places.[53]

---

[53] Ibid.

Only two weeks later, Halima was raped again by three shiftas who attacked her in her hut around midnight on April 25, 1993. "They raped me and beat me with the back of their guns and their boots," Halima said.

> After all three had raped me, they threatened to kill me if I did not give them everything I owned. I was so scared after the second rape, I went to UNHCR and the police. I told them that I did not want to stay. I had lost everything including my food ration card.

Halima was finally transferred to Marafa camp by the UNHCR in July 1993. Meanwhile, she had become pregnant as a result of the rapes and then suffered a miscarriage. When we interviewed Halima, she had been hemorrhaging for a number of weeks but had not seen a doctor.

Rape by Kenyan Police and Security Officials

While most refugee women had various complaints about the Kenya police, they said that the police were generally not responsible for widespread sexual assault.[54] Some Kenyan police or soldiers, however, have raped Somali refugee women. Seven of 192 rape cases reported to UNHCR between January and August 1993 involved Kenyan police.

At the time of our investigation in 1993, no police officer implicated in a rape case had been disciplined by police authorities or by the courts. Largely as a result, refugee women who were raped by Kenyan police were extremely reluctant to report the violation to police, and also feared being penalized or repatriated back to Somalia should they decide to do so.

Khadija was a twenty-year-old woman from the Marehan clan. The conflict in Somalia disrupted her university studies, forcing her to flee to Kenya in 1991. She and her family lived first at Liboi camp and then at Ifo. On May 17, 1993, as she was walking back to her hut at dusk, a white police pick-up truck passed her. These cars had been donated by the UNHCR to the Kenyan police to enable them to provide better protection to the refugee camps. As the car passed by, one of the policeman called to her in Kiswahili.

---

[54] There have been numerous complaints, however, by Somali refugees in the capital of Nairobi, of constant harassment for bribes by the Kenyan police. Somali women who are unable to pay the police for their release from a police cell often have to provide sex. Africa Watch interview with a group of Somali women, Nairobi, Kenya, July 24, 1993.

Since Khadija did not understand, she ignored them. They stopped the car, and one policeman grabbed Khadija by the wrist trying to force her into the car. She fought back and, after other refugees crowded around shouting *"askari, askari"* ["guards, guards"], they left and drove back to the police station.

The refugees stood around the area for about fifteen minutes telling Khadija how lucky she was not to have been taken by the police. Then, the car returned. The refugees began to run away, fearing a reprisal as two policemen jumped out of the car and began chasing them. Terrified, Khadija tried to run. She told us:

> I was so afraid that I couldn't move. My legs were stuck to the ground. Then I started to run, but he had seen me. I was wearing a white scarf. Two of them got out of the car and then caught me by the arms and legs and dragged me into their car. All the refugees came out and watched, but they were too scared to do anything. I was screaming and crying, and I scratched one man badly. They put me in the car between them and drove to the place where the police sleep. They dragged me into a tent, and three men raped and beat me. After a while I stopped screaming because I was afraid.[55]

Khadija's ordeal ended when another policeman discovered what his colleagues were doing and stopped them. He picked Khadija up saying, *"pole, pole"* ["sorry, sorry"]. Then he walked her to the gate of the police compound and told her in English, "Go and don't tell anyone about this." By the time Khadija got to her hut, it was midnight. Her neck was swollen to twice normal size because they had held her in a chokehold in the car, and her head was bruised from being kicked. Khadija's mother wanted to complain to the police station about the behavior of their officers, but the other refugees convinced her this was unwise.

Not knowing what to do, Khadija decided to return to Somalia. However, she did not have enough money, and the bus stop was near the police camp. Finally, she notified the UNHCR that she could not stay at the camp anymore. She was taken to see a doctor by the UNHCR and then transferred to the Dagahaley camp, located nearby. At Dagahaley, Khadija

---

[55] Interview at coastal camp, Kenya, July 23, 1993.

saw the police who had raped her visit the camp several times. Scared that they were hunting for her, she began sleeping in different places each night.

In July 1993 she was transferred to another camp. Although Khadija has found the new camp much safer than Ifo and Dagahaley camps, she told us that she is still afraid of the Kenyan police after two months in Nairobi. She noted, "They treat refugees how they want and you can't do anything because you are a refugee. Even now I am scared. What if the police that raped me are transferred from Ifo camp?"

While rape of Somali refugee women by Kenyan police and security officials did not appear to be frequent, when it happens, there is no recourse for Somali refugee women. Khadija could easily identify her assailants, but there was nowhere for her to complain without fearing reprisals. Ultimately, a UNHCR protection officer raised the case with the police inspector at Ifo camp, who stated that he had investigated the incident and that the alleged victim had gone into the tent willingly. The police never interviewed Khadija. The case was closed by the police.[56]

The Stigma of Rape

Somali women who have been raped face not only the physical and psychological trauma of rape but also the likelihood of rejection by their families. A strong cultural stigma is attached to rape in Somalia, as elsewhere. In numerous cases, families have begged UNHCR officials to take their young daughter to another camp after she has been raped because of the stigma on the family.[57] In other cases, once a woman is raped she is ostracized by her husband and isolated from her family.

Hibaq, a forty-year-old woman, was raped by three unknown assailants in the middle of the night at Liboi camp in March 1993. She was sleeping in her hut with her three children ages twenty-one, ten and eight years. She told us:

> I live in a compound with my husband and his second wife,
> and I was woken up by a torch shining in my face. I asked
> who it was, and they told me to shut up. There were three
> men dressed in black with white scarves around their heads.
> One of them had a gun. They dragged me out of the house
> and then searched the house for money. They couldn't find

---

[56] Interview with UNHCR relief worker, Dagahaley camp, Kenya, July 26, 1993.
[57] Interview with UNHCR official, Nairobi, Kenya, July 16, 1993.

any so they dragged me back inside and began beating me.
I started crying and screaming "God is great, God is great
and my God is watching you." They said "Fuck your God."
They slapped me on my ears, and even now I can't hear in
one ear. No one came out to help me. They were too
scared. Then all three raped me in my own house while my
children were there. One of them held a gun at my throat
while the other raped me, and then they changed places. For
one hour they raped me, and then they left and went to
another house.[58]

When Hibaq's husband discovered that she had been raped, he sent
her out of the compound where the family was living and took her belongings,
including her food ration card. For approximately one month, she was
sleeping in different places, unable to collect her food ration, and forbidden by
her husband from seeing her children. When the UNHCR learned of this case,
its personnel convened a meeting in April 1993 with the committee of elders
at the camp and negotiated the return of Hibaq's food ration card and access
to her children.[59] Hibaq's husband, however, refused to have anything to do
with her, and she now lives alone in a separate hut in Liboi camp. At the time
of our interview, she still suffered from sleeplessness and sharp pains in her
ribs where she was beaten.
    For fear of being stigmatized, Somali women refugees who are victims
of rape often refuse to acknowledge publicly that they have been raped, even
when medical evidence indicates that the attack occurred. In other cases,
women do not seek medical assistance or file a police report because they do
not want it known that they were raped. Between July 18 and 24, 1993, four
refugee women who were raped refused to allow a doctor to examine them.[60]
In the medical center at Liboi camp, the hospital documented thirty-nine cases
of rape from late 1992 to mid-1993. The UNHCR's consultant on sexual
violence documented thirty other cases that took place during the same period
that never came to the attention of the medical center.
    Most women who have been raped only go to a doctor if they suffer
other injuries from being beaten, knifed or shot, and even then, many do not
mention that they were raped. In some cases, the women do not perceive the

[58] Interview, Liboi camp, Kenya, July 19, 1993.
[59] Interview, Fauzia Musse, Liboi camp, Kenya, July 19, 1993.
[60] Ibid.

rape itself as an injury. Hibaq told us that she saw a doctor after she was raped, but only because she had been beaten so badly that she could not hear. However, she never told the doctor that she had been raped.

On occasion, if a rapist is identified as another refugee, the families settle the case through the elders with the rapist's family paying "blood money" in compensation for the crime committed. Unfortunately, the settlement is usually negotiated on behalf of the woman by her male relatives, sometimes against her wishes, and the settlement money often remains with the male relatives.

Response of the Kenyan Government and the UNHCR

In 1993 Human Rights Watch found that the Kenyan government's response to the rampant incidence of rape had been woefully inadequate. The government provided inadequate security around the camps and made no concerted effort to arrest or prosecute those responsible for the widespread rape. In part, this was due to the general insecurity in the area and the fact that the police authorities were themselves targets of attack by the local bandits. However, the government's failure to investigate and prosecute rape is also a direct result of law enforcement officials' refusal to treat such claims seriously.

One year later, Human Rights Watch found during a follow-up mission that the situation had changed for the better, due to efforts by the UNHCR and the Kenyan government. In September 1994 Human Rights Watch visited the camps in North Eastern Province and interviewed UNHCR officials, Kenyan police, relief workers and a Kenya organization of women lawyers.[61] The UNHCR had introduced fencing around the refugee camps and cooperated with the Kenyan police to promote greater physical safety. With financial assistance from the international donor community, the UNHCR had also established counseling and medical services for rape victims and had contracted FIDA, a women lawyers' organization, to assist refugee women to seek legal redress. For its part, the Kenyan government augmented police presence in the camps, ordered more frequent police patrols (including bi-monthly helicopter patrols), and had the UNHCR provide limited training in humanitarian and human rights law for police. As a result of these combined preventive efforts, the number of reported rapes of Somali refugee women and

---

[61] In 1994, the UNHCR would not permit Human Rights Watch individual interviews with the refugee women themselves.

girls had fallen significantly from more than 200 cases in 1993 to approximately fifty reported rapes through August in 1994.

To date, there are important problems remaining, however, which the UNHCR and the Kenyan government have not yet tackled. First, although the number of night-time attacks has decreased, young refugee girls constitute a higher percentage of all rape victims than ever. Somali girls are traditionally responsible for fetching firewood and herding goats, activities that require them to leave the relative security of the camps. The UNHCR has yet to take steps to lessen the need for women and girls to leave the camps.

Second, justice continues to elude rape survivors, since impunity for rapists remains the norm rather than the exception. Even with legal counsel for the victims, the odds of convicting the perpetrator are distressingly slim. While police response to allegations of rape has been poor generally, the Kenyan police have been particularly reluctant to investigate cases implicating members of their own rank and file.

Third, the long distance to the nearest court in Garissa (over one hundred kilometers), coupled with an overburdened court calendar, has caused long delays in prosecution. According to Kenyan lawyers, unless the Kenyan government upgrades the police post in the Dadaab area to a full-fledged police station, no magistrate can be assigned to hear cases in the area.

Lastly, there are no women police officers posted in the Dadaab area. Despite assurances from the Kenyan government that it would build adequate police barracks for policewomen to be assigned to the camp area, police officers have told Human Rights Watch that a police housing shortage continues to be the reason why there is not a single woman officer protecting the refugee population made up largely of women and children.

As these continuing problems indicate, despite the reduction in the overall incidence of rape, the Kenyan government and UNHCR must remain vigilant in carrying out their protection duties towards refugees in Kenya. While violence against refugees in the Somali refugee camps in North Eastern Kenya is by no means eradicated, the improvements in the situation indicate that decisive action by the international community and the host government can improve the lives of refugee women. The international community should recognize the efforts made to date by the Kenyan government and UNHCR and assist them to address the remaining problems.

GENERAL RECOMMENDATIONS

To the United Nations High Commissioner for Refugees:
As noted in the introduction to this section, the UNHCR has developed two sets of guidelines for refugee protection: (1) Guidelines for the Protection of Refugee Women and (2) Sexual Violence Against Refugees: Guidelines on Prevention and Response. We call on the UNHCR to step up efforts to implement these guidelines fully and vigorously in all refugee camps. In particular, we emphasize that:

- The UNHCR should ensure physical security in the refugee camps.
- The UNHCR should organize inter-agency meetings with other relief organizations and relevant government agencies, as well as the refugees themselves, to develop a plan of action to prevent sexual violence. Priority should be given to the protection needs of unaccompanied refugee women and girls, who are often the most vulnerable groups.
- The UNHCR should ensure that appropriate medical care, including psychological counseling, is provided to refugee women and girls, with particular emphasis on female rape survivors, including those who have become pregnant as a result of rape. These health providers should be women, if at all possible, given cultural sensitivities that may inhibit a woman from seeking medical assistance from male health care workers. Health care workers should be sensitized to the fact that women will often be reluctant to speak of sexual assault. In areas where female genital mutilation is practiced, health care providers should be trained to address the specific medical complications which may ensue to raped women who have undergone the practice.
- The UNHCR employees and the staff of private relief agencies under contract to the UNHCR must be made aware, through appropriate training, of the widespread sexual violence against refugee and displaced women, and all protection programs should address this issue. Female staff should be employed to work with women refugees to identify their concerns. Refugee and displaced women who have been raped should be treated in a confidential and sensitive manner.
- Refugee protection programs should include community education within refugee camps to protect rape survivors from further stigmatization, ostracism or punishment by their own communities.

Women's experience of rape can be rendered even more traumatic by cultural or religious views that blame the victim.

- The UNHCR should assign a higher percentage of female protection officers, field interpreters, health workers and counselors to the camps.
- In collaboration with other humanitarian relief agencies, the UNHCR should provide relief provisions directly to women, especially women heads of households, to reduce the potential for sexual extortion.
- Where possible, the UNHCR should identify and promote alternatives to refugee camps.
- The concept of international protection should be broadened to provide greater protection to internally displaced persons, including women.   The UNHCR should work with other U.N. agencies to ensure that standards are developed for the protection of internally displaced persons.   These standards should include protections to ensure that displaced women are not the object of sexual violence.

To Host Governments:
- Governments should ensure that national laws against sexual violence are diligently enforced in refugee camps in their territories, in accordance with the relevant international legal obligations. Governments should also vigorously investigate all allegations of abuse of power by government employees and promptly punish those found responsible. To facilitate effective prevention and investigation of sexual violence against refugee women and girls, female police officers and immigration officials should be assigned to refugee camps and border crossing points.
- Governments should take steps to ensure that their asylum adjudicators recognize gender-based persecution, including sex-specific abuse, as grounds for political asylum under refugee law. Asylum should be granted in cases where there is well-founded fear of persecution that constitutes a type of harm that is particular to or due to the applicant's gender, as discussed above.
- Governments should adopt guidelines to assist asylum adjudicators to evaluate gender-related persecution as a basis for asylum.   The adjudicators should be trained, among other things: to recognize the sensitivity of interviewing victims of sexual violence; to be patient with female applicants to overcome inhibitions, particularly regarding sexual abuse; to interview women separately from men and privately; recognize that women who have been sexually assaulted may suffer

from Rape Trauma Syndrome and that these symptoms may influence how an applicant responds during the interview.

3
ABUSES AGAINST WOMEN IN CUSTODY

For many women prisoners, being held in detention or in custody deprives them of more than just their liberty, but also their physical security and dignity. Male jailers often sexually and physically abuse and mistreat women held in custody, especially those held without access to the courts, to counsel, or to their families.[1] These abuses—forced vaginal, anal and oral sex; inappropriate sexual touching and fondling; beatings; excessive pat-downs and strip searches; and the use of vulgar, sexualized language by guards toward women prisoners—are facilitated by the power of male guards in the daily lives of women prisoners and by official tolerance of abusive guard behavior. In addition, prison guards and staff hold over women prisoners the threat of further abuse or retaliation should the women report misconduct or seek redress. As a consequence, incarcerated women are intimidated into silence, and their attackers are rarely called to account for their crimes against women in custody.

Human Rights Watch has documented and published reports on violence against women in custody in the United States, Pakistan, and Egypt. Even societies as apparently disparate as these three, have in common that women in custody are subjected to official mistreatment that ranges from humiliation to torture, although the specific countries' situations determine variations in mistreatment and in the remedies that are available. In Pakistan and the United States, as the population of women in custody has increased, so have the possibilities for abuse because prison authorities do not adequately train and oversee their staff. We found that women in custody are frequently subjected to a range of abuses by their jailers from the time of their arrests throughout their incarceration.

Women are incarcerated for numerous reasons, some of which violate international human rights law. Many are arrested and detained or imprisoned as a result of either discriminatory laws or the discriminatory application of laws. For example, in Pakistan, penal laws that criminalize fornication outside of marriage are discriminatory in application. One section of Pakistan's Islamic penal laws, known as the Hudood Ordinances, defines the offense of

---

[1] While there have been some instances of female jailers abusing female prisoners or detainees, Human Rights Watch investigations found that in the overwhelming percentage of cases of custodial violence, the alleged abuser is male.

zina in part as "sexual intercourse without being validly married," and is routinely applied to imprison the victims of rape.[2] A woman who reports rape to the authorities risks being accused of zina and incarcerated, having "confessed" to unlawful intercourse, should her accusation not be believed or proved under criminal laws. Many Pakistani women find rape extremely difficult to prove under criminal laws that simultaneously set a high standard of proof for rape and undervalue women's testimony as witnesses or victims.

State agents also detain women in place of or to punish their absent male family members or in an effort to coerce male relatives hiding from authorities to turn themselves in. In Egypt, internal security forces have detained female family members of suspected Islamist militants who are wanted by the authorities, in order to force the militants to turn themselves in. These arbitrary detentions, themselves violative of international human rights standards, are frequently accompanied by threats of sexual and physical abuse, as well as sexualized verbal degradation. These abuses are used to compel the men in hiding to give themselves up in exchange for the release of their female family members. The act or threat of rape and other sexual mistreatment of women are perceived in Egypt to be profound offenses against a woman's individual honor as well as the honor of her family and male relatives. Consequently, when security forces threaten to rape or otherwise sexually assault a detained woman, they understand that they are committing a grave offense against not only the woman herself, but also against an entire family or community.

Once imprisoned, both male and female prisoners suffer violence at the hands of abusive guards. However, male jailers often abuse women prisoners for different reasons than those for which male prisoners are harmed. Often, because male guards bring to their jobs discriminatory attitudes about male dominance and female submissiveness, women prisoners are treated in ways that punish them for not meeting their male guards' expectations about female comportment. For example, some state-level prisons in the United States discipline women prisoners more severely for more petty infractions than their male counterparts. In other cases, the mistreatment of women in detention appears to target their sexuality in a deliberate attempt to degrade them and, by extension, their male family members. Egyptian security forces, for instance, have compelled female relatives of suspected Islamist militants to strip naked, and then placed them in a closed room with naked male detainees in an effort to degrade them.

---

[2] Offense of Zina (Enforcement of Hudood) Ordinance, 1979, Section 4.

Women held overnight in pretrial detention at police lockups, often with no access to legal representation and without being officially charged, are in many ways the most vulnerable to physical and sexual assault. These women are invisible in the criminal justice system. Many times, no official, apart from the arresting officers, knows that the women are being held.

Women who are mistreated, threatened and harassed while in custody often find that reporting such abuse achieves negligible results and may lead to retaliation. Reflecting an institutional bias against prisoner testimonies, prison officials are disinclined to believe a woman prisoner's allegations of abuse by a guard simply because of her prisoner status. In numerous cases we have investigated, prison officials favor the word of a guard over that of the prisoner even in the face of compelling evidence to the contrary. This failure to credit women's allegations and to provide an impartial grievance mechanism denies prisoners their right to due process, reinforces the prisoner's sense of powerlessness, condones the guard's behavior, and results in impunity for abusive prison staff. The virtual absence of accountability hinders attempts at redress for custodial abuse.

When confronted with documentation of widespread violence against women in custody in their countries, governments have often denied or ignored the role of state agents, or, as in the case of Pakistan, accused the women prisoners of lying about their ordeals. In Egypt, the government has denied the detention of innocent citizens and ignored allegations of sexual assault and mistreatment, or it has characterized the allegations as attempts by Islamist militants to slander the government. The United States federal government claims to have instituted protections for female prisoners, in particular to safeguard their privacy; in practice, however, these procedures appear to have offered women little protection from sexual misconduct and other inhuman and degrading treatment by guards who work in state-level prisons.

Actual or threatened reprisal by prison staff also contributes to the sense of powerlessness among women in custody. In the United States, guards have retaliated against women who complained of harassment or abuse by citing them for such violations as "refusal to follow an order," or by threatening to postpone their parole. In Pakistan, implicated policemen have visited former female detainees at their homes to intimidate them into withdrawing allegations of custodial abuse. The threat of retaliation often succeeds in stopping women prisoners from making complaints.

Even in cases where prison officials investigate allegations of assault by guards against women prisoners, the investigations seldom result in dissuasive punishment of the offending officer. For example, in the countries examined below, too often police and guards who assault women prisoners get the equivalent of a slap on the wrist in the form of a suspension or written reprimand. Prison guards found guilty of assault after internal investigations are rarely fired or criminally prosecuted. Rather, they may be allowed to resign or transfer to another prison facility; neither form of punishment limits the officers' ability to work in a supervisory position over other female prisoners.

International Legal Protections

International human rights norms provide extensive protections for prisoners and detainees, including women in custody. Among numerous other international instruments, the International Covenant on Civil and Political Rights (ICCPR), the Convention against Torture and Other Cruel, Inhuman or Degrading Treatment or Punishment (hereafter Torture Convention), the Standard Minimum Rules for the Treatment of Prisoners, and the Body of Principles for the Protection of All Persons under Any Form of Detention or Imprisonment, together weave a blanket of protections against the mistreatment of prisoners.

Torture and Other Cruel, Inhuman or Degrading Treatment

Torture and other cruel, inhuman, or degrading treatment of prisoners constitute gross violations of human rights. Both the ICCPR and the Torture Convention condemn such mistreatment and obligate states to prevent and remedy instances of torture and other cruel, inhuman or degrading treatment or punishment. In fact, the right not to be subjected to such abuse ranks as one of the most fundamental of all human rights, and is considered part of customary international law, guaranteed to all persons without distinction of any kind, including discrimination based on gender.[3]

Article 7 of the ICCPR and Article 5 of the Universal Declaration of Human Rights proscribe torture and other cruel, inhuman or degrading treatment or punishment. Under the Torture Convention, a given act is torture when it: (1) causes severe physical or mental suffering; (2) is committed for the purpose of obtaining information, punishment, intimidation or coercion;

---

[3] See ICCPR, Part II, Article 2(1) and Part III, Article 7.

and (3) is inflicted or instigated by or with the consent or acquiescence of any person acting in an official capacity.[4]

To establish cruel, inhuman or degrading treatment, which is prohibited by Article 7 of the ICCPR and Article 16 of the Torture Convention, it must be shown that a particular act or condition caused mental or physical suffering rising to a particular level of severity, although below that of torture, and was inflicted by or at the instigation of a government actor.[5] The critical difference between torture and other cruel, inhuman and degrading treatment, according to one interpretation, is "the duration of the treatment, its physical or mental effects and, in some cases, the sex, age and state of health of the victim."[6]

The inherently coercive nature of the prison environment and the unequal and authoritarian relationship between prison employees and prisoners vitiate the usual notions of consent in sexual relations. Where sexual intercourse between officers and prisoners involves the use or threat of force, punishment or retribution, or involves the promise or provision of reward, it constitutes rape. Sexual touching with these elements constitutes sexual assault. Both rape and sexual assault in custody amount to a form of torture. Even where no overt act or threat of force or retribution or offer of reward can be demonstrated, sexual contact between a prison employee and a prisoner is still an abuse of power and should be criminalized.

Article 10(1) of the ICCPR further provides that "all persons deprived of their liberty shall be treated with humanity and respect for the inherent

---

[4] Torture is defined in Article 1 of the Torture Convention as: "any act by which severe pain or suffering, whether physical or mental, is intentionally inflicted on a person for such purpose as obtaining from him or a third person information or a confession, punishing him for an act he or a third person has committed or is suspected of having committed, or intimidating or coercing him or a third person, or for any reason based on discrimination of any kind, when such pain or suffering is inflicted by or at the instigation of or with the consent or acquiescence of a public official or other person acting in an official capacity." Convention Against Torture and Other Cruel, Inhuman or Degrading treatment or Punishment, adopted and open for signature, ratification and accession by General Assembly resolution 39/46 of December 10, 1984.

[5] In the *Greek Case*, the European Commission defined degrading treatment as treatment or punishment which "grossly humiliates one or drives him to act against his will or conscience." See *The Greek Case* in the *Year Book of European Convention on Human Rights* (European Commission on Human Rights, 1969) p. 186.

[6] Nigel Rodley, *The Treatment of Prisoners Under International Law* (New York: Oxford University Press, 1987), p. 93.

dignity of the human person." These provisions not only prohibit torture and ill-treatment but also impose a positive duty on state parties to treat prisoners humanely.[7]

In addition to the international treaties that protect individuals from torture and other cruel, inhuman or degrading treatment, two key U.N. resolutions—the Standard Minimum Rules for the Treatment of Prisoners[8] and the Body of Principles for the Protection of All Persons under Any Form of Detention or Imprisonment[9]—provide further authoritative guidance. The Standard Minimum Rules are a set of guidelines for prison administrators to interpret and apply the international protection against cruel, inhuman or degrading treatment or punishment. They also assist in the interpretation of the more general requirements in Article 10(1) of the ICCPR mandating the humane treatment and respect for the human dignity of prisoners.[10]

The Standard Minimum Rules prohibit discrimination against prisoners based on several grounds, including sex, require that prisoners have necessary information at their disposal regarding prison regulations and procedures for filing complaints, and instruct prison personnel to conduct themselves professionally.[11] While the Standard Minimum Rules do not purport to be a literal manual for corrections officials, they are intended as an elaboration of

---

[7] "Compilation of General Comments and General Recommendations Adopted by Human Rights Treaty Bodies," General Comment 7 to Article 7, U.N. Document HRI/GEN/1/Rev.1, July 29, 1994, p. 7.

[8] Standard Minimum Rules for the Treatment of Prisoners, approved by the Economic and Social Council by resolutions 663 C, July 31, 1957, and 2076, May 13, 1977, reprinted in U.S., *A Compilation of International Instruments: Volume I (Part 1) Universal Instruments* (New York: United Nations Press, 1993), pp. 243-262. The Standard Minimum Rules, while not itself a binding agreement, is considered an authoritative explanation of standards in the ICCPR, other treaties, and customary law that are binding.

[9] Adopted and proclaimed by General Assembly resolution 45/111 of December 15, 1990. Similar to the Standard Minimum Rules, the Body of Principles is not legally binding on governments, but recognized to offer authoritative guidance.

[10] Standard Minimum Rules, Rule 31, reiterates the prohibition on cruel, inhuman or degrading treatment or punishment within the particular context of punishment within the prison itself. Rule 31 provides that "corporal punishment, punishment by placing in a dark cell, and all cruel, inhuman or degrading punishments shall be completely prohibited for punishment for disciplinary offenses."

[11] Ibid., Rule 35 (1); Rule 6 (1), and Rule 48.

what is "generally accepted as being good principle and practice in the treatment of prisoners and the management of institutions."[12]

The Body of Principles for the Protection of All Persons under Any Form of Detention or Imprisonment also requires humane treatment of all prisoners; prohibits torture, or other cruel, inhuman or degrading treatment; and recognizes prisoners' right to due process, including the right to appeal disciplinary action before it is taken.[13]

Privacy

Article 17 of the ICCPR provides for the right of every person to be protected against arbitrary or unlawful interference with her privacy. The right to privacy in international law is not absolute. Detention and confinement pursuant to lawful prosecution or punishment is one of the situations in which the right to privacy can be legitimately curtailed. But the person who is incarcerated does not by that fact lose her entire claim to privacy. On the contrary, the state can only restrict her exercise of that right only to the extent strictly made necessary by security concerns incidental to the situation of incarceration. Invasions of privacy cannot be arbitrary and cannot be used as an opportunity for abusive treatment. It is the state's obligation to fulfill its responsibility to provide a secure environment with the minimal possible invasion of the prisoner's privacy. To that end, international law limits the role of male officers in women's prisons, preventing them from participating in the strip search or pat-frisk of women prisoners.[14] Abusive cross-gender pat-frisks not only subject women prisoners to degrading treatment, but also constitute a violation of a prisoner's right to privacy.

The Standard Minimum Rules stipulate that incarcerated women should be supervised by female officers.[15] Further, these rules require that officers be trained on how to carry out their professional duties, to ensure the humane treatment of women prisoners.[16] The Human Rights Committee has

---

[12] Ibid., preliminary observations.

[13] Body of Principles for the Protection of All Persons Under Any Form of Detention, Principle 1, Principle 6, Principle 30(3), and Principle 38.

[14] General Comment 16 to Article 17 states that, "Persons being subjected to body search by State officials, or medical personnel acting at the request of the State, should only be examined by persons of the same sex." General Comment 16 to Article 17, "Compilation of General Comments . . . "

[15] Standard Minimum Rules, Rule 53.

[16] Ibid., Rule 47.

interpreted Article 17 of the ICCPR to guarantee that body searches, for example, ". . . are carried out in a manner consistent with the dignity of the person who is being searched."[17]

Due Process

These international instruments further obligate states to ensure effective redress for women victims of custodial violence, whether they are imprisoned or held in police lockups.[18] Articles 9 to 16 of the ICCPR and Article 2 of the Torture Convention guarantee, among other things, freedom from arbitrary arrest or detention; presumption of innocence; right to non-discriminatory treatment; and the right to an impartial, speedy trial. Other international instruments, such as the Standard Minimum Rules for the Treatment of Prisoners, and the Body of Principles for the Protection of All Persons under Any Form of Detention or Imprisonment establish general rules and procedures for management of prisons, including: the establishment of a fair, speedy, process for the investigation of a prisoner's complaint; a right of a prisoner to appeal disciplinary measures before action is taken; a right to be informed of a detailed code of regulations by which a prisoner's behavior will be judged; a right to respond to charges; a right to appeal to a higher administrative authority; a right to have a court review the sanction for abuse of administrative discretion; and a right to cooperate with an investigation, offer evidence and to know the results.

International standards have failed to protect women in custody because they are seldom enforced. The types of abuse reported below illustrate the range of violence women in custody face. Governments must take urgent steps to ensure that their corrections officials and security forces strictly adhere to international standards guaranteeing due process, protection from torture and cruel, inhuman or degrading treatment or punishment, and the right to privacy in their treatment of women in custody. Further, they must create and implement effective mechanisms for redressing alleged official violence and other forms of misconduct against women in custody, including prompt and impartial investigation, prosecution, and punishment of those found

---

[17] General Comment 16 to Article 17, "Compilation of General Comments . . ."

[18] Although designed to regulate instances of lawful arrest, the international standards governing prison conditions also apply, by logical force, to unlawful situations such as cases of arbitrary, irregular and even clandestine detention to which governments subject detainees in some situations.

responsible, including the prison administrators who preside over institutions in which abuse is rampant and unchecked.

POLICE ABUSE OF WOMEN IN PAKISTAN

In Pakistan, more than 70 percent of women in police custody experience physical abuse, including sexual abuse, at the hands of their jailers, according to local human rights lawyers.[19] Reported abuses include beating and slapping; suspension in mid-air by hands tied behind the victim's back; the insertion of foreign objects, including police batons and chili peppers, into the vagina and rectum; and gang rape. Yet despite these alarming reports, police officers almost never suffer criminal penalties for such abuse, even in cases in which incontrovertible evidence of custodial rape exists.[20] One senior police official told a delegation of local human rights activists that "in 95 percent of the cases the women themselves are at fault."[21]

This attitude is reflected in the way police handle allegations of rape brought by the victims. Police routinely refuse to register such complaints, particularly if they implicate a fellow officer. Police officers also illegally detain women in a police lockup for days at a time without formally registering a charge against them or producing them before a magistrate within the required 24-hour period. Women thus can be held indefinitely without the knowledge of the courts. It is during these periods of "invisibility" that most sexual abuse of female detainees occurs.

Many of the women detained in Pakistan should not be in custody in the first place. Between 50 and 80 percent of all female detainees in Pakistan are imprisoned under the Islamic Hudood Ordinances, penal laws introduced in 1979, which in law and in practice discriminate against women. Prior to the

---

[19] The following material was adapted from the Women's Rights Project and Asia Watch, *Double Jeopardy: Police Abuse of Women in Pakistan* (New York: Human Rights Watch, 1992).   See also Asma Jahangir and Hina Jilani, *The Hudood Ordinances: A Divine Sanction?* (Lahore: Rhotac Books, 1990), p. 137.

[20] Human Rights Watch investigated police abuse of women in Pakistan during a mission in October 1992. The Human Rights Watch team interviewed victims of custodial rape and other abuse, lawyers, activists and police and government officials. In Lahore, Human Rights Watch interviewed Deputy Inspector General Maqbool, who told us that to his knowledge "not a single officer had been convicted" of custodial rape.

[21] Human Rights Commission of Pakistan, *Newsletter*, October 1991, p. 7.

passage of the Hudood Ordinances, women were not directly involved with the criminal justice system in any significant number; since their introduction, thousands of women have been imprisoned under these laws alone. The steep rise in the number of female prisoners in turn increased the opportunity for police misconduct toward women.

The Hudood Ordinances criminalize, among other things, adultery, fornication and rape, and prescribe punishments for these offenses that include stoning to death, public flogging and amputation. Human Rights Watch does not object to laws founded on religion, provided that human rights are respected and the principle of equality before the law is upheld. However, the Hudood laws, as written and applied, clearly conflict with these rights and principles. Not only do they prescribe punishments that are cruel and inhuman under international law, but they clearly discriminate on the basis of gender.[22] The laws also conflict with the Pakistani Constitution, which guarantees the right to equality and non-discrimination on the basis of gender.

Discrimination under the Hudood Ordinances

Under the Hudood ordinances, proof of rape for the maximum (*Hadd*) punishments of stoning to death or 100 lashes in a public place requires the testimony of four male Muslim witnesses to the act of penetration. The testimony of a woman—not only the victim but *any* woman—carries no legal weight for this maximum punishment. This requirement means that women who have been sentenced to the maximum punishments, deemed cruel and inhuman under international law, have been so sentenced under a law that prevents them from testifying on their own behalf. Men have also been cruelly sentenced under these laws, although in general men accused of rape are effectively exempted from the maximum Hadd punishments, because women can neither testify nor is any person likely to be able to produce four male Muslim witnesses to the act of penetration. Although no Hadd sentences have been carried out to date, nothing impedes the state from carrying them out in the future. Human Rights Watch recommends that these laws be repealed and that all other obstacles to a woman's right to testify equally with a man in a court of law be removed.

The majority of rape and adultery or fornication cases attract the lesser (*Tazir*) punishments, which entail public flogging, rigorous imprisonment, and fines. While the testimony of women is admissible at this level, Pakistani

---

[22] The Hudood Ordinances have also been shown to discriminate on the basis of religion, but this issue falls outside the purview of this report.

courts still exhibit a bias against women. The courts tend to see women as complicit in sexual offenses, despite a lack of evidence or evidence to the contrary, and require from female rape victims extraordinarily conclusive proof that the alleged intercourse was forced.[23] Moreover, many women who alleged but were unable to prove rape have themselves been charged with adultery or fornication for consensual sex, although a failure to prove rape does not prove that consensual sex occurred.[24] Since the Hudood Ordinances were promulgated in 1979, many rape victims no longer attempt to prosecute their rapists for fear of prosecution themselves. Such was the case of five women in Larkana who were gang-raped in January 1994 and revoked their allegations when they were threatened with prosecution under the Hudood Ordinances. In another case from 1991, eighteen-year-old Majeeda Mujid was abducted by several men and raped repeatedly by her abductors over a two-month period, until they finally turned her over to the police. Although she complained that she had been raped, the police charged her with illicit sex, imprisoned her pending trial, and let the men go free.

In some cases, when medical evidence has been introduced in support of a rape charge in which forcible intercourse cannot be proved, men have also been charged with adultery or fornication. However, medical evidence implicating accused males often cannot be obtained, so they are frequently released for lack of evidence while their women victims are imprisoned

---

[23] Under Pakistan's Evidence Code, whether a woman sought immediate assistance following her rape can be a factor in determining whether her complaint is true. This rule, known as the "fresh complaint rule," has been widely discredited in the United States and Europe because it has been used to support the presumption that women who fail to report rapes may not have been raped. The rule fails to acknowledge the many sound reasons why women might fail to report rape, including, in the context of Pakistan, the risk of criminal prosecution if they fail to prove their case. In addition, in the absence of physical evidence of resistance, such as bodily injuries, courts are prone to disbelieve the woman's testimony that the act was non-consensual. Pakistan's highest religious court, the Federal *Shariat* Court, has successfully overturned rape convictions and reduced sentences on such grounds.

[24] According to the International Commission of Jurists, "there have been many reported cases where a complaint of rape has been made and the court has convicted and punished both parties for adultery or fornication." International Commission of Jurists, *Pakistan: Human Rights After Martial Law* (Geneva, 1987), p. 128. Human rights lawyers Jahangir and Jilani documented four cases which occurred between 1980 and 1987. See Jahangir and Jilani, *The Hudood Ordinances* . . . , pp. 90-92. Human Rights Watch documented one such case in our 1991 mission.

pending trial based on their own allegations of forcible intercourse. For example, in 1983, an eighteen-year-old blind woman, Safia Bibi, became pregnant allegedly as a result of rape. Her pregnancy was cited by the prosecution as proof that she had engaged in extra-marital sex, and her assailant was acquitted due to "want of evidence." In response to national and international protests, Safia Bibi was acquitted on appeal. In 1983, fifteen-year-old Jehan Mina became pregnant after allegedly being raped by her uncle and his son. When she filed the complaint with the police, she was charged with fornication. In sentencing her, the court stated that "the basis of conviction is her unexplained pregnancy coupled with the fact that she is not a married girl."[25]

The discriminatory provisions of the Hudood laws are exacerbated by their discriminatory application by the police and judiciary. According to several Pakistani legal aid attorneys who represent indigent women charged with Hudood offenses, the vast majority of Hudood cases (most of which are registered by the woman's husband or father) are not supported by the evidence and should not have been prosecuted. In many cases, women are wrongfully prosecuted for Hudood offenses because they refuse to marry men chosen by their families, decide to leave home or marry men against their parents' will, or seek to separate from or divorce abusive husbands. Norwal,[26] a twelve-year-old girl whom we interviewed at the Kot Lakhpat prison in Lahore in October 1992, was charged with zina (adultery) after eloping with her cousin.

In part, judges hear ill-founded Hudood cases because they, like the police, are eager to show that they are tough on crime. But, wrongful prosecution of women also reflects a tendency on the part of the police and judiciary to see women as guilty until proven innocent. In effect, the Hudood laws have given legal sanction to biased social attitudes towards women, thus not only legitimizing the oppression of women in the eyes of the state but also intensifying it: women who seek to deviate from prescribed social norms now may not only be subject to societal censure, but also to criminal penalties. It is this enforcement of state power in the name of religion and its use as a tool to legitimate abusive state power, rather than religion itself, that is at issue. Although acquittal rates for women in Hudood cases are estimated at over 30 percent, by the time a woman has been vindicated she will have spent months,

---

[25] *Pakistan Law Journal* 1983 Federal Shariat Court 134.

[26] Last names of interviewees are withheld by Human Rights Watch unless otherwise indicated.

and possibly years, in prison. In most case, she will have been subjected to police abuse while in custody.

Even in cases in which no formal charge is brought against a woman, judges often suspect that if she was abducted or raped she must have been behaving inappropriately to begin with and was in some way complicit in the offense. In lieu of filing a formal charge against the women in such cases, judges frequently remand female rape and abduction victims to private detention facilities for indefinite periods to await the outcome of the cases lodged against their alleged abusers. Such facilities often function like prisons, but are subsidized by private philanthropies. Officials attempt to justify such prolonged detention as a form of "protective custody" for the women, but in effect it amounts to the punitive detention of innocent women for the crime of being an alleged victim. Local human rights organizations have filed habeas corpus petitions on behalf of such women, and some have been freed. However, the cases had no effect on the underlying problem of private detention of women accused of no offense. We interviewed several women confined to one "protective" facility, Darulaman, in Lahore. In one typical case, Farznan, a twenty-year-old, was detained at Darulaman after running away from home when her parents tried to force her to marry against her will.

Police Abuse of Women in Custody

During our October 1992 mission, we interviewed a number of women who had been tortured and mistreated in police custody. According to them, attorneys, and Pakistani human rights groups, common methods of torture included beating and slapping; suspension in mid-air by hands tied behind the victim's back; the insertion of foreign objects, including police batons and chili peppers, into the vagina and rectum; and gang rape.

In one well-publicized case, Aasia Ayoub was detained at the Banni police station in Rawalpindi on September 3, 1991, after a neighbor alleged that Ayoub had stolen a purse. Ayoub was arrested without warrant, and no formal charges were filed. According to subsequent inquiries, she was held overnight in the police lockup where the station house officer and other police present slapped her, threatened to insert chilies into her vagina, kissed her, and fondled her on the breasts, legs, and genitals. The police also threatened to molest her fourteen-year-old daughter. Widespread publicity about the case forced the government to take action. The police officers were suspended, but charges against them were only filed after a local human rights activist filed a writ requesting the High Court to intervene. A judicial inquiry concluded that the police had sexually tortured Ayoub. The magistrate who conducted the inquiry was transferred after he refused to grant the officers bail. The police were eventually acquitted for lack of evidence.

The Human Rights Commission of Pakistan, an independent monitoring organization, reported in 1994 that an assistant sub-inspector of police in the Gujarpura district of Lahore raped a woman in police custody in the presence of her eighty-year-old mother, who was also molested. An inquiry determined that the officer was guilty and recommended that he be dismissed. In Kharian, a young woman who was reportedly raped by a police constable and three of his accomplices was herself charged with a crime when she reported the rape. After a magistrate heard the story, the case against the woman was dropped and the rapists arrested. We do not know whether they have been tried. During a 1994 raid on the village of Kadianwala, in Narowal district, police severely beat villagers, including several women, one of whom was pregnant.[27]

Barriers to Justice

It is extremely difficult for women prisoners to seek redress for sexual and physical abuse by police. They must confront rape and evidence laws that overtly discriminate; they face the possibility of criminal prosecution or—at a minimum—social ostracism if they fail to prove their rape allegations; they must combat police and judicial attitudes that are clearly biased against them; and they must overcome procedural obstacles to prosecuting the police that affect all victims of custodial abuse, including the absence of any independent body to investigate and prosecute abuses of police power.

The possibility of obtaining equal justice in Pakistan has been further reduced over the past decade by the steady erosion of judicial independence, mainly through the government's retention of undue influence over the judiciary and through the establishment of parallel religious and "speedy trial" courts, which apply summary procedures that restrict fair trial guarantees. While Human Rights Watch does not oppose religious courts or speedy-trial rules per se, both the religious and speedy trial courts in Pakistan have been shown to weaken the independence and jurisdiction of the civil courts and to violate due process. This trend culminated in the adoption of the 1991 Shariat Act, which subjects the constitution and the law-making authority of the legislature to the revisional authority of Islamic religious leaders, many of

---

[27] Human Rights Commission of Pakistan, *State of Human Rights in 1994* (Lahore, 1995), pp. 44-45, 49.

whom, according to local human rights activists, "have been known to take positions against women."[28]

The discriminatory treatment encountered by women who enter the criminal justice system reflects the treatment of women as second-class citizens in Pakistani society generally. From birth, the life of the average Pakistani woman is characterized by her economic, social, cultural and political subordination. She will receive less food, medical care, and education, be paid and inherit less, have fewer opportunities to participate in civil society, and live a shorter life than her male counterparts.[29] Even in comparison with women in many other parts of the world, she will on average marry earlier, bear more children, be more likely to die in childbirth, and work more hours without compensation. Like women everywhere, she will be at risk of violence in the home and, in some areas of Pakistan, she may face violence by the community, particularly if she engages in behavior seen to deviate from prescribed social norms.

Given this subordinate status, once a woman is in prison she is unlikely to know how to secure even the minimal protections due to her under law, or to make herself heard if she tried to secure those protections. Eighty percent of all female prisoners in Pakistan are illiterate, and nearly 90 percent live on a monthly family income equal to less than US$40. According to a survey conducted in 1988, over 90 percent of the ninety women prisoners interviewed in two prisons in Punjab were unaware of the law under which they had been imprisoned. Over 60 percent had received no legal assistance whatsoever.[30]

The Response of the Pakistani Government

In response to international and domestic pressure, the Pakistani government has initiated some measures to address the problem of widespread abuses against women. These steps, while welcome, will do little to curb these abuses unless the government takes effective action to hold its own police and

---

[28] A representative of the Women's Action Forum (WAF), a nongovernmental, national women's rights organization, quoted in Women Living Under Muslim Laws, "WAF Rejects Shariat Bill," *Special Bulletin on the Erosion of the Judiciary and Human Rights Legislation* (Lahore, 1992), p. 7.

[29] For more on this, see Farida Shaheed, *Pakistan's Women: An Analytical Description* (Lahore, 1990), pp. 20-22.

[30] Jahangir and Jilani, *The Hudood Ordinances* . . . , pp. 134-136.

other security forces accountable for torture, rape and illegal detention, and change the laws under which women are wrongfully detained.

For more than twelve years, human rights and women's rights advocates in Pakistan have been campaigning for the repeal of discriminatory laws, including the Hudood Ordinances, good faith prosecution of abusive police, greater adherence to the fundamental principles of due process and equality before the law, and increased legal services for women. Some members of Pakistan's judiciary, particularly at the High Court level, have recognized the epidemic proportions of violence against women in custody and have initiated investigations.

Late in 1994, the Senate set up a commission of inquiry for women, headed by a Supreme Court judge and including senators and prominent private citizens, to examine the laws that discriminate against women and to suggest amendments and other remedial measures. At the same time, a tribunal was established to look into abuses against disadvantaged segments of the populace, including women. It is too soon to tell whether these bodies have had any effect in ameliorating conditions for women.

Police stations staffed entirely by women police officers were functioning in several cities in Pakistan by the end of 1994. The stations are tasked to deal with cases in which women have been the principal victims. In 1994 the government also passed a law prohibiting the detention of women in police stations for questioning, except in cases of murder or robbery. Under this law, the police are required to take women directly into judicial custody. However, it remains to be seen whether these laws will be observed in practice. Police regulations prohibiting the overnight detention of women were on the books for years and were frequently disregarded.

Despite these welcome measures, the government's response remains woefully inadequate. While the government gained media attention in 1994 for prosecuting one man, Maulvi Mohammad Sharif, in a case in which he was charged with inserting electrified iron rods into his wife's vagina, it did not seek to implement legislative reforms to protect women. The Hudood Ordinances, as applied in Pakistan, continue explicitly to discriminate against women.

Pakistan is obliged under international law and its own constitution to refrain from torture and ill-treatment of prisoners in custody and to provide female victims of such abuse with equal protection under the law. But the government has failed to eliminate the overtly discriminatory laws and practices that promote the wrongful prosecution of women and result in their prolonged imprisonment. And, rather than remove procedural obstacles to justice for the victims of police abuse, the government has adopted policies that perpetuate police impunity and erode judicial independence.[31]

As Pakistan bids to be a significant regional and international power, the government must take immediate steps to adopt and adhere to international human rights standards and to end all forms of violence against women and gender discrimination. Its failure to do so will only perpetuate the oppression of women in Pakistan and further diminish the country's stature as a nascent democracy in the eyes of the international community.

SEXUAL ABUSE OF WOMEN PRISONERS IN THE UNITED STATES

Women incarcerated in United States state prisons face a serious and potentially pervasive problem of sexual misconduct by prison officials.[32] Human Rights Watch found that male officers have engaged in rape, sexual assault, inappropriate sexual contact, verbal degradation and unwarranted visual surveillance of female prisoners in eleven prisons in five states and the District of Columbia.[33] Two prison systems that Human Rights Watch investigated, in Georgia and the District of Columbia, have taken initial steps to address this problem. But most states are failing to address custodial sexual misconduct adequately and have yet to train officers to avoid such misconduct or to put in place administrative measures and, where appropriate, to apply criminal sanctions to prohibit and punish this egregious human rights abuse.

Our findings are based on an eighteen-month investigation, from 1993 to 1995, of state prisons in California, Georgia, Illinois, Michigan, New York,

---

[31] Despite the government's stated intention to eliminate custodial violence and gender discrimination, it has yet to ratify most of the relevant international human rights instruments, including the International Covenant on Civil and Political Rights and the Convention on the Elimination of All Forms of Discrimination Against Women. Although Pakistan is a signatory to the Convention for the Suppression of the Traffic in Persons, it has largely failed to meet its obligations under this agreement.

[32] The following material is part of an upcoming report from Human Rights Watch on sexual misconduct in U.S. state women's prisons.

[33] Each of the fifty states operates and maintains its own prison system. These systems are separate and distinct from the federal prison system, which is overseen by the Federal Bureau of Prisons. Thus, the applicable law will be different for each state. Most crimes are prosecuted in state courts, under state criminal law, and prisoners are sentenced to terms in state institutions.

and the District of Columbia.[34]   Our interviews with prisoners posed a
number of initial problems, primarily as a result of the prisoners' pervasive
fear that they would be retaliated against for speaking with us.[35]   At the
prisoners' request, and for their protection, we have withheld their real names
and the exact place, date and time of their interviews.

Our findings, while profoundly troubling, scratch only the surface of
the problem of sexual misconduct in the state correctional systems that we
investigated and, perhaps, in United States' women's prisons as a whole. We
found not only evidence of serious state violations, but also warning signs of
a grave and potentially explosive national problem of custodial sexual
misconduct in women's prisons.   The need to address this problem is
particularly urgent given that the female prison population in the United States
is increasing at almost double the rate of the male population.[36]   Absent

---

[34] The respective correctional systems generally cooperated with our investigation
and permitted us to conduct unsupervised interviews of female prisoners in their
facilities' visiting or attorney rooms. However, the official tendency to downplay or
even deny reports of sexual misconduct made this an extremely difficult problem for
us to investigate. While no state correctional officials flatly refused to speak with us
concerning sexual misconduct in their facilities, such interviews were often
unnecessarily difficult and, in some cases, impossible to arrange.

[35] In rare instances, prisoners came forward for the first time upon learning of our
visit to their facility. But in the majority of cases, we interviewed prisoners who lodged
complaints of sexual misconduct prior to our investigation. In addition to the female
prisoners and the relevant corrections authorities in the facilities where they were being
held, we also interviewed the prisoners' attorneys, volunteers who work in women's
facilities, local and national women's and civil liberty organizations with prison
expertise, current and former corrections employees, and U.S. Department of Justice
officials responsible for overseeing state correctional systems.

[36] According to the Department of Justice, Bureau of Justice Statistics (BOJS), the
population of incarcerated women in the United States has increased from 14,000 in
1980 to 40,556 in 1989, an increase of approximately 200 percent. This increase is
nearly double that of men, whose population rose 112 percent in the same period.
Greenfield and Minor-Harper, Bureau of Justice Statistics, *Special Report: Women in
Prison* (Virginia: Bureau of Justice Statistics, 1991). As of March 1995, there were
over 1,900 women in the Illinois prison population, a number which has nearly
quadrupled since 1983, while the male population has doubled. California's prison
population increased by 450 percent between 1980 and 1993, while, in roughly the same
time period, the overall prison population, including men and women, grew at 346
percent. California Department of Corrections, *Commission Report on Female Inmates
and Parolee Issues* (California: California Department of Corrections, 1994), p. V.

significant reform by state corrections and criminal justice systems the potential for custodial sexual misconduct in U.S. women's prisons can only increase.

The Custodial Environment in U.S. State Prisons

The United States differs from most prison systems in the world in that it employs male staff in positions involving unsupervised contact with female prisoners. The United Nations Standard Minimum Rules for the Treatment of Prisoners prohibit such employment, but the United States nonetheless allows male officers to hold contact positions in women's prisons.[37] It has done so largely to satisfy national labor laws and as a result of numerous anti-discrimination suits.[38]

The increased presence of male officers and staff in female prisons—at times male officers now outnumber their female counterparts in women's prisons by three to one—places important and fairly unique responsibilities on the U.S. federal and state corrections systems. The corrections administrations must ensure that violations of the basic human rights of female prisoners are not the price paid to satisfy U.S. labor laws. In virtually every prison that we visited, state prison authorities allowed male officers to hold contact positions over female prisoners without the benefit of any clear definition of sexual misconduct, any clear rules and procedures with respect to it, or any meaningful training in how to avoid it.[39] Prison officials

---

[37] Standard Minimum Rules for the Treatment of Prisoners, approved by the Economic and Social Council by resolutions 663 C, July 31, 1957, and resolution 2076, May 13, 1977, reprinted in U.S., *A Compilation of International Instruments: Volume I (Part I) Universal Instruments* (New York: United Nations Press, 1993), pp. 243-263, Rule 53.

[38] Under Title VII, Civil Rights Act of 1964, 42 United States Code Section 2000e *et. seq.* an employer may not discriminate on the basis of sex, unless an employee's sex is a Bona Fide Occupational Requirement (BFOQ), i.e. reasonably necessary to perform the specific job. In the absence of specific circumstances, U.S. federal courts have been unwilling to characterize a person's sex as a BFOQ.

[39] Men comprise the majority of corrections officers in New York's women's prisons, including the evening and night shifts in the housing units. Nonetheless, the New York department of corrections does not provide specific training for male officers assigned to work with women, even though it agreed to do so as an element of the settlement in the class action lawsuit *Blackman v. Coughlin.* 84-CIV 5698, September 1993 (District Court, New York) (the suit covered only Bayview Correctional facility).

(continued...)

also were failing to equip female prisoners to deal with the potential abuse in the cross-gender guarding situation. They rarely, if ever, informed female prisoners of the risk of sexual misconduct in custody. Nor did they advise them of the mechanisms available—to the extent that they exist—to report and remedy such practices.

The states' failure fully to inform female prisoners about the risks of and remedies for sexual misconduct is particularly negligent, given that female prisoners often enter the U.S. correctional system with a prior history of sexual abuse.[40] Although no national statistics in this regard yet exist, attorneys and volunteers in every state that we visited told us that the female prisoners often have such personal histories.[41] According to Christina Kampfner, a clinical psychologist working in Michigan's women's prisons, women's past abuse renders the women particularly vulnerable to exploitation by the male officers once they enter prison. Kampfner stated that many women with this history are easy targets for sexual abuse—"the women are so needy and in need of

---

[39](...continued)
In Illinois, where male officers out-number female officers two to one, few written instructions apply to male corrections officers' responsibilities over female prisoners. The only exception occurs at Dwight Correctional Center, where there appears to be some limits on male guards' roles, and, according to some prisoners, male officers are not assigned regularly to the overnight shift on the lower security units, although they may substitute for the regular officer. Michigan's department of corrections allows both men and women to work within the housing units and makes no distinction between male and female corrections officers in conducting pat-frisks or searches of the shower and toilet areas.

[40] Statistics indicate that anywhere from 40 to 88 percent of incarcerated women have been victims of domestic violence and sexual or physical abuse prior to incarceration, either as children or adults. A study of women in Oklahoma's state prisons found that 69 percent reported physical and/or emotional abuse after the age of eighteen. Before eighteen, nearly 40 percent reported being sexually abused—raped or otherwise molested—and 44 percent reported emotional or mental abuse. Sargent, Marcus-Mendoza and Ho Yu, "Abuse and the Women Prisoner," in *Women Prisoners: A Forgotten Population* (Westport, CT: Praeger, 1993). According to testimony presented in *Jordan v. Gardner*, 85 percent of women incarcerated in Washington state have reported a history of serious abuse, including rapes, molestation and beatings. *Federal Reporter, Second*, Volume 986, p. 1525 (Ninth Circuit, 1994).

[41] Telephone interview, Rebecca Jurado, professor of law, Western State University, Irvine, California, March 21, 1995; interview, Bob Cullen, attorney, Atlanta, Georgia, August 4, 1994.

love, they are set up for oppression. The only way they know is to exchange their bodies [to meet this need]."[42] While this may not always be the case, it appears that prior sexual abuse is a significant risk factor for custodial sexual misconduct and one which, in our experience, prison authorities generally and mistakenly ignore.[43]

In women's prisons across the United States, ill-trained male officers guard female prisoners with little appropriate guidance or oversight regarding sexual misconduct. The result is a custodial environment that is highly sexually charged. Both prisoners and advocates told us consistently that male officers regularly comment on the female prisoners' body parts and treat them to a barrage of degrading physical references and gestures. It is in this context that the officers further step over the line with the prisoners and engage in rape, sexual assault, other forms of sexual contact and inappropriate visual surveillance of the women while they are dressing, showering or using the toilet.

Sexual Misconduct and U.S. Law

The United States' obligation to prohibit and punish custodial sexual misconduct derives in part from U.S. constitutional law. The Eighth Amendment of the U.S. Constitution prohibits cruel and unusual punishment, which has been interpreted to include rape and sexual assault of prisoners by officers in prison.[44] Despite this constitutional prohibition, few state laws expressly criminalize custodial sexual misconduct by prison staff toward prisoners. To our knowledge, only thirteen states and the District of Columbia expressly criminalize all sexual intercourse with or sexual touching of a prisoner by prison staff.[45] The federal government also has criminalized

---

[42] Interview, Christina Kampfner, psychologist, Ann Arbor, Michigan, May 17, 1994.

[43] Interview, Bob Cullen, attorney, Atlanta, Georgia, August 4, 1995.

[44] *Women Prisoners of the District of Columbia Department of Corrections v. District of Columbia*, 1994 LEXIS 19222 (District Court, District of Columbia, December 13, 1994).

[45] The states are Colorado, Connecticut, Georgia, Idaho, Iowa, Louisiana, Maine, Michigan, Nevada, New Jersey, North Carolina, North Dakota and Ohio. These conclusions are based upon a memorandum provided to us by the Georgia Department of Corrections. It was prepared by Melissa Manrow, attorney at law, for W. Davis Hewitt, Special Assistant Attorney General, in December 1993. Only two states that we visited, Michigan and Georgia, contain provisions in their respective penal codes

(continued...)

sexual intercourse and touching between a prisoner and prison employee on federal land, which includes federal correctional facilities.[46]

Although states are required to respect a prisoner's Eighth Amendment rights, the amendment generally is enforced only through litigation, primarily individual lawsuits filed by prisoners alleging personal harm. To receive redress under the Eighth Amendment for physical abuses, a prisoner must prove that a prison official or officials acted "sadistically and maliciously."[47] This standard is more specific than that required for torture under international law.

The U.S. Department of Justice (DOJ) also has the authority to enforce the Eighth Amendment. It may do so by bringing criminal charges against prison officials or civil suits for civil rights abuse against incarcerated persons, but its resources for pursuing such cases have been limited greatly by Congress.[48] The DOJ may criminally prosecute a person "acting under the

---

[45](...continued)
criminalizing sexual contact with a prisoner, but they categorize the crime quite differently. Michigan classifies all sexual contact (including both intercourse and touching) with a prisoner as a misdemeanor offense in its rape law. Michigan Penal Code, Section 750.520e. This provision does not prevent state prosecution for felony rape, instead of under the misdemeanor provision. But, in Georgia, the prohibition against sexual contact with prisoners is not contained within the state's rape law. Rather, Georgia has categorized sexual contact with a prisoner as sexual assault. Georgia Criminal Code, Section 16-6-5.1.

[46] Under 18 United States Code Section 2241, it is a felony offense to knowingly cause in a federal prison a person to engage in sexual intercourse by using or threatening the use of force. Under 18 United States Code Section 2243 it is also a criminal offense for a person with "custodial, supervisory or disciplinary" authority to engage in sexual intercourse with or touch a prisoner sexually in a federal correctional facility. The only defense specified for the latter crime is for the defendant to prove that he is married to the victim.

[47] Human Rights Watch and the American Civil Liberties Union, *Human Rights Violations in the United States*, (New York: Human Rights Watch, 1993), p. 99. See *Hudson v. Mcmillan*, 112 Supreme Court Reporter, p. 999 (U.S. Supreme Court, 1992); *Whitley v. Albers*, 475 United States Reports, p. 320 (U.S. Supreme Court, 1986).

[48] Paul Hoffman, "The Fed, Lies and Videotape: The Need for an Effective Federal Role in Controlling Police Abuse in Urban America," *Southern California Law Review*, vol. 66 (1993), p. 1522.

color of state law"[49] for violating a prisoner's constitutional rights under 18 United States Code Sections 241 and 242.[50]   But the DOJ must meet a high evidentiary burden to establish a violation of these statutes; in addition to the standard of proof required for violating the Eighth Amendment, the DOJ also must prove beyond a reasonable doubt that the public official had the "specific intent" to deprive a prisoner of a constitutional right.[51]

The DOJ's authority to investigate and institute civil suits against state institutions for violating the civil rights of prisoners is found under the Civil Rights of Institutionalized Persons Act (CRIPA).[52]   Before suing a state pursuant to CRIPA, the DOJ first must have "reasonable cause to believe" that a state institution engages in a pattern or practice of subjecting prisoners to "egregious or flagrant conditions" that violate the U.S. Constitution. The DOJ also may enforce the constitutional rights of prisoners under the Violent Crime Control and Law Enforcement Act of 1994,[53] which allows the DOJ to sue law enforcement officers civilly if there is reasonable cause to believe they engaged in a pattern or practice of denying constitutional or federal rights.[54]

Beyond these statutes, the U.S. has ratified two international treaties that protect the human rights of prisoners—the ICCPR and the Torture Convention—and thus is bound to uphold the standards set forth in these

---

[49] "Under color of state law" means that a state official must be using her authority as a government official when the violation occurs. A state official may be acting under color of state law even if her conduct violates state law. *Screws v. United States*, 325 United States Reports, p. 109 (U.S. Supreme Court, 1945).

[50] Sections 241 and 242 are both general civil rights provisions, and their application is not limited exclusively to abuses within prisons.

[51] *Screws v. United States*, 325 United States Reports (U.S. Supreme Court, 1945), p. 103, (regarding 18 United States Code Section 242); *United States v. Guest*, 383 United States Reports, p. 760 (U.S. Supreme Court, 1966) (regarding 18 United States Code Section 241).

[52] 42 United States Code Section 1997 *et. seq.*

[53] 42 United States Code Section 14141.

[54] DOJ representatives take the position that the new law applies to corrections officers because they are law enforcement officials. Telephone interview, Department of Justice, May 8, 1995.   Little analysis exists interpreting this law, but it appears to require a lower standard of proof than CRIPA to challenge abusive treatment by law enforcement officials.   CRIPA requires a showing that a pattern or practice of "egregious or flagrant conditions" exist that cause grievous harm before the DOJ may file suit. By contrast, the new statute requires only a showing that there is a "pattern or practice of conduct" depriving a person of her constitutional rights.

documents. The U.S. is also bound by the principles set forth in the Universal Declaration of Human Rights and customary law. In ratifying the two treaties, however, the U.S. attached extensive reservations, declarations and understandings that undermine the protections ostensibly offered U.S. citizens. The U.S. declared that Articles 1 through 27 of the ICCPR and the provisions of the Torture Convention are "non-self-executing" or, in other words, that without enabling legislation, the provisions cannot be invoked by U.S. citizens in U.S. courts.[55] In addition, the U.S. indicated its unwillingness to comply with Article 7 of the ICCPR by entering a reservation that limits U.S. recognition of the right to be free from torture or other cruel, inhuman or degrading treatment or punishment to that standard already recognized by the Supreme Court relative to the Eighth Amendment.[56] While international law does permit governments to make reservations to international treaties, they cannot be incompatible with the object or purpose of the treaty.[57] In our view, these reservations, declarations and understandings are incompatible with the object and purpose of the treaty, and thus, we hold the U.S. to the full terms of both treaties.[58] The international human rights standards set forth in these treaties have been elaborated by additional international documents that provide further authoritative guidance for U.S. law.[59]

---

[55] Thus far, the U.S. has not enacted legislation to implement the ICCPR. The only legislation enacted to implement the Torture Convention allows only those individuals who claim that they were tortured outside the United States to file charges in U.S. courts. 18 United States Code Section 2340 *et. seq.*

[56] United States government, "U.S. Reservations, Understandings, and Declarations to the International Covenant of Civil and Political Rights," October 3, 1992, Reservation 3.

[57] Vienna Convention on the Law of Treaties, Article 19(3).

[58] Human Rights Watch and the American Civil Liberties Union memo, "Comments to the United Nations Human Rights Committee Concerning the First Periodic Report of the United States on Compliance with the International Covenant on Civil and Political Rights."

[59] See U.N. Standard Minimum Rules for the Treatment of Prisoners; U.N. Body of Principles for the Protection of All Persons Under Any Form of Detention or Imprisonment, adopted by General Assembly resolution 45/111, December 14, 1990; and the U.N. Basic Principles for the Treatment of Prisoners, adopted by General Assembly resolution 43/173, December 9, 1988. In *Lareau v. Manson*, 507 Federal Supplement, p. 1177 (District of Connecticut, 1980), *affirmed in part, remanded in part on other grounds,* 651 Federal Reporter, Second, p. 96 (Second Circuit, 1981), the court

(continued...)

Because international treaties are part of the supreme law of the U.S., the president or executive branch must ensure that they are executed faithfully, both on the federal and state levels. The fifty states also are bound by these international laws and norms by virtue of their obligation to act consistent with the supreme law of the United States, which includes customary international law and all international treaties ratified by the U.S.[60] Where state practices or laws are inconsistent with international treaties to which the U.S. has acceded, the state must change such practices or laws, or the federal government must force the state to comply with the international treaties.[61]

Thus, although U.S. law offers female prisoners some protection from sexual misconduct by officers, these protections are inconsistent across states and their enforcement at both the state and federal levels has been woefully inadequate. Instead of encouraging and assisting states vigorously to address this problem in their women's prisons, the United States government has allowed custodial sexual misconduct to fall into a kind of legal and political vacuum where neither international, nor federal, nor state law is seen to apply. Moreover, when confronted with this problem, many senior-level state officials not only fail to acknowledge sexual misconduct in state prisons, but also deny women seeking to report such abuse their internationally guaranteed rights to due process of law, to freedom from undue punishment or reprisal and, ultimately, to justice. As a result, not only are rape, sexual assault, criminal sexual contact, verbal degradation and inappropriate visual surveillance of female prisoners by male officers disturbingly common in a number of state women's prisons in the United States, but this fact also remains largely hidden from public view.

Rape, Sexual Assault and Criminal Sexual Contact

As noted above, the sexual misconduct that we investigated in women's prisons in the United States often occurs in a custodial environment that is highly sexually charged. Explicit and degrading verbal abuse of the female prisoners is commonplace. Women consistently told of being referred

---

[59](...continued)
described the Standard Minimum Rules as ". . . establishing standards for decent and humane conduct by all nations" or as "[c]onstituting an authoritative international statement of basic norms of human dignity and of certain practices that are repugnant to the conscience of mankind." 507 Federal Supplement, pp. 1192, 1188.

[60] Restatement (Third) of Foreign Relations, Section 111(1) (1987).

[61] Ibid., Section 111, comment d.

to as bitches, whores, and prostitutes by the male officers.[62]   They said that the officers would routinely proposition them or make lewd suggestions such as, "When you gonna' break off some of that for me," or "When you gonna' suck my dick," or "I want to fuck you."[63]   The women spoke of being subjected to constant commentary on their body parts and to a barrage of degrading physical references and gestures.

The officers' sexual misconduct does not stop at degrading language, but extends to rape and sexual assault.   In every state that we visited, we investigated cases of male corrections officers and nonsecurity prison staff who used overt physical force or other forms of physical restraint to compel female prisoners to engage in vaginal, anal or oral sexual intercourse, sometimes repeatedly.   Prisoners recounted how they were trapped by officers and forced to have sex with them in isolation units, in their own cells, or in administrative areas under the officers' control.[64]   Such misconduct often resulted in severe physical and psychological harm to the prisoner.[65]

In one case we investigated, Zelda, an inmate at Dwight Correctional Center in Illinois, was allegedly raped repeatedly by a corrections officer in retaliation, she believes, for exposing a sex for drugs ring inside the prison.[66]

---

[62] In an example from Dwight Correctional Institute in Illinois, male corrections officers reportedly hung a pair of women's underpants on the window in the housing unit and posted on the fan the words "ho [whore] patrol," implying the officers were responsible for supervising whores or prostitutes. Interview, Illinois, May 1994. All names withheld by Human Rights Watch unless otherwise indicated.

[63] Tammy, a prisoner in California, told us that an officer reportedly grabbed her vagina and asked, "Do you think I could have a piece of that?"   The officer also propositioned women on her work detail and commented on their bodies. According to Tammy, he would say, "How big do you like 'em?" or "is it big enough for you?" Interview, California, July 1994.

[64] Disciplinary hearings in Georgia showed that a deputy warden raped at least one inmate in his office. He had called her to his office to discuss problems she was having. *Stanley v. Department of Corrections,* before the State Personnel Board for the State of Georgia, Number 93-53, p. 3. We found examples of women prisoners being trapped by officers forced to have sex in every state we investigated.

[65] For example, two women in Illinois were so agitated that prison doctors prescribed sedatives or psychotropic medication after they came forward with allegations of sexual misconduct. Interview, Gail Smith, attorney, Chicago, Illinois, May 10, 1994. Another female prisoner was described by her mother as crying and unable to sleep after her alleged rape. Interview, Illinois, June 22, 1994.

[66] Interview, Illinois, May 1994.

In November 1993 a male corrections officer entered Zelda's room late at night while she was asleep and, according to Zelda:

> He came in and woke me up. He hit me in the nose. There was blood everywhere. Then he put cuffs on me. Even when I stopped fighting he kept hitting me. He raped me vaginally, then he turned me over and raped me anally, then he turned me over again. Then his watch went off and he went really quickly. He took the cuffs off and left. I just laid there.

Zelda was taken to an outside hospital the next evening, where the doctor examined her and wrote "sexual assault" on her medical record, in the box marked "Diagnosis."[67] Zelda was reportedly raped by the same officer on two subsequent occasions, on December 5, 1993, and January 30, 1994. Following the second alleged rape, however, Zelda did not receive immediate medical treatment by prison officials. Zelda's attorney, Margaret Byrne, visited her four days after the second alleged incident and told us that "she [Zelda] was bruised, battered and completely beat up."[68] After the third alleged rape, Zelda did receive medical care that revealed several physical injuries down most of her right side. Despite the medical evidence, the Illinois Department of Corrections has closed its investigation into the rapes. It appears they have done so primarily because Zelda did not identify her attacker immediately.

A prisoner in California, Uma, told us that an officer raped her after a long period of harassment. Uma stated that he watched her while she was taking a shower; "cornered" her in the prison laundry room; and hit her on the buttocks and grab her breasts as she walked by. Eventually, the officer entered Uma's cell while her cellmates were at breakfast. She told us:

---

[67] Lab results from a culture prepared from a vaginal swab later reportedly yielded the growth of a certain microbe commonly found in the rectum. Despite this finding, prison officials sent another female inmate to segregation for possible sexual misconduct with Zelda. Prison officials, furthermore, told Zelda she was being placed in temporary custody for possible sexual misconduct. Zelda was cleared of the sexual misconduct charges days later.

[68] Byrne described Zelda's injuries as follows: "She had bruises up her arms, inside her thighs, on her shins, her ribs, the side of her face, one eye was purple." Interview, Margaret Byrne, attorney, Chicago, Illinois, May 11, 1994.

I felt fear real quick. I knew something was wrong and I
didn't want to look. [the officer] pulled the blanket. I sat up
and tugged at the blanket. Then the whole blanket came off
. . . He just tore my whole shirt. That's when he assaulted
me sexually. I was screaming, yelling and crying. Martha
across the hall was banging on her window. While he was
still in the room, I went into the shower. I felt dirty.[69]

Officers also have employed less overt and thus less detectable means
of coercion to pressure prisoners into sexual relations. Rather than physically
compelling the prisoners to engage in such conduct, the officers have
threatened them with physical force or with punishment or retaliation should
the women fail to comply. For example, a former corrections employee in
New York told us that male staff in women's prisons would threaten to put the
female prisoners in segregation or to make their lives a "living hell" by
intercepting their packages or stopping their visits if the women did not agree
to sexual relations.[70] Similar practices were reported in every correctional
system that we investigated.[71] In another example, according to a prisoner
in Michigan, Lisa, Officer Bernard Rivers entered her cell in April 1988 and
told her that he thought she was cute and that he liked her. He reportedly told
her that he could positively or negatively affect her parole, depending on how
she responded to his sexual advances. She said she involuntarily submitted to
his sexual advances.[72]

Officers deployed equally coercive means to touch female prisoners
in inappropriate sexual ways. Female prisoners spoke of being "cornered" and
rubbed up against by male officers and of being forced to manipulate the

[69] Interview, California, July 1994. Additional cases are documented in a
forthcoming Human Rights Watch report.

[70] Interview, former corrections employee, New York Department of Corrections,
January 17, 1995.

[71] Additional cases are documented in a forthcoming Human Rights Watch report.

[72] Lisa came forward eighteen months later, after Rivers was again assigned to her
housing unit, out of fear that he would force her to have sexual relations with her again.
The Michigan Department of Corrections largely ignored Lisa's allegations until she,
with the help of her attorney, Deborah LaBelle, obtained a court order and wore a wire
[hidden microphone] inside the prison. She successfully taped a conversation with
Rivers. His statements acknowledged the sexual assault and resulted in the sheriff's
office recommending prosecution. He committed suicide before trial. Telephone
interview, Deborah LaBelle, attorney, Michigan, February 27, 1995.

men's sexual organs.[73]   They also told us of having male officers aggressively pinch or grope their nipples, breasts, buttocks, and vaginal areas.[74]

In the majority of cases that we investigated, the officers did not coerce the prisoners with actual or threatened force, punishment or retaliation. Instead, officers promised or provided otherwise unobtainable goods and services to the prisoners in exchange for various forms of sexual intercourse or sexual touching. The officers abused their authority to assign the prisoners a coveted work detail or put money in their accounts or provide them with bubble gum or cigarettes or stamps or drugs in exchange for sexual favors. In one case that we investigated a female prisoner engaged in repeated oral sex with an officer in exchange for a pair of cheap earrings.[75] Rachel, a prisoner in New York, told Human Rights Watch that she felt obliged to allow a corrections officer to kiss and grope her. According to Rachel:

> He used to bring me stuff . . . I felt I owed him. He did
> everything for me. I was away from my family and kid,
> upstate. I felt like he deserved it, but he did it for a reason
> . . . He did it because he wanted to get into my panties.[76]

Of all the abuses that we investigated, this exchange of sex for favors in women's prisons was the most common and, in our view, the least addressed by prison authorities. Such conduct appears for both officers and prisoners alike to function as a kind of custodial quid pro quo. The officers obtain desired sexual relations and the women secure valuable favorable treatment. Rebecca Jurado, a law professor and attorney who works with

---

[73] Interview, Michigan, March 1994; *Samuel F. Evans v. Department of Corrections*, before the State Personnel Board for the State of Georgia, Number 93-29.

[74] According to a statement by a prisoner in Michigan, Raymond Raby, a corrections officer, entered her cell at night and woke her up. He took her into a visiting room where he grabbed her and kissed her, then fondled her breasts and put his finger in her vagina. After the prisoner reported the assault, Raby was interviewed by the police and admitted that he was having sex on a nightly basis with women prisoners. In another case, a prisoner in New York stated in her affidavit to Prisoners' Legal Services that an officer came into her room and groped her breasts after she asked him for a cigarette. When escorting her later that day to the hospital, he kissed her and put his hands up her dress. Interview, Ruth Cassell, Prisoners' Legal Services, New York, April 19, 1994.

[75] Interview, Christina Kampfner, psychologist, Michigan, May 17, 1994.

[76] Interview, New York, August 1994.

female prisoners in California, told us that the women may often see nothing out of the ordinary or abusive in this exchange.[77] She told us that given the women prisoners' personal histories, which as noted above often involve a pattern of physical or sexual abuse, the women simply accept such exploitation as a condition of incarceration. As one male officer from New York put it, these female prisoners are "used to being used."[78]

Many prisoners and advocates in the states we visited told us that this informal trade in sex for favors permeates the prisons with which they are familiar.[79] This suggests a level of official tolerance for such abuse that amounts to complicity in the officers' fundamentally abusive and exploitative conduct. Any exchange between officer and prisoner depends on and is fueled by the decidedly unequal relationship between the two parties. The officer can provide the prisoner with favorable treatment exclusively because he has the power to do so. His decision to provide such treatment in exchange for sex with a prisoner is much more than what one state official described to us as "giving in to temptation." It constitutes a serious abuse of the officer's custodial authority, resulting in coerced sexual contact with the prisoner that amounts to rape or sexual assault.

The circumstances in which a female prisoner can consent to sexual relations with an officer in authority over her are extremely rare. In applying state rape and sexual assault laws to instances of sexual contact between officers and prisoners, prison officials and prosecutors need to take into much greater account the fact that the relationship between these two parties is by definition unequal and authoritarian and not in any way conducive to free and informed consent on the part of the prisoner.

Not all forms of sexual contact between officers and prisoners in their custody involve coercive pressures on the prisoner by the officer and thus amounting to rape or sexual assault. Female prisoners in several states told us

---

[77] Telephone interview, Rebecca Jurado, professor of law, March 21, 1995.

[78] Interview, former corrections employee, New York Department of Correctional Services, January 17, 1995.

[79] Interview, Christina Kampfner, psychologist, Michigan, May 17, 1994; telephone interview, Rebecca Jurado, professor of law, March 21, 1995. One corrections official reported being approached by women prisoners who viewed sexual relations as a necessary means to obtain certain items. Interview, Elaine Lord, Superintendent, Bedford Hills Corrections Center, New York, June 22, 1994.

of "going after" male officers and of "initiating" sexual relations with them.[80] Such encounters can occur without ever involving any apparent coercive element. However, several cases that we investigated that initially involved nonforcible sexual contact between an officer and a prisoner ultimately escalated into increasingly abusive and violent situations.

Pam, a prisoner in New York, was involved with two different officers at one prison. Pam became involved with an officer after he put money in her account and started writing her letters and sending her packages. But the officer became increasingly possessive and violent as the relationship progressed:

> Nobody could talk to me. He became violent with his hands.
> If I was talking to another man he would hit me. He had the
> impression I was gay. He would [give a disciplinary citation
> to] another [woman] whenever I talked to her. There's no
> leaving an officer. You will have problems.[81]

Nancy, a former prisoner who has served in two California prisoners, told us that she was sexually involved with a corrections officer at California Institution for Women in the mid-1980s. She said the officer "was always bringing me stuff, cologne, money." She told us that she had sexual intercourse with the corrections officer on two occasions, but met him several times, in her words, "to mess around." Then after Nancy refused to continue sexual relations, he continued his practice of appearing outside her door.[82] In such cases the female prisoners told us that they learned much too late that the person with whom they believed themselves to be on equal footing in the relationship was in fact an officer by whom they could be and were totally controlled. It is by virtue of this inherent and inescapable inequality between the two parties that sexual contact between officers and prisoners that is not forced or coerced, and thus does not amount to rape or sexual assault, should still constitute a distinct and serious criminal offense and be prosecuted as a felony. No matter what the circumstances, it is always the officers' professional duty to refrain from sexual relations with persons in their custody. Unfortunately in those states that have already expressly outlawed

---

[80] Telephone interview, July 1994; interviews, New York, August 1994; and interviews, Georgia, March 1994.

[81] Interview, New York, August 1994.

[82] Telephone interview, July 1994.

sexual contact (or a similar offense) between officers and prisoners, we have found that there is a tendency to treat this crime as a lesser offense than rape or sexual assault and then to prosecute all instances of custodial sexual contact, including those involving coercion by the officer, under it.

At times, female prisoners become pregnant as a result of sexual misconduct in custody. This can be an intensely traumatizing experience, often compounded by the tendency of prison authorities to treat women in these circumstances in a cruel way. Iris, a prisoner in New York, was charged with sexual intercourse and sentenced to nine months or 270 days in segregation, after she tested positive for pregnancy. Within a few hours after they confirmed her pregnancy, prison authorities transferred Iris to Bedford Hills and placed her in segregation in the special housing unit. At Bedford Hills, staff pressured her repeatedly to have an abortion. Then, over four months into her pregnancy, Iris began bleeding and stopped feeling movement of the fetus. This occurred, according to Iris, after her cell was sprayed with insecticide. Despite her symptoms, medical staff refused to see her immediately. Two weeks later a sonogram taken at an outside hospital confirmed that the fetus was dead.[83]

Irrespective of whether women's pregnancies resulted from rape or from non-forcible sexual intercourse with an officer, prison officials have punished such prisoners by placing them in administrative segregation.[84] Once they were removed from the general population, which could also lead to their reduced access to counsel or other outside monitors, the women uniformly reported that corrections authorities pressured them to reveal the name of the father and to undergo an abortion. For example, in 1993 Anne, a prisoner in Michigan, reported that she had been sexually assaulted by a corrections employee and requested a pregnancy test. Almost immediately after the test result returned positive, the authorities removed her from the prison and placed her in a segregated cell at Huron Valley Men's Prison (HVM) infirmary. While at HVM, Anne was in her cell for nearly twenty-four hours a day and denied access to a phone. According to Anne, investigators repeatedly interrogated her about the circumstances of her pregnancy. One investigator threatened to keep her in segregation throughout her pregnancy, take away her accrued good time and return her to the facility where she was assaulted unless she assisted with the investigation. Anne also told us that this

---

[83] Interview, New York, July 1994.
[84] Interviews, California, July 1994; interviews, Michigan, March 1994; and interviews, New York, July 1994.

investigator pushed her to have an abortion and asked her repeatedly, "Don't you think it'd just be better for you and the child to just have an abortion?" She resisted the pressure and carried her pregnancy to term.[85]   The involuntary segregation of pregnant prisoners wrongfully punishes victims of custodial rape or criminal sexual contact and may subject them to wholly inappropriate or even harmful conditions. Such punishment, moreover, also deters many prisoners from reporting sexual misconduct in general.

Abusive Body Searches and Privacy Violations
         Human Rights Watch found that male corrections employees inflicted cruel, inhuman and degrading treatment on women prisoners through abusive pat-frisks and strip searches. These body searches, when conducted by male guards on female prisoners, also constitute violations of prisoners' right to privacy. Prisoners in every state that we visited reported that, in conducting pat-frisks—out of respect for the prisoners' privacy rights, the officers are required to use the back of the hand, rather than the palm when searching the prisoner's chest and genital areas—male officers often use their hands or fingers to grope or grip the women's breasts, nipples, vaginas, buttocks, anus, and inner thighs. A prisoner in Michigan told us, "The male officers sit by the door to the kitchen and shake the women down [frisk] as they leave [the kitchen]. We watch the way they do it and who they pick. I watched one who felt a woman down in front of everyone as she left. It's always the male officers at the door who do the shakedowns."[86]
         Moreover, we found that strip searches of female prisoners, while usually conducted by female officers in order to protect the women's privacy, at times took place in the presence of one or more male officers as well. New York's department of correctional services videotaped strip searches of women entering segregation from January or February 1994 until July 1994. According to Betsy Fuller, an attorney with Prisoners' Legal Services, approximately one hundred to 200 women were searched. Fuller reviewed between six to eight tapes, which she described to us as "images I will never forget." When asked to strip, according to Fuller, one woman was frightened by the camera and hysterical throughout the strip search.[87] Allowing male officers to view, if not participate in, such searches and conducting strip searches in a degrading manner violates prisoners' rights to humane treatment

---

[85] Telephone interview, Deborah LaBelle, attorney, February 27, 1995.
[86] Interview, Michigan, March 1994.
[87] Interview, Betsy Fuller, Prisoners' Legal Services, October 4, 1994.

and to privacy, as defined by the U.N. Human Rights Committee. Nonetheless, corrections authorities consistently fail to sanction and have at times even condoned such conduct.

Prisoners also spoke consistently of discomfort caused by inappropriate visual surveillance by male officers, particularly in their living areas. They reported that officers watched them while they were dressing, showering, or using the toilet and that male officers frequently entered their housing units without first announcing their presence. In Michigan, male corrections officers have reportedly roamed the shower and toilet facilities and freely abused their authority to conduct searches. Officers have pulled back the shower curtain on inmates to comment or stare. It has reached a point, one prisoner said, where prisoners have learned to shower when certain corrections officers are not on duty.[88] Prisoners in Central California Women's Facility also reported that male corrections officers walk into the showers and talk to them.[89] Similarly, women incarcerated in Illinois's Logan Correctional Institute reported that officers did not announce themselves when coming onto the housing units and occasionally enter shower areas when women are undressed.[90]

The Response of the State Governments

Of the correctional systems that we investigated, only those in Georgia and the District of Columbia have made visible and significant efforts to address the problem of custodial sexual misconduct. In both cases, these actions resulted from class action suits filed against the respective departments of corrections following long histories of unrecognized and unremedied custodial sexual misconduct. Corrections officers in both systems were found to have engaged in rape, sexual assault, inappropriate viewing and verbal degradation of female prisoners in their custody.[91] The two correctional systems were found to have failed consistently to train officers and prisoners to identify and avoid such misconduct. Both state systems failed to pursue complaints of sexual misconduct and to ensure that officers who engaged in such abuse were disciplined and, where appropriate, prosecuted.

---

[88] Interview, Michigan, March 1994.

[89] Interviews, California, July 1994.

[90] Interviews, Illinois, May 1994.

[91] *Cason v. Seckinger*, Civil Action No. 84-313-1-MAC (Georgia), *Women Prisoners of the District of Columbia Department of Corrections v. District of Columbia*, 1994 U.S. Dist. LEXIS 19222 (District of District of Columbia, December 13, 1994).

Subsequent to the class action suits, both correctional systems have begun to take long overdue remedial measures and to undertake a number of potentially important reforms.   For example, Georgia created and hired investigators for a new investigative procedure to monitor compliance with the state's criminal law ban on sexual contact between corrections staff and prisoners.[92]   Pursuant to a court order, the District of Columbia Department of Corrections wrote and instituted a policy, which went into effect on May 15, 1995, prohibiting any sexual contact with prisoners by any employee or agent of the department.[93]   However, most departments of corrections that we investigated have taken no similarly notable remedial or preventative actions to address custodial sexual misconduct in their facilities.   Some states prefer to deny that the problem exists at all.   The state of Michigan, for example, continues to deny that it has a sexual misconduct problem and to state publicly that it has "zero tolerance" for such abuse,[94] despite two state-sponsored investigations indicating custodial sexual misconduct in its women's facilities and a 1995 United States Department of Justice determination that echoed these findings.[95]

No state that we visited currently has in place the requisite combination of prison rules and procedures and criminal law and practice to combat custodial sexual misconduct in women's prisons.   In fact, rather than working to expose and address custodial sexual misconduct, correctional systems often contribute to its perpetuation.   They fail not only to put in place adequate prison rules or criminal laws to prohibit such abuse (or do not enforce such provisions where they already exist), but also to establish procedures whereby abuse can be reported, investigated and punished without the complainants fearing retaliation and, in some cases, undue punishment.

---

[92] Georgia Department of Corrections Standard Operating Procedures, "Investigations of Allegations of Sexual Contact, Sexual Abuse and Sexual Harassment," November 9, 1994, draft.

[93] District of Columbia Department of Corrections, "Sexual Misconduct Against Inmates," Department Order 3350.2A, May 15, 1995.

[94] Press Release, Michigan Department of Corrections, January 7, 1993.

[95] The DOJ found "that the sexual abuse of women prisoners by guards, including rapes, the lack of adequate medical care, including mental health services, grossly deficient sanitation, crowding and other threats to the physical safety and well-being of prisoners violates their constitutional rights."   Letter from Deval Patrick, Assistant Attorney General, Civil Rights Division, U.S. Department of Justice, to John Engler, governor, State of Michigan, March 27, 1995.

The Lack of Clear Prison Rules and Appropriate Criminal Law

One of the key factors in creating a U.S. women's prison environment ripe for sexual misconduct is the lack of clear prison rules and, where appropriate, criminal laws that prohibit such abuse. As a result of this political and legal indifference to the problem, states routinely fail to deter, discipline or criminally sanction incidents of custodial sexual misconduct adequately. This directly contributes to the prevalence of such abuse.

All state departments of corrections assured us that sexual misconduct was something that they treated as a serious matter and would not tolerate. However, we found little concrete evidence of such commitment. Prison rules in the majority of correctional systems that we investigated only vaguely discourage "overfamiliarity" or "personal dealings" with prisoners and are too euphemistic for officers to understand that the proscribed conduct includes not only all sexual contact with prisoners, but also the use of sexually explicit comments and gestures and unwarranted invasions of their privacy.[96] Even where rules clearly prohibiting such conduct do exist, corrections authorities simply fail to emphasize them enough.[97] As a result of the states' failure to train officers to recognize and refrain from sexual misconduct, male officers engage in such misconduct with female prisoners without any informed sense of the prohibitions on and likely consequences of such behavior.

Most states we investigated lack any clear policy or procedure for punishing officers who engage in sexual misconduct of whatever form. With respect to actual sexual contact between officers and prisoners, the appropriate sanction should be dismissal, but this is not always made clear. We found that even in those instances where such misconduct is proven, the culpable officers are rarely dismissed. Instead correctional authorities have engaged in disciplinary half-measures, such as the officers' reassignment, transfer or voluntary resignation, the last of which often terminates the department of corrections investigation into the prisoner's complaint. These approaches are highly problematic, primarily because by failing to prevent work in other

---

[96] In Michigan, department of corrections policy appears to prohibit both degrading language toward and degrading treatment of prisoners, but the provisions seem to apply only to the conduct of other prisoners. A later clause does prohibit "personal abuse" of prisoners by corrections staff, but does not define the term. Michigan Department of Corrections Policy directive 03.03.130, "Rights of Clients to Humane Treatment and Living Conditions," June 7, 1982.

[97] For example, in New York, when the employee manual addresses "overfamiliarity" it portrays it as a problem initiated by prisoners.

prison areas or facilities or later re-employment, they risk exposing more prisoners to misconduct by the abusive officer. For example, in Michigan, a corrections officer was rehired after he resigned voluntarily rather than face an investigation into allegations of sexual misconduct. He was then suspended three months later for "overfamiliarity" with another prisoner.[98] Women prisoners in Illinois consistently raised the same names of officers who were known to be physically aggressive and abusive.

Both state department of corrections and criminal justice systems have left sexual misconduct unremedied. Our investigation indicates that states prosecute very few cases of sexual intercourse or sexual touching between officers and prisoners. The majority of the states that we investigated have no criminal law that deals directly with this abuse and those that do often decline fully to enforce such prohibitions. When an attorney in Illinois contacted the local district attorney's office to inquire how to file a criminal complaint, she was informed that his office did not have jurisdiction—it had to be referred from the Illinois Department of Corrections.[99] Thus, prisoners are denied the right to file criminal complaints for alleged crimes committed against them. In Georgia, it was the district attorney's policy until 1992 not to enforce that state's criminal statute outlawing sexual contact between an officer and a prisoner as a felony offense. It took the class action suit filed in 1992 on behalf of all the female prisoners in that state to reverse this trend and secure criminal indictments of officers suspected of such misconduct. In most cases, the actual prosecution of these indictments has yet to occur. In fact, the district attorney responsible for the prosecutions told us that, in his view, custodial sexual misconduct was "a crime without a victim."[100]

If states where custodial sexual contact is not expressly prohibited pursue such cases at all, they do so under existing rape and sexual assault laws, which often do not take into account the circumstances of incarceration or the officer/prisoner relationship as possible elements of these crimes. In these states, the simple fact that the custodial sexual contact occurred at all—no matter what the circumstances—is not considered a crime. Thus, unless the female prisoner who complains of such misconduct can show the presence of severe physical force, grave bodily injury or other recognized

---

[98] Telephone interview, Deborah LaBelle, attorney, February 27, 1995.

[99] Interview, Margaret Byrne, attorney, Illinois, May 9, 1994.

[100] Interview, Joe Briley, district attorney, March 24, 1994. He was forced to resign in August 1994 on suspicion of sexually harassing his female staff. "Ocmulgee DA was told to quit, GBI report says," Atlanta Constitution, October 11, 1994.

elements of the crimes of rape and sexual assault (and sometimes even then), prison officials and prosecutors are likely to presume that she consented to sexual contact and, thus, that no rape or sexual assault occurred. If the female prisoner cannot prove rape or sexual assault, not only will her complaint of sexual misconduct go unprosecuted, but it is likely that she will be punished for what is seen as her own participation in a breach of prison rules. In some cases that we investigated, the female prisoner was punished severely while the male officer escaped sanction altogether.   According to Ruth Cassell, a prisoners' rights advocate, an inspector general in New York brought charges against a young woman for sexual misconduct after determining that she was pregnant. At the hearing, she was sentenced to 730 days, or two years, in segregation and a twenty-four month loss of good time credit, because the inspector general believed the prisoner was lying about who impregnated her. After two and a half months in segregation, all charges against the prisoner were dropped except the charge for engaging in sexual relations, for which she was sentenced to time served. She was punished even though she testified that she was coerced into having sex by her supervisor.[101]

All states that we investigated sanction female prisoners for sexual misconduct as a matter of practice and two states, New York and Illinois, do so as a matter of policy.[102] Even prisoners whose allegations seemingly are credited by prison officials effectively are punished by authorities by being placed in administrative segregation pending the outcome of the investigation into their complaints. While such segregation could, if voluntarily requested by the prisoner, function as a form of protective custody, we found that in most instances prison officials used it to punitive effect. For example, in California, women housed in administrative segregation pending an investigation have been kept there for extensive periods of time and denied access to the telephone and visits with their attorneys.[103] A women prisoner in Michigan was sent involuntarily to segregation while charges that an officer raped her were investigated. She was subsequently transferred to a higher-security facility. The officer, to our knowledge, was never disciplined in any way, even though the prisoner passed a polygraph test that the officer refused to take.[104]   Even in those instances where the presumption of official

---

[101] Telephone interview, Ruth Cassell, Prisoners Legal Services, January 26, 1995.
[102] Rule 101, New York Department of Corrections Inmate Handbook; 20 Illinois Administrative Code, §504, Table A.
[103] Interview, Carrie Hempel, attorney, California, July 25, 1994.
[104] Interview, Michigan, March 1994.

coercion is not supported by the evidence, we believe that whatever state interests might be served by punishing the prisoner for sexual misconduct are insufficient to outweigh the deterrent effect of such punishment on the willingness of women to report such abuse. The fear of punishment prevents many women from reporting any sexual misconduct by guards.

Failure to Investigate

Prisoners rarely volunteer to come forward with a complaint of sexual misconduct. Should a prisoner choose to report such abuse, or be compelled to do so by bodily injury, pregnancy or other factors, she not only faces potential punishment, but more often than not confronts a prison system that discourages such complaints, curtails their investigation, treats the complainant with a combination of indifference and suspicion and exposes her to the risk of retaliation from both officers and fellow prisoners.

All of the states that we visited provide internal grievance mechanisms that are available in theory to female prisoners for a wide variety of complaints. However, these grievance mechanisms often have not functioned effectively for prisoner complaints of sexual misconduct. Grievance forms have not been consistently made available to prisoners, nor have prisoners been informed about the rules and procedures governing their use. Moreover, the procedures generally lack even a pretense of confidentiality. Officers have been told not only of complaints against them but also of the identity of the complainant. For instance, in Illinois, the first statement a woman prisoner wrote about an alleged rape reportedly was provided to the implicated officer. Subsequently, according to the prisoner, the officer and his colleagues harassed her for submitting the statement.[105] At least three of the states that we visited, Michigan, California and, to a lesser extent, New York, require the prisoner to confront informally the corrections officer implicated in her complaint before filing a formal grievance. This effectively denies her the right to complain.

Even if a prisoner surmounts these obstacles and manages to make a complaint of sexual misconduct, no guarantee exists that the prison authorities will investigate her complaint. No prison that we investigated has published clear guidelines for investigating custodial sexual misconduct, nor were the prisoners that we interviewed aware of such guidelines when they did exist. On at least two occasions, Michigan has assigned an officer to

[105] Interview, Illinois, May 1994.

investigate himself; not surprisingly both officers cleared themselves of the charges.[106]

No state that we investigated routinely refers custodial sexual misconduct complaints to independent investigators or, where appropriate, state police or prosecutorial authorities. In our experience, prison administrators generally prefer to handle such matters internally, away from the heightened public scrutiny that often accompanies allegations of custodial sexual misconduct by correctional officers or staff. In the opinion of the deputy counsel for the Illinois department of corrections, there was no need to contact the state police about rape allegations because "in a rape case, there's probably nothing the state police can do that we wouldn't be doing."[107] In some cases, the prisoner's attorney and even her family members are kept in the dark about the course of an internal investigation or are shut out of the investigative process altogether.[108] This not only leaves the state departments of corrections in the dubious position of investigating themselves but also denies to female prisoners legal remedies that may be available to them outside the correctional system.

The inability of female prisoners successfully to file complaints of sexual misconduct and to see such complaints fully and fairly investigated is attributable in no small measure to a bias against prisoner testimony that pervades all levels of the U.S. corrections and criminal justice systems that we investigated. This bias is particularly crippling in cases of custodial sexual misconduct, because, absent severe physical harm to the prisoner, the availability of evidence other than her own testimony with respect to sexual abuse is extremely limited. For example, officials usually view testimony by other prisoners as insufficient; as prisoners, their veracity also is in doubt. Moreover, professional solidarity often plays a role in derailing investigations into staff sexual misconduct. Prison staff not directly involved in sexual

---

[106] Interview, Michigan, March 1994.

[107] Interview, Susan O'Leary, deputy counsel of Illinois department of corrections, Illinois, September 27, 1994.

[108] In New York, attorneys have had difficulty obtaining statements that their clients may have made to prison officials or investigators. Telephone interview, Ruth Cassell, Prisoners legal Services, January 26, 1995. The mother of a prisoner allegedly raped in an Illinois prison repeatedly contacted the warden in her efforts to pursue an investigation of her daughter's rape. Her phone calls were not returned until she contacted an attorney. She was never notified about the outcome of the investigation. Telephone interview, June 22, 1994.

misconduct often turn a blind eye to such abuse and will rarely testify in support of a prisoner's charge of such misconduct against a fellow officer.[109]

Punishment and Retaliation

The states' failure clearly to prohibit sexual misconduct and ensure that such abuse is reported and investigated whenever it occurs largely keeps custodial sexual misconduct in women's prisons in the United States hidden from public view. As noted above, the added possibility that prisoners might themselves be punished for such misconduct only drives the problem further underground. In addition, while prison authorities administratively segregate female prisoners pending allegations of sexual misconduct, they routinely fail to take any administrative action against the officers who are also implicated in such allegations. Thus, while prisoners alleging sexual abuse are in fact or effect being punished, in no state that we investigated does a guarantee exist that an officer accused of sexual abuse will be removed from authority over or contact with the complainant pending the investigation's outcome.

Instead, a prisoner who files a sexual misconduct complaint may come into direct contact with the implicated officer and be unduly exposed to retaliation by him or his cohorts. Uma, a prisoner in California, told us that, after she came forward with allegations of sexual misconduct, she was repeatedly harassed by staff as well as prisoners sympathetic to the staff. Corrections officers, she reported, repeatedly questioned her about her role in the investigation and called her out of her cell to tell her things, such as, "You think that was bad, now you're in my unit. Wait until you see what we do with you here."[110] Our interviews in Georgia revealed that the women involved in the *Cason* suit have been retaliated against by corrections officers and prisoners.[111]

As a matter of policy, most states outlaw such retaliation, which also is clearly prohibited under international human rights law. Nonetheless and without exception, prisoners in every state told us of being terrified that if they registered a complaint of sexual abuse the officers would find out about it and seek retribution against them. In every prison that we visited, such retaliatory acts by officers frequently occurred. Attorney Brenda Smith of the National

---

[109] For example, one former employee of the Georgia department of corrections told us, "That's the way the system was—you keep your mouth shut about the rumors and allegations." Interview, former employee, Georgia, March 1994.

[110] Interview, California, July 1994.

[111] Interview, Georgia, March 1994.

Women's Law Center told us that in her experience retaliation against prisoners who complain of sexual abuse takes several forms: prisoners can be sent to administrative segregation, be targeted for disciplinary reports that affect their parole, or be taken out of favored educational programs or work assignments.[112]

The Need for Enhanced Federal Oversight

The U.S. government appears, by and large, to underestimate grossly the problem of rape, sexual assault, criminal sexual contact and other custodial abuse of women in U.S. prisons. For example, in its report to the United Nations Human Rights Committee pursuant to its obligations under the International Covenant on Civil and Political Rights, the U.S. State Department said that the "important underlying issue of sexual abuse [by male guards in women's prisons] is addressed through staff training and through criminal statutes prohibiting such activity."[113] Based upon our investigation of sexual misconduct in five states, they have vastly understated the problem of sexual abuse in the women's prisons in the U.S. and greatly overstated the degree to which it is being remedied.

When questioned further by a member of the Human Rights Committee about respect for female prisoners' privacy rights, the United States responded that, in order to protect the privacy of female prisoners, "only female officers are allowed to conduct strip or body cavity searches, except in emergency situations."[114] The U.S. government representative added that "male officers work in the women's housing units, but they are admonished to respect the inmates' privacy by not intentionally observing them in states of undress."[115] In contrast, our research indicates that male guards routinely participate or view strip searches in nonemergency situations and there is little instruction that could be called "admonishing." Thus, these answers do not at all address, and in fact obscure, male correctional officers' routine practice of inappropriately touching and viewing female prisoners under their supervision.

---

[112] Interview, Brenda Smith, senior staff counsel, National Women's Law Center, February 27, 1995.

[113] U.S. Department of State, First Periodic Report of the United States on Compliance with the International Covenant on Civil and Political Rights. U.N. Document, HRI/CORE/1/ADD.49, August 17, 1994.

[114] Press Release, General Assembly, "Human Rights Committee Concludes Consideration of Initial Report of United States," HR/CT/405, March 31, 1995, p. 4.

[115] Ibid.

The federal government is not utterly indifferent to this problem. United States federal law expressly criminalizes custodial sexual abuse when it occurs in federal facilities. In addition, our interviews with the Department of Justice (DOJ) Civil Rights Division, which has responsibility for overseeing the civil rights of incarcerated persons, and our observations of this division's intervention in at least one of the state correctional systems that we investigated, lead us to conclude that DOJ is keenly aware of the problem and does make efforts, albeit limited, to address it. For example, their investigation in Michigan last year shed much-needed and long-overdue light on the serious problems of sexual abuse and other violations in that state's women's prison. In addition, the DOJ reportedly is pursuing similar inquires in women's prisons in Arizona and Alabama.

The DOJ's presence continues to be negligible to nonexistent in the other state prison systems considered in this report, all of which have cases of custodial sexual misconduct similar to those found in Michigan. Of those other states—California, Illinois, New York and Georgia—only the latter appears to have caught the attention of the DOJ.

Even though the DOJ Civil Rights Division, and in particular the unit that deals with civil litigation, is short on financial and human resources and long on pressing problems in the many institutions of a custodial nature over which it has oversight, concerted, consistent and full federal attention to the problem of rape, sexual assault, and other abuse of female prisoners in United States state prisons for women is long overdue.

Ultimately, the main cause of the problem of custodial sexual misconduct in the United States is the failure of official political will. As the cases of Georgia and the District of Columbia demonstrate, when public officials want (or are compelled) to do something about the problem of sexual misconduct in custody, something gets done. The widespread absence of official resolve to address this problem both creates and perpetuates an extremely volatile situation in U.S. women's prisons that is characterized by the rise in the number of female prisoners being guarded by ill-trained male officers, the absence of appropriate prison rules and criminal law, the lack of adequate reporting and investigatory mechanisms, and the routine failure to discipline or punish offending officers. Taken together, these factors have produced a custodial environment in the United States' women's prisons that is ripe for sexual abuse.

There can be no doubt in the mind of any U.S. public official who cares about the integrity of the penal and criminal justice systems that something needs to be done about custodial sexual abuse of women in U.S. prisons and done now. Given the steadily rising female prison population, the United States can no longer afford for the rape, sexual assault, and other sexual misconduct in its women's prisons to be what one attorney called the "dirty little secret of corrections." The secret is out. The U.S. government must uphold its international human rights obligations to prohibit and punish custodial sexual abuse by its own agents and urge them to assist this country's state governments and departments of corrections to devote the necessary financial and human resources to secure the speedy eradication of this problem.

SEXUAL ASSAULT BY U.S. BORDER PATROL AGENTS

Human Rights Watch has published three reports since 1992 describing serious human rights violations committed by U.S. Border Patrol agents, including unjustified shootings, serious beatings, and sexual assaults.[116] Despite extensive, publicly available documentation of these abuses, little has been done to hold abusive agents accountable. Grossly inadequate complaint, review and disciplinary procedures allow agents to continue their assaults on undocumented persons, permanent residents, and U.S. citizens with impunity. In its reports, Human Rights Watch has made detailed recommendations to improve these procedures, but the Immigration and Naturalization Service (the parent agency of the Border Patrol) has failed to implement meaningful reforms.

U.S. Border Patrol agents stationed along the southwest border with Mexico have sexually assaulted women while they are in custody and following interrogations. Victims of abuse by Border Patrol agents often do not know they can file a complaint, however, nor do they believe filing a complaint will result in any sanction against an abusive agent, and they often fear reprisals should they submit a formal complaint. Because of the many deterrents to filing a complaint in these cases, local advocates believe the number of rapes and other gender-related crimes perpetrated is much higher than reported.

---

[116] The following material was adapted from Human Rights Watch/Americas, "Crossing the Line: Human Rights Abuses Along the U.S. Border with Mexico Persist Amid Climate of Impunity," *A Human Rights Watch Short Report*, vol. 7, no. 4 (April 1995).

Cases of Sexual Assault
The cases described below illustrate the types of abuses Border Patrol agents have committed:
On September 3, 1993, twenty-two-year-old "Juanita Gómez"[117] was reportedly raped by a uniformed Border Patrol agent in a remote area near Nogales, Arizona.[118] She had crossed through a hole in the border fence between Nogales, Sonora, and Nogales, Arizona, with her cousin to shop on the U.S. side when she was stopped by Border Patrol agent Larry Dean Selders. He ordered them into his vehicle and then propositioned them, stating that if one agreed to have sex with him he would not return them to Mexico. When the women declined his offer, Gómez was told to remain in the agent's vehicle while her cousin was ordered to leave. The agent then drove with Gómez into the desert, where he reportedly raped her.
Gómez reported the incident to the Mexican consulate in Nogales, Arizona, and Border Patrol and local officials questioned her, with the Nogales police accusing her of being a liar and a prostitute. She was examined at a hospital and provided detectives with samples of semen and blood for their investigation. The local police made several mistakes in collecting evidence, and the accused agent did not provide the semen and blood samples requested by the county attorney.
Agent Selders was originally charged with rape and kidnapping, but the county attorney offered to drop these charges in exchange for a "no contest" plea to "attempted transporting of persons for immoral purposes . . . while he was married," a crime which is the lowest class of felony. He was sentenced to one year in prison and would be eligible for parole after six months. From the time he was charged with rape and kidnapping until the plea was accepted, Selders was on paid administrative leave from the Border Patrol; he resigned in August 1994. In negotiating his plea agreement with the county attorney, Selders unsuccessfully sought immunity from prosecution on federal charges as well. On April 5, 1995, Selders was indicted on federal civil rights, bribery and other charges. Attorneys for Gómez have also filed a civil suit against the Border Patrol for injury and damages.
As frequently happens once a Border Patrol agent commits a serious abuse that attracts attention, information about Agent Selders' prior misconduct has begun to emerge. In this case, an attorney familiar with Gómez's case

---

[117] Real name withheld by request.
[118] This account is based on interviews with the victim, her lawyer, the Justice Department's Office of the Inspector General, and press reports.

recalled a sexual assault incident reported to her years ago in which the assailant used a similar *modus operandi*. In January 1995 she was able to locate the alleged victim, who identified Selders as her assailant.

On October 18, 1993, Haime Flores's van was stopped at the San Clemente checkpoint.[119] She was the only passenger and was ordered out of the vehicle. A Border Patrol agent examined her documents (she had a valid temporary visa) and determined they were invalid. The agent took her into the station, where a supervisor determined her documents were valid.

The agents decided she needed to be searched, however, and summoned a female agent. In front of three male agents, the female agent allegedly examined Flores's brassiere and inserted a finger into Flores's vagina; no contraband was found. The male officers reportedly laughed and joked as they watched the search.

On September 26, 1994, an attorney filed a US$2 million civil lawsuit on Flores's behalf against the U.S. and five unnamed Border Patrol agents, alleging sexual assault and battery, false imprisonment, infliction of emotional distress, and violation of her civil rights.

In October 1989, a woman was stopped by Border Patrol agent Luis Santiago Esteves,[120] who had followed her after he questioned her at a checkpoint north of Calexico, California. She and her boyfriend complained to Esteves's supervisor that Esteves made sexually explicit, harassing phone calls to the woman in the days following their encounter with him. The agent was not punished, but instead was transferred to another inspection station at the border crossing. There, he was twice arrested for allegedly raping two women he met while on duty during a two-year period. He was suspended after his arrest in the first reported rape, in December 1989, but was reinstated after the alleged victim failed to appear in court for the agent's preliminary hearing, despite this and the earlier allegation. His reinstatement underscores the Border Patrol's reluctance to investigate misconduct, and apply disciplinary sanctions, after criminal cases falter.

In July 1991, after the second alleged attack, Esteves was arrested and the following year was tried on twenty-three felony offenses against both women.[121] He was found guilty on three counts of felonious sexual

---

[119] This account is based on information collected by the American Friends Service Committee's U.S.-Mexico Border Program and information included in the alleged victim's lawsuit.

[120] *People v. Esteves* (Case No. 14866, Imperial County, California, 1992).

[121] Ibid.

misconduct, and sentenced to twenty-four years in prison. Esteves appealed his conviction and was re-tried and acquitted on all charges in December 1994. His attorneys argued successfully that the conviction had to be reversed due to "prejudicial admission of improper rebuttal evidence."[122]

Lack of Adequate Mechanisms for Accountability

The three cases of sexual misconduct described in this chapter are rare because the victims have brought civil or criminal charges against the accused agents. It is far more common for alleged victims of abuse by immigration law enforcement agents not to file complaints or lawsuits against the offending agents. As described above, even in cases that victims and their attorneys initiate, the results are rarely satisfactory.

In its investigations into the problem of human rights violations committed by Border Patrol agents, Human Rights Watch has confirmed many of the findings of a 1980 U.S. Civil Rights Commission report on this subject; to this day, the INS has failed to implement the recommendations made by the commission. Because the INS has been unwilling to correct its flawed complaint, review, and disciplinary procedures, Human Rights Watch has recommended the creation of an independent review commission. The commission would receive complaints of abuse directly from victims or witnesses, investigate those complaints, and recommend disciplinary sanctions or criminal prosecution, where appropriate. The commission would hold public hearings and include a community outreach office to educate members of the public about their rights and the complaint procedures.

Human Rights Watch has made recommendations to improve reporting and training procedures regarding the proper use of firearms and other equipment; to ensure medical attention is provided to wounded detainees; to improve the complaints and investigatory procedures; and, generally, to enhance public transparency of the agency's actions regarding abuse complaints and investigations. We have also called for an elimination of strip searches and body-cavity searches unless there is probable cause to suspect that a person possesses contraband, and we have emphasized that such searches should never be used to intimidate, harass, or humiliate. We have also called for human rights training that includes the topics of sexual assault and harassment, which should be supplemented by periodic review and reinforced by management. While some of our specific recommendations have

---

[122] *The People v. Luis Santiago Esteves*, D017689, Super. Ct. No. 14866, Fourth Appellate District, Division One, State of California, February 22, 1994.

been incorporated during the past year into a revised I.N.S. firearms policy (now awaiting approval by the Border Patrol's union) and a new non-deadly force policy, the agency has failed to recognize that lack of enforcement—rather than the lack of policies—remains the primary obstacle to improving the human rights record of the Border Patrol.

WOMEN DETAINED IN EGYPT

Since 1992 Egypt has faced continuing political violence and a corresponding rise in human rights abuses committed by both government security forces and Islamist militants.[123] Shootings and bombings by the military wings of Islamist opposition groups have resulted in the deaths and injury of members of security forces, Egyptian civilians and government officials, and foreigners. The clandestine Islamic Group, an organization that advocates the creation of an Islamic state in Egypt, has claimed responsibility for many of these attacks. The deliberate targeting of civilians violates one of the basic principles of international humanitarian law, and Human Rights Watch condemns in the strongest terms such actions by the Islamic Group.

But human rights abuses by one party in a situation of internal strife never justify violations by another party. Acts of murder and attempted murder committed by armed opposition groups do not give the state license to abandon the human rights standards it has pledged to uphold under Egyptian and international law. In disregard of these standards, Egyptian security forces, particularly State Security Investigation (SSI), the internal security apparatus attached to the Ministry of Interior, have been permitted to operate in a lawless manner. Their human rights abuses include arbitrary arrest, incommunicado detention, and torture of suspects during interrogation.

One particularly reprehensible security force practice is the detention and intimidation of innocent family members—including women, children and the elderly—in order to pressure fugitive relatives to surrender to authorities, frighten families into silence about human rights abuses, and discourage them from pursuing complaints or speaking to journalists and human rights investigators. These actions are part of the arsenal of techniques used by the security forces to safeguard their impunity.

---

[123] The following material was adapted from Human Rights Watch/Middle East, "Egypt: Hostage-Taking and Intimidation by Security Forces," *A Human Rights Watch Short Report*, vol. 7, no. 1 (January 1995).

The victims of "hostage-taking," the term used by victims and Egyptian lawyers to describe the arrest of family members for the purpose of forcing fugitive relatives to give themselves up, have since 1992 primarily been the relatives of known or suspected Islamist militants who are wanted by the authorities on suspicion of carrying out violent crimes against the state. Family members of both sexes and all ages have been targeted and detained with no legal basis. Local authorities typically denied that these individuals were in custody. Since many of the victims were blindfolded and detained incommunicado, it was often difficult if not impossible to ascertain the actual place of detention.

The detention and ill-treatment of female family members is a powerful tool for intimidating communities and coercing men to surrender to security forces. The threat of rape and the sexually degrading treatment of women are perceived to be profound offenses against a woman's individual honor as well as the honor of her family and male relatives. In societies around the world, including Egypt, men define their honor in part by their ability to protect and control women's sexual purity. Preying on men's sense of responsibility for their female family members, security forces use or threaten mistreatment, particularly sexual mistreatment of women to pressure fugitives to surrender.

Hostage-taking cannot be dismissed as isolated actions carried out by lawless local officers. The arbitrary and punitive detention of family members in locations as diverse as metropolitan Cairo and towns and villages in Upper Egypt indicates that the practice has become systematic and therefore undoubtedly is sanctioned, if not ordered, at a high level within Egypt's security apparatus.

Hostage-taking is only one manifestation of the pervasive and ongoing problem of arbitrary arrest and incommunicado detention in Egypt. Lawyers interviewed by Human Rights Watch registered uniform frustration at the inaction of local prosecutors in the face of such abuses, arguing that there is no effective oversight of police and security forces' conduct. Other lawyers concurred that Egypt's prosecutorial system lacks independence and is thoroughly compromised and functions, in effect, as an arm of police and security forces. Many lawyers believe that this breakdown of the rule of law has its origins at the top and blame prosecutors for inaction. For example, Prosecutor General Ragaa el-Araby has not discharged one of the key duties of his office—independent investigation of abuses and prosecution of abusers. This lack of will to hold state agents accountable permeates the entire system, influences the behavior of prosecutors at the local level, and allows security forces to operate with impunity, in defiance of the law and the Egyptian government's obligations under international human rights treaties.

Hostage-Taking and Abuse of Female Detainees

Human Rights Watch has collected information about cases of arbitrary detention of family members by security forces, in violation of Article 9(1) of the ICCPR, which protects the right to liberty; these cases date back to 1990. Once detained, family members—including mothers, wives, daughters, and sisters—have been subjected to torture or inhuman or degrading treatment. These incidents have occurred in major cities, including Cairo, and in towns and villages throughout the country.

In 1990, for example, a fifty-three-year-old mother of seven was illegally detained for six days at the local police station in Minya, a city south of Cairo. The security forces lashed her with a whip that cut her skin while arresting her. She was detained because her sons were suspected of involvement with militant Islamist groups. "I was a hostage," she told us. "They did this to me because they wanted my son Hamdi, who was not yet sixteen years old. My son Sayyid came to visit me on the fourth day of my detention. They took him to SSI and beat him and then detained him for six months. . . . It was all done to threaten us. They told me that my sons should not have contact with Islamic groups."[124]

In December 1991, in Domyat, on the northeast Mediterranean coast, relatives of suspects were detained following an attack that wounded security officer Major Mutawwi Abu al-Naja. According to the written report of a local lawyer, security forces "went on a rampage" in the village of al-Wasil after the attack, raiding houses and rounding up many youths. "If they entered a house and did not find anyone they wanted," the lawyer wrote, "then they would . . . arrest whomever they found—a wife, a mother, a sister, a daughter, and would hold them as hostages until [the suspect] surrendered himself.[125]

Hostage-taking and other forms of pressure of families increased in 1992, when authorities began an all-out crackdown on militant Islamists. As political violence mounted in Upper Egypt that year—with police and security forces, Christians and tourists attacked by armed Islamists—families of those suspected of involvement in this violence were increasingly targeted and mistreated in detention.

---

[124] Interview, Minya, February 1992.

[125] This report was obtained in February 1992, when Human Rights Watch representatives visited Domyat.

Hostage-taking in the oasis city of Fayoum, southwest of Cairo, followed the killing of an SSI officer there on March 3, 1992. According to the Egyptian Organization for Human Rights (EOHR), relatives of the wanted suspects were detained at the al-'Azab prison and the paramilitary Central Security Forces camp located fifteen kilometers from Fayoum, for periods of from twenty-four hours up to ten days. At the camp, security forces degraded wives of fugitives by forcing them to strip naked and placing them in a closed room with naked, male detainees. They abused the women in order to coerce from them information about the hiding places of fugitives.[126]

On April 28, 1992, forty-year-old police officer Mukhtar Ahmad Dawud was shot dead in an ambush in Isna, in Upper Egypt, as he was riding home on his motorcycle. After the officer's killing, security forces laid siege to Mat'ana, a village just north of Isna, and took hostages, "starting with the heads of every big family, old men, sixty and seventy years old," according to a lawyer from the area. "Then they came back and took the women, about fifteen of them, old and young." He said that the women were insulted and cursed, kicked in the legs, and spat upon if they asked to use a bathroom.[127]

In December 1992 family members were taken hostage when a massive number of security forces moved on Imbaba, the densely populated Cairo slum where Islamist militants maintained a strong and visible presence. The EOHR cited hostage-taking as one of the abuses carried out by security forces, in addition to mass arbitrary arrests, temporary disappearances and widespread torture. The EOHR reported that wives, mothers and sisters of wanted suspects were detained and, in some cases, degraded or tortured. "Some of the women held were subject to severe torture by the police officer of Imbaba police station for the whole duration of their detention which included beatings with [sic] rod and the handling of the genitals and forcing them out of their clothes."[128] The latter form of mistreatment causes great mental anguish in a culture that highly values female modesty.

Abuse of female family relatives of suspected Islamist militants taken hostage by security forces continued in 1993 and 1994. In a 1993 case of hostage-taking in a town in Upper Egypt, "The mother was tied with her hands behind her back. They threatened to rape her if her [wanted] son did not show

---

[126] EOHR, "Torture in Egypt/Central Security Forces Camps" (Cairo, December 10, 1992), p. 11.

[127] Interview, Cairo, February 1993.

[128] EOHR, "Imbaba: An Intense Image of the Deterioration of the State of Human Rights and Respect of the Law in Egypt" (Cairo, March 20, 1993), p. 6.

up in two days."[129]   The brothers of the wanted man and their wives also were detained. According to a local lawyer, the women were blindfolded, bound, slapped, beaten with a heavy leather whip, and threatened with rape. The wives were held for one day and then released.

The Response of the Egyptian Government
Despite repeated complaints by Egyptian lawyers and documentation by local and international human rights organizations, the Egyptian government continues to deny that security forces take and abuse hostages. In a June 1993 document prepared for Human Rights Watch, the Ministry of Foreign Affairs maintained that Egypt "does not waver in its dedication to the respect of human rights and basic freedoms." The Foreign Ministry stated that the Interior Ministry fully complies with Egyptian and international law in carrying out its activities.

The Foreign Ministry denied that family members were detained as hostages. It asserted that "security agencies, when carrying out arrest orders, do not target any person other than those designated for arrest by the orders. Only in cases where opposition, aggression or resistance are exhibited toward the commissioned force by a family member or a neighbor would someone other than the intended be presented before the [prosecutor] in a legal context." The Foreign Ministry further wrote: "The stirring up of allegations about the detention of women as hostages and their exposure to disgrace, torture and the violation of their virtue in some regions of Upper Egypt comes as part of a broad plan on the part of terrorist groups to arouse popular sentiment against security operations, whereby they take advantage of the special role that the woman plays in eastern society."

GENERAL RECOMMENDATIONS

To Governments:
- Governments should criminalize and publicly condemn violence, especially sexual abuse by prison or jail officials, against women in custody. They should investigate thoroughly and without undue delay accusations of such abuse and fully punish those found guilty.
- Consistent with the U.N. Body of Principles for the Protection of All Persons under Any Form of Detention or Imprisonment, governments

---

[129] Interview, Upper Egypt (name of town withheld), July 1994.

should ensure that prison and jail staff treat all prisoners humanely and with respect for their inherent dignity.

- Consistent with the U.N. Standard Minimum Rules for the Treatment of Prisoners, governments should ensure that prison and jail staff apply prison rules impartially, without discrimination based on sex, among other grounds.
- Governments should enact and strictly enforce statutes that make it a criminal offense for prison officials to engage in any kind of sexual contact with prisoners.   Even where force, coercion, threat of punishment or offer of reward cannot be demonstrated, female prisoners should not be punished for such contact.   The inherently coercive nature of the prison environment and the unequal relationship between prison employees and prisoners is a factor in any such contact, while the penalogical interest served by such punishment is far outweighed by the deterrent effect it is likely to have on prisoners' willingness to report custodial abuse.
- Governments should establish independent investigative units with the authority to receive complaints and initiate investigations of alleged physical, including sexual, abuse of women prisoners by prison and jail staff or police.
- Governments should ensure that a prison's internal procedural rules and regulations, as well as state and federal laws, governing the treatment of prisoners are consistent with international standards. They should expressly define and prohibit sexual misconduct, including rape, fondling, inappropriate touching, the use of sexualized, demeaning language or gestures, and inappropriate observation of prisoners' bodies.   The condition of incarceration should be seen as a factor aggravating the seriousness of custodial sexual misconduct, particularly rape, rather than as a mitigating factor as often occurs.
- Governments should eliminate discriminatory laws and practices that contribute to the wrongful incarceration of women.   This should include a review of rules of evidence in order to eliminate norms that discriminate on the basis of sex.
- Governments should ensure that women enjoy full equality before the law.   To that end, they should eliminate gender bias in the administration of justice. Judges should be appropriately trained in non-discriminatory application of the law.
- Governments should vigorously enforce laws and rules governing the treatment of women in police custody or prison. Specifically, laws and regulations should punish prison and jail staff who humiliate or degrade women prisoners and require respect for the privacy of

women in custody. To this end, governments should, among other things: ensure that women prisoners are not subjected to strip searches unnecessarily or for the purposes of humiliation or punishment; restrict the role of male guards or police in such searches, except in cases of emergency; protect women prisoners from inappropriate observation by male personnel while being searched and while in the showers, bathrooms, and other personal areas where the dignity of a prisoner requires privacy in all but extraordinary circumstances.

- Governments should ensure that women prisoners are effectively informed upon entering a custodial situation, about jail or prison policies, their rights as prisoners under international law, and the means available to exercise those rights. Consistent with the U.N. Standard Minimum Rules for the Treatment of Prisoners, women prisoners who cannot read should be given this information verbally.

- Governments should prevent and enforce sanctions for any form of punishment or retaliation against women prisoners for filing complaints of custodial abuse against prison or jail officials.

- Governments should ensure that prisons and jails implement procedures to facilitate the safe reporting of abuse by women prisoners. The identity of women inmates filing complaints against guards or other prison or jail personnel should remain confidential, so as to prevent retaliation and to facilitate safe reporting, until revelation of the identity of the accused is absolutely necessary to the investigation of the charges.

- Governments should ensure that all state-imposed deterrents to the reporting of sexual and other forms of physical abuse by prison or jail staff or police are eliminated, such as requirements that women prisoners confront their alleged assailants prior to filing a formal complaint. Nor should women face punitive sanctions if the allegations are not proven.

- Governments should ensure that guards and other prison or jail personnel accused of sexual or other misconduct are removed immediately from having any contact with the accusing prisoner, until the accusation has been fully investigated and a judgment has been issued and executed.

- Governments should ensure that prison services maintain up-to-date data on sexual misconduct charges for all prisons under their direction. To ensure accountability, they should further create

independent review mechanisms to monitor the handling and outcome
of cases of alleged sexual abuse.

- Governments should ensure that guards, police, and other prison or
jail personnel are expressly forbidden to take part in any capacity
whatsoever in investigations in which they stand accused of
misconduct.

- Governments should ensure that jail and prison personnel are
effectively trained to know that physical abuse of and sexual
misconduct with prisoners by prison and jail staff is strictly prohibited
and will not be tolerated. Such training should specify that all such
abuse and misconduct will be punished administratively and, where
appropriate, criminally.

- Government compliance reports to CEDAW should include
information on steps taken to eradicate violence and discrimination
against women in custody, including measures taken to sanction
prison or jail personnel found guilty of such abusive behavior.

To Donor Governments:

- Donor governments should review the human rights records of
recipient governments and, in doing so, examine the treatment of
women in custody.

- Donor governments should call upon recipient governments to:
implement effective prohibitions against sexual misconduct in
custodial situations by prison and jail officials, including
implementation of clear laws criminalizing such misconduct; provide
evidence of mandatory training programs for prison personnel
regarding prohibitions on sexual misconduct; demonstrate the
existence and enforcement of transparent, impartial mechanisms to
investigate allegations of sexual misconduct by prison and jail guards
and police; and demonstrate the vigorous prosecution of guards and
other prison and jail personnel found guilty of such abuses.

- Donor governments should ensure that assistance for judicial reform
assure that laws that discriminate against women in the administration
of criminal justice are identified and repealed.

To the United Nations:

- The U.N. Special Rapporteur on Torture should consistently address
the issue of sexual abuse of women in custody as integral to his or
her mandate to document, investigate and condemn torture or cruel,
inhuman or degrading treatment. In his or her reporting, the special
rapporteur should identify and denounce in particular torture or cruel,

inhuman or degrading treatment that takes the form of sexual abuse; investigate allegations of physical, including sexual, violence against women prisoners by police and prison or jail staff; and call for governments to provide effective remedies for such abuse.

- Consistent with its mandate to investigate "cases of detention imposed arbitrarily or otherwise inconsistently with the international standards set forth in the Universal Declaration of Human Rights or in the relevant international legal instruments accepted by the States concerned," the U.N. Working Group on Arbitrary Detentions should investigate cases in which women have been wrongfully detained as a result of discriminatory laws, in violation of their rights to equal protection before the law and to freedom from discrimination.
- The U.N. Human Rights Committee should continue to monitor the treatment of women in custody, in order to ensure respect for their rights to privacy, physical integrity, and freedom from torture, and other cruel, inhuman or degrading treatment.

4
TRAFFICKING OF WOMEN AND GIRLS INTO FORCED PROSTITUTION AND COERCED MARRIAGE

In any given year, many thousands of young women and girls around the world are lured, abducted or sold into forced prostitution and involuntary marriage. They are bartered at prices that vary depending on their age, beauty and virginity, and exploited under conditions that amount to a modern form of slavery. Women and girls who have been trafficked can rarely escape or negotiate the conditions of their employment or marriage. In countries where Human Rights Watch has investigated the problem of trafficking, we have found that many police officers and other local government officials facilitate and profit from the trade in women and girls: for a price, they ignore abuses that occur in their jurisdictions; protect the traffickers, brothel owners, pimps, clients and buyers from arrest; and serve as enforcers, drivers and recruiters. If a woman is taken across national borders, immigration officials frequently aid and abet her passage.

The burgeoning trade in women and girls is linked fundamentally to women's unequal status. On the supply side, adverse socioeconomic conditions in many regions increase the likelihood that women and girls will be lured into forced prostitution or involuntary marriage. In most parts of the world, most notably in rural areas, women and girls have fewer educational and economic opportunities than males. The attraction of a big city, better-paying jobs, and a better life cause women and girls who have few options at home to accept alleged job or marriage offers far away. Moreover, even if the woman or girl herself is not tempted, the preference for sons in many societies (both to carry on the family name and as social insurance in old age) and the promise of immediate payments often lead families to sell their daughters.[1] Because many agents are local people familiar with local conditions, they strategically recruit in the lean period before harvests or target families with financial difficulties. The recruiters' timing, coupled with the traditional responsibility of women to care for their families, make offers of employment or marriage difficult to resist.

---

[1] Report of South Asia Regional Workshop on Protecting the Rights of Women and Children with Special Reference to International Trafficking and Labour Migration (Dhaka, Bangladesh, June 2-4, 1992), p. 3.

On the demand side, the growth of sex tourism has in some cases accelerated the forced trafficking in women and girls. Our research found, however, that local demand for prostitutes or wives is at least as important as tourism, if not more so. Additionally, in countries such as Thailand and India, which have a high prevalence rate of the human immunodeficiency virus (HIV), the clients' fear of infection has led traffickers to recruit younger women and girls, sometimes as young as ten, from remote areas perceived to be unaffected by the acquired immunodeficiency syndrome (AIDS) pandemic, in order to ensure their "purity" or virginity.[2]

Although the traffic in women and girls possesses distinct characteristics in each country or region where it occurs, certain patterns have emerged that cut across geographical boundaries. In a typical situation, a woman or girl is first recruited by an agent with promises of a good job in another country or province. For instance, Bangladeshi and Nepali women and girls are promised the opportunity to escape poverty at home to the relative prosperity of Pakistan and India, respectively. Women and girls have also been abducted outright, as some testimonies from southern Thailand indicate. Yet another mode of recruitment is through false marriage offers, with the "bride" later sold off to a brothel. If the women are taken across national borders, immigration officials frequently abet their illegal passage.

Once recruited or abducted, virtually all women and girls trafficked into forced prostitution are controlled through debt bondage. The initial debt is usually a payment to the woman's family at the time of recruitment, which she must repay, with interest, by working in a brothel. This "debt" mounts as the brothel owners add on the costs of food, clothes, medicine and other expenses. Escape is virtually impossible without repaying the "debt," since leaving the brothel puts the woman at risk of punishment by the brothel owner, his employees or the police, retribution against her parents and other relatives for defaulting on her debt, and/or arrest as an illegal immigrant. Women trafficked or sold into forced marriage are also held captive through financial obligations. Distance from home, lack of familiarity with the local language or dialect, and inability to find local support networks further reinforce the women's and girls' dependence on the brothel owners, pimps or "husbands."

Victims of forced prostitution in particular are exposed to health risks, especially sexually transmitted diseases (STDs), because they are not allowed to negotiate the terms of sex. Aside from risk of infection through sexual

---

[2] Marlise Simons, "The Sex Market: Scrouge on the World's Children," *The New York Times*, April 9, 1993.

intercourse with many clients, the growing popularity of contraceptive injections in brothels also contributes to the spread of disease, since brothel owners often use the same and possibly contaminated needle several times. For women who develop AIDS, forced prostitution is ultimately fatal. Other women have become infertile due to other STDs and, thus, unmarriageable in cultures where the primary purpose of marriage is procreation. Shunned by their own families and communities, many of these women must return to prostitution in order to support themselves.[3]

Because prostitution is illegal in most countries, and prostitutes are scorned in virtually all, victims of forced prostitution face legal and moral isolation. Human Rights Watch takes no position on prostitution per se. However, we strongly condemn laws and official policies and practices that fail to distinguish between prostitutes and victims of forced trafficking, treating the latter as criminals rather than as persons who deserve "temporary care and maintenance" in accordance with international human rights standards. We also oppose laws and policies that punish women who engage in prostitution but not the men who operate and profit from prostitution rings and who patronize prostitutes: such policies are discriminatory on the basis of sex. Moreover, we are extremely concerned that absent effective law enforcement and social services for the victims, such attitudes toward prostitutes exacerbate the problem of trafficking. Out of fear of social ostracism, women are reluctant to speak about their experiences of abuse and thus to warn others who might also be vulnerable.

Although trafficking in women and girls has become a lucrative and expanding cross-border trade, it routinely escapes effective national and international sanctions. Trafficking for the purposes of forced prostitution has frequently been mischaracterized by governments and human rights organizations alike as a voluntary act, presuming the women's consent, even when ample evidence exists to the contrary. Both forced prostitution and coerced marriage also have largely been dismissed as crimes perpetrated by private individuals for which states have no responsibility under international human rights law. In fact, governments do have specific international legal duties to take steps to eradicate trafficking and related abuses.

---

[3] Preliminary Report submitted by the Special Rapporteur on violence against women, its causes and consequences, U.N. Document E/CN.4/1995/42, (Geneva: United Nations, November 22, 1994), p. 50.

International Legal Protections

Trafficking in persons and related abuses are prohibited under international human rights law. Governments are specifically obligated to take appropriate steps to eradicate forced trafficking in persons, exploitation of prostitution, slavery-like practices, forced labor, and coerced marriage. Despite these obligations, governments have allowed the practice of forced prostitution of women and girls to flourish.

Trafficking and Forced Prostitution

From the start, efforts to create human rights norms regarding trafficking have focused on punishing traffickers rather than the victims, in stark contrast to government practice described in the case studies in this chapter. International human rights instruments that prohibit trafficking and exploitation of prostitution address these practices in broad terms. Human Rights Watch is particularly concerned that many state parties have failed to protect women and girls from coerced trafficking and forced prostitution, or have failed to prosecute vigorously those who commit such abuse. The international community first denounced trafficking in persons in the 1949 Convention on the Suppression of Traffic in Persons and the Exploitation of the Prostitution of Others (the Trafficking Convention). Under the terms of this treaty, state parties "agree to punish any person who, to gratify the passions of another, procures, entices or leads away, for purposes of prostitution, another person . . ."[4] In addition, the Trafficking Convention requires state parties to sanction any person who runs or finances a brothel; in our view, law enforcement agencies should focus particularly on individuals who operate, aid or abet forced prostitution operations.[5] States should further "adopt or maintain such measures as required . . . to check the traffic in persons . . . for the purposes of prostitution."[6]

With regard to persons who have been trafficked, the convention emphasizes their protection and safe repatriation. It calls on state parties "so far as possible" to "make suitable provisions for [trafficking victims'] temporary care and maintenance"; to repatriate such persons "only after agreement . . . with the State of destination"; and, where persons cannot pay

---

[4] Trafficking Convention, Article 1.

[5] Ibid., Article 5.

[6] Ibid., Article 17. This includes making "such regulations as are necessary" to protect immigrants, in particular women and children, and all persons in transit.

the costs of repatriation, to bear the cost "as far as the nearest frontier."[7]
While we recognize the right of governments to make and enforce laws
regulating national borders, they must distinguish between those who
purposefully violate immigration laws and others who are victims of forced
trafficking.

The obligation of state parties to take all appropriate measures to
suppress the traffic in women was later reiterated in the 1979 Convention on
the Elimination of All Forms of Discrimination Against Women (CEDAW).[8]
CEDAW does not, however, elaborate upon specific steps.   Like the
Trafficking Convention, CEDAW links trafficking to the exploitation of
prostitution, but fails to address trafficking for other exploitative ends, such as
coerced marriage and forced labor.

Slavery-like Practices and Forced Labor
In addition to treaty provisions that address trafficking particularly,
other human rights instruments apply to practices commonly associated with
the trafficking industry. The 1956 Supplementary Convention on the Abolition
of Slavery, the Slave Trade and Institutions and Practices Similar to Slavery
(Supplementary Slavery Convention) bans all slavery-like practices, including
debt bondage and forced marriage. Debt bondage is defined as:

> the status or condition arising from a pledge by a debtor of
> his personal services or of those of a person under his control
> as security for a debt, if the value of those services as
> reasonably assessed is not applied towards the liquidation of
> the debt or the length and nature of those services are not
> respectively limited and defined.[9]

Forced marriage, too, is condemned as a slavery-like practice under
the Supplementary Slavery Convention. Article 1 prohibits "any institution or
practice whereby . . . a woman, without the right to refuse, is promised or
given in marriage on payment of a consideration in money or kind."[10] This
provision reinforces the guarantee, under the International Covenant on Civil

---

[7] Ibid., Article 19.
[8] CEDAW, Article 6.
[9] Supplementary Slavery Convention, Article 1(a).
[10] Ibid., Article 1(c)(ii).

and Political Rights (ICCPR), of marriage only with "the free and full consent of the intending spouses."[11]

The uniformity of international treaties' and national governments' condemnation of slavery and slavery-related practices have made the prohibitions against these abuses part of customary international law.[12] All nations, therefore, are required to prosecute and punish individuals who engage in slavery and slavery-related practices, regardless of whether they have ratified the relevant conventions.

Illegal confinement of women and girls contribute to the slavery-like conditions of the brothel or marriage. Not only are they not permitted to leave their immediate surroundings but also, in many cases, the women and girls are unable even to communicate with anyone outside of the brothel or home. Their unlawful confinement frequently is enforced with the help or tacit consent of police or other officials, in violation of Article 9 of the ICCPR, which provides that no one shall be arbitrarily deprived of liberty. Even where there is no official complicity, the state is obligated to investigate this practice and to prosecute alleged offenders.

The combination of debt bondage and illegal confinement in situations of forced prostitution is tantamount to forced labor, defined by the International Labor Organization as "All work or service which is exacted from any person under the menace of any penalty and for which the said person has not offered himself voluntarily."[13] Freedom from forced labor is recognized by the International Labor Organization as one of seven labor standards that constitutes a basic human right and is also guaranteed by the ICCPR.[14] Despite these protections, thousands of women and girls are compelled into prostitution in many countries.

Torture

Similar to the right to be free from slavery and forced labor, freedom from torture is one of the peremptory norms of the international human rights regime. Both human rights treaties and customary international law prohibit torture and impose obligations on governments to prevent and punish acts of

---

[11] ICCPR, Article 23(3).

[12] M. Cherif Bassiouni, "Enslavement as an International Crime," *New York University Journal of International Law and Politics*, vol. 23 (1991), p. 445.

[13] International Labour Organization Convention (No. 29) Concerning Forced or Compulsory Labor, Article 2.1.

[14] ICCPR, Article 8(3)(a).

torture.[15]   The Convention Against Torture and Other Cruel, Inhuman or
Degrading Treatment or Punishment defines torture as:

> any act by which severe pain or suffering, whether physical
> or mental, is intentionally inflicted on a person for such
> purposes as obtaining from him or a third person information
> or a confession, punishing him for an act he or a third person
> has committed or is suspected of having committed, or
> intimidating or coercing him or a third person, or for any
> reason based on discrimination of any kind, when such pain
> or suffering is inflicted by or at the instigation of or with the
> consent or acquiescence of a public official or other person
> acting in official capacity.[16]

Under this definition, state agents—police, border officials, prison guards—
who participate, instigate, or acquiesce in the rape, beating, or severe
psychological abuse of women and girls held in bondage in brothels should be
held liable for torture, or cruel, inhuman or degrading treatment.

Failure to Ensure Equal Protection and Nondiscrimination
    The case studies in this chapter also show that governments rarely
arrest or prosecute the men—the brothel owners, clients, buyers, and recruiters,
including state agents—responsible for forced trafficking. For example, police
raids on brothels in Pakistan, Thailand and India, when they occurred, more
often resulted in the arrest and prosecution of the women and girls than of the
brothel owners. This discriminatory arrest pattern is rendered that much more
offensive by the fact that trafficking victims are entitled to protection, not
sanction, under international treaties. Not only have anti-prostitution
immigration laws been largely useless in curbing the trafficking of women and
girls, but they have been enforced in ways that compound the harm to the
trafficking victims. The wrongful application of these statutes has been an
important means by which traffickers and pimps intimidate and control women

---

[15] Universal Declaration of Human Rights, Article 5; ICCPR, Article 7; Convention
Against Torture and other Cruel, Inhuman or Degrading Treatment or Punishment
(Torture Convention); Nigel Rodley, *The Treatment of Prisoners Under International
Law* (New York: Oxford University Press, 1987), pp. 63-64.
    [16] Torture Convention, Article 1.

and girls, and in some cases a way by which corrupt officials profit from their plight.

The discriminatory and arbitrary arrest of trafficking victims violates women's rights to be free from discrimination on the basis of sex and to the equal protection of the law. Article 3 of the ICCPR requires that "State Parties . . . undertake to ensure the equal rights of men and women to the enjoyment of all civil and political rights."[17] In addition, CEDAW requires state parties to "take all appropriate measures, including legislation, to modify or abolish existing laws, regulations, customs and practices which constitute discrimination against women" and to "accord women equality with men before the law."[18]

International Initiatives

Local, regional and international nongovernmental organizations (NGOs) have been at the forefront of efforts to raise awareness of trafficking and to press for accountability. NGOs, particularly local groups, are carrying out desperately needed programs to warn girls and their families of the dangers of trafficking, shelter those who have managed to escape, provide urgent medical and psychological care, assist in repatriation, and press governments to strengthen domestic laws against trafficking.

The work of NGOs has filled the gaps left by government inaction and, at times, has led to governments' improving their behavior. For example, in Thailand, NGOs have sheltered Burmese women and girls and found safe, unpublicized ways to return them home over the border. In addition, Thai NGOs have advocated that their government adopt the necessary legislation and ratify the relevant international instruments on trafficking. Similarly, NGOs in Pakistan have been instrumental in improving protections for trafficking victims. By raising public and official awareness of the trafficking of Bangladeshi women and girls into Pakistan, the private group Lawyers for Human Rights and Legal Aid has pressured the Pakistani government to take additional steps to protect trafficking victims. The Edhi Center in Karachi and Lahore, too, has helped to bail women out of jail and provide otherwise unavailable shelter to more than a hundred women at a time.

Given the failure of governments to suppress the traffic in women, some observers have suggested that NGOs take on a larger role in addressing

---

[17] ICCPR, Article 3. In addition, Articles 2(1), 2(3)(a), and 26 prohibit discrimination on the basis of sex.

[18] CEDAW, Articles 2 and 15.

the problem. But nongovernmental groups should not be expected to make up for shortcomings of the state. While governments could and should consult with NGOs to improve their response to the illicit trade in persons, they cannot abdicate their duty to protect human rights.

Largely due to the demands of NGOs, which often operate with limited resources and at considerable risk to their staff, intergovernmental organizations, particularly the United Nations, have begun to address international trafficking in persons. In March 1994 the United Nations Commission on Human Rights adopted Resolution 1994/45 calling for the elimination of trafficking in women for the purposes of prostitution. The appointment of a U.N. Special Rapporteur on Violence Against Women and the work of the U.N. Special Rapporteur on the Sale of Children, Child Prostitution and Child Pornography, in particular, have helped put pressure on the U.N. and its member states to recognize the seriousness of the trafficking problem.[19] U.N. specialized agencies, including UNICEF, UNDP and WHO, have begun to analyze the issue of trafficking and prostitution in relation to their education, development and relief work. The International Police Organization (INTERPOL) has also held several conferences on trafficking and has attempted to coordinate cross-border efforts of law enforcement agencies to curb trafficking in children.

Unfortunately, these limited efforts do not constitute an effective, coordinated campaign against trafficking in women and girls. The problem is increasingly complicated and multifaceted, with roots in socioeconomic and gender inequities that are exploited by ever more sophisticated, organized criminal networks. Law enforcement alone will not end the abuse, but it would at least be the start of a long-term solution. At a minimum, governments must shake off their indifference to official complicity. Beyond this, they should develop and collaborate in bilateral and multilateral efforts to contain trafficking's further expansion.

---

[19] Vitit Muntarbhorn, who had served as U.N. Special Rapporteur on the Sale of Children since 1989, resigned his post in late 1991 citing personal reasons and lack of support from the United Nations.

BURMESE WOMEN AND GIRLS TRAFFICKED TO THAILAND

"Lin Lin" was thirteen years old when she was recruited by
an agent for work in Thailand. Her father took 12,000 baht
(equivalent to US$480) from the agent with the
understanding that his daughter would pay the loan back out
of her earnings. The agent took "Lin Lin" to Bangkok, and
three days later she was taken to the Ran Dee Prom brothel.
"Lin Lin" did not know what was going on until a man came
into her room and started touching her breasts and body and
then forced her to have sex. For the next two years, "Lin
Lin" worked in various parts of Thailand in four different
brothels.   The owners told her she would have to keep
prostituting herself until she paid off her father's debt. Her
clients, who often included police, paid the owner one
hundred baht (US$4) each time. If she refused a client's
demands, she was slapped and threatened by the owner. She
worked every day, except the two days off each month she
was allowed for her menstrual period.   Once she had to
borrow money to pay for medicine to treat a painful vaginal
infection. This amount was added to her debt. On January
18, 1993, the Crime Suppression Division of the Thai police
raided the brothel in which "Lin Lin" worked, and she was
taken to a shelter run by a local nongovernmental
organization. She was fifteen years old, had spent over two
years of her young life in forced prostitution, and tested
positive for the human immunodeficiency virus or HIV.[20]

"Lin Lin" is just one of thousands of Burmese women and girls in
Thailand who have been trafficked into what amounts to female sexual
slavery.[21] Burmese trafficking victims are subjected to a range of violations

---

[20] The following material was adapted from Asia Watch and Women's Rights
Project, *A Modern Form of Slavery: Trafficking of Burmese Women and Girls into
Brothels in Thailand* (New York: Human Rights Watch, 1993). The names of
interviewees are withheld by Human Rights Watch unless otherwise indicated.

[21] As of January 1994, estimates of Burmese girls working in brothels in Thailand
ranged from 20,000 to 30,000, with approximately 10,000 new recruits brought in each
year.

of internationally recognized human rights, including debt bondage, illegal confinement, arbitrary detention, discriminatory arrests, and numerous due process violations. In three visits to Thailand in 1993, Human Rights Watch gathered evidence that government officials, particularly the Thai police, are involved directly in every stage of trafficking and forced prostitution. Our information gathered since then indicates that there has been no substantial change in the conditions we documented in 1993.

The Socioeconomic Context
        The number of Burmese women and girls recruited to work in Thai brothels has soared in recent years as an indirect consequence of political repression in Burma (Myanmar) by the ruling State Law and Order Restoration Council (SLORC) and of improved economic relations between Burma and Thailand.[22] Most donor countries responded to the 1988 crackdown on the pro-democracy movement by the Burmese military, and subsequent human rights abuses in Burma, with economic sanctions and withdrawal of foreign aid. SLORC, desperate for foreign exchange, turned to Thailand, offering a range of economic concessions. Such economic links led to official openings along the Thai-Burmese border, allowing both Thai and Burmese citizens to cross the common border more easily.[23] This opening of trade and border crossings has facilitated the rise in trafficking of Burmese men, women and children, with the same routes as are used to transport drugs and goods being used to transport people.
        A border boom brought about by the increased trade with Burma, together with the profitable tourist industry in Thailand, has increased the demand for women in the sex industry, especially for young girls.[24]

---

        [22] Burma was officially renamed Myanmar on June 8, 1990 by SLORC. While the new name has been adopted by the United Nations, many Burmese understand the use of "Myanmar" as *de facto* recognition of SLORC's authority and prefer to use "Burma." For a more in-depth discussion of the political situation in Burma, see Asia Watch and Women's Rights Project, *A Modern Form of Slavery*, pp. 10-20; and Human Rights Watch/Asia, "Burma: Entrenchment or Reform?—Human Rights Developments and the Need for Continued Pressure," *A Human Rights Watch Short Report*, vol. 7, no. 10 (July 1995).
        [23] "New Border Checkpoints Open," *Bangkok Post*, October 7, 1992.
        [24] Both Thailand and Burma began promoting tourism to the Golden Triangle area, and the Thai press reported plans for the construction of a major new road through China, Burma and Thailand. The new road would link Mae Sai on the Thai side with
(continued...)

According to one source, tourism generates some US$3 billion annually, and sex is one of its "most valuable subsectors,"[25] employing anywhere from 800,000 to two million persons throughout the country.[26]   However, the tourist trade is less a factor in the sex industry than local demand.   It is estimated that 75 percent of Thai men have had sex with a prostitute.[27] Therefore, despite the expenses incurred in employing a network of agents to recruit new workers, paying protection money to police, and giving minimum allowances to the women and girls, the brothel owners can make substantial profits.   Agents, local police and others involved in the business also benefit.

If the Burmese women and girls are deported to Burma, they face not only the possibility of forced conscription as porters for the SLORC military but also arrest on charges of leaving the country illegally and engaging in prostitution.   To avoid deportation, many look for any way to stay in Thailand—which makes them particularly vulnerable to continued exploitation. Burmese trafficking victims' legal situation is made even more precarious by the fact that Thai deportation decisions often ignore the likelihood of persecution by the SLORC authorities upon return to Burma.

Thai Legal Context

Thailand first addressed the problem of trafficking of women into Thailand in 1928 by passing the Trafficking in Women and Girls Act (Anti-Trafficking Act).[28]   The statute specifically exempts trafficking victims in

---

[24](...continued)
Keng Tung in Burma—an area from which many of the women and girls we interviewed for *A Modern Form of Slavery* originally came. "Thailand-Burma-China Road Link Nearer Reality," *Horizons* (Bangkok), June 1993. The Golden Triangle refers to the area where the borders of Thailand, Burma and Laos meet, and is well known for opium and heroin production.

[25] Steven Schlosstein, *Asia's New Little Dragon* (Chicago: Contemporary Books, 1991), pp. 196-197.

[26] "Prostitution: Looking Beyond the Numbers," *The Nation* (Bangkok), July 11, 1993.

[27] Hnin Hnin Pyne, "AIDS and Prostitution in Thailand: Case Study of Burmese Prostitution in Ranong," unpublished thesis, May 1992, p. 19.

[28] The Anti-Trafficking Act was adopted in response to the presence of large numbers of foreign nationals in Thai brothels. Many were women who were initially brought into Thailand as slaves. The abolition of slavery in 1905 by King Rama V brought about an immediate increase in prostitution, as former women slaves were

(continued...)

Thailand from imprisonment or fine, but they must be sent to a state reform institution for at least thirty days. At this time, prostitution was still legal in Thailand. Thailand criminalized prostitution in 1960 through the Suppression of Prostitution Act. Still in effect, this law prohibits prostitution and penalizes both prostitutes and those who procure them or benefit from their exploitation, but not the clients.[29]   It does not explicitly exempt persons forced into prostitution from punishment.   Similar to the Anti-Trafficking Act, the Suppression of Prostitution Act views prostitutes as women in need of "moral rehabilitation."

Despite the passage of the Suppression of Prostitution Act, the Thai government's commitment to eradicating prostitution was called into serious question six years later with the introduction of the Entertainment Places Act of 1966, which regulates nightclubs, dance halls, bars and places for "baths, massage or steam baths which have women attend to customers." The use of such licensed establishments for prostitution is outlawed, but police enforcement is lax and many "places of service" fail to register altogether. The Thai Penal Code, adopted on November 13, 1956, also criminalizes procurement for the purpose of prostitution. In fact, the penal code assigns higher penalties to this offense than does the anti-prostitution law.

Therefore, by 1990, Thailand had four separate legal regimes, addressing different but sometimes overlapping elements of both trafficking and prostitution. The resulting inconsistencies, while not insurmountable, have undermined the development of clear legal sanctions on forced prostitution and trafficking. But the Thai government's failure to combat forced prostitution and trafficking results primarily from its unwillingness to enforce even the most straightforward provisions, such as the prohibition against trafficking in women and girls. Worse still, not only has the Thai government failed to protect trafficking victims, but its agents are directly complicit in many of the human rights violations against Burmese women and girls.   Thai law enforcement officials routinely profit from non-enforcement of the law by extorting protection fees from brothel owners and subject trafficking victims to discriminatory and abusive treatment.

---

[28](...continued)
drawn into the sex trade.   Sukanya Hantrakul, "Prostitution in Thailand," paper presented at the Women in Asia Seminar Series, Monash University, Melbourne, July 22-24, 1983.
[29] Suppression of Prostitution Act, 1960, Sections 6, 9 and 10.

The Anand Panyarachun administration, installed in 1991, attempted to respond to the rising problem of forced and child prostitution. Most notably, Prime Minister Anand established an anti-prostitution task force within the Crime Suppression Division, a division of the Central Investigation Bureau that has jurisdiction over the entire country. Unfortunately, this task force has been plagued since its inception with problems of understaffing and inadequate funding. Responding to growing international and local pressure, Anand's successor, Chuan Leekpai, announced a stepped-up campaign against child and forced prostitution in November 1992, two months after his election.

Despite the highly publicized police crackdown on brothels under the Chuan administration, the trafficking of Burmese women and girls continues virtually unchecked. Although evidence exists that members of Thai police and border patrol forces are directly involved in the flesh trade, to our knowledge, none has ever been punished for trafficking or forced prostitution. Brothel owners, pimps and recruiters also have been largely exempt from punishment. The main targets of the Chuan administration's crackdown on forced and child prostitution have been the victims themselves; thus, the government's high profile "rescues" in reality have been arrests.

Since our investigation in 1993, the Thai government has made limited efforts toward legal reform. In July 1994 the Thai Cabinet approved a draft anti-prostitution bill that would increase penalties against procurers and brothel owners and, for the first time, punish clients who patronized a prostitute between fifteen and eighteen years old. The sanctions would be significantly harsher for clients of prostitutes under age fifteen. As of June 1995, this law had not been passed by parliament.

Trafficking in Women and Girls

Recruitment

The first phase of the illicit trade in Burmese women and girls is their recruitment and sale into brothels throughout Thailand. The actions of the recruiting agent and the brothel owners violate not only international norms against trafficking and forced labor, but, as noted above, also domestic Thai laws prohibiting trafficking and prostitution. Human Right Watch interviewed in-depth thirty women and girls from all over Burma, twenty-six of whom had been trafficked into Thailand through Mae Sai province in the northwest, one through Mae Sot, also in the northwest, and three through Ranong in the south. They ranged in age from twelve to twenty-two, with the average around seventeen; only four had been to school and could read and write in Burmese.[30]

The process of recruitment by agents working for brothel owners necessarily is covert because of laws restricting the freedom of Burmese citizens to leave their country and laws in both Thailand and Burma that criminalize prostitution. Brothel owners rely on a network of "small agents" and "big agents," acting in concert—and for a price—with Thai and Burmese officials to keep a steady supply of Burmese women and girls coming across the border. All but one of the women Human Rights Watch interviewed were lured from their homes on a promise of economic benefits. However, data from other sources, including police records, indicate that in Ranong in particular, the use of physical force is common.[31]

Only four of the twenty-nine who went to earn money knew that they were going to be prostitutes. Of the thirty women and girls, eleven had been brought into Thailand by family members. The network for finding work in Thailand appears to be well-known in the rural areas of Burma. Of the remaining nineteen women and girls, eight were recruited by women returning from brothels, who usually believe their escape is contingent on their ability to find successors.

In most cases, the girl, accompanied by a parent, brother, aunt, friend or teacher, met the agent on the Thai side of the border, where the agent gave the girl's companion a sum ranging from 1,000 to 20,000 baht (US$40 to US$800). The terms of the payment were never explained to the girl herself. It only became clear once she was in the brothel that the owner regarded the payment as a loan, with interest, against future earnings that she must repay.

Even before they reached the brothels, the Burmese women and girls were subjected to sexual abuse, including rape. In general, rape during recruitment may be discouraged by the fact that virginity increases the value of the women and girls. Of our thirty interviewees, three reported being raped en route to the brothel. "Chit Chit" told us:

---

[30] We received documentation on additional cases from Ranong area in the Southern area from other nongovernmental organizations.

[31] For example, in June 1991 police from the Crime Suppression Division raided a brothel in Ranong and "rescued" twenty-five women, most of them Burmese. Two of the women were sisters who, intending to go shopping, had hired a motorcycle to take them to the Ranong market. The motorcycle driver abducted the two and sold them to a brothel. According to a police report filed by the girls' uncle, they were forced to work and threatened with death by the pimps if they tried to escape.

When she left her village in Taichelek in 1990 at the age of eighteen she was taken directly to a policeman named Bu Muad, in Mae Sai, who himself was a brothel agent. He gave her 10,000 baht (US$400) and drove with "Chit Chit" and another woman from the same village to Chiangrai in a police van. Another agent drove the truck. The two women stayed for eleven days with the policeman and his wife. While they were in Chiangrai, the policeman raped "Chit Chit" while his wife and the other women were away at the market. He warned her that if she ever told anyone, he would beat her. According to "Chit Chit," this policeman was a regular visitor to the brothel in Chiangmai, beating girls for the owner if they did not cooperate or were recalcitrant in any way.

The initial destinations of trafficking victims rarely are final. While some women stay in one brothel for a year or more, many of those interviewed were frequently moved around by the owners. One woman was moved to four different brothels over an approximately ten-month period.

The Brothel

Although brothels are illegal in Thailand, they continue to flourish. Brothels vary from seven or eight girls in the back of a noodle shop to a multi-story building with over a hundred workers. Brothel owners use a combination of threats, force, debt bondage and illegal confinement to control the women and girls, force them to work in deplorable conditions, and eliminate any possibility of negotiation or escape. Those women and girls seeking to flee legitimately fear capture and punishment by the owners or agents, arrest for illegal immigration or prostitution, or abduction and resale to another brothel owner.

Despite international legal prohibitions against debt bondage, every Burmese woman and girl we interviewed reported this abuse. For most of the interviewees, their debt appeared to consist of the initial amount their families or companions received from the agents, plus transport, protection money or payoffs to police and other officials, and any advances provided for clothing or other personal items. The money given by the agent typically was doubled by the brothel owner to include "interest." Many of those interviewed had no idea how much money was exchanged and as a consequence had no idea how much they owed. In addition, some women never knew how much they earned, how much they were supposed to earn, or what were the terms for repayment of the debt.

"Tar Tar" knew that the going rate in her brothel in Bangkok was 110 baht (US$4.40) per hour. She was told by the other women in the brothel that her share was 30 percent, or thirty-six baht, plus any tips. "Tar Tar" figured of the thirty-six baht, half went toward payment of her original cash advance, which was 10,000 baht (US$400, doubled to include interest), and half was ostensibly for rent and food, so "Tar Tar" was never actually able to keep any of it. The owner gave her and the other workers thirty baht a day to buy food, but this amount also was deducted from her earnings. She assumed that she and the owner would settle the accounts at the end of the year.

Some of the women had a vague understanding that they would have to work for a specific length of time to pay off the debt. The women and girls were never told the terms of their debts, which differed for every worker. Further, no consistent share of the customers' payments accrued to the workers within a brothel; often, they were permitted to keep only the tips. They simply waited to be told that their debts were paid and hoped they would have extra money saved from tips to pay for their transportation home. The Burmese women and girls we interviewed were determined to pay off their debts as quickly as possible, knowing it was the only way to get home.

"Yin Yin" was told by the brothel owner that she could go home after 1,000 clients. Most of her clients were police, soldiers, border patrol and other men in uniform as the brothel was located in Borai (along the Thai-Cambodian border). "Yin Yin" worked hard and served 1,000 clients in three months. She saved about 3,000 baht (US$140) in tips. Then the agent told her that her mother had taken another 5,000 baht (US$200) from the agent. As a result, "Yin Yin" believed that she was in debt again, even though she had no way of knowing whether her mother really did take more money, and no idea what to do if the owner was lying. The owner then transferred her to another brothel where she had to work for another six to seven months before she was arrested.

The debt bondage of the Burmese women and girls is enforced by their near-total confinement to the brothel premises. According to sources interviewed in Bangkok and Chiangmai, Burmese women and girls were not allowed to leave the brothel or its immediate surroundings without escorts. The brothel owner often reminded the women and girls of the extent of his network and the support of the police who could trace the women if they left before their debts were paid. With few exceptions, the Burmese were unable to communicate with anyone outside of the brothel and its clients. In many cases, telephone and mail communication were banned by the brothel owners. For example, "Kyi Kyi," who worked in the Old Victoria brothel in Ranong for three years, said she was beaten whenever she tried to listen to the BBC or send letters through clients.

The primary concern of every Burmese woman and girl we interviewed was to avoid arrest, detention and deportation as an illegal immigrant. Those interviewed claimed their fears were constantly exploited by the brothel owners, agents and pimps. They were told of the terrible conditions in the Thai immigration jails, abuse during deportations, and frequent arrests by Burmese officials upon return to Burma. The Burmese women and girls believed that only the owner and his network, which included the police, could get them home safely. It should be noted that unlike brothel owners in Bangkok who played on the women's and girls' fears to keep them under control, brothel owners in Ranong reportedly used armed force and other instruments of physical control.

This combination of debt bondage and illegal confinement renders the employment of the Burmese women and girls tantamount to forced labor, which is prohibited under international law and the Thai Constitution.[32]

In large measure, the brothel owners profit from the repeated rape and sexual assault of the Burmese women and girls, sometimes over long periods of time. Because refusal to service clients often results in beatings, warnings about punishment for defaulting on the debt, or threats of arrest as illegal immigrants, the women cannot be considered willing participants in the sexual intercourse that occurs within the brothels. Yet, Thai legal prohibitions against rape and sexual assault have been rarely, if ever, enforced by the Thai government against the attacks that take place within the brothels.[33]

Many of the Burmese women and girls talked at great length about losing their virginity by rape in the brothels. Those who had been in a brothel for years still spoke in detail about their first days there, how they tried to resist, the force used against them, how much it hurt, and how they could not stop crying.

"Myo Myo" had been in the brothel for five days when she had to take her first client, a Thai who paid 1,500 baht (US$60) for her virginity. She tried to escape, but the client slapped her and held her back. She finally ran out of the room. Two pimps and the owner came and caught her. All three beat her. Another Burmese there told her to be quiet and try to do as she

---

[32] Constitution of the Kingdom of Thailand, Section 31, December 22, 1978.
[33] Thai Penal Code, Section 276.

was told so she did not get killed. After that the owner beat "Myo Myo" often, and she said she had to agree to everything.

For girls fifteen years old or younger, the sexual intercourse they experience in the brothels always constitutes statutory rape under Thai law, and clients should be held accountable.[34] Brothel owners also are liable under the penal code for having assisted or facilitated the commission of this offense and should be punished for two-thirds of the penalty for statutory rape.[35]   In practice, however, the government's crackdown on child prostitution has not resulted in clients or brothel owners being prosecuted and punished for statutory rape.

The repeated threat or use of force by brothel owners to compel the women and girls to have sex with the clients not only renders them in some instances accomplices to rape or statutory rape, but in every single case constitutes a clear violation of the penal law prohibiting procurement for the purposes of prostitution.   This law not only penalizes the initial act of procurement, with or without force, but also punishes such procurement "to service the wanton desires of another . . .   irrespective of whether or not a number of such acts have been committed on different occasions."[36]

Nearly every Burmese women and girl interviewed had to work between ten and fourteen hours a day, with only a few days off each month during menstruation. Some interviewees explained that they could get time off only if they were very sick or sore, and they only dared to do so if absolutely necessary. Those interviewed had an average of ten clients a day (some with as many as twenty on weekends) with no power to negotiate who their clients were or what they did with them. The women and girls could also be hired out for the entire day or night if the client left a deposit and/or identification. They talked of feeling vulnerable and frightened when leaving the brothel with a client. However, because of the owner's fear that his girls could be stolen and sold elsewhere, he was usually careful about which clients he allowed to take the women or girls out of the brothel. Often it was only police officers and other law enforcement officials who were accorded this privilege.

Provision of health care in the brothels is sporadic at best, and in most cases nonexistent. In six of the nineteen different brothels where women we interviewed had worked, they reported routine contact with health care providers, but primarily this was to provide birth control and test for STDs,

---

[34] Ibid., Section 277.
[35] Ibid., Section 86.
[36] Ibid., Sections 282-283.

including AIDS. Most brothels had basic medications and creams available for their employees, frequently for a price. Serious illnesses usually went untreated.

All of the women and girls we interviewed were provided contraceptives by the brothel owners; it was clearly in the owners' interest to ensure that their workers did not get pregnant. The women and girls themselves appeared to have no choice of which contraceptive they would be given, nor did they understand how the contraceptives worked. None of the women and girls we interviewed had become pregnant.[37]

Many were more likely to contract HIV than to become pregnant. Nineteen of the thirty women and girls we interviewed had been tested for HIV. Of these, fourteen were found to be HIV positive. Since most, if not all, of the women and girls had come to Thailand as virgins, they were most likely infected by their clients.

Public health officials have distributed condoms to brothels throughout Thailand, usually free of charge. The women and girls interviewed said that condoms were often given to the client, with their price included in the rate. None reported any insistence by the brothel owners on condom use; the choice was entirely up to the client. The women and girls themselves did not know about AIDS or the benefits of condom use while in the brothel. Those interviewed also said that using condoms was often too painful because of the additional friction condoms caused, especially when they had to service a minimum of seven or eight men a night. The Thai Penal Code provides that whosoever by negligence "causes bodily or mental harm to another person shall be punished with imprisonment not exceeding one month or 1,000 baht or both."[38] Brothel owners are in a position to prevent the "mental and bodily harm" from both the forced prostitution and the resulting exposure of trafficking victims to the AIDS virus, and they should be held criminally negligent for failing to do so.

The Role of the Thai Government
Our investigation revealed official involvement in every stage of the trafficking process, yet the Thai authorities have made little concerted effort to investigate and punish abuse by their own agents. While the abusers have

---

[37] However, this appeared to be less true in Ranong. In July 1993 a highly publicized raid in Ranong led to the "rescue" of 148 Burmese women and girls. Twenty of them were found to be pregnant.

[38] Thai Penal Code, Section 390.

enjoyed near-impunity, the victims have met with the full force of the law. The Thai government, rather than "rescuing" the women and girls as pledged, is in fact wrongfully arresting them, either as prostitutes or as illegal immigrants. Where the Burmese women and girls are concerned, this unlawful arrest inevitably leads to their summary deportation and a range of additional abuses in violation of both international and domestic law.

Official Involvement
            Procurement and trafficking for the purposes of forced prostitution are not only widespread in Thailand, but in many instances occur with the direct involvement of the Thai police or border guards. It is extremely difficult for Burmese to cross the border and travel any distance without the knowledge and involvement of the Thai police. Ten of our thirty interviewees were willing and able to identify police who had been involved in transporting them from the Thai-Burmese border into northern Thailand or directly to a brothel. The situation in Ranong is particularly alarming because of the large extent to which the local police and government authorities condone and at times collaborate in the systematic abuse of Burmese women and girls. For example, a Ranong merchant stated that "anyone who hopes to win a seat as Ranong's [member of parliament] must publicly announce a clear policy supporting border trade . . . and that means easing restrictions on illegal migrant labor, and on foreign prostitutes."[39]
            Police involvement in forced prostitution persists after the women and girls are in the brothel. Brothels routinely operate with police knowledge and police protection. On July 26, 1993, the Crime Suppression Division of the police force raided houses suspected to be brothels in Bangkok. The police found account books listing protection payments to Thai government officials.[40] Fifty percent of the Burmese women and girls we interviewed reported having police as clients. Of these, most told of special privileges the police received from brothel owners. For instance, "Aye Aye" told Human Rights Watch that police came often to her at the Dao Kanong brothel in Bangkok where she worked. They usually came in uniform in groups of two to five men and were very friendly with the owner. The police were the only ones allowed to take girls out of the brothel, and they never had to pay. "Aye

[39] "Ranong's 'Constructive Engagement' Poses Big Dilemma," *Bangkok Post,* September 13, 1992.
[40] "89 Suspected Call-girls Arrested," *The Nation,* July 28, 1993.

Aye" had to go out with policemen on two occasions. Both times the men were in full uniform with walkie-talkies and guns.

Once a woman or girl is arrested, local police frequently allow brothel owners access to her in custody. Several of our interviewees had been arrested previously by local police and returned to the brothel after the owner paid their fine. The amount paid by the brothel owner was then added to their debts and increased their bondage.

Another example of the depth of official involvement in protecting the brothel owners' interests was the widely-reported murder in Songkhla province of Passawara Samrit, a Thai woman from Chiangmai, who had apparently been forced into prostitution. Her murder was discovered on November 2, 1992, the same day that Prime Minister Chuan Leekpai announced his crackdown on child prostitution. According to witnesses, Passawara was threatened by police and the brothel owner, after the brothel owner discovered her escape plans. Passawara fled to a provincial hospital for protection, but the staff turned her over to the welfare office which planned to turn her over to the police. The next morning she was found dead in the bathroom. The official investigation revealed that two police officers to whom Passawara initially turned for help had tried to convince her to return to the brothel and work off her "debt." They reportedly threatened to arrest her for prostitution if she did not return to the brothel. The Songkhla police investigating the murder announced six murder suspects, including two police officers and two provincial officers. In late December 1993 four of the suspects were sentenced for Passawara's murder; the two police officers received the death penalty.[41]

Following the investigation, twenty Songkhla policemen reportedly were transferred but were not charged with any crime. Another sergeant was charged with accepting bribes from the brothel owner. In January 1993 Assistant Police Chief Pracha Prommok warned that any "policemen discovered taking kickbacks will face tough and punitive action."[42] However, with the exception of the Passawara Samrit case, not a single Thai police officer has been charged or prosecuted for prostitution-related crimes. In a September 1993 interview, Prime Minister Chuan acknowledged that government officials continued to be negligent in suppressing prostitution;[43]

---

[41] "Four Receive Sentences for Thai Prostitute's Murder," United Press International, December 31, 1993.

[42] "Chavalit Wants All Brothels Closed," *The Nation*, January 30, 1993.

[43] "Chuan Declares All-Out War on Child Prostitution," *The Nation*, September 28, 1993.

at the same time Police Maj. Bancha Netinan indicated that the police department was "cracking down on staff involvement of the flesh trade."[44] Netinan told reporters that 302 inactive positions had been created for police officials involved in prostitution.   While any effort to curtail official involvement in child and forced prostitution is welcome, Human Rights Watch believes that transfers cannot substitute for prosecution and punishment.

Failure to Enforce Laws

A pattern of impunity also applies to brothel owners, pimps and recruiters whom the Thai police and courts have largely exempted from arrest or punishment. Several of the known brothel raids occurring in 1991, 1992 and early 1993 did involve the arrest of pimps and brothel owners, but these efforts have been extremely limited. Impunity for all but the women appears to be the rule rather than the exception. For example, a July 8, 1993 raid in the Muang district of Kanchanaburi province involved the arrest of thirty-two Burmese women and girls, but the pimps and the brothel owner escaped.[45]

When the police arrest agents, pimps or brothel owners, they are routinely charged under the Suppression of Prostitution Act, which carries lesser penalties than those provided under the Penal Code. In two interviews in 1993, one with Human Rights Watch and one with the press, Police Col. Surasak Suttharom, deputy commander of the Crime Suppression Division, explained that not only did the current laws contain many loopholes for the brothel owners, but the judicial system has not prosecuted brothel owners vigorously and has fined them rather than give jail sentences.

Brothel owners not only escape punishment for procurement and brothel operations, but also for the range of abuses committed in the course of these illicit practices. To our knowledge not a single brothel owner has been investigated or punished for debt bondage, illegal confinement, forced labor or criminal negligence. Similarly, neither clients who engage in the statutory rape, nor the brothel owners who aid and abet them, have been sanctioned, despite the clear prohibition in the penal code on sex with girls under age fifteen.

Discriminatory and Arbitrary Arrest of Trafficking Victims

Whereas the Chuan administration has failed to arrest the largely male state agents, brothel owners, pimps, recruiters and clients involved in forced

---

[44] Ibid.
[45] "Police Save 79 Burmese Women from Five Brothels," *The Nation*, July 9, 1993.

prostitution, it has engaged in a routine practice of arresting the female victims. This discriminatory arrest pattern constitutes a violation of the Thai government's obligations under CEDAW, which Thailand ratified in August 1985, to "accord to women equality with men before the law."[46]

To some extent, this discrimination is embedded in the Suppression of Prostitution Act, which penalizes prostitutes, who are predominantly female, but exempts their male clients from sanction. However, even when the law is neutral on its face, as in provisions that penalize both prostitution and procurement, it is applied by the Thai authorities in a discriminatory manner that directly contradicts both domestic and international law. Thailand's Anti-Trafficking Act explicitly exempts trafficking victims, while the Trafficking Convention calls on states to make "suitable provisions for [trafficking victims'] temporary care and maintenance."[47] The Anti-Trafficking Act also requires Thai authorities to arrange and pay for the victims' repatriation to their country of origin, a provision that is consistent with the Trafficking Convention. Thai authorities, however, routinely ignore this requirement as well.

Violations of Due Process

The arrest of the Burmese women and girls is not only discriminatory and without legal justification, but frequently violates basic principles of due process as provided in international treaties and Thailand's Code of Criminal Procedure.[48] In the case of the Burmese women and girls, principles of due process appear to be honored more in the breach than in their observance.

The Crime Suppression Division and local police officers seem unable to establish a consistent rationale for arrests and, according to our research, often conduct them without warrant. Those arrested in police raids are taken to local police stations. Some are subsequently released to nongovernmental shelters, but the majority are taken to police lockups. The Burmese women and girls we interviewed reported major inconsistencies in the procedures followed by the authorities with regard to where and how they were detained;

---

[46] CEDAW, Articles 2 and 15.

[47] Trafficking Convention, Article 19.

[48] Thailand has not yet acceded to the ICCPR, but its provisions, like those in the U.N. Body of Principles for the Protection of All Persons under Any Form of Detention or Imprisonment, establish an internationally recognized framework for due process protection.

if and how they were charged; if they were tried; the fine and length of sentence; and the procedure followed for their release or deportation.

Many of the women and girls said that once arrested they were not informed of the charges against them. In some instances, our interviewees told us that they were routinely asked questions in Thai, which they did not understand. Often the women and girls were given papers to sign, in Thai, which they could not read. And not a single woman or girl we interviewed reported being given an opportunity to explain before a judge or authority how she came to Thailand, what abuses she suffered in the brothels, or what she might have to fear in returning to Burma. These actions and omissions are in violation of due process protections set forth in the ICCPR and the Body of Principles.

Prolonged Detention
In addition to the requirements under the U.N. Body of Principles for the Protection of All Persons under Any Form of Detention or Imprisonment, both the Thai Code of Criminal Procedure and the Immigration Act prohibit the holding of detainees for over forty-eight hours, unless necessitated by the investigation or other exigencies. Under no circumstance is detention for over seven days allowed without permission from the court. The Suppression of Prostitution Act further requires that persons charged with prostitution be tried in a court of law. Despite these requirements, most of the women and girls we interviewed had suffered prolonged detention, often in abusive conditions, for several days and, in some cases, months without any judicial hearing or access to legal counsel. Those in the penal reform institution, Pakkret, had been there for one to six months without being charged, appearing before a judge, or having the benefit of counsel.

Our extremely restricted access to the local jails and to Pakkret made it hard to determine whether Burmese women and girls arrested on charges of prostitution were tried properly before being detained or sent to reform institutions. For those Burmese women and girls arrested under the Immigration Act, the requirements for trial and judicial oversight also appeared to be minimal. The Immigration Act provides that an alien who is found to have engaged in prostitution can be deported. No trial is required, although aliens in this category have the right to appeal, with the exception of those who entered the country without a passport or visa.[49] To our knowledge, Burmese women and girls trafficked to Thailand, often with official

---

[49] Immigration Act of 1979, Section 22.

complicity, do not have valid travel documents and have not been able to exercise their right to appeal.[50]

The detention of those held in the Immigration Detention Center (IDC) is often prolonged arbitrarily by the fact that illegal Burmese immigrants rarely have the resources to pay fines and for transportation to the border. Thus, they must stay in the IDC to pay off the expense by working at the IDC at a rate of seventy baht a day.

In addition to the fines and deportation costs, IDC detainees can be forced to pay numerous "fees" to move their papers through the bureaucracy. Although NGOs try to help by paying transport costs to the point of deportation, it often happens that the more the detainees pay, the more the officials demand from them. There are many women and girls in the IDC whose "fines" and transportation costs are negotiated and paid by brothel owners, who then have the women released to them by the police.

Custodial Abuse

In the course of their detention in the various institutions, the Burmese women and girls uniformly reported custodial abuse, ill-treatment and abusive prison conditions, with conditions varying depending on the institution. The Burmese women and girls who were taken to local jails and to the IDC reported being held in overcrowded cells and subjected to sexual abuse by the police. Conditions at the IDC, in particular, fall far short of the U.N. Standard Minimum Rules for the Treatment of Prisoners. The IDC is severely overcrowded; with the exception of a few beds in the women's cell reserved for "room leaders" (women used by immigration officers to control other detainees), all detainees sleep on the floor so close together that they cannot roll over. The hygienic facilities are limited and few supplies are available unless brought from the outside. From the day the women and girls were detained at the IDC until the day they are deported, they were not allowed to leave the room.

An extensive underworld run by the room leaders pervades the IDC. The room leaders, themselves illegal immigrants, are extremely powerful and feared. They reportedly have a collaborative relationship with the officials to

---

[50] Again, without free access to the local jails or the Immigration Detention Center (IDC) in Bangkok it is difficult to state this with certainty.

handle the necessary transportation fees and other business transactions.[51] Although we do not have direct evidence, many of the women and girls we interviewed told us that prostitution inside the detention center is common.

There were also frequent reports of sexual abuse and beatings by immigration officers, guards and police associated with the IDC. "Muyar" told us she was taken out of her cell with about twenty other women and girls to be fingerprinted. Two Burmese and one Chinese girl were taken aside and in front of others, several policemen grabbed their breasts and touched their bodies. They did this while calling out the names of the other girls and women who were to come forward. If they hesitated, they would be hit hard with a stick. To our knowledge, there are no female guards or officers assigned to the women's cell.

Most of the women we interviewed had been detained at Pakkret, which they referred to as a prison. Communications with the outside world from Pakkret were extremely limited and always monitored. "Tar Tar," a former inmate, told us that all the mail coming in or going out was opened, and that detainees were not allowed to use the phone. Disciplinary measures included public humiliation and/or beatings. "Tar Tar" also reported witnessing a warden returning girls to the brothel owner. One of the most disturbing elements of the reports of arbitrary detention, poor conditions and ill-treatment in Pakkret is that Thai authorities have blocked all outside efforts to investigate or monitor conditions there. NGOs simply are denied access.

Summary Deportation

Both Thai law and international anti-trafficking norms establish mechanisms by which trafficking victims can return to their countries of origin without any menace of penalty from either government. But summary deportation has been the rule, and the process is as corrupt and abusive as every other aspect of the Burmese women's and girls' ordeal in Thailand.

Under the Immigration Act, illegal immigrants are responsible for paying their own transportation expenses to the border for deportation.[52] The wording of the law suggests they have some choice regarding the point of deportation, if they are willing to pay their transportation expenses. Burmese

---

[51] The room leaders in the women's cells appeared to receive contraband in exchange for collaboration with officials: they were well-dressed, with fancy hair barrettes, make-up and fingernail polish. Business transactions include purchasing of coffee, food and drugs as well as selling and buying of release papers among inmates.

[52] Immigration Act of 1979, Section 56.

generally want to return to minority-controlled or disputed territories in war zones to avoid capture by the SLORC authorities, and they are willing to pay exorbitant fees to be taken to such areas.

Women and girls from brothels in the Ranong area who were arrested as illegal immigrants but not brought to the IDC in Bangkok had no choice about where they were deported—they went straight into the arms of SLORC officials in Kawthaung in Burma. On July 14, 1993, raids in Ranong resulted in the arrest of 148 Burmese girls and women, of whom fifty-eight were reportedly returned to SLORC officials in Kawthaung. According to reliable sources in Kawthaung, the women were sentenced to three years in prison for illegally leaving Burma. The remaining ninety women are believed to be back in Ranong after brothel owners negotiated their fines with the Thai authorities.

Most IDC detainees preferred to be deported through Kanchanaburi Province, because the Thai-Burmese border there is controlled mostly by minority militia who generally are helpful to the deportees. Nevertheless, even deportation from Kanchanaburi is marked by such chaos, extortion and fear that women and girls were often tempted to succumb to pressure to take offers for work in Thailand, even knowing that such jobs will most likely return them to the brothels, rather than proceed into Burma.

Prior to deportation the deportees remained in the Kanchanaburi immigration jail for an average of seven days. This is the only province where deportees routinely are detained, and the Kanchanaburi immigration jail is known among the Burmese as the most abusive and corrupt jail along the border. Women and girls reported paying extra to be put into a cell together with male inmates for safety against harassment from Thai police and immigration officers. One Burmese male described the experience of a group of women who were held with him for eight days in the Kanchanaburi jail: Thai policemen came each night to the cell to call a woman or girl down to wash dishes, as a pretext for sex. Those who refused to go were hit; eventually they all had to go.

Women faced additional problems when they reached the deportation point, including abductions and solicitations from prostitution agents. In many cases, police officers themselves offered (for a price) to take the deportees back into Thailand. Since deportees rarely had money, they become dependent upon an agent willing to advance them the fee. This typically became the start of a new cycle of debt bondage.

If the deportees withstood the initial onslaught of brokers and began walking away, they realized over the next few days that they had little choice but to find some arrangement for work or at least transport back into Thailand.

Most deportees could not begin to find their way back into Burma on their own, due to the war along the border and often their own disorientation. For instance, "Maw Maw" was deported from the Kanchanaburi jail on January 27, 1993, after having stayed there one week. She was taken with a group of 120 deportees to Panang Htaw, an abandoned refugee camp. From there, the police pointed out the direction to the border and ordered the deportees to start walking. They were escorted by armed Thai uniformed soldiers. She said that ten other women had been deported with her. On the first day, seven of them left with people offering jobs around the deportation site. "Maw Maw" did not know what kind of jobs they had been promised.

Deportees delivered to Burmese authorities upon arrival in Burma reportedly were arrested on charges of illegal departure. In addition, since prostitution is illegal in Burma, Burmese women and girls who were suspected of having been prostitutes in Thailand also could have been charged with prostitution and given lengthy sentences. Although no official procedures are in place for monitoring the welfare of deported Burmese, consistent reports come back to Thailand of people, including deportees, being routinely arrested, detained, subjected to abuse and forced to serve as porters for the SLORC military.

The Thai government has on occasion recognized that no sound legal justification exists for arresting, detaining and summarily deporting the Burmese trafficking victims. For a brief period in 1992, rather than arresting and imprisoning the girls as illegal immigrants, then Cabinet Minister Saisuree Chutikul arranged for at least one group of ninety-five women and girls to be officially repatriated to Burma. But little information has been available on their status after their return. U Ye Myint, a Burmese Embassy spokesman, later claimed that forty-three of the returnees remained in Rangoon for medical treatment, as they were found to be HIV positive, while fifty-two were returned to their towns and villages.

Although the official repatriation process was problematic, in large part because it lacked an official effort to monitor the safety of the returned women and girls, it appeared to have enabled many of the women to return home safely. Yet, rather than improving this approach by establishing official repatriation procedures for trafficking victims, including mechanisms to monitor the welfare of the returnees, the Chuan administration appears to have abandoned it entirely.

Forced Prostitution and HIV/AIDS

For the majority of Burmese women and girls trafficked into forced prostitution in Thailand, the human rights abuses they experience will ultimately prove fatal. Of the nineteen Burmese woman and girls we interviewed who had been tested for HIV, fourteen were found to be infected with the virus that causes AIDS.[53] In our view, the high rate is directly attributable to the Thai government's abdication of its obligation to protect the Burmese women and girls against forced prostitution and related abuses, and the government's failure to investigate and prosecute the abusers, including Thai officials.

Awareness of AIDS among potential customers has driven the Thai sex industry to recruit more and more young girls from remote villages perceived to be untouched by the AIDS pandemic. Young girls, sometimes only thirteen or fourteen years old, may be particularly at risk for HIV infection. Not only are they often too intimidated even to attempt to negotiate the terms of sex, but preliminary medical research suggests that the younger the girl, the more susceptible she may be to HIV infection, for physiological reasons.[54] After the initial period when the women and girls are sold as virgins to just a few men, the number of customers multiplies, sometimes to as many as ten to fifteen a day, any of whom could be a source of infection. What emerges from our interviews is a pattern of transmission from male customers to young girls.

The Thai government has long been aware of the existence of illegal brothels, but has been slow to address the health risks to the women and girls within them. This delay is probably due to denial, since AIDS at first was perceived as a "foreigners' disease," and to a desire to protect the tourism industry, of which sex tourism is a major component. In fact, this denial continues as the Thai government's two-fold strategy for combatting AIDS—law enforcement and health intervention—for the most part targets

---

[53] In 1991 HIV infection trends among female prostitutes generally in Thailand was said to be 21.6 percent, according to World Health Organization, "AIDS/HIV Infection in Southeast Asia," November 7, 1992, p. 4.

[54] Because the mucous membrane of the genital tract in girls is not as thick as that of a grown women, medical researchers have hypothesized that it is a less efficient barrier to viruses. Moreover, young women may be less efficient than older women in producing mucous, which has an immune function. United Nations Development Program, "Young Women: Silence, Susceptibility and the HIV Epidemic" (undated) [hereinafter "Young Women"], pp. 3-4.

Burmese women and girls as illegal immigrants and sources of transmission, while largely exempting procurers, brothel owners, pimps and clients from punishment under the law.

It was not until February 1991, under then Prime Minister Anand, that the government began a serious and aggressive AIDS prevention and education campaign. Anand took several steps to control HIV/AIDS, including setting up a national AIDS Committee. Since the change in government in September 1992, however, the HIV/AIDS program appears to have stalled, and budget allocations for combatting AIDS have decreased.

The official Thai AIDS control and prevention program heavily emphasized condom promotion and distribution. But condom availability is irrelevant when the Burmese women and girls have no capacity to negotiate condom use or the number of customers.[55] Whereas their clients can choose to use condoms or to abstain from sex, the women and girls have no such choice: they are captive partners. Those who attempted to refuse customers often faced retaliation. Sometimes, the owners and pimps threatened them with physical harm or allowed the customers to do so.

"Kyi Kyi" worked every day and had at least four to five clients a day. If she did not agree to a client or his demands, she was beaten by the owner. She tried to escape in 1991, but the owner beat her with a very thick wooden stick. The owner told her if she tried to escape again, he would shoot her. He then took a pistol out and put it to her head and said, "Like this."

The refusal of the central government to enforce laws against trafficking and forced prostitution put local health officials in a difficult position. If they refused to enter the brothels, they may have knowingly contributed to the spread of a grave public hazard and failed to provide medical care to those in need. If they entered in their official capacities and declared the women and girls either "clean" or "infected," they would have appeared to legitimate an illegal industry. That provincial health authorities had to make the onerous choice between providing health care and exposing human rights abuses is intolerable. Absent genuine law enforcement, there is little incentive for health officials to report suspected abuse.

Our 1993 investigation indicated that not only has the Thai government failed to protect Burmese women and girls from human rights

---

[55] Moreover, condom use is a questionable strategy for women and girls in forced prostitution who are forced to have sex with many customers each day, because condom use often leads to friction sores which may facilitate viral transmission. See, generally, UNDP, "Young Women."

violations that render them vulnerable to HIV infection, it has inflicted additional abuses on them on account of their actual or perceived HIV status. Frequently, HIV testing was imposed on a mandatory basis, sometimes by public health officials, and without informed consent, on women and girls working in Thai brothels and, for a period in 1992, in detention at Pakkret. Mandatory testing without informed consent is condemned by the U.N. Human Rights Center and the World Health Organization[56] as an unjustifiable interference with the individual's basic right to privacy.[57] Governments may derogate from that right to protect public health, but only if three stringent conditions are met: mandatory testing must be required legally; serve a legitimate, urgent public purpose; and be strictly proportional to the benefit to society.[58] Mandatory testing of the Burmese women and girls failed to meet any of these conditions.

To begin with, Thai law does not authorize mandatory testing of prostitutes. In fact, Thailand's 1992-1996 National AIDS Plan includes human rights protection guidelines that explicitly rule out testing under any circumstances unless informed consent is given by the individual concerned or by her legal representative.[59] In addition, mandatory testing is neither strictly required nor effective; public health experts worldwide appear to have reached a consensus that mandatory HIV screening is not an effective method of slowing the spread of this infection and may even be counterproductive.[60] Finally, by opting to test on a compulsory basis all the Burmese who were "rescued" from brothels and placed in Pakkret and some women and girls in brothels, the Thai government has selected one of the most intrusive and least effective measures for AIDS control.

---

[56] United Nations Human Rights Center (UNHRC) and World Health Organization, *Report of an International Consultation on AIDS and Human Rights, Geneva, July 26-28, 1989* (New York: United Nations, 1991)[hereinafter *AIDS and Human Rights*], p. 55.

[57] Universal Declaration of Human Rights, Article 12.

[58] UNHRC and WHO, *AIDS and Human Rights*, p. 15.

[59] The only exceptions are military and police officials who have to enter combat situations or confront dangerous persons. In addition to the ban on compulsory testing, the human rights guidelines also require pre- and post-test confidentiality and strict confidentiality of medical records. National Economic and Social Development Board, AIDS Policy and Planning Coordination Bureau, Office of Prime Minister, "Thailand's 1992-1996 National AIDS Prevention Plan," 1992, p. 23.

[60] UNHRC and WHO, *AIDS and Human Rights*, p. 42.

Because implementation of the National AIDS Plan is not monitored carefully, forced HIV testing of women and girls in brothels without their informed consent depended on the inclination of the local authorities. For instance, "Chit Chit" was tested four times in her first brothel in Chiangmai. Then she was tested twice while in another brothel in Bangkok. After her arrest by a plainclothes policeman, she was tested again in Pakkret. She was not given the results of any of these tests. At the IDC, there was no systematic testing or treatment for sexually transmitted diseases nor for the HIV virus. However, when the women were sent for emergency health services it became routine practice to test for the HIV virus without informing the patients, requesting their consent, or informing them of the results. During government campaigns against child and forced prostitution in June and July 1992, approximately 150 Burmese women and girls were "rescued" and sent to Pakkret, where they were mandatorily tested for the HIV virus. Although they did receive AIDS information, the testing was done without pre- and post-test counseling.

After forcible testing, authorities subjected the Burmese women and girls to the further indignity of withholding their test results, even from those who, aware that they had been tested for HIV, requested to know their status. Even more troubling is that although the results were withheld from the women and girls, public health staff and, at times, government officials, had access to the medical records. Internationally accepted guidelines, as well as the Thai National AIDS Plan, emphasize confidentiality as an imperative ethical norm in dealing with HIV/AIDS. In addition, the Thai Penal Code holds   health   professionals   criminally   liable   for   breaching   patient confidentiality.[61]

In flagrant violation of these legal and ethical standards, Thai health officials consistently failed to hold the HIV test results in strictest confidence. It is particularly reprehensible that brothel owners who had repeatedly demonstrated their callous disregard for the women's health were sometimes given the test results. Brothel owners could exploit their knowledge of the women's HIV status in two ways: by maximizing profit from "clean girls" by charging higher prices for them, or by expelling those found to be infected.

Mandatory testing also resulted in de facto discrimination against prostitutes. The official policy for mandatory testing was determined by the goal to make female prostitutes safe for their clients. Yet, the customers, pimps, and brothel owners associated with the brothel from which the women

---

[61] Thai Penal Code, Section 323.

were "rescued" were not subjected to mandatory screening, even though male-to-female transmission is at least three times as efficient as female-to-male transmission.[62]   The different medical confidentiality standards that applied to prostitutes, versus men selected for national sentinel surveillance of HIV/AIDS, who were tested at clinics for sexually transmitted diseases, also had a disparate impact on women, who are the overwhelming majority of prostitutes.   Under the National AIDS Plan, men are tested on an unlinked confidential basis, providing the highest assurance of confidentiality, whereas the women's results frequently are revealed.[63]

In addition, Burmese women and girls received very limited information about the AIDS virus.   AIDS education for the Burmese would help them assert some control over their lives by informing their later decisions about marriage and children.   The Thai government thus far has failed to summon the necessary political will and financial resources to reach Burmese women and girls in closed brothels.   Our findings indicate that only a small percentage of the Burmese women and girls had any knowledge about HIV/AIDS.   Given the high rates of HIV infection among Burmese women and girls forced into prostitution, and Thai police complicity in protecting the trafficking rings, the Burmese deserved far more public health attention from the Thai government than they received.

The ordeal of the Burmese women and girls continued on the Burmese side of the border.   In addition to fears of punishment by SLORC for unauthorized emigration and involvement in prostitution, the returnees had reason to be concerned about persecution against persons with HIV or AIDS. According to a report by the Burmese Department of Health, some population groups in Burma are tested on a mandatory basis, including "Myanmar [Burmese] citizens returning from abroad."[64]

Burmese women and girls lured into Thailand for the purposes of prostitution face a wide range of violations of international human rights norms.   These abuses are perpetuated by the failure of the Thai government to meet its protection obligations under international law and to enforce its own

---

[62] Jonathan Mann, Daniel J.M. Tarantola, and Thomas W. Netter, eds., *AIDS in the World* (Cambridge, MA: Harvard University Press, 1992), Appendix 6.1A.

[63] In unlinked anonymous testing, the blood or saliva sample is identified by a number or other code rather than the name of the patient.

[64] Myanmar's Department of Health in collaboration with WHO, UNDP and UNICEF, "A Joint Review of Myanmar's Medium Term Plan for the Prevention and Control of AIDS," October 12-16, 1992, p. 4.

laws in an impartial and non-discriminatory manner. The Thai government punishes female trafficking victims while allowing the brothel owners, agents, pimps, clients and local officials involved in recruitment and brothel operations to go free.   While the stiffer penalties against traffickers and the criminalization of clients in the pending anti-prostitution bill are steps in the right direction, they will be only as effective as their enforcement. As this section highlights, the root of the problem lies not in the absence of legislation but in the lack of political will to enforce the law.

NEPALI WOMEN AND GIRLS TRAFFICKED TO INDIA

At least hundreds of thousands, and probably more than a million women and children are employed in Indian brothels.[65] Many are victims of the increasingly widespread practice of trafficking in persons across international borders. In India, a large percentage of these victims are women and girls from Nepal. While Nepalis are trafficked into many Indian cities, Human Rights Watch chose to focus on Bombay because it appears to have the highest concentration of Nepali girls and women in prostitution. In Bombay, according to the calculations of an organization of Nepali brothel staff,[66] there are about 20,000 Nepalis in the city's flesh trade; other agencies estimate that the actual number is closer to 50,000. Most of these women and girls work for Nepali *gharwalis* (madams), and almost all are illiterate. Seventy percent are thought to belong to ethnic minority groups such as the Tamang, Gurung, Magar, and Sherpa. Women and girls from Nepal's Hindu majority communities constitute about 10 to 15 percent. Twenty percent of Bombay's brothel population is thought to be girls under the age of eighteen, and at least half of them may be infected with HIV.[67]

---

[65] The following material was adapted from Human Rights Watch/Asia, *Rape for Profit: Trafficking of Nepali Girls and Women to India's Brothels* (New York: Human Rights Watch, 1995).

[66] Shodhak Sanyukta Nepali Satya Pidit Mahila Sangh (United Nepali Organization for the Relief of Suffering Women), an organization of Nepali brothel staff.

[67] According to press reports, the Indian government's Human Resource Development Ministry released a report in May 1994, based on a survey conducted in 1991-1992 in six Indian cities. The study found 70,000 to 100,000 sex workers, of whom 15 percent were under fifteen years of age when they entered prostitution; 25

(continued...)

Based on research conducted in Nepal and India in 1994, Human Rights Watch found that trafficking victims in India are subjected to conditions tantamount to slavery, and to serious physical abuse. Besides being held in debt bondage for years at a time, women and girls in the brothels suffered rape and other forms of torture, severe beatings, exposure to AIDS, and arbitrary confinement. Women and girls who manage to survive the system of debt bondage and return to Nepal face few choices. Some become recruiters to fulfill their owners' requirement that they find other girls to take their places. Women who escape the brothels before they have paid off their debts, who return without money, or who are sick and cannot work, are shunned by their families and communities. Many of these women will return to India for lack of other alternatives. Those lucky enough to have managed to earn money are more easily accepted back into their communities, and may eventually marry.[68]

Both the Indian and Nepali governments are complicit in the abuses against trafficking victims. In India, police and local officials protect brothel owners from police raids and traffickers, and both policemen and civilian officials patronize the brothels. Meanwhile, Nepali women and girls who complain to the Indian police about rape or abduction, or who are arrested in raids or for vagrancy, are held in detention euphemistically called "protective

---

[67](...continued)
percent were between sixteen and eighteen years. The study found that nearly 12 percent reported being tricked into entering the industry, and that 50 percent of all earnings went to brothel owners, pimps, police and local crime bosses. Most women surveyed reported being indebted for sums ranging from Rs. 10,000 to Rs. 15,000 (US$333 to US$500). Central Social Welfare Board, *Prostitution in Metropolitan Cities of India,* submitted to the Human Resource Development Ministry in August 1993, released May 1994, cited in *Pioneer* (Delhi), June 15, 1994; *Statesman* (Delhi), June 8, 1994; *Sunday Observer* (Delhi), October 3, 1993.

Although it is difficult to verify statistics on women in the sex trade in India (estimates range from hundreds of thousands to over ten million nationwide) it is clear the percentage of Nepali girls in Indian brothels is very high, that their numbers appear to be increasing, and that the average age at which they are recruited is significantly lower than it was ten years ago, dropping from fourteen to sixteen years in the 1980s to ten to fourteen years in 1994.

For HIV prevalence estimates, see Indian Health Organisation, "Tulasa and the Horrors of Child Prostitution" (Bombay: IHO, July 1993).

[68] However, the marriages rarely last longer than the money, and diseases contracted in the brothels have often left the women sterile.

custody."   In Nepal, traffickers similarly bribe border police to allow traffickers to transport women and girls into India.

Existing laws in both countries have had virtually no effect on curbing trafficking. While there has been some official acknowledgment in both India and Nepal of the magnitude of the problem, neither government has taken serious measures to stop trafficking. The burden of responsibility, however, rests primarily with India—to combat forced trafficking and to protect the women and girls whose rights are violated in its territory.

Profiting from Rape

In India's red-light districts, the demand is growing for Nepali women and girls as prostitutes, especially virgins with fair skin and Mongolian features. Nepali women and girls are largely segregated in brothels located in what are known to their Indian counterparts and their customers as "Nepali *kothas*" or compounds. The concentrations of Nepali prostitutes vary from city to city but appear to be highest in the Bombay neighborhood of Kamathipura. Brothels vary by size, physical configuration, ethnicity of sex workers, and price. But in all cases, movement outside the brothels is strictly controlled, and the sex workers are subjected to both physical and psychological abuse. The cheapest brothels, nothing more than dark, claustrophobic rooms with cloth dividers hung between the beds, are known among Nepalis as "pillow houses."

Most girls and women start out in these cheap brothels, where they are "broken in" through a process of rapes and beatings. They are then frequently resold to other brothels where they can bring in more money for the owner. Some women are also resold as punishment for escape attempts. About one-fifth of all Bombay's brothel workers, or approximately 20,000 women, work in squalid brothels like these on numbered lanes (or *gallis*) in Kamathipura. Certain lanes, like the 11th and the 13th, are known particularly as Nepali gallis.[69]   This segregation of Nepali girls and women exposes them to a wider range of clients, and a wider and more unpredictable range of sexual expectations, mistreatment, and sexually transmitted disease because many

---

[69] Some activists in Bombay's red-light districts believe that the auspicious number "7" in the building number, often attached to a neon sign saying, "Welcome," also signifies a Nepali kotha. Accordingly, this "welcome system" is designed to highlight the segregation that already exists and to attract customers with a special preference for Nepalis.

customers, both Indians and foreigners, seek out Nepali prostitutes for their "golden" skin and their reputation for sexual compliance.[70]

Brothels are big business. Despite expenses incurred in employing a network of agents to recruit new workers in Nepal (some procurers are reportedly paid up to Indian Rs.6,000, or US$200, per trip) and paying bribes weekly to police and local crime bosses (said to total Rs.200, or US$6.60, per brothel inmate per week), even the cheapest of brothels can turn a substantial profit, generally collecting from Rs.50-Rs.100 (US$1.66-US$3.33) per client, with much more for special services. A brothel may employ anywhere from four to fifty workers, and an inmate may serve more than fifteen clients a day, on an average of twenty-six to twenty-eight days a month.

The owner, who frequently owns more than one brothel, clearly stands to make a profit, but agents, local police and others involved in the industry also benefit. As one former prostitute told Human Rights Watch, "Police, doctors, *dalals* [agents or pimps], they are all fed by the brothels." In stark contrast, the Nepali women and girls earn extremely little, if anything. Most workers are allowed to keep only the tips from their clients, Rs. 2 to 5 (US$0.15 or less) per man. With these meager resources, they must cover their own expenses for food, clothing, and personal effects. The cost of medical care is typically paid by the owner and added to a woman's "debt."

The Women and Girls

The Nepali girls and women whom we interviewed were forcibly trafficked into India. They did not work as prostitutes voluntarily but were held in conditions tantamount to slavery. Promises of jobs and marriage are common techniques by which recruiters entice their victims to leave home. But some victims described other, more overtly coercive tactics such as kidnapping. Girls who are already in debt bondage in other industries, particularly carpet factories, are particularly vulnerable.

The following cases, based on interviews conducted by Human Rights Watch in March 1994 with young women in Nepal who had returned from

---

[70] Although tourism is an important industry in both countries, and sex tourism appears to be on the increase in India, tourism is less a factor in the sex industry than the local demand. All of the women Human Rights Watch interviewed reported that most of their customers were Indian. Some were also Nepali, although in at least one case Nepali customers were discouraged, for fear they would help Nepali girls escape.

Bombay, and in July 1994 with women still employed in Bombay's brothels, describe some of the patterns typical of forced trafficking from Nepal to India.

"Maya's" experience reflects a case of simple abduction.[71]   Maya is from a small village in Nuwakot district. She is twenty-three, but looks much older, with dark circles under her eyes, and dry, lined skin. She said she first left her village when she was eighteen and returned there in July 1993, after three years in an Indian brothel.

She was married at around thirteen. Soon after, her husband began seeing someone else. He moved out when Maya was sixteen, married a second wife and took her to Kathmandu. Maya had lived alone for two years when her father-in-law told her she should follow her husband to Kathmandu. At her husband's house she was beaten and treated very badly.

In 1990 a fellow villager began visiting the house. The second time he came to visit, he brought another man along. They invited Maya and her husband to come out to see a movie. Maya's husband told her to go ahead without him. The three of them boarded a bus, which Maya said kept going farther and farther from Kathmandu. Eventually, they went through the border at Kakarbhitta. They were never stopped or questioned by the police.

After two days traveling by bus, they reached Bombay and the men left Maya at a house and told her they would pick her up the next day. They never came back. Maya realized she was in a brothel when she saw that the house was occupied by about twenty-five women, all but three of whom were from Nepal. Two or three were girls she had known from her own village. The brothel where Maya worked was called a "pillow house." It was a large building, with several rooms where the women lived, slept and worked. There were eight beds in each room and curtains dividing the beds. All of the girls' and women's earnings were turned over to the brothel owner, a woman named Renu Tamang from Urleni in Nuwakot district. The women worked from noon to 1:00 a.m. They were given no days off. After a year, the owner told Maya that the broker had been paid for her and that she was responsible for paying back her purchase price, but she was never told how much she owed. The owner told her she could go home only after she paid off her debt. Maya noted that another brothel inmate, a woman from Trisuli, had worked there for thirteen years and had never managed to pay off her debt.

Maya was beaten severely for the first four or five days she was held in the brothel because she refused to have sex with customers. They continued

[71] The names of Nepali and Indian women and girls in the sex industry have been withheld by Human Rights Watch unless otherwise indicated.

to beat her until she submitted. Later on, she was battered with bottles and sticks because she was not earning enough. She said that all the brothel inmates were beaten if they did not earn enough. Her customers included Indians and foreigners—Germans, Singaporeans, Filipinos and Saudi Arabians. The customers would select the woman they wanted, and the women could not refuse, or they would be beaten.

In the three years Maya was held in the brothel, she never received any form of contraception. Girls who became pregnant would receive abortions. The brothel did not provide condoms, but occasionally customers brought their own. Maya said that she never asked clients to use condoms because she did not know they could prevent AIDS. Because she stayed in the brothel only a short time, she did not know the symptoms.

After one year in Bombay, Maya began to get sick. She developed a high fever and was taken to a doctor who gave her an injection, but she did not know what it was. She then returned to work. Maya told us that she and two other girls, one from Sindhupalchok who was sick, and one from Gorkha, decided to escape from the brothel. All of them had been beaten often and feared for their lives. Maya said that while some police officers often came as clients to the brothel, one branch of the police force frequently raided the brothel looking for child prostitutes. The three women appealed to these police to help them escape, and the police took them to the border and handed them over to the Hanuman Dhoka police station in Kathmandu. Maya was sent on to the police in Ranipowa and then Trisuli, where she was held in detention for ten days. From there it took her six days to reach Nuwakot. As Maya understood the police policy on returnees, the police inform the girl's family by letter and then hold her until the relatives come to collect her.

Maya and the two other women filed complaints at the Hanuman Dhoka police station in Kathmandu, and the police told them that they would be informed once the traffickers were found, but as far as she knows, no one was arrested.

Maya's health deteriorated after her return. She lost weight and suffered from diarrhea, high fevers and stomach aches. After returning to the village, her health improved slightly. In January 1994, she was treated with traditional medicine and felt that she had been cured, although she remained very tired and weak and could not work. Local health workers suspected Maya might not have escaped but rather was ejected from the brothel in India because she had contracted HIV.

"Tara," at thirty-four or thirty-five years old, is one of the oldest women in a brothel in Bombay. A local activist described her as the "in-charge" of the younger brothel inmates. Senior women like Tara are frequently used by gharwalis to keep track of newer inmates. Our interview with Tara was instructive because it reflected both her experiences as a young trafficking victim and her attitudes now, which are closer to those of brothel management.

Tara arrived in Bombay eighteen or nineteen years ago when she was sixteen years old. She told Human Rights Watch that she grew up in Nuwakot district and was trapped in prostitution when she went with two girlfriends to see the cigarette factories at Janakpur, on the Nepal/India border.

> We fell into the clutches of a *dalali* [agent]—a Nepali dalali at that. We were three girls together, in the beginning. We spent two years together, but then we were separated. When I was captured, I could not escape or return to my home: they would have caught me for sure. If I had known what was to happen to me, I would have killed myself halfway. [But] leaving this life is not an option for me, I simply cannot think about it. My purity was violated, so I thought: why go back, go back to what? I may as well just stay here. If I ever catch that damn dalali, I don't know what I would do to her.

Tara described her bewilderment upon arrival in Bombay.

> When they brought me here, it was in a taxi. Everywhere I looked, I saw curtained doorways and rooms in this area. Men would go and come through these curtained entrances. People on the street would be calling out, "Two rupees, two rupees." I asked the other Nepali women if these were offices; it seemed the logical explanation. In two days I knew everything. I cried.

The building in Bombay where Tara lives and works has two floors, and houses about fifty women. There are two *maliks* [bosses] for the building. She said that when she first came, there were mostly Nepali girls working there, and a Nepali gharwali. Now both Indians and Nepalis work together.

Despite the fact that Tara was herself an unwilling victim of the industry, she was caught in the system for nearly twenty years and is now a senior woman with management responsibilities. Her testimony, bitter when referring to the past or to women who have managed to escape, was generally sympathetic to her gharwali—with whom she probably shares a similar history. The fact that she has not attempted to return to Nepal or to open her own establishment suggests that she has not escaped the cycle of debt. According to Tara:

> Many girls return to their home area, build houses. Money is everything. It gets you acceptance in the village. There is no one in Nepal who does not know about Bombay and this business, not one person in Nepal. The gharwali is good to the girls and does not harm them. She makes the food arrangements, takes care of their needs. It is when a girl falls into the clutches of bad men, *goondas* [thugs], that she is defiled by them, and ill treated in many ways.

Tara's testimony reflects some of the most persistent myths of the trafficking industry: that all prostitution is voluntary and driven by economic hardship, and that many prostitutes become rich and return home. Brothel inmates report being coached to give stock answers to questions from investigators and curious customers, and oft-repeated success stories help keep inmates striving to earn money. "Santhi," a woman whose case is described below, told Human Rights Watch, "In the brothels we were told by the owner to tell the police we came by ourselves because we didn't have food. We were told to say we were twenty-five years old. If we didn't say that we would be beaten."

The Traffickers

Traffickers are most typically men in their twenties or thirties or women in their thirties and forties who have travelled the route to the city several times and know the hotels to stay in and the brokers to contact. Traffickers frequently work in groups of two or more. Male and female traffickers are sometimes referred to as dalals and dalalis [commission agents], who are either employed by a brothel owner directly or operate independently. Professional agents who recruit for the bigger brothels reportedly may be paid up to Rs.6,000 (US$200) per girl. But most traffickers are small-time, local recruiters who earn considerably less. In either case, to stay in business they need the patronage of local bosses and the protection afforded by bribes to the police.

Female traffickers are referred to as *didi* or *phupu didi* (literally, paternal aunt). In Nuwakot district, according to local activists, the majority of didis are returned prostitutes from five or six village development committees (VDCs) in eastern Nuwakot.[72] The peak trafficking months in Nuwakot and Sindhupalchowk are between June and late August or early September when the didis return to the villages to participate in local festivals and to recruit girls to bring back to the cities. These months precede the harvest, when poverty is felt most acutely, making it easy to recruit.

Family members—uncles, cousins, stepfathers—also act as trafficking agents. Of seven trafficking victims interviewed by Human Rights Watch in March 1994, six were trafficked to India with the help of close family friends or relatives. In each case, the victim complained of deception. According to a report by two concerned NGOs:

> Girls are recruited in a number of ways. Village girls and their families are often deceived by smartly dressed young men who arrive in the village claiming to have come from Kathmandu and offering marriage and all the comforts of modern urban life. They go through a local ceremony and leave the village never to be seen again. The girls end up in Indian brothels. Sometimes older men promise the girls employment in the city. Another avenue is through distant relatives or friends who pretend to arrange a marriage with relatives or friends in another village, but instead abduct the girl and send her to India. Sometimes a trusted individual abducts the girl on the pretext of educating her in India.[73]

---

[72] Nepal is divided into five development regions, fourteen zones and seventy-five districts. Under the *panchayat* system, these zones were administered by "zonal panchayats," which fed into the Rastriya Panchayat, but since 1990, zones no longer function as administrative units. Districts are broken down into subsectors called "village development committees," (VDCs) and "municipalities." There are 3,995 VDCs in Nepal and thirty-six municipalities. VDCs are the smallest local administrative unit. The village development committees of Betini, Bal Kumari, Sikharbeshi, Gyanphedi, Samundratar and Gaunkharka are noted as centers for trafficking. Urleni VDC is also the alleged home village for several brothel owners.

[73] Omar Sattur, Anti-Slavery International and Child Workers of Nepal Concerned Centre, *Child Labor in Nepal,* No. 13 (Kathmandu: ASI's Child Labour Series, 1993), p. 60.

Trafficking appears to be on the increase throughout Nepal, growing most rapidly in areas where it has so far received the least attention—towns and villages along the east-west highway, border towns, tourist centers, and according to some reports, the camps that house Bhutanese refugees in Jhapa district in eastern Nepal.[74]

Local women who have returned from India are also employed as recruiters. These women are exceptionally well placed to identify potential trafficking victims because they already know the local girls and their families. Women who are already in the sex trade and have graduated to the level of brothel keepers, managers or even owners travel through the villages of their own and neighboring districts in search of young girls.[75]

These local agents buy girls from their families, sometimes for as little as Nepali Rs.200 (US$4), or tempt them with promises of future earnings, and take them to the Indian border where they are sold to a broker or for anything from Indian Rs.1,000-Rs.8,000 (US$22-US$266). These middlemen then sell them to brothel owners in Bombay and elsewhere for Rs.15,000-Rs.50,000 (US$500-US$1,666), depending on the girl's age, beauty and virginity. This purchase price, plus interest (reported to be 10 percent of the total), becomes the "debt" that the women are told they must work to pay off through prostitution. Because only the brothel owner knows the terms of the debt, and most women and girls have no idea how much they owe or the terms for repayment, they often "pay back" indefinitely.

Carpet Factories

Carpets are Nepal's most important export and, along with tourism, one of its most essential industries. Besides being notorious in their own right

---

[74] Dr. Aruna Upreti of the Women's Rehabilitation Centre, a relief organization in Calcutta, told a journalist with the *Telegraph* in December 1993 that the number of Nepalis in Calcutta's brothels had doubled in the past year. She said that besides a large number of Tamang girls from Nepal's hill districts, Bhutanese girls from the refugee camps in eastern Nepal were arriving in India and that girls from the southern town of Butwal had been found in places as far away as Hong Kong. "Nepal Girl-runners Turn to City," *Telegraph*, December 1, 1993.

[75] Jyoti Sanghera, Federation Internationale Terre des Hommes, "Prevention of Traffic in Persons and the Exploitation of the Prostitution of Others; Trafficking and Sexploitation of Nepali Girl Children and Women in the Sex Industry," presentation at the session of the U.N. Working Group on Contemporary Forms of Slavery, Geneva, July 29 to August 2, 1991, p. 7.

for appalling working conditions, the pervasive use of child labor and debt bondage, Kathmandu carpet factories have been important recruitment centers for Indian brothels.[76]   Brokers working within the carpet factories select likely girls and entice them into leaving the factories with offers of better jobs elsewhere—a relatively easy task since many carpet workers are themselves caught in a state of debt bondage and receive no wages.   The brokers then arrange for their transport to India, frequently with the complicity of friends and   family   members.[77]   According   to   children's   rights   advocates, underground   brothels   sometime   operate   out   of   some   of   Nepal's   carpet factories.

[S]ome carpet factory brokers . . . roam in the villages to lure young girls to work in the carpet factories of Kathmandu where many of them are forced into prostitution and even trafficked to Bombay. These girls are abused and exploited by storekeepers, loom masters and checkers before they give up and agree to do the "night shifts."   And they sell themselves for Rs.20-50 (US$.40-US$1.00) per sex act. The customers are arranged by the pimps in the factory who take commissions from the girls. In Kathmandu's many garment factories, too, the girls do one kind of work during the day and another kind at night.[78]

"Neela's" experience demonstrates the link between the carpet industry and trafficking. In 1989 "Neela"s stepfather took her from their village in Sindhupalchowk to Bhaktapur, a suburb of Kathmandu, where a friend of his got her a job in a carpet factory. She was fourteen years old. A few months later, in January 1990, a young male co-worker who had been introduced to Neela as her "cousin" suggested that they leave the Bhaktapur factory and go to Kakarbhitta, a town on the Indian border, where, he claimed, working

[76] U.S. Department of Labor, *By the Sweat and Toil of Children: The Use of Child Labor in American Imports, A Report to the Committees on Appropriations, United States Congress*, July 15, 1994, pp. 119-122.   Between July and November 1994, Nepal's export of carpets dropped by 36 percent when sales to Germany, Nepal's largest importer, slowed after a television broadcast aroused public concern over the carpet industry's use of child labor. Child Workers In Nepal Concerned Centre (CWIN), a Kathmandu-based organization dedicated to the rights of children, reported in January 1995 that the use of child labor in the organized sector began to decrease as a result of international pressure.

[77] CWIN reported in 1994 that of 300 Nepali prostitutes interviewed in Bombay, 40 percent had been trafficked from carpet factories.

[78] Rupa Dita, "Child Prostitution in Nepal," *Voice of Child Workers*, Issue Numbers 15 and 16 (Kathmandu, December 1992), p. 57.

conditions were better and they could earn more money. Neela agreed and was taken out of the factory by her stepfather, her stepfather's friend and this young man. After traveling six days by bus and by train, they arrived in Bombay.

There, Neela was taken to the grounds of a temple where the men introduced her to two women. Neela went with the women to a house that she later discovered was the home of the brothel manager. She stayed there overnight. The next morning she was taken to another house where sixteen or seventeen girls were asleep on the floor. Because she was so young, Neela was taken to a separate "training" room where she was kept for three months, after which she was told she had been sold for Rs.15,000 (US$500) and would have to work there until she paid off her debt. Her first customer was a middle-aged man who paid Rs.5,000 (US$166) for her because she was a virgin. Neela said the manager always charged more money for new girls, but she was never told how much the regular customers paid; all the money was given directly to the owner. Nor was she told how long it would take to repay her debt.

As the youngest in the brothel, Neela received better treatment than many of the girls and women working there. She was not beaten, even when she was caught trying to escape one night by pretending to go to the toilet which was outside behind the brothel. However, she was insulted and threatened, and saw others frequently beaten severely, "until blood came from their mouths," for trying to escape and for fighting.

Many other girls in the brothel were under-age, and all were Nepali. Neela told Human Rights Watch that the brothel was frequently raided by police in search of under-age girls and that when the police came, the brothel owners would try to hide the newcomers, because "not all police were the same." Sometimes the same police who came in civil dress as paying customers and sought her out would raid the brothel later.

Neela said condoms were not available in the brothel where she worked, although customers sometimes brought their own. She never asked a customer to use a condom.

After about a year in the brothel, Neela was picked up in a police raid and taken to a shelter for children because she was under-age. In the shelter she tested positive for HIV. After two years at the shelter, when Neela was eighteen, the police offered to send her home. With her consent, the Indian police informed the Nepali police, and she was taken to Kathmandu. She was brought first to Hanuman Dhoka police station in Kathmandu, then to Bhaktapur police station, where she was held for eight days. During that time the police took her to Teku Hospital for what she later learned was an HIV test.[79]   Afterwards, she was told she had tested positive.   Neela said a journalist interviewed her while she was still in police custody and published her photo and story in a local paper.   Because she felt ashamed she decided not to try to locate her family and now lives in a shelter.

Fraudulent Marriage Offers

Fraudulent marriage offers are another common ruse of recruitment. In some cases, the traffickers actually go through a wedding ceremony.   In others, the marriage offer itself is enough to lure a woman away from home. A police officer in Butwal told Human Rights Watch that in 1989 he arrested a very handsome youth in Jhapa district in eastern Nepal who had trafficked nine girls to Bombay by marrying them.   He took each to Bombay and abandoned her in a crowd.   An accomplice would then approach the girl, offer to help her find the missing young man, and lead her to a brothel.   The following case is typical of this kind of deception.

"Sita," thirty-one, returned to Nepal from India in October 1993 after working for ten years in a Bombay brothel.   She is a high-caste Hindu from a small village in Tanahu District, near Pokhara.   She was married when she was fourteen.   After two years of marriage, she became pregnant, and her husband went to India in search of work.   Because her in-laws mistreated her, she returned to her parents' home.   In 1983, when she was twenty and her son was four, a neighbor commented that her husband had been gone a long time and probably was not coming back.   She told Sita that a man from India wanted to marry her if she was willing to remarry. Sita told her family she was going to the fields to work and went instead to meet the man with her son.

They caught a bus to Pokhara, the nearest town.   In Pokhara he offered Sita a cigarette.   She remembered very little after smoking the cigarette and thought she may have passed out.   Sita said she remembers boarding another bus and then waking up in a large room with three beds with curtains around them.   There were six or seven other women in the room.   She asked them where she was, but they replied in a language she did not understand.

The man who brought her there took Sita's son and said he would show him around town. They never returned.   Sita was frantic.   She wanted to go out and search for them, but the owner, a woman from eastern Nepal,

---

[79] The Nepal Ministry of Health's AIDS control program is located in Teku Hospital.

told her she had been sold to a brothel and could not leave. Sita did not see her son again.

She escaped to Nepal in October 1993 with the help of a Nepali vegetable seller she befriended in the brothel. Everyone in her village had thought she was dead. She now lives in her parents' home.

Abductions

To a lesser extent, some Nepali women are abducted outright. Several women we interviewed mentioned that they, or other women in the brothels where they worked, had been drugged by their abductors.

"Devi" was taken to India by two female neighbors, whom she knew quite well. They told her to go along with them to a market far from their village to pick up something. They travelled a long way and eventually arrived at a village. She was led to a room, and the door was locked. Devi had no idea where she was.

The two women who kidnapped her did not return. After three nights, another woman, called Nithu, made Devi travel with her to another town. Devi pleaded with her to let her go, but was told, "No, you have been sold and have to work. All Nepali girls have to work."

Devi was taken to a room where she saw five girls from Pokhara whom she knew and four others. She asked the other girls there to help her escape, and eight days later when the brothel owner found out, Devi was sold to another brothel. After three or four days she attempted to escape again, this time by appealing to a Nepali customer for help. Unfortunately, another girl in the brothel overheard her and informed the owner, and Devi was again sold late that night to a third brothel. There were under-age girls in all the brothels in which she worked. Devi was not told how much the first two owners paid for her. The last owner told her she had paid Rs.40,000 (US$1,333) for her and that she would have to work it off by taking customers.

"Kamala," twenty-six, returned to Nepal in September 1993 after spending nine years in India. She was given drugged milk and abducted by her stepfather's elder brother and his son while on a trip with them, and trafficked to India when she was seventeen. She woke up in a big hall with a lot of lights, which turned out to be a hotel lobby, but she does not know the name of the hotel.

Her cousin and uncle were with her. They told her that they needed to go to the bank and left her alone in the hotel lobby. While they were gone two men told her she had been sold. She started to cry in disbelief. They asked her if she could read, and they showed her a receipt for Rs.40,000.

When the men tried to put her in a taxi, she said she had to go to the toilet first. She locked herself in and would not come out. She hid in the toilet until about 4:00 a.m., then she slipped out of the hotel and escaped. She was taken in by a woman who lived in a nearby slum who got her a job as a domestic servant in the home of a couple who worked at a hospital. But, as is the case with many domestic workers in India, her employers "held" her salary for her so that when she left their service, she had no money. It took Kamala nine years working as a domestic servant in two different households to make her way back to Nepal.

Official Complicity
    Despite the fact that both Nepal and India have numerous laws criminalizing trafficking and prescribing severe penalties for abusers, trafficking in women and girls flourishes between the two countries. Human Rights Watch's investigation reveals the involvement of police and other government officials at various points along the trafficking routes, but there has been little effort on the part of either government to investigate charges of official complicity or to punish those responsible.
    Police demand bribes in order not to arrest traffickers and brothel owners, or are themselves involved in trafficking. Government officials protect traffickers who are politically influential. The Bharatiya Patita Udhar Sabha (Indian Association for the Rescue of Fallen Women), a voluntary organization dedicated to the welfare of the country's sex workers, in a 1993 letter to the union home minister alleged that police regularly extorted large sums of money—up to Rs. 26,000 (US$866) per day in Delhi alone—in red-light areas as protection money. The organization's president, Khairati Lal Bhola, charged that on a daily basis, the local police station received payoffs according to rank: a constable could expect Rs.25 (US$0.83), a head constable received Rs.40 (US$1.33), and an assistant sub-inspector (ASI) received Rs.80-Rs.100 (US$2.66-US$3.33). The group alleged that the station house officer (SHO) received Rs.500 (US$16.66) per month, and that the district special branch police, which addresses special categories of crimes, collected monthly payments of about Rs.300 (US$10) per kotha [brothel compound] of ten girls, and Rs.500 (US$16.66) for larger kothas.[80]

---

[80] *The Statesman*, (Delhi), August 30, 1993; *Pioneer*, (Delhi), December 30, 1993. Bharatiya Patita Udhar Sabha also charged that to set up a new brothel, large amounts of money ranging from Rs. 50,000 (US$1,666) and Rs.200,000 (US$6,666) had to be

(continued...)

In the case of recently trafficked girls and women, the organization alleged that police were involved in a fraudulent process called "registering" the victims, whereby a madam of a brothel would notify the police of the arrival of a new victim in her establishment and pay a bribe for their silence. A madam routinely paid between Rs.5000 and Rs.25,000 (US$166-US$833) to the police station depending on the price she paid for the woman. In the case of a minor, the police took their bribe from the madam, kept the girl for a day in a police lockup, and produced her in court the next day along with a falsified first information report (FIR) attesting to her adult status. This document protects the brothel owner from being charged in future with the prostitution of a minor. The under-age girl, falsely registered with the authorities as twenty-one years of age or older, would then be handed back to the madam. For this service, the madam paid the police Rs.500-Rs.1000 (US$16-US$33). In other cases, a girl would be given falsified papers and brought before the magistrate on a false charge of seduction in a public place, and handed back to the madam on payment of a fine of about Rs.1,000 (US$33) for her release. Thus, for a fee, the madam is assured of police collusion in keeping the trafficking victim captive, while the performance of a few legal routines protects the police from complaints of negligence.

The testimony of women interviewed by Human Rights Watch supported charges of police collusion with pimps and brothel owners to profit from the trafficking and arrest of minor girls. Based on interviews with women who worked in Bombay, the police there also appear to participate in "registration" or "licensing" charades similar to that described in Delhi's red-light areas.

Debt Bondage

In addition to international legal prohibition against debt bondage, Nepali and Indian laws also include similar injunctions. India enacted the Bonded Labour System (Abolition) Act in 1976 to outlaw all forms of bonded and slave labor. Article 374 of the Indian Penal Code further makes it a crime to unlawfully compel any person to labor against his or her will.

Every Nepali girl or woman with whom we spoke, however, said that the brothel owner or manager forced her to work by invoking her indebtedness. The supposed debt, along with threats and beatings, stood between her and the

---

[80](...continued)
paid to the police. The purchase of a new kotha of fifty or more inmates by a well-to-do owner required a police payoff as high as Rs.300,000 (US$10,000).

possibility of freedom. For most of the women interviewed, the debt was the amount of money that the brothel owner said he or she paid a broker when the girl was purchased, plus the costs of medical care, protection money or payoffs to police and local thugs, and 10 percent interest.

The Delhi-based welfare organization Bharatiya Patita Udhar Sabha charged in the above-mentioned 1993 letter to the union home minister that some madams in Delhi even compelled girls to sign forms stating that they were voluntarily working as maid servants or as bonded laborers until they repaid the loans they had purportedly taken. Although occasionally the gharwali may pay for food, clothes and medicine, these costs are frequently added to the debts. In any case, a girl's indebtedness to the gharwali is based on the gharwali's own expenses. For example, a gharwali who has paid Rs.15,000 (US$500) to purchase a girl, plus an additional Rs.5,000 (US$166) to the police so that she will not be arrested under the Immoral Traffic (Prevention) Act of 1986 (ITPA), would calculate the girl's "debt" at Rs. 20,000 (US$666), plus interest. The owners then take 100 percent of her earnings until that amount is paid off.

A woman's earnings depend on the type of brothel in which she is employed, her age and appearance, and the nature of the sex acts she is compelled to perform. Devi said that all the women and girls where she worked were dependent on tips for food to supplement the meager meals provided by the brothel. As a newcomer without regular customers, and an older woman at that, Devi received few tips. She told Human Rights Watch that although she was never allowed to handle any money in the "pillow houses" where she worked, she heard from other women that the owners charged Rs.30 (US$1) for five minutes. In the "bungalow"—common name for a fancier brothel—where she took the money from customers beforehand and turned it over to the management, the rate was Rs.110 (US$3.66), again for a very short time.

A villager in Nuwakot district who had travelled to Bombay several times told Human Rights Watch that in his experience a prostitute might have more than twenty-five customers a day, earning small tips of Rs.2-5 (US$0.05-US$0.15) from customers. Customers can also pay extra to take women outside.[81]

---

[81] In the evenings, informants described jeeps full of girls heading toward the suburbs of Bombay, en route to beer halls, restaurants, clubs, and hotels. Although the streets are lined with police, they rarely interfere.

A girl who has managed to escape, but finds that she has no way to support herself, may negotiate her return to a gharwali, resulting in a fifty-fifty division of her earnings. Sometimes the woman attaches herself to a local thug to support her in her negotiations with the gharwali. However, this type of an agreement frequently results in indebtedness of a different sort, since the girl is often convinced to take a loan from the gharwali to see herself through.

None of the Nepali girls or women we interviewed knew about the monetary arrangements between the brothel owner, the agents and their families. Because the women did not know how much money had been exchanged or how much they earned, they had no idea about the extent to which they were indebted. But all were frequently reminded that they had to work to pay off their debts, and many were threatened or beaten for not earning enough. We were told by both returnees from brothels and other people from their villages that there were rules in Bombay brothels about how long girls should work and how much they would be paid. Despite this persistent rumor, none of the girls with whom we spoke earned anything like the amounts typically mentioned, or knew anyone who had.

"Santhi" said she worked in three low-grade brothels or "pillow houses" and a "bungalow." In the pillow house she had fifteen to twenty customers a day and, except for regulars, customers paid Rs.15 (US$0.50) for five minutes. She also worked for four months in a bungalow that charged Rs.100-Rs.300 (US$3-US$10) per hour. Some customers would pay to take the girls out all night, or sometimes for days at a time. If they were taken out to a hotel they were paid at least Rs.1,000 (US$33). Although Santhi does not know how much she was originally sold for, she was told that each time she was sold it was for a higher price. None of the owners ever told her how much she had to repay, but the brothel managers kept track of how many customers each girl served per day and claimed to figure that against their debt. Santhi had heard there was a rule that the brothel can keep you three years, but after three years they have to give you Rs.20,000 (US$666), gold and clothes.[82] But they did not give her anything like that. Most of the money she brought out with her was her tips, and she managed to send a box of clothes to her father. After she was there seven years, her father came to

---

[82] A villager we interviewed in Sikharbeshi said he had heard that a women's group in Bombay has gotten agreement from brothel owners that after a girl has worked eight years, she should get Rs.20,000 (US$666), a box of clothes, and a certain amount of gold. Within those first eight years all the money is taken by the gharwali. If she goes back after eight years the money is supposed to be split fifty-fifty with the gharwali.

see her, but the owner said she had to stay another two years before she could leave. After two more years, her father came to the brothel and brought her out. When she left the brothel she was given Rs.5,000 (US$166), which she turned over to her father.

Besides the money earned by parents from the sale of their daughters (a few hundred rupees if she is sold to a local recruiter, or several thousand if the family sells her directly to a broker), male relatives also make periodic trips to India to collect the girls' earnings. In Nepali villages in places like Nuwakot and Sindhupalchowk, which have several women in Bombay brothels, a prominent member of the village may be appointed to travel to India, collect the money they earn and bring it back to their parents. For the women and girls, this means that not only are they under pressure to pay off their debts to the brothel owners, but out of whatever earnings they do receive, primarily in tips, they are expected to help support their families.

Illegal Confinement

There are other aspects of the work in brothels which reinforce its non-voluntary nature, including illegal confinement.[83] The women and girls we interviewed explained that they would be beaten severely if they were caught trying to escape. Fear of the police also deters escape attempts. With few exceptions, the Nepali women are unable to communicate with anyone outside of the brothel, and some are even forbidden to go out with Nepali clients for fear that the latter might be likely to help the women escape. Even conversation with customers is sometimes forbidden. A villager in Nuwakot who was familiar with Bombay's brothels told Human Rights Watch, "Only girls who pay off their 'loan,' have gone on a holiday to their village and come back, are allowed to leave the brothel alone. Before that they are not allowed out alone."

In Sita's case, no one in the brothel was allowed to leave unescorted. Everything was brought by vendors into the brothel to sell: food, clothes, even videos. They were allowed no contact with their families. Sita, who could not read or write herself, said that none of the women in the brothel was permitted to write or to have pens and paper.

Applicable Indian and Nepali Law

Trafficking in human beings and the abuses associated with it are explicitly prohibited under many of India's domestic laws, including the Indian

---

[83] Article 9 of the ICCPR guarantees the right to liberty.

Constitution, specific anti-trafficking acts, the Indian Penal Code, and in state and local ordinances. The problem, therefore, lies not in absence of legal sanctions but in the lack of consistent enforcement.

The Indian Constitution specifically bans the traffic in persons. Article 23, in the Fundamental Rights section of the constitution, prohibits "traffic in human beings . . . and other similar forms of forced labour." Article 39 guarantees equal treatment of men and women and obligates the state to ensure "that the health and strength of workers, men and women . . . and children are not abused . . . and that children and youth are protected against exploitation . . ." Article 42 protects against inhumane working conditions.

The two principal Indian laws that address trafficking and prostitution in particular are the Suppression of Immoral Traffic in Women and Girls Act of 1956 (SITA) and the Immoral Traffic (Prevention) Act of 1986 (ITPA), colloquially called PITA, an amendment to SITA. Neither law prohibits prostitution per se, but both forbid commercialized vice and soliciting.[84] Aside from lack of enforcement, SITA is problematic in several ways. One of its chief drawbacks is that the prescribed penalties discriminate on the basis of sex: a prostitute, defined under SITA as always a woman, who is arrested for soliciting under SITA could be imprisoned for up to a year, but a pimp faces only three months.[85] SITA allowed prosecution of persons other than the prostitutes only if the persons involved "knowingly" or "willingly" made women engage in prostitution. Accordingly, pimps, brothel owners, madams,

---

[84] SITA, a penal law, was passed in 1956 and enforced in 1958 as a consequence of India's signing the Trafficking Convention, rather than as a result of any mass social welfare movement. SITA did not seek the "abolition of prostitutes and prostitution as such and to make it *per se* a criminal offence or punish a person because one prostitutes oneself." Its stated goal was "to inhibit or abolish commercialised vice, namely the traffic in persons for the purpose of prostitution as an organised means of living." Prostitution was defined as the act of a female who offers her body for promiscuous sexual intercourse for hire. Accordingly, the engagement by a woman in individual, voluntary, and independent prostitution was not an offense.

[85] The law permitted penalization of a woman found to be engaged in prostitution under certain conditions. For example, Section 7(i) penalized a woman found engaged in prostitution in or near a public place. Section 8(b) did the same for a woman found seducing or soliciting for purposes of prostitution. The law also permitted a magistrate to order the removal of a person engaged in prostitution from any place and to punish the person upon refusal. Offenses under SITA were bailable, but a woman picked up from the street by the police usually did not have either the money or the influence to keep herself out of custody or free from fines.

and procurers could feign ignorance of prostitution and escape punishment. The client, moreover, was not viewed as an offender and could not be sanctioned under SITA.[86] Finally, SITA only addressed street prostitution; prostitution behind closed doors was left alone—a loophole that actually promoted the establishment of brothels.

The Immoral Traffic (Prevention) Act of 1986 (ITPA)[87] amended the 1956 SITA in important ways. However, its basic goals and premises remain much the same as those of SITA.[88] Although prostitution as such is not prohibited under ITPA, this statute contains nine punishable offenses, including operating a brothel, abetting in brothel keeping, living off brothel earnings, procuring, detaining, activity in vicinity of public places, seducing or soliciting.[89] Ironically, ITPA does not authorize the police actually to close

---

[86] Indeed, clients sometimes were called as witnesses against women accused of prostitution. Police could arrest clients only by applying the indecent behavior and obscenity sections of local laws, or the Indian Penal Code. For example, Section 110B of the Bombay Police Act penalizes indecent behavior and allows for the arrest of pimps and prostitutes.

[87] The changes in the title of the act represented important conceptual as well as policy shifts, most importantly, the recognition of the range of victims was extended from women and girls to persons. Various other definitions were reworked in the 1986 act.   Prostitution, which had been "the act of a female offering her body for promiscuous sexual intercourse for hire," became "the sexual exploitation or abuse of persons for commercial purposes."   The shift in emphasis from promiscuity to exploitation was particularly significant, especially for Nepali women whose abuse was justified on the basis of their reputed "promiscuity."

[88] Many of the amendments ITPA made to the 1956 law endeavored to broaden the act to include both men and women as the exploited parties, and all parties involved in prostitution. But in some cases the amendments actually served to further discriminate against women in prostitution. For example, according to ITPA, whoever attempts to solicit "by words, gestures, wilful exposure of her person . . . for the purpose of prostitution," shall be subject to up to one year imprisonment (six months for a first offense) and a fine of up to Rs. 500 (US$16). But a 1986 amendment to the law adds that if the offense is committed by a man, the mandatory sentence ranges from only seven days to three months.

[89]   In the case of soliciting, women are subject to much longer terms of imprisonment than men found guilty of the same offense. Procurers of prostitutes or those found guilty of inducing someone to undertake prostitution are subject to a prison sentence of three to seven years and a fine of Rs.2,000 (US$66); a second conviction carries a mandatory prison sentence of seven to fourteen years. A first conviction for
(continued...)

brothels.[90] Unlike SITA, ITPA recognizes that men and children can also be sexually exploited for commercial purposes, and introduces stiff penalties against those who profit from the prostitution of minors and children.[91]

---

[89](...continued)
brothel keeping under ITPA carries a mandatory prison term of one to three years and a fine of Rs.2,000 (US$66). A second conviction is punishable by two to five years' rigorous imprisonment and a Rs.2,000 fine. Anyone convicted of living on the earnings of a prostitute is subject to seven-year imprisonment and a fine of Rs.1,000 (US$33) or ten years if the prostitute is a child. Any person who engages in prostitution in a public place and any customer with whom the prostitution is carried out are subject to up to three months in prison. If the offense involves a minor, the prison term can range from seven years to life.

[90] Under ITPA a brothel was redefined broadly as any place where sexual exploitation or abuse occurred. Accordingly, under Section 3 of ITPA, the keepers of any place where sexual abuse occurred could be prosecuted. In the case of trafficked women, this would now cover the houses and room where the newly-trafficked girls and women were physically and psychologically broken, in the process called "training." ITPA also attempts to eliminate the loophole of lack of knowledge which SITA afforded brothel keepers and owners by placing the burden of proof on the landlord conditionally. However, the primary condition under which ITPA can presume that a landlord has knowledge of the illegalities on his premises is extremely unlikely to be met and therefore effectively useless: that a newspaper report names his premises as used for prostitution.

[91] Girls and women are treated differently under SITA, although their exploiters are not. SITA had defined adulthood as twenty-one years. Accordingly, an adult woman prosecuted for soliciting or prostituting in a public place would be tried in court and, if convicted, sent to a protective home or institution, whereas a girl was immediately referred for rehabilitation. However, the punishments for exploiters of women and girls were the same. Now, ITPA makes distinctions between "major," "minor," and "child." The act defines as a "child" anyone who is under sixteen years of age. Persons between sixteen and eighteen years are considered "minors," and anyone eighteen or older is an adult or "major." Those who exploit minors or children are subject to prison terms of not less than seven years and not more than ten years.

Contrary to the internationally recognized right to equal protection of the law, ITPA reverses the burden of proof for adults. While children and minors arrested under the act are presumed innocent, those over eighteen are required to prove their innocence. ITPA's additional clause addressing the offense of procuring carries rigorous imprisonment of seven to fourteen years in the case of a minor and seven years to life in the case of a child. Similarly, prostitution of a minor or child in a public place is punishable with seven years to life, or up to ten years along with a fine. However,
(continued...)

ITPA also expands police power to prevent trafficking, but at the same time attempts to curb the potential abuse of power by the police during raids—such as verbal, physical and sexual harassment. Whereas SITA empowered a special police officer to conduct a search of any premises without a warrant, ITPA extends these powers to the accompanying trafficking police officers who enter the premises. However, ITPA prohibits male police officers from conducting a search unless accompanied by two female police officers. Interrogation of women and girls also has to be undertaken by female police officers. If this is not possible, the women and girls can be questioned only in the presence of a female member of a recognized welfare organization. Additionally, the act mandates rehabilitation of prostitutes in "protective homes," shelters or reformatories where education and living facilities are to be provided.[92]

---

[91](...continued)
these measures are effectively weakened by the discretionary powers given by the ITPA to the court to reduce the term of imprisonment to below the seven-year minimum for offenses such as detaining a person for prostitution or seduction of a person in custody.

The implications of this provisions are particularly serious for women and girls trafficked over long distances, as in the case of Nepali women and girls. Not only does the exercise of the court's discretionary power dilute the general legal threat to persons who traffic women from abroad, but it also reduces the effective impact of laws against other abductors and kidnappers who imprison women and girls in brothels far from their homes. Women and girls transported over long distances and detained for prostitution face greater obstacles in attempting to escape from the brothel system, due to distance and differences of language and culture. Even if they manage to escape from their original captors they risk falling prey to other abductors and kidnappers who do not fear long jail sentences for their actions. ITPA introduces another clause whereby if a person is found with a child in a brothel it is presumed, unless proved to the contrary, that the child has been detained for prostitution.

[92] However, a Supreme Court review of one such facility in Delhi between 1979 and 1981, and subsequent independent studies conducted in 1990 of the same home and of the Liluah home in Calcutta, found that inmates of "protective homes," including former brothel inmates, women charged with criminal offenses and "non-criminal lunatics," were housed together in appalling conditions, denied adequate food and clothing and provided with no vocational training. There were also reports of forced prostitution and bonded labor. In the Liluah Home for Destitute Women, in Calcutta, a survey by university students found the institution to be severely overcrowded. Inmates complained of grave mistreatment, including branding with hot irons, rapes, and sexual assaults. Almost all inmates were suffering from malnutrition. Many also had chronic
(continued...)

Aside from statutes that address the traffic in persons particularly, other existing legislation, including the Bonded Labour System (Abolition) Act and Article 376 of the Indian Penal Code (IPC), explicitly forbid the purchase and sale of human beings, forced labor and all forms of bonded labor. The IPC also prohibits the trafficking and sale of minors.[93] In addition, existing rape, assault, and abduction laws can be used to address the systematic abuse of women and girls in brothels described in previous sections.[94] Article 375 of the IPC defines rape as the act of engaging in sexual intercourse with a woman when the act is against her will; without her consent; with her consent, when her consent has been obtained by putting her or any person in whom she is interested in fear of death or injury; with her consent when she is incapable of understanding the consequence of her consent; or when she is under sixteen years of age. Rape laws are applicable to both brothel staff and customers.[95]

---

[92](...continued)
skin diseases and tuberculosis. See, *Telegraph*, "House of Horror; The Liluah Home: Where inmates are starved, assaulted, degraded, molested and humiliated," July 29, 1990. See also Arun Bhandari et al., *Women and AIDS: Denial and Blame; A Citizen's Report* (New Delhi: Saraswati Art Press, November-December 1990), pp. 46-49.

[93] In addition, Sections 372 and 373 of the IPC state that anyone who buys, sells or obtains possession of any person under the age of eighteen for prostitution, illicit intercourse, unlawful or immoral purposes, or knowing that such use at any age is likely, is subject to up to ten years' imprisonment. The IPC also contains prohibitions against indecent assaults on women (Section 354), kidnapping, abduction, and wrongful confinement (Sections 359-368), and mandates imprisonment of up to ten years for the procurement or import of minors for the purposes of illicit intercourse, kidnapping and abduction leading to grievous hurt, slavery or subjection to "unnatural lust" (Section 367).

[94] In the case of sexual assault by police or police complicity in sexual abuse of trafficking victims, the Criminal Law (Amendment) Act of 1983, enacted as a result of a 1983 case of custodial violence against women in police lockups in Mathura, provides for the offense of custodial rape and prescribes a mandatory ten years' imprisonment for any police officer who rapes a woman in custody. Custody is customarily understood to include situations where the victim is effectively under the control of the police or security forces; it is not limited to conditions of detention in a prison or lockup.

[95] Male brothel staff who use rape to "break in" new girls are clearly subject to these laws. Under the IPC a minimum term of seven years' imprisonment may be imposed for rape. In addition, Section 376 of the IPC states: "Where a woman is raped by one or more in a group of persons acting in furtherance of their common intention,
(continued...)

The Indian Ministry of Human Resources Development's (HRD) Central Advisory Committee on Prostitution[96] released a report in May 1994 that acknowledged the organized and international nature of the trafficking industry and the use of coercion and force in procuring women and girls for prostitution. The report called for paramilitary forces to check the entry of females from abroad and advocated implementation of Section 13(4) of the ITPA which authorizes the appointment of a centralized anti-trafficking force with interstate jurisdiction. In June 1994 the Central Bureau of Investigation (CBI) responded to the HRD Ministry's invitation and agreed to assume responsibility for trafficking enforcement, pending additional funding.[97]

Nepal's 1990 Constitution, its civil code and several specific laws forbid the trafficking and sale of women and children and other forms of slavery-like practices. Article 20 of the Nepali Constitution states, "Traffic in human beings, slavery, serfdom or forced labour in any form is prohibited. Any contravention of this provision shall be punishable by law . . . "

The constitution is supplemented by a national legal code called the *Muluki Ain*, which contains provisions against interstate and domestic trafficking in human beings.[98] Section 1 of the law governs "traffic in human beings," while Section 3 forbids slavery and all other "transactions in human beings."[99]

Article 4 of the Traffic in Human Beings (Control) Act of 2043 (1986/1987) expressly forbids the sale of "human beings with any motive; the transport of "any person abroad with intent of sale," the act of "compel[ling] any woman to take to prostitution through allurement or enticement, deceit,

---

[95](...continued)
each of the persons shall be deemed to have committed gang rape within the meaning of this subsection."

[96] Part of the Human Resources Ministry's Department of Women and Child Development.

[97] *Pioneer* (Delhi), June 28, 1994.

[98] The Muluki Ain was first codified in 1854. It was promulgated anew after the adoption of the 1962 Constitution, has been amended many times since then, and remains in effect today.

[99] The Muluki Ain decrees prison sentences of twenty years for international trafficking cases where the victim has already been sold, and sentences of ten years' imprisonment for attempted sale, plus fines equivalent to the amount of the transaction. In cases where the purchaser is found within Nepal's borders, he or she is subject to the same punishment as the seller. *Muluki Ain (Jiu Masne Ko)*, amended October 2, 1964, and December 19, 1975.

threats, intimidation, pressures or otherwise; and "conspiracy for committing any of the acts mentioned." The act applies the same penalties to these offenses regardless of whether they are committed inside or outside Nepal's territorial boundaries and makes no distinction between crimes committed by Nepalis and by foreigners. The law dictates prison terms of ten to twenty years for trafficking in human beings and, disturbingly, reverses the burden of proof, requiring the accused in a trafficking case to disprove the charges.[100]

With regard to minors, Section 2 of the Muluki Ain prohibits the enticement and separation of children under sixteen from their legal guardians. Pimping and solicitation of prostitutes is forbidden under Section 5 of a law titled "Intention to Commit Adultery."[101] Intercourse with a child under fourteen is considered rape, regardless of consent.[102]

In May 1992, two years after Nepal ratified the U.N. Convention on the Rights of the Child, it passed the Children's Act 2048. This law, which defines a child as any person under sixteen years of age, prohibits torture and cruel treatment, the use or involvement of any child in an "immoral profession," child pornography, the sale of girl children as religious offerings to temple deities, and child labor.[103]

---

[100] The presumption of innocence is a fundamental principle laid down in Article 14(2) of the ICCPR. Reversing the burden of proof in trafficking cases is therefore a breach of international law. Note: Trafficking cases are prosecuted by a government prosecutor, and traffickers retain private defense. This has meant that activists and human rights lawyers who follow trafficking as an issue of concern have had little access to court documents or information about the process of ongoing legal cases. Likewise, women who have made complaints against traffickers, assert that they were not kept informed about the progress of these cases.

[101] Muluki Ain, "Intention to Commit Adultery" (Asaya Karani Ko), amended December 19, 1975. Section 5 states: "In cases where a person entices a woman with the intention of arranging sexual intercourse with himself or with any other person, or arranges contacts and affairs with prostitutes, he shall be punished with imprisonment for a term ranging from six months to two years, or with a fine ranging from Rs. 500 to Rs. 6000, or both."

[102] Muluki Ain, "On Rape," (Jabarjasti Kavani Ko), Section 1, amended December 19, 1975.

[103] The Children's Act 2048; A Bill to Provide for Safeguarding the Interests of Children, was signed by the king on May 20, 1992. Section 15 states: "Children [shall] not be made involved in immoral professions"; Section 13 prohibits "offering of girl child in the name of God or Goddess"; Section 5 prohibits discrimination between sons and daughters; and Section 7 forbids torture and cruel treatment.

Enforcement Problems

The failure of the criminal justice system to enforce laws against trafficking and related crimes has been a serious problem in both Nepal and India. In India a lucrative patronage system has developed between corrupt police and brothel owners that ensures unequal law enforcement. Women and girls are reportedly arrested by the thousands under those sections of the law designed to curb public prostitution and solicitation. Their arrests allow the police to promote a public image of vigilance against prostitution while rarely arresting and prosecuting brothel owners and traffickers responsible for forced prostitution. The owners and traffickers are, in fact, protected from prosecution for some of the most serious offenses by local police who receive regular payment for their services, warn brothel owners of impending raids, and patronize brothels as customers.

In Nepal the failure of the police to act against traffickers appears to be due as much to poor training and lack of political will as to corruption or intimidation. When interviewed by Human Rights Watch, Nepali police and government officials at all levels characterized trafficking as a social malaise rather than a problem for law enforcement. They tended to blame ethnic communities for greed and moral laxity and to charge Nepal's burgeoning NGO community with the task of solving it through "social awareness."[104] Logistical complications posed by Nepal's very limited infrastructure, a 500-mile-long open border with India, and its lack of any system to screen cross-border travellers also complicate prevention measures.

The 1993 report of then U.N. Special Rapporteur on the Sale of Children Vitit Muntarbhorn was particularly important in outlining the complicity of official forces in trafficking and in drawing the link between industrial recruiting, bonded labor and forced prostitution in Nepal. The report found that, in general, legal remedies were not easily accessible to the victims of abuse and that law enforcement agencies lacked both training and the will to confront child exploitation. The special rapporteur called for improved law enforcement, investigation and punishment of corrupt officials; better international cooperation to control trafficking, including national cooperation

---

[104] Some local police also stated that the way to stop trafficking was to arrest and prosecute victims.

with Interpol; and the establishment of national policy bodies to deal with child exploitation.[105]

The special rapporteur's findings correspond with those of Human Rights Watch. Despite the abundance of legislation aimed at preventing trafficking and other forms of slavery, neither India nor Nepal has adequately enforced existing laws, investigated reports of official complicity in the trafficking industry or prosecuted officials found profiting from the trade.

BANGLADESHI WOMEN AND GIRLS TRAFFICKED TO PAKISTAN

Hidden in the slums of Karachi, Pakistan is a flourishing trade in young women and girls from Bangladesh.[106] The forced trafficking of Bangladeshi women and girls into Pakistan for the purposes of domestic or sexual slavery has been going on for at least ten to fifteen years.[107] A 1991 study by the National Council for Social Welfare in Pakistan estimated that one hundred to 150 Bangladeshi women and girls are brought into Pakistan each year and many are sold against their will into prostitution, marriage or domestic servitude.[108] The average age of the trafficking victims is fifteen.[109] The majority have been lured from Bangladesh to Pakistan with promises of jobs, decent pay and a better life. Others were abducted from

---

[105] Muntarbhorn's report stated that Nepal's "[l]aw enforcement authorities are often weak, understaffed, undertrained and corrupt . . ." and that "[t]here is an expansive web of criminality which exploits children and which abuses the open border with India . . . . There is still insufficient transfrontier cooperation both to prevent child exploitation and to ensure safe return and rehabilitation of children subsequently." *Rights of the Child; Sale of children, child prostitution and child pornography,* U.N. Document E/CN.4/1994/84/ADD.1, (Geneva: United Nations), January 20, 1994, report submitted by Vitit Muntarbhorn, Special Rapporteur, in accordance with Commission on Human Rights resolution 1993/82, Addendum, Visit by the Special Rapporteur to Nepal, pp. 7-8.

[106] The following material was adapted from Asia Watch (now Human Rights Watch/Asia) and Women's Rights Project, *Double Jeopardy: Police Abuse against Women in Pakistan* (New York: Human Rights Watch, 1992).

[107] *Daily Star* (Dhaka), editorial, September 1, 1991.

[108] "Promises of Decent Living Lure BD Women to Come to Pakistan," *Dawn* (Karachi), November 2, 1991, p. 7.

[109] Beena Sarwar, "Victimizing the Victims," *Weekend Post* (Lahore), November 15, 1991.

outside their homes and then sometimes drugged. The Bangladeshi women and girls are brought by bus and train through India to Pakistan or, in many cases having been transported to India, they walk across the border into Pakistan.[110] They often end up in brothels in Bangladeshi *paras* (slums) in Karachi, although as their numbers have grown, brothels have been found in small towns throughout Pakistan.[111]

In the early days of the female slave trade in Pakistan, when the number of victims was smaller and the crime less well-known, the sale of women and girls was advertised blatantly. A Bangladeshi journalist who witnessed an auction described it:

> At night, girls were brought to the slum and [the] auction took place indoors. There was not bidding as such because there was an understanding between the procurers and the customers before the auction. Usually the younger and more beautiful girls were sold quickly and at higher prices. The unmarried and virgin girls were sold for 15,000 to 20,000 taka [U.S.$1 = 33.20 taka]. Some girls were kept aside before the auction to be taken separately to hotels for wealthy buyers who were given the opportunity to inspect the girls individually. Those who were sold went with the buyers. The rest returned to the place they came from. Everyone remained silent. It seemed that the girls were helpless and speechless.[112]

In recent years, as the number of Bangladeshi women and girls trafficked into Pakistan has increased and the problem has drawn additional

---

[110] Lawyers for Human Rights and Legal Aid, *The Flesh Trade: Report on Women's and Children's Trafficking in Pakistan,* (Karachi: Lawyers for Human Rights and Legal Aid, 1991)[hereinafter *The Flesh Trade 1991*].

[111] Macsoon Hussain, *Contemporary Forms of Slavery in Pakistan* (unpublished report, 1991), p. 6. The author is a Pakistani sociologist who has studied the problem of trafficking.

[112] Muhammad Ali, "Trafficking in Women, part II," *Weekly Detective* (Dhaka), October 21, 1983.

public attention, the practice of selling females has become more clandestine.[113] By the early 1990s, agents acting on behalf of pimps kept the women in dens within Karachi's teeming slums and quietly traded them from these hostels.[114]

The Bangladeshi women and girls are held under terrible conditions. According to a 1993 report, the women are not given proper food and are kept in crowded rooms. They are given chores to do while they are in the den, such as washing and cooking.[115] To compel the women and girls to provide the desired services, the pimps threaten to expose the women's status as illegal immigrants or denounce them under the *Hudood* laws, which penalize, among other things, sex outside of marriage and impose long prison terms and severe corporal punishment.[116] Those who resist are beaten or worse.[117]

---

[113] According to social worker Abdul Sattar Edhi, who runs the largest refuge for Bangladeshi women in Pakistan, as of 1989 fifteen to twenty women crossed the borders each month. By 1992 the monthly number had risen to 150 to 200. According to *The Flesh Trade 1991*, over 200,000 Bangladeshi women and girls altogether were in Pakistan as a result of trafficking.

[114] The 1991 report by the Lawyers for Human Rights and Legal Aid notes that "the girls, women and children are brought to Karachi and are kept in the dens of these *touts* [pimps] whose wives and daughters help them in keeping a hawk's eye on these women. In the meantime, the pimps arrange buyers for these girls." Lawyers for Human Rights and Legal Aid, *The Flesh Trade 1991*, p. 7.

[115] Lawyers for Human Rights and Legal Aid, *The Flesh Trade: Report on Women's and Children's Trafficking in Pakistan* (Karachi: Lawyers for Human Rights and Legal Aid, 1993), p. 4 [hereinafter *The Flesh Trade 1993*].

[116] The Hudood Ordinances criminalize, among other things, adultery, fornication and rape, and prescribe punishments for these offenses that include stoning to death, public flogging and amputation. The Hudood laws, as written and applied, clearly conflict with principles of human rights. Not only do they prescribe punishments that are cruel and inhuman under international law, but they clearly discriminate on the basis of gender. For a more complete discussion of the Hudood Ordinances, see the Pakistan section in the chapter on "Abuses Against Women in Custody" from this volume.

[117] Bhagwandas, "Bengali Women: Paradise Lost?" *Tuesday Review* (Karachi), January 29-February 4, 1991. Bhagwandas interviewed several women who were detained after an August 1990 police raid on a brothel in Karachi. One of the women told him, "All the women in the den were forced to live in sin. None of them including me were spared. First the den keeper's men used me and then later other men used to come." The woman told the reporter that any women who resisted was badly beaten, so that the women had to give in to the requests of the operators.

Rather than continue to auction the Bangladeshi women and girls openly, as publicity about the abuses grew the pimps took to marrying them off, sometimes to the pimps themselves. These forced marriages protect the pimps from being charged under the Hudood laws. In an interview with a local Karachi daily, an infamous pimp, Sher Khan, who denied selling girls but was later arrested for running a brothel, claimed, "I assist in the arrangements of a girl's marriage. It is a good deed. I collect the money from the bridegroom's parents and pay it to the girl's parents. The priest pronounces marriage and a simple ceremony takes place."[118]

Bangladeshi women who were picked up during police raids of prostitution dens, or who escaped, reported that they were "married" rather than sold and that the exchange of money between the pimp and the buyer took the form of dowry. A 1988 story in a Karachi newspaper documented the sale of a Bangladeshi woman in which an Islamic judge charged 500 rupees (US $19) to "marry" the girl to her buyer. Reportedly, these "husbands" often bought the girls and then sold them again at a small profit. Depending on the virginity, beauty and health of the women and girls, a sale could bring anywhere from US$800 to US$1,600.[119]

Instead of protecting the Bangladeshi women and girls by arresting those accountable for their illegal sale and forced prostitution or forced marriage, the Pakistani government has imprisoned the women and girls while allowing most brokers and pimps to go free. According to the 1990 National Welfare Survey by the Human Rights Commission of Pakistan, 1,400 Bangladeshi women and girls were imprisoned in Pakistan, ostensibly for entering the country illegally or for offenses under the Hudood Ordinances.[120]

In many cases Bangladeshi women and girls arrested by police in raids on brothels suffered prolonged detention, usually because they lacked legal counsel or the financial resources to pay bail or surety. In other cases, the police allowed pimps to bail out the women and take them back to the prostitution dens. Meanwhile, the pimps went free. At the time of our investigation, some pimps involved in the sale of Bangladeshi women and girls had been arrested by the police, not one had been prosecuted or punished by

---

[118] Zulqarnin Shadid and Bushra Jabbar Khan, "The Slave Trade," *Mag* (Pakistan), August 1990, p. 57.

[119] In 1988 the going rate was 30,000 to 50,000 rupees, and before that the price was 5,000 to 10,000 rupees. Sarwar, "Victimizing the Victim," *Weekend Post*.

[120] *Dawn*, November 2, 1991, p. 69.

the government for trafficking or for any of the other abuses resulting from trafficking and forced prostitution. Speaking in 1991, one local activist noted that the Pakistani government, instead of dealing with the problems, seemed intent on "victimizing the victims."[121]

The Women and Girls

Human Rights Watch interviewed several Bangladeshi women in Lahore and Karachi who had been brought to Pakistan by traffickers and ended up being imprisoned, either on Hudood charges or for violations of Pakistan's immigration law. We interviewed these women after they had been released from prison. In a Lahore case, the woman was awaiting the outcome of a Hudood case that had been filed against her by her buyer, from whom she had escaped. In Karachi, we spoke to three young women in a local welfare center who were hoping to be repatriated to Bangladesh.

Human Rights Watch interviewed Shamim Akhtar, a twenty-year-old woman from Dhaka, Bangladesh, in Lahore, Pakistan. Akhtar told us that several men abducted her from outside her aunt's home and took her by train to New Delhi, India. Akhtar believes that she was given drugs, because she was unconscious for the entire trip. From New Delhi, they took a bus to an unknown place, then got off and started walking toward Pakistan. At the Pakistani border, there was a police station with two other Bangladeshi women in it. The men spoke to the police but Akhtar did not understand what they said. They then crossed the border.

Akhtar was then locked in a room in Karachi for about fifteen days, until her captors found a buyer. The buyer took Akhtar to his house, and she was made to put her thumb print on a blank piece of paper, which later was made into a marriage certificate. Akhtar lived with the buyer for about a year, until the mother of the buyer told Akhtar that she had been sold to someone else. Akhtar tried to drown herself that night but was saved by a passerby. She married the uncle of her rescuer and lived with him until her buyer's brother discovered that she was still alive and tried to get money from her new family. After refusing to pay, Akhtar and her husband moved to Lahore. In August of that year, police came to their house in Lahore saying that she had been married twice. The police took Akhtar and her husband to the police station and charged them with adultery under the Hudood Ordinances. Akhtar

---

[121] Advocate Nausheen Ahmed, cited in Sarwar, "Victimizing the Victims," *Weekend Post.*

and her husband both made bail, and ultimately they were acquitted of the *Zina* (adultery) charge.[122]

Human Rights Watch also interviewed several Bangladeshi women at the Edhi Center in Karachi. The Edhi Center was founded by Abdul Sattar Edhi, a well-known Pakistani social worker and philanthropist. Edhi has frequently supplied bail and surety for women accused under the Hudood Ordinances, and the Edhi Center is the largest refuge for Bangladeshi women in Pakistan.

We interviewed Neelofar at the Edhi Center in Karachi. Neelofar told us that she had been working at a mill in Chittagong, Bangladesh, when a woman told her that she could earn much more money in Bombay. The next day the woman took Neelofar and her younger sister, Jasmeen to meet a man who was a pimp. The pimp told both sisters that they would receive jobs as domestic servants. They went from Chittagong to Jessore, Bangladesh by bus, took a train to India, and then walked across the border to Pakistan. It took them a month to reach Karachi. Altogether there were more than twenty women and four younger girls in the group. In Karachi they were brought to the pimp Bachuu's house in Ayesha Manzil. Forty to fifty women were living in the house. Women who complained or tried to return home were beaten, although Neelofar said she was not beaten. Men came to the house to buy the women.

The police raided the house after Neelofar had been there ten days. She was kept in a police lockup for four days, and then taken before a magistrate and transferred to the Karachi Central Jail, to be charged with illegal immigration. All the Bangladeshi women and girls were kept together in the prison separate from the Pakistani women. The police arrested one man in the raid but not the pimp. The pimps would come to jail and tell the women and girls that only they could get them bail. While Neelofar was in prison, other Bangladeshi women were brought there under arrest.[123]

In two separate reports on the trafficking of women and children into Pakistan, the Lawyers for Human Rights and Legal Aid (LHRLA), a nongovernmental organization, documented cases of Bangladeshi women and girls who were brought to Pakistan against their will and sold into forced

---

[122] Interview, Shamim Akhtar, Lahore, Pakistan, October 1991.

[123] Interview, Neelofar, Karachi, Pakistan, October 1991. All names of interviewees are withheld by Human Rights Watch unless otherwise indicated.

prostitution and marriage.[124] The testimonies that this organization collected suggest a pattern of illegal inducement, transport, abuse, sale and forced sexual and domestic servitude of women, in some cases with police complicity, in violation of Pakistan's obligations under international law.

> One day a close friend of mine came to my house with a man and said that he has come from Pakistan with a letter to me from my father. The man was actually a pimp and he had paid my friend 15,000 taka to do the job. I took the letter to my uncle. He read that my father was very ill and he wanted to see me before he died. I panicked and agreed to go with this man called Anwar, the pimp. He brought me to India with nine other women. The border guards made them cross at night into Pakistan. In Karachi I was given to Mohammed Ali Pagla where I remained for a few days. One day it was my turn to take a bath and I tried to run. But the guards tried to stop me and force me back into the house when an old man saw me fighting and intervened. He took me to the police station and from there to the Edhi home.[125]

Another woman reported:

> I am from Hajipur, Dhaka. One day my father's stepbrother came from Pakistan and was very nice to us. He wanted to take me to visit my sister who was married in another city. Instead he took me to a house where there were twelve girls and eight boys. We all crossed the border into India and finally came to Karachi via Lahore. He sold me to an old man called Ilyas for Rs. 80,000 and he took me to Punjab. He raped me and ill-treated me, and his relatives were abusive too.[126]

---

[124] The interviews with the women and girls contain only general information, since the researchers "tried not to disturb them too much as this was not an interrogation." Lawyers for Human Rights and Legal Aid, *The Flesh Trade 1991*, p. 10.

[125] Testimony of Sahana, eighteen years old. Lawyers for Human Rights and Legal Aid, *The Flesh Trade 1993*, p. 6.

[126] Testimony of Marjina, seventeen years old. Ibid., p. 8.

The Role of Law Enforcement Agencies
There is some indication that in 1990 and 1991 the Pakistani police began to crack down on the trafficking dens. According to newspaper reports, on August 16, 1990, the Gulberg police in Karachi arrested sixteen Bangladeshi woman and men in a raid on a known prostitution den near Ayesha Manzil. All thirty-two were charged under the Hudood Ordinances. On April 2, 1991, Karachi police arrested forty-nine Bangladeshi girls and eighteen agents. The women and men were charged with prostitution and illegal immigration.

In general, however, police raids on prostitution dens appear to be few and far between, and the women and girls arrested in the raids continue to be charged as illegal immigrants and prostitutes. The police raids are ineffective, since the pimps rarely are arrested and, are therefore free to run their brothels. Local observers report that the police are bribed to leave the pimps alone and, most of the time, the women and girls as well.[127] When the police do arrest the women and girls, the pimps often pay the police to receive access to them while they are in custody. The pimps use that access to attempt to persuade the women and girls to be bailed out by them, and return to the brothels.[128]

In one case documented by the LHRLA in 1991, twenty-four-year-old Rahena was arrested in a police raid on the den where she was forced to work. Rahena said that the pimps visited her several times in prison. The pimps told her that they were the only ones who could secure her bail and release.

In another case documented in the same report, twenty-nine-year-old Pyara Bibi and her mother were brought to Karachi by an agent who promised that they would earn a lot of money. They went with him and traveled in a bus with several other women to the border, which they crossed at night. They reached Lahore and were sent by train to Karachi, where they were taken to Ayesha Manzil. Pyara Bibi says she was sexually abused by the pimp and his brother. One night they were arrested in a police raid. Not long after their

---

[127] According to interviews with the Bengali women detained in the August 1990 raid, the police "are in connivance with the traffickers, pocketing money from the sale of women and sending the women to prison when the amount of the bribe does not satisfy them." "Rescued Slaves Handed Back to Masters," *Dawn,* January 10, 1991.

[128] *Submission of the Anti-slavery Society to the United Nations Economic and Social Council, Commission on Human Rights, Sub-Commission on Prevention of Discrimination and Protection of Minorities, Working group on Contemporary Forms of Slavery,* Sixteenth Session (Geneva, 1990), p. 2.

arrest, pimps visited them in jail. According to LHRLA, Pyara Bibi and her
mother have been released on bail and have not been seen since.

LHRLA Director Zia Awan told Human Rights Watch in 1991 that
the pimps have better access to his clients than he does. Of the eighty
Bangladeshi women and girls in Karachi Central Jail at the end of 1991, Awan
estimated that by February 1992 thirty of them had been released by the police
to the pimps. Once freed, and without any assistance from the Pakistani
government, the women and girls legitimately believe they have no place to
go other than back to the brothels. Usually, the only alternative is to be bailed
out by the private Edhi Center, which has meager resources.

Police in Pakistan frequently detain Bangladeshi women and girls
illegally and for long periods in police lockups on charges of Hudood
violations.[129] There have been several reports of police abuse of Bangladeshi
women and girls in their custody, although these allegations are not well-
documented. Fatima, an eleven- or twelve-year-old girl interviewed by
National Public Radio in 1991, said that she had been detained for two weeks
by police in a lockup and badly beaten before she was taken to Karachi
Central Jail. A 1990 newspaper report on trafficking in women alleges that the
police operating in the Bangladeshi slums often violate the police rules and
illegally detain Bangladeshi women overnight or longer in police lockups.[130]
On September 21, 1991, Agence France-Presse reported a case of three
Bangladeshi women arrested in a police raid in Karachi who were later raped
in police custody.

Although little documentation exists of the abuse that Bangladeshi
women encounter in police custody, one thing is clear: the women and girls,
not the pimps, bear the brunt of police raids. The Karachi pimp, Sher Khan,
reportedly was arrested before the January 1991 raid, but as of May 1995 he
had not been prosecuted and punished and, unlike many of the women arrested
in his dens, he was released on bail.[131]

The discriminatory enforcement of Pakistan's prostitution laws has
disastrous consequences for the Bangladeshi women, but a deeper problem lies

----

[129] Arbitrary detention is not limited to Bangladeshi women and girls; it is also
applied against Pakistani women detained on charges of Hudood violations. See the
Pakistan section from the "Abuses Against Women in Custody" chapter in this volume.

[130] Shadid and Khan, "The Slave Trade."

[131] Letter from Zia Awan, president, Lawyers for Human Rights and Legal Aid, to
Human Rights Watch Women's Rights Project, July 26, 1995; telephone interview, Zia
Awan, July 25. 1995.

in the misconception of the underlying crime itself. Though in some cases the Bangladeshi women arrested in police raids may be willing participants, their stories point to a consistent pattern of compulsion that often takes the form of physical and sexual violence. In such cases, by arresting the women and girls and charging them with Hudood offenses, the police are penalizing the victim and, in effect, absolving the criminal.

The Karachi police officer Dig Javed Iqbal, who led an August 2, 1990 raid on a prostitution den in Karachi filled with approximately forty-nine Bangladeshi women, told reporters that the police had raided the hostel because they had heard that the local pimp "had smuggled some Bangladeshi girls into the country for the purposes of prostitution." When asked by reporters why the women and girls were arrested if they had been trafficked into prostitution, the officer replied, "since they had given their consent, they were involved in the racket."[132]

Arrest on presumption of consent—despite ample evidence to the contrary—is a precursor to charges under the Hudood Ordinances. Charging women and girls with Hudood offenses has the effect of making it nearly impossible for the women to serve as witnesses against the den operators for the crimes of trafficking, physical and sexual abuse and in many cases, illegal confinement, because they exclude women's testimony. As noted by Awan:

> Prosecution of Bangladeshi women and girls for Hudood offenses turns the witnesses to a crime into the accused. It serves to protect and shield the big fish, the real culprits, even if the small fries, the local procurers are brought to book. During detention the pimps are generally allowed to meet the women and girls; they are left at the mercy of the pimps and traffickers. If the women are acquitted, which happens often because of weaknesses in the prosecution's case, they are forced to go back to the flesh trade. Above all, such trials and even convictions do not help end trafficking in women, which continues to flourish. It might treat the symptom, but it does not treat the disease.[133]

---

[132] "Dreams of Better Life Turn into Nightmare," *Dawn*, April 3, 1991.
[133] "Special Laws to Handle White Slave Trade Demanded," *News* (Islamabad), April 5, 1991.

This significantly reduces the odds that such abuses will be prosecuted and eliminated, even when, as in the August 1990 raid, lower-level agents also are arrested and charged under the Hudood Ordinances.

After the August 1990 raid, all the women and agents were released for lack of evidence after having been charged with Hudood offenses. No other criminal prosecution was pursued. A report by a Pakistani sociologist, *Contemporary Forms of Slavery in Pakistan*, suggests that "there are reasons to believe that a weak case against the den operators is deliberate by police, who stand much to gain from continued trafficking."[134]

Even if, as many local observers note, the Bangladeshi women and girls usually are acquitted of Hudood offenses, they often spend prolonged periods in pre-trial detention. In particular, for women who are charged with illegal immigration under the Foreigners Act, for which the minimum sentences are shorter than those provided under the Hudood Ordinances, their pre-trial detention often exceeds the likely sentence by as much as one to three years.[135]

In sum, trafficking of Bangladeshi women and girls into Pakistan is a thriving and growing business. The police are aware of it, but they disproportionately and unfairly penalize the female victims, perversely assume their consent to forced prostitution and coerced marriages, subject them to prolonged and often illegal detention, and fail to punish the criminals adequately. Despite these obvious injustices and disastrous consequences for the women and girl victims, the Pakistani and Bangladeshi governments have done little to address the problem.

The Response of the Pakistani and Bangladeshi Governments

Both the Pakistani and Bangladeshi governments have ratified the 1926 Slavery Convention and the 1956 Supplementary Slavery Convention, and thus have undertaken obligations to suppress slavery in all its forms. Both governments are aware of the rising flesh trade between their countries, yet neither has taken sufficient measures to stem it in any significant way. A 1992 U.S. State Department human rights report concluded that "the government of Pakistan with the help of the government of Bangladesh took steps in 1990 to

---

[134] Hussain, *Contemporary Forms of Slavery in Pakistan,* p. 6.
[135] Sarwar, "Victimizing the Victims," *Weekend Post.*

document and repatriate some of the women, but the problem remains largely unsolved."[136]

A review of available materials suggests that the Bangladeshi government has taken some steps, including periodic raids, to arrest traffickers operating within its own borders.[137] But the government has made little consistent effort to assist the Bangladeshi women and girls who are already in Pakistan.

The 1991 BBC documentary "The Flesh Trade" included an interview with the Bangladeshi High Commissioner in Pakistan, who stated that to his knowledge only one Bangladeshi woman had been reported to his commission as being forcefully trafficked into Pakistan and she was repatriated immediately. In the documentary, the BBC reporter took the high commissioner to the Edhi Center, where he met with the many Bangladeshi women and girls staying there. The Bangladeshi women and girls pleaded with the high commissioner to send them home, and he agreed to do so. However, according to Zia Awan of LHRLA, since the high commissioner's visit, the high commissioner has not repatriated a single Bangladeshi woman.[138]

The response of the Pakistani government has been no better. On April 10, 1991, soon after an April 2 police raid on a brothel described above, Interior Minister Chaudry Shujaat Hussain announced that the Ministry of Interior had asked the provincial governments and border authorities to tighten security to guard against illegal entry, and Hussain proposed enhancing the punishment for illegal entry.[139] However, to our knowledge, the Pakistani government has made little visible effort to punish the traffickers; nor has it

---

[136] U.S. Department of State, *Country Reports on Human Rights Practices for 1991*, (Washington, D.C: Government Printing Office, 1992), p. 1561 [hereinafter *1991 Country Reports*].

[137] According to newspaper reports in Bangladesh dailies, on August 9, 1991, federal police rescued seventy-five persons, including women and children, at a border area with India and arrested four traffickers. On August 13, Bangladesh Federal Police reportedly arrested two traffickers in a border village who "confessed they were members of an international women trafficking group." On August 23, federal police rescued fifteen women and thirty children as they were being smuggled across the border to India and detained three traffickers.

[138] Sarwar, "Victimizing the Victims," *Weekend Post*. Letter from Zia Awan, president, Lawyers for Human Rights and Legal Aid, to Human Rights Watch Women's Rights Project, July 26, 1995.

[139] "Provinces Asked to Check Infiltration of Bangladeshi," *News*, April 10, 1991.

adopted any measures to check the traffic in persons, to provide facilities for
the many victims of trafficking who languish in prison, or to make lasting
arrangements for their repatriation. The LHRLA turned their 1991 report, *The
Flesh Trade*, into a Constitution Petition to Pakistan's Supreme Court and it
is still pending.[140] In addition, Pakistan's interior minister announced in
1993 that the government would discuss the trafficking problem with the
Indian government and tighten security at the borders, but no action has yet
been taken.[141]

In fact, Pakistani officials have largely ignored the problem of
trafficking in women, although they cannot claim to be unaware of it. The
Pakistani government should be well informed about the issue, given the
regular articles in the national press; reports by the U.S.-based National Public
Radio and the BBC, both of which were repeatedly broadcast in Pakistan;
detailed reports by reputable national nongovernmental organizations, including
the National Social Welfare Agency, the Human Rights Commission of
Pakistan, Lawyers for Human Rights and Legal Aid; and several national and
regional conferences on trafficking designed to improve the regional
governments' response. Nonetheless, in a February 1992 public address in
Washington, Pakistan's ambassador to the United States, Abida Hussain,
stated, "When a woman whose family has been left behind in Bangladesh
arrives in Pakistan, what happens to her may not be very kind, but I am not
aware of any organized trafficking going on."[142]

The reasons for the Pakistani and Bangladeshi governments' passive
response to the problem of trafficking in women are no doubt complex.
However, trafficking victims have little, reason to expect fair treatment from
the criminal justice system. The police are pre-disposed unfairly, and often
corruptly, to judge the trafficking victims and to presume their consent to
abuses committed against them while excusing the offenses committed by their
abusers. The reality remains that in the absence of any family or financial
support, these women are unlikely to receive the protection from the system
that they are due as a matter of right under both domestic and international
law. It is incumbent upon the Pakistani government to investigate and
prosecute forced prostitution and coerced marriage and related abuses.

---

[140] Letter from Zia Awan, president, Lawyers for Human Rights and Legal Aid, to
Human Rights Watch Women's Rights Project, July 26, 1995.

[141] *The Flesh Trade 1993*, p. 23.

[142] Ambassador Abida Hussain, address at the Asia Society, New York, February
1992.

Moreover, the Pakistani and Bangladeshi governments must collaborate to fulfill their international legal obligations to protect women and girls from forced trafficking.

GENERAL RECOMMENDATIONS

To Governments:

- All governments that have not yet done so should accede to the international instruments relevant to the trafficking in women and girls, including the International Covenant on Civil and Political Rights, the Convention on the Elimination of All Forms of Discrimination Against Women, and the Convention for the Suppression of Traffic in Persons and the Exploitation of the Prostitution of Others.

- All governments should move as quickly as possible to reform their prostitution and trafficking laws to make them consistent with international human rights standards, particularly those designed to protect victims of forced trafficking.

- Governments should monitor their borders closely against trafficking in women and girls, including by inspection of vehicles. Special training should be given to law enforcement officials at the borders about trafficking and their obligation under international human rights and domestic criminal law to protect forced trafficking victims and investigate and arrest those suspected of engaging in such abuse.

- In accordance with Article 20 of the Trafficking Convention, governments should monitor and investigate employment agencies or recruitment networks operating in known trafficking centers, which might serve as fronts for recruitment for coerced prostitution.

- Law enforcement training should include trafficking issues and relevant laws. Police at all levels should be given clear directives indicating their responsibility to investigate and arrest traffickers and warning that police found guilty of participating in trafficking and forced prostitution will be prosecuted.

- In countries from which significant numbers of women and girls are trafficked, the governments should undertake campaigns to educate women in their own language—using, for example, workshops, pamphlets and posters—about the dangers of trafficking, the various ways to recognize a trafficking agent, women's basic rights to be free from torture, to physical integrity and to freedom of movement under

national and international law, and the channels of redress should their
rights be violated overseas, including assistance from their embassies.

- Governments should actively investigate and prosecute to the full
extent of the law all those involved in trafficking and forced
prostitution, with particular attention to their own police and officials
who may aid and abet the illegal entry of woman and girls, receive
pay-offs or protection money from brothel owners and/or agents,
patronize illegal brothels, have financial holdings in, collect rent from,
or in any other way are complicit in the operations of such brothels.

- Governments should further prosecute the abuses associated with
forced prostitution and coerced marriage, such as debt bondage, illegal
confinement, and rape.

- Consistent with international law, governments should not arrest or
prosecute forced trafficking victims for illegal immigration. Women
and girls who have been rescued from forced prostitution should be
placed in non-penal institutions pending their repatriation or
normalization of their immigration status. In those refuges, women
should be informed of their due process rights under national and
international law, including rights to appeal deportation orders, to
contact their embassies and, in the event they face criminal charges,
to access to legal counsel and to a fair trial.

- In cases where the immigration status of a woman or girl is unclear
and she is arrested, her due process rights must be fully protected.
Law enforcement agencies should ensure that she understands the
nature of the charges against her, has access to an interpreter, if
necessary, and legal counsel. She should enjoy the right to a fair and
impartial trial without undue delay.

- Governments should ensure that police lockups, immigration detention
centers and prisons strictly conform to the U.N. Standard Minimum
Rules for the Treatment of Prisoners. Governments should investigate
any report of extortion and sexual abuse in detention and prosecute
those responsible to the fullest extent of the law.

- In keeping with the Trafficking Convention, countries of destination
should coordinate with countries of origin for the safe repatriation of
forced trafficking victims. In the case of indigent women, the country
of destination should bear the cost of repatriation to the border and
arrange with the country of origin to cover any additional costs. The
agreement should include a guarantee that women and girls who have
been trafficked against their will or knowledge will not be arrested,

fined or in any way held accountable for illegal departure or
prostitution upon repatriation.

- Governments of origin should maintain a central registry of missing
persons. Cooperation with nongovernmental organizations who are
helping trafficking victims would be extremely valuable in this regard.
- Governments should prosecute those who conduct and facilitate forced
marriages, and governments should not prosecute women forced into
marriage for bigamy, adultery and other similar crimes.
- Governments should vigorously protect the human rights of trafficked
women and girls who have or may have contracted the AIDS virus.
Consistent with World Health Organization guidelines, HIV testing
should be conducted only with the full and informed consent of the
individual, and test results should be kept strictly confidential. All
women who are tested should be informed of the results if they so
request.

To the United Nations:
- The U.N. secretary-general and the U.N. high commissioner for
human rights should ensure that all U.N. agencies consistently address
issues related to trafficking and forced prostitution that fall within
their mandates by developing programs and strategies designed to
curb such abuse and ensure accountability. They should cooperate
with the U.N. Special Rapporteur on violence against women, its
causes and consequences, in this regard.
- U.N. agencies that have AIDS programs, including the World Health
Organization, the U.N. Development Program and UNICEF, should
address the human rights implications of the AIDS pandemic in
relation to the forced sexual activity of trafficking victims. Such
programs should, among other things, encourage governments to train
their health and law enforcement officials to respect the human rights
of women and girls who have been trafficked, including the right to
be free from discrimination on the basis of sex, ethnicity and national
origin.
- In light of the resignation in 1994 of the Special Rapporteur on the
Sale of Children, Child Prostitution and Child Pornography, the
United Nations should appoint a new special rapporteur on these
issues as soon as possible. In addition, the United Nations should
evaluate the concerns of the former special rapporteur, Vitit
Muntarbhorn, and reform its system in order to provide the new
special rapporteur more substantial and useful support.

- The Human Rights Commission should call on the Working Group on Contemporary Form of Slavery to investigate cases of forced prostitution.

To Donor Countries:
- Donor countries should encourage recipient countries to adopt the recommendations outlined above and should use every opportunity to raise the issue of trafficking both publicly—at international meetings, congressional or parliamentary hearings, and press conferences—and privately, in meetings with relevant officials. They should also work to develop programs and strategies for bilateral and multilateral aid programs to affected countries that would make funds available for certain kinds of training, education, information dissemination and legal reform programs related to trafficking. Some of this assistance should be conditioned on evidence of effective prosecution of officials, brothel owners, agents and pimps.
- Donor countries should also ensure that loans financed through bilateral or multilateral lending institutions for construction on borders include a system for monitoring the impact, direct or indirect, that such a project would be likely to have on trafficking in women. As a part of their efforts to promote the rule of law, donor countries and international financial institutions should insist that recipient countries with a significant trafficking and forced prostitution problem accept administration of justice loans to improve their law enforcement and judicial capabilities in this area, as a condition for the disbursement of loans for development projects in regions where trafficking of women and girls into forced prostitution is widespread.

5
ABUSES AGAINST WOMEN WORKERS

Women throughout the world confront physical and sexual violence as well as sex discrimination in the workplace. Public and private sector employers discriminate with impunity against women, as women and as mothers or potential mothers. Sex discrimination in the workplace often is motivated by the frequent perception that women are less reliable than men and that women's productive capacity is compromised by their reproductive function. Although discrimination on the grounds of sex or maternity is prohibited under international human rights law and barred by the domestic laws of most countries, it is nonetheless routinely tolerated by many governments. Aside from the problem of nonenforcement of laws against sex and maternity discrimination, the labor statutes and regulations of some countries are themselves discriminatory in that they exclude women from particular job and training opportunities.

Women workers also experience sexual and physical violence at the hands of their employers with little or no legal redress. Human Rights Watch investigations have documented violence against women workers that includes rape and other forms of sexual assault, beating, kicking, slapping and burning. In addition, women workers have reported being subjected to illegal confinement, extremely long working hours and nonpayment of wages. Sex discrimination in the workplace and in the criminal justice system frequently compounds the effects of violence. Numerous women workers, particularly those who are female heads of households, remain silent in the face of abuse by employers. Some fear that by complaining they would lose their jobs in shrinking labor markets that are increasingly hostile to women workers. Other female employees do not report abuse for lack of faith that the criminal justice system will respond to gender-related abuse. Their concerns frequently are borne out by police and judges who dismiss their allegations or, in some cases, even detain the complainants.

Violence and discrimination against women in the workplace, though of long standing, have received little attention in traditional human rights documentation and advocacy, which has focussed on government crackdowns against predominantly male union organizers. Women workers constitute only a small percentage of rank-and-file union membership and an even smaller percentage of union leadership. While women union organizers and members have not escaped repression that is committed or tolerated by government officials, most women workers are more likely to be abused because of their gender, class, immigration status, or a combination of these factors, than because of their union activism. Yet, governments and human rights groups have directed much less scrutiny and condemnation at abuses that occur on the job than those that happen on the picket line.

Several global trends have increased the risk of abuse to women workers. These trends include burgeoning labor migration, large-scale economic transformation, and rising competition for capital investment. First, increased knowledge of income disparities, the demand for cheap labor in the wealthier countries, and the dramatic collapse of barriers to cross-border movement since the end of the Cold War have greatly increased the flow of labor migrants.[1] It has been estimated that, since the 1980s, the female migrant population has outnumbered the male migrant population,[2] in some cases by wide margins.[3] Governments of both sending and receiving countries sometimes actively promote labor migration.[4] Aside from assisting their own

---

[1] International Organization for Migration intervention at U.N. General Assembly, Ninth U.N. Congress on the Prevention of Crime and the Treatment of Offenders, Report of the Asia and Pacific Regional Preparatory Meeting, U.N. Document A/CONF.169/RPM.1, Bangkok, 17-21 January 1994. [U.N. General Assembly, 48th Session, Third Committee, Agenda Item 110, A/C.3/48/L.9/Rev.2.]

[2] Of international female migrant workers, 72 percent are found in Asia, 11 percent in Europe, 8 percent in North America, and 9 percent elsewhere. "Preliminary Report of the Special Rapporteur on Violence Against Women," U.N. Document E/CN.4/1995/42, November 22, 1994, at Paragraph 220, citing "Advancement of Women: Violence Against Migrant Women Workers," Report of the [U.N.] Secretary General, U.N. Document A/49/354.

[3] For example, a 1990 airport survey in Sri Lanka found that 65 percent of migrant workers were female, of whom the majority were domestic servants. Of the migrant workers who have left Indonesia officially in 1988, 78 percent were women. Peter Stalker, *The Work of Strangers: A Survey of International Labor Migration* (Geneva: International Labor Organization, 1994), p. 106.

[4] The Philippines provides one example: "The late President Ferdinand Marcos set off the exodus in 1974 when, facing economic disaster, he mobilized Filipinos to go abroad to earn hard currency and reduce unemployment. Of a population of nearly seventy million, some 3.5 million Filipinos now work overseas, according to the government. Nongovernmental organizations put the figure at more than 4.5 million. . . . The Philippines is the world's largest labor exporter, and remittances are Manila's principal source of foreign currency. Economic migrants sent home $2.6 billion in the first eleven months of 1994, the government says, a 29 percent jump over the same period a year earlier. And that's just what came in through the banking system." "A New Kind of Hero," *Far Eastern Economic Review*, March 30, 1995.

families, female migrant workers often serve the economic interests of both receiving and sending countries. By sending money to their families back home, they provide their home country with needed foreign exchange. At the same time, by freeing women in the receiving countries from housework to participate in paid work, or by taking jobs that locals do not want, female migrant workers fuel the economy of the receiving country. But, having encouraged the migration of women workers, many countries then abdicate responsibility for protecting the fundamental human rights of migrant workers. While alarm over the perceived economic threat of migrants is growing in many receiving countries around the world, scant attention has been given to the abuse they encounter outside their country of origin.

As the Kuwait case study in this chapter shows, female migrant workers are a particularly vulnerable group because of their frequent lack of familiarity with the laws, language and systems of the country of destination. They cannot appeal to their home country's labor protections since the labor laws of most countries do not extend beyond national borders.[5] At the same time, the labor laws of some receiving countries exclude either migrants generally or categories of work—e.g., domestic service—in which female migrant workers predominate. Or when labor laws are adequate on paper, they may not function in practice for lack of enforcement. Women employed as domestic workers in individual homes, such as those in Kuwait, may have an especially difficult time claiming protection of the law. Their "invisibility" also offers employers ample opportunity to evade labor protection laws.[6] Our investigation found that many work in situations of illegal confinement that severely curtail their ability to organize and seek help. Others who lack the proper legal documentation risk sanctions for immigration law violations if they turn to the authorities.

Aside from women who migrate through official channels, countless women and girls are trafficked by criminal elements that operate illegally with

---

[5] For example, the U.S. Supreme Court ruled that the Civil Rights Act of 1964 does not protect U.S. citizens working for U.S. companies abroad from discriminatory employment practices. *EEOC v. Arabian American Oil Co.,* 111 Supreme Court 1227 (1991). The labor laws of most countries relate to persons, including foreign nationals, working within their territories, but do not apply to their own nationals working overseas. The major exception is the rights of seamen, primarily because they are often in international waters. Phone interview, Pharis Harvey, International Labor Rights Fund, July 17, 1995.

[6] Stalker, *The Work of Strangers,* p. 109.

the active cooperation or tacit tolerance of the authorities. Trafficking victims rarely have full knowledge of the conditions that await them; sometimes, they are simply abducted. Many of those who are trafficked for work end up in forced prostitution. (See chapter "Trafficking of Women and Girls into Forced Prostitution and Coerced Marriage" in this volume.)

Another international trend that has increased the risk of abuse to women workers is massive economic restructuring in former communist states since the end of the Cold War. The privatization and reduction of state-owned enterprises has led to large-scale layoffs, even as social assistance programs funded by the state are withdrawn. As the Russia and Poland case studies illustrate, women workers have borne the brunt of economic dislocation. Women workers are fired from public sector employment in disproportionate numbers, are discriminated against in retraining opportunities and job placement by government agencies, and remain chronically unemployed for longer periods than men because of blatant sex discrimination by both public and private employers.

The existence of protective legislation for women sometimes exacerbates the problem of sex discrimination. Protective legislation is intended to shield women from hazardous work or to enable women to balance their responsibilities at work and at home. Employers often use it, however, as an excuse to discriminate with impunity against women workers on the grounds that they are too expensive or their rate of absenteeism is too high relative to male workers.[7]

Intense global competition for foreign investment is another factor that renders female workers vulnerable to human rights violations. For many developing countries, the abundance of cheap labor is their chief competitive advantage. To ensure that wages remain low, some of these governments retaliate against union organizers, neglect to enforce minimal labor standards, and ignore abuses committed by employers, including those in the export-oriented sectors. Factory owners and managers in special export zones have also discriminated against women with impunity by requiring them to undergo pregnancy examinations as a condition of employment.[8]

---

[7] The Committee on Standards of the International Labor Organization is reviewing certain protective labor standards that may have a discriminatory impact on women workers, including, for example, restrictions on women in night work.

[8] As detailed in a forthcoming report by the Human Rights Watch Women's Rights Project, Mexico's *maquiladora* sector is one example of where such discrimination occurs.

Some governments—including Singapore, Indonesia and China—have advanced the specious argument that civil and political rights, including worker rights, are incompatible with the right to economic development. This thesis fails to consider the impact on individual workers of the kind of economic development that sacrifices rights. As one law professor put it, "If development is to be more than a hollow achievement benefiting only foreign investors and local elites, then worker rights must progress simultaneously with economic development."[9] Repression of individual rights can often have devastating consequences for the economically underprivileged, by denying them the opportunity to speak out and organize themselves in order to seek better wages, avert impending famine, combat environmental hazards, or defend against arbitrary deprivation of their property.[10] Moreover, labor rights codified by the International Labor Organization (ILO)—the main intergovernmental agency responsible for articulating and protecting worker rights—are adopted by a two-thirds majority of individual delegates from all member states at annual conferences, and thus cannot be dismissed as reflecting only the interests of Western, industrialized nations.

International Legal Protections

Women workers have the right to be protected from violations of their civil and political rights, as enshrined in the International Covenant on Civil and Political Rights. In addition, the ILO recognizes several worker rights codified in various conventions as basic human rights. These include the rights to freedom of association (including the rights to organize unions and to bargain collectively), freedom from forced labor, and equality of opportunity and treatment on the basis of sex.[11] Under its complaints mechanism, the

---

[9] Lance Compa, "International Labor Standards and Instruments of Recourse for Working Women," *Yale Journal of International Law*, vol. 17 (1992), p. 161.

[10] For further discussion, see *Indivisible Human Rights: The Relationship of Political and Civil Rights to Survival, Subsistence and Poverty* (New York: Human Rights Watch, 1992).

[11] These include Convention (No. 11) on the Right of Association (Agriculture), 1921; Convention (No. 87) on Freedom of Association and Protection of the Right to Organize, 1948; Convention (No. 98) on Right to Organize and Collective Bargaining, 1949; Convention (No. 135) on Workers' Representatives, 1971; Convention (No.141) on Rural Workers' Organizations, 1975; Convention (No. 151) on Labor Relations (Public Service), 1978; Convention (No. 29) on Forced Labor, 1930; Convention (No. 105) on Abolition of Forced Labor, 1957; Convention (No. 100) on Equal

(continued...)

ILO can also receive and investigate petitions alleging labor rights violations in member countries. Its reports and findings are an important point of reference in bilateral discussions on labor standards. ILO conventions and decisions are binding on governments. Where governments refuse to abide by them, other countries can and should take such recalcitrance into account and include compliance among conditions for trade and other economic relations.

International protection for workers can be further augmented through other channels, such as labor rights conditionalities in the global trade regime, regional trade pacts, or national trade laws. Unfortunately, the Uruguay Round of multilateral trade negotiations, the only internationally recognized regime for global trade regulation, did not result in a labor rights clause that requires member states to respect basic workers rights.[12] More progress has been achieved at the regional and national levels. Both the United States[13] and the

---

[11](...continued)
Remuneration, 1951; Convention (No. 111) on Discrimination, 1958; and Convention (No. 156) on Workers with Family Responsibilities, 1981. *International Labor Conventions and Recommendations 1919-1981* (Geneva: International Labor Organization, 1982). Nonetheless, debate continues regarding what constitutes a "basic" or "core" set of labor rights. Theresa A. Amato, "Labor Rights Conditionality: United States Trade Legislation and the International Trade Order," *New York University Law Review,* Volume 65 (April 1990), footnote 2.

[12] "Final Act Embodying the Results of the Uruguay Round of Multilateral Trade Negotiations" (Office of the U.S. Trade Representative, Executive Office of the President, Washington, D.C., December 15, 1993). A committee has been formed to discuss the possibility of attaching such a provision to the World Trade Organization.

[13] For example, since 1983, the U.S. Congress has passed four pieces of legislation that conditions access to the U.S. market on the basis of respect for labor rights. These include the Caribbean Basin Initiative (also known as the Interest and Dividend Tax Compliance Act of 1983); the 1984 amendments to the Generalized System of Preferences (GSP); the 1985 amendments to the Overseas Private Investment Corporation (OPIC) Act; and the 1988 Omnibus Trade and Competitiveness Act. Each of these statutes contains a labor rights clause that permits the U.S. to suspend the trade benefits of any beneficiary country that violates or fails to take steps to accord workers "internationally recognized worker rights." U.S. law does not, however, include invidious sex discrimination as a violation of an "internationally recognized labor right." By contrast, the Clinton administration recently promoted a set of "model business principles" for U.S. businesses with overseas operations. These principles include, among other things, "avoidance of discrimination based on . . . gender . . ." This code of conduct, unfortunately, is purely voluntary and too general to be effective.

European Union,[14] for example, condition trade benefits to beneficiary countries under their Generalized System of Preferences on respect for labor rights. These mechanisms, however, have not been rigorously and consistently applied to uphold women workers' rights, including freedom from invidious discrimination on the basis of sex or maternity.

Among regional trade pacts, the 1993 North American Free Trade Agreement involving Canada, Mexico and the U.S. does require parties to the agreement to promote, among other things, the elimination of employment discrimination on the basis of sex[15] and equal pay for women and men.[16] Of the eleven labor principles covered under the side agreement on the protection of worker rights, three—occupational safety and health, child labor, or minimum wage technical labor standards—are deemed to be of sufficient importance that their violation would merit monetary penalties against the

---

[14] Under the European Union's Generalized System of Preferences, among other things, "practice of any form of forced labor" or "export of goods made by prison labor" may lead to a suspension of GSP status following "hearings" on such alleged violations. In addition, the European Union's GSP also provides for "special incentives" in the form of an additional margin on tariff reductions to encourage beneficiary countries to conform to internationally recognized standards. Systematic sex discrimination is not one of the grounds for suspension of GSP status. European Commission, "Proposal for a Council Regulation concerning the new GSP scheme for the period 1995-1997," COM(94)337 final.

[15] North American Agreement on Labor Cooperation, Supplemental Agreement to the North American Free Trade Agreement, Annex 1, Principle 7: "Elimination of employment on such grounds as race, religion, age, sex or other grounds, subject to certain reasonable exceptions, such as, where applicable, bona fide occupational requirements or qualifications and established practices or rules governing retirement ages, and special measures of protection or assistance for particular groups designed to take into account the effects of discrimination."

[16] Ibid., Principle 8: "Equal wages for women and men by applying the principle of equal pay for equal work in the same establishment." The other principles include: freedom of association and protection of the right to organize; the right to bargain collectively; the right to strike; prohibition of forced labor; labor protections for children and young persons; minimum employment standards, such as minimum wages and overtime pay; prevention of occupational injuries and illnesses; compensation in cases of occupational injuries and illnesses; and protection of migrant workers.

offending country, after a review by a duly convened panel.[17] This enhanced level of enforcement does not, however, extend to either of the gender-specific protections. Moreover, the effectiveness of the side agreement is seriously undermined by a cumbersome petition process and a lack of transparency at the ministerial stage of adjudication.

Given the growing percentage of women in the labor force in most countries and among migrant worker populations, an urgent need exists to strengthen both domestic and international legal protections for women workers. Governments and the International Labor Organization must actively investigate and publicly condemn violations of the rights of women workers. Of equal importance, they should work, in conjunction with trade unions and women's organizations, to educate and train women workers to be agents in securing better protection of their own rights.

Finally, governments and international financial institutions are increasingly recognizing the rule of law and good governance not only as important goals in themselves, but as critical to the development of successful economic systems. In promoting these principles, they should ensure that the basic rights of all workers, including women, are fully protected.

ASIAN DOMESTIC WORKERS IN KUWAIT

Every year since the liberation of Kuwait in March 1991, nearly 2,000 women domestic workers, mainly from Sri Lanka, the Philippines, Bangladesh and India have fled the homes of abusive Kuwaiti employers and sought refuge in their embassies.[18] The embassies of these Asian countries report a daily average of four to five runaway maids. According to the former labor secretary at the Sri Lankan embassy in Kuwait, L. Ariyadasa, "Most of them

---

[17] A review panel convened under the terms of the agreement may impose a "monetary enforcement assessment" of not more than $20 million against a party with "a persistent pattern of failure" to enforce occupational safety and health , child labor or minimum wage technical labor standards. Ibid., Part Five, Article 27(1) and Annex 39.

[18] The following material was adapted from Middle East Watch (now Human Rights Watch/Middle East) and Women's Rights Project, "Punishing the Victim: Rape and Mistreatment of Asian Maids in Kuwait," *A Human Rights Watch Short Report*, Volume 4, Issue 8, August 1992. It was updated during fact-finding missions in 1993 and 1994.

are severely beaten, . . . raped or even burned." In April 1995 he said that the problem was "getting worse and worse every day."[19]

Our investigation—based on fact-finding missions in 1992, 1993 and 1994 and subsequent updates—has found that while most domestic servants in Kuwait do not suffer at the hands of their employers, in a significant portion of households there exists a pattern of rape, physical assault and mistreatment of Asian maids that takes place largely with impunity. Debt bondage and illegal confinement are also common. Kuwaiti law exacerbates the problem by excluding domestic workers from the country's labor law protections.

While abuse of maids is common in other countries, the situation in post-war Kuwait is especially critical. In 1993 the Philippines' Overseas Workers Welfare Administration (OWWA) reported that it had never before seen a problem on the scale of that in Kuwait. According to David Corpin, head of OWWA, "There was a distinct trend for violence, and molestations and beatings increased after the war."[20]

Origins of the Problem

Kuwait has long depended on foreign workers to provide the backbone of its labor force.[21] By 1990, prior to the Iraqi invasion of Kuwait, foreign workers and their dependents, also referred to as expatriates, accounted for nearly 62 percent of Kuwait's population.[22] Many of these workers come from India, Sri Lanka, Bangladesh and the Philippines. The number of expatriate workers in the private sector reached 600,000 in January 1994,[23] nearly 90 percent of private sector employment. The maids are almost all expatriates, mostly from Asian countries. Over the past ten years, the number

---

[19] Agence France-Presse (AFP), April 13, 1995, dispatch from Kuwait. Ariyadasa added, "Our embassy is sheltering more than 150 runaways, all of them are either physically or sexually abused." In a May 1995 interview with Human Rights Watch, Ariyadasa agreed to be identified publicly.

[20] Belinda Rhodes, "Filipinas tell of their nightmare in Kuwait," *San Francisco Examiner*, August 8, 1993.

[21] Ian J. Seccombe, "Economic Recession and International Labor Migration in the Arab Gulf," *The Arab Gulf Journal*, vol. 6 (April 1986), p. 46.

[22] Population Estimates, Ministry of Planning.

[23] Bassam al-Qassas, "Transfer of residence open," *Arab Times*, January 22, 1994. This figure is for the private sector only. According to a Kuwaiti economist quoted in the article, expatriates constituted 95 percent of the pre-war private sector work force and Kuwaitis accounted for only 30 percent of the total work force.

of Asian maids has more than doubled, from about 72,000 in 1985 to nearly 135,000 in 1994.[24]

Although abuse was prevalent before the Iraqi occupation,[25] the treatment of Asian maids took a turn for the worse following liberation,[26] a trend now acknowledged by Kuwaiti officials.[27] Every year since liberation, over 2,000 Asian maids have sought shelter in their embassies. Most who fled their employers complained of rape, physical abuse, mistreatment or non-payment of wages, according to information we obtained from foreign embassies in Kuwait, Kuwaiti government officials, journalists, U.S. State Department officials and others. In April 1995 over 200 maids were sheltered at the Philippines embassy, 150 at the Sri Lankan embassy and smaller numbers at other embassies. Without offering alternative shelters, the Kuwaiti government repeatedly asked embassies not to offer refuge to runaway maids.

Prompted by reports of abuse in Kuwait, the Philippines government banned Filipinas from going to work in Kuwait as maids. Nonetheless, many Filipinas still travel to Kuwait to work as housemaids, although some are lured by false promises of other kinds of jobs. Currently, some 30,000 work as maids in Kuwait. The Gulf remains the most popular destination for Filipino overseas workers whose remittances constitute their country's largest source of foreign exchange.[28]

---

[24] Ibid., pp. 464, 466-67. Seccombe, "Economic Recession . . . ," pp. 44-45. *See also* Frank Eelens and J.D. Speckmann, "Recruitment of Labor Migrants for the Middle East: The Sri Lankan Case," *XXIV International Migration Review* (Summer 1990), p. 299.

[25] The abuse of domestic workers in Kuwait prior to the invasion is recorded in Reda Helal, Al-Sira' ala al-Kuwait (Struggle Over Kuwait), (Cairo, 1992), p. 41 (in Arabic); U.S. Department of State, *Country Reports on Human Rights Practices for 1988* (Washington, D.C.: U.S. Government Printing Office, 1989), p. 1407; U.S. Department of State, *Country Reports on Human Rights Practices for 1989* (Washington, D.C.: U.S. Government Printing Office, 1990), p. 1464.

[26] See Middle East Watch, *A Victory Turned Sour: Human Rights in Kuwait since Liberation*, (New York: Human Rights Watch, 1991); Middle East Watch and Women's Rights Project, "Punishing the Victims. . . "

[27] Mohammad Khobaizi, head of the Deportation Center at Dasma Police Station, told a Kuwaiti newspaper that there had been an "increase after liberation" of maid abuse. Betty Lipphold, "Kuwait continues to depend on expatriate manpower," *Arab Times*, December 30-31, 1993.

[28] Ibid. The article cites a Philippines government estimate that 5,000 (or 17 percent) of the 30,000 total in Kuwait may be abused.

Patterns of Abuse

Our investigation revealed a significant and pervasive pattern of rape, physical assault and mistreatment of Asian maids by some Kuwaiti employers, who act largely with impunity. During a 1992 mission, we investigated sixty cases, one-third of which involved the rape or sexual assault of maids by their employers or a man with access to the employer's house. Well over two-thirds of these cases involved physical assault, including kicking, beating with sticks, slapping and punching. Almost without exception the women we interviewed spoke of non-payment of salary, passport deprivation, and near-total confinement in their employers' homes. Asian embassy officials and other sources reported to us that these findings held true for the larger population of maids who fled their employers. Subsequent investigations by Human Rights Watch in 1993 and 1994, found that the patterns remained roughly the same as in 1992.

We also found indications that such abuses are under-reported.[29] Maids face numerous obstacles to reporting abuse or mistreatment. Many women are confined in their employers' homes. Others confront police refusal to investigate their complaints. In addition, the social stigma attached to certain types of abuse, particularly sexual assault, deters many women from reporting employer abuse to the authorities.

Only a handful of the charges against abusive employers are investigated or prosecuted every year. In an April 1993 letter to Human Rights Watch, the Kuwaiti government stated that between February 1991 and February 1993, only fifteen sexual assault cases against maids were prosecuted. In an interview with Human Rights Watch in April 1995, a Kuwaiti official conceded that many sexual assault offenses go unprosecuted because prosecutors too frequently exercise their discretion to close the investigation of these crimes without ever filing charges.

In addition to denying abused domestic workers justice under applicable criminal and civil law, the government explicitly excludes them from the protection of the country's labor law. The law covers most other workers (including expatriates), regulates working conditions, and provides for civil arbitration in employment disputes. In the April 1993 letter to Human Rights Watch, the Kuwaiti government maintained that "exempting domestic servants from labor regulations is consistent with international labor legislation.

---

[29] Domestic violence and rape are two of the most under-reported crimes internationally. See United Nations, *Violence Against Women in the Family* (New York: United Nations, 1989), p. 17.

Since the work of these individuals is directly connected with their employers, it is necessary to enact a separate legal regime for them to take these conditions in consideration."[30]   Although the government of Kuwait hosted an International Labor Organization delegation in the fall of 1994 to investigate this and other labor issues, no legislation has been adopted to regulate the work of domestic servants.

Except in the most egregious cases of abuse, employers are rarely prosecuted. Public prosecutors, in practice, do not pursue charges of employer abuse absent vigorous pressure from the victim, her family, embassy and lawyers. In most cases, the victim and her family cannot afford the services of lawyers, whose fees average several years' of a maid's salary. Foreign embassies are reluctant to intervene for fear of adverse reactions from the Kuwaiti government. Nor, in many cases, do they have sufficient resources to enlist the help of lawyers.

Abused maids have had little alternative but to flee to their embassies or to shelter with friends while they seek to settle their disputes, find new jobs, or return home. But most of these options have been foreclosed by the government. Arbitration is unavailable, job transfer exceedingly difficult to secure, and the government denies exit visas to the maids seeking to leave without their employers' permission. The result has been that, unless the maids can find informal means of resolving their difficulties, as some do, they languish in increasing numbers at the deportation centers or their countries' embassies.

The abuse of Asian maids is not limited to sexual or physical assault. Debt bondage, passport deprivation, and confinement are also common and create conditions for the maids to suffer assault in near total isolation. The maids' exclusion from the labor law paves the way for this isolation and denies them even minimal protection against unfair practices.

Exclusion from the Labor Law

Kuwait's Private Sector Labor Law No. 38 of 1964 (the labor law) governs working conditions for most workers, including expatriates, in the private sector. It explicitly excludes domestic servants from its provisions.[31]

---

[30] Letter, Nasser Mohamed El-Nasr-Allah, Ministry of Justice, April 10, 1993.

[31] Law No. 38 of 1964 Concerning Labor in Private Sector (as amended through 1989), Chapter 1 (Scope of Implementation), Article 2(e) (hereinafter "Law No. 38") provides that "domestic servants and those having their status" shall "not be subject to the applications of this law's provisions."

Meshari al-Osaimi, a member of the National Assembly's Legislative Committee and former head of the Kuwaiti Lawyers' Association, told Human Rights Watch that many of the problems facing the maids in Kuwait stem from this exclusion: "It affects the atmosphere of work and the sense of what treatment maids are entitled to. In 1964 there were only a few hundred maids, today there are 200,000. Now their exclusion from the law is a human rights issue."[32]

The labor law governs the maximum daily and/or weekly hours an employee can be required to work,[33] employees' entitlement to overtime,[34] and provisions for weekly and annual leave.[35] If employers violate these requirements, the labor law provides workers with access to the Ministry of Social Affairs and Labor to air their grievances about working conditions and have them investigated or arbitrated by the ministry.[36]

The law's exclusion of domestic servants has fueled a widespread attitude that the maids are not entitled to the same rights as other workers. As a group, women domestic servants have no right to organize,[37] and no power either to bargain for fair employment terms or to enforce the terms their employers agreed to when they were hired. Nor do they have access to the government facilities for arbitration of employment disputes. This has created an atmosphere in which the maids can be, and often are, overworked and ill-treated by their employers with little expectation that the state will intervene. The establishment of a government office in 1993 to deal with maids and servants has not improved matters for the maids. Little known and with no legal mandate, the office has had no perceptible success in combating abuse or reporting it.

Rape, Sexual and Physical Assault

Our investigation revealed a disturbing prevalence of rape and sexual assault claims, which require the immediate attention of the Kuwaiti

---

[32] Interview, Attorney Meshari al-Osaimi, president of the Kuwait Lawyer's Association, Kuwait City, April 1992.

[33] Law No. 38, Article 33.

[34] Ibid., Article 34.

[35] Ibid., Articles 35-39.

[36] Ibid., Chapter XV (General Provisions), Articles 95 and 96.

[37] Maids are denied the right to organize because labor organizations are only authorized under Law No. 38, from which the women are excluded. In addition, all foreign workers must satisfy stringent conditions to join existing unions.

authorities.   We interviewed Asian maids who were raped or sexually assaulted, and were beaten during a rape or attempted rape by their employers. Others were beaten when they refused to consent to sex with an employer or his male relative. Still others were subjected to violence or its threat to coerce them into sexual intercourse.

It is impossible to say what percentage of all the maids working in Kuwait have been sexually assaulted by their employers.   Women face enormous obstacles to reporting abuse and to leaving difficult or abusive work situations. Women who do escape risk arrest for being out without a passport or for other offenses. Increasingly, escaping an employer's home also involves the possibility of deportation. Furthermore, even if the maids do manage to overcome all these obstacles, they may be personally reluctant to report that they had been raped or sexually assaulted.[38]

In several cases we investigated, the physical and emotional trauma was so severe that the women became catatonic and psychologically, as well as physically, injured. In some cases, the woman received appropriate medical care, but a number of escaped maids whom we interviewed in their embassies or the Kuwaiti government's deportation center showed unmistakable signs of trauma that had not received any medical attention.

S. B., a twenty-year-old Sri Lankan, told us that on the day she was admitted to the hospital, her employer had followed her into a room she was cleaning, locked the door and raped her. After he raped her, he threw her off the balcony and she landed on the ground several stories below.[39] When S.B. was admitted to the hospital, both her ankles were broken, she was bleeding vaginally and had lacerations on her labia and rectal area that required stitches. She was catatonic and unresponsive to verbal cues for weeks following her admission to the hospital.[40]

L., a twenty-two-year-old Filipina, ran away from the same employer three times. After she ran away the first time because her employer pressured her for sex, she was arrested for being out without her passport and taken to

---

[38] The social barriers to reporting rape and sexual assault are tremendous. Many women have families and children whom they do not want to find out. Others, especially younger, single women, told us they found it difficult to report being raped because they were virgins before the assault and came from countries in which their virginity was a prerequisite to marriage.

[39] Interview, Kuwait City, May 1992. Full names of interviewees withheld by Human Rights Watch unless otherwise indicated.

[40] Interview, Kuwait City, May 1992; interview, Washington, D.C., June 1992.

Dasma police station, where she was detained for a month until her employer obtained her release. He brought her back to his home in the Salmiyah district of Kuwait City, where he again asked her to have sex with him. She told us that when she refused, "he punched my face [and] said he would kill me." She told us that thereafter the employer raped her repeatedly. L. escaped again and this time stayed with a friend, only to be tricked into returning to her employer's home, from which she finally fled to the embassy. [41] To our knowledge, no case was pursued against her employer, and L. was deported to the Philippines during the first week of May 1992.[42]

W. T. came to Kuwait from Sri Lanka in September 1991. She worked for a couple in the town of Jahra. She told us that her employers' son raped her repeatedly: "Before I came here I was a virgin. . . . Now no one in Sri Lanka will marry me. I have been ruined." On one occasion her female employer threw boiling tea at her, causing blisters on her shoulders and breasts.[43] When she complained to her employer about being raped, the woman kicked her in the stomach and beat her before taking her to see a gynecologist at al-Jahra Hospital. W.T. fled her employer and sought refuge at her embassy, but the embassy officials sent her to the police station, where we interviewed her in May 1992. The police told us that although they called the son and his father to the police station for questioning, the two men were released immediately. W.T., however, was detained at the Dasma Police Station Deportation Facility and later deported. We received no information on the outcome of the investigation of the rape and assault charges.

---

[41] From her friend's home, L. later called her employer to request her passport so she could go home. He agreed to give it to her, but when he brought her back to his home, he beat her, punching her in the face repeatedly. He then took her to Mubarak Hospital, where she received three stitches under her left eye. "I did not tell the doctor [how I got hurt] because I was afraid. I also did not tell the doctor I was raped and might be pregnant." After she received treatment, the employer took her back to his home. A week later, L. again ran away, this time to the Philippines Embassy. When we interviewed her moments after her arrival, the entire left side of her face was swollen and bruised and the three stitches on her left lower eyelid were leaking blood. She said that her employer had beaten her again and that she ran away after he punched her in the face where the stitches were. Interview, April 1992.

[42] Many of the women who were deported during the last week of April and first week of May 1992 left Kuwait voluntarily. In other cases, however, women who wanted to stay and continue working were denied this option. See Middle East Watch and Women's Rights Project,"Punishing the Victims . . ., " Section III.

[43] Interview, Kuwait City, May 1992.

Shaikha, a thirty-year-old Indian woman, stated that she was raped and beaten by her employer, who left bruises on her chest and thighs. After she was raped, Shaikha escaped from the house and walked alone to al-Razi Hospital, where she fainted in the entrance at 6:30 a.m.[44] Shaikha was later repatriated to India by her embassy. To our knowledge, no action was taken against her employer.[45]

Ambia K. told us that her male employer repeatedly attempted to rape her. She said that on one occasion, "Baba[46] wanted to have sex with me, and he took a knife and put it to my throat. That time he broke my thumb. My madame came and took the knife so he wouldn't cut me." She also described her employer's unwanted fondling of her genital area. She said, "My madame wanted to send me home, but the baba refused." She said that sometimes her male employer also beat her with a plastic water pipe that left her legs bloody. We noted visible scars on her legs. One day, her male employer beat her and threw her out the front gate, locking it behind her. She eventually met a group of Bangladeshis who took her to a safe place.[47]

Mumtaz S., a nineteen-year-old Sri Lankan woman who worked for a family in the Suleibikhat District, was sexually assaulted by her employer's son. She was also punched in the head repeatedly by her employer whenever the infant she took care of misbehaved. After two months of this treatment, she told us she drank two tall glasses of bleach to try to kill herself. Her employers took her to Suleibikhat Hospital for treatment; there she was arrested for attempted suicide following her treatment.[48] Unspecified charges were filed against the son, but were ultimately dismissed.

In interviews with runaway maids in December 1993 and January 1994, nearly one-third cited rape or sexual assault as the main cause for their

---

[44] Interview, Kuwait City, April 1992.

[45] Interview, Kuwait City, April 1992.

[46] Asian maids often referred to their male employers as "baba" and their female employers as "mama" or "Madame."

[47] The family also employed a Bangladeshi man as a driver. Ambia K. told us that when the employer threw her out the gate, the driver came and beat her, trying to convince her to have sex with their employer. When she refused, the driver put her in the car and took her to a Pakistani man who also wanted to have sex with her. She fought with the Pakistani, got out of the car and ran away. She found a bus stop and met an Indian boy who told her to take the bus to the airport. She did that, and at the airport she met the group of Bangladeshis who took her to safety. Interview, Kuwait City, May 1992.

[48] These charges were ultimately dropped, and she was sent to her embassy.

flight from their employers' homes. Kuwaiti officials conceded privately that there is a serious problem with sex crimes against the maids. One official suggested strengthening the procedures for investigating and prosecuting sex crimes, including imposing judicial oversight over prosecutors' decisions to discontinue investigations of these crimes.[49]

Physical abuse was even more widely reported by maids than sexual assault and appears to be pervasive. Over two-thirds of the cases we investigated involved complaints of physical assault, including kicking, beating with sticks and pipes, slapping, punching and pulling of hair. Foreign embassy officials and local human rights activists independently corroborated this finding, noting that most of the Asian women who have run away to their embassies since liberation claim to have been beaten or otherwise physically assaulted in some manner. In some cases physical assault was severe enough to require the victims' hospitalization.

We also spoke to some women who had not run away from their employers but reported being slapped in the face, hit on the back of the head with a shoe, or kicked in the shins for "transgressions" as minor as not moving fast enough. Male and female employers of every social background were cited as assaulting their maids. The cases detailed here exemplify the nature and type of physical abuse perpetrated by employers in Kuwait.

N. G., a twenty-five-year-old from Bangladesh, told us she worked for a relative of the Emir and that she was repeatedly beaten if she was late or otherwise violated the rules set for her work. As a consequence of this mistreatment, N.G. carries scars on her forehead, stomach, arms and thighs, and reported partial loss of hearing.[50] To our knowledge, no action was taken against her employer.[51] She was later repatriated with the help of friends.

Fatima, a forty-five-year-old from Bangladesh, had worked in Kuwait for six years before the occupation. She returned to Kuwait after liberation to work for a different employer, who stopped paying her after the first few months. She said her new employer frequently kicked and beat her, sometimes "with a piece of wood about one foot long and two to three inches thick." On one occasion, she said her employer kicked her down a flight of stairs. In another incident, the employer's twenty-five-year-old son "hit me on the head with the toilet cover as I was cleaning the toilet."[52]

---

[49] Interviews, Kuwait, December 1993-January 1994; New York, April 1995.
[50] This was confirmed by an embassy official.
[51] Interview, Washington, D.C., June 1992.
[52] Interview, Kuwait City, May 1992.

Illegal Employment Practices

Debt bondage, prohibited under international human rights law, occurs when a debtor pledges to provide personal services in payment of a debt, but the person to whom she or he is indebted fails to deduct the value of the debtor's services from the debt, or the length and nature of those services are not limited and defined.[53]

Kuwait's labor law requires that no more than 10 percent of wages due may be deducted for settlement of debts owed the employer.[54] But, because domestic servants are excluded from this law, they cannot invoke this provision. Consequently, employers often do not honor the 10 percent limitation. In many cases we investigated, a large percentage or, in some cases, the entirety of maids' salaries had been withheld by employers, allegedly to settle the maids' debts.[55] The women workers appeared to have no say in the amount attributed as loaned to them or in the decision regarding salary proportions to be deducted towards their debt. In many cases we investigated, debt had the effect of placing women in bondage to their employers. It was used as a means of forcing the women to endure long working hours, inadequate food and sleep, no days off, and no time to attend a place of worship,[56] for fear of never getting paid or of losing their jobs.

---

[53] 1957 Supplementary Convention on the Abolition of Slavery, the Slave Trade, and Institutions and Practices Similar to Slavery, Article 1(a). Kuwait has ratified this convention.

[54] Law No. 38, Chapter VII (Wages), Article 31. It also requires that employment of all covered workers must be made under a contract, which may or may not be written. Ibid., Chapter IV (Contracts), Article 12.

[55] In cases investigated by Human Rights Watch the debts appeared to have been incurred under questionable circumstances. Employment agents, based either in Kuwait or in an Asian country, charge the Kuwaiti employer a commission—sometimes as high as US $1,200 to $2,000—as well as the cost of airfare to find and bring the maid over to Kuwait. Employers are told that they can recoup these fees from the maids. However, maids have usually already paid duplicate fees to the agents (and they or their families have often gone into debt to do so) and only upon arrival in Kuwait do many learn that employers will deduct their own payments to the agent from the maid's salary. Thus maids find themselves indebted involuntarily to their employers from the outset. Maids are usually recruited through employment agencies that are illegal under seldom-enforced Kuwaiti laws. Interviews, Kuwait, January 4, 1994 and May 21, 1994.

[56] Interviews with six Indian women at church, Kuwait City, May 1992; Interview, Mary, Kuwait City, May 1992; Interview, January 1994.

Many maids told Human Rights Watch that they worked long hours, frequently eighteen to twenty hours a day with no formal rest periods.[57] In many cases corroborated by police investigations, they stated they were not paid for months. In one case, no salary was paid for nineteen months. Withholding wages robs maids of the means to leave abusive situations. It is extremely difficult for the women to escape debt bondage. First and foremost, they and their families depend on their salaries. Relative to what they can earn in their home countries, maids earn high wages in Kuwait. The average Asian maid earns between US $75 and $120 per month and sends most, if not all, of her earnings to support her family at home. For this reason, after incurring the considerable expense of coming to Kuwait, she cannot afford to return home without being paid. Even if maid do wish to leave, the lack of money is a significant obstacle to escape. They can neither afford a ticket home nor support themselves while attempting to find another job, which in any case is nearly impossible to do without their previous employer's consent. Furthermore, employers often threaten maids with arrest should they leave without satisfying their debt.

The effective bondage of the women workers is further enforced by employers' taking their passports. Kuwaiti Undersecretary of Foreign Affairs Sulaiman al-Shaheen told Human Rights Watch that "the employers keep the passports to put pressure on the girls [to pay their debts]."[58] Almost every maid's passport is taken from her by her employer upon arrival in Kuwait.[59]

Passport deprivation by employers is illegal. According to a 1972 decision by the Superior Appeals Court of Kuwait:

> [A] person may not be deprived of their passport nor denied access to it without a legally sanctioned reason...[A]ssuming the [employer] withheld it because of a dispute he had with the [employee] and that [the employer] had substantive reasons to believe that the [employee] might flee, there are other means available to him to prevent his escape by filing

---

[57] Middle East Watch and Women's Rights Project, "Punishing the Victim . . . ," pp. 8-10.

[58] Interview, Ministry of Foreign Affairs, Kuwait City, May 5, 1992.

[59] Interview, Brigadier Yagoub al-Muhaini, Ministry of Interior, Director of Police Investigations, Kuwait City, May 1992; Interview, Attorney Meshari al-Osaimi, president of Kuwait Lawyer's Association, Kuwait City, April 1992; Interviews, maids and human rights activists, January 1994.

> a motion with a court of law. *Confiscation of the passport,*
> *which by necessity leads to illegal restriction of the freedom*
> *of its holder, is a consequence that the [employer] does not*
> *have the right to effect and is against the law.*[60]

Yet, despite the court's unambiguous decision directly linking passport deprivation to "illegal restriction of the freedom of its holder," the government appears to accept this practice when applied to Asian maids. The Ministry of Interior's director of police investigations, Brigadier al-Muhaini, told us,"I'm not concerned with the passports, as a matter of fact. If an employer keeps the passport, it is only so the employee won't lose it, not to keep her in custody. It is just as we treat our children at home—it's the same thing with the maids."[61]

At the same time that the government tolerates the taking of the maids' passports, it rigorously enforces the Aliens Residence Law, which requires foreigners to carry their passports or other papers confirming their legal status at all times or be subject to immediate arrest and fine or detention.[62] Thus, if a maid flees without her papers or residency documents, she is very likely to be arrested or detained.[63] We found that Asian women walking in the streets are subjected to random questioning by police or military officials.[64] If a maid cannot produce the required documents, she can be

---

[60] Superior Appeals Court, 1st Circuit Commercial, No. 638 (1972), August 5, 1972. Emphasis added. See, also, Superior Appeals Court, 1st Circuit Commercial, No. 662 (1972), August 5, 1972 ("Since a passport is a personal document indispensable for an individual for identification and secure and safe movement within the country...a passport may not be withheld from the person to whom it has been issued.") (All translations by Human Rights Watch.)

[61] Interview, Kuwait City, May 1992.

[62] Aliens must present their passports and other identity and residence documents "whenever requested" by appropriate authorities. Aliens Residence Law, Section II, Article 8. Violation of the requirement to produce these documents may be punished by imprisonment for not more than three months and/or a fine of KD 200 to 400. Ibid., Article 24. This is equivalent to approximately US $600 to $1,400, or many times the usual monthly salary of most Asian maids.

[63] We did not come across any cases in which the escaped maid was fined, although that penalty is prescribed by the law.

[64] Checkpoints continue to be erected in Kuwait, but the frequency of their use fluctuates, depending on security and administrative considerations. Non-Kuwaiti
(continued...)

detained.[65] In a 1994 visit to the makeshift deportation facility at the Dasma police station, a Human Rights Watch representative found that many of the maids kept there had been detained after being stopped on the street by police. Some women were stopped while fleeing alleged abuse to seek shelter at their embassies.[66]

Passport deprivation was also a barrier to maids' ability to leave Kuwait. As described below, the Kuwaiti government requires an exit visa to be stamped on the passport of all departing aliens. Most maids who flee abusive employers do not have their passports and cannot obtain the necessary exit visa. Thus, the government prevents them from leaving Kuwait, in violation of the internationally guaranteed right to leave any country.[67]

Debt bondage coupled with passport deprivation permits employers illegally to confine their Asian maids. Confinement may be limited or total. A maid may be permitted to accompany the family on an excursion or go to a public place of worship. Or she may be forbidden any contact whatsoever with the outside world, including by phone or mail. In many of the cases we investigated, the abused women had experienced such total confinement, sometimes including being locked in the room in which they slept. One woman described to us how when her employers left home, they unplugged the phones and locked her into one room. Then they locked all the windows and the front door behind them. The woman eventually escaped early one morning by climbing over the wall of the garden when her employers were just waking up.

The effect of isolating the maids from the outside world is that few are aware of employers' abusive practices, and it is nearly impossible for a woman to report abuse to the police—presuming they would be responsive—or to her embassy, unless she is able (and courageous enough) to take the drastic step of running away. In some cases, the maids became so desperate they jumped out of windows or off balconies two or more stories high to get away

---

[64](...continued)
residents found without proper papers are usually immediately detained, as a Human Rights Watch representative observed during a December 1993-January 1994 visit.

[65] Interview, Kuwait City, April 1992.

[66] Interviews, Kuwait City, January 1994.

[67] Article 12, International Covenant on Civil and Political Rights: "Everyone shall be free to leave any country, including his own." The government has deported the women *en masse*. In April 1992, some 800 were deported at government expense; a group of 400 were deported in July 1993.

from abusive employers. Others tried to commit suicide following intolerable abuse. These women often were taken to hospitals with injuries such as broken ankles and heels, fractured pelvises, broken vertebrae, and paralysis.

Paramedics at Mubarak al-Kabir Hospital told to us that Helen D., a Filipina maid, was admitted with her hands bound behind her back and a gag in her mouth. She told hospital personnel that she was raped by her employer and had jumped from a fourth-story window to escape.[68] After receiving treatment at Mubarak and al-Razi Orthopedic Hospital, Helen was arrested pursuant to a police order on unspecified felony charges and taken to al-Nugra Police Station.[69] According to our information, the police then returned her to the same employer.

On January 28, 1994, Ratanayake Upasenage, a twenty-six-year-old Sri Lankan maid, fell to her death from the fifth-floor apartment of her employers. Mrs. Upasenage had arrived in Kuwait the previous December, leaving her husband and four children in Sri Lanka. Neighbors testified that on more than one occasion before her death, Mrs. Upasenage had been severely beaten by her employers and that once before her death, she had attempted to run away but was forcibly returned to her employer by the building's guard. Her death was ruled a suicide, but her family's requests for an independent autopsy were rejected. Her body was repatriated by the Sri Lankan embassy after her employer refused this responsibility and rejected requests by her family to return her belongings and back pay. There has been apparently no investigation of the assault on Mrs. Upasenage before her death or of her reported forcible return to her abusive employer.[70]

The Response of the Kuwaiti Government

Despite the number of credible claims, only a few employers have been prosecuted for the physical and sexual abuse of domestic workers. To our knowledge, no legal action has been taken against any employer for debt bondage, illegal confinement or passport deprivation. We found a consistent

---

[68] Interviews, Kuwait City, May 1992. We were unable to obtain or examine her hospital records to determine if her rape allegation was medically substantiated. For more discussion of this case, see Middle East Watch and Women's Rights Project, "Punishing the Victims . . .", p. 19.

[69] Al-Nugra Police Station Arrest Order, signed by Lt. Col. Adel Muhammed al-Sabbagha, for Hawalli District Commander, Hawalli Province Investigations Administration, Ministry of Interior, dated April 14, 1992, Ref. J 3/4/14.

[70] Phone interviews, New York, February and March 1994.

pattern of law enforcement agencies' refusing to credit women's allegations and failing to investigate or prosecute rape, physical assault, debt bondage, passport deprivation and confinement. In addition, police often wrongfully detained women seeking to report abuse or arrested abused women for supposed violations of Kuwaiti law without investigating the context in which those supposed violations, such as being out without a passport, occurred. In general, Kuwait's response to abuse of Asian women servants has been characterized by a tendency to abdicate responsibility for the problem, extend undue protection to Kuwaiti employers, and deny the abused women available remedies.

In some instances, individual Kuwaiti law enforcement officials have attempted to provide the abused maids with some assistance. We discovered cases in which police officers attempted informally to arbitrate employment disputes with employers or secure new jobs for maids, rather than return them to abusive employers or process them for deportation. These individual efforts are laudable. However, such ad hoc solutions to the maids' problems have served to undercut vigorous enforcement of existing criminal law and to obscure the necessity for legal reforms that would provide more effective protection than informal procedures. Without such enforcement and reform, abused women without good, informal connections were (and still are) left with little alternative but to return home. Initially, the government foreclosed even that opportunity. And, once they agreed to deport the women, they did so without investigating the abused women's complaints or resolving their claims.

Abdication of Responsibility

Three years after we released our report, the government still publicly denies that the problem exists on a significant scale, accuses maids of fabricating their stories, and charges the press and human rights organizations with exaggeration and misrepresentations. In an April 1995 report from Kuwait, Minister of Social Affairs Ahmed al-Kulaib dismissed concern about the problem, saying that the number of abused maids was negligible compared to the numbers living in Kuwait. He was responding to a statement that Mahinda Raiapakase, Sri Lanka's labor minister, had made during a March 1995 visit to Kuwait indicating that "there is a problem" concerning the plight of the maids.[71]

---

[71] AFP, April 13, 1995.

The government of Kuwait also attempted to evade responsibility for the problem and for coming up with a solution. One official said that the "problems facing the Asian servants and maids in Kuwait were due to . . . the irresponsibility of the servants' offices in their [own] countries."[72] In the same vein, Kuwait's chief public prosecutor told us he thought it was the responsibility of the embassies to pursue claims on behalf of the women.[73] Undersecretary of Foreign Affairs Sulaiman al-Shaheen publicly called on the Asian embassies in Kuwait to "play a bigger role to protect the rights of their citizens."[74]

The Asian embassies' willingness to advocate on the maids' behalf is limited by their perception that such activism jeopardizes their national economic self-interest. At a time when Kuwait is attempting to rid itself of many foreign workers it perceives as undesirable,[75] the Asian ambassadors expressed concern that if they put pressure on the Kuwaiti government regarding the treatment of the maids, Kuwait might retaliate by limiting the employment of both the maids and other nationals from that country, including those working in more skilled-labor positions.[76]

The remittances potentially at risk are significant. An average wage of KD 30 to 40 per month (approximately US $90 to $120) could, for instance, supports three to four people in Sri Lanka or Bangladesh.[77] One Asian

---

[72] "Indian envoy urges maids law, fires broadside at dream agents," *Arab Times*, March 24, 1992. "Servants offices" refers to the employment agencies that recruit maids for jobs in Kuwait and other Gulf countries, many of which operate illegally in Asia. It should be noted that Kuwaiti employment agencies also exist and reportedly are soon to be regulated by the state.

[73] Interview, Chief Public Prosecutor Mohammed al-Bannay, Kuwait City, May 1992.

[74] Jack Kelley, "Kuwait rape reports to be probed," *USA Today*, March 3, 1992, p. 4A.

[75] See Middle East Watch, "Nowhere to Go: Palestinians in Kuwait," *A Human Rights Watch Short Report*, vol. 3, no. 12 (October 1991).

[76] This threat is in fact real. Saudi Arabia, a strong influence on Kuwait's government, responded to the Philippines' 1988 ban on domestics taking up positions in the Kingdom by imposing a five-month freeze on work permits for all Filipino workers. Philip Shehadi, "Asian, Gulf governments take action against maid abuse," *Reuters Library Report*, March 31, 1989.

[77] Interview, Kuwait City, May 1992. There is also some competition between Asian governments to provide the largest number of expatriate workers, including

(continued...)

official told us that "women maids send home far more money than all the educated people we send away and then lose to the brain drain."[78]   A Sri Lankan diplomat told us that the foreign exchange remittances his country receives from women laboring abroad as domestic workers is the highest source of all his country's export earnings, accounting for more revenue than tea, rattan or coconut.[79]   In the Philippines, overseas workers' remittances constitute the country's largest source of foreign exchange, accounting for $1.72 billion in 1992.[80]

Failure to Provide Due Process and Equal Protection
Kuwait has an international obligation to provide Asian maids with due process[81] and equal protection[82] under its criminal law, which prohibits rape, assault and illegal confinement.   National law also extends protections including the constitution, which precludes restricting the right to freedom of movement, including through the deprivation of passports;[83] and civil law,

---

[77](...continued)
maids.   Several sources alluded to a "price war" for maids: one source said that while Sri Lankan maids get KD 40 (approximately US $120 in May 1992) per month, Bangladeshi or Indian women would work for KD 25 (approximately US $75 in May 1992), while another source complained that Bangladeshi women make more than Filipinas.

[78] Interview, Kuwait City, May 1992.

[79] Ibid.

[80] Belinda Rhodes, "Filipinas tell of their nightmare in Kuwait," *San Francisco Examiner*, August 8, 1993, citing central bank figures.

[81] The right to due process is the right to be treated fairly and in a non-arbitrary manner.   It flows from Article 8 of the Universal Declaration of Human Rights, which guarantees that "[e]veryone has the right to an effective remedy by the competent national tribunals for actions violating the fundamental rights granted him by the constitution or by law;" and Article 10, which states that "[e]veryone is entitled in full equality to a fair and public hearing by an independent and impartial tribunal, in the determination of his rights."

[82] The right to equal protection is articulated in Article 7 of the Universal Declaration of Human Rights, which states: "All are equal before the law and are entitled without any discrimination to equal protection of the law."

[83] Constitution of the State of Kuwait, Part III (Public Rights and Duties), Article 31 states that "nor shall...[any person's] liberty of movement be restricted, except in accordance with the provisions of law."   The Kuwaiti courts have interpreted this provision to mean that employers may not unilaterally withhold an employee's passport.
(continued...)

which requires employers to pay their employees according to the terms of the employment contract.[84]   The fact that most of the abuses in question were committed by private individuals does not relieve the Kuwait government of its responsibility under international law to provide due process and equal protection to Asian maids.[85]

Under Kuwaiti law, rape and sexual assault are felonies. Rape by use of force, threat or deception, is punishable by death or life imprisonment. A mandatory death sentence is prescribed if the perpetrator is someone who has authority over the victim.[86] In a March 1993 letter to Human Rights Watch, the Ministry of Justice stated that this provision applies to domestic workers in private homes. A number of other articles set forth the sentences for other situations of rape and sexual assault.[87]

---

[83](...continued)
See Middle East Watch and Women's Rights Project, "Punishing the Victims. . . ," Section II, on passport deprivation.

[84] The problem of unpaid wages that underlies debt bondage also violates Kuwait's Civil Code, which maids could invoke to sue their employers. Civil Code, Law No. 67 of 1980, Article 209 ("In a contract . . . if one side does not fulfill his obligation after he is notified to do so, the other side may [receive] compensation if warranted . . .") (translation by Human Rights Watch).

[85] Section 702 of the Third Restatement of the Foreign Relations Law of the Foreign Relations Law of the United States sets forth the binding principle of state responsibility for the acts of private individuals: "A government may be presumed to have encouraged or condoned acts prohibited...if such acts,...have been repeated or notorious and no steps have been taken to prevent them or to punish perpetrators."

[86] Penal Code, Law No. 16 of 1960 (as amended), Part II: Crimes Against Individuals, Section 2 (Crimes Against Honor and Reputation), Article 186 (hereinafter "Penal Code"). Human Rights Watch strongly condemns the imposition of the death penalty for any act.

[87] Ibid. Article 188 sentences to fifteen years of imprisonment anyone who has intercourse with a woman between the ages of fifteen and twenty-one, or to life, if the perpetrator has authority over the woman. Article 191 punishes anyone who sexually violates the honor of another by use of force, threat or deception with fifteen years in prison, or with life imprisonment, if the perpetrator has authority over the woman. Article 199 also criminalizes "a disgracing act committed in private, but less than dishonor" that is committed against a woman without her consent, and perpetrators can be sentenced to prison for up to one year.   "Dishonor" in this article is usually understood to mean sexual intercourse.

Assault resulting in bodily harm is punishable by two years of imprisonment and a fine,[88] while if someone is assaulted by a person using a knife or other weapon, or if the assault results in permanent disability to the victim, the perpetrator can be sentenced to ten years in prison and a fine.[89] Assault resulting in severe physical pain or temporary disability is punishable by up to five years in prison and a fine.[90]   Threatening someone with violence or death is also punishable by a two- or three-year sentence, respectively.[91]

Passport deprivation by employers has been clearly outlawed under the constitution, and confinement is a felony punishable by three years in prison.[92]   As detailed above, non-payment of salary is a civil violation, and debt bondage violates both Kuwait's international human rights obligations[93] and its labor law, although, as noted, the government has excluded the maids from the latter protection.

According to attorneys, human rights activists, Asian officials and women domestic servants we interviewed, despite these legal protections, it is rare that an employer is prosecuted for debt bondage or illegal confinement of an Asian domestic servant.   The above-cited case from 1972 held passport deprivation by employers to be illegal.   However, the decision does not appear to have been applied to any of the Asian maids' cases.   Thus, these pervasive abuses occur with near-total impunity.   In interview after interview, maids cited non-payment of salary, passport deprivation and confinement as prominent aspects of the conditions under which they worked.

Moreover, the Kuwaiti government has largely failed to apply rape and battery laws to abusive employers or to provide the prescribed criminal and civil remedies to the maids.   We are aware of only a handful of cases in the past three years in which the police or public prosecutor have investigated and prosecuted rape or assault of a maid by her employer, and only a few resulted in punishment.   In 1993, a Kuwaiti employer and his Lebanese wife

---

[88] Ibid., Article 160.

[89] Ibid., Articles 161 and 162.

[90] Ibid., Article 162.

[91] Ibid., Article 173.

[92] Ibid., Article 184. The penalty for confinement is enhanced to seven years if the action is accompanied by physical torture or threats of killing.

[93] Kuwait is a signatory to the 1957 Supplementary Convention on the Abolition of Slavery, the Slave Trade, and Institutions and Practices Similar to Slavery that outlaws debt bondage. See Article 1.

were sentenced to seven years each for the murder of their maid. In 1994, a female employer was sentenced to three years of imprisonment for beating her Filipina maid to death. The sentences were relatively lenient in comparison to other cases of murder, which is usually punished by the death penalty or life in prison.

Police in Kuwait are generally reluctant to believe maids' allegation of abuse. Most of the abused women with whom we spoke who had attempted to report incidents of violence or mistreatment to the police, said the officers did not appear to believe their accusations, made light of their claims, and frequently refused to register their complaints. Sometimes police return maids seeking to register complaints to abusive employers, a practice that can expose the employee to retaliatory violence.

There have also been credible reports of police abuse of Asian maids who sought their protection.[94] In one case we investigated, a maid complaining of sexual assault was detained at the police station and was allegedly beaten and threatened with prosecution for running away if she refused to return to work.[95]

In another case we investigated, a Sri Lankan woman was stopped by a police officer who asked for her identification and took her into custody when she could not produce her passport. He took her in his car to the desert, where he allegedly raped her. He then left her in a restaurant in Kuwait City. She returned to her employers, who took her to the police station to register a rape complaint. At the police station, she identified one of the officers there as the rapist. She told us that he was not prosecuted, however.[96]

Police abuse of Asian women workers was also reported to us by Asian embassy officials who told us they heard numerous complaints from

---

[94] Police in Kuwait, as mentioned above, have a reputation for torturing and otherwise mistreating foreigners. Especially in the aftermath of the Gulf War, the police were responsible for serious and ongoing human rights abuses, including rape, torture, arbitrary arrest and detention. *See* Middle East Watch, *A Victory Turned Sour* (New York: Human Rights Watch, September 1991). The maids' fear of the police stems in part from the fact that aliens accounted for the largest number of victims of those abuses. Ibid., p. 1.

[95] Interview, Mumtaz S., Kuwait City, May 1992.

[96] Interview, Kuwait City, May 1992. See also *A Victory Turned Sour*, for more details on rape and mistreatment of maids by security forces.

runaway maids who sought shelter at the embassies instead of complaining to the police.[97]

When a Human Rights Watch representative visited the severely crowded Dasma police station in early 1994, several women reported being abused physically and sexually by the guards.

Although several senior government officials told us that the women should go to the police and register their complaints,[98] one of those same officials conceded that "the police generally don't do it [investigate]."[99] Our research revealed some cases in which the police failed entirely to investigate criminal complaints; in most cases, they had conducted cursory investigations, after which the files were closed. Only in a few cases did prosecutors conduct credible inquiries leading to formal charges and arrest. In an interview with Human Rights Watch in April 1995, a Kuwaiti official conceded that many sexual assault offenses go unprosecuted. He said that most occur in the outlying areas of Kuwait and that prosecutors too frequently exercise their discretion to close the investigations of these crimes without ever filing charges. He called for limiting the discretion given to prosecutors in this matter and for judicial supervision of prosecutors' decisions.[100]

While Kuwaiti law enforcement officials have repeatedly shown themselves to be reluctant to investigate and subsequently prosecute employers, they often detain abused employees. We have documented numerous cases in which maids who registered (or attempted to register) complaints against employers were detained by the police, pending the investigation or other "resolution" of the complaint. In some instances, the police apparently viewed the detention of these complainants without charge as a form of "protective" custody. Brigadier al-Muhaini, the Interior Ministry director of police investigations, confirmed that "if the police are afraid to send [a maid] to the employer or she has no place to go, they will keep her at the station."[101] The wrongful arrest of Asian maids stems, in part, from Kuwait's lack of an alternative place to house the women while their cases are being investigated,

---

[97] Interview, Kuwait City, April 1992.

[98] Ibid..

[99] Interview, Undersecretary Abdul Aziz Dikheel al-Dikheel, Ministry of Justice, Kuwait City, May 1992.

[100] Interview, April 17, 1995.

[101] Interview, Kuwait City, May 1992. Brigadier al-Muhaini's statement comports with our findings that there are occasions on which police do not force maids to return to abusive employers.

short of sending them back to abusive employers. Kuwaiti law mandates the detention of maids not carrying the appropriate documents and does not provide alternatives to detention for maids who do not want to return to their employers' homes. The government should not penalize women who seek to exercise their right to police protection. Rather, reasonable alternatives must be established such as providing a neutral shelter or allowing the women to reside at their embassies.

In still other cases, abused women workers who have fled without their passports or have attempted suicide have been arrested for violating Kuwaiti law requiring maids to carry their passports at all times.[102] These women are arrested and charged by the police, despite Kuwait's Penal Code, which provides that people are not criminally responsible for acts they commit under threat of violence or in order to protect themselves from physical harm.[103] In several cases we investigated, maids who reported that they had been raped by their employers were arrested for not having their passports or residency papers.[104] The police did not investigate the possibility that they had broken the passport law to escape further physical harm (nor did they investigate the alleged rape).

The most egregious examples of the Kuwaiti government's tendency to penalize the victims, without reasonably investigating the context in which their seeming misdemeanors occur, are found amongst the suicide attempts we documented. For example, out of a total of thirty-nine registered felonies committed by all domestic servants, both male and female, between January and April 1992, nearly half were suicide cases in which the servants were accused of trying to kill themselves.[105] In each of the attempted suicide cases involving Asian maids that we investigated, the woman tried to kill herself only after suffering extreme mistreatment or abuse at the hands of her employer.

---

[102] The residence permit of a servant who leaves her employer's service before the end of her contract is deemed canceled. Ministerial Order No. 84 of 1977 (Regulating the conditions and Formalities of Private Servants Ordinary Residence), Article 3. Without a residence permit, an expatriate cannot legally reside in Kuwait, and she is subject to immediate arrest and deportation. Ibid.

[103] Penal Code, Articles 24 and 25.

[104] Interview, Kuwait City, April 1992.

[105] Letter from Ministry of Interior, International Organization Liaison Office to Middle East Watch and the Women's Rights Project (May 20, 1992), p. 3. This letter lists attempted suicide as a felony.

Instead of filing charges against abusive employers, the police frequently summon the employers to caution them or threaten them with criminal prosecution, as a means of resolving the situation. This acts, to some extent, as a substitute for the formal arbitration of employment disputes by the Ministry of Social Affairs and Labor that has been precluded by the maids' exclusion from the labor law.

If the differences cannot be resolved, the police sometimes try to find a new employer for the maid. Officials at Dasma Deportation Center described several cases in which they had successfully assisted the transfer of a maid from one employer to another.

The adverse effect of this informal approach is that the police view it as a substitute and often feel justified in doing nothing to enforce the relevant criminal or civil law to protect Asian maids. Moreover, informal resolution of the maids' problems obscures the need to institute legal reforms and provide better protections.

For example, under the present Aliens Residence Law, if a maid wishes to work for a different employer, her first employer must approve the transfer of her residence permit to the second employer.[106] If her previous employer does not consent—as was often the case with abused women servants who fled—and she nonetheless terminates her contract, her residence permit is considered revoked and she is subject to immediate deportation.[107] Ad hoc police intervention has apparently worked in some instances to encourage previous employers to consent to transfer, but such intervention is not available to the vast majority of abused maids, who are left to face deportation should they attempt to transfer employers without consent.

---

[106] Law No. 55 of 1982, Amending Some Provisions of Aliens Residence Law, Article 1: "In the event of leaving service of his employer, the alien's residence permit shall be canceled...and the alien shall leave the country...Unless the consent of the employer is secured in writing, it is impermissible to employ...any alien whose residence permit was canceled in accordance with [these provisions]." (All translations by Human Rights Watch.)

[107] See Aliens' Residence Law, Article 20 ("an alien shall be expelled from Kuwait...if the period of his residence permit has expired") and Ministerial Order No. 84 of 1977, Regulating the Conditions and Formalities of Private Servants Ordinary Residence, Articles 3 ("If a servant leaves the service of his employer before the expiry of his service contract term, his residence permit shall be canceled"), and 4 ("In the event of [a servant's] residence permit cancellation . . . an order shall be issued for deportation of such servant").

Deportation is highly likely, especially now that the government is beginning to deport people without valid residence permits.[108]

The government's policy of deporting workers who choose to terminate their contracts in advance of closure may be justified in cases where the worker chooses to leave a job and thus violates a contract. However, if a woman terminates her contract early because of abuse by her employers, it is inappropriate to revoke her residence permit and order her immediate deportation, in the event she cannot receive a legal job transfer. These sanctions typically result in the denial of due process and equal protection. All Asian women servants found to have fled as a result of abuse should have, at a minimum, the opportunity to find another job, if they so desire, without risk of deportation. In addition, women should be permitted to reside in Kuwait in order to pursue their civil or criminal claims against their abusive past employers.

Moreover, extending the protection of the labor law to domestic workers would immediately address and protect maids against some of the abuse and mistreatment they experience—such as the non-payment of wages, debt bondage and oppressive conditions—and provide a workable arbitration mechanism that would help all maids to resolve employment disputes. Many of the maids with whom we spoke would have appreciated this opportunity; without it, they had little choice but to return to abusive employers or to their countries of origin.

Refusal to Repatriate and Subsequent Deportation

As a rule the Kuwaiti government does not allow abused Asian women domestic servants wishing to leave to do so until they satisfy their employers' financial claims. Kuwaiti employers in many cases refused to relinquish their workers' passports, and the government would not issue exit visas to the women without their passports.[109] Some embassies tried to eliminate this obstacle by providing the maids with replacement passports or *laissez-passers*, but found that, despite the fact that the law requires them to

---

[108] "Hold on family visit visas confirmed," *Arab Times*, May 1, 1992.

[109] To further complicate matters, maids who ran away often had no idea of the name or address of their employers (or did not wish to say for fear of being forcibly returned to them). This made it impossible for their embassies or the police assist with the return of their passports.

honor such documents,[110] the Kuwaiti government refused to issue exit visas to women holding them. The government usually insists that the maid must secure her employer's consent indicating that he has no financial claims against her. Such consent is difficult to obtain in contentious cases. Moreover, many employers refuse to pay for their maids' repatriation, leading to a limbo during which maids are detained until funds are secured for their repatriation.

The government's request for travel fees from the maids was inconsistent with Kuwait law that requires the government to shoulder the deportation expense in cases where the government decides to deport a person and that person cannot pay the cost.[111] Moreover, under the implementing regulations of the Aliens Residence Law, in cases where an employment contract has been terminated[112] in advance of the agreed-upon date, the employer—not the employee—is required to pay repatriation costs.[113]

Over four years after the liberation of Kuwait, the plight of Asian maids remains critical. Attracted by the promise of higher wages and secure employment, many Asian women continue to migrate to Kuwait in hopes of finding paying work to support themselves and their families. Instead what many of them find is a life of misery—forced to work long hours with no pay, confined to their employers' homes, and subjected to physical and sexual abuse that is almost never investigated or punished. The pervasive mistreatment of these women will not cease unless Kuwaiti authorities extend labor protections to foreign maids, and end the impunity for employers who abuse their employees.

---

[110] Kuwaiti law states: "A laisser-passer or any other document, issued by competent authority... may substitute the passport." Minister of Interior Order No. 22 of 1975, Promulgating the Implementing Regulations of Aliens Residence Law, Article 1.

[111] Although the minister of interior may order the alien to bear her or his own costs of deportation if she or he has money available (Aliens Residence Law, Article 21), the comments to the Aliens Residence Law state that the government will undertake to pay such expenses if the deportee cannot. Ibid., Explanatory Memoranda.

[112] To the extent that these regulations do not explicitly specify that sexual or physical abuse constitutes termination of contract, they should be reformed to so indicate.

[113] Implementing Regulations of Aliens Residence Law, Minister of Interior Order No. 22 of 1975, Article 20.

DISCRIMINATION AGAINST WOMEN WORKERS IN RUSSIA

Economic and political changes in Russia have left many Russians staggering under the burdens of rising unemployment, high rates of inflation, disappearing social services and the threats of corruption and organized crime.[114] Women in particular are suffering the consequences of such change: they face widespread employment discrimination that is practiced, condoned and tolerated by the government. Government employers have fired women workers in disproportionate numbers—over two-thirds of Russia's unemployed are women[115]—and refuse to employ women because of their sex. According to a 1992 report in *The Guardian*, "When factories take on workers they announce that they want men, and when women are rejected it is their sex which is entered on their application forms as the reason."[116] When women challenge such discrimination, they either are ignored by their employers and by state agencies responsible for enforcing anti-discrimination laws or are told that priority should be given to men seeking jobs.

Far from attacking sex discrimination, the government actively participates in discriminatory actions and fails to enforce laws that prohibit sex discrimination. When asked about the problem of women's unemployment in February 1993, Russia's labor minister, Gennady Melikyan, responded, "Why should we employ women when men are out of work? It's better that men work and women take care of children and do housework. I don't think women should work when men are doing nothing."[117]

In March 1994 the Women's Rights Project of Human Rights Watch sent a mission to Russia to investigate government participation in illegal

---

[114] The following material was adapted from Human Rights Watch Women's Rights Project, "Neither Jobs Nor Justice: State Discrimination Against Women in Russia," *A Human Rights Watch Short Report*, vol. 7, no. 5 (March 1995).

[115] Statistics indicate that, until recently, women have made up approximately 50 percent of the Russian workforce. Zoya Khotkina, "Gender Aspects of Unemployment and the System of Social Security" (unpublished article), March 1994.

[116] Anne Sailas, "No Place for Women," *The Guardian* (London), May 1, 1992, p. 22.

[117] H. Womack, "Why Employ Women When There Are Men Out of Work?" *The Independent*, March 21, 1993, p. 11.

discrimination against women.[118] This is the second report by Human Rights Watch to examine how political and economic changes in Central and Eastern Europe and the former Soviet Union have affected women's ability to exercise their rights.[119] The assumption that the introduction of democratic processes and a market economy will improve the protection of human rights generally in Russia has proven to be true in some aspects, such as people's ability to exercise their freedom of association or speech. But women's human rights, far from being better protected in a rapidly changing Russia, are being violated and denied.

During the Soviet period, equality between the sexes was part of the official ideology, and discussion of women's issues was controlled by officially-sponsored women's organizations. Despite official Soviet rhetoric, women and men were not afforded equal rights in practice and, in some areas, the law explicitly curtailed women's rights. Because the state sought to control the issue of women's rights just as it did all other social issues, independent women activists and women's organizations were suppressed and forced underground.[120] As a consequence, the independent women's movement in Russia has been visible only since the end of the 1980s, and many Russians, both men and women, reject the concept of women's equality

---

[118] During our investigation we interviewed researchers examining the causes and consequences of women's unemployment through individual interviews and statistical analysis as well as over twenty-five unemployed women, all of whom have tried with no success to find new jobs. We also visited state unemployment agencies in Moscow, St. Petersburg and Kaluga.

[119] See also Helsinki Watch and Women's Rights Project, "Hidden Victims: Women in Post-Communist Poland," *A Human Rights Watch Short Report*, vol. 4, no. 5 (March 1992).

[120] For nearly half a century, the Soviet Women's Committee, in effect an organ of the Communist Party, was the only women's organization allowed to exist in the Soviet Union. In the early Soviet years, many women's councils were created to promote communist ideas among women, especially in Central Asia and other non-Russian areas. A few of these councils survived into the later Soviet period. From the time of the Bolshevik revolution, women's issues were considered only in the context of the overall class struggle. Thus, the state maintained that women's oppression would be solved with the implementation of a communist society and presented no gender-specific issues. In 1980, the Soviet Union expelled four of six contributors to an underground feminist publication, *Almanac: Women and Russia*. During the late 1970s and early 1980s, other *samizdat* (underground) publications addressing women's issues were officially restricted.

as vehemently as they spurn state policies and social programs linked with the Soviet era.[121] This rejection of the commitment to protect women's rights, combined with new political, economic and social pressures, threatens to undermine the legal protections that do exist for women and to create obstacles to women's participation in the economic and political future of their country.

Discrimination against women in the workplace by Russian state agencies, enterprises and agents violates both international human rights and domestic laws guaranteeing freedom from discrimination.[122] The Russian government is directly responsible for the discrimination committed by its agents, either as employers or as employees of state unemployment offices, and also is responsible for its failure to enforce laws prohibiting sex discrimination and to sanction employers engaging in discrimination.

Although equality between the sexes was a central tenet of the Bolshevik revolution, and the Soviet constitution guaranteed equal rights for women and men, Soviet women's actual experience in no way resembled sexual equality. The Soviet state often sacrificed its commitment to women's equality in the workplace in the name of other government policies and priorities. Women were pushed into the labor force when economic expansion was a national priority, such as during the industrialization in the 1930s and war and reconstruction during the 1940s.[123] As workers, however, women were denied access to high-paying, prestigious occupations and high-level positions.[124]

Vocational training schools in the Soviet Union segregated girls and boys and provided them with different kinds of training to prepare them for work. Thus, for example, girls and not boys were trained for jobs in "female"

---

[121] See, e.g., Isobel Montgomery, "Equality: Union City Blues," *The Guardian*, April 23, 1993, p. 10.

[122] Sex discrimination is prohibited by they Universal Declaration on Human Rights, Articles 2 and 7; the International Covenant on Civil and Political Rights (ICCPR), Article 2; and the Convention on the Elimination of All Forms of Discrimination against Women (CEDAW), Article 2. Russia is a party to both CEDAW and the ICCPR. Russian law explicitly prohibits discrimination on the basis of sex, pregnancy and maternity in hiring and firing decisions (Articles 16 and 170, Code of Labor Laws of the Russian Federation).

[123] Natalia Mirovitskaya, "Women and the Post-Socialist Reversion to Patriarchy," *Surviving Together* (Washington, ISAR), Summer 1993, p. 44.

[124] Under the Soviet system, women also tended to be concentrated in lower-paying industries considered "women's work" such as the textile and food industries.

sectors such as clothes making and food preparation.[125] During periods of economic reform, on the other hand (e.g., after the 1965 Kosygin reforms and in the context of current reforms), women were and are encouraged to focus on their responsibilities to home and family rather than on their work outside the home.[126] In the 1970s, the Soviet government, trying to increase low birth rates, promised women a financial bonus for the birth of their first, second and third child, and taxed childless couples.[127]

Despite the government's shifting position regarding women's role in the workplace, state policy and social norms consistently reinforced motherhood as women's primary contribution to Soviet society. In 1981 the twenty-sixth congress of the Communist Party decided "that reinforcement of the traditional maternal role was needed for the betterment of the state."[128] This emphasis on women's "biological destiny" as mothers shaped women's legal status and undermined efforts to pursue social equality for women.[129] Women struggled under what became known as the "double burden" of working outside the home as well as shouldering most if not all child care and household management responsibilities. As one activist stated, "Our society thinks children are children of women, not children of men."[130] As another Moscow women's rights activist has observed, "The new catch-phrase is: 'Let's return women to their natural destiny.'"[131]

---

[125] Vocational training schools in the Soviet Union segregated girls and boys in order to provide them with different kinds of training, thus steering them into different sectors and occupations. Women held a disproportionate number of jobs as unskilled laborers and were underrepresented at the upper end of the occupational hierarchy. Women also experienced a lesser degree of upward occupational mobility, even where women made up the majority of workers in a field. Laurie Essig, "Meticulously Observing CEDAW: A Critique of the USSR's Second Periodic Report to the Committee," (unpublished paper), January 1989.

[126] Rosalie B. Levinson, "The Meaning of Sexual Equality: A Comparison of the Soviet and American Definitions," *New York Law School Journal of International & Comparative Law,* Volume 10 (1990), p.157.

[127] Ibid.

[128] Ibid.

[129] Janet Hunt-McCool and Lisa Granik, *The Legal Status of Women in the New Independent States of the Former Soviet Union* (Washington, D.C.: U.S. Agency for International Development, May 1994).

[130] Zoya Khotkina, discussion at Moscow Gender Studies Center, March 18, 1994.

[131] "Russia's women face a new reign of fear," *The Financial Times* (London), Aug. 21, 1993, quoting Marina Baskakova [sic] of the Moscow Gender Studies Center.

In today's Russia, many women share the view that "we were told for seventy-five years that we were equal, so what good did that do us?"[132] Many Russian women and men spurn the principle of sexual equality as empty Soviet rhetoric. They justify sex discrimination and the differential treatment of women in terms of discarding the legacies of the Soviet era and asserting Russian traditions. After years of state regulation of every aspect of their lives, many Russians regard with suspicion the notion that the state should play a role in protecting women's rights in the workplace.

In this context, many policymakers have emphasized their desire to protect women's traditional role in the family and, in ways strongly reminiscent of the Soviet state, to relieve women of the burden of working both in and outside the home. In late 1993, members of the Russian Federation parliament introduced a family law that threatened women's rights on a number of fronts. First, the Draft Principles of Legislation on the Protection of the Family, Mothers, Fathers, and Children vested rights with the family unit and not with the individual members of the family. Under this draft law, it was the family, and not its individual members, that could own real and personal property. Further, the personal income of each family member was to be put into a common family budget. The draft law also granted the family the right to decide whether to have children.[133] An early version of the legislation restricted the working hours of mothers with children under age fourteen to thirty-five hours per week.

Russian women's activists expressed concern that if the family were recognized as the fundamental unit of society, women would have no recourse in situations of domestic violence because they would be limited in asserting their individual rights in a way that disrupts family life. Moreover, if women have no individual claim to their earnings or property, their ability to leave an abusive situation would be greatly compromised.

Although the draft family law was discarded, women's rights activists fear that some form of this law, combined with the government's intent to

---

[132] Danny Reuvekamp, "The Urgent Need for Quality Improvement in Russia," International Planned Parenthood Federation newsletter (New York), 1994, pp. 22-23.

[133] The draft law contained provisions recognizing a child's "right to life" from the time of conception and granting men and women "equal rights in deciding all issues of family life, including issues of family planning." "Russia's women face a new reign of fear," The Financial Times (London), August 21, 1993. Women's rights advocates fear that such legislation would require women to seek permission from their partners before seeking abortions.

carry out a "progressive demographic policy" to reverse negative population growth, will result in government restrictions on women's access to family planning and abortion services and ability to work. In many parts of Russia, women's ability to practice family planning already is greatly restricted, because family planning services other than abortion—including access to contraceptives—are non-existent. And the government has demonstrated its interest in taking steps to limit access to abortion services. In March 1994 the Ministry of Health proposed excluding abortion services from the basic medical insurance coverage provided by the state. According to the director of Moscow's Gender Studies Center:

> Forcing women to pay for abortion is a direct consequence of the government's desire to increase the Russian population. This isn't the first time we have seen negative population growth as a reason to push women out of their jobs. The nationalists and some other government figures want to limit a woman's right to determine how many children she has.[134]

Their fears may well be justified; Russian legislators expressed to Human Rights Watch their intent to adopt some provisions of the law as part of, for example, the draft labor law proposed in early 1994. The former head of President Boris Yeltsin's Commission on Women, Family and Demography, Yekaterina Lakhova, told Human Rights Watch, "We would like to have the family recognized as a juridical unit. And we want to reduce the marriage age from eighteen to sixteen."[135]

Cutbacks in social services traditionally provided by the state add to the pressures on women to leave work to care for their families. Five thousand government day care centers closed in 1993.[136] According to Ludmila Zavadskaya, a member of the Duma (the lower house of parliament), the

---

[134] Interview, Anastasia Posadskaya, director of the Moscow Center for Gender Studies, Moscow, March 17, 1994. Unless otherwise noted, all interviews cited in this report were conducted by Human Rights Watch/Women's Rights Project. Women in Russia are still able to obtain abortions free of charge, but, as was the case during the Soviet era, women must pay to have anesthesia during the procedure.

[135] Interview, Yekaterina Lakhova, former head of the Presidential Commission on Women, the Family and Demography, Moscow, March 21, 1994.

[136] Ibid.

drastic reduction of social services has helped force women out of the workplace:

> Women have to leave work as preschools are closed. In 1993 almost 6,000 preschools were closed and many of their buildings became commercial structures. In 1993 payment for keeping a child in preschool increased twenty to thirty times compared to 1992. Many families cannot afford it. It is especially difficult for single-parent families, which make up 14 percent of the population.[137]

These changes—both legal and social—combined with rising unemployment and the backlash against concerns with women's equality threaten to undermine Russian women's ability to maintain in law and to enforce their fundamental rights. The Russian government has given life to this threat by participating in and failing to act against violations of women's human rights. Russian women are pushing their government to meet its international human rights obligations so that Russia's transition to a more democratic society and market-based economy does not deprive women of their rights to freedom from discrimination and equal protection of the law.

Employment Discrimination

> The problem of women's labor is not an abstract problem. It's a question of our survival.
> —Marina Gordeyeva, Administrative Officer (otvets vennyi sekretar), Union of Women of Russia

Women in Russia face widespread employment discrimination that is practiced, condoned and tolerated by the government. Women have been fired in disproportionate numbers by government industries, agencies and ministries that are reducing their workforces or privatizing their operations. Researchers examining the causes of women's unemployment in 1994 found that when the government defense industry reduced the number of working days per week (and hence the amount of compensation) for a large part of its workforce, it

---

[137] Ludmila Zavadskaya, presentation in panel discussion on gender issues in transitional economies, presentation at the World Bank, Washington, D.C., March 1994.

put only women on the new work schedule. In the same factories, men
continued to work full-time and to receive their usual wages.[138]   A news
report from May 1992 notes, "The release of women in those branches in
which they traditionally constituted a majority of workers is proceeding at a
rapid pace. But, in addition, today's employers are trying specifically to cut
back and hire fewer women."[139]

In contrast to men, women remain chronically unemployed upon
losing their jobs. Official statistics indicate that, across Russia, two out of
three unemployed Russians are women.[140]   In many regions, over 85 percent
of the unemployed are women.[141]

Women's   disproportionately   high   representation   among   the
unemployed is attributable in significant part to government practices that
openly discriminate against women. In a variety of professions, employers,
many of them government enterprises, have fired women in large numbers and
retained male employees. In a number of recorded cases where government
enterprises conducted mass dismissals, they fired significantly more women
than men. In May 1993, 90 percent of the workers fired by government
enterprises in the Alexandrov region were women. The workers were fired not

---

[138] Khotkina, "Gender Aspects of Unemployment..." The defense industry factories
are located in the Alexandrov, Vladimir region and the Dubna, Moscow region.

[139] Mikhail Borodulin and Irina Gulchenko, "The Labor Market: The Fair Half on
the Verge of Stress," *Nezavisimaya Gazeta* (Moscow), May 16, 1992, p.2.

[140] Until recently, women made up approximately half of Russia's work force. The
overall dislocation of the Russian economy has left many Russians unemployed and
searching for work in a market that no longer values their skills. Official statistics
indicate that 2.3 million people applied to be registered as unemployed in 1993. Of
these, 67.3 percent were women. In many regions of Russia, women's unemployment
exceeds 80 percent. Scholars monitoring the rates and causes of unemployment maintain
that actual unemployment is much higher. Zoya Khotkina, "The Gender Aspects of
Unemployment . . . ," (unpublished article). A sociologist in St. Petersburg who
interviewed close to seventy unemployed women found that only "a handful" had
registered as unemployed. According to the federal Department of Employment, only
25 percent of the unemployed even try to register as unemployed. Interview, Tatyana
Prokhorova, federal Department of Employment, Moscow, March 14, 1994.

[141] Khotkina, "Gender Aspects of Unemployment . . ." In one-third of the regions
of the Russian Federation, the percentage of the unemployed who are women is over
85 percent, and in several regions (Tverskaya, Tumenskaya, Amurskay, Sahalinskaya,
Volgogradskaya regions and the autonomous republics of Adigea and Buriatyaya)
women constitute over 90 percent of the unemployed.

only from the female-dominated textile industry, but also from machine-building plants where men and women made up equal percentages of the workforce.[142]   In 1993 officials in the unemployment office in Saratov, a large industrial city in southern Russia reported that 90 percent of the newly unemployed were women.[143]   According to the founder of Women of St. Petersburg, an association that helps unemployed women, "Women are less protected than anyone in this society. In government enterprises, they aren't afraid to fire women because they know women aren't able to defend their rights."[144]   Government and private employers, openly expressing their preference for hiring men, advertise job vacancies for men only and deny positions to women because of their sex. Women interviewed by Human Rights Watch reported that discrimination is on the rise and the government is doing virtually nothing to stop it.

        Moreover, the Soviet legacy of occupational segregation left women concentrated in certain industries and levels of employment—women are under-represented in supervisory, managerial and mechanized jobs—that have experienced the most drastic cutbacks.[145]   According to a St. Petersburg sociologist who researches the causes and consequences of women's unemployment, "Women are being pushed out of the workplace because under the socialist system, women were tracked into superfluous jobs, and these jobs are disappearing as the economy is restructured."[146]

        Women's unemployment in Russia is even more acute than official data suggest given the growing problem of "hidden unemployment." Hidden unemployment refers to those who are in fact without work but not officially

---

[142] Ibid.

[143] Lisa Granik, "The Legal Status of Women in Post-Soviet Russia," in Hunt-McCool and Granik, *The Legal Status of Women in the New Independent States of the Former Soviet Union* (Washington: USAID, May 1994), p. 83.

[144] Interview, Lydia Shemaeva, founder of Women of St. Petersburg, St. Petersburg, March 28, 1994.

[145] According to different sources, many of the sectors experiencing the most significant reduction in the workforce were "feminized" during the Soviet era. In other words, many workers are being fired from superfluous jobs that were held by women because women workers, even during Soviet era, not viewed as efficient because of the demands of child care and housework.   Elena Zdravomyslova, "Strategies of Unemployed Women in the Transition to the Market Economy: The Case of Russia" (unpublished paper), July 1994; Khotkina, "Gender Aspects of Unemployment in the Transition to the Market Economy: The Case of Russia" (unpublished paper), July 1994.

[146] Interview, Elena Zdravomyslova, St. Petersburg, March 28, 1994.

registered as unemployed, as well as to those who remain on the roster of workers but have no work to do and receive little or no pay. One researcher asserted that official statistics overlook at least one-third of those who are actually unemployed but not officially registered as such.[147] Some government enterprises do not fire workers, including female workers, outright. Rather, in an attempt to maintain women's access to social services received through the workplace, such employers refrain from firing workers and instead require them to take extended holidays without pay or at the minimum wage, which is equal to less than one-quarter the cost of subsistence. These practices are particularly widespread in industries where women make up most of the workforce, such as textile manufacturing and clothing production. As demonstrated above, even in industries that employ both men and women, reports indicate that women are more frequently forced off the payroll or onto part-time schedules.[148] In 1993 as much as 30 percent of the working population of Russia experienced some form of hidden unemployment.[149]

The consequences of sex discrimination in employment are profound. Women struggling to provide for themselves and their families are prevented, because of their sex, from competing for the shrinking number of available jobs. At the same time, reforms designed to usher in a market economy have resulted in a reduction of the number of social programs available to support families, children and the unemployed.[150] Unable to find work and virtually without the protection of social services, single women, especially those with children, sink into poverty. Figures from 1992 indicate that 55 percent of Russian female-headed households with children under the age of six years live below the poverty line.[151]

---

[147] Khotkina, "Gender Aspects of Unemployment..." Khotkina's research shows that only 73.3 percent of the individuals who contacted the state employment service for job opportunities and who had no job at the time of that contact were registered officially as unemployed.

[148] Ibid.

[149] Ibid. For many individuals, the prospect of remaining employed in name only and thus continuing to receive certain benefits and services is more desirable than outright dismissal. Human Rights Watch does not challenge this practice per se. Rather, we are concerned that women are disproportionately affected by such practices in part because employers, acting on gender stereotypes, view men's wages as families' primary income and women's income as supplemental.

[150] Ibid.

[151] Ibid.

Although women's poverty in Russia is not solely attributable to employment discrimination, such discrimination creates an obstacle to women finding work that men do not face. Many married as well as single women face economic hardship when they lose their jobs, thus causing their families to lose half or more of their income. The women who run the greatest risk of chronic unemployment are young women with small children and women over the age of forty-five. A study conducted by Russia's Central Institute of Labor found that between 30 and 50 percent of the directors of state employment offices regard small children as a major barrier to women finding work.[152]

The Russian government denies women's constitutionally guaranteed right to equality and freedom from discrimination on the basis of sex, pregnancy and maternity by allowing and participating in blatantly discriminatory employment practices. This failure violates both internationally-guaranteed human rights and Russian prohibitions against sex discrimination. Sex discrimination is prohibited by the Universal Declaration on Human Rights, the International Covenant on Civil and Political Rights, and the Convention on the Elimination of all Forms of Discrimination Against Women (CEDAW).[153] In addition, Article 11 of CEDAW specifically calls upon governments to "take all appropriate measures to eliminate discrimination against women in the field of employment."[154]

Legislative Restrictions on Women's Employment

Labor legislation, held over from the Soviet era, continues to restrict women's participation in the workforce. Soviet and Russian legislation historically prohibited women from working in particularly unhealthy or strenuous posts, such as underground jobs, or in positions that interfered with their responsibilities as mothers, such as night or weekend jobs.[155]   The

---

[152] Ibid.

[153] Universal Declaration, Articles 2 and 7; ICCPR, Article 4; CEDAW, Article 2.

[154] Article 11(1) of CEDAW requires that women have, on an equal basis with men, employment opportunities and free choice of profession and employment, and receive vocational training and retraining. Article 11(2) further prohibits discrimination on the basis of pregnancy and motherhood, and requires states party to prohibit dismissal on the grounds of pregnancy or maternity leave.

[155] The 1922 Labor Code of the Soviet Union listed occupations in which women were not permitted to work, including "heavy and dangerous occupations" such as mining. In 1932, the list of prohibited occupations was extended to include work

(continued...)

Soviet legislature justified such limits on women's labor as necessary to protect women's ability to have and to raise children. The Council of Ministers of the USSR issued numerous decrees barring women from various occupations.[156] By January 1981, 460 occupations, primarily those requiring physical labor in the construction, chemical and metal industries and driving large vehicles, were closed to women on the grounds that such work harmed women's health.[157]

In addition to the restrictions on where and when women can work, Russian law extends—as did Soviet law— numerous protections and benefits to pregnant and nursing women as well as women with small children.[158] Such parental benefits are extended only to women because Russian government policies reflect society's expectation that women are and should be the parents primarily responsible for child care. Men are prohibited by statute from taking advantage of these benefits unless they are raising children alone.[159]   Much of this protective legislation prevents women from competing on an equal basis in the labor market and perpetuates the stereotype of women as unreliable and expensive workers.

---

[155](...continued)
underground, involving molten metal or requiring contact with dangerous chemicals. In 1978, the State Committee on Labor and Social Questions promulgated the most extensive list of prohibited occupations to date. Miriam B. Gottesfeld, "The Worker's Paradise Lost: The Role and Status of Russian and American Women in the Workplace," 14 *Comparative Labor Law Journal* 68, p. 86 (1992).

[156] Granik, "The Legal Status of Women . . . ," p. 82, citing Peers, "Workers by Hand and Womb," *Soviet Sisterhood* 135 (B. Holland, ed. 1985). An extensive list of "industries, professions, and jobs with difficult and harmful work conditions," in which women may not be employed, as passed by the State Committee on Labor and Social Questions on July 25, 1978, is reproduced in *Trud zhenshchin i molodezhi: Sbornik normativnykh aktov,* pp. 24-61 (Moscow, 1990).

[157] Levinson, "The Meaning of Sex Equality . . ." p. 167.

[158] For example, by law, women were and are entitled to special daytime rest periods while nursing and should be transferred to lighter work at the same salary if their jobs required physical exertion. Women receive a paid maternity leave of fifty-six days before and after childbirth and the option of taking a year's unpaid leave before returning to work.

[159] In April 1990 the Soviet government extended the benefits granted to women in connection with maternity (restriction on night work and overtime, additional leave, etc.) to fathers raising children without their mothers (due to death, deprivation of parental rights, extended periods of medical treatment, etc.).

Where protective legislation is, by its terms, discriminatory, e.g. mandated for women and forbidden to men, or has a discriminatory effect on women, it clearly violates women's right to freedom from discrimination. Regardless of their motivation, employment practices and laws that deny or limit women's employment opportunities on the basis of sex violate international and domestic prohibitions against sex discrimination. Similarly, excluding women with childbearing capacity from certain jobs creates a barrier to employment based on gender and thus explicitly discriminates against women on the basis of sex. Although Human Rights Watch does not take a position on protective legislation *per se,* we do condemn such legislation to the extent that it discriminates or promotes discrimination on the basis of sex.

Currently, both gender-specific protective legislation and mandated benefits in Russia deny women the ability to compete for work on equal terms with men. Rather than allow women to choose where to work, the state has determined that women are unfit for certain jobs, or that certain types of employment are inappropriate for women. In theory, the benefits extended to women workers should enhance their ability to bear and raise children while remaining employed, if they so choose, and to support their families. In Russia today, however, many employers use the cost of such gender-specific regulations to rationalize pressuring women to leave the workplace. According to a Russian lawyer interviewed by Human Rights Watch:

> These privileges are bad for women. Privileges given to women should be given to both parents or else employers won't be interested in hiring women. If we have a law limiting the work week for women with children, today they will fire all the women with children, and tomorrow they will fire all the women who might have children.[160]

With regard to the actual term of pregnancy and childbearing, international standards require that women have protection against being fired for reasons of pregnancy or maternity leave.[161] The Convention on the Elimination of All Forms of Discrimination Against Women also calls upon states "to provide special protection to women during pregnancy in types of work proved" harmful. Where, however, the state creates statutory protections

---

[160] Interview, Svetlana Polenina, Union of Russian Jurists, Moscow, March 22, 1994.

[161] CEDAW, Article 11(2)(a).

for women, it must ensure that such protections do not have adverse employment consequences for women; nor should such regulations be used to justify discriminatory labor practices. Women always should be entitled to choose whether to take advantage of such protective legislation and, under no circumstances, should they be punished for utilizing statutory benefits.

Thirty-five-year-old Tatyana Alioshina, a design engineer, lost her job with a government engineering office on January 25, 1994. She went to the unemployment office to look for a new position, "but they offered me nothing in my field. The problem is that I have three children and live far away. They offered me retraining in a specialty in which I would have a hard time finding a job—hairdressing." Alioshina told Human Rights Watch:

> Having children is the first barrier for a woman in finding a job. If a manager takes a woman for a job and she has children, she will be taking time to care for her children. Plus, women have many benefits, and managers don't want such workers. In our organization, they started two years ago to pay us benefits for children. Then a manager came in who said, "Why should we pay these benefits? It's easier just to fire these workers."[162]

Russian officials also acknowledge employers' refusal to hire women, especially women with children. A member of the Duma told Human Rights Watch:

> Women are well-qualified. Their unemployment is not due to being uneducated, but to discrimination. Women here are protected. They receive maternity leave, special benefits for children, child care leave. These protections result in discrimination because it's more efficient to hire men. We are facing a situation where women's privileges work against them.[163]

Asked to explain the higher rate of unemployment for women, a representative of the federal Department of Employment asserted that the

---

[162] Interview, Kaluga, March 23, 1994.

[163] Interview, Galina Klimantova, member of the Duma and chair of the Committee on Women, Family and Youth Affairs, Moscow, March 15, 1994.

"special regulations" that are available only to women—extended paid maternity leave, vacation time when children are small, sick child leave—make women uncompetitive as employees: "Employers prefer men because women cost so much."[164]

Employers, both government and private, explicitly refuse to hire or retain women employees when they can employ men who are not entitled to parental benefits and special protections. In addition, as highlighted by the above quotations, employers continue to perceive all women as mothers or potential mothers and hence as liabilities they cannot afford in an increasingly competitive economy. Thus, women in unemployment offices have been turned away by placement officers and potential employers who told them that their parental responsibilities make them unreliable employees.[165]

Some Russian officials recognize the problems that protective legislation, combined with the state's failure to enforce anti-discrimination laws, are creating for women. Ludmila Zavadskaya, chair of the Duma Subcommittee on Human Rights and Current Laws, told Human Rights Watch that she and others are working to draft laws that will guarantee women and men equal opportunities in the workplace and will strengthen enforcement of anti-discrimination provisions.[166] According to Yekaterina Lakhova, a member of the Duma and former head of President Yeltsin's Commission on Women, Family and Demography:

> The supportive measures [protective legislation] that we had are no longer respected. Women are discriminated against in the sphere of employment. When men are trying to find jobs, no one asks them whether they have children. Women should have an equal chance to make decisions. Now we want to create a law that will provide equal opportunities in the job sphere.[167]

Despite some officials' stated commitment to equal opportunity for women workers, the Russian state has failed to enforce existing prohibitions

---

[164] Interview, Tatyana Prokhorova, federal Department of Employment, Moscow, March 14, 1994.

[165] Granik, "The Legal Status of Women...", p. 83.

[166] Interview, Ludmila Zavadskaya, chair of Duma Subcommittee on Human Rights and Current Laws, Moscow, March 16, 1994.

[167] Interview, Moscow, March 21, 1994.

on sex discrimination and instead clings to protective legislation as the means to women's equality. Thus, for example, Duma member Lakhova simultaneously advocated amending the labor law to abandon protective legislation that hinders women's employment, and increasing women's paid maternity leave to three years. Her proposal demonstrates the persistent belief that the way to solve Russian women's problems in reconciling family and work responsibilities is to enable them to stay home full-time. As Kaluga Mayor Vitaly Chernikov stated, "Today we have more unemployed who are women. This is connected to women's nature: they have children and need to be with them. We have some special protections for women, but we need to do a better job of protecting women."[168]

The above proposals virtually ensure that women with young children will not be able to find work. As long as the law mandates that mothers of young children be granted extensive paid leave to stay home with their children and simultaneously fails to enforce prohibitions on sex discrimination, employers will see men as more desirable employees. The government's failure to enforce anti-discrimination laws allows employers to exercise such discriminatory preferences without sanction.

Thus far, the government's proposed solutions to employment discrimination merely duplicate existing problems. In 1994 the Ministry of Labor drafted a new labor law that it claimed would address the problem of women's unemployment. The Labor Ministry's vice minister for social problems further claimed in early 1994, "We want to see equal opportunities for women in the sphere of hiring, especially when they are pregnant or have children."[169] Yet the revised law retained most of the previous restrictions on women's labor. In fact, the only changes in the draft code actually added to the special protections and benefits for women that—when combined with government failure to enforce anti-discrimination laws—undermine women's ability to find work. Nowhere did the proposed reforms confront the need for stricter enforcement of anti-discrimination laws.[170]

---

[168] Meeting with Human Rights Watch and local activists, Kaluga, March 24, 1994.

[169] Interview, Vice Minister for Social Problems Valerii Yanvariov, Ministry of Labor, Moscow, March 25, 1994.

[170] Ibid. The Vice Minister stated: "The draft labor law has a chapter that deals with women and guarantees equality in hiring. There are limits on the jobs in which women can work, including jobs on weekends or at night. Pregnant women have a right to maternity leave for seventy working days. If they have problems they can take

(continued...)

After active lobbying by women's organizations opposed to such legislation, the draft law ultimately was scrapped by the Duma, which plans to revise the existing labor law rather than propose sweeping new legislation.

Discriminatory Dismissals

I think when employers review the issue of reducing the number of workers in an enterprise and have the choice as to whom to keep, they have practical reasons for firing women. Women often have ill children. They worry about their households and other traditional women's issues. Employers may think it better to hire slightly less-qualified men.
—Valerii Yanvariov, Vice Minister for Social Problems, Ministry of Labor[171]

Overt sex discrimination has prompted many dismissals by government employers. Employers have frequently fired women first because they view them as "more expensive to employ and less reliable" than men.[172] As described above, these employer biases against women are often grounded in the belief that women with children or of child-bearing age will require expensive benefits and will sacrifice job performance to family responsibilities. One Russian lawyer who has represented a number of women in challenging discriminatory employment practices recalled a court hearing in 1993 in which

---

[170](...continued)
eighty-six days. Women can take maternity leave for one and a half years and receive one hundred percent of the minimum wage. They may take a leave of an additional one and a half years at fifty percent of the minimum wage which is paid by the enterprise."

[171] Ibid. However, Yanvariov also stated, "Employers may decide that they need men rather than women, but this is contrary to the law. It will take some time for employers to understand the importance of societal goals regarding equality."

[172] Elena Zdravomyslova, "Strategies of Unemployed Women in the Transition to the Market Economy: The Case of Russia," paper presented at the Second Feminist Conference in Graz, Austria, July 1994, p. 4. Zdramyslova based her comments and paper on sixty-five interviews she conducted with unemployed women in St. Petersburg. Her interview subjects either were or had been unemployed during the recent period of economic reforms. She interviewed women with and without higher education, women of ages ranging from twenty to fifty-three, single and married women, women with and without children, and women belonging to different income groups.

the employer stated, "I would fire all women if I could. Women have children who are always getting sick. They take off too much time."[173]

The following cases provide examples of women losing their jobs because of illegal discrimination based on sex, pregnancy, and maternity.

An unemployed electrical engineer from Kaluga, a city south of Moscow, told Human Rights Watch:

> I recently lost my job when they reduced the number of employees in our defense plant. They reduced the workforce overall by 30 percent. I worked in a department that was all women, about one hundred of us, and they let go about thirty. It's hard to find work in my field, especially for women. Employers prefer to hire men in these specialties.[174]

Angela Mavrina was fired from her job as an ecological researcher with a government organization when she was pregnant:

> I lost my job one and a half years ago. I am still unemployed. When they were reducing the number of workers, they fired me. I told my boss I was pregnant, and he said, "We don't need workers like you." I went to the local [state-run] employment office, but they had nothing for me. They said, "It's impossible for you to find work because you're pregnant and soon will be taking maternity leave. No one wants to hire such workers. There's no point in even trying."[175]

When Mavrina went to the local department of employment office to ask about unemployment benefits, "They told me I was fired illegally and said they would help me file a complaint. The lawyer who took my case wouldn't pursue it because my employer hired my lawyer's boss. I missed several court hearings because I didn't know when to go." The Kaluga City Court later

---

[173] Interview, Lubov Mikhailova, Kaluga, March 24, 1994.

[174] Interview, Kaluga, Russia, March 24, 1994.

[175] Interview, Kaluga, Russia, March 23, 1994.

ruled that Mavrina's complaint had been filed too late and dismissed her case.[176]

In Moscow, an attorney interviewed by Human Rights Watch related the case of a client whose employer, a government research institute, attempted to force her out of her job while she was on maternity leave.

> She wasn't paid even the little sum that is required. They called her all the time and told her to come and sign a statement that she wanted to resign. I helped her write a letter complaining of the mistreatment to the directors of her department and of the government institute. We argued that they could be punished for trying to force her to resign while she was on maternity leave. After that, they stopped bothering her.[177]

Also in Moscow, a metals engineer looking for work at a state-run employment fair told Human Rights Watch:

> I am a metals engineer and have been unemployed for two years. Our plant started to privatize, and they fired many people. Most of the people fired were women. I've been looking for work for two years, but I can't find a job in my field.[178]

As the above case illustrates, once women lose their jobs, they become chronically unemployed, going for months and even years without being offered a new job. Men, by contrast, are unemployed for shorter periods of time.[179]

Discriminatory Hiring

> Everybody is looking for men as workers. When I left my place at the plant, they said I could have my job back if I

---

[176] Angela Mavrina currently is represented by activist and lawyer Lubov Mikhailova, who has written an appeal of the lower court decision.

[177] Interview, Karina Moscalenko, attorney, Moscow, March 17, 1994.

[178] Interview, Moscow, March 17, 1994.

[179] Khotkina, "Gender Aspects of Unemployment..."

was a man. They only want men. Women are tied down
with children so employers don't want to hire them. I don't
know how we will survive.
—Unemployed woman in Moscow[180]

Women also confront sex discrimination when they seek new
employment. Government employers openly express their preference for hiring
men.[181]   At the request of employers, government employment offices
frequently advertise jobs for men only and refuse to refer women to jobs if the
employer has indicated a preference for men.[182] Public sector employers
often ask women about children and marital status in job interviews and reject
applicants on the basis of their sex, maternity or potential maternity. Female
job seekers interviewed by Human Rights Watch in state unemployment
offices identified being a woman, and particularly a woman with children, as
the greatest barrier to finding work.

A thirty-four-year old engineer and mother of two interviewed in a
government unemployment office told us:

I have been unemployed since December 1993 when I lost
my job. They reduced the labor force by many. Our plant
was mostly women, so most of those fired were women.
This is my fifth time in this office. I registered in December,
and I have had interviews for jobs as an electric engineer.
But I haven't had any job offers, because they want to hire
men. This is a man's specialty. When I go for the
interviews, they ask me if I have children. Children are often
ill, and I would have to take time off to care for them.[183]

---

[180] Interview, Moscow, March 18, 1994.

[181] According to a 1992 report in *The Guardian*, "When factories take on workers
they announce that they want men, and when women are rejected it is their sex which
is entered on their application forms as the reason." Anne Sailas, "No Place for
Women," *The Guardian*, May 1, 1992, p. 22.

[182] Russia has established a federal department of employment that maintains local
departments by region. The federal office in Moscow documents the rate and causes
of unemployment; local offices provide referrals to job opportunities, register the
unemployed for state benefits, and refer registered unemployed to job training.

[183] Interview, Kaluga, March 24, 1994.

Another women looking for work in the Kaluga unemployment office
stated:

> I registered one month ago. I haven't found any
> opportunities. I come here every day. They offered me a
> job on an assembly line, but it wasn't enough money to
> support my children. I have two children, ages four and two.
> Nobody wants to hire me, because I'm young and have
> children. Employers usually say they don't want women
> with small children.[184]

Human Rights Watch gathered evidence that employers prefer to hire
men during several visits to state-run unemployment offices in Moscow, St.
Petersburg and Kaluga. In a government unemployment office in Kaluga, for
example, announcements posted on the walls described positions available,
salaries and qualifications for jobs that blatantly included the specification that
only men need apply. All the positions advertised were in the government
sector.

We also visited an employment fair sponsored by the Department of
Employment in downtown Moscow, where both government and private sector
employers had set up booths to meet with prospective employees. Many of the
employers specified in printed job announcements that they were seeking male
employees for certain jobs and females for others. For example, at a table
where two men sat representing a state-supported Moscow machinery factory,
job offerings listed on paper were divided by sex. The jobs for women
consisted almost entirely of menial, poorly-paid work—as cleaners, security
guards, or assembly line workers. These jobs ranged in monthly salary from
30,000 to 200,000 rubles (US$10 to US$67 in December 1994) per month, and
most were at the lower end of the spectrum. The men's jobs were largely in
specialized fields and ranged in salary from 80,000 to 400,000 rubles (US$26
to $133 in December 1994) per month.

Discrimination in Retraining

Women who try to improve their chances of finding work with
retraining have had their opportunities limited because of their sex. Many of
the training programs offered by government employment offices direct women
into courses that prepare them for work in "women's jobs" that arc usually

---

[184] Interview, Kaluga, March 24, 1994.

poorly paid. A number of women interviewed by Human Rights Watch stated that the retraining opportunities offered by the state employment office were limited to low-paying, low-skill jobs, such as housekeepers, seamstresses, typists and hairdressers, even for women with higher academic and/or professional backgrounds. In a January 1993 interview, Moscow Employment Department Chief V. Ovsyannikov described the retraining efforts of his agency:

> Our department allocated funds to train unemployed women in new occupations in demand on the labor market. Since May [1992] the center has been offering free courses in fabric-cutting and sewing, knitting, hair styling, secretarial work, and in work at children's kindergartens.[185]

A spokesperson for the federal Department of Employment confirmed that women continue to receive training primarily to work as governesses or child care providers, housekeepers, seamstresses or bakers.[186]

Five women interviewed by Human Rights Watch in one of Moscow's local unemployment offices all were fired from government enterprises and institutes. The employment office offered the women retraining in secretarial and sewing skills. One woman, a forty-four-year-old widow who spent her career working on engineering projects told us, "My situation is terrible. I have been unemployed for two years. I was trading in the streets to survive. Here they offered me retraining in sewing."[187]   Human Rights Watch supports the efforts of the Russian Department of Employment to provide training to unemployed women and men, but is concerned that women are being offered training only in fields considered appropriate for women and thus are being denied the opportunity to receive training for jobs opening up in developing sectors of the economy.

A forty-year-old unemployed electrical engineer explained her difficulty in finding work:

---

[185] C. Yerisova, "Combatting Unemployment: Incubator for Businessmen," *Moskovskaya Pravda* (Moscow), January 27, 1993,   Foreign Broadcast Information Service, February 27, 1993, FBIS-USR-93-022.

[186] Interview, Tatyana Prokhorova, federal Department of Employment, Moscow, March 14, 1994.

[187] Interview, Moscow, March 18, 1994.

I'm registered at the local unemployment office. They haven't offered me any jobs. They advised me to take a retraining course in hairdressing or sewing. That's all they offer for women. Even to get into those courses, you have to wait for half a year. I won't find a job in my field. Industry is shrinking, and it's especially difficult for women to get these jobs.[188]

To the extent that state-sponsored training programs for women are limited to certain fields, the Russian government denies women on the basis of their sex the opportunity to acquire the skills that would enable them to pursue new employment opportunities in the fields of their choosing. Further, state efforts to direct women toward such training programs could contribute to the creation of a segregated workforce in which women populate the low-paying, low-skill jobs.

Government Failure to Enforce Anti-Discrimination Laws

International standards prohibiting sex discrimination require states to outlaw both private and public discrimination on the basis of sex and to establish adequate remedies for victims of such discrimination. Although Russian law prohibits sex discrimination in employment and creates a process for challenging discriminatory employment actions, Russian authorities are enforcing neither the ban on discrimination nor, generally, the remedy. Since the beginning of *perestroika*, both public and private employers have flouted laws that prohibit discrimination on the basis of sex and maternity with impunity.[189] One lawyer told Human Rights Watch, "As privatization

---

[188] Interview, Moscow, March 17, 1994.

[189] Russian law prohibits sex discrimination in employment. Article 16 of the Code of Labor Laws of the Russian Federation provides, "Any kind of direct or indirect restrictions of rights or establishment of direct or indirect advantages to hiring based on sex...is not permitted." Under the Russian Constitution of 1993, men and women are guaranteed "equal rights and equal freedoms as well as equal opportunities for their realization" (Article 19, Para. 3). "These guarantees, however, are not enforced. Popular notions that women are unfit for many positions of authority or supervision, for example, continue to inhibit women from having the same upward professional mobility as men. Women do not receive equal pay for equal work." Granik, "The Legal Status of Women . . . ," p. 72. Russian labor law also includes specific provisions banning discrimination against pregnant women in both hiring and firing. Article 170 of the code

(continued...)

started, the owners of businesses indulged openly in discrimination. They don't feel bound by the legal system."[190] Recently married and pregnant women suffer discrimination by both government and private employers trying to avoid the expense of paid leave and other maternity benefits.[191]

State officials are aware of the causes and degree of women's unemployment, but, to our knowledge, the state is doing almost nothing to enforce anti-discrimination laws and, in some instances, government officials refuse to condemn the state's role in violations. Instead, the Russian government emphasizes the importance of employing men rather than women and "extol[s] the virtues of a female return to [the] home."[192]

To our knowledge, in only one instance has a government body denounced sex discrimination as illegal and impermissible. In March 1994 a special court reviewed a challenge to the widespread publication by newspapers of job advertisements that specify that men only need apply for certain professional positions. Jobs for women are listed separately and many specify that applicants should be young, blonde, long-legged and "without inhibitions" (willing to have sex with their bosses).[193] The court ruled that sex-specific job advertisements violated the Russian constitution's guarantee of equal rights and freedoms:

> Restrictions by indication of gender constitute an infringement of Article 19 of the Constitution of the Russian Federation establishing that men and women have equal rights and freedoms and equal opportunities for their realization and Article 16 of the Code of Labor Laws of the

---

[189](...continued)
states, "It is forbidden to refuse to hire women and take away their pay for reasons connected with pregnancy or the existence of children."

[190] Interview, Svetlana Polenina, Russian Union of Jurists, Moscow, March 22, 1994.

[191] Ibid.

[192] Zdravomyslova, "Strategies of Unemployed Women . . .," p. 4.

[193] A 1993 Reuter report told the story of Natasha Belyayeva, an unemployed university graduate looking for work. During an interview for a job as an office secretary, she stated, "The director...looked me up and down and said, 'Okay, you look good, you're sexy enough. But if you want to work as a secretary your salary will be very low.' He said I could earn as much in a day as I would in a month as a secretary, if I offered clients sexual services." Fiona Fleck, "Russian Women Squeezed Out of Job Market into the Home," *Reuter European Business Report*, February 18, 1993.

Russian Federation, which forbids "any kind of direct or indirect restriction of rights, or the establishment of direct or indirect advantages to hiring on the basis of sex.[194]

Yet, as of March 1995, little had been done to enforce the ruling and to stop such advertisements from being published.

State failure to enforce anti-discrimination laws has particularly deplorable consequences for women compelled by widespread discrimination in the government sector to look for work in the private sector.[195]   Sex discrimination, sexual abuse and harassment are rampant in Russia's developing private sector.[196]   In some instances, women have reported being raped when they appeared for job interviews.[197]

Although the government is not directly responsible for the discriminatory or abusive actions of private employers, its failure to enforce anti-discrimination laws and to punish individuals responsible for sexual abuse violates its international obligations to protect women's rights to freedom from discrimination and to bodily integrity.

Private employers' mistreatment of women ranges widely, from advertising for sexually compliant employees to actual sexual assault.   As described above, private companies run newspaper advertisements seeking female employees prepared to have sex with their bosses to keep their jobs. A research fellow at the Center for Independent Social Research who has

---

[194] The decision that sex-specific jobs advertisements violated the Russian constitution's guarantee of equal rights and opportunities for men and women was reached by the Judicial Chamber on Information Disputes in Moscow on March 11, 1994. This court is attached to the office of the President of the Russian Federation. The case was brought against several newspapers—*Izvestia*, *Finansovaya Izvestia*, *Ekonomika i Zhizn*—that had carried advertisements for specifying that men only need apply for certain professional positions including lawyers, accountants, and securities specialists.

[195] Article 18 of the Russian Criminal Code, titled "On Forcing a Woman to Engage in Sexual Relations," prescribes a three-year prison sentence for those convicted of sexual harassment in the workplace.

[196] The Moscow-based Fund for Protection from Sexual Harassment at Work has a list of approximately 300 private businesses where employers regularly abuse or harass their employees. Dmitry Babich, "Workplace Harassment," *Moscow Times*, July 5, 1994. Director of the fund Valery Vikulov told the *Moscow Times* that a number of women in Moscow informed him they were raped by potential or current employers.

[197] Ibid.

conducted extensive research into the causes and conditions of women's unemployment in St. Petersburg found that, in some cases, women are offered jobs only if they are willing to perform "intimate services." She stated, "This is a big problem in private businesses, and there is no regulation of this. Sexual abuse is not considered abuse. People think it is a part of our culture."[198] One woman who rejected the sexual advances of her employer told Human Rights Watch that she consequently left her job:

> I am a single mother. I can't work at night because I don't have a husband to care for my baby. I experienced sexual harassment in the private sector, so I had to leave my job. I was working as an accountant, and, on the second day, my boss wanted me to sleep with him. So I had to leave. This happens to many women.[199]

In a similar incident reported by *The New York Times* in April 1994, a twenty-three-year-old graphic designer quit her job because her employer repeatedly grabbed her and pressured her to have sex with him.[200]

Much as the Russian government has turned a blind eye to sex discrimination in the workplace, it also has, to our knowledge, largely ignored reports of widespread sexual harassment of female employees by both Russian and foreign private companies. According to an April 1994 press report, "Sexual harassment in the workplace is rampant in today's Russia, and the sexism that thrived under the Communists is growing worse, aggravated . . . by the new lawlessness that rules the business world."[201]   With few exceptions, the Russia government has not acted against such lawlessness by denouncing or investigating allegations of sexual harassment [202]   On the

---

[198] Interview, Elena Zdravomyslova, St. Petersburg, March 28, 1994.

[199] Interview, Moscow, March 18, 1994.

[200] Alessandra Stanley, "Sexual Harassment Thrives in the New Russian Climate," *New York Times*, April 17, 1994.

[201] Ibid.

[202] In early 1994, the first known sexual harassment case in Russia was brought in the southern Siberian city of Barnaul. Thirty-five-year-old Tatyana Smyshlayeva complained that her supervisor at the municipal health clinic threatened to fire her if she did not respond to his repeated groping of her in his office. Prosecutors on the case, which was later dismissed in the February 1994 general amnesty, could find no precedent of such a case being tried. Ibid.

contrary, prohibitions against sexual harassment, like those against sex discrimination, are not enforced even when such incidents are reported. As a consequence, many employers feel free to grope their female employees and demand sex on the job without fear of being held to account for their actions. The Russian government must end the impunity for employers who discriminate against, sexually harass and physically assault their female employees by enforcing provisions in the criminal and labor codes that penalize such behavior.

EMPLOYMENT DISCRIMINATION IN POST-COMMUNIST POLAND

Since 1989 Poland has undergone dramatic political and social changes that brought about, among other things, extraordinary improvements in certain areas of human rights that had been routinely violated in the past.[203] For instance, the rights to political representation, due process, freedom of association, free expression, and conditions in prisons have improved significantly. These changes, along with the Polish constitution's guarantee of equal protection to women, suggest that Polish women enjoy the protection of their fundamental rights. In reality, many Polish laws blatantly discriminate against women and the post-communist government has done little to safeguard and enhance women's human rights. During the transition from communism to a more democratic society, past discrimination and current political, social and economic pressures have combined to result in a growing risk of sex discrimination in the workplace. Even the limited gains for women under communist rule have been threatened. This case study examines the early changes in the situation of women workers in Poland since the fall of communism.

Legal Situation
During the communist era, equality between the sexes was part of the official ideology and women ostensibly were granted the same basic rights as men. When the communist regime was overthrown in Poland in 1989, many of the laws perceived to be a legacy of the communists were also rejected. One major target of the backlash against communism-era laws was the

---

[203] The following material was adapted from Helsinki Watch and Women's Rights Project, "Hidden Victims: Women in Post-Communist Poland," *A Human Rights Watch Short Report*, vol. 4, no. 5 (March 1992).

principle that men and women have equal rights. The belief in women's equality was challenged by many who advocate returning to "traditional Polish ideals," which were defined to encompass the notion that women's proper place is within the home.

The Polish constitution, which was promulgated under the communist regime, is the principal law in Poland guaranteeing equality of the sexes, including equal pay for equal work.[204] Article 78 of the constitution ensures equal rights for women in every field of political, economic, social and cultural life. Aside from the constitution, most Polish law either does not explicitly uphold sexual equality or in some cases, laws explicitly distinguish between men and women.

Many Polish employment laws take a paternalistic or protective stance toward women by treating women as physically weaker than men. These laws work to the detriment of women by preventing them from taking many jobs and shortening their careers involuntarily. For example, one decree states that "It is prohibited to employ women in jobs particularly arduous and detrimental to their health."[205] This decree lists more than ninety occupations in twenty fields of employment in which women may not work. The jobs unavailable to women, including various branches of industry, health care, forestry service, agriculture, and transportation, usually are better paid than those that women commonly hold.[206]

Another law makes the retirement age for women five years lower than for men—sixty and sixty-five, respectively. Under communism, this law was perceived as a woman's privilege because she could retire and begin receiving a pension earlier than her male counterpart. However, the enormous economic upheaval that followed the fall of communism, involving massive layoffs and rising unemployment, resulted in this law being used to force women to retire earlier than they otherwise would choose. The cost to women of forced early retirement was compounded by the fact that post-retirement economic security in Poland has decreased dramatically since communist rule ended. The Polish Ombudsman, who is appointed by Parliament to protect

---

[204] Article 67, Part 2, published in *Rzeczpospolita* (*Republic*), May 23, 1991.

[205] Rozporzadzenie Rady Ministrow z dn. 19 stycznia 1971 (Council of Ministers Directive, January 19, 1971), Dz. U. 4/1979, poz. 18.

[206] Amendments in Rozporzadzenie Rady Ministrow z dn. 5 wrzesnia 1984 (Council of Ministers Directive, September 5, 1984), Dz. U. 44/1884, poz. 235.

civil rights through legal action,[207] successfully contested the application of the law to university teachers, but it continues to apply in all other cases.

Besides laws created ostensibly to protect women, other laws are designed to promote women's role as the primary family caretaker. These laws discriminate against women because they often result in shorter work hours for women and decrease employers' willingness to hire women workers; not only are women given significant leeway to perform family responsibilities, but men are given almost no opportunity to do the same. For instance, one law granted long-term leave benefits to care for a sick child only to the mother and not to the father, unless the father is a single parent or in some other exceptional situation.[208] In addition to establishing different legal treatment for men and women, this law made employers more eager to employ men than women. In March 1995 new regulations went into effect that would also grant sick-leave benefits to the father, but the regulations reduced the benefit to 80 percent of full salary.

Many of these discriminatory employment laws were promulgated prior to 1989, but in contrast to numerous other statutes that originated in the communist era, laws that discriminate against women have largely been immune from reform. The post-communist Polish government has continued to enforce these laws, even though they have their origin in the communist era, while the current ombudsman has refused to challenge these laws as violating the Polish constitution's equality provision.

De Facto Employment Discrimination

In addition to the discriminatory employment laws currently in force, Polish women confront sex discrimination in practice from which the law offers no specific protection. For example, no law prohibits sex discrimination in hiring practices. Consequently, employers who choose a man over an equally or better qualified woman for a particular position face no legal sanction. Human Rights Watch found that employers frequently deny women employment simply because of their sex. The reasons often are given openly: women get pregnant; have children; use maternity leaves and sick leaves to

---

[207] The role of the ombudsman depends heavily on the approach taken by the appointed individual. For instance, when Ewa Letowska was ombudsman she included issues of sex discrimination within her reports. In contrast, the current ombudsman, Tadeusz Zielinski, has been less active in protecting women from sex discrimination. "Women's Rights: Privilege or Prejudice," *Warsaw Voice*, November, 1994.

[208] Law of December 17, 1974.

care for children; and thus, it is economically advantageous to hire men rather than women. This discrimination has become more pronounced since the fall of communism and has occurred even though Polish women, in general, are better educated than men. For instance, although men constitute a slight majority of those with a college education in Poland, women represent a significant majority of those with high school diplomas.[209]

Even under communism, the impact of job discrimination against women was apparent. According to official Polish data, as of 1988 more than 50 percent of Polish women had jobs, and women accounted for about 45 percent of all employed Poles. But relatively few women held managerial positions. Moreover, women's salaries have been significantly lower than those of men employed in substantively similar jobs: women receive on average between 70 to 80 percent of the pay received by men holding the same jobs.[210] In addition to the specific legal restrictions on the kinds of jobs women may hold, some jobs, such as teaching, nursing, janitorial work, and clerical duties, traditionally are overwhelmingly female and among the lowest paid. As a result, Polish women's average income is significantly lower than that of men.

Although Polish women confronted consistent discrimination under communism, they experienced virtually no unemployment until its demise. Since 1989 unemployment has become a steadily growing feature of the Polish economy,[211] with a disproportionately negative impact on women workers. In December 1994 women constituted more than half of the unemployed (52.8 percent).[212] In fact, in public discussions on unemployment in the early 1990s, people have suggested that one way to decrease the level of unemployment is to encourage mothers to stay home and take care of their children. At the same time, Solidarity, the worker's union that was instrumental in the democracy movement, proposed a "family wage" designed to encourage women to stay home. Under this proposal, a man would collect substantial supplements to his salary for each child if his wife did not work,

---

[209] Glowny Urzad Statstyczny, *Kobieta w Polsce,* (Main Statistical Office, *The Woman in Poland*) Warsaw, November 1990, p. 18.

[210] Ibid., pp. 13-14.

[211] As of 1994, unemployment in Poland averaged about 16 percent. In certain areas of the country, unemployment approached 35 percent. Polish Committee of NGOs Beijing 1995, "The Situation of Women in Poland," p. 35.

[212] Ibid.

thus making it economically inadvisable for some women to work. This "family wage" proposal was never brought to a vote in Parliament.[213]

Based on interviews with women in Poland in 1991, Human Rights Watch also found that women were more likely to be fired than men. In mass layoffs there was a tendency to protect the "main supporter" of a family, who was usually presumed to be a man. Once fired, women also found it much more difficult to get new jobs because job openings mostly were gender-specific and targeted at men. The state-run employment agency, which everybody seeking to collect unemployment benefits must use, encouraged sex discrimination by having separate employment offices for men and women, resulting in fewer job opportunities for women. For example, in January 1990 there were three unemployed women for each job offered for women while the number of unemployed men equaled the number of offers available to men. A mere ten months later, in October 1990, for each job offer requesting a woman there were thirty-seven unemployed women, while for men the proportion was one to ten.[214]

In a study done in May to June 1993 entitled "The Warsaw Job Market for Women," the Center for the Advancement of Women, a Polish nongovernmental organization, interviewed 407 employers from both the public and private sector to explore sex discrimination in employment. The study found that men were hired for twice as many new jobs as women, and that the group most vulnerable to layoffs were women over forty in state sector office jobs.[215]

Government action regarding child care, whether intentionally or not, also has operated to keep women out the workforce. Under communism, day care was affordable and generally, although not universally, available. Since the end of communism, more than half of all day care centers have closed down. The Polish government has delegated responsibility for public day care to local governments, which are even more impoverished than the national government. Many local governments have had to raise public day care fees significantly; of those that managed to stay open, most have become extremely

---

[213] Telephone interview, Ursula Nowakowksa, director, Women's Rights Center, Warsaw, Poland, June 21, 1995.

[214] *Kobieta w Polsce* (The Woman in Poland), p. 25.

[215] Polish Committee of NGOs Beijing 1995, "The Situation of Women in Poland," p. 17 (summarizing the findings of the "The Warsaw Job Market").

expensive. Women with more than one child often find that it no longer makes economic sense to work.[216]

The post-communist Polish government has done little to remedy the legal and increasing *de facto* discrimination women experience in the job market. Moreover, in some cases government action has contributed directly to the problem. The result has been women's increasing disenfranchisement from the rapidly changing economic structure. Without active efforts by the government to change this, women will find themselves effectively locked out of the Polish economy.

GENERAL RECOMMENDATIONS

To Governments:
- All incidents of violence against women workers should be fully and fairly investigated.
- Debt bondage, passport deprivation, and illegal confinement should be prohibited by law and such laws should be enforced.
- Labor standards should be assessed with a view to amending any provisions that discriminate on the basis of sex, pregnancy, maternity, or national origin. All governments should further take measures to prohibit labor practices that have discriminatory impact on the basis of sex, maternity, national origin or job category. Victims of employment discrimination on the basis of sex should be afforded an appropriate forum to challenge the practice and to obtain an effective remedy.
- To the extent that parental benefits are provided or required by the government, men and women should equally be eligible to receive them, with the exception of childbirth leave.
- Legal restrictions on the freedom of association of women workers, including migrant workers, and in particular domestic workers, should be removed.
- International labor standards, particularly those recognized by the International Labor Organization as basic human rights, should be strictly enforced in export processing zones and export-oriented industries. Such standards should also be applied to women workers who are homeworkers or subcontractors.

---

[216] Ibid., p. 34; Malgorzata Pomianowska, "Wraca Ola z przedszkola" ("Ola Comes Back from the Nursery School"), *Polityka* (*Politics*), June 8, 1991.

- Governments should uphold the due process rights of women workers, including female migrant workers and irrespective of their immigration status, who seek to report abuse by employers. Governments should not wrongfully arrest women workers whose passports or other identity papers have been confiscated by their employers for violations of immigration laws. Host governments should under no circumstances retain the lawful passports of foreign migrant workers. Migrant women, regardless of their immigration status, should be granted the right to stay in the country pending the outcomes of criminal or civil suits against allegedly abusive employers or of labor disputes. During this period, they should be provided shelter in non-penal facilities.

- The governments of countries that either send or receive significant numbers of migrant workers, including women, should develop bilateral agreements to protect the rights and security of these migrants. Such agreements should include, among other things, procedures for the safe repatriation of migrant workers.

- Both sending and receiving countries should also closely monitor recruitment and employment agencies to ensure that they are legitimate operations that do not engage in abuses against female migrant workers. Sending countries should provide special training to migrant workers to inform them prior to departure of their rights in the country of destination. Such training should be provided in the workers' own language.

To the International Community:

- The United States and the European Union should amend their General Systems of Preferences legislation to require beneficiary countries to take meaningful steps toward addressing invidious sex discrimination as one of the conditions for receiving trade benefits.

- International assistance, both public and private, to support labor movements should develop programs to promote the participation of women in unions and workers associations, both as leaders and rank-and-file members, and to provide information to women about their rights in the workplace.

- International financial institutions, such as the World Bank, as well as donor governments should extend the concept of "good governance" to include a firm commitment to the protection of human rights, including basic worker rights.

- Businesses—along with their affiliates and subcontractors—should fully respect, at a minimum, the labor standards recognized by the

International Labor Organization as basic human rights, with particular emphasis on the rights to nondiscrimination, freedom from forced labor and free association.

6
DOMESTIC VIOLENCE

Domestic or family violence is one of the leading causes of female injuries in almost every country in the world and it accounts in some countries for the largest percentage of hospital visits by women.[1] It primarily affects women and operates to diminish women's autonomy and sense of self-worth. Domestic violence usually involves the infliction of bodily injury, accompanied by verbal threats and harassment, emotional abuse or the destruction of property as means of coercion, control, revenge or punishment, on a person with whom the abuser is involved in an intimate relationship. The assailant frequently blames the attacks on the victim and her behavior.[2] He may also use the attacks to control his partner's actions.[3] A battered woman may become isolated with little community or family support and be afraid to leave her home. She may also begin to believe that her inability to avoid abuse in an intimate relationship demonstrates that she is a failure and deserves or is powerless to escape the abuse.[4] Human Rights Watch's investigations found, unfortunately, that law enforcement officials frequently reinforce the batterer's attempts to demean and control his victim.

---

[1] A 1993 national survey of domestic violence in Japan by the Domestic Violence Research Group found 58.7 percent of the sample reported physical abuse by a partner and 59.4 reported sexual abuse. In a detailed family planning survey from 1990 in the Kissi district of Kenya, 42 percent of women said they had been beaten by their husbands; in Papua New Guinea, 67 percent of rural women and 56 percent of urban women have been victims of wife abuse, according to a national survey conducted by the Papua New Guinea Law Reform Commission in 1986. These studies were set forth in Lori L. Heise, *Violence Against Women: The Hidden Health Burden* (Washington, D.C.: World Bank, 1994), pp. 6-9, 14, 18. "Each of the studies is individually valid, but they are not directly comparable because each uses a different set of questions to probe for abuse." Ibid., p. 5.

[2] Joanne Fedler, *"I've got a Problem with my Husband . . ." Lawyering Domestic Violence through the Prevention of Family Violence Act 1993 - An Evaluation After a Year in Operation.* (South Africa: unpublished manuscript, 1995).

[3] Ayuda, *Domestic Violence: A Manual for Pro Bono Lawyers* (Washington, D.C.: Ayuda, 1994), Introduction, pp. 21-24. Ayuda is a nongovernmental organization that provides legal services to immigrant women in Washington, D.C.

[4] United Nations African Institute for the Prevention of Crime and the Treatment of Offenders, *Report of the Training Workshop on Law, Women and Crime in Africa,* (Kampala, Uganda: United Nations, 1994), p. 7.

341

The police and judicial authorities often dismiss domestic violence as a "private" matter rather than a widespread scourge that demands urgent state action. The forms of violence that women experience in the home, including rape, murder, assault and battery, are condemned by the criminal laws of virtually all countries. However, when committed against a woman in an intimate relationship, these attacks are more often tolerated as the norm than prosecuted as crimes, even when laws exist on the books that specifically condemn domestic violence. In many places, those who commit domestic violence are prosecuted less vigorously and punished more leniently than perpetrators of similarly violent crimes against strangers.

At every step of the process to obtain legal protection from domestic assault, women face barriers that prevent them from prosecuting their batterers and make a mockery of the justice system. Legislatures pass laws that exempt marital rape from criminal sanction; police refuse to arrest men who beat their wives, and in some cases even intimidate women into withdrawing complaints of spousal abuse; prosecutors fail to charge men with domestic assault; court clerks turn away women who seek restraining or protection orders; and judges accept "honor" and "heat of passion" defenses that allow wife-murder based upon "legitimate provocation," usually adultery.

For instance, in Brazil, even after the highest court of appeal rejected the honor defense as illegitimate in 1991, lower courts continued to exonerate men who killed their wives or lovers if they acted to defend their honor against the women's alleged infidelity. Similarly, in Pakistan, men who have killed their allegedly adulterous wives have invoked the "grave and sudden provocation" defense successfully to mitigate their sentences.[5] The "heat of passion" defense in the United States also has operated to reduce the punishment of men who murdered their wife if they had witnessed (or in some cases discovered) her adultery.[6]

---

[5] Asia Watch (now Human Rights Watch/Asia) and Women's Rights Project, *Double Jeopardy: Police Abuse of Women in Pakistan,* (New York: Human Rights Watch, 1992), p. 46.

[6] Donna K. Coker, "Heat of Passion and Wife Killing: Men Who Batter/Men Who Kill," *Southern California Review of Law and Women's Studies*, Volume 2, Number 1, 1992, pp. 71-130. In recent years, this defense has been accepted less frequently, but cases still appear intermittently. For example, Kenneth Peacock, who murdered his wife in Maryland several hours after discovering her with another man, was allowed to plead guilty to the lesser charge of manslaughter, which carries a recommended sentence of

(continued...)

International Legal Protections

Although domestic violence by definition is committed by private individuals (although some state agents also abuse their wives, girlfriends or children), states nonetheless are bound by numerous international laws and norms that oblige them to protect women's lives and physical security. Where states routinely fail to prosecute domestic violence against women because of the sex and status of the victim, in contrast to their efforts to prosecute other criminal violence, they deny women equal protection of the law. Under international law, governments are obligated to guarantee equality before the law for all of its citizens, without regard to sex. The ICCPR prohibits sex discrimination in three different articles. Article 2(1) of the ICCPR states that,

> Each State Party . . . undertakes to respect and to ensure to all individuals within its territory and subject to its jurisdiction the rights recognized in the present Covenant, without distinction of any kind, such as . . . sex.

Article 3 of the ICCPR provides for the right of men and women to the enjoyment of all civil and political rights." Article 26 further guarantees that,

> all persons are equal before the law and are entitled without any discrimination to the equal protection of the law. In this respect, the law shall prohibit any discrimination and guarantee to all persons equal and effective protection against discrimination on any grounds such as . . . sex.

In addition to the ICCPR, the Convention on the Elimination of all Forms of Discrimination Against Women (CEDAW) also prohibits sex discrimination by requiring state parties "to pursue a policy of eliminating

---

[6](...continued)
three to five years. On October 17, 1994, Judge Robert Cahill sentenced Peacock to only eighteen months in jail and stated "I seriously wonder how many married men . . . would have the strength to walk away without inflicting some corporal punishment. I'm forced to impose a sentence . . . only because I think I must do it to make the system honest." Megan Rosenfeld, "Mercy for a Cuckolded Killer: Women Outraged over Judge's Light Sentence," *Washington Post*, October 19, 1994; Karl Vick, "Md. [Maryland] Judge Taking Heat in Cuckolded Killer Case," *Washington Post,* October 30, 1994.

discrimination . . . [and] to ensure that public authorities and institutions shall act in conformity with this obligation."[7] Almost all regional treaties contain similar prohibitions.[8]

Where states respond to evidence of murder, rape or assault of women by their intimate partners with inaction, they send the message that such attacks are justified or, at a minimum, will not be punished. In doing so, states fail to take the minimum steps necessary to protect their female citizens' rights to physical integrity and, in extreme cases, to life. The International Covenant on Civil and Political Rights (ICCPR) contains several prohibitions against violence that implicate domestic violence. Article 6(1) provides that "Every human being has the inherent right to life. This right shall be protected by law. No one shall be arbitrarily deprived of his life." Article 7 states that "No one shall be subjected to torture or to cruel, inhuman or degrading treatment." And Article 9(1) guarantees that "Everyone has the right to . . . security of person." While the ICCPR does not explicitly refer to private violence, including domestic violence, the broad language in the above provisions clearly can encompass such abuse. State parties are obligated to combat domestic violence by virtue of having undertaken "to respect and to ensure" the rights recognized in the covenant.

International law applies to the actions of states or individuals acting as agents of the state. But, the concept of state responsibility has developed to recognize that states are "obligated to investigate every situation involving a violation of the rights protected by [international law]."[9] For example, the Inter-American Court on Human Rights in the late 1980s[10] offered commentary on the scope of states' duty under Article 1 of the Inter-American Convention on Human Rights "to ensure" the rights within the treaty to all person within their jurisdiction. The same requirement "to ensure" rights

---

[7] CEDAW, Article 2.

[8] African Charter on Human and Peoples' Rights, Articles 2, 3; American Convention on Human Rights, Articles 1, 24; and European Convention for the Protection of Human Rights and Fundamental Freedoms, Article 14.

[9] *Velásquez Rodríguez* (July 29, 1988), Inter-American Court of Human Rights (series C) No. 4, para. 176 (specifically discussing rights contained within the Inter-American Convention of Human Rights).

[10] Ibid. The court offered this commentary in three cases decided in 1988-1989. The tribunal found in these cases that the government of Honduras was responsible for a series of forced disappearances carried out between 1981 and 1984 by members of the Honduran military. It extended its commentary to cover the full scope of Article 1(1).

protected by a treaty is found in Article 2 of the ICCPR. The court stated that a state "has failed to comply with [this] duty . . . when the State allows private persons or groups to act freely and with impunity to the detriment of the rights recognized by the Convention."[11] Moreover, the court required governments to:

> take reasonable steps to prevent human rights violations and to use the means at its disposal to carry out a serious investigation of violations committed within its jurisdiction, to identify those responsible, to impose the appropriate punishment and to ensure the victim adequate compensation.[12]

This includes "ensur[ing] that any violations are considered and treated as illegal acts."[13] Consistent with this reasoning, Human Rights Watch believes states should be held accountable for consistent patterns of discriminatory enforcement of criminal law. If the state persistently fails to take reasonable measures to prevent, investigate, prosecute or punish acts of domestic assault, particularly wife-murder, when committed by private actors, this violates their female citizens' right to physical integrity. Thus, what would otherwise be wholly private conduct is transformed into a constructive act of the state, "because of the lack of due diligence to prevent the violation or respond to it as required by the [Inter-American Convention.]"[14]

Elaborating on the due diligence standard, the court clearly stated that a single violation of human rights or just one investigation with an ineffective result does not establish a state's lack of diligence. Rather, the test is whether the state undertakes its duties seriously. Such seriousness can be evaluated through the actions of both state agencies and private actors on a case by case basis. This due diligence requirement encompasses the obligation both to provide and enforce sufficient remedies to survivors of private violence. Thus, the existence of a legal system criminalizing and providing sanctions for domestic assault would not be sufficient; the government would have to

---

[11] *Velásquez Rodríguez,* para. 176 (referring to the Inter-American Convention).
[12] Ibid., para. 174.
[13] Ibid., para. 175.
[14] Ibid., para. 172.

perform its functions so as to "effectively ensure" that incidents of family violence are actually investigated and punished.[15]

The Committee on the Elimination of Discrimination Against Women in 1992 affirmed government accountability for the routine nonprosecution of domestic assault. The committee's General Recommendation 19 condemns gender-based violence as a form of sex discrimination that greatly inhibits a woman's ability to enjoy rights and freedoms on a basis of equality with men.[16] The recommendation specifically noted that "States may also be responsible for private acts if they fail to act with due diligence to prevent violations of rights, or to investigate and punish acts of violence."[17]

In another significant step towards enhancing state accountability for gender-based violence, the United Nations Commission on Human Rights appointed the first Special Rapporteur on Violence against Women in 1994.[18] The special rapporteur is tasked to carry out and follow up on missions, undertaken either separately or jointly with other special rapporteurs or working groups, on all forms of violence against women and to recommend ways of eliminating such violence. The special rapporteur's first report set forth the international legal framework condemning domestic violence and detailed actions that were currently being pursued by governments to reduce the occurrence of domestic assault. With regard to state responsibility for domestic violence, she wrote:

---

[15] Ibid., para. 167 (applies this test to the question of disappearances).

[16] General Recommendation 19, Committee on the Elimination of Discrimination Against Women, January 29, 1992.

[17] Ibid., Article 10.

[18] The U.N. Commission on Human Rights, at its fiftieth session on March 4, 1994, adopted resolution 1994/45, entitled "The question of integrating the rights of women into the human rights mechanisms of the United Nations and the elimination of violence against women." In this resolution, the commission decided to appoint, for a three-year period, a special rapporteur on violence against women, including its causes and consequences. The special rapporteur is obligated to: "(a) Seek and receive information on violence against women, its causes and consequences . . .; (b) Recommend measures, ways and means . . . to eliminate violence against women . . .; (c) Work closely with other special rapporteurs, special representatives, working groups and independent experts of the Commission on Human Rights . . . in the discharge of its functions." Commission on Human Rights, "Further Promotion and Encouragement of Human Rights and Fundamental Freedoms, Including the Question of the Programme and Methods of Work of the Commission," U.N. Document E/CN.4/1995/42, p. 3.

In the context of norms recently established by the
international community, a State that does not act against
crimes of violence against women is as guilty as the
perpetrators. States are under a positive duty to prevent,
investigate and punish crimes associated with violence
against women.[19]

The special rapporteur, moreover, asserted that countries should not use
tradition or custom as an excuse for abdicating their responsibilities to prevent
violence against women.[20]

Besides appointing the Special Rapporteur on Violence Against
Women, the United Nations has also engaged in standard-setting activities to
address violence against women, including family violence. The U.N.
Declaration on the Elimination of Violence Against Women, adopted in
December 1993, is a comprehensive statement of international standards with
regard to the protection of women from violence. The declaration denounces
violence against women, including violence in the home, as "a violation of the
rights and fundamental freedoms of women." It provides that:

states should condemn violence against women . . . [and]
exercise due diligence to prevent, investigate and, in
accordance with national legislation, punish acts of violence
against women, whether those acts are perpetuated by the
State or by private persons."[21]

At the regional level, the 1995 Inter-American Convention on the
Prevention, Punishment and Eradication of Violence Against Women is the
first regional human rights treaty to focus exclusively on gender-based violence
and to prohibit explicitly violence within the home.[22] Article 2 of the
convention defines violence against women:

---

[19] Preliminary Report Submitted by the Special Rapporteur on Violence Against
Women, its causes and consequences, U.N. Document E/CN.4/1995/42, November 22,
1994, p. 18.

[20] Ibid., p. 16.

[21] Declaration on the Elimination of Violence Against Women, U.N. Document
A/Res/48/104, February 23, 1994, Article 4.

[22] Inter-American Convention on the Prevention, Punishment and Eradication of
Violence Against Women, entered into force on March 5, 1995.

to include physical, sexual and psychological violence: a. that occurs within the family or domestic unit or within any other interpersonal relationship, whether or not the perpetrator shares or has shared the same residence with the woman, including, among others, rape, battery and sexual abuse. . .

Not only does the convention require state parties to condemn, prevent and punish violence against women,[23] it also calls on governments to undertake progressively specific positive measures to address the root causes of gender-based violence, such as mass education programs to counter gender stereotypes, as well as to create protective and social services for victims of violence.[24]

As the following case studies show, domestic violence that goes unpunished is endemic in many countries. It is a problem that persists even when other areas of human rights protection have improved. Whereas previously, international human rights standards had been applied to strictly public action, this is no longer true. The United Nations, regional human rights bodies and governments have begun to acknowledge, in principle, state accountability for abuses by private actors. It now remains for governments to summon the political will to end impunity for domestic violence through the justice system, and for the international community to hold governments that fail to do so fully accountable under human rights law.

VIOLENCE AGAINST WOMEN IN BRAZIL

A 1991 Human Rights Watch investigation in Brazil revealed that Brazilian women receive little or no justice when they reported physical abuse by their husbands or partners to the police.[25] In spite of the approximately 125 specialized police stations (Delegacias De Defesa Da Mulher) established in Brazil to deal exclusively with violence against women, many women in rural and urban areas have found police to be unresponsive to their claims and have encountered open hostility or incredulity when they attempted to report

---

[23] Ibid., Chapter III, Article 7.
[24] Ibid., Chapter III, Article 8.
[25] The following material was adapted from Americas Watch (now Human Rights Watch/Americas) and Women's Rights Project, *Criminal Injustice: Violence Against Women in Brazil* (New York: Human Rights Watch, 1991).

domestic violence. Some delegacias are chronically underfunded and their staff poorly trained. The Brazilian Penal Code, in spite of indefatigable lobbying on the part of Brazilian women's rights activists, remains biased and discriminatory in its letter and in its implementation.

The continued application of the honor defense, which has no basis in law,[26] is inherently biased, and is almost exclusively applied to wife-murder. The emphasis on "provocation" by the victim even in pre-meditated wife-murder crimes; the near total failure to prosecute battery and rape in the home; and the prejudicial treatment of rape victims both in law and in fact, represents a pattern of discriminatory treatment by the criminal justice system of female victims of domestic violence. This pattern demonstrates that Brazil does not meet its international obligations to guarantee to its female citizens the equal enjoyment of their civil and political rights and the equal protection of the law.

Brazil has taken limited steps toward meeting these obligations. In 1991 Brazil's highest court rejected the defense of honor for the crime of wife-murder in its *Lopes* decision.[27] The 1988 constitution reflects a concern for familial violence and specifically calls for states to establish mechanism to impede domestic violence. And, the creation of the women's police stations also indicates Brazil's recognition both of the wide-scale problem of violence against women and its obligations to take positive steps toward eradicating such abuse.

Nonetheless, in 1991 a Human Rights Watch investigation and subsequent monitoring of the state response to violence against women in Brazil revealed that these changes have had very little impact. In 1991 the organization's Women's Rights Project issued its first report on domestic violence and state responsibility in Brazil. They responded to the severity of

---

[26] It is still possible in Brazil for a man to kill his allegedly unfaithful wife and be absolved on the grounds of honor, particularly in Brazil's interior, where one state prosecutor told Human Rights Watch the honor defense is successful 80 percent of the time.

[27] On August 5, 1988, in the Brazilian city of Apucarana, Joa Lopes murdered his wife and her alleged lover. The defense argued that Lopes acted in legitimate defense of his offended honor. An all-male jury accepted the argument and absolved him of the double homicide. A state appellate court in Parana upheld this decision. On March 11, 1991, the Superior Tribunal of Brazil overturned the lower court's ruling and ordered a new trial, thereby declaring that murder cannot be conceived of as a legitimate response to adultery.

Brazil's domestic violence problem, made visible largely by the campaigning of the women's movement, and the degree to which such abuse continues to receive both the explicit and implicit sanction of the Brazilian government. The report concluded that impunity prevails for men who beat, rape and kill their wives and girlfriends, as epitomized in the use of the honor defense to exculpate men accused of killing their wives or partners. The Brazilian criminal justice system has failed generally to investigate and prosecute in a nondiscriminatory manner crimes of domestic violence against women, in contravention of Brazil's obligations under international law.

This failure continues in 1995. While the government has created approximately six shelters for battered women throughout the country, the criminal justice system remains largely unresponsive to women's complaints of abuse, except where, as one women's rights activist and attorney told Human Rights Watch "[the battered woman] has lots of money to hire a very good lawyer to defend her case and push it through the Brazilian legal system. She went on to add that in many domestic violence cases, judges simply file away the complaints and they are rarely investigated"[28]

The Role of the Women's Movement
The Superior Tribunal's rejection of the honor defense in Lopes followed a decade-long struggle by Brazilian advocates of women's rights to debunk the "legitimate defense of honor" and to force the state to prosecute wife-murder and other domestic violence crimes to the full extent of the law. This movement against domestic violence emerged, in part, against the background of Brazil's military dictatorship and in the context of the gradual liberalization which began in the late 1970s and culminated in the 1985 indirect election of a civilian president and the creation of the new Brazilian Republic. Reports of sexual abuse, torture and murder of political prisoners during the dictatorship led to a national debate about violence and, in the mid-1970s, to the creation of a number of nongovernmental human rights organizations in which women were very active.

Active women in both urban and rural areas and across racial and economic divides seized on domestic violence and used it successfully to propel gender concerns into the broader public policy debate. A series of local demonstrations led to several nationwide protests against domestic violence from which emerged the slogan that became the *crie de coeur* of the Brazilian women's movement: "Those who love don't kill."

---

[28] Telephone interview, Dr. Leila Linhares, July 17, 1995.

A major goal of both the state and national councils was combatting violence against women. The National Council for Women's Rights (CNDM) president Jacqueline Pitanguy put gender-specific violence at the top of the council's political agenda, launching a "say no to violence against women" campaign and compiling several documents detailing violence against women and criticizing the inadequate penal and judicial response.

By late 1985 eight women's police stations had opened in the state of São Paulo, and by 1990 there were seventy-four throughout the country.[29] The women's delegacias represented an integrated approach to the problem of domestic violence. They were designed to investigate gender-specific crimes, and to provide psychological and legal counseling.

By the mid-1980s, the now active and institutionalized women's movement began to focus on legal reform to consolidate their hard-won gains. Women were granted the franchise in 1932, but until a 1962 civil code reform they were considered perpetual subordinates, legally equated with "minors, spendthrifts and backwoodsmen"[30] and could not, for example, work outside the home without their husband's permission. The constitution enacted in 1988 reflects many of the national women's movement's demands.[31]   In particular, Article 226, Paragraph 8 provides that "the state should assist the family, in the person of each of its members, and should create mechanisms so as to impede violence in the sphere of its relationships." Similar provisions have been adopted in state constitutions throughout Brazil.

Domestic Violence
Available statistics show that over 70 percent of all reported incidents of violence against women in Brazil take place in the home. In almost all of these cases the abuser was either the woman's husband or her lover. Over 40 percent involved serious bodily injury caused by, among other things, punching, slapping, kicking, tying up and spanking, burning of the breasts and

---

[29] Jacqueline Pitanguy, "Violence Against Women: A Global Problem," report to the Ford Foundation, 1991.

[30] Romy Medeiros de Fonseca, "Law and the Condition of Women in Brazil," cited in *Law and the Status of Women*, Columbia Human Rights Review (New York: 1977), p. 14.

[31] Women's rights advocates secured, for example, maternity and paternity leave, improved prison conditions for women, and improved labor and health standards. Their efforts to decriminalize abortion failed. Abortion is currently illegal in Brazil, except in cases of rape or risk to maternal health.

genitals, and strangulation.[32] Brazil's 1988 census, conducted by the Brazilian Institute for Geography and Statistics (IBGE), includes the first national statistics broken down by gender on crimes of physical abuse and the extent to which they are reported to the police and prosecuted in the courts. The IBGE study found that from October 1987 to September 1988, 1,153,300 people declared to the IBGE that they had been victims of physical abuse. A marked difference emerged in the nature of violence suffered by women as opposed to men. For Brazilian men, murder and physical abuse primarily involve acquaintances or strangers and occur outside the home. For Brazilian women, the opposite is true. The 1988 census showed that men were abused by relatives (including spouses) only 10 percent of the time, while women are related to their abuser in over half of the cases of reported physical violence.

After battery and serious threat of death or physical harm, rape is the third most reported form of violence against women, although by all accounts the "under-registration of sexual occurrences is significant."[33] Of those cases that are reported, rape appears to occur less frequently in the domestic context than it does outside the home. A study of reported rapes in the state of Minas Gerias found that over half were perpetrated by strangers.[34] However, researchers point out that these limited statistics do not support the conclusion that marital rape does not frequently occur. They stressed that prevailing attitudes that marital rape is not a crime may substantially reduce both reporting and investigation.

Neither the census nor the various police studies examine the incidence of homicide in which females are victim. Such crimes are handled by special police stations which deal exclusively with this type of offense and which do not provide murder statistics broken down according to gender. In addition, the number of homicides in which females are victims is difficult to

---

[32] *Jornal do Commercio,* April 28, 1990.

[33] Fundação SEADE, Conselho Estadual Da Condição Feminina, *Um Retrato Da Violência Contra A Mulher* (*A Portrait of Violence Against Women*) (CIP International, 1987).

[34] Maria da Conceição Marques Rubinger, et al., *Crimes Contra A Mulher: A Violência Denunciada,* (provisional title) forthcoming report prepared with funding from the Ford Foundation, 1991, Table 17.

determine accurately because they are often unreported, particularly in the poorer or more remote areas of the country.[35]

Wife-Murder

Although national homicide statistics broken down by gender are not available, existing information indicates that wife-murder is a common crime.[36] A 1991 study of more than 6,000 violent crimes against Brazilian women from 1987 to 1989 found that 400 incidents involved murders of women by their husbands or lovers.[37]

The Legal Context

Under Brazilian law, homicide is defined as a crime against life (*crime contra a vida*). It is the only crime that requires a jury trial. The Penal Code, passed in 1940, differentiates between unintentional murder (*homicídio culposo*) and intentional murder (*homicídio doloso*). In cases of intentional murder, Article 121 of the code makes a distinction between simple homicide (*homicídio simple*) which carries a penalty of six to twenty years and qualified homicide (*homicídio qualificado*) which carries a penalty of twelve to thirty years.[38]

Article 121, Section 1 of the Penal Code describes attenuating circumstances which can result in the reduction of penalties (*diminuição de*

---

[35] According to interviews conducted by Human Rights Watch, wife-murders go unreported largely because they happen "behind closed doors." An October 30, 1990 *Miami Herald* article also notes that Brazil's "vast territory often shrouds many killings in impunity" and quotes the former president of the national council of women saying that "nobody has any idea how many women are being killed in Rio's slums."

[36] We discuss both homicides and attempted homicides as well as cases in which the female victim is not the wife but the live-in lover of the accused. Statistics usually separate these two groups but show little differentiation of behavior between them.

[37] Letícia Lins, *Jornal do Brasil*, April 1, 1991. The article cites a study prepared by Viva Mulher!, a group based in the northeastern capitol of Recife which monitors crimes of violence against women.

[38] A qualified homicide involves aggravating factors such as a spousal relationship between the aggressor and the victim. Aggravating factors under Article 121, Section 2 of the Penal Code include a base (*torpe*) motive (i.e., one which causes general repugnance, like a murder for money or pleasure), a futile (*fútil*) motive (i.e., one which is so insignificant that it does not constitute an acceptable explanation for the crime), the use of insidious or cruel means, or the use of actions, like a surprise attack, which prevent the victim from defending him or her self.

pena) by up to one-third. These include, among other things, being under the influence of violent emotion (*violenta emoção*) caused by an unjust provocation by the victim (*injusta provocação da vítima*).[39]   Murders to which this reduction are applied are known as "privileged homicides" and carry an optional sentence of one to six years.

A homicide is not considered a crime in Brazil if, among other things, it was committed in legitimate self-defense (*legítima defesa*).   Under Article 25 of the Penal Code, self-defense is defined as "the case of one who using the necessary means with moderation reacts against unjust aggression present or imminent to his right or someone else's."

Charges in homicide cases are brought by the prosecutor (*Promotor*) who is under the jurisdiction of the state attorney general (*Procurador Geral*), head of the Public Ministry (*Ministério Público*). Following receipt of the police report, the prosecutor conducts his own investigation and recommends to the judge whether and on what charge to try the suspect. The victim or her family may retain independent counsel to accompany the prosecution during this phase. This attorney does not have the same authority as the prosecutor, but can assist in the gathering of evidence and in questioning, though not subpoenaing, witnesses.

During the pre-trial phase, which begins once the judge receives the prosecutor's recommendation, the judge hears the accused and witnesses on both sides and may subpoena additional witnesses or seek additional evidence. There is no grand jury. The judge alone determines whether there is sufficient evidence for a jury trial for homicide or attempted homicide—the only crimes in Brazil which merit a jury trial.

After hearing the arguments of both the prosecution and defense and reading the testimony of witnesses, the jury makes its final decision based on answers to a series of questions posed by the judge at the behest of the opposing sides. The questions follow a standard format, although their content reflects the specific facts of the case. The jurors only answer "yes" or "no." They do not consult with one another and convey their answers by secret ballot. Under Article 5 of the Brazilian Constitution, the sovereignty of the

---

[39] Article 28 of the Brazilian Penal Code says that "emotion or passion does not exclude anyone from penal responsibility." However, one Brazilian sociologist has pointed out that the committee in charge of reviewing the Penal Code took a somewhat lenient attitude towards crimes of passion. That is why passion is included as an attenuating circumstance in the articles concerning homicide.

jury's decision is guaranteed.[40] The judge determines the sentence based on the jury's verdict.

The Honor Defense

Prior to Brazil's independence in 1822, Portuguese colonial law allowed a man who caught his wife in the act of adultery to kill her and her lover, although the reverse was not true.[41] Brazil's first post-independence penal code was enacted in 1830 and did away with this rule. Brazil's second penal code, enacted in 1890, included an exemption from criminal responsibility for those who committed a crime "under a state of total perturbation of the senses and intelligence." Wife-murder cases soon came to be defended as "crimes of passion" in which the wife's adulterous behavior occasioned such strong emotion in the accused that he experienced a kind of "momentary insanity" resulting in the crime. The emphasis in such cases was placed not on the nature of the crime itself, but on the degree to which the husband intended to commit it.

For the next fifty years, defense attorneys successfully used the "crime of passion" argument to obtain acquittal of husbands accused of murdering their wives and, on occasion, though far less frequently, of wives accused of murdering their husbands.[42] It proved so effective in obtaining acquittal that Brazil's third penal code, which remains in force today, explicitly states that "emotion or passion does not exclude criminal responsibility."[43]

As a result of this change in the penal code, acquittal in wife-murder cases became more difficult to obtain. Defense attorneys, unhappy with this development, devised the legitimate defense of honor as a new exculpatory strategy. Like the crime of passion argument, the honor defense shifts

---

[40] Article 5, Section 38 of the Brazilian Constitution states "the institution of the jury is recognized in such forms as may be organized by law, the following being assured (a) full defense; (b) confidentiality of the balloting; (c) sovereignty of the verdicts; and (d) jurisdiction to try felonious crimes against life." The Jury Tribunal, commonly known as the popular jury, was first instituted in Brazil in 1822 and has seen several changes in composition and jurisdiction since. At present, state pools of between 300 and 500 potential jurors are chosen each year. Every three months 21 names are chosen by the judge from this larger group, of which seven become the sentencing council. Jury trials continue until a verdict is reached; they are not adjourned.

[41] Mariza Corrêa, *Os Crimes Da Paixão*, (São Paulo: Editora Brasiliense, 1981).

[42] Ibid., p. 22.

[43] Brazilian Penal Code, Article 28.

attention from the killing itself to the absence of intent on the part of the murderer.   However, rather than focusing on the accused's "momentary insanity" as vitiating criminal intent, the honor defense characterizes the accused as having acted spontaneously in legitimate self-defense against an imminent aggression, though against his honor rather than his physical being.

The notion that a man's honor can be gravely threatened by his wife's adulterous action reflects proprietary attitudes towards women deeply rooted in Brazilian society.   When Brazil's first civil code was passed in 1914, women were considered perpetual wards, like minors and the elderly.   The 1988 constitution grants full equality to women, but the civil code has yet to be changed.

This subordinate status is the basis for the belief that the wife is the husband's property and any action by her that does not fall within the prescribed conjugal norm, especially adultery, constitutes an offense against his honor.   In many cases, a successful honor defense depends less on showing the accused's passion or lack of intent to kill than on demonstrating the husband's honor and the wife's dishonorable behavior within a recognized conjugal relationship.[44]   For example, in one 1972 case, the couple had been married for sixteen years.   All was well in the marriage until she got a job, began coming home late and, according to testimony from the accused, refused to pay her "conjugal debt."   The husband killed her and was acquitted, again on legitimate defense of honor.   The decision was upheld on appeal.[45]

As this case demonstrates, the honor defense has been successfully invoked in Brazil as if it were the equivalent of legitimate self-defense, with the defendant's resulting acquittal.   Yet at no point does the law equate a threat to a man's honor with the danger posed by an imminent physical attack.

---

[44] As noted in Conselho Nacional Dos Direitos Da Mulher, *Quando A Vítima É Mulher* (When the Victim is a Woman),(Brasilia: CEDAC, 1987), a study prepared for the National Council on the Rights of Women, the jury "doesn't evaluate the crime in itself, but instead evaluates the victim and the accused's life, trying to show how adapted each one is to what they imagine should be the correct behavior for a husband and wife . . . . The man can always be acquitted if the defense manages to convince the jury that he was a good and honest worker, a dedicated father and husband, while the woman was unfaithful and did not fulfill her responsibilities as a housewife and mother . . . . This way the ones involved in the crime are judged distinctly.   Men and women are attributed different roles, in a pattern that excludes citizenship and equality of rights."

[45] Ibid., p. 126.

The legitimate defense of honor accepts not only that a wife's adultery constitutes such an "imminent threat," but also, as in the case described above, that her merely alleged adultery or desire to separate or refusal to engage in sexual relations constitute such a threat as well.

A key aspect of the self-defense rule is proportionality of the means employed. The accused must "use the necessary means in moderation" in responding to an imminent threat. Even assuming that a wife's act of adultery tarnished her husband's honor, homicide, or in some cases double homicide, is obviously not a proportionate response. Yet, the Brazilian courts repeatedly legitimated such disproportionate responses.

As early as 1955, Brazil's high court began to overturn cases involving acquittal on the grounds of honor. In one 1968 decision, the court found that the "legitimate defense of honor does not exist in a homicide committed by a husband during a crisis of indignation, when the wife has threatened the conjugal honor."[46] Although by Brazilian law the high court's decisions refer only to the specific case being judged and have no precedential value, its decisions in practice carry significant jurisprudential weight and are expected to establish precedent, particularly at the appellate court level. In honor defense cases, however, the high court's decisions have had no such unifying effect and, consequently, a history of contradictory jurisprudence has evolved.

For example, a review of appellate court records for the state of Rio de Janeiro from 1978 to 1987 reveals this long-standing contradictory trend. Of twenty cases involving the legitimate defense of honor, eight contained outright and principled rejections of the defense. In one 1979 case, the tribunal found that "the Penal Code doesn't allow a man to decree the death penalty to an unfaithful wife or lover." In a 1983 case, the court found that, as quoted above, "recognizing legitimate defense of honor is equivalent to establishing the right to kill, once social prejudices are accepted."[47]

However, another five cases upheld the honor defense. In one 1984 case involving an attempted murder, the appellate court found:

---

[46] Records of the Superior Tribunal Federal, the appellate court of last resort prior to the 1988 constitutional amendments creating two high courts of appeal, one for civil and criminal cases and one for constitutional matters.

[47] Tribunal of Justice of Rio de Janeiro, Division of Jurisprudence, records for 1978 to 1987.

[the victim,] who was in matrimonial litigation with the defendant, demanded he pay alimony. That should have made her adopt a more strict behavior to justify the onus she wanted to put on her ex-husband. However, she showed up in the company of an ex-employee said to be her lover, and caused a completely legitimate reaction on the part of the defendant under the point of view of the defense of his hurt honor.[48]

The ongoing tension in Brazilian jurisprudence concerning the honor defense expressed itself in conflicting judicial decisions in the case of João Lopes, a bricklayer who stabbed to death his wife and her lover after catching them together in a hotel room in the city of Apucarana. On March 11, 1991, the Superior Tribunal of Justice, Brazil's highest court of appeal in criminal and civil cases, overturned lower and appellate court decisions acquitting Lopes of the double homicide on the grounds of legitimate defense of honor.

The court nullified the lower courts' decisions on the grounds that they were against all facts in the case. It found that "honor is a personal attribute which is the property of each spouse. There is no offense to the husband's honor by the wife's adultery. There is no such conjugal honor." In addition, the high court found that "homicide is not an appropriate response to adultery" and "given that there was no proof of revenge on the part of the wife, the adultery does not place the husband in a state of self-defense as contemplated by the penal code."[49] Finally, the court proclaimed that what is defended in such cases "is not honor but the pride of the Lord who sees his wife as property."[50]

However, when the *Lopes* case was re-tried on August 29, 1991, the lower court ignored the high court's ruling and again acquitted Lopes of the double homicide on the grounds of honor. The lower-court judge who presided over the second trial ruled that the honor defense was "essentially the heart" of the matter. The judge told reporters that "one decision of the

---

[48] Ibid.

[49] The Court's emphasis on the absence of revenge on the wife's part served to negate the possibility that her actions were consciously designed to attack her husband thereby causing him to defend himself.

[50] Decision of the Superior Tribunal of Justice, March 11, 1991.

Supreme Court does not necessarily form a national precedent."[51] The lower court's ruling is particularly significant because the second jury's decision is definitive and cannot be appealed again, unless on other grounds.

The Response of the Courts

Several criminal justice officials interviewed by Human Rights Watch argued that, in the absence of precedential authority at the high court level, lower court judges cannot be held accountable for the honor defense's continued success. A prosecutor in Pernambuco stated that "the jury doesn't want to know about the law. She demeaned him. So to wash his honor, he killed her. The patriarchal concept is very strong." In his view, "the citizens don't judge correctly. In the interior [juries] don't conform to the expectations of society. Justice is limited. A man kills his wife and goes back on the street."[52] He estimates that in the country's interior the honor defense is still successful 80 percent of the time.

The defense attorney in *Lopes* told Human Rights Watch in April 1991 that "it's not the legal system, but macho society that acquits wife-killers. . . . Society talks louder than the courts."[53] He was certain that the high court's decision would have no impact on the jury tribunal and, as it turned out, rightly expected that the honor defense would be upheld by the jury when the case was re-tried in the lower court in August 1991.

The argument that juries, not judges, are responsible for the continued success of the honor defense has some basis in Brazilian law. In all criminal and civil cases, except homicide, the judge is the sole adjudicator. In homicide cases, however, the popular jury assumes the responsibility for deciding cases, and the judge has remarkably little control over the legal or factual basis for its verdict. Judges can dismiss cases for lack of evidence[54] or acquit defendants when convinced that there was no intention to commit a crime,[55] but they have limited authority to impede the arguments of either party and almost no authority to exclude evidence.[56] The lower court judge in the

---

[51] State Judge Luis Fernando Araujo, quoted in Associated Press, September 2, 1991.

[52] Interview, State Prosecutor Avilar Caribe, April 1991.

[53] Interview, Attorney João Batista Cardoso, May 1991.

[54] Criminal Procedure Code, Article 409.

[55] Ibid., Article 411.

[56] Any and all evidence presented by counsel is admissible in homicide cases as long as it was not obtained by illicit means and is relevant.

Lopes decision told reporters that "unless the defense's strategy is completely absurd or irrelevant, I can do nothing to impede it."[57]

Several attorneys handling constitutional and criminal cases interviewed by Human Rights Watch stressed the limited authority of trial court judges. Under Article 483 of the Criminal Procedure Code, the judge cannot interfere in the jury's decision in any way and is largely restricted to posing the questions which the jury will answer in deciding the case. The jury's verdict is sovereign, and can only be appealed if it is against all material evidence in the case or if procedural irregularities occurred in the course of the trial or sentencing. The *Lopes* case, for example, having been appealed once on the merits, cannot be appealed again unless procedural irregularities are discovered.

In principle, Human Rights Watch does not dispute the desirability of the jury's sovereignty. Rather, we are concerned about the propensity of judges in honor defense cases to defer to that sovereignty even when the jury's verdict is not supported by the law or the facts. While the jury is sovereign, its sovereignty does not extend to deciding contrary to law or against all material evidence. The Superior Tribunal in *Lopes* reversed the verdict on both grounds. Although its decision is not binding, it does constitute an interpretation of the law that should guide lower court decisions in specific cases. The judge presiding at Lopes's second trial should have instructed the jury in the law consistent with the high court's decision. By permitting the jury to acquit Lopes on the grounds of honor a second time, the judge subordinated his role as guardian and explicator of the law to the whim of a jury ignorant of the law and motivated by social prejudice. To ignore a landmark ruling by the nation's highest court in the very same case makes a mockery of the appellate process and the administration of justice in Brazil.

Privileged Homicide

Even when the honor defense is not invoked, Human Rights Watch found ample evidence that the Brazilian courts treat defendants in wife-murder cases more leniently than others arrested for murder, largely through the misuse of the "violent emotion" exception to mitigate sentences. The penal code explicitly states that "emotion or passion does not preclude criminal responsibility," but "violent emotion right after the unjust provocation of the

---

[57] State Judge Luis Fernando Araujo, quoted in Associated Press, September 2, 1991.

victim"[58] is a mitigating circumstance in cases of homicide or attempted homicide. For the violent emotion exception to apply, the accused must have acted under the influence of spontaneous emotion resulting from some provocation of the victim. Such crimes are deemed "privileged homicides" and carry a sentence of one to six years. By contrast, intentional homicides carry a twelve to thirty year sentence.

In principle, the extent to which a crime was premeditated or the result of momentary passion should be weighed in determining the crime's severity. The violent emotion exception however, is often misapplied to benefit defendants in wife-murder cases who have shown substantial premeditation. In addition, it is often accepted with little or no evidence of an "unjust provocation" by the victim. Thus, murderers who should have received a minimum sentence of twelve years sometimes serve as little as eighteen months.

In the wife-murder cases investigated by Human Rights Watch, the courts seemed unusually willing to overlook evidence of intentional homicide on the part of the accused and focus instead on the behavior of the victim and its alleged provocative effect. For example, in the 1989 *Aníbal Maciel de Abreu e Silva* case, the court granted the violent emotion mitigation despite clear evidence that the crime was both deliberate and premeditated. Moreover, the alleged provocation was never actually proven in court.

On June 3, 1985, Aníbal Maciel de Abreu e Silva shot and killed his ex-wife Nícia de Abreu e Silva, from whom he had been separated for three months. He shot her four times, once in the back. Several days after the murder, Aníbal presented himself to the police. In his deposition he said he had waited to see Nícia outside the school where she was studying. He was carrying a gun "as usual." He testified that when she came out of the building they got into an argument and he "lost his senses" and killed her. He said he did not plan the crime and did not suspect her of having any lovers.[59]

The prosecution charged Aníbal with qualified homicide, aggravated by surprise (medical records showed that Nícia did not physically anticipate the assault) and by base motive, due to his unwillingness to pay the alimony asked for by Nícia pursuant to their separation. This crime carries a minimum sentence of twelve years. The defense asked that the aggravating factors regarding motive be dropped and that Aníbal be charged with simple homicide.

---

[58] Penal Code of Brazil, Article 28.
[59] Aníbal Maciel De Abreu e Silva, statement to the police, June 13, 1985.

In classifying the crime the judge retained only the aggravating factor of surprise.

In the trial, according to the victim's sister, Aníbal's attorney argued that the murder was a privileged homicide committed in a state of violent emotion provoked by the victim. He contended that Aníbal had committed the crime out of jealousy prompted by the fact that Nícia had had three lovers and a lesbian affair with the family's maid.[60] The prosecution contested this defense, pointing out that the accused himself did not suspect a lover. The lovers were never produced, nor was any evidence regarding the maid. The prosecutor further argued that the crime was premeditated. No witness was produced to verify that Aníbal normally carried a gun.

The jury accepted the violent emotion defense. In 1989 Aníbal was convicted of privileged homicide and sentenced to four and one half years. Because he was a first-time offender with good behavior he served eighteen months in an "open" prison and then was released. The state prosecutor in the case told Human Rights Watch that the jury's decision was against all facts in the case.[61] Thus, even though there was ample evidence that Abreu e Silva had planned the crime and no evidence to support the defense's claim of provocation by the victim or that the claimed provocation had immediately preceded the murder, the court sentenced the defendant according to the violent emotion exception.

In one 1981 case examined in the National Council on the Rights of Women (CNDM) study, Francisco Carlos Neto stabbed to death his wife Marinete from whom he had been separated for two years. Testimony in the case indicated that Francisco had threatened to "finish with Marinete" in the past because she had sought alimony after their separation. The defense sought Francisco's absolution on the grounds that he was not in full possession of his mental faculties at the time of the crime. However, a psychological report ordered by the judge determined that Francisco was criminally responsible and aware of the consequences of his act. Nonetheless, the jury found that he was not mentally responsible and acquitted him.[62]

A criminal court judge who frequently presides over wife-murder trials acknowledged the influence of gender biased social norms in wife-murder cases, although he stated that such prejudices do not influence his own

---

[60] Interview, Cecília Barbosa, April 1991.

[61] Interview, Prosecutor Jorge Vacite, May 1991.

[62] Conselho Nacional Dos Direitos Da Mulher, *Quando A Vítima É Mulher* (When the Victim is a Woman), p.76.

decisions. In speaking of the application of the violent emotion defense, he said "the rule in these cases is established by custom. From a society of Latin origins there always prevailed superiority of man over woman. . . . There exists perhaps in all of us a bit of machismo. This evidently influences how such crimes are viewed. . . . The woman has to fight to present alternative facts to society."[63]

Many women's rights advocates feel that without considerable public attention Brazilian courts will remain extremely resistant to such "alternative facts." They have witnessed so many wrongful applications of the violent emotion defense in wife-murder cases that they have come to view it, like the honor defense, as inherently discriminatory against women.

According to several prosecutors and judges the violent emotion defense is rarely used in cases in which wives kill their husbands. One state prosecutor told us that "in general, women who kill their husbands are always sentenced to a higher sentence than men who kill their wives. . . . Most men who are accused of killing their wives get simple homicide. Many of the women accused of killing their husbands get qualified homicide."[64] One judge stated that the difference in sentencing between men and women "is related to the fact that men kill their wives in the heat of the moment while women in the great majority plan. Men normally act in an impetuous moment, although it is important to stress that they also plan."[65] The implications of such discriminatory treatment are devastating. When wife-murder cases reach the courts there is considerable risk that female victims will not receive equal justice and that their murderers—if only because of undue reduction of sentence—will receive the implicit sanction of the judiciary. Despite this disturbing history of misapplication of the violent emotion defense, Human Rights Watch does not advocate its elimination, since we have understood that there are valid reasons for its application in certain cases. Rather, we urge

---

[63] Interview, Judge Roberto Ferreira Lins, April 1991.

[64] Interview, State Prosecutor Avelar Caribe, April 1991.

[65] Interview, Judge Roberto Ferreira Lins, April 1991. Judge Lins noted that women often plan to murder their husbands because it would be fatal to them if they did not. He pointed out that many of the husband-murder cases he has judged involved a long history of battery prior to the homicide. In the United States, in some states prior incidents of battery can be cited as evidence that the accused, even if she killed her husband when he was asleep, for example, was acting in legitimate self-defense. Human Rights Watch is unaware of any husband-murder cases in Brazil which have been successfully argued along these lines.

narrowly defined judicial standards to ensure that it is applied only in appropriate circumstances and in a non-discriminatory manner consistent with equal protection requirements of international law.

Preferential Treatment of Offenders

The reportedly lenient treatment accorded assailants in wife-murder cases is especially troubling because a large majority of defendants are already "privileged" under Brazilian law as first-time offenders.[66] As one defense attorney interviewed noted, "You don't kill your wife twice."[67] Because such offenders are often people of good standing with no prior record, the large majority not only defend their cases while at liberty but also receive reduced penalties.

The principle of first-time offender was introduced in Brazil in a 1977 penal code reform which became known as the *Lei Fleury* (Fleury Law, named after a notorious police chief who was one of its early beneficiaries). The Fleury Law affects all forms of imprisonment for first-time offenders awaiting trial, sentencing or a decision on appeal. It gives judges discretion at any of these stages to grant liberty to first offenders pending a judicial decision on the merits, so long as there is no cause for preventive detention. Preventive detention is only used by judges to preserve the public order and to ensure the appearance of the accused at trial or pending appeal. The 1990 heinous-crimes law modified the Fleury Law, exempting from its benefit first-time offenders accused of heinous crimes, including rape.

Criminal defendants should be accorded reasonable bail. However, social prejudices lead judges to release offenders in wife-murder cases far more often than in other homicide cases, even when there is a legal basis for their detention. According to several defense attorneys and judges interviewed by Human Rights Watch, an estimated 90 percent of the defendants who are

---

[66] Several activists interviewed by Human Rights Watch pointed out that first-time-offender status would be denied to any perpetrator who had a previous record, and that many wife-murder crimes culminate a long period of domestic abuse. Unfortunately, as detailed in the section of this report on battery, such crimes often are not reported to the police, or, more important, when reported, are not always registered in an official police bulletin. And, even when registered, they are rarely prosecuted. Thus a wife-murderer who is a "first time offender" might actually have a history of committing domestic abuse, but it would not necessarily have been registered with the authorities.

[67] Interview, Clóvis Sahione, attorney, April 1991.

convicted in wife-murder cases pursue their case without ever spending a night in custody until they are finally sentenced, which is often years later.

In the *Anibal Abreu e Silva* case discussed above, the prosecution requested the preventive detention of the accused on the grounds that he had fled the scene of the crime and retained ample means to flee the country. The judge denied the prosecution's request, leaving Anibal to pursue his case while at liberty, a status which benefits the accused in several ways, which includes exacerbating the judicial system's already chronic delay. As one defense lawyer noted, "time gained by being at liberty works in favor of the accused. Society begins to forget."[68] Moreover, according to judges and prosecutors with whom we spoke, offenders in wife-murder cases often take advantage of their freedom to flee, thereby rendering prosecution—which in Brazil requires the presence of the accused—practically impossible.

First-offender benefits are also invoked after conviction. One criminal court judge asserted:

> Our law is loose and sloppy. Somebody's condemned to six years for killing his wife and he's a first-time offender with a good background, he won't even serve eighteen months. He usually goes to a semi-open prison and then one year later is granted conditional liberty (*liberdade condicional*) which is not linked to anything. We don't even watch him.[69]

The benefits of provisional liberty for deserving candidates should be preserved, but judges should weigh such liberty against the gravity of the crime, the desirability of speedy justice, and the potential for injustice resulting from flight—and should not allow social prejudice about the crime to influence their judgment. The Brazilian government is not per se responsible for deeply rooted social prejudices which underlie the honor defense, misapplication of the violent emotion defense, unwarranted reduction of charges in wife-murders and preferential treatment of offenders. Nor are such discriminatory attitudes unique to Brazil. However, insofar as Brazil's police and judges legitimate such prejudices by routinely allowing them to influence their disposition of wife-murder cases, the government is responsible for failing to fulfill its

---

[68] Interview, Zulaiê Ribeiro, April 1991.
[69] Interview, Judge Roberto Ferreira Lins, April 1991.

obligations under both domestic and international law to guarantee equal protection to its citizens without regard to sex.

Battery: The Legal Context

Under the Brazilian Penal Code, physical abuse falls into the category of causing bodily injury (*lesão corporal*), defined in Article 129 as an offense "to someone's physical integrity or health." Such crimes carry a sentence of three months to a year. The penal code distinguishes between minor and serious injuries, with the seriousness determining the length of the sentence. Serious abuse can result in a prison sentence of from one to eight years. Beatings which end unintentionally in death carry a four to twelve year prison sentence. Crimes of physical abuse are not tried by juries. They are decided by judges pursuant to police reports and the investigations of the prosecution, defense and judge. As with homicide, penalties are reduced in corporal-lesion cases when the crime is committed unintentionally or immediately after an unjust provocation of the victim. Prison sentences can be replaced by fines when the nature of the offense is not serious.

A woman seeking to report a physical attack or sexual abuse to the police follows a standard procedure. After reporting to the police station, the complaint is registered in a Bulletin of Occurrence by a detective and the woman proceeds to the Medical-Legal Institute (IML) for an examination. After receiving the IML's report the police investigation begins and is overseen by a detective inspector. The results of the inquiry are forwarded to the police chief for review and summation and then passed on to the justice system for prosecution. Though the system works in theory and provides for adequate oversight, Human Rights Watch found evidence of reports to the police which were never officially registered, registered complaints which were never fully investigated and investigated cases which, despite their apparent merit, were never prosecuted.

In addition to criminal penalties, the law provides such remedies for domestic abuse as separation orders and divorce. However, of primary concern for this report is the application of criminal law to physical abuse of women in the home. In general, although the creation of women's police stations has greatly enhanced the public visibility of crimes of domestic violence, the formal criminalization of such abuse is the exception rather than the rule.

The Response of the Police and the Courts

At the time of our investigation, female victims had little reason to expect that their abusers—once denounced—would ever be punished. A police chief in Rio de Janeiro told Human Rights Watch that to her knowledge, of more than 2,000 battery and sexual assault cases registered at her station in 1990, not a single one had ended in punishment of the accused. The São Luis women's police station in the northeastern state of Maranhão reported that of over 4,000 cases of physical and sexual assault registered with the station, only 300 were ever forwarded for processing and only two yielded punishment for the accused.

Prior to the creation of the women's police stations in 1985, police stations rarely investigated crimes of violence against women which occurred in the home. In many cases, police officers were actively hostile towards female victims seeking to report such abuse. A 1983 study in Minas Gerais by the Center for the Defense of Women's Rights found that the police often turned female victims away, on the grounds that domestic violence was "a private problem." When police did register domestic abuse crimes, they frequently failed to follow standard procedures, leaving out pertinent information about the circumstances of the abuse. In addition, they often subjected the victim to abusive treatment aimed at implicating her in the crime.[70]

Brazil's 1988 census, coupled with reports gathered from the women's *delegacias*, revealed a high level of domestic abuse among reported crimes of physical violence against women. A 1987 study of over 2,000 battery cases registered at the São Paulo delegacia from August to December 1985, found that over 70 percent of all reported crimes of violence against women occurred in the home. Almost 40 percent of these registered incidents involved serious bodily injury, usually committed by the accused's own feet or fists.[71] The 1988 census generally corroborates these figures. These statistics gave the first in-depth picture of domestic violence in Brazil.

In the ten years since their creation, the delegacias have succeeded not only in expanding the definition of criminal activity in Brazil to include violence against women, but also in altering the traditional perception of wife-

---

[70] Maria da Conceição Marques Rubinger, et al., *Crimes Contra A Mulher*, Introduction.

[71] Fundação SEADE, Conselho Estadual Da Condição Feminina, *Um Retrato Da Violência Contra A Mulher* (CIP International, 1987)

beating as socially acceptable. According to former National Council of Women President Jacqueline Pitanguy:

> The existence of the delegacias means that certain acts (which were not and still are not in many cases) perceived as criminal behavior by the regular police, by the accused and frequently by the victim are now qualifying as criminal behaviors. And they are being punished as such. In this sense the delegacias not only combat crime but also its definition, changing the border of accepted/non-accepted social behavior.[72]

Despite the delegacias' considerable accomplishments in responding to women victims and raising the visibility of domestic violence, as of 1991 the actual criminalization of such abuse had not markedly increased. Sociologists, researchers, attorneys and women's rights advocates interviewed by Human Rights Watch estimated that only 20 to 50 percent of the domestic-abuse cases reported to the delegacias were ever investigated. Figures from the main São Paulo delegacia show that of 2,573 bodily injury cases registered in 1989, only 1,135, or less than 50 percent, were ever investigated by the police.[73]

The reasons for these low investigative rates are complex and vary from police station to police station and state to state. However, general trends have been discernible. Most people familiar with the delegacias attributed this problem less to the failings of the delegacias themselves (although they are a contributing factor) than to the limitations imposed on the delegacias by the institutional and social context within which they operate. Many people we interviewed, including *delegadas* (women police officers), attribute low investigation rates primarily to shifting and often diminishing economic and political support from the state and federal governments, low police morale, and lack of training about domestic violence at the police academy.

The effectiveness of the delegacias has depended on the importance local authorities ascribe to them. They are not equally distributed throughout

---

[72] Pitanguy, "Violence Against Women, Addressing a Global Problem," report to the Ford Foundation, 1991, p. 5.

[73] Assessoria Especial Das Delegacias De Defesa Da Mulher Do Estado De São Paulo, General Statistics, 1989.

the country. In fact, there are no delegacias in Brazil's rural areas.[74] Nor do they receive equal support vis-á-vis each other or the regular police stations. Pitanguy notes that "the prestige of the women's police stations inside police structures varies, but in general they are not given the importance of traditional specialized police stations like those for homicide or drugs."[75]

Several delegadas we interviewed spoke of the discriminatory treatment they experience from many of their police colleagues as a result of choosing to work in the women's police stations. One delegada told us that the delegacias are treated like "the kitchen of the police." A women's rights activist who works closely with the delegacias stated "the delegacias are not a career police thing. There is a stigma attached to working in a delegacia. The delegadas do not like the work because of discrimination in the police force."[76]

While diminishing resources and poor morale are key factors in low investigative rates by the police, the most regularly cited problem is that many women police serve in the delegacias without receiving adequate specialized training. Sonia Alvarez points out that although "in some cases feminist scholars and activists were brought in to train female police at these specialized precincts, feminists were marginalised from most, as the selection and training of staff was entrusted to the local force."[77] In São Paulo and Rio for example, early attempts to have material on domestic violence incorporated into the police training manuals, while successful at first, suffered from both lack of institutional support and financial cutbacks, and were ultimately dropped.

In some delegacias, particularly in the early years, lack of police training was offset by the presence of social workers who were trained to respond in domestic violence cases. However, financial cutbacks and lack of internal support have scaled down the capacity of the delegacias to provide psychological aid as originally intended. Some cities and states, like São Paulo and the small city of Santo Andre outside of São Paulo, continue to retain social workers in the delegacias to assist victims. In the states of Belo

---

[74] U.S. Department of State, *Country Reports on Human Rights Practices for 1994* (Washington, D.C.: Government Printing Office, 1995), p. 337.

[75] Pitanguy, "Violence Against Women, Addressing a Global Problem," p. 6.

[76] Interview, Cida Medrado, April 1991.

[77] Sonia E. Alvarez, *Engendering Democracy in Brazil* (New Jersey: Princeton University Press, 1990), p. 246.

Horizonte and Rio de Janeiro, however, delegacias no longer provide this service. Overall, the counseling services provided at the delegacias is minimal.

These institutional constraints have limited the capacity of the delegacias to move beyond raising the visibility of domestic violence, by receiving and tabulating complaints, to increasing the actual criminalization of such abuse. Attorneys with whom we spoke believe that, in particular, the delegadas' lack of training perpetuates a reluctance by police authorities, regardless of their gender, to see domestic violence as a crime. According to Pitanguy, "Police women still need to perceive certain violent behavior as crimes."[78]   As one attorney who frequently represents domestic violence victims in civil cases noted, "the delegacias normally don't register the crime. . . . There doesn't exist any mentality in the delegacia that a crime has occurred. . . . Even the delegacias don't consider domestic violence a crime. Even registered cases don't go forward; they get shelved. It's a question of mentality. It's family, it's not a crime."[79]

Even when domestic abuse is perceived as a crime, these attitudes carried over into the police's choice of the crime to be charged and resulted in reduced charges in cases of domestic abuse. In the 1987 São Paulo study cited above, for example, researchers noted that in 30 percent of the cases classified as "serious threats" and 36 percent of those classified as "misunderstandings," the police record included complaints of physical abuse which apparently had not been reflected in the crime charged.[80]

These reduced charges are to some extent attributable to lack of training. Detectives, who are often the first to interview the victim, are not always versed in the law pertaining to the classification of domestic abuse offenses. Although police chiefs are required to have legal degrees and should correct improper classifications before they are forwarded for prosecution, this is not always the case.

Available data indicates that reduced charges are also due to the police's reluctance to investigate reports of domestic abuse. Researchers at the University of São Paulo Center for the Study of Violence found that "the women police showed a lot of disrespect for the victims. They were not sympathetic, sort of fed-up. They ended up blaming the victims for their own

---

[78] Interview, Jacqueline Pitanguy, April 1991.
[79] Interview, Cecília Teixeira Soares, Pró-Mulher, April 1991.
[80] *Um Retrato Da Violência Contra A Mulher*, p. 44.

fate."[81] One researcher noted that certain "informal mechanisms" exist to file lesser charges in cases of domestic abuse so that they can be registered as private action crimes which depend on the initiative of the victim, not the state, for prosecution.

This reluctance to investigate is often due to the delegadas' assessment that domestic abuse will not be prosecuted. As one scholar noted, "the delegadas are in a double bind. They want to help the victim but they do not want to mislead her about the likelihood that her assailant will be punished."[82] One victim of domestic violence interviewed by Human Rights Watch had just come from a delegacia where the delegada told her "it would not do any good to register the crime because 70 percent of such cases are dropped."[83]

Brazil's first chief of a women's police station, Rosemary Correa, who later became a deputy in the São Paulo State Legislature, estimates that 40 percent of domestic abuse cases are prosecuted. However, the main delegada in Rio told Human Rights Watch that, of the over 2,000 battery cases she investigated in 1990, none resulted in punishment of the accused. Similarly, the U.S. State Department's human rights report for 1990 noted that in the main delegacia in São Luis, Maranhão, of over 4,000 complaints registered by women from 1988 to 1990, only 300 were forwarded for processing by the court and only two men were convicted and sent to prison.[84] The U.S. State Department's human rights report for 1994 noted that one delegacia in Rio de Janeiro reported that "more women were submitting complaints, which increased from 80 per month in 1993 to 300 per month in 1994, and that 80 percent of the complaints involved spousal abuse."[85]

Women police officers in several cities reported that even when they investigate cases in a timely manner and forward them for prosecution they do not hear from the prosecutor for months, and then he or she is usually seeking

[81] Interview, Nancy Cardia, sociologist, University of São Paulo's Center for the Study of Violence, April 1991.

[82] Interview, Silvia Pimentel, professor, April 1991.

[83] Interview, name withheld by Human Rights Watch, at Pró-Mulher, a legal and social assistance office in Rio de Janeiro, April 1991.

[84] U.S. Department of State, *Country Reports on Human Rights Practices for 1990,* (Washington, D.C.: Government Printing Office, 1991), p. 531.

[85] U.S. Department of State, *Country Report on Human Rights Practices for 1994,* p. 337.

additional information.[86]   One delegada said the prosecutors often sent the files back to the police "due to a back-log in the courts. It's sent back [to the delegacia] to buy time." One police chief admitted that in cases where "it takes a long time, the case can kind of go away."[87]   According to one criminal court judge "someone commits a crime and it takes an eternity for it to get a response. This is a great discredit to judicial power." The day before our visit he was presiding in the trial of a case which occurred seventeen years ago.   While he was quick to point out that this kind of delay "is the exception," he noted that "a lot of these trials go on for years. It's really a structural problem."[88]

The failure to prosecute can also be attributed in part to the nature of domestic violence.   In the first place, both prosecutors and judges have dropped cases when they believe the couple will reconcile. Moreover, in the courts as with the police, there is a persistent failure to see domestic battery as a crime. Judges receive no training on domestic violence. A defense lawyer representing domestic violence victims in Rio de Janeiro stated that the "judiciary takes a benign view towards violence against women."[89] Professor Silvia Pimentel added, "Domestic violence is not sufficiently followed by the state. We are seeking improvements in the law and its implementation, but it requires more than a change in legal framework. It requires a whole change of attitude. A man should not be able to beat and/or kill his wife with impunity."[90]

---

[86] Under the law, police have thirty days to complete an initial investigation when the suspect is not detained, and the prosecution has another thirty days to conduct its own investigation and recommend charges. However, these limits are regularly exceeded, often without the required judicial authorization.

[87] Interview, Detective Inspector Mary May da Silva Porto, April 1991.

[88] Interview, Judge Roberto Ferreira Lins, April 1991.

[89] Interview, Attorney Leila Linhares, April 1991. Linhares is a criminal defense attorney who works for CEPIA, an organization which monitors, among other things, penal and judicial response to crimes of violence against women.

[90] Interview, Professor Silvia Pimentel, April 1991.

VIOLENCE AGAINST WOMEN IN RUSSIA

The law doesn't protect women. If a woman goes to the
police and tells them that she is being beaten by her husband
or partner, the police say, "But he didn't kill you yet."[91]

The Russian government, and particularly its law enforcement
agencies, have denied women's right to equal protection of the law by failing
to investigate and prosecute violence against women, including domestic
violence and sexual assault.[92] According to victims and activists working on
their behalf, local law enforcement officials scoff at reports of violence by
domestic partners and refuse to intervene in what they identify as "family
matters." In some instances, police themselves mistreat and harass women
who report such crimes as a way to intimidate them and stop them from filing
complaints.

In March 1994 the Women's Rights Project of Human Rights Watch
sent a mission to Russia to investigate government participation in illegal
discrimination, including in the administration of criminal justice, against
women.[93] The assumption that the introduction of democratic processes and
a market economy in Russia will improve the protection of human rights
generally in Russia has in some aspects, such as people's ability to exercise
their freedom of association or speech, proven to be true. But women's human
rights, far from being better protected in a rapidly changing Russia, are being
violated and denied.

Women's rights activists, lawyers and even government officials
recognize that violence against women is prevalent in Russia. Spousal abuse,
in particular, is not only widespread but also largely accepted. Official
statistics indicate that every fifth person killed in Russia is killed by a spouse,

---

[91] Interview, Marina Pisklakova, coordinator of Moscow Trust Line for battered
women, Moscow, March 14, 1994.

[92] The following material was adapted from Human Rights Watch Women's Rights
Project, "Neither Jobs Nor Justice: State Discrimination Against Women in Russia," *A
Human Rights Watch Short Report*, vol. 7, no. 5 (March 1995).

[93] We interviewed several women who had tried unsuccessfully to report domestic
or sexual abuse to the police. The counselors of newly established crisis hotlines in
Moscow, St. Petersburg and Yekaterinburg provided us with further documentation on
both the scale of domestic violence and sexual assault and the police's lack of
responsiveness to women's reports of such attacks.

and the majority of those killed by their spouses are women.[94]   Despite recognition of the problem, the state, and particularly its law enforcement agencies, have done little to denounce domestic violence as a crime or to investigate allegations of domestic violence.   Wanda Dabasevich of the recently established St. Petersburg Human Rights Center told Human Rights Watch about a woman who "complained to the police for one year [about her husband's attacks], and they never even talked to her husband."[95]   In March 1994 the Center was pursuing two cases of victims of domestic violence. According to Ms. Dabasevich, "Both women went to the police. The police said they would talk with their husbands, but they didn't. The police never even wrote out a formal complaint."[96]

Domestic violence is not the only form of violence against women that has been overlooked rather than investigated by the Russian criminal justice system. Women who have suffered sexual assault and rape, whether at home, on the job or in the streets, have reported police indifference and even hostility toward their claims.[97]   According to Natalia Gaidarenko,

---

[94] Statistics cited by a representative from the Ministry of Social Welfare, meeting at the Union of Russian Jurists, the Commission on Women's Issues, March 22, 1994.

[95] Interview, St. Petersburg, March 27, 1994.

[96] Ibid.

[97] At least one cause of the failure to respond to reports of rape is the widespread belief among Russian police that women are often to blame for such attacks. Interview, Natasha Khodireva, psychologist and founder of St. Petersburg hotline, St. Petersburg, March 27, 1994. Worse still, a study conducted at the end of the Soviet period offers evidence that members of the judiciary share the tendency to blame the victim in cases of sexual assault, resulting in a criminal justice system biased against rape victims. Valerie Sperling, "Rape and Domestic Violence . . .," pp. 16-22. The founder of Moscow's sexual assault hotline told Human Rights Watch about the case of a woman who called her in December 1993: "She had called a private firm to inquire about a job opening. The director [of the firm] made an appointment with her at the end of the day. When she arrived in his office, he locked the door and tried to force her to perform oral sex. He ripped her clothes and hit her. When she went to the police, they told her it was hopeless to file a complaint because it would be impossible to prove her allegations. Then the police suggested that, if she bribed them, they would conduct an investigation.   She didn't file a complaint with the police." Interview, Natalia Gaidarenko, Moscow, March 22, 1994. In every instance of sexual assault reported to the police that Human Rights Watch gathered from hotlines in Moscow and St. Petersburg, women were similarly taunted or harassed by police.

founder of the independent Moscow Sexual Assault Recovery Center, "One lawyer admitted that the police rarely believe a rape victim."[98]

Russian authorities' failure to investigate and prosecute effectively battery and rape in the home and their biased response to rape victims establish a pattern of discriminatory treatment by the criminal justice system of female victims of domestic violence and sexual assault. Such treatment violates Russia's international obligations to guarantee that its female citizens enjoy equal protection of the law and civil and political rights without discrimination. Article 3 of the International Covenant on Civil and Political Rights provides for "the equal treatment of men and women to the enjoyment of all civil and political rights . . . ." Article 26 further provides that "all persons are equal before the law and are entitled without any discrimination to the equal protection of the law." Furthermore, the Convention on the Elimination of All Forms of Discrimination Against Women (CEDAW) obligates states parties "to pursue a policy of eliminating discrimination . . . to refrain from engaging in any act of discrimination...[and] to ensure that public authorities and institutions shall act in conformity with this obligation."

Such biased treatment of female victims of domestic violence and sexual assault also is prohibited by the terms of the Russia Constitution, which guarantees all Russian citizens equality under the law. The constitution states that, "Men and Women have equal rights and freedoms and equal possibilities for their implementation."[99]

Domestic violence and sexual assault and the state's unresponsiveness to such attacks on women are far from new. During the Soviet era, the problem of spousal abuse was ignored by the press and seldom was raised in public fora. Soviet police reflected societal attitudes by refusing to intervene in cases of domestic violence.[100]

Police refusal to investigate claims of domestic violence persists in today's Russia. As the cases below indicate, police also have failed to investigate claims of sexual assault. As police officials point out, crime in general is on the rise in Russia; police are overwhelmed, and law enforcement in general is lagging. But, women who are turned away by police are not told that investigating their claims may take a long time due to the backlog of

---

[98] Natalia Gaidarenko, "'Moscow Does Not Believe in Tears': Sexual Assault in Russia," *Initiatives in the New Independent States* (newsletter), Spring/Summer 1994.

[99] Russian Constitution, Article 19.

[100] Valerie Sperling, "Rape and Domestic Violence in the USSR," *Response*, Volume 13, Number 3 (1990).

work.   Rather, they are told by police that the attacks against them are not problems for law enforcement officials at all.

Although officials claim and press reports record that violent crime against both women and men is increasing in Russia,[101] the testimonies in this section reveal that the state has refused to protect women from violence because it does not take crimes against them seriously.

Domestic Violence

> In most cases, police say this is a family matter. If a woman
> is beaten and calls the police, they ask who is beating her.
> If she says her husband, the police tell her it's a private
> affair.   Now that crime is increasing, police say they don't
> have time for family matters.[102]

Despite official acknowledgment that domestic violence affects the lives of thousands of women in Russia, the official and societal response to women's reports of spousal abuse indicates that such assault is considered a "family affair" rather than a problem for law enforcement.   Reports gathered by Human Rights Watch indicate that individual police share the widely-held view that spousal abuse is a private matter in which the police should not or need not intervene.   As a consequence, police often fail to respond to reports of domestic violence, or, if they do respond, take no action against the abuser.   A founder of a St. Petersburg hotline for women told us:

> It's traumatizing for women to go to the police. We've been
> studying the police and their responses to violence against
> women.   They have very sexist attitudes.   They think of

[101] Steven Erlanger, "Russia's New Dictatorship of Crime," *New York Times*, May 15, 1994; Aleksandr Golov, "Crime and Safety in the Public Consciousness," *Izvestia* (Moscow), July 23, 1993, p. 4.

[102] Interview, Natalia Rimashevskaya, director of the Institute for Socioeconomic Population Studies at the Russian Academy of Sciences, Moscow, March 14, 1994. The institute houses the Moscow Gender Studies Center and Moscow's first hotline for victims of domestic violence.

domestic violence as the problem of women, that women provoke violence with their behavior.[103]

The generally dismissive attitude of the police toward reports of domestic abuse permits men to beat their wives or domestic partners with impunity. In an interview with Human Rights Watch, Yevgenii Riabtsev, the head of the ministry of the interior's public relations section, admitted that domestic violence is a serious problem in Russia and that the police have not treated the problem as one for law enforcement. Rather than accept police responsibility for the failure to investigate such violence, Riabtsev suggested that police are thwarted in their efforts by women's failure to report assault. He thus suggested that women victims of domestic violence, and not the police who disregard and mistreat them, are the main obstacle to police investigations of such assault. Riabtsev also shifted the blame for the violence itself to its victims, stating, "After marriage, many women don't look after themselves. They let themselves go physically, and their husbands lose interest."[104] Similarly, Acting Minister of Social Security Ludmila Bezlepkina, who is responsible for preparing Russia's report to CEDAW, stated, "Problems of family violence are very urgent for us now." She asserted, however, that abusive family members should not be punished:

> I don't agree that police should be used in situations of domestic violence. This is not productive and just makes people more cruel. It depends on the tradition of the country. We should be able to choose how we deal with this problem. Restricting measures involving the police should be the last resort.[105]

---

[103] Interview, Natalia Khodireva, psychologist and founder of the St. Petersburg hotline for victims of domestic and sexual violence, St. Petersburg, March 27, 1994. The hotline has ten psychologists trained to offer counseling and hopes to link with other health care providers in order to offer a full range of services to survivors of violence.

[104] Interview, Yevgenii Mikhailovich Riabtsev, chief of section, Ministry of Internal Affairs, Center for Public Relations, Moscow, March 25, 1994.

[105] Interview, Ludmila Bezlepkina, acting minister, Ministry of Social Security (also called the Ministry of Social Protection of the Population), Moscow, March 25, 1994.

Domestic violence is a seriously underreported crime in Russia.[106] Experts in Russia, as in other countries, attribute women's reluctance to report such attacks to women's awareness that police will not respond to their complaints,[107] and also to societal pressures that encourage women to hide family violence from everyone, even neighbors.[108] In addition, women fear that reporting domestic abuse will provoke their attackers without actually securing protection from the authorities. A counselor for victims of domestic violence in Moscow told us:

> Women don't call the police because they are afraid it will make the situation worse for them and their children. Also, everyone thinks it is shameful to discuss family problems with the police. Some women don't call because they think it's no use. In some cases, they have friends who have contacted the police to no avail.[109]

A psychologist who works with victims of domestic and sexual violence further stated:

> Domestic violence is a huge problem. But no one will talk about it. I have a friend whose husband rapes her, and she can't even cry because her children sleep in the same room. She has never gone to the police.[110]

The government contributes to the lack of information about rates of domestic violence by not keeping statistics about those individuals who do

---

[106] Sperling, "Rape and Domestic Violence...," pp. 17, 21.

[107] Russian law does not require mandatory arrest for batterers and "police tend not to take domestic violence complaints seriously." Ibid, p. 21.

[108] See, for example, Americas Watch and Women's Rights Project, *Criminal Injustice*, pp. 50-52.

[109] Interview, Marina Pisklakova, Moscow Trust Line, Moscow, March 14, 1994. Pisklakova is the sole full-time staff member of the Moscow Trust Line, a hotline for victims of domestic violence. Pisklakova attempts to provide counseling and services to victims of domestic violence and maintains records of the phone calls and personal visits she receives. The hotline provided Human Rights Watch with its records on numerous cases for the four months preceding our March 1994 visit.

[110] Interview, Natalia Khodireva, St. Petersburg, March 27, 1994.

report their assaults to the authorities. The Ministry of the Interior keeps no data about domestic violence separate from general records of hooliganism (disturbing the peace) and physical assault.[111] The lack of relevant data about violence against women by family members has the effect, whether intended or not, of concealing such abuse. Official recognition of the scale of domestic violence in Russia would be a particularly important step toward eliminating the barriers that keep women from reporting such assault.

Currently, the data on violence against women is collected only by the private sexual assault and domestic violence hotlines that have opened in several Russian cities. They keep records of how many women contact them, the reasons for the call or visit, and the details of women's individual problems. Increasingly, they also ask women whether they have sought help or reported attacks against them to the police. The hotline staffs in Moscow, St. Petersburg and Yekaterinburg report a steady volume of calls and visits from women abused by spouses and partners.[112] The testimonies that follow are drawn from reports collected by these hotlines as well as Human Rights Watch interviews.

Svetlana is in her early thirties and lives with her infant son in the Moscow apartment she shared with her former husband. Svetlana divorced her husband in early 1994 after he abused her and threatened to kill her. Svetlana recalled that the first eight months of her marriage were "pretty good," but then he started to threaten her:

> He said that he would break my legs or my teeth so that no one else would want me, so that he could take care of me and I would understand that he really loved me. I was really

---

[111] Russia has no criminal statute that specifically prohibits domestic violence, but such crimes can readily be prosecuted under statutes prohibiting hooliganism (defined as a disruption of public order) and light or grave bodily injury. Valerie Sperling, "Rape and Domestic Violence in the USSR," *Response*, Volume 13, Number 3 (1990), p. 19.

[112] The hotline in Yekaterinburg receives between five and fifteen calls per week during "quiet periods" and over twenty calls per week after they advertise their service. About two-thirds of the callers are reporting domestic violence and sexual assault. Telephone interview, Olga Zayarnaya, director of the Yekaterinburg hotline, St. Petersburg, March 28, 1994.

> scared. Once someone threatens to hurt you, one day he will
> do it.[113]

Soon after the threats started, Svetlana discovered that she was pregnant. Her pregnancy was complicated, and she was bedridden, during which time her husband taunted her with the fact that she was under his power and refused to feed her unless she begged. In August 1993, several months after the birth of their son, Svetlana's husband resumed a steady stream of verbal abuse. On one occasion, she told us, he grabbed her by the arm, threw her to the floor and threatened her: "'If you say something bad to me again, I'll kill you. You must submit to me completely. You have nothing, no money.'" Svetlana fled the apartment with her baby, but he followed them, threatening to kill her if she sought a divorce. Svetlana returned to the apartment out of concern for her child's health. Later that night:

> I was in the bathroom. He started banging on the door,
> screaming that he would beat me and kill me. He broke the
> handle on the door. I waited about forty minutes before
> coming out. He was in a terrible state. He said, "I'm going
> to kill you and no one will do anything to me for it." I was
> so scared.

After more beatings and death threats, Svetlana called the police. A policeman promised that he would speak with her husband, and he did. But the police took no action against her husband, and Svetlana believes that the police simply told her husband that he had a right to live in the apartment even if she did not want him there. When she returned to the police station, Svetlana said a policeman told her, "As long as you are not divorced, there's nothing for the police to do. That's between a man and wife, it's a family matter."

---

[113] Interview, all names withheld by Human Rights Watch unless otherwise indicated, Moscow, March 20, 1994.

After their divorce, her husband continued to come to the apartment against Svetlana's wishes and to threaten her.[114] She again sought help from the police:

> I went to the police and one said, "What do you want from me?" I asked him to talk to my ex-husband and stop the threats. The policeman said he would talk to him. But later I learned that he never did. Soon after that, my ex-husband and his brother came to the house and moved my things out of my rooms. I went with my baby to the police. Three policemen came to the apartment after one hour, but the men had left. The police shrugged and said, "What you're telling us is just talk. You have no witnesses. Nobody saw what happened; nobody heard anything. You have no proof of what you say. I have talked with your husband, and he is a calm, nice man. He has a right to live here."
>
> I gave him the name and number of my friend who had overheard the threats, but she told me the police never called. I felt defeated. I couldn't expect any help from the police. I am a hostage in my own apartment. I'm afraid to go to the police now. They didn't help me before, and I don't want to provoke my husband's family.[115]

The full-time counselor on the Moscow Trust Line emphasized the lack of recourse for female victims of domestic violence with another recently recorded case:

> I got a call from a woman who told me that her husband is a policeman and that he beats her all the time. She says he

---

[114] Even though Svetlana divorced her husband in February 1994, by law he still has the right to live in the apartment they shared during their marriage. As a consequence, she cannot deny him access to the apartment and lives in fear that he may return and continue his physical attacks and death threats. Russia's chronic housing shortage, inherited from the Soviet era, forces many couples to continue to live together even after being divorced.

[115] Svetlana reported her husband's attacks to the Aporni Punkt police station in the Perovski district of Moscow, the 102nd precinct.

beats her "like a professional." He knows how to do it so
that the bruises don't show. She told me that he calls his
friends at the police station before he beats her and tells them
that she is provoking him with her behavior. He says, "So
if something happens to her, you know that she is provoking
me with her behavior."

I asked her if she could call another police station. She said
that she can't because they refer the case to the local station,
and her husband works there, and all of the police there are
his friends. She's still with her husband. We have no way
to protect her.[116]

In another case reported to the Moscow Trust Line in February 1994,
fifty-four-year-old Ludmila called after her husband beat her badly. The
hotline counselor told Human Rights Watch:

After he beat her, she left the house and called the police
from the street. She met a policeman near her house and
told him about the violence. She told me that the policeman
responded, "But he didn't kill you yet. You should go home.
He's your husband."[117]

When police do respond to a report of a domestic dispute, they seldom
arrest the man responsible for spousal assault.   One woman who called the
Moscow Trust Line for victims of domestic violence said that her neighbors
called the police because her husband beat her. On one occasion, the police
came to the apartment, but they did not arrest her husband. The fact that law
enforcement seldom acts against the aggressor in a domestic dispute
discourages victims from calling them at all. Domestic violence victims thus
are caught in a vicious cycle. Authorities' failure to respond to allegations of
abuse deters women from registering complaints, and their silence is used by
the police to excuse official inaction.
    As Russia undergoes major social, economic and political upheaval,
Russian women are fighting to achieve greater respect for their rights and, in
particular, protection from violence in the family and in the street. In doing

---

[116] Interview, Marina Pisklakova, March 16, 1994.
[117] Ibid.

so, they confront deeply-entrenched attitudes about women's status in society, such as those that accept violence against women in the home and even blame the victim for her husband's attacks, and the widespread rejection of women's equality as a legacy of the Soviet era. To prevent such attitudes from translating into a denial of women's rights, the Russian government must publicly condemn crimes of violence against women, in particular domestic violence, and increase the vigor and effectiveness of its response to violence against women.

VIOLENCE AGAINST WOMEN IN SOUTH AFRICA

My husband has always abused me. He has a drug and alcohol problem. I stayed because I am Catholic and because we have six children, until he kicked me out. He used to tie me to the bed so I couldn't go out. I wasn't allowed to answer the phone. One time, he beat me so bad, he cracked my head and broke one of my fingers. Another time, he burned me with boiling water. Once he put an electric shock through my fingers. I got a peace order [restraining order] against my husband while I was married, but when they came to the house, the police said all they could do was warn my husband. Since my divorce four years ago, my husband harasses me all the time. He follows me. He steals my and my children's clothes from the line. He comes around the house in the middle of the night. The police arrested him for trespassing three times, but he was immediately released. The police told me that they could not do anything more since we were divorced. In January 1995, I went to get an interdict and the court clerk told me that they couldn't give me one because "everybody's free to walk the streets and live their lives." Soon after, he threw a burning towel through the window of the house which burnt the curtains and started a fire. Now he is in prison for two months for damaging property.[118]

---

[118] Interview, all names withheld by Human Rights Watch unless otherwise indicated, Durban, February 3, 1995.

In April 1994 sweeping political changes following the first multiracial general election held in South Africa brought an end to the repressive apartheid policies of the past and ushered in a new government that has pledged to respect human rights and uphold the rule of law.[119]   This recently elected government of national unity, led by the African National Congress (ANC), is legally committed, under the interim constitution brought into effect on the first day of the elections, to the achievement of full equality for women.   At the highest policy-making levels the government   has specifically expressed a commitment to addressing the problem of violence against women.   The Reconstruction and Development Programme (RDP), which sets out government priorities, states that the RDP must focus on "the reconstruction of family and community life by prioritizing and responding to the needs of. . .women and children who have been victims of domestic and other forms of violence."[120]

Despite these pledges, as the above testimony illustrates, the South African judicial and law enforcement system often responds more promptly to property damage than to women at risk from their violent partners.   While women's organizations note that, compared to a decade ago, the response of police and judicial authorities to violence against women has improved to a certain extent, they stress that situations similar to the one cited above are not uncommon.

In January 1995 the Women's Rights and Africa divisions of Human Rights Watch sent a mission to South Africa to investigate the problem of domestic violence and evaluate the state's efforts to stem such abuse.   In addition to interviewing women survivors of domestic violence in Johannesburg, Durban and Cape Town, Human Rights Watch met with police officials, magistrates, prosecutors, district surgeons, government social workers, nongovernmental advocates for women's rights, and staff of privately operated shelters for battered women.

Despite the new government's pledge to prioritize the problem of violence against women, Human Rights Watch found that an enormous gap exists between policy and practice.   The legacy of the state violence that

---

[119] The following material is part of an upcoming report from Human Rights Watch on violence against women in South Africa.

[120] The Reconstruction and Development Programme of the Government of National Unity sets out the policy goals and strategies of the new government. Government of National Unity, *The Reconstruction and Development Programme*, (African National Congress: 1994), Section 2.13.15.

underpinned the apartheid state has resulted in extremely high levels of violence throughout society, including in the home. Staggering numbers of South African women of all races and income levels face violence as a daily reality, often at the hands of men they know and on whom they rely. South African women's organizations estimate that perhaps as many as one in six South African women is being abused by her partner.[121]

In 1993 new legislation, the Prevention of Family Violence Act, improved women's access to protection from domestic violence by simplifying and expediting the procedure for obtaining interdicts (restraining orders) against abusive partners. Women's organizations report that magistrates' courts in many areas have used the act effectively. However, the law is still limited in several important regards. In particular, it does not apply to certain types of intimate relationships, lacks specificity on the types of abuse that may result in the grant of an interdict, and has limited jurisdiction. Besides these shortcomings in the law itself, indigent women often experience delays in obtaining interdicts as a result of delays by the Justice Department in the payment of their court fees.

Moreover, women survivors of domestic violence, regardless of race, still face a police and judicial system that is unsympathetic, and sometimes even hostile, to women who seek redress. Frequently, police officers and court clerks are unaware of the law and consequently misinform or turn away women complainants. In other cases, the police are well-aware of the law, but choose not to respond promptly and decisively. Police officers commonly either fail to respond to calls for help or merely warn abusers. Prosecutors frequently discourage women from bringing charges; and many court clerks are ignorant of the laws that protect women. Such mistreatment appears in large part to be due to entrenched attitudes among police and court officials who view domestic violence directed against women as a "private" matter which need not be taken seriously by the state.

Human Rights Watch recognizes that the new South African government is confronted with numerous political, social and economic problems caused by the legacy of apartheid. However, lasting political and social transformation towards a democratic South Africa can be genuinely achieved only if the ANC-led government shows the same commitment toward eradicating gender-based violence as it does toward racial oppression.

---

[121] For a more detailed discussion of the statistics on domestic violence, see the following section.

The Magnitude of the Problem

While South African women's organizations acknowledge the difficulty of collecting accurate data on domestic violence, all agree that the levels of domestic violence are staggering. These nongovernmental organizations (NGOs) working with battered women explain that the figures they use are estimates extrapolated from their caseload and surveys. No systematic government studies have been carried out with the aim of establishing the extent of the problem nationally.

The Cape Town-based NGO Rape Crisis estimated in 1992 that one in every three women is assaulted by her male partner.[122] The Women's Bureau estimates that approximately one in four women is abused by her partner.[123] The Advice Desk on Abused Women, located in Durban, estimates that one in every six women is regularly assaulted by her partner, and that one in four women is at some time forced to flee because of life threatening situations in their home.[124] In Johannesburg, People Opposing Women Abuse and Co-ordinated Action for Battered Women also estimate that one in six women is being abused by their partner.[125]

The types of abuse that South African women face in the home include physical abuse such as hitting, choking, burning, stabbing, the use of electric shocks, and confinement; verbal humiliation and degradation by their partners; and emotional abuse through threats of violence, economic deprivation or restricted access to their children.[126] A 1993 study of 398

---

[122] Rape Crisis (1992), as quoted in Desiree Hansson and Beatie Hofmeyr, *Women's Rights: Towards a Non-Sexist South Africa*, Number 7, Developing Justice Series, Documentation Center, Center for Applied Legal Studies, University of Witwatersrand (undated), p. 20.

[123] "One in Four Women is Abused," *Citizen* (South Africa), June 21, 1994.

[124] Advice Desk for Abused Women mission statement (undated), p. 4.

[125] "Women Fight for Rights," *Northeast Tribune* (South Africa), July 13, 1993.

[126] In South Africa, domestic violence is often fatal. Between 1986 and 1988, 223 family murders were reported, during which time there was approximately one incident per month in which a family member (usually the husband) would kill his wife and/or children, often before committing suicide. Approximately 90 percent of these types of family killings involved Afrikaans-speaking families. These statistics do not distinguish between the murder of a spouse or child and the killing of the whole family. See V. Vall, "Family Murders in South Africa," Psychology Honors paper, University of Witwatersrand, unpublished (1988); *The Star*, November 18 and November 22, 1988, as quoted in Graeme Simpson, "Jack-Asses and Jackrollers: Rediscovering Gender in
(continued...)

battered women in Alexandra township near Johannesburg, found that intimate partners inflicted physical injuries with fists, knives, bricks, the traditional knobkerrie [club-ended stick], bottles, hammers, axes and screwdrivers. [127] The most common injuries requiring hospitalization were fractures of the head, limbs, sternum and ribs, followed by scalp and facial lacerations as well as penetrating chest wounds involving the lungs. In addition to the physical injuries sustained from such abuse, battered women often develop somatic symptoms such as headaches, backaches, fatigue, abdominal and pelvic pain, recurrent vaginal infections, sleep and eating disorders, sexual dysfunctions, and other signs of moderate or severe depression. [128]

The difficulty in determining the exact extent of the problem stems from the fact that the majority of domestic violence survivors do not seek official help, but rather rely on an informal network of family and friends. A 1993 survey of 111 women conducted by a well-established women's organization found that 50 percent sought assistance from their extended family; 22 percent went to friends or neighbors; 12 percent went to the church; 8 percent went to street committees or councils; and 2 percent went to social workers. Only 6 percent went to the police. [129]

Indifference and hostility toward domestic violence on the part of police and judicial authorities, combined with the distrust of the police carried over from the apartheid era, have made women victims of violence, particularly black women, [130] reluctant to seek redress. Although the new national police commissioner has pledged to transform the police force into a

---

[126](...continued)
Understanding Violence," Center for the Study of Violence and Reconciliation (1992), p. 7.

[127] Mmatshilo Motsei, *Detection of Woman Battering in Health Care Settings: The Case of Alexandra Health Clinic*, Women's Health Project, Paper Number 30, January 1993, p. 14.

[128] Ibid., p. 2.

[129] Daniel Nina and Stavros Stavrou, "Violence in the Home," *Sash*, January 1994, p. 27. Black Sash is a well-established South African women's organization with networks of advice offices. *Sash* is their publication.

[130] In this report, "black" will be used to refer to all South Africans previously classified as "African" or "Black" (of purely African ancestry), "Indian" (mostly the descendants of indentured servants brought to South Africa by the British to work in the sugar plantations), or "coloured" (of mixed race). "White" will refer to South Africans of European ancestry. The subcategories will also be used, since their previous classification continues to affect the living circumstances of South African .

government body that will service the needs of the whole community, regardless of race or gender, there has been only negligible change in the manner in which women who report domestic violence are treated by many police officers.

Fear of social stigma and reprisal from their abusive partners further compounds women's reluctance to report abuse. Often, battered women's own relatives discourage them from reporting assault because of the shame that disclosure may bring to the entire family. Absent faith that the justice system will handle their claims in an impartial, nondiscriminatory manner, many women do not believe that reporting their cases is worth the humiliation they will face within their community. A survey of 10,697 women (with a mean of 8.2 years of abuse), conducted by the Advice Desk for Abused Women and the National Women's Coalition, found that women's reluctance to report abuse to the police and government legal and social services stemmed directly from their negative experiences with police; the inadequacy of the legal system in dealing with domestic violence; and the fragmentation of social services.[131]

Limitations of the Law and A Lack of Implementation

International human rights and South African law prohibits discrimination on the basis of sex and guarantees equal protection of the law for all citizens. Accordingly, police and judicial officers are bound under international law to act decisively to prevent, investigate and punish domestic abuse. Domestic violence survivors, like other assault victims, are entitled to immediate and effective police protection and judicial relief through equal enforcement of the laws. The government is obligated to coordinate among the police forces, judicial system and social services agencies to ensure effective enforcement of the law.

Under South African law since 1994, all persons are equal before the law. Although there is no specific crime of wife or partner beating, battered women can seek legal redress for domestic abuse by laying assault charges for injuries suffered at the hands of their lovers, boyfriends or husbands.[132]

---

[131] Anshu Padayachee, "The Prevention and Treatment of Abused Women in South Africa: A Game of Trivial Pursuit," Advice Desk for Abused Women (undated), Durban, p. 2.

[132] There is no specific crime of wife or partner beating. Intrafamily offenses can include arson, assault, assault with intent to do grievous bodily harm, threats to do

(continued...)

Women seeking to prevent future violence can also seek an interdict (restraining order), pursuant to the 1993 Prevention of Family Violence Act, which allows women to obtain an interdict to permit the police immediately to arrest an abusive partner who violates the order. In both cases, the police investigate and decide whether to arrest or not. Similarly, the decision to prosecute is within the court's discretion.

The law protecting women from domestic abuse, while greatly improved with the passage of the 1993 Prevention of Family Violence Act, is still not as comprehensive as it could be. However, the major impediment is not the law itself,· but the implementation of the law by the police and judiciary. South African judicial and police authorities often fail to uphold women's rights because of their reluctance to intervene in domestic abuse cases. In large part, this inaction is due to entrenched attitudes within the law enforcement and judicial systems which perpetuate the myth that violence in the home is a private affair.

These attitudes within the government institutions that are responsible for preventing and punishing domestic abuse are due to a number of factors. The apartheid policies of the previous government in South Africa involved extreme levels of interference in private life, including a prohibition on interracial marriage or sex and onerous restrictions on freedom of movement that often prevented families from living together. Such interference, however, related only to the enforcement of the policies of apartheid. As in many other countries, the family was viewed as a private entity when it came to preventing abuse between partners. The government considered the protection of a woman suffering family violence by arresting her partner or ordering him not to contact her to constitute extreme state interference in a private relationship; this view continues to shape official responses to violence against women today.

In other cases, police and judicial officers do not understand the complexity of domestic abuse and may refuse to offer protection to a battered

---

[132](...continued)
bodily harm, obstructing justice, cruelty to children, incest, kidnapping, murder, culpable homicide, rape, forced prostitution, unlawful entry on to property, malicious damage to property, theft, robbery, unlawful possession of a firearm, sodomy, extortion, blackmail and sexual assault. Joanne Fedler, *"I've got a problem with my husband .": Lawyering Domestic Violence Through the Prevention of Family Violence Act 1993—An Evaluation After a Year in Operation* (South Africa: forthcoming publication, 1995), p. 2.

woman who repeatedly returns to an abusive spouse. Battered women often seek reconciliation with their abusive partners for various reasons, including distrust of the ability of the legal and law enforcement system to offer effective protection, economic dependence on their spouse[133], fear of retaliation, sense of shame and self-blame, children, or even love. They often want only the abuse to end, not the relationship.[134] South African police and judicial officers receive virtually no training to enable them to understand the dynamics of family violence and to ensure that they know that they are required to enforce the law regardless of the number of times a woman chooses to return to an abusive relationship.

However, by not acting decisively to prevent, investigate and punish domestic abuse, South African police and judicial officers are failing to enforce the law equitably across gender lines in violation of international human rights law which prevents discriminatory application of the law on the basis of gender.

The Prevention of Family Violence Act

In October 1993 the former National Party government passed the Prevention of Family Violence Act.[135] The act introduced an improved, expedited procedure that makes it easier and cheaper for a woman to seek an interdict against an abusive partner.[136] An abused woman can file for an interdict at the nearest magistrates' court. If the magistrate believes that the woman is in danger of abuse, he or she may grant an interdict, accompanied by a suspended warrant of arrest, in order to prevent the abuser from further assaulting or threatening the woman. Once the abuser is served notice by the

---

[133] For example, in all of the cases that Human Rights Watch came across, the abused wife or girlfriend, rather than her abusive partner, had to move out of their joint residence in order to escape from family violence.

[134] See Joanne Fedler, *"I've got a problem with my husband ..."*

[135] Prevention of Family Violence Act, No. 133 of 1993, *Government Gazette,* October 6, 1993.

[136] The Prevention of Family Violence Act was promulgated at a time when it was politically expedient for the National Party government to be seen to be doing something for women in order to attract the female vote in the April 1994 election. Its enactment was not accompanied by government funding for support structures nor by programs to address gender bias in the police and court system. Joanne Fedler, *"I've got a problem with my husband ...",* p. 7.

sheriff's office, a governmental agency separate from the Department of Justice and the Police Services, the interdict comes into effect.

In the event that the woman possessing an interdict is threatened with abuse, she can call the police, who should immediately arrest the abuser using the suspended warrant of arrest. The apprehended partner should be brought before a magistrate within twenty-four hours and charged with violating the interdict. The penalty is a fine or imprisonment not exceeding twelve months, or both.

Women's rights activists told Human Rights Watch that the cheaper, simplified application procedure and the immediate arrest provisions are significant improvements from the past.[137] Until 1993 abused women could only seek to stop abuse through a "peace order," which merely constituted a warning, and had no provision for automatic arrest or prosecution if breached.[138] If a woman complained of abuse, the court would have to hold an enquiry to determine whether the order had been contravened. Only then could the abuser be prosecuted for contempt of court and fined.[139] A survey conducted by the Advice Desk for Abused Women found that the old procedure was ineffective as a remedy for battered women.[140] Battered women could also apply to the Supreme Court (the next court up from magistrates' courts in the South African judicial hierarchy) for an interdict, but this was an expensive prospect, requiring the retention of an attorney and an advocate and high legal fees.

---

[137] Other legal remedies which women can seek include divorce, a claim for money damages, an order to commit the abuser to a mental institution and an order for compulsory substance abuse treatment. Apart from divorce, the other remedies are almost impossible to obtain and rarely used by abused women. Anshu Padayachee, "The Prevention and Treatment of Abused Women in South Africa: A Game of Trivial Pursuit," The Advice Desk for Abused Women (undated), pp. 12-13.

[138] Section 344(1) of the Criminal Procedure Act 51 of 1977.

[139] Section 384, Criminal Procedure Act 56 of 1955.

[140] The Advice Desk for Abused Women found that of ninety-three peace orders obtained between January to June 1993, less than one quarter of the women found it acted as a deterrent to further abuse. Seventy-one women reported that the violence increased after they obtained the order and threats of divorce and deprivation of financial support were made to them. These threats, they claimed, prevented them from making reports to the police regarding breaches of the peace order. They were further deterred because the courts could not provide them with any protection other than a warning to the abuser. Padayachee, "The Prevention and Treatment of Abused Women...", p. 11.

Over a year and a half after its promulgation, the 1993 Prevention of Family Violence Act appears to have had mixed results. While interdicts are still granted only at the magistrates' discretion, they are now cheaper, quicker and simpler to obtain. The form can be filed without the assistance of a lawyer. Most South African women's groups that we interviewed agree that magistrates have generally been responsive to women's applications for interdicts. For example, in one year and two months, the seven magistrates courts designated to deal with interdicts in the Cape Town area granted 90 percent of the applications before them.[141] In a four-month period between April and July 1994, the total number of interdicts granted for the whole of South Africa was 2,118 while 169 applications were denied.[142]

While the interdict cannot provide complete protection to a victim from a spouse intent on battering, the order does set limits that are immediately enforceable. For some battered women, this new law has made a positive difference in ending domestic abuse. One woman told Human Rights Watch, "Since I got the interdict the fighting and screaming have stopped because my husband is afraid of going to jail."[143] Another woman said that the interdict had made "quite a difference. After fifteen years of abuse it stopped. He now knows that I can go to the police."[144] In one case, the interdict forms alone had been sufficient to cause a violent husband to stop his abusive behavior.[145] A number of battered women surveyed by the NGO the National Institute for Crime Prevention and Rehabilitation of Offenders (NICRO), noted similar experiences and stated in telephone interviews that the interdict had changed their lives for the better.[146]

---

[141] The breakdown for 4,869 interdict applications, between December 1, 1993 and January 1995, is as follows: (1) Bellville: 699 granted, fifteen denied; (2) Cape Town: 452 granted, twenty denied; (3) Goodwood: 630 granted, eight denied; (4) Kuilsriver: 322 granted, two denied; (5) Mitchell's Plain: 1,568 granted, thirty denied; (6) Simonstown: eighty-seven granted, none denied (only until July 1994); (7) Wynberg: 1,035 granted, one denied (only until mid-December 1994). *Magistrate's Liaison Report on the Implementation of the Prevention of Family Violence Act*, unpublished report, June 1994 (for figures between December 1, 1993 to July 1994), and interview with paralegal, National Institute for Crime and Rehabilitation of Offenders (NICRO), Cape Town, February 8, 1995 for figures between August 1, 1994 to January 15, 1995.

[142] "Statistics on Family Violence," Law, Race and Gender Project, CIV-1.

[143] Interview, Johannesburg, February 17, 1995.

[144] Interview, Cape Town, February 8, 1995.

[145] Interview, Johannesburg, February 15, 1995.

[146] Telephone survey forms of clients, NICRO, Cape Town, February 8, 1995.

Despite improvements, the Prevention of Family Violence Act has far from eliminated domestic violence.   First, it applies to only certain relationships: married women (by civil or customary law); women living with an abusive boyfriend; and women who at one time lived with their abusive husband or boyfriend. The law excludes women harmed in other relationships. Women being abused by a male relation other than a husband or boyfriend, or by a non-live-in sexual partner, must still resort to the more expensive and complicated interdict procedure applicable in the Supreme Court.   Other excluded relationships in which women's safety may be at risk include partners in a lesbian relationship and teen-age girls living with their parents.[147]

In the South African context, the exclusion of women who have never lived with their abusers in a "marital" relationship is particularly problematic. Due to former apartheid policies, numerous black families have been forced to live apart. Many black men who work as migrant laborers reside in all-male hostels in the urban areas, and may maintain a lover in the township while their "official" families remain in the rural areas. Meanwhile, black women who work as domestic servants also often live away from their families on their employer's premises. There are approximately one million domestic servants in South Africa, or approximately one in every five black adults in the labor market.[148] Women workers in these situations may be involved in abusive relationships; but because they have not lived with their spouses, cannot apply for an interdict.

Second, the act does not specify the range of abuses for which a woman may be granted an interdict. Rather, individual magistrates have wide discretion to determine whether a particular abuse qualifies under the act's broadly worded terms, including "assault or threaten" as well as "any other act."[149] As a result, there is no consistency as to what actions would merit an interdict. For example, it is unclear whether most magistrates would view severe emotional harassment not coupled with physical violence or threats of violence as abuse. The act's silence in this regard leaves open the possibility that women who are abused emotionally, but not physically, would not qualify for protection.

Third, the act only provides protection to women in expressly stated areas. If a woman is physically distant from the man who is abusing her, the

---

[147] Joanne Fedler, *"I've got a problem with my husband ..."*, p. 14.
[148] "Hard Life is Getting Harder for South Africa's Domestics," *New York Times*, October 17, 1994.
[149] Prevention of Family Violence Act 1993, Section 2(1).

interdict does not authorize the police to arrest and charge the abuser immediately. Even service of interdicts by the sheriff's office is restricted to certain areas. One woman told Human Rights Watch, "I specifically asked the sheriff's office to serve the interdict on my husband at work, because I knew if he received it while I was around at home, he would give me a thorough beating. But they told me it was out of their jurisdiction."[150]

Fourth, although the courts can and do waive the fee for the interdict to be served on the abuser, impoverished women report long delays in the serving of the interdict. It appears that the sheriff's office, which is responsible for serving the abusive partner, does not act until it receives the fee from the Department of Justice.[151] Human Rights Watch heard of cases where women who had been granted an interdict by a magistrate had waited up to six weeks for the sheriff to act on the order, instead of the usual one to two days. Yasmeen, of Indian origin, who has been assaulted regularly since her marriage nine years ago, applied for an interdict on January 4, 1995. However, the sheriff's office did not serve the interdict for two weeks while awaiting payment from the state.[152]

Fifth, the act does not extend protection through the interdict to advocates who assist abused women. Men have been known to threaten or stalk counselors in order to intimidate them and, through them, the partner they are abusing. In these cases, no expedited protection order exists for counselors to protect themselves from the aggression that violent husbands deflect to them. In July and August 1994, counselors at the NISAA Institute for Women's Development who were stalked by client's husband reported that initially the police denied them assistance.[153] In Johannesburg, a lawyer with People Opposing Women Abuse was stalked for two days in 1994 by one client's husband and threatened by another woman's spouse for "destroying his marriage."[154]

In addition, some South African lawyers have pointed out that the act is also problematic from the perspective of the abusive husband or partner.

---

[150] Interview, Johannesburg, February 15, 1995.

[151] The cost is the distance from the court to the house. The sheriff's office charges by the kilometer. Costs can be up to 100 Rand [U.S.$35.00].

[152] Interview, Durban, January 31, 1995.

[153] Interview, Jubi Dangor, NISAA Institute for Women's Development, Johannesburg, February 15, 1995.

[154] Interview, Joanne Fedler, attorney, People Opposing Women Abuse, Johannesburg, February 14, 1995.

They argue that since the interdict can be granted in the absence of the accused, the act is unconstitutional because it denies the accused abuser the opportunity to oppose the application, thus violating their rights to due process and the South African *audi alteram partem* legal principle, requiring a court or other adjudicator to hear both sides of any case before giving a judgment. However, Human Rights Watch believes that the act does provide due process protections because an aggrieved husband can, under the act, immediately petition the court to amend or set aside the interdict before he is subjected to any restrictions to his liberty. Concerns about the unspecified duration of the interdict can be similarly addressed by seeking a court amendment.[155]

Police Ignorance of the Law

In practice, the greatest obstacle to the effective implementation of the Prevention of Family Violence Act appears to lie with the police, many of whom are ignorant about the law, despite a memorandum issued by the Department of Justice to the police and courts in 1993. Consequently, a woman possessing a valid interdict may nonetheless receive little protection from law enforcement agents. One counselor told Human Rights Watch of a case in Soweto in which an abusive husband locked his wife in the house, intending to set it on fire. Her screams alerted the attention of the neighbors and eventually the police arrived. Although she possessed an interdict, the police did not know what it was and were unwilling to help. When the organization People Opposing Women Abuse complained to the station commander, he reportedly said, "Of course they [the police officers sent to the scene] don't know about interdicts, next time send her directly to me."[156]

---

[155] Critics have also noted that the interdict may allow the court to exclude an abusive husband from access to his house, thus depriving him access to his own property. See "The Prevention of Family Violence Act: Innovation or Violation?" *De Rebus*, March 1994, p.212 and "Family Violence Act causes 'Nightmarish' Problems," Fiona Stewart, Letter to the Editor, *De Rebus*, October 1994, p. 721. As far as Human Rights Watch was able to determine, this fear appears to be unfounded because most magistrates appear not to grant applications that ask for men to be prohibited from entering the marital home. The National Institute for Crime and Rehabilitation of Offenders has found that only 2 percent of interdict applications seeking this remedy were granted. Interview, Jane Keen, National Institute for Crime and Rehabilitation of Offenders (NICRO), Cape Town, February 8, 1995.

[156] Interview, Debbie Brent, shelter administrator, People Opposed to Woman Abuse (POWA), February 17, 1995.

One station commander who was personally knowledgeable about the Prevention of Family Violence Act told Human Rights Watch that, "Frankly, the way in which this Act was publicized through the [police] stations was poor."[157] Another police officer interviewed by Human Rights Watch, while also aware of the act, was completely ignorant of the police role. He mistakenly described the interdict procedure as follows:

> Women who have been beaten by their husbands can get an interdict with the court. When this interdict is violated by the husband, she must go back to the courts again and return to us with a letter from the magistrate before we can do anything. The problem is many women come in here before that without real interdicts.[158]

When we challenged his misperception of the interdict procedure, he stated:

> We have a different type of interdict here [in Alexandra]. Maybe what you are describing happens elsewhere in the country. Over here, we don't even get notified of some laws because we are in a township. So maybe the station commander has not been told of this new law.[159]

In a July 1994 study conducted in KwaZulu-Natal, by the South African human rights organization Lawyers for Human Rights, paralegals were sent to fourteen area police stations to speak with police officers.[160] The paralegals were to find out if women were able to access the protections under the Prevention of Family Violence Act, and if the application forms for interdicts were available at the police stations. The results of this survey indicated that barely 60 percent of the station commanders were even aware of the one-year-old act and few stations had the forms available for women to

---

[157] Interview with Major J. Koobair, station commander, Sydenham police station, Durban, February 2, 1995.

[158] Interview, Officer Nguchane, Alexandra police station, Alexandra, February 17, 1995.

[159] Ibid.

[160] Police stations at the following locations were visited: Chatsworth, Hammarsdale, KwaDabeka (Clermont), Kwamashu, Lamontville, Msinsini, Nagina, Pinetown, Pungashe, Umlazi, Umsinsini, Umzumbe, Vela and one unnamed.

fill out. In only one case had the station commander held lectures for the staff of the station to inform them about the provisions of the law.[161]

The current procedure for notifying police of new laws is clearly inadequate. The Police Services must take steps to ensure that all police officers at all stations are systematically informed of the Prevention of Family Violence Act and of the police's duty to enforce its provisions. The police response to domestic abuse calls must be standardized to ensure that all stations respond promptly and decisively to assist women who are being abused.

Unsympathetic or Hostile Police Attitudes

Unfortunately, problems with the police are more complex than just lack of adequate information about the Prevention of Family Violence Act. The police frequently fail to act in domestic violence complaints because they hold discriminatory views about women. "Police culture works against women," noted a counselor at the Cape Town organization Rape Crisis, "the attitudes and assumptions that the police have about women undermine the proper functioning of the law."[162] These attitudes were expressed blatantly in a number of interviews conducted by paralegals for Lawyers for Human Rights in 1994. Police station commanders were outright hostile when informed of the provisions of the Prevention of Family Violence Act.[163] Sergeant Gwamanda of the police station at Hammarsdale, near Durban, who had never heard of the act, reportedly said after being shown a copy of the act that it would "make wives be rude to their husbands and cases of divorce will be more if women know about that gazette [which contained the Act]."[164]

Women of all races told Human Rights Watch that they were unwilling to report incidents of domestic violence to the police, due to the widespread knowledge that the police are often unhelpful and even hostile. Advocates for abused women confirmed frequent police indifference.

Janet, a white woman who does temporary work, has been abused intermittently by her husband. She stated:

---

[161] Paralegal report of interview with Captain Martin Marais, station commander, KwaDabeka police station, August 5, 1994.

[162] Interview, Denise Washkansky, counselor, Rape Crisis, Cape Town, February 10, 1995.

[163] Paralegal reports submitted to Lawyers for Human Rights, 1994.

[164] Paralegal report of interview with Sergeant Gwamanda, Hammarsdale station commander, KwaDabeka police station, July 26, 1994.

The last time in December [1994], he fractured my nose by hitting me with a pipe and tried to rape me in front of our child. But I didn't bother to go to the police because they won't do anything. I'm filing for a divorce.[165]

Molly, a mixed race or "colored" housewife, married for eighteen years, was granted an interdict because her husband regularly became violent when he was drunk. She told the Women's Rights Project:

My husband beats me when he is drunk. I always call the police. They come and warn my husband, but then they say that they can't do anything more because it is a domestic affair and leave. I did get an interdict, but I think my husband destroyed it.[166]

Sally, a "colored" woman and a housewife married for sixteen years, has been regularly abused by her husband, who had been convicted for armed robbery in the past. "At first," she said:

I thought that it was part of the marriage. My husband comes home drunk all the time and abuses me. Many times, he has forced me to have sex with him. He threatens me with his gun if I do not give him oral sex. I am now hiding at my mother's house. I am too scared to get an interdict. What will the police do? Nothing.[167]

Pumla Ngewu, a counselor at the Cape Town-based organization Ilitha Labantu noted that in Guguletu township the police were completely unhelpful except for one officer: "When Sergeant Adonis is there, the women who go in are helped. Otherwise, they face problems."[168]

Women who are the partners of police officers or their friends often have a particularly difficult time getting help from law enforcement agencies. According to Anshu Padayachee of the Durban-based Advice Desk for Abused

---

[165] Interview, Durban, February 3, 1995.

[166] Ibid.

[167] Interview, Durban, January 31, 1995.

[168] Interview, Pumla Ngewu, counselor, Ilitha LaBantu, Guguletu, February 8, 1995.

Women, "Police husbands, from captain to major, are armed and feel they are a law unto themselves." She said:

> There have been a number of cases in which women have been driven to suicide. There was one case in which a woman married to a policeman complained to her husband's senior officer. He would not believe her because the man is a good policeman. Around November 1994 she shot herself.[169]

In another case, documented by the Advice Desk, a battered woman who had been married for three months to a police officer shot herself in December 1994. She had reported the beatings to the station commander who had allegedly told her that "she mustn't worry about it."[170] Jane, an black woman married to a police officer, tried to charge her husband with assault and to file for a divorce. However, the police station has lost all traces of her complaints. She believes that her husband's friends at the station destroyed her file.[171] Laila, a woman of Indian origin married for thirty-five years, told Human Rights Watch that she has been unable to get help from the police:

> [My husband] beats me sometimes until I am bruised all over. I have an interdict, but the police are not helpful. My husband is friends with the station commander. I don't think that I could ever get assistance from the police.[172]

Another battered woman reported that the police refused to help her and instead admonished her by saying, "How could you do this to your husband," a traffic policeman.[173]

One counselor at the Advice Desk on Abused Women recounted the experience of one of her clients seeking an interdict against her boyfriend. A police officer at the Sydenham Police Station in Durban discouraged her from filing the application, allegedly telling her not to "waste her time with those

---

[169] Interview, Anshu Padayachee, Advice Desk on Abused Women, February 1, 1995.

[170] Ibid.

[171] Interview, Durban, January 31, 1995.

[172] Interview, Durban, February 3, 1995.

[173] Interview, Debbie Brent, People Opposed to Woman Abuse (POWA), February 17, 1995.

people [the Advice Desk on Abused Women] and to return to her husband."[174]   In December 1994 when a representative of the NISAA Institute for Women's Development went to the Lenasia police station, near Johannesburg, after receiving a telephone call from an abused woman, the police officer behind the charge desk, S. B. Naidoo, reportedly said, "Here come those anti-male women again."   When confronted, Officer Naidoo threatened, "This is a police station. If you don't talk quietly, we will lock you up."[175]

Black women living in townships report routine police delays in responding to domestic violence calls. In Alexandra township, one resident told Human Rights Watch that delays of up to twenty-four hours by the police in response to calls of domestic abuse are common. In many cases women are informed that there are no available police vehicles for the police to come to the residence. However, the same woman noted, "when the police need to find a vehicle to transport a drunken driver for a breath test, then a vehicle is always found. It is a matter of priorities."[176] According to another woman in Alexandra township:

> I called them [the police] to stop my husband from beating me. I had an interdict so they could arrest them. It took the police one hour to come to my house. By that time, my husband had left. I told the police where my husband had gone. But they were unwilling to go there and arrest him.[177]

Police inaction is not confined to the townships. In Johannesburg, an abusive husband followed his daughter in March 1994 and discovered the location of shelter where his wife and children were living. Upon seeing the husband, the wife, who had an interdict, called the police in fear. The police

---

[174] Interview, counselor, Advice Desk for Abused Women, Durban, February 1, 1995. Commendably, station commander Colonel P. Naidoo expressed concern upon receiving a complaint from the Advice Desk and asked for the woman concerned to meet with him directly in the future.
[175] Interview, Jubi Dangor, NISAA Institute for Women's Development, Johannesburg, February 15, 1995.
[176] Interview, Alexandra Community Center, Alexandra, February 17, 1995.
[177] Interview, Capetown, February 8, 1995.

arrived, but did not take any action against the husband because, in their view, it was a domestic affair. When they left, the police confiscated the interdict, leaving the woman not only at risk of harm from her abusive spouse, but also without the legal document to which she was entitled. The police did not return the interdict until the organization People Opposed to Women Abuse contacted a magistrate. By that time, any confidence that the woman might have had that the interdict would provide her with protection was destroyed.[178]

In another particularly notorious case in June 1994, the South African police brought an abusive husband to a battered women's shelter in Durban and threatened to break in on behalf of the husband, who claimed that his wife had been abducted by the Advice Desk on Abused Women. A police officer from Sydenham police station, accompanied by the abusive husband, demanded entry into the shelter. The woman had previously sought and been granted an interdict following two years of abuse from her husband, who in the past had threatened to harm her children and family members if she left him.[179]

A shelter staff-person attempted to explain the woman's situation to the police, including the fact that an interdict had been issued. The police officer, however, refused to listen or to give the name of his superior. He insisted that the staff open the door to allow the husband to retrieve his wife. When the shelter employee refused, the police officer left promising to return. Several hours later, around midnight, three detectives from Sydenham police station returned and insisted that the shelter allow the husband to speak with his wife to verify that she was not being held against her will. The accompanying police officers became abusive, threatening to break the door and to arrest the shelter staff.

The woman, in the meantime, had locked herself in her bedroom upstairs. She agreed, however, that she would go to the police station in the morning, but was terrified of going outside to speak with anyone in the dark while her husband was nearby. The shelter staff-person later noted that the police were:

> totally insensitive to the abuse the woman had suffered and
> her fear. In fact, in choosing to believe the husband (who

---

[178] Interview, Debbie Brent, People Opposed to Woman Abuse, February 17, 1995.

[179] Interview, Rashida Manjoo, attorney, Advice Desk for Abused Women, Durban, January 31, 1995.

had been served with an interdict that morning), they sent a strong message to her that the police, like so many other members of society, are going to take the man's word and treat the woman's rights as ancillary.[180]

Rather than acknowledge discriminatory attitudes within the police force, some police officials blame other factors for the uneven implementation of the Family Violence Prevention Act. One police commander, for example, expressed the opinion that the success of the law was limited both because the black community is reluctant to pursue legal remedies. He also said that the area housing shortage deterred women from pursuing legal action against an abusive spouse if they cannot later find separate residences for themselves and their children.[181]   The station commander of Umsinsini station in the Umzumbe area noted that in rural areas such as his, the lack of telephones impeded women from reporting battering.[182]   While these are important obstacles that cannot be remedied by the police alone, the police authorities must, at a minimum, ensure that their officers are properly trained to respond to those complaints that are filed.   Unfortunately, such training is at best inconsistent, and at worst non-existent.

The station commander at Sydenham police station explained that although his police station received daily complaints of domestic abuse and approximately one rape report a week the police officers do not know what to do: "We are unwilling to go further, because we are untrained in this area and not sure of what to do."[183]   Until there is standardized training nationally about the act, with an emphasis on women's rights to equal protection of the law, police officers will continue to dismiss incidents of domestic violence.

Judicial Impediments
While the interdict application procedure has been simplified and expedited, not all courts are authorized to issue interdicts. Accordingly, many

---

[180] Letter from Susan Garvey, shelter staff-person to station commander, Sydenham Police Station, Domerton, June 20, 1994.

[181] Paralegal report of interview with Captain Martin Marais, station commander, KwaDabeka Police Station, August 5, 1994.

[182] Paralegal report of interview with Warrant Officer C.J. van Vuuren, Umsinsini police station, July 11, 1994.

[183] Interview, Major J. Koobair, station commander, Sydenham police station, Durban, February 2, 1995.

women, particularly in the rural areas, are deterred by the long distance they must travel to the nearest court in order to file for an interdict. For example, in early 1994 the Umlazi court outside Durban was not empowered to issue interdicts, forcing predominantly women of the black population there to travel approximately forty kilometers to Durban to apply to the court for protection. Similarly, the Amanzimtoti court, in a white and Indian area in KwaZulu-Natal province, did not handle interdicts, requiring women to travel approximately fifty kilometers to Durban. The Wentworth court in a "colored" area near Durban also referred all interdicts to the Durban magistrates' court thirty kilometers away.[184] Women in more isolated areas may have to travel even greater distances. If this interdict procedure is to be effective and equitable, it needs to be more readily accessible to all women.

Even when women have travelled to the appropriate court, they may be unable to secure relief. Women have complained about interference by court clerks when they tried to apply for an interdict. The duty of the court clerk is to distribute the correct forms to abused women—and nothing more. It is not their job to determine the merit of the application or to vet women before handing them a form. However, there have been a number of cases in which court clerks have refused to give women the forms to file an interdict because "I can't see any bruises," "you aren't married" or "he's not beating you at the moment."[185] Further, similar to the police, the clerks in some courts are not even aware of the existence of the law. One paralegal discovered that the court clerk at the Umzumbe magistrates' court had not heard of the act one year after its passage.[186]

Prosecutors have wide discretion on whether to prosecute once an interdict is violated. Prosecutors note that unless the woman agrees to the prosecution, it is unlikely that a charge will be brought. Although they can technically proceed without the battered woman's consent, practically, it is impossible to get a conviction without the woman's testimony. One prosecutor interviewed by Human Rights Watch noted that her court received approximately five to six interdict applications a day. Many of those applications were later withdrawn because of threats by abusive partners to

---

[184] Interview, Rashida Manjoo, Advice Desk for Abused Women, Durban, January 31, 1995.

[185] Interview, Yasmin Bacus, coordinator, Advice Desk for Abused Women, Durban, January 31, 1995.

[186] Paralegal Report of interview with court clerk Mr. Gwala, Umzumbe magistrates court, July 27, 1994.

withhold financial support. Similarly, many charges against men who had violated the interdict are withdrawn by the abused woman. The prosecutor stated:

> If the complainant wants to withdraw the case we oblige, because it is a domestic setting. Sometimes, too, when I think that the abuse is not severe and it's the first time, I urge them to get back together and to drop the charges.[187]

When asked what sort of abuse she considered not serious enough for charges to be brought, she replied, "If it's a slap or a kick and its the first time and he is sorry, then I do not encourage her to file charges."[188]

While Human Rights Watch does not oppose informal efforts by judicial officials to facilitate reconciliation per se, we emphasize that women must be informed of their right to pursue criminal and civil charges against an abusive spouse, and should never be coerced into withdrawing complaints. Further, there should be uniform standards to guide prosecutors regarding what kinds of abuse warrant prosecution.

When an individual has violated an interdict or committed another criminal offense, an early step in the proceedings will be an application for the accused to be released on bail. Since the new constitution has come into effect, the right to bail is protected as a constitutional right. Previously, the burden was on the accused person to show that bail should be granted; this burden has been reversed, so that the presumption is now in favor of the grant of bail and a prosecutor must demonstrate that bail is inappropriate in a particular case. Given South Africa's past history of unlimited powers of detention without trial, the presumption in favor of release on bail is an important human rights achievement. However, many prosecutors are not properly trained to recognize cases in which bail should be opposed and are insufficiently prepared for the court hearing at which bail is determined. In many domestic assault cases, men with a history of violent assault are being released on bail, without adequate protection for their partners who are placed in danger. In one 1994 case reported to Human Rights Watch, a man was released on bail after violating an interdict on a Friday. He was scheduled to appear in court the following Monday to be charged. Upon release, he sought out his partner and beat her, violating an interdict a second time. When he

---

[187] Interview, prosecutor (name withheld on request), Durban, February 3, 1995.
[188] Ibid.

appeared in court on Monday, he was facing two counts of assault.[189] In another July 1994 case, a man was arrested for violating an interdict after he stabbed his wife. He was released on bail immediately by the police and later stabbed his wife six times as she got off a bus.[190] While the right to bail must be protected, the South African government should also train prosecutors and magistrates to recognize cases in which bail should be denied, especially those involving a history of violent assault or violation of bail conditions.

Inadequate and Uncoordinated Government Services

While some of the limitations of the Prevention of Family Violence Act can be fixed through legislative action, legal remedies for domestic abuse can never on their own eradicate the problem. Protection of abused women in a domestic setting often requires greater government intervention than a legal penalty against an abuser. Given entrenched social attitudes and the diffused nature of domestic violence, in many cases, an interdict is simply not sufficient to end the abuse. Joanne Fedler, a lawyer with People Opposing Women Abuse, noted from her experience that there are some abusive husbands who will not hesitate to harm their partners if sufficiently angered, despite the legal penalties: "If a man is intent on harming his wife, the interdict will not stop him. In fact, it may even infuriate him sufficiently to kill her."[191] Rashida Manjoo of the Advice Desk for Abused Woman knew of a case in which an abusive husband had forced his wife to eat the very interdict granted to protect her.[192] In cases such as these, the government should provide services that enable women to leave domestic situations that endanger their physical security.

One of the major impediments to dealing effectively with the problem of domestic violence has been the lack of coordination among government services, particularly the Departments of Justice, Welfare, Health, Safety and Security, and the Police Services. The haphazard and often inadequate assistance that abused women receive from the government contributes to their reluctance to leave such violent relationships and to the likelihood that they will return home, for lack of options rather than as a result of any

---

[189] Ibid.

[190] Group interview with staff from the Advice Desk for Abused Women, Durban, February 1, 1995.

[191] Interview, Joanne Fedler, People Opposed to Women Abuse (POWA), Johannesburg, February 14, 1995.

[192] Interview, Rashida Manjoo, Advice Desk for Abused Women, February 1, 1995.

improvement in the relationship. As noted previously, some police officers have cited this as an excuse for their failure to respond. According to Anshu Padayachee of the Advice Desk for Abused Women:

> Abused women need many diverse services: emergency shelter, medical care, protection, financial assistance and counseling services. One agency alone cannot offer all these services, therefore it is imperative that services are well coordinated and that the various professionals understand how other agencies view the problem and deal with it. . .Today, women in South Africa are experiencing great difficulty in securing adequate treatment. . . the lack of collaboration between agencies results in services for abused women being prone to fragmentation, discontinuity and inaccessibility.[193]

Joanne Fedler concurred:

> Battered women do not need the law's sympathy. Nor do they need to become the symbol of the extent to which a particular government cares for the disempowered. They need safety. They need maintenance. They need a roof over their heads. They need work. They need legal advice that is responsive to the unique circumstances in which they find themselves. A commitment to ending violence in the home must deliver to women the means of survival. Only then will legislative improvements to the Prevention of Family Violence Act be a measure of the extent to which women's lives are valued.[194]

Yet, these kinds of government services for abused women are largely non-existent. The above-mentioned departments do not coordinate at the national level, and government funding for programs to address family violence appears to be negligible. None of the eleven privately run shelters

---

[193] Anshu Padayachee, "Inter-Agency Liaison: A Problem in the Treatment and Prevention of Wife Abuse," *ACTA Criminologica*, Volume 5, Number 1, 1992, pp. 66-67.

[194] Joanne Fedler, *"I've got a problem with my husband ..."*, p. 33.

assisting abused women in South Africa receives any state funding.[195] Tamina echoed the dilemma of other abused women when she said, "I am treated very shabbily. He comes home very late at night and uses foul language against me. He has thrown his shoes at me and has hit me with a belt and broomstick. But I am still with my husband because I have nowhere to go."[196] As Tamina's testimony vividly illustrates, coordinated legal, protective, and social services are urgently needed to help women leave violent relationships. The South African government should commit, or encourage others to provide, resources for programs that address the specific needs of domestically abused women. Until then, they will have nowhere to go and no viable options to rebuild a life without violence.

GENERAL RECOMMENDATIONS

To Governments:
- Governments should denounce domestic violence as a crime as one step toward fully upholding the right of women to equal protection under the law.
- In order to comply with their due diligence requirement under international law, states must take reasonable steps to prevent domestic violence. These steps should include, at a minimum, criminalizing all forms of domestic assault, investigating allegations of domestic assault, and prosecuting and punishing those identified as responsible.
- Governments should provide their law enforcement agencies with adequate resources and instructions to investigate and prosecute domestic violence. For example, state prosecution offices should have a division, or some attorneys, specifically assigned to prosecuting domestic violence cases.
- In addition, governments should ensure that all police officers are trained to respond to and investigate reports of domestic violence. Governments should commission individuals or nongovernmental organizations with expertise in addressing domestic violence to develop and implement such programs nationwide.
- Judges and prosecutors should be similarly trained to recognize domestic assault as a crime and the social prejudices that often

---

[195] There are six shelters in Johannesburg, one in Port Elizabeth, one in Cape Town, one in Kimberly and two in Durban. Law, Race and Gender Project, CIV-3.

[196] Interview, Durban, February 1, 1995.

contribute to its acceptance. The honor defense is not an acceptable excuse for spousal abuse and should not be equated with the "heat of passion" defense.

- Governments should publicly denounce and legislate against the defense of honor as an excuse for the crime of murder. The police and judges should be trained accordingly. Where appropriate, the government should appeal judicial decisions that exonerate domestic abusers on the basis of honor.

- Governments should provide a civil remedy for domestic violence survivors in the form of a legally enforceable protection order (or interdict) that is easily accessible and readily available. Courts should issue such orders to direct the alleged batterer to refrain from contacting, approaching, harassing and assaulting the complainant. The police must enforce these protection orders diligently.

- Civil and criminal remedies for domestic violence also should not be limited to live-in spouses or lover but should also be available to women who have never married or lived with their abusive partners.

- Governments should create an independent mechanism to monitor and oversee police treatment of domestic violence survivors. The mechanism should be able to receive individual complaints from the general public and should be empowered to take steps to discipline police officers who do not investigate allegations of domestic assault.

- In order to strengthen mechanisms to combat domestic violence, governments should compile reliable and comprehensive national statistics on domestic violence, broken down by gender and with a separate section for wife-murder. Such statistics should include, but should not be limited to, the frequency of such violence, rates of prosecution, and types of punishment. Efforts should be made to survey the extent to which domestic assault is not reported to the police.

- The police should provide domestic violence victims with information about the names and ways of contacting shelters and groups that assist survivors of domestic violence. This information should be available in all languages commonly spoken in the station's region.

- National and state authorities should provide funds for public shelters for victims of domestic violence and their dependent children. These funds should not include restrictions on the basis of marital status, race, language, or sex of batterer.

- Governments should include information about the incidence of domestic violence and their efforts to eradicate it in their official reports to the Committee on the Elimination of Discrimination

Against Women in compliance with the Committee's General Recommendation 12 (Eighth Session, 1989).

To the United Nations:
- The United Nations Human Rights Commission should support, by providing sufficient resources, the efforts of the Special Rapporteur on Violence against Women to investigate domestic violence. It should also facilitate her communication with other United Nations agencies, including the Human Rights Committee, and should further disseminate her findings widely.
- The Human Rights Committee should request states to include information in their periodic reports to the committee about any steps they have taken to combat domestic violence as a part of their overall efforts to ensure the physical integrity of individuals within their territories. In addition, the committee should investigate any communications received under the Optional Protocol to the ICCPR that indicate a pattern of state nonprosecution of domestic assault.

To Donor Governments:
- Donor countries should ensure that any bilateral police training program they sponsor includes information on the proper handling of domestic violence and sexual assault allegations.
- As part of their administration of justice programs, donor countries should seek to eliminate gender bias in the judicial handling of domestic violence cases by providing appropriate training for judges and court clerks.

7

REPRODUCTION, SEXUALITY
AND HUMAN RIGHTS VIOLATIONS

Issues of reproductive and sexual autonomy lie at the core of passionately held ideological, religious and cultural notions of female gender identity. Because this is often contested ground, reproductive and sexual issues frequently present the context for the trampling of women's rights by or with the deliberate acquiescence of the state. Such abuse includes, among other things, violence against women, coercion, sex discrimination and unequal protection of the law, restrictions on the rights to free expression and movement, and intrusions upon women's privacy.[1] In addition to violations against individual women, states have also perpetrated or condoned abuses against health care providers, women's rights advocates, journalists, and others because of their particular views on these heated issues.

In numerous instances, the state is directly responsible for abuses in the course of implementing policies or projects that regulate women's sexual and reproductive decision-making and actions. For example, the Turkey section in this chapter documents how the police and state doctors have physically compelled Turkish women and girls to undergo virginity examinations. Concerns over population size and its perceived relationship to state interests—e.g., economic development, national security, environmental conservation—have given rise to population control strategies that incorporate gross abuse of women's rights. During the communist era in Czechoslovakia, for example, the government forced numerous Romany women to be sterilized, some while they were unconscious, in an effort to reduce what it considered a "high unhealthy population."[2] Numerous sources have also reported that local Chinese officials have frequently used or condoned physical, psychological and economic coercion to enforce China's official one-child

---

[1] The issue of whether or not reproductive and sexual autonomy is or should be guaranteed under international law is a complex and important subject. Human Rights Watch does not currently have a position on it, but recognizes it to be an emerging area of international human rights law deserving of profound consideration.

[2] See "Sterilization of Romany Women," in Helsinki Watch (now Human Rights Watch/Helsinki) *Struggling for Ethnic Identity: Czechoslovakia's Endangered Species* (New York: Human Rights Watch, 1992), p. 20.

policy.[3] In 1994 China further adopted the Law of the People's Republic of China on Maternal and Infant Health Care, essentially a eugenics law, that threatens to undermine the right of couples with a "serious hereditary disease" to found a family.[4]

States have also interfered with women's ability to access information regarding family planning by restricting the right to freedom of expression, as happened in Ireland when its courts handed down injunctions preventing clinics and student groups from publicizing information on abortion services abroad. In still other situations, state complicity is largely found in the government's failure to ensure women's right to equal protection of the law and nondiscrimination on the basis of sex, by not enforcing domestic law that guarantees women's rights related to reproduction and sexuality. In Poland, for example, the post-communist government blatantly though indirectly denied to women equal protection of the law; while abortion was legal at that time, the government allowed the Polish Medical College to abuse its physician licensing powers to sanction doctors who chose to perform abortions.

Even where there is no direct state involvement, governments have frequently been complicit in abuses against women that are carried out in the name of tradition, culture or religion, by purposefully turning a blind eye toward them. Societies in all regions of the world create social arrangements to order interaction among members of the community; these arrangements almost always include distinct gender roles. International human rights

---

[3] See, for example, Immigration and Refugee Board Information and Research Branch, "The People's Republic of China: The One-Child Family Policy," *Human Rights Briefs* (Ottawa, Canada: Immigration and Refugee Board, June 1989); Maria Hsia Chang, "Women," in Yuan-Li Wu et al., eds., *Human Rights in the People's Republic of China* (Boulder, CO: Westview Press, 1988).

[4] Law of the People's Republic of China on Maternal and Infant Health Care, adopted at the Tenth meeting of the Eighth National People's Congress Standing Committee on October 27, 1994. Translated in Foreign Broadcast Information Service (FBIS), "Law on Maternal, Infant Health Care," FBIS-CHI-94-211, November 1, 1994. Article 10 of the law states: "When either one of the couple is diagnosed to have a serious hereditary disease, which is medically deemed unsuitable for reproduction, . . . [t]he couple may marry if they agree to take long-lasting contraceptive measures or give up child bearing by undergoing ligation . . . [emphasis added]" "Serious hereditary diseases" is defined in Article 38 as: "congenital diseases caused by hereditary factors, which are medically deemed as not suitable for child bearing because such diseases make patients lose total or partial ability to live independently and have a high potential to be passed to the next generation."

standards require states not to enforce, or condone the enforcement of, reproductive and sexual norms through violent or sexually discriminatory means. Yet, states often flout their international legal obligations in this regard. For example, Turkish state officials routinely tolerate and sometimes perform forced gynecological examinations on women and girls to maintain the ideal of female virginity. Numerous African as well as Asian and Middle Eastern governments condone involuntary female genital mutilation or circumcision—which is carried out in part to suppress female sexual desire—even in countries where this traditional practice has been outlawed.[5] The failure to ensure that women remain within the boundaries of their socially defined sexual and reproductive roles, which are sometimes codified in law, is widely considered to tarnish not only the woman's reputation, but also her family's or even her entire community's honor. Thus, women, but not men, who engage in "immodest" behavior are attacked by state agents or punished with impunity by their husbands or families, sometimes with fatal consequences.[6]

---

[5] For information on female genital mutilation (also known as female circumcision), see, for example, UNICEF, "Guidelines for UNICEF Action on Eliminating Female Genital Mutilation," Executive Directive from James P. Grant, executive director, CF/EXD/1994-009, October 31, 1994; Nahid Toubia, *Female Genital Mutilation: A Call for Global Action* (New York: Women, Ink., 1993); Asma M. A'Haleem, "Claiming Our Bodies and Our Rights: Exploring Female Circumcision as an Act of Violence," in *Freedom from Violence*, Margaret Schuler, ed., (OEF International, 1992); Fran Hosken, *The Hosken Report*, 3rd ed. (Massachusetts: WIN News, 1983); Olayinka Koso-Thomas, *The Circumcision of Women: A Strategy for Eradication* (London: Zed Books, 1992).

[6] One example of the role of state agents: on June 24, 1993, the state-controlled *Jomhuri Eslami* newspaper in Tehran reported that a number of women were rounded up and sentenced to flogging for being badly covered ("bad-hejab," the hejab is a loose garment which covers the shape of the body and shows no more than the face and hands). Tehran's police chief "vowed the campaign would be pursued decisively and unreformable offenders treated 'harshly'." The report did not make clear if the sentences were carried out. "Iranian women sentenced to flogging for dress," *Reuters, Limited,* June 24, 1993. Under Iranian law, a woman can be flogged up to seventy-four times for inappropriate dress.

See also, the discussion of the *Hudood* Ordinances in "Police Abuse of Women in Pakistan" and of the "honor defense" in "Domestic Violence Against Women in Brazil," in this volume.

The international community has been timid about condemning abuses cloaked in terms of cultural, traditional or religious imperatives, especially when they affect the sensitive and controversial domain of female sexuality. In doing so, governments have failed to uphold the principle of the universality of human rights, a cornerstone of the international human rights regime. The 1993 World Conference on Human Rights declared that "While the significance of national and regional particularities and various historical, cultural and religious backgrounds must be borne in mind, it is the duty of States, regardless of their political, economic and cultural systems, to promote and protect all human rights and fundamental freedoms."[7]

Cultural defenses for violations of women's rights in the context of reproduction and sexuality also warrant careful scrutiny for another reason. Rather than reflecting a true concern for the public or social order, they have often been exploited by factional interests to preserve or to achieve political dominance. Nowhere is this more apparent than in the rhetoric and actions of political, religious or other extremists who use the preservation of tradition and culture as a rallying cry to incite violence, particularly violence against women portrayed as transgressing social and sexual norms, as a means of consolidating popular support. Authorities have often supported the violent actions of extremists or have abdicated responsibility for curbing them because they fear alienating a segment of the public that sympathizes with those elements. States should be held fully accountable when they conspire in, encourage, condone or tolerate such acts.[8]

---

[7] World Conference on Human Rights, "The Vienna Declaration and Program of Action," adopted June 25, 1993, Paragraph 5.

[8] For example, on March 22, 1995, the women's branch of the Popular Police to the Director of the Libyan Cultural Center in Khartoum, Sudan, sent a letter to the center warning against certain female behavior. The letter reportedly stated: ". . . since woman is the bases [sic] of good and useful society, we took upon ourselves to protect women against herself [sic] . . . through the following measures: 1. All (women) have to dress in a decent and not dishonorable, not transparent, not tight but ample and wide dress. 2. It is forbidden that girls stand with men in streets and doubtful places and in a manner not approved by Shari'a. 3. It is forbidden that girls ride with men who do not have family or alliance relationship with them. 4. Idleness in the street and loud speaking to a degree are forbidden (for women). Whoever (girl/woman) does not abide by this regulation [sic] would render herself subject to legal questioning from Police of Manners and General Discipline through the Murabitat of Popular Police." Similar letters of intimidation and verbal threats allegedly are routinely sent to officials in

(continued...)

International Legal Protections

International human rights norms ensure to women the right to receive information regarding sexuality and reproduction and to make decisions in these matters free from violence and sex discrimination. The constellation of applicable civil and political rights includes, among others, the rights to physical integrity, freedom of expression and association, nondiscrimination and equal protection of the law, and privacy.

The United Nations Human Rights Committee's General Comment 19 on the right to found a family stated that "When state parties adopt family planning policies, they should be compatible with the provisions of the Covenant [on Civil and Political Rights] and should, in particular, not be discriminatory or compulsory."[9]   Consistent with this comment, the 1994 United Nations-sponsored International Conference on Population and Development (ICPD) recognized that reproductive rights are embodied in "certain human rights that are already recognized in national laws, international human rights documents and other relevant U.N. consensus documents."[10] Drawing upon existing human rights norms, the ICPD condemned in particular the use of violence, coercion, and discrimination in family planning programs.

In addition to these violations singled out by the ICPD, states have also infringed upon women's right to privacy in the pursuit of demographic, eugenic or other state objectives that affect women's reproductive or sexual lives.[11]   While the right to privacy is not absolute, it does impose additional limitations on the ways in which states can regulate a range of issues, from contraceptive use to choice of sexual partner.[12]   In particular, governments

---

[8](...continued)
charge of education establishments and other public places. Report on file at Human Rights Watch.

[9]   United Nations, "Compilation of General Comments and General Recommendations Adopted by the Human Rights Treaty Bodies," U.N. Document HRI/GEN/I/Rev.1, July 29, 1994, pp. 29-30.

[10] Report of the International Conference on Population and Development, Paragraph 7.3, U.N. Document A/Conf.171/13, 1994.

[11] ICCPR, Article 17; American Convention on Human Rights, Article 11; European Convention for the Protection of Human Rights and Fundamental Freedoms, Article 8.

[12]   For example, the European Court of Human Rights in Strasborg has on three occasions upheld the rights of gays and lesbians against state regulation on the basis of a right to private life. See *Dudgeon v. The United Kingdom* (1981), *Norris v. Ireland* (1988), and *Modina v. Cyprus* (1993).

may not derogate from their duty to uphold individual privacy in an "arbitrary and unlawful" manner.[13]

Similar to many of the other abuses documented in this volume, those which occur in the context of women's reproductive and sexual lives often are not perpetrated by state agents, but rather by private individuals, including family members. Human rights law recognizes that "the family is the natural and fundamental group unit of society and is entitled to protection by society and the State."[14] Governments, however, must balance this duty with its obligation to uphold the competing rights of constitutive members of the family as individuals. States may not legitimize, condone or tolerate intra-familial activities that involve violence or threat of violence, regardless of whether they are motivated by notions of female sexuality and reproduction or any other consideration. The Nigerian government's acquiescence in forced marriages orchestrated by parents is an example where the state should be held accountable under international law for privately perpetrated abuse.[15]

Human Rights and Reproduction

The International Covenant on Civil and Political Rights (ICCPR) directly address the realm of reproduction in one provision. Article 23.2 of the ICCPR declares, "The right of men and women of marriageable age to marry and to found a family shall be recognized."

Over the past three decades, the right of couples and individuals to found a family—and therefore to decide on the number and spacing of children—has been further elaborated in the Convention on the Elimination of All Forms of Discrimination Against Women (CEDAW) and various international declarations and plans of action.[16] Article 16(1) of CEDAW provides that:

---

[13] ICCPR, Article 17.1.

[14] ICCPR, Article 23.1. Article 17 also prohibits "arbitrary and unlawful interference" with family.

[15] This situation is discussed in a forthcoming report by Human Rights Watch/Africa and the Women's Rights Project.

[16] This right has been affirmed in various United Nations-sponsored conferences. It initially appeared in the 1968 Teheran Declaration, and subsequently in the Declaration on Social Progress and Development (1974), the World Population Plans of Action of Bucharest (1974) and Mexico City (1984), and the Women's Conference of Mexico City (1975) and Nairobi (1985).

> States parties shall take all appropriate measures to . . .
> ensure on a basis of equality of men and women . . . the
> same rights to decide freely and responsibly on the number
> and spacing of their children and to have access to the
> information, education and means to enable them to exercise
> these rights.

This article introduces three important points. First, women are
entitled to make, and not simply to acquiesce to, decisions regarding
reproduction on an equal basis with men. Second, this decision is to be made
freely and responsibly.[17] The state's authority to ensure that individuals make
"responsible" decisions is subject to the caveat that it must not do so in any
way that is violative of internationally recognized human rights. Of the range
of potential abuses, discrimination may be the most elusive to human rights
monitoring. The requirement that women (and men) should make reproductive
decisions responsibly is, at first glance, beyond reproach; but it is, in fact,
fraught with the potential for discrimination because female responsibility is
almost always defined and evaluated in a context of unequal power relations
between men and women. On the other hand, the phrase "freely and
responsibly" implies that in order for women (and men) to act responsibly, the
state should provide, or ensure the provision of, "information, education and
means" to women to formulate their decisions.

Third, although Article 16 does not mention specifically family
planning, it can be understood to include family planning information,
particularly when it is read in conjunction with other provisions of CEDAW.
Articles 10(h), 12(1) and 14.2(c) of the Women's Convention explicitly refer
to the state's obligation to ensure access to family planning information.[18]

---

[17] Interpreting this article, the Committee on the Elimination of Discrimination
Against Women has stated: "Decisions to have children or not, while preferably made
in consultation with spouse or partner, must not nevertheless be limited by spouse,
parent, partner or Government." General recommendation 21, "Report of the Committee
on the Elimination of Discrimination Against Women," Thirteenth session, April 12,
1994, Supplement No. 38 (A/49/38).

[18] Article 10(h) of CEDAW calls on state parties to ensure equality between men
and women in "[a]ccess to specific educational information to help to ensure the health
and well-being of families, including information and advice on family planning; Article
12(1) calls on state parties to ensure, "on a basis of equality of men and women, access

(continued...)

Human Rights and Sexuality

International human rights law does not address directly or indirectly the issue of sexuality per se outside the context of reproduction. Under Article 16 of CEDAW, women at a minimum have the right to know the reproductive consequences of sexual intercourse, and to decide, on an equal basis with men, whether or not to engage in sexual intercourse that could lead to pregnancy. Beyond this, the fundamental rights to physical security and inherent dignity of the human person[19] defend individuals from violence and coercion.[20] Even at times when certain important rights can be legitimately suspended, the emergency measures that governments can then adopt restricting those rights may not be applied in a manner that involves discrimination on the basis of sex.[21] These rights extend to private, consensual sexual activity among adults. States may not breach these rights to compel women to conform to

---

[18](...continued)
to health care services, including those related to family planning"; and Article 14.2(c) requires state parties to ensure to women the right "to have access to adequate health care facilities, including information, counseling and services in family planning."

[19] Article 3 of the Universal Declaration of Human Rights and Article 9.1 of the ICCPR guarantees to everyone "liberty and security of person." This right, although traditionally applied to conditions of arrest or detention, has been expanded over time to cover non-custodial situations. For example, CEDAW's Recommendation No. 19 defined sex discrimination to include gender-based violence, regardless of where it takes place, that impairs or nullifies women's rights and freedoms under international law. The committee stated, "These rights and freedoms include, *inter alia*, . . . the right to liberty and security of person." Similarly, the Inter-American Convention on the Prevention, Punishment and Eradication of Violence Against Women condemns such violence "whether in the public or private sphere" (Article 1) and affirms the right of a woman "to have the inherent dignity of her person respected . . ." (Article 4(e)). The 1993 World Conference on Human Rights also concluded that "gender-based violence and all forms of sexual harassment and exploitation, including those resulting from cultural prejudice . . ., are incompatible with the dignity and worth of the human person, and must be eliminated." Vienna Declaration and Program of Action, U.N. Document A/Conf.157/24 (Part I), Paragraph 18.

[20] Universal Declaration on Human Rights, Article 3; ICCPR, Article 9; African Charter on Human and Peoples' Rights, Articles 4 ,5 and 6; American Convention on Human Rights, Articles 5 and 7; and the European Convention on Human Rights, Article 5.

[21] ICCPR, Article 4(1). Discrimination on the basis of sex is also explicitly barred under the UDHR, Articles 2 and 7; the African Charter, Article 2; the American Convention, Article 1; and the European Convention, Article 14.

particular sexual norms, or to engage in or refrain from sexual activities, whether for the purposes of reproduction or other ends. Moreover, they are obligated "to take the necessary steps, . . . to adopt such legislative or other measures as may be necessary to give effect" to these rights.[22]

Whether or not civil and political rights can be interpreted to include an underlying principle of sexual autonomy has been widely contested. Whereas the governments that convened for the ICPD in 1994 embraced the concept of reproductive rights, they failed to reach consensus on the notion of sexual rights. Their omission was, in large part, due to concerns that recognition of sexual rights would promote extramarital and premarital sex as well as gay and lesbian relationships. However, just as governments have condemned the use of violence, coercion and discrimination to achieve family planning objectives, the use of these abusive tactics to control female sexuality would also violate human rights standards, to the extent that they are committed or routinely tolerated by the state.

FORCED VIRGINITY EXAMS IN TURKEY

This problem had become horrifying. Virginity exams were often done by police taking women to forensic medicine or state hospitals. This practice is contrary to universal laws of humanity and to medical ethics. We have let doctors know that they are not required to perform this exam. But we know some doctors still do it, just as some doctors take a prisoner's heartbeat during torture.[23]

In a mission to Turkey in July 1993, Human Rights Watch investigated the prevalence of forced virginity control exams and the role of the government in conducting or tolerating such exams.[24] Although the

---

[22] ICCPR, Article 2(2).

[23] Interview, Dr. Nesrin Cobanoglu, M.D., Ankara, July 12, 1993.

[24] This material was adapted from Human Rights Watch Women's Rights Project, "A Matter of Power: State Control of Women's Virginity in Turkey," *A Human Rights Watch Short Report*, vol. 6, no. 7 (June 1994). The terms "virginity control" and "virginity control exam" are used to refer to gynecological examinations undertaken to determine the status of the hymen. According to Prof. Dr. Ozdemir Kolusayin, M.D.,

(continued...)

actual extent of the abuse is unknown, interviews with doctors, lawyers and local women's and human rights activists revealed that the threat of such exams follows women through their lives. Virginity exams are forced by law enforcement officials upon female political detainees and common criminal suspects charged with "immodest" behavior or alleged prostitution.[25] Evidence also exists of such exams being performed on hospital patients, state dormitory residents and women applying for government jobs. Families subject their female children to virginity exams, often at the hands of state medical professionals.

At the root of the pervasive imposition of virginity control exams in Turkey, whether at the hands of the state or private individuals, is the presumption that female virginity is a legitimate interest of the family, the community and, ultimately, the state. As a result, forced examinations to verify female virginity are not only deemed justifiable, but also are seen as legitimately overriding the individual rights of women to bodily integrity, privacy and equality before the law.

---

[24](...continued)
Director of Istanbul Forensic Medicine, the purpose of such examinations is to establish whether the hymen was broken as a result of sexual intercourse and when the hymen was broken. Some exams are performed upon women accused or suspected of prostitution for the purpose not only of determining whether they are virgins but also whether they have had recent sexual intercourse. In such cases, a ruptured hymen and evidence of recent sexual activity are both potential evidence of prostitution. Dr. Kolusayin specified that it is important to have virginity exams performed by specialists because only they are familiar with the many possible appearances of the hymen. He also acknowledged that there are "technical problems involved" in assessing the status of the hymen because it is very soft tissue that usually heals itself within seven to ten days. Interview, Istanbul, July 9, 1993. Other gynecologists indicate that an examination of the hymen should not be considered conclusive evidence of lost virginity. Interview, Dr. Nahid Toubia, M.D., New York, January 1994. The terms "vaginal" or "gynecological" exams are used to refer to the general medical procedure whether undertaken for health or other reasons.

[25] The Turkish police, or Security Department, is divided into divisions with different responsibilities. The first division is the Anti-Terror Department which monitors illegal political activities. The second division is the Public Order Department which is responsible for policing prostitution and offenses described by the Turkish criminal code and the police duty and authority law as violating public order.

Social Context

> This is a way for men to control women. Why do men want
> women to be untouched? It is a matter of power.[26]

For many women in Turkey, a damaged reputation virtually ends any possibility of marriage. The behavior of unmarried women therefore is guarded closely in order to protect them from even the suggestion of inappropriate sexual activity. In addition, any physical rupture of the hymen, regardless of its connection to sexual activity, is considered evidence of lost virginity. According to an Istanbul forensic physician who is critical of virginity exams, "Hymens are sacred. If she has a torn hymen, that's what matters, regardless of how she got that way."[27] Doctors examining women at the direction of the police prepare reports in which they equate signs of a ruptured hymen—regardless of its cause—with loss of virginity. Medical reports obtained by Human Rights Watch indicate that where doctors found signs of old breaks in the hymen, the cause of which could not be determined, they labeled the women being examined: "not a virgin."[28]

Families act to protect the honor of their female members, and girls and women are expected to preserve both their physical virginity (i.e. an intact hymen) and their reputation for chastity. No such emphasis is placed on male virginity. Nor does family honor in any way rest on the preservation of male virginity prior to marriage. The application of these different standards to men and women results in women's behavior being assessed for its sexual implications by family members when men's behavior is not so scrutinized. This assumes its most extreme form as a forced virginity exam.

Social norms encourage families to act in defense of their honor, and legal norms protect their ability to do so.[29] Both female and male honor are

---

[26] Interview, Canan Arin, attorney and activist, Istanbul, July 1993.

[27] Interview, Dr. Sebnem Korur Fincanci, M.D., Istanbul, July 8, 1993.

[28] Human Rights Watch has on file copies of medical reports prepared after a raid by the Urla Security Department on an Izmir hotel in July 1991. In the raid, several women were detained by the police for suspected prostitution. The women were taken to a state hospital and forced to undergo vaginal exams to determine their virginity and whether they had had recent sexual intercourse.

[29] Turkish law, for example, reduces the penalty for murder if it is committed "against a newly born child with the purpose of protecting the dignity and reputation

(continued...)

linked to the maintenance of female chastity, although not to male chastity. Thus female sexual conduct comes within the "legitimate" purview of male control. Paramount importance is placed on female virginity.

The link between the concept of honor condoned by the state and the discriminatory control of women's virginity establishes a context in which a woman's right to bodily integrity and privacy, and therefore not to be subjected to a forcible and invasive bodily exam, is subordinate to the family's interest in maintaining its honor. Thus, at the request of family members, state and private physicians perform virginity exams on women, whether they are adults or minors. In many instances, parents believe their actions protect their daughters' reputations either by (1) providing tangible "proof" that the girl or woman remains a virgin despite allegations to the contrary,[30] or (2) establishing with medical evidence that the girl or woman's hymen was ruptured in an accident and not as a result of extramarital sexual activity.[31]

Where adult women are concerned, family monitoring of women's modesty is so prevalent in Turkish society that they rarely exercise their right to refuse virginity exams. According to a doctor who has performed numerous virginity exams at the behest of both state agents and family members, "Women accused of not being virgins, they have no choice but to consent [to virginity exams] because otherwise it is understood to mean that she is admitting that she is not a virgin. There is no real consent because of family and police pressures."[32]

Thus, a woman may be deterred from exercising her right to refuse because she sees it as a choice between vindicating her reputation by agreeing to the exam or tacitly admitting her loss of "honor" by refusing. In many instances, according to local activists, the woman may not be aware that she

---

[29](...continued)
of the offender or of his wife, mother, daughter, grandchild, adopted daughter or sister." (Turkish Criminal Code, Article 453.) Similarly, the punishment for the crime of leaving children unattended is reduced when committed "against an illegitimate child with the intention of preserving one's reputation for chastity, or that of one's wife, mother, descendant or sister." (Turkish Criminal Code, Article 475.)

[30] If, for example, an unmarried woman's honor is challenged by members of the community on her wedding night, a previous virginity exam provides evidence establishing her virginity.

[31] "People believe this [virginity control] is done for the good of the girl. It is not, and this should be made clear." Interview, Dr. Selma Gungor, M.D., Ankara, July 12, 1993.

[32] Interview, Dr. Umit Biger, M.D., Istanbul, July 9, 1993.

has a right to refuse. Even doctors are not assured of being allowed to respect a woman's right to refuse an exam, particularly when the exam is being conducted at the instigation of the state. To our knowledge, only limited efforts by individual doctors have been made to ensure that women are aware of their right to refuse virginity exams and are able to assert that right.

Legal Context

Rather than challenging the discriminatory emphasis on female virginity, Turkish criminal law and, ultimately, state practice reinforce it. Turkish criminal law makes female honor the state's business.[33] Many sex crimes are defined by Turkey's criminal code in terms of their impact on women's virginity and honor. In fact, sexual assaults against women are classified by law as "Felonies Against Public Decency and Family Order." In contrast, other forms of battery are considered "Felonies Against Individuals."

Crimes against public decency and family order include rape,[34] acting "indecently in public" or engaging in sexual intercourse in public,[35] removing "the virginity of a girl who has completed fifteen years of age, with a promise of marriage,"[36] and abducting an adult woman through force, violence, threats or fraud and "under lascivious feelings or with the intent of marriage."[37] The statutes defining many of these crimes explicitly refer to the virginity of the victim. For example, causing a woman or girl to lose her virginity after falsely promising to marry her is a felony. Medically documented loss of virginity is considered evidence of the crimes of seduction, statutory rape and removing virginity with a promise of marriage.

A man charged with any of these crimes can escape criminal liability by marrying the women bringing charges.[38] If family members suspect or know that a woman has had sexual intercourse, they may attempt to force a

---

[33] The Turkish criminal code is based on the Italian criminal code of 1889, which was adopted by Turkey in 1926. The code has been greatly amended and over half of its articles changed. In addition to the criminal code, there are numerous penal statutes which pertain to specific crimes and regulate special fields of criminal law. Dr. Feyyaz Golcuklu, "Criminal Law," in *An Introduction to Turkish Law*, Tugrul Ansay and Don Wallace, Jr., eds. (Deventer, Netherlands: Kluwer Law and Taxation Publishers, 1987).

[34] Turkish Criminal Code, Article 416.

[35] Ibid., Article 419.

[36] Ibid., Article 423.

[37] Ibid., Article 429.

[38] Ibid., Articles 423 and 434.

marriage between a daughter and her sexual partner by filing criminal charges with the police who then take her for an exam. Thus, if statutory rape or "removal of virginity" is charged by family members, a girl may be required to submit to a virginity exam.

The designation of sex crimes as violations of community or family morality has two consequences. First, it identifies the community and not the individual woman as the party that suffers harm consequent to the crime. Second, it defines the harm done in terms of a woman's honor rather than her physical integrity. The investigation and prosecution of sex crimes thus stress not the physical harm to the woman but rather her honor and thus public decency and family order that may have been compromised.[39] Consequently, sex crimes committed against non-virgins are perceived to be less serious offenses than those committed against virgins because the potential damage to family order is less grave. Until the late 1980s, for example, Article 438 of the Turkish Criminal Code provided reduced penalties for men convicted of rape and abduction where the victim was proved to be a prostitute.[40] The emphasis on public decency and family order in codifying sex crimes lays the groundwork for women's honor—rather than the physical harm suffered—to be the central question at issue in such investigations.

Virginity or lack thereof is not relevant to and does not determine the legitimacy of a claim of sexual abuse or assault. Nonetheless, prosecutors and judges may unfairly deem evidence of a woman's virginity to be relevant to any charge of sexual assault, even though loss of virginity is not an element of the crime of rape.[41] Thus, women alleging sexual assault are judged in light of the invidious notion that a woman's sexuality, as indicated by her mode of dress, lifestyle or status as a virgin, implies consent to sexual relations or a lack of credibility. Assessing a woman's credibility as a witness and as

---

[39] The law even provides a remedy for the perceived harm of lost honor by creating an incentive—suspension of criminal prosecution—for a man charged with certain of these crimes to marry his "victim" and thus minimize the consequences of her loss of honor.

[40] Article 438 was challenged in Turkey's constitutional court as violatory of the Constitution, but the court rejected the claim on the grounds that dishonest women, i.e. prostitutes, should not be treated the same as honest women. After much public debate, the Turkish parliament repealed the provision in 1988/89. Canan Arin, Report on Women's Status in Turkish Law (unpublished paper), September 27, 1991.

[41] Interview, Istanbul, July 8, 1993.

a victim in light of her reputation for modesty, or lack thereof, reinforces the different standards by which men and women's sexual behavior are judged.

Nonetheless, gynecological exams are performed in the course of investigating most sex crimes, in part for the purpose of determining whether the woman involved is a virgin.[42] This not only invites discrimination in the adjudication of such crimes, but also is inconsistent with the Turkish criminal code. Local doctors, activists and lawyers concur that vaginal exams may be performed at the state's behest only (1) consequent to the filing of criminal charges and then only with the woman's willing participation in collecting evidence to support her charge, or (2) as a part of regular health checks for working prostitutes pursuant to Turkey's present law on prostitution. Moreover, gynecological exams pursuant to criminal charges may be performed only at the request of a prosecutor or judge.[43] Despite such regulations, state officials compel women to submit to vaginal exams without their consent and when no criminal charges have been filed alleging a sex crime.

The Turkish authorities' involvement in or tolerance of forced virginity control exams violates rights expressly guaranteed by the Turkish constitution. Forced virginity exams violate women's right to privacy as protected by the Turkish Constitution.[44] Sexual intercourse between consenting adults is not illegal in Turkey, thus the consensual sexual conduct

---

[42] When a woman files a criminal complaint alleging a sex crime, the court or prosecutor may direct that an examination be conducted for the purpose of gathering forensic evidence. The doctors responsible for performing gynecological exams in such cases are forensic physicians employed by the ministry of justice to act as court consultants. The police, however, have no independent authority to send women to forensic medicine for gynecological exams. A doctor asked by the police to perform such an exam is required to send the case back for authorization from a judge or prosecutor. Interview, Prof. Dr. Ozdemir Kolusayin, director of Istanbul Forensic Medicine, Istanbul, July 9, 1993. Doctors referred to in this report as forensic physicians are employees of the ministry of justice.

[43] Interview, Dr. Ozdemir Kolusayin, director of Istanbul Forensic Medicine, Istanbul, July 9, 1993.

[44] Article 17 of the Turkish Constitution provides, "The physical integrity of the individual shall not be violated except under medical necessity and in cases prescribed by law." The Turkish Constitution also specifically protects individuals' privacy. Article 20 states that "[e]veryone has the right to demand respect for his private and family life. Privacy of individual and family life cannot be violated. Exceptions necessitated by judiciary investigation and prosecution are reserved."

of unmarried women is protected against the unwanted scrutiny of police and other state officials.   Police have no legal justification for harassing women in their homes or on the street for suspected sexual conduct.   Such scrutiny violates women's right to be free from arbitrary interference with their privacy and homes.   The exams themselves violate the right to privacy by subjecting women's bodies to unwarranted and invasive searches.

The infliction of virginity exams also violates the Constitution's guarantee of freedom from discrimination.[45]   As the testimonies below demonstrate, the state discriminates against women by acting to control women's private, sexual practices with the threat or imposition of abuse to which men are not subjected.[46]   Thus, although both men and women may suffer torture or cruel and degrading treatment while in police custody or be detained for improper behavior, only women are subject to degrading and abusive treatment pertaining to their sexual conduct.   Moreover, the bias that maintains the legitimacy of the state's interest in women's sexuality is imbedded in laws and state practices that attempt to monitor women's, and not men's, sexual conduct.   For example, if an unmarried couple staying in a hotel is detained for suspected prostitution, it is the woman who is questioned about her sexual conduct and examined for evidence of lost virginity.   In other words, her virginity or lack thereof may be considered evidence in an investigation of illegal prostitution whereas his sexual practices are not considered relevant to the investigation.   Nor is he threatened with or subjected to comparable invasions of his privacy and physical integrity.

The detention of women for suspected illegal prostitution and their subjection to virginity exams also raise questions regarding due process.   The ICCPR states that "[n]o one shall be deprived of his liberty except on such

---

[45] Article 10 of the Turkish Constitution provides that "[a]ll individuals are equal without any discrimination before the law, irrespective of language, race, colour, sex, political opinion, philosophical belief, religion and sect, or any such consideration."

[46] Although it may be argued that the status of men's virginity cannot be ascertained with a medical examination, neither can the status of women's virginity be determined conclusively with a gynecological examination. Yet only women are questioned about their virginity and selected as targets for invasive and degrading exams. Interview, Dr. Nahid Toubia, M.D., January 13, 1994. As a Turkish doctor told Human Rights Watch, the fact that a woman's hymen is torn or damaged "is not necessarily evidence of sexual intercourse." Nonetheless, the perception is "if her hymen is ruptured, then she is not a virgin." Interview, Dr. Sebnem Korur Fincana, M.D., Istanbul, July 8, 1993.

grounds and in accordance with such procedure as are established by law."[47]
The Body of Principles for the Protection of All Persons under Any Form of
Detention or Imprisonment (Body of Principles) provides a number of due
process protections relevant to the arbitrary detention of Turkish women
accused of illegal prostitution. First, it specifies that no one shall be detained
without an effective and prompt opportunity to appear before a judicial or
other authority and an opportunity to defend herself. A detained person has
the right to know why she is being detained as well as the terms of her
detention. Further, detained persons should not be denied the opportunity to
communicate with family and counsel. Finally, the Body of Principles
mandates that detainees be treated humanely and with respect for their dignity.
"No circumstance whatever may be invoked as a justification for torture or
other cruel, inhuman or degrading treatment or punishment."[48]

Turkish officials operate in flagrant violation of these principles.
Evidence indicates that police detain women for suspected illegal prostitution
or immoral activity without justification and without first conducting any kind
of investigation to support their accusations. These women are not charged
with the crime of practicing prostitution illegally. Nor are they brought before
a prosecutor or judge. Instead, they are held without charge and forced to
submit to gynecological exams, which we previously described as a form of
cruel and degrading treatment. Some women are then held against their will
and forced to undergo treatment if they are diagnosed with a sexually
transmitted disease.

Abuse of Women in Custody

Press reports from 1986 through 1992 recount instances in which: (1)
a fifteen-year-old girl detained by gendarmes in Diyarbakir was sent to a state
hospital with a letter from the police requiring a virginity examination;[49] (2)
Mete Altan, the head of the Security Department in the city of Adana,
defended the practice of sending female political detainees for virginity exams

---

[47] ICCPR, Article 9.

[48] Article 90 of the Turkish constitution provides that international treaties ratified
by the Turkish government have the force of domestic law. Thus, the human rights
instruments ratified by Turkey strengthen domestic protections for victims of human
rights abuse. Principles 1, 6, 11, 12, 13, 15 of The Body of Principles for the
Protection of All Persons under Any Form of Detention or Imprisonment, U.N. General
Assembly Resolution 43/173 of December 9, 1988.

[49] "15 yasindaki kiza bekaret kontrolu," *Ozgur Gundem* (Turkey), June 20, 1992.

and stated that police send "militant girls" for virginity exams to avoid future accusations of police abuse during interrogation;[50] (3) the director of a girls' dormitory attempted to force residents to undergo virginity exams;[51] and (4) police searching for the husband of a Kurdish woman forced her to undergo a vaginal exam ostensibly to determine whether she had had recent sexual relations with her husband.[52]

Turkish women's activists are convinced that reported cases of virginity exams are but a small number of those actually conducted under state authority.[53] However, collecting more evidence is exceedingly difficult. First, social pressures encourage women not to reveal such treatment. Women do not want their families to know that they were subjected to an invasive and humiliating vaginal exam, or that their "honor," as represented by their reputation for chastity, has been challenged.[54] If a woman's family knows that she has been examined, they guard the information from other members of the community.

Second, women are not likely to report abusive, compulsory examinations to the authorities who, in many instances, are responsible for their mistreatment. Police or other officials who participate in abuse are likely to suppress reports of abuse and subject the complainant to further harassment.

---

[50] Tekin, "Kiz militanlara bekaret kontrolu," *Cumhuriyet*, June 24, 1992.

[51] "Urperten Diyalog," *Gunaydin*, (Turkey) March 16, 1989; "kizlara cirkin soru," *Gunaydin*, March 15, 1992.

[52] "Kocasi aranan kadina cinsel temas kontrolu," *Cumhuriyet*, Sept. 3, 1986.

[53] In Ankara, the women's division of the Human Rights Association as well as a group of doctors opposed to virginity control staged campaigns to combat virginity control. As part of their efforts they established support groups for women to discuss their experiences of forced virginity exams and attempted to use their contacts to document the extent of the problem. Although women frequently spoke of past experiences or their knowledge of forced exams being performed on others, they consistently refused to reveal specific information about their own experiences. Interviews, Fevziye Sayilan, Human Rights Association, Ankara, July 13, 1993 and Dr. Nesrin Cobagnolu, M.D., Ankara, July 12, 1993.

[54] H., who was forced by security police to undergo virginity exams prior to and following her interrogation, stated that her family knew she had been detained but she would not tell them that she had been examined forcibly to determine her virginity. "I didn't want to tell my mother about this because she is of a mind that says a woman's virginity is sacred and private. She would have gone crazy if she had known. Kurdish women won't talk about this because it is a matter of honor." Interview, Istanbul, July 8, 1993. All names withheld by Human Rights Watch unless otherwise indicated.

Other officials may dismiss claims of abuse as unimportant, thus demonstrating the state's apparent acceptance of the legitimacy of virginity exams.

Recently adopted legal reforms—the Criminal Trials Procedure Law (CMUK)—require physical examinations of detainees prior to and following interrogation so that doctors may examine detainees and report signs of torture.[55] Although the CMUK does not require virginity exams, police assert that women checked for their virginity will be protected against sexual assault in the same way that they are protected against other forms of torture or other cruel, inhuman or degrading treatment by a general physical examination. The fact that the state does not recognize that the forced exams themselves constitute cruel, inhuman or degrading treatment testifies to the degree that this particular violation of women's rights is condoned by the state.

Moreover, even if one accepted that the exam might, in theory, have some protective value, in practice that has not proven to be the case. The testimonies of victims of custodial abuse,[56] as well as doctors' allegations,[57] indicate that, in order to mask the abuse of detainees, police often force doctors to prepare false reports stating that they detect no signs of torture or mistreatment. In other cases, doctors working for the state agree to falsify their medical reports. Medical exams have thus provided no incentive for police to refrain from rape or other forms of torture.

Political Detainees

Turkish women and men are subject to torture, including rape and other forms of sexual assault, and other gross violations of their human rights while in custody for political or ordinary crimes. For women detainees, threats of rape often are compounded by police taunts that rape will deprive women of their virginity and their honor, prevent them from marrying and cause them

---

[55] Adopted in November 1992, the Criminal Trials Procedure Law (CMUK) purports to enhance protection of detainees from torture, incommunicado detention and arbitrary arrest. CMUK does not apply to individuals detained under the Anti-Terror Law. Among other things, CMUK requires that detainees be examined by physicians before and after interrogation in order to identify where torture occurs.

[56] *See, e.g.*, Helsinki Watch, *Broken Promises: Torture and Killings Continue in Turkey* (New York: Human Rights Watch, 1992).

[57] Interview, Dr. Mahmut Ortakaya, M.D., Diyarbakir Doctors' Association, Diyarbakir, July 15, 1993.

to be ostracized by their families and communities. Detained by village guards[58] on June 29, 1993 and accused of supporting the Workers' Party of Kurdistan (PKK), S. was taunted by her captors that rape would rob her of her virginity and leave her unmarriageable.

> When they took us to the local station, they put each of us in separate rooms. Then they told me that we shouldn't help the PKK; that they would kill us and rip us apart if we helped the PKK. When they were asking me questions they said, "If you don't talk, we'll rape you. Now you're engaged, but after we rape you no one will marry you." Then they took me to the torture place. They took off my clothes and put me in a tire and rolled it around the room. Then they gave me pressured water. I was blindfolded and naked. After that, one of them made me lie down. For four or five minutes he got on top of me. I felt pain and I was bleeding. Then he told me to get dressed. All I saw was that he was wearing soldier's pants. He didn't say anything, and he covered my mouth.

S. was released after three days. "They took me to a hill, and the village guard who took me said not to tell anyone what happened because they would kill me, and it would be bad for me if anyone knew."[59]

A., a young female member of Ozgur-Der, an extremist political party that advocates political violence, told Human Rights Watch that during each of the eleven times she has been detained since 1990, she was threatened with rape, stripped and sexually abused. She stated that police repeatedly harassed her about whether she was a virgin. On July 12, 1991, the Anti-Terror Police raided the Istanbul office of Ozgur-Der and detained sixty-one people, including A. On the second day of her detention, A. stated that she was blindfolded and dragged by her hair from her cell to an interrogation room.

---

[58] The village guard system forces villagers to choose between acting as armed guards at the service of the security forces, thus becoming targets for the PKK, or abandoning their villages. *See* Helsinki Watch, *The Kurds of Turkey: Killings, Disappearances and Torture* (New York: Human Rights Watch, 1993).

[59] After her release, S. filed a complaint with the prosecutor's office. A gynecological examination conducted after she filed her complaint revealed evidence of rape. Interview, Diyarbakir, July 15, 1993.

I think there were ten to fifteen of them. They pushed me
from man to man. I think they were standing in a circle.
They said, "While we are fucking her we will close our eyes
because she is so ugly. You are an old maid." They told me
to take off my clothes and asked, "Are you still a girl? We
will make you lose your virginity. We'll stick our fingers in
you, and you won't be a virgin anymore. Don't worry if we
take your virginity, then we'll fuck you and marry you or
give you to the prostitutes where you can get fucked all you
want." I was naked. They tried to kiss me and touched my
body. Then they suspended me. They put me on a stick
between two filing cabinets like a crucifix. They were
touching all over my body. They were touching my body
with a truncheon and said they would stick it inside my
vagina. One said, "OK, boy, take your clothes off so you can
fuck her." I tried to resist, but what could I do. They put a
wire on my nipple, one on each of my hands, and one on my
toes. They were saying, "Her body is really pretty. Her cunt
is really pretty. Let's not give electricity. Let's rape her."
Then they started the electricity.[60]

Police emphasis on virginity in the harassment and abuse of female
detainees also has led them to use the threat or performance of forced virginity
exams to humiliate, intimidate and frighten women detained for alleged
political activity, violations of Turkish standards of public conduct, or illegal
prostitution.

H., a twenty-one-year-old journalist, was traveling in southeastern
Turkey with her colleague, also a young, female journalist, and working as a
stringer for a Turkish newspaper. Both women were detained by the Mus
Bulanak Security office on January 23, 1993. After being held overnight and
before being questioned, H. and her friend were taken by the police to the
back door of the Mus State Hospital. There:

---

[60] After her interrogation, A. was taken by the police to a state forensic physician
who issued her a "ten-day report." Such reports are known by the number of days the
doctor authorizes a patient to take off from work due to physical injury or illness.
Interview, Istanbul, July 10, 1993.

the doctor took me into his office to the table where women give birth. I was shocked, and I turned to leave, but the doctor was standing between me and the door. I realized that they were going to do virginity control. I said that I wanted to see a lawyer, that I was detained for no reason. Then the Anti-Terror Police stood up and said, "Why don't you want virginity control? We do this to all of the women we detain to protect ourselves. Why do you refuse? Are you not sure of yourself?" Then the doctor said, "You better do this or they will force your legs apart for you." He pulled me apart and looked. He opened me with his fingers and looked with a tool in his hand.[61]

H. identified the doctor as Alper Gumesalan. She asserts that he also forcibly examined her companion.

The police questioned H. and her companion for two days about their presence in Mus and whether they had connections to the PKK. After their interrogations, the women were taken again to the state hospital for virginity exams. Again they protested and begged the doctor not to perform the exam. H. even offered to sign a statement that she was not tortured in order to avoid the exam. But both H. and her colleague were forced to undergo a second examination.

In October 1993, *Ozgur Gundem*, a left-wing, pro-Kurdish newspaper, reported that Nilufer Koc was detained in Sirnak on September 29, 1993, while working as a translator for a German delegation investigating the situation in the emergency zone region. A state of emergency applies in much of southeastern Turkey. The emergency provisions allow the police to detain persons suspected of "terrorist" activity for thirty days without being charged or presented to the prosecutor. Koc alleges that she was detained, immediately taken to the health center in Sirnak and subjected to a forcible virginity examination. Police then returned her to the offices of the Sirnak Security Directorate where, she states, they interrogated and tortured her for six days.[62]

---

[61] Interview, Istanbul, July 8, 1993. H. asked Human Rights Watch not to identify her by name lest her family discover that she was subjected to a virginity control exam during her detention. She also asked us not to identify her traveling companion by name.

[62] This case was reported by the Human Rights Foundation of Turkey on October 9, 1993 in a report citing *Ozgur Gundem*.

Police in some instances use the findings of virginity exams to harass women. If an exam "establishes" that a woman is not a virgin, "this is used to taunt her, humiliate her."[63] If, on the other hand, the exam shows that a woman is a virgin, police may threaten to rape her and destroy her "honor." Forced virginity exams also have been used by police in some cases as punishment. In April 1993, eight women prisoners in Nevsehir Prison were discovered attempting to dig a tunnel with male prisoners. The prison director ordered the women to be taken for virginity control exams. The women resisted, but were examined nonetheless. The women called the press to protest their treatment. Despite calls for action from these women and the Human Rights Association, no investigation into the women's allegations has been initiated.[64]

As noted, police and other government officials claim that virginity exams, abusive in themselves, protect women from being abused while in police custody. This argument maintains that forcible virginity examinations before and after interrogation act as a deterrent against sexual assault of detainees by police. Police also argue that forced virginity exams before and after interrogation are necessary to defend police against subsequent claims of custodial rape. Police assert that an exam that finds that a woman is not a virgin is evidence against a claim of rape because it establishes that she is sexually active and that her "loss of honor" is not attributable to custodial rape. This argument rests on the assumption that only women who can prove their virginity prior to an alleged incidence of rape can successfully bring rape charges against the police. One woman forced to undergo a virginity control exam told Human Rights Watch that the police told her that they regularly submit women to such treatment: "We do it to everyone, even if they are detained only for two hours. We do it two times—when we detain women and again before we release them—in order to protect ourselves. We do it so that you won't say we raped you."[65]

As a matter of law, however, gathering forensic evidence by means of a gynecological examination is permissible under Turkish and international law only when criminal charges already have been filed, and, even then, a woman always has the right to refuse an exam. Moreover, the finding that a

---

[63] Interview, Dr. Sahika Yuksel, M.D., Istanbul, July 8, 1993.

[64] Interview, Eren Keskin, attorney and branch secretary of Istanbul Human Rights Association, Istanbul, July 8, 1993. Keskin has a number of clients currently incarcerated in Nevsehir Prison.

[65] Interview, H., Istanbul, July 8, 1993.

female detainee is not a virgin in no way negates the validity of the accusation that she was raped while in custody and thus should offer no protection to police against such charges.

Police Duty and Prostitution Detainees

The use of forced virginity control exams is not limited to political detainees, but extends to those detained under police duty and prostitution laws as well. Turkish police not only abuse their power to enforce the criminal law, but also arbitrarily interpret Turkish regulations regarding public conduct and morality to allow for virginity control exams.[66] The police duty law requires Turkish police to protect life, chastity or honor and property.[67] This law explicitly authorizes police to detain those who act against public morality and rules of modesty, those who do "shameful actions," and those who act in ways "not approved by the social order."[68] The law, however, does not define which actions qualify as violations of public order. Interpretations of this provision vary, thus creating arbitrary and inconsistent standards for judging women's public conduct.

The police duty law does not provide for virginity control exams as a means of enforcement. Nonetheless, police interpret the power to monitor public behavior as allowing them to threaten and use virginity exams against women who violate individual policemen's standards of morality. Turkish women have been stopped by police for driving cars alone late at night,[69] and threatened with virginity control for sitting on a city park bench after dark with male friends.[70]

Police also rely on their authority to regulate prostitution to detain women and subject them to virginity exams. Prostitution is legal in Turkey, but to work legally as a prostitute, a man or woman must be registered and carry an identity card indicating the dates of his or her health checks. Legal prostitutes are required to undergo frequent exams to check for sexually transmitted diseases. Police are authorized to check the cards of registered prostitutes to determine whether they have been examined regularly and to take them to the health authorities for an exam if they have not gone on their own.

---

[66] Polis Vazife Ve Selahiyet Kanunu, Law No. 2559 (Turkey), [Laws on the Duties and Authority of the Police] [hereinafter Police Duty Law].

[67] Ibid., Article 2(B)(II).

[68] Ibid., Article 11.

[69] Interview, New York, June 10, 1993.

[70] Interview, Istanbul, July 11, 1993.

Police also have the power to raid places of illegal prostitution and to detain women working illegally as prostitutes.[71] This law does not grant police the power to subject detained women to virginity exams.

In applying the prostitution laws as well as the police duty law, police often do not distinguish between different kinds of activity. Instead, women detained for public immodesty are subjected to the same treatment as are suspected prostitutes and are forcibly examined for evidence of virginity or recent sexual activity. In many instances, the line between immoral public behavior and suspected prostitution blurs so that the rationale for detention is not always clear. For example, women dining alone may be seen as immodest and be detained as suspected illegal prostitutes. The director of state forensic medicine in Ankara told Human Rights Watch that state doctors perform virginity exams at the request of the police when women are accused of prostitution or of "abnormal" behavior in parks.[72] Moreover, if police suspect a woman of prostitution for any reason, and she has no certificate of registration, they detain her and bring her to forensic medicine to check for recent sexual intercourse.

The enforcement of Turkish prostitution regulations by the police is highly arbitrary. Instead of adhering to established procedures, police and state health care providers arbitrarily detain women without conducting a preliminary investigation to support allegations of illegal prostitution and then force them to undergo gynecological exams.[73] Although the stated purpose of such exams is to check prostitutes for sexually transmitted diseases, doctors examine women not only for signs of disease but also for evidence of virginity and/or recent sexual activity. The latter evidence is taken as evidence of prostitution by both doctors and police, even though neither a ruptured hymen nor evidence of sexual activity in itself constitutes proof of prostitution.

---

[71] Genel Kadinlar Ve Genelevlerin Tabi Olacaklari Hukumler Ve Fuhus Yuzunden Bulasan Zuhrevi Hastaliklarla Mucadele Tuzugu [Regulation Pertaining to Public Women and Whorehouses and on Fighting Venereal Diseases Transmitted through Prostitution] art. 96 (Turkey) [hereinafter Regulation on Prostitution].

[72] Interview, Dr. Esen Kaynak, M.D., state medical forensic, Ankara Group director, Ankara, July 12, 1993.

[73] Further, a dermatologist specializing in venereal diseases and who has worked extensively with prostitutes, states that even the regular health checks are done roughly and in ways intended to punish and humiliate the women for working as prostitutes. Interview, Dr. Turkan Saylan, M.D., Istanbul, July 17, 1993.

In a widely reported incident on July 23, 1991, several Turkish women and a German tourist, Angelika Wittwer, were detained in a raid by the local Security Department on a hotel in the city of Urla in the southwestern province of Kutahya. The police accused the women of prostitution, took them to the state hospital and demanded that the doctors examine them to determine whether they were prostitutes. The women were examined by state doctors, who reported their medical findings on one in the following terms:

> Old breaks in various parts of her hymen were found. She
> is not a virgin. In her vaginal exam, no live or dead sperm
> were found. . . The concrctc evidence of prostitution—the
> presence of sperm—was not found.[74]

According to press reports, Angelika was detained for fifteen hours. Shortly after this incident, the ministry of tourism reportedly expressed regret that a foreigner had been ill-treated. But, instead of investigating the police abuse of authority and punishing those responsible, the authorities merely transferred two of the police officers involved in taking the women for exams.

Women who claim that they are not prostitutes and refuse to undergo exams have been held at the state hospital until they undergo an exam, because, according to Dr. Ozdem Gerikalmaz, director of the Istanbul Hospital of Venereal Diseases, "Maybe they don't want it at first, but they come the next day and agree to the exam. If a woman said no, I would tell her to solve her problem with the police. The police know who is a prostitute."[75]

On August 28, 1992, Hatice Seckin, age thirty-nine, was dining with two of her friends in the Camlica Restaurant in Istanbul.[76] While the women were eating, police entered and conducted an identity check of everyone in the restaurant. The police took the six women in the restaurant, including Seckin, her eating companions and three others, into custody.

All six women were held overnight at the Umraniye Central precinct. The police repeatedly asked them questions about whether they were working for the owner of the restaurant and if they were "working illegally," i.e., as prostitutes. On Monday, the police took Seckin and her friends to the Istanbul

---

[74] Urla, Devlet Hastanesi, Tek Tabib Raporu (report of the doctor at the state hospital in Urla), July 24, 1991.

[75] Interview, Dr. Ozdem Gerikalmaz, M.D., director, Istanbul Hospital of Venereal Diseases, July 10, 1993.

[76] Telephone interview, Hatice Seckin (her real name), November 1993.

Venereal Diseases Hospital, where they were compelled to undergo vaginal exams. The examining doctors told the women that the exams were required because they were suspected of working illegally in the restaurant. The women were kept, allegedly for purposes of treatment, against their will in the hospital for one week. Hospital officials allowed Seckin to phone her family and lawyer from the hospital. The lawyer came to the hospital and spoke to the doctors, but Seckin did not see him. Seckin's daughter contacted a member of parliament for help. After the parliamentarian's call to the director of the hospital, and after six nights and seven days in the hospital, the women were released. Although the women believe they were detained under the law against prostitution, they were held for ten days without charge, which is not authorized by that law.

The Contemporary Lawyers' Association filed a complaint with the prosecutor's office alleging police abuse of authority on the women's behalf. Because, however, the complaint was against government employees, the prosecutor was obliged first to inform the relevant administrative unit and allow it to conduct an internal investigation.[77] In this case, the Istanbul Governor's Office conducted the administrative investigation and informed the prosecutor—without providing a rationale for its conclusions—that there was no need to bring any action against the police.[78]

Turkish authorities argue that public health interests in monitoring prostitutes for sexually transmitted diseases and providing them with treatment in order to check the spread of such diseases justify forced gynecological or virginity exams. This argument is contrary to international standards for determining when human rights may be restricted by the need to protect public health. Limits on privacy, freedom of movement, or individual liberty—all of which are implicated by the detention of women and their subjection to forced exams—cannot be justified simply by the state's claim that such exams are required for public health.

Governments may derogate from fundamental human rights in order to protect health only where three stringent conditions are met. According to a report on AIDS and human rights prepared by the U.N. Center for Human Rights and the World Health Organization, there must be "a specific law which is accessible and which contains foreseeable standards as opposed to administrative policy or individual discretion not based on legal rules." The

---

[77] Mamura Muhakemet Kanunu [Law on Suing Civil Servants].

[78] Interview, Ali Riza Dizdar, attorney with Contemporary Lawyers' Association in Istanbul, November 1993.

law must be shown to be strictly required to serve a legitimate purpose of society for which there is a pressing need. And the measures adopted must be the least intrusive available and strictly proportional to the urgent purpose they are designed to serve.[79] Forced virginity or vaginal exams fail to meet any of these conditions.

The police practice of detaining women and submitting them to exams serves no legitimate societal purpose that supersedes women's rights not to be arbitrarily detained and subjected to cruel and degrading treatment. The exams are often conducted with no discernible public health purpose. Vaginal exams are performed on women detained for even minor instances of "public immodesty" to determine not whether they have sexually transmitted diseases, but whether they are virgins or have engaged in recent sexual intercourse. The doctors' findings regarding virginity or sexual activity are used by police as evidence of prostitution.

Even if such exams were defensible on urgent public health grounds, the requirement that they be unintrusive and strictly proportional would mean that only women proven to be, and not just suspected of, working as prostitutes could be required to undergo testing for sexually transmitted diseases. Under no circumstances would concern for public health legitimate forcible exams undertaken for the purpose of determining whether a woman is a virgin or has had recent sexual intercourse.

Abuse by Other State Agencies

According to lawyers involved in the campaign against virginity control exams, other state officials, such as directors of state-run dormitories for female university students and state orphanages, require virginity exams of women when they enter the facility initially and after nights spent elsewhere.[80] In separate incidents in the spring of 1992, two female high school students killed themselves after school authorities ordered them, along with several other female students, to submit to virginity control exams. On April 27 in the town of Kutahya, four girls were taken by school authorities and family members to Simav State Hospital to have their hymens examined

---

[79] U.N. Center for Human Rights and World Health Organization (WHO), *Report of an International Consultation on AIDS and Human Rights*, Geneva, July 26-28, 1989 (New York: United Nations, 1991). For a discussion of this, see Asia Watch and Women's Rights Project, *A Modern Form of Slavery: Trafficking of Burmese Women and Girls into Brothels in Thailand* (New York: Human Rights Watch, 1993).

[80] Interview, Fahrunnisa Akbatur Ekren, attorney, Ankara, July 13, 1993.

after being spotted picnicking in the woods with boys. On a separate occasion in May 1992, a girl ran away from home in Mugla-Ula upon learning that the director of her school had urged her father to take her for a virginity exam. She was found dead several days later. Her father had a virginity exam performed upon his dead daughter.[81]

Press reports of the deaths briefly caught the attention of the Turkish public.[82]   Women's groups in Ankara publicly denounced the practice of forcibly examining girls and women in order to establish their virginity.[83] Some government officials condemned the involvement of the school directors in the forced exams. Turkan Akyol, Minister of Women's Affairs, was quoted as saying, "I find this very ugly, very humiliating. I'm going to do everything I can on this subject. . . .With precautions, we can avoid the repetition of these kinds of incidents. All of the officials who dare to create these incidents will be punished."[84]

Despite Minister Akyol's commitment to do everything she can on this subject, the Turkish government has failed adequately both to prohibit the use of forcible virginity control exams, including by its police, or to punish those state agents who engage in it. The Mugla school director was suspended, but he reportedly was reinstated to his post in August 1992, just three months after his suspension and in time for the start of the next school year.[85]

In February 1995, the Turkish Ministry of Education proposed regulations authorizing virginity exams for schoolgirls under eighteen when

---

[81] "Olduren bekaret," *Cumhuriyet* (Turkey), May 9, 1992.

[82] See, e.g. Nadire Mater, "Sexual Control on Girl Students Leads to Suicide," Interpress Service Third World News Agency, May 15, 1992; "Bekaret kontrolune bir intihar daha," *Cumhuriyet*, (Turkey) May 8, 1992; "Hepimiz Guzide'nin atladigi yerdeyiz," *Cumhuriyet*, (Turkey) May 1, 1992; "Bir engizisyon cinayeti," *Aktuel* (Turkey).

[83] The women's section of the Ankara Human Rights Association held a press conference in front of the Ministry of Education because school officials were involved in forcing the girls to submit to virginity exams. The statement included a demand for action against the involved school officials.

[84] "Minister Akyol: 'Those who check virginity are going to be punished,'" *Cumhuriyet*, May 12, 1992. Vali Lale Aytaman, the female governor of the Mugla province, also spoke out against virginity exams in a newspaper interview. "Kadin Vali kendini de sucladi," *Sayfa*, (Turkey) May 13, 1992.

[85] Interview, F., Human Rights Association, Ankara, July 13, 1993.

required by school authorities. Only after women's organizations generated public outcry over the proposal did the government withdraw it.[86]

A psychiatrist in Istanbul who works with victims of torture and domestic violence told Human Rights Watch that some state hospitals have written rules permitting them to examine all female patients for their virginity upon their entry to the hospital.[87] In one widely reported incident, the Istanbul provincial health director, his assistant and two gynecologists arrived at Bakirkoy Mental Hospital, a state hospital in Istanbul, on May 10, 1991, to investigate allegations of staff sexual misconduct with female patients. The doctors went directly to the ward from which the complaint had emanated, interrupted a group therapy session with female patients, separated the unmarried from the married women, and began subjecting the unmarried women to gynecological exams without their consent.[88]

At least one patient, a medical student,[89] refused to submit to an exam. The doctors ignored her protests and compelled her to be examined in front of the other people in the room.[90] The student told a journalist interviewed by Human Rights Watch that the doctors forced her onto a table and spread her legs apart. She claimed that the first doctor forced his hand inside her, and then called another doctor over. The second doctor reportedly examined her roughly, causing her pain, and then inserted his finger so forcefully in her rectum that she screamed. He pronounced her a virgin.[91]

The Istanbul Doctors' Chamber, a professional medical association and the regional chapter of the Turkish Medical Association, responded to the allegations by initiating an investigation into the ethics of the medical professionals involved in the incident.[92] No other government inquiry was conducted. The findings of the Istanbul Chamber, which have not been were

---

[86] Musa Akdemir, Pas de test de virginité pour les lycéennes en Turquie, Libération (Paris), Feb. 15, 1995.

[87] Interview, Dr. Sahika Yuksel, M.D., Istanbul, July 8, 1993.

[88] Interview, Istanbul, July 1993. Human Rights Watch interviewed a doctor familiar with the details of this case who spoke on the condition of anonymity. This information also was reported in the Turkish press.

[89] The name of the student is on file with Human Rights Watch.

[90] The student complained to her aunt about the exam. The aunt then made a public complaint with the prosecutor's office denouncing the doctors and identifying the Istanbul provincial health director and his assistant as among those responsible.

[91] Interview, Filiz Kocali, Istanbul, July 7, 1993.

[92] Interview, Istanbul Doctors' Chamber, Istanbul, July 10, 1993.

challenged by the medical professionals involved and were submitted to the ethics council of the Turkish Medical Association for review. Should the Turkish Medical Association find the accused medical professionals guilty, the maximum punishment for their ethical breach would be six months suspension from the profession.

The rationale for virginity exams performed on hospital patients is a variation of the protection defense offered by the police: that compulsory virginity exams are justified because they serve the victim's interest in being protected from rape and sexual abuse. In this instance, doctors justify the exams as necessary to establish the veracity of allegations of staff sexual misconduct. The argument that the exams are justified by the protective function they serve is no more legitimate under these circumstances than it is when applied to police practices. It is inconsistent with both domestic law and international standards for state actors, whether police, hospital administrators or school authorities, to subject women to nonconsensual and discriminatory virginity exams to search for possible evidence of sexual activity or abuse.

Further, as is the case with exams compelled by police, virginity exams in this context do not serve their alleged purpose of protecting women from and gathering evidence of sexual assault. Because the hymen and surrounding tissue heal quickly, an exam conducted days or weeks after an assault would not offer evidence of rape in the form of either tears of the inner vaginal tissue or sperm that could be used to identify the assailant.[93] The exams thus are meaningless as a deterrent.

State Participation in Family-Initiated Virginity Exams

Evidence of the imposition by families of virginity exams is difficult to gather, both because the women are reluctant to come forward and because the exams are often conducted by private physicians. Family initiation of virginity exams clearly contributes to the widespread nature of the problem. Our interviews with both private and government doctors and local activists suggest that the use of such exams is not uncommon. The main emphasis of this report is state participation in virginity exams. Given, however, the invasive and degrading character of the exams and the fact that, where adult women are concerned, exams often are conducted without their consent, we are concerned that the government has not acted to discourage private individuals from initiating virginity exams or to stop state doctors from participating in the practice.

---

[93] Interview, Dr. Ozdemir Kolusayin, M.D., Istanbul, July 9, 1993.

According to doctors interviewed by Human Rights Watch, family members bring both adult and minor daughters directly to state or private doctors for virginity exams to obtain proof of virginity, or take their daughters to the police to file criminal charges alleging illicit sexual activity with the intent of using evidence of sexual activity to pressure a woman's sexual partner to marry her. According to a forensic medical specialist:

> Families have the power to bring daughters for virginity exams because under the penal code, they [the parents] can claim the girls were raped and that an investigation is required. I know there is a problem here because from time to time, prosecutors delegate their authority to the police. So the police act on behalf of the prosecutor and often make very different decisions than a prosecutor would. The police are much more likely just to order virginity control.[94]

A gynecological exam might constitute a legitimate means of gathering evidence to establish sexual assault. For a gynecological exam performed on an adult woman to be justifiable, however, it should be conducted only with her informed consent and pursuant to the basic requirements of due process. In the case of the minor girl, the parents may deem it in her "best interest" to pursue such an allegation through mandating a virginity exam. Human Rights Watch does not dispute the parental authority to act in the "best interest" of the child and supports state efforts to investigate allegations of statutory rape. But, to the degree that parental decisions made on behalf of minors conflict with minors' fundamental right to bodily integrity, such decisions should be carefully scrutinized. Virginity control exams are invasive and degrading. Moreover, it should be emphasized that virginity per se is not relevant to a finding of sexual assault nor is it, according to many gynecologists, medically verifiable.

In Istanbul, a doctor and professor of forensic medicine asserted that families frequently bring women and girls to the state forensic medical department for virginity exams. This doctor stated that during her residency in forensic medicine, at least one woman was brought for a virginity exam every time that she worked the nightshift. Many of these women allegedly were attempting to force men to marry them. The doctor recalled two cases of women over eighteen who, when asked for their consent, refused to undergo

---

[94] Ibid.

an exam. In both instances, the women's families agreed not to pursue a virginity exam.[95] This underscores the fact that doctors who respect women's right to refuse virginity exams can effectively prevent this abuse from occurring.

The Roles of the Turkish Government and Medical Profession

The Turkish government participates in and tolerates the subjection of women to unwanted virginity exams. Following the suicides of girls forced to undergo virginity control in Kutahya and Mugla-Ula in the spring of 1992, Minister of Women's Affairs Turkan Akyol denounced virginity control and vowed to punish officials responsible for such abuse. Yet the only action taken against officials responsible for the girls' virginity exams was the temporary suspension of a single school director. To our knowledge, the Turkish government has taken no steps to stop the performance of virginity control by state actors. Nor has it investigated allegations of such abuse by police and state health care providers. Turkish officials deny their participation in this abusive practice and claim that, where virginity control exams are performed, they are not compulsory.

Turkey's then-minister of human rights, Mehmet Kahraman, responded initially to reports of forced virginity exams by denying government involvement in such violations and pledging that any specific complaint about virginity exams would be investigated. Nonetheless, the minister argued that, in certain cases, virginity exams might serve a protective function and thus would be legitimate. He asserted that medical evidence of rape may be required either to help the victim obtain evidence against her attacker or to establish the truth of her claim.[96] Although it is accurate to note that medical evidence is important to corroborate reports of sexual assault, this provides no justification for *compulsory* virginity exams. Nor, as noted above, does virginity per se have any relevance to a finding of sexual assault.

The government's denial of reports of nonconsensual virginity control is inconsistent with testimony of abuse gathered for this report including the statements of female political detainees, women held as suspected illegal prostitutes, female hospital patients and women taken to state hospitals by family members. While we appreciate the Turkish government's stated commitment to stopping such abuse, evidence shows that virginity control

---

[95] Interview, Dr. Sebnem Fincanci, M.D., Istanbul, July 8, 1993.

[96] Interview, Ankara, July 14, 1993.

exams continue to be forced on women, and the government must take much more concerted and aggressive action to eliminate the practice.

The participation of medical professionals—whether state or private—in forced virginity exams is also of concern because it violates basic tenets of medical ethics. The Principles of Medical Ethics adopted by the U.N. General Assembly state:

> It is a gross contravention of medical ethics as well as an offence under applicable international instruments, for health personnel, particularly physicians, to engage, actively or passively, in acts which constitute participation in, complicity in, incitement to or attempts to commit torture or other cruel, inhuman or degrading treatment or punishment.[97]

Medical practitioners must do no harm without the expectation of compensating benefit to the patient. "Thus, medical intervention is ethical only when expected benefits outweigh the harm, pain, and risks attendant upon the procedure." Medical intervention also should have the informed consent of the patient. "The patient, except when he or she is reasonably presumed to be mentally incapacitated, determines the applicability of harm and risk and decides whether the expected benefits are worthwhile."[98]

Forensic medical practitioners are taking some steps to end the participation of state and private doctors in impermissible virginity exams. The state department of forensic medicine plans to increase the number of forensic specialists throughout the country. These doctors would be thoroughly trained in their field as well as educated specifically about where and when to perform gynecological exams.

---

[97] Principle 2, Principles of Medical Ethics Relevant to the Role of Health Personnel, Particularly Physicians, in the Protection of Prisoners and Detainees against Torture, and Other Cruel, Inhuman or Degrading Treatment or Punishment; adopted by the U.N. General Assembly, December 18, 1982. Principle 4 further provides: "It is a contravention of medical ethics for health personnel, particularly physicians: (b) ...to participate in any way in the infliction of any such treatment or punishment which is not in accordance with the relevant international instruments."

[98] Albert R. Jonsen and Leonard A. Sagan, "Torture and the Ethics of Medicine," in Eric Stover and Elena O. Nightingale, eds., *The Breaking of Bodies and Minds: Torture, Psychiatric Abuse, and the Health Professions* (New York: W.H. Freeman and Company, 1985), p. 36.

Many Turkish doctors do oppose virginity exams and refuse to perform any gynecological examination without women's informed consent. Some doctors, appalled by the widespread and frequent use of virginity exams, have organized campaigns to stop the practice. Evidence indicates, however, that, despite growing awareness of virginity exams as an illegitimate practice, many doctors continue to participate in exams, fail to ask women for their consent, and even use the threat of force to compel women to submit.

The Turkish government bears the responsibility for the actions of its agents and for its failure to act against forced virginity exams conducted by non-state actors. Instead of denouncing virginity exams as abuse, however, the government denies or dismisses the problem. Even when government and medical officials acknowledge such abuse, they often blame families for the problem and attribute the abusive practice to traditional cultural norms.

THE ABORTION DEBATE AND VIOLATIONS OF CIVIL LIBERTIES IN IRELAND

In 1983 an amendment to the Irish constitution recognized the fetus's right to life as a specific right.[99]   Since then the Irish government has infringed on women's rights to information and to travel freely outside their country in efforts to prevent women from receiving abortion services in other countries where they are legal by . Irish women's organizations successfully challenged these restrictions in European courts and at the polls. Their efforts led to new legislation that guarantees individuals the right to disseminate information about family planning options outside of Ireland, but significant restrictions to the freedom of expression remain in place.

Freedom of Expression and Movement

In 1983 the Irish government adopted an amendment, approved by popular referendum, to the Irish constitution. The amendment stated: "The state acknowledges the right to life of the unborn and, with due regard to the right to life of the mother, guarantees in its laws to respect and as far as practicable, by its laws to defend and vindicate that right."[100]   This amendment has been interpreted by Irish courts to allow abortions only in

---

[99] Abortion has been illegal in Ireland since 1861. Offences Against the Person Act, Section 58.

[100] Constitution of Ireland, Eighth Amendment.

cases where the mother's life is in immediate danger, for example, in ectopic pregnancies and in cases of pre-eclampsia.[101] Abortion is permitted only when the health of the pregnant woman is at risk. However, since abortions continued to be available under more lenient standards in England and other nearby countries, Irish women seeking an abortion almost immediately began to travel overseas in increasing numbers.[102]

In order to prevent Irish women from having abortions in countries where it was legally available, anti-abortion groups petitioned the courts to block the release, either publicly or privately, of information about family planning services in other countries.[103] The first challenge to the freedom of expression occurred in 1986. The Society for the Protection of the Unborn Child (SPUC), an extremely active, private anti-abortion group, successfully sued two family planning clinics to prevent them from providing nondirective pregnancy counseling.[104] Following the Irish Supreme Court's refusal to overturn an injunction against the clinics issued by a lower court, the clinics appealed the supreme court ruling to the European Court of Human Rights.[105] In 1992 the European Court of Human Rights held that the injunction against the clinics violated the right to freedom of expression in the European Convention for the Protection of Human Rights and Fundamental Freedoms.[106]

Prior to the decision of the European Court of Human Rights, some student unions in Ireland defied the 1988 Irish Supreme Court decision by publishing information about British family planning clinics in student handbooks. When SPUC subsequently sued these student groups in 1989, the students argued that the right under European Community law to receive medical services legally provided in another member state includes the right

---

[101] *Attorney General v. X,* 1992 Irish Reports 1 (Irish Supreme Court).

[102] Irish counseling networks estimate the number of women travelling to Britain for abortions at approximately 4,000 a year. But, since that number is based upon women giving Irish addresses, the actual number is believed to be much higher.

[103] Jo Murphy-Lawless, "Fertility, Bodies and Politics: The Irish Case," *Reproductive Health Matters,* Number 2, November 1993, p. 56.

[104] Nondirective pregnancy counseling involves a discussion of all pregnancy options, including abortion, without advocating any particular choice.

[105] The European Court of Human Rights has jurisdiction to adjudge Ireland's compliance with the European Convention of Human Rights based upon Ireland being a party to that convention.

[106] *Open Door Counseling v. Ireland,* 246 European Court of Human Rights (Series A) (1992).

to receive information about such services.[107] Before issuing any rulings, the Irish High Court—the court immediately below the Supreme Court—asked the European Court to decide whether abortion constituted a medical service and, if so, whether the students have the right to distribute information about abortion clinics in other member states. Meanwhile, the Irish Supreme Court, on appeal from SPUC, barred the student groups from continuing to disseminate information about abortion services overseas.[108]

In 1991 the European Court of Justice ruled that abortion qualified as a service under Article 60 of the European Treaty.[109] But the court also held that because the student groups were not associated with abortion clinics overseas, they were not qualified to challenge the prohibition on the distribution of information as an obstruction to the free flow of services. As a result, the court never addressed the ban's compatibility with European Community law and the injunction remained. Despite the court's silence in this regard, the injunction against the student groups clearly interfered with their right to freedom of expression under international human rights law, consistent with the above-mentioned 1992 decision of the European Court of Human Rights in *Open Door Counseling v. Ireland.*

---

[107] The Treaty of Rome, which established the European Community (now European Union), requires that citizens of any country within the European Community be allowed to travel between member states to receive services. Article 59 provides, "restrictions on freedom to provide services within the Community shall be progressively abolished during the transitional period in respect of nationals who are established in a State of the Community other than that of the person for whom the services are provided." Article 62 prohibits the introduction of new restrictions. Under Article 60, services include "(d) activities of the professions."

[108] *SPUC v. Grogan,* 1989 Irish Reports 760 (Irish Supreme Court). The student groups argued that the high court had not made an appealable decision. The supreme court found that the high court had made two decisions, one to refer the questions to the European Court of Justice, and another not to issue the injunction. Leaving the referral untouched, the supreme court decided that the failure to issue an injunction was an appealable decision. Comment, "*Society for the Protection of Unborn Children (Ireland) Ltd. v. Grogan*: Irish Abortion Law and the Free Movement of Services in the European Community," *Fordham International Law Journal*, Volume 15, 1991-1992, p. 501.

[109] Case 159/90, *SPUC v. Grogan,* 62 Common Market Law Reporter 849 (1991). Because Ireland is a member of the European Community (now European Union), the European Court of Justice is empowered to evaluate whether Ireland's domestic laws are in conformity with European Community law.

The "X" Case

In 1992 the Irish government's attempt to interfere with the right freedom of movement provoked a national and international outcry. "X," a fourteen-year-old girl who had reportedly been impregnated through rape, went to Britain for an abortion in early February 1992. After learning of her trip, the Irish attorney general obtained an injunction prohibiting the girl from leaving Ireland to have an abortion, even though she had already left. When the girl and her parents returned to Ireland to contest the ban, the Irish High Court forbade them from departing Ireland for the duration of the girl's pregnancy. This injunction violated the girl's right to leave her country as guaranteed in Article 12(2) of the ICCPR, which Ireland has ratified.[110]

At the same time that the high court was considering the "X" case, the Irish attorney general threatened Irish newspapers with contempt of court if they continued to report on the lawsuit. In February 1992 Human Rights Watch wrote to then Prime Minister Albert Reynolds to protest the attorney general's effort to silence the press. We also urged the Irish government "to refrain from any such future stifling of speech about abortion or any related issue," similar to the prior restraints on free expression placed upon family planning clinics and student unions.[111] Meanwhile, Irish newspapers spurned the restriction by continuing to report on the "X" case, and the attorney general did not act on his threat to hold them in contempt of court.

The intense international scrutiny and political pressure from the Irish public, numerous nongovernmental organizations, and newspapers prompted then Prime Minister Reynolds to make a public statement in the Irish Parliament encouraging the girl's parents to appeal the ruling to the Irish Supreme Court.[112] Her parents did so; on March 5, 1992, the supreme court ruled that the girl could seek an abortion on the grounds that because the girl was suicidal, her life was in danger. However, the court's narrow ruling failed to address whether a woman has the right to leave Ireland to seek an abortion if her life was not in danger, and thus, implicitly left in place the restriction on the right of pregnant women to leave the country in cases where their lives are not at risk.

---

[110] Article 12 of the ICCPR states "Everyone shall be free to leave any country including his own."

[111] Letter from Human Rights Watch to Albert Reynolds, prime minister of Ireland, February 14, 1992.

[112] Telephone interview, Ruth Riddick, director, Irish Family Planning Association, Dublin, Ireland, June 13, 1995.

The "X" case created an "emotional tidal wave" in Ireland over the government's attempts to curb civil liberties,[113] which, combined with the European court decisions, persuaded the Irish government in November 1992 to present three new constitutional amendments for a public vote. The amendments proposed changing the 1983 anti-abortion amendment and removing the controls on the rights to freedom of expression and movement. The first proposal, designed to satisfy the anti-abortion movement, explicitly rejected the threat of suicide as a valid justification for abortion. The other two proposals, which were intended to bring Ireland into compliance with international human rights norms and the recent European courts' decisions, guaranteed that the right to travel[114] and freedom of expression[115] would be preserved despite the prohibition against abortion in Ireland. The electorate rejected the first proposal and adopted the latter two.

Abortion Information Bill

In spite of the clear results of the referenda, the Irish government did not implement their provisions for several years.[116] Not until March 1995, two and a half years after the referenda, did the Irish parliament approve a draft Abortion Information Bill establishing the right to provide information on overseas abortion clinics. Before signing the bill into law, President Mary Robinson requested the Irish Supreme Court to decide on the constitutionality of the draft legislation on March 18, 1995.

The proposed bill guaranteed the right to provide any information, verbally or in print, likely to be required by a woman for the purposes of having a legal abortion in another country.[117] The law, however, limited this

---

[113] Ibid.

[114] "This subsection shall not limit freedom to travel between the state and another state." Constitution of Ireland, Thirteenth Amendment.

[115] "This subsection shall not limit freedom to obtain or make available, in the state, subject to such conditions as may be laid down by law, information relating to services available in another state." Constitution of Ireland, Fourteenth Amendment.

[116] The Irish Family Planning Association immediately commenced giving out abortion information, but the previously injuncted clinics were unable to distribute the relevant information until they went through the formal court process of having the injunction lifted. Telephone interview, Ruth Riddick, March 23, 1995.

[117] It permits the publication of any such information in a book, newspaper, or any other document, in film or recording, by means of radio or television, or by any other means. The Regulation of Information (Services Outside the State for Termination of
(continued...)

right in two significant ways. First, persons may provide information on abortion only if the recipient requests it.[118] Second, they must provide such information without any advocacy of abortion.[119] By dictating when and what kind of information may be provided, these conditions interfere with the right of individuals freely to impart information, as guaranteed in Article 19 of the ICCPR. This right should be reasonably construed to include information that offends the public, or a portion of the public (who oppose abortion).[120] Moreover, although the ICCPR permits states in certain circumstances to restrict the exercise of free expression in order to protect, among other things, "morals," this argument can hardly apply to the private exchange of information between a doctor and a patient.

Because both anti-abortion and pro-abortion groups believed the bill was unconstitutional, the chief justice appointed a team to each side—"counsel for the rights of the mother" and "counsel for the rights of the unborn"—to argue against the constitutionality of the bill.[121] The attorney general presented the case in its favor. The counsel for the rights of the mother protested the constitutionality of the bill on the grounds that it was more restrictive than the referendum on free expression had envisioned and actually reduced the level of information services that had become available since the public passed the referendum on freedom of expression. Women's rights activists also believed that the bill's restrictions against advocating abortions could prevent a doctor from advising a patient that her life could be in danger

---

[117](...continued)
Pregnancies) Bill 1995, Section 3 [hereinafter Information Bill]. Information may be provided by "a person who engages in, or holds himself, herself or itself out as engaging in, the activity of giving information, advice or counselling to individual members of the public in relation to pregnancy." Ibid., Section 1.

[118] Ibid., Section 3.

[119] Ibid., Section 4.

[120] The European Court of Human Rights had ruled that: "Subject to paragraph 2 of Article 10 [of the European Convention on Human Rights], [the right to freedom of expression] is applicable not only to 'information' or 'ideas' that are favorably received or regarded as inoffensive or as a matter of indifference, but also to those that offend, shock or disturb the State or any sector of the population. Such are the demands of that pluralism, tolerance and broadmindedness without which there is no 'democratic society.'" *Handyside Case*, European Court of Human Rights, Volume 24, Series A (1976), p. 23.

[121] Geraldine Kennedy, "Judgment Likely to be a Landmark," *Irish Times*, April 1, 1995.

if she did not terminate her pregnancy.[122] In addition, they were concerned that the limitation on referrals by doctors could prevent doctors from discussing relevant medical records and conditions with the overseas health provider that may be necessary to the treatment of the patient.[123] For example, doctors were not permitted to send letters of referral or make appointments for their patients.[124]

On the other side, the counsel for the rights of the unborn essentially argued that any information provided would promote abortion and thus should be banned based on the primacy of natural law, which they claimed prohibits abortion under any circumstances.[125]

On May 12, 1995, the Irish Supreme Court held that the Abortion Information Bill is constitutional. The court specifically remedied two of the major free expression concerns of the counsel for the rights of the mother. It stipulated that the bill does not prevent a doctor from informing a woman that her life or health is in danger if she continues her pregnancy.[126] The court also interpreted the prohibition on doctor referrals to apply only to the actual making of appointments for abortions. Once an appointment is made, the woman's doctor may provide medical information to, and communicate with, the overseas physician as much as necessary for proper treatment.[127]

The Irish Supreme Court decision significantly advances Irish women's ability to receive information decisions regarding reproductive choices, but falls short of fully vindicating the right to impart information on abortion services overseas. Human Rights Watch does not take a position on the right to abortion, nor do we advocate that doctors should be required to provide medical advice against their moral or religious convictions. We believe, however, that the right to impart information means that health care providers who wish to give advice about overseas family planning options,

---

[122] Submission on Behalf of Counsel Assigned by the Court to Argue with Particular Reference to the Rights of the Mother [hereinafter Submission for Rights of Mother], p. 3.

[123] Ibid., pp. 3-4.

[124] Ibid., Section 8.

[125] Submission on Behalf of Counsel Assigned By the Court in Particular Reference to the Rights of the Unborn Child, pp. 2-4.

[126] Supreme Court of Eire, Decision in the Matter of Reference to the Court of the Regulation of Information (Services Outside the State for Termination of Pregnancies) Bill, May 12, 1995, p. 69 [Decision].

[127] Ibid., p. 72.

including abortion, should not be prevented from doing so simply because the patient did not know to request the information specifically. The condition that information may be distributed only when a person requests it limits the ability of clinics and physicians to notify the general public about abortion services abroad.

ABORTION POLICY AND RESTRICTIONS ON WOMEN'S RIGHTS IN POST-COMMUNIST POLAND

Shortly after the fall of communism in Poland in 1989, the public debate on abortion law heated up.[128] This debate, at times, resulted in the Polish government violating women's rights to equal protection and freedom of association. On March 16, 1993, after steadily increasing the restrictions on abortion, the Polish government's new abortion law, which essentially banned abortion, went into effect. Human Rights Watch documented abuses, including violations of the rights to equal protection and freedom of association, by the Polish government between 1989 and 1993 in the context of regulating women's access to abortion.

Denial of Equal Protection

Poland's first post-communist government acted quickly to reduce women's access to abortion. During the communist regime, a woman could receive an abortion in a state hospital if she presented a note from a doctor attesting to her adverse social or medical circumstances. Obtaining such a note was a formality, and abortion generally was available on demand in the first trimester of pregnancy.

The situation in Poland changed significantly in the spring of 1990, shortly after the fall of communism, when a new official directive required women seeking an abortion in a state facility to obtain approval from a psychologist and two doctors.[129] Moreover, a doctor could refuse to issue the necessary document without reason. Poland's ombudsman, who is

---

[128] The following material was adapted from Helsinki Watch (now Human Rights Watch/Helsinki) and Women's Rights Project, "Hidden Victims: Women in Post-Communist Poland," *A Human Rights Watch Short Report*, vol 4, no. 3 (March 1992).

[129] Rozporzadzenie Minsitra Zdrowia i Opiecki Spolecznej z dn. 30 kwietnia 1989 (Dz. U. Nr 29 poz. 178) (Directive of the Minister of Health and Social Security of April 30, 1989).

supposed to protect the civil and political rights of Polish citizens through legal action,[130] sued in the constitutional tribunal challenging a doctor's arbitrary power to refuse to issue such a document, but the tribunal held that the regulation was constitutional.[131]

Furthermore, the Polish government discriminated against women by imposing a fee—about one-fourth of an average monthly salary—for all abortions in state facilities. While abortion remained legal, it became the only medical procedure (other than cosmetic surgery without medical indications) for which a fee was charged.[132]

Reflecting the changed political climate with respect to abortion, the Polish Medical College promulgated, with the acquiescence of the government, a medical ethics code in 1991 that contradicted the Polish abortion law existing at that time. The code was approved by the Polish Medical College during its national convention held in mid-December 1991. The Medical College, created in 1989, is a private institution to which all Polish doctors must belong in order to practice medicine, and which has the right by law to revoke a license to practice medicine.

Under the 1991 medical ethics code, abortion was the only procedure, besides euthanasia, that was specifically prohibited. The code forbade doctors from performing an abortion unless the pregnancy endangered a woman's life or health or resulted from a felony. Moreover, it proscribed, except in very limited circumstances, prenatal tests that could potentially jeopardize the life of the fetus or the mother.[133] The medical ethics code stated that a woman carrying a damaged or malformed fetus, due to a hereditary disease or other factors, could not terminate her pregnancy. Doctors who violated the code risked being disciplined by the Medical College with a number of sanctions, including the revocation of their medical licenses.

Even though some provisions of the medical ethics code contradicted and vitiated the abortion law then in effect, the Polish government did not challenge them expeditiously or take meaningful steps to ensure that the abortion law could have effect. Only the Government Plenipotentiary for

---

[130] The ombudsman is appointed by the parliament. She receives complaints from citizens and decides which complaints to pursue.

[131] Decision of the Constitutional Tribunal of January 15, 1991.

[132] With some exceptions, health care is free for all Poles.

[133] Some prenatal tests, such as amniocentesis, which are performed routinely in many countries if the mother requests, can pose risks to the fetus in a small percentage of cases and therefore a doctor in Poland can refuse to perform them.

Women's and Family Affairs objected to the discriminatory provisions of the medical ethics code, in response to a petition from a small group of members of parliament. Her comments, contained in a letter to the Medical College's national convention, were largely ignored.[134] The ombudsman filed suit in the constitutional tribunal on January 7, 1992, but the case was dismissed on a technicality.

In 1993, following the adoption of a new abortion law, the ombudsman again challenged the code. The ombudsman claimed that the code conflicted with the new abortion law, because the new law permitted abortions in cases of fetal defects whereas the code allowed no such exception. That March, the constitutional tribunal ruled that the Medical College cannot penalize a physician who performed an abortion in violation of the code if he or she obeyed the new abortion law.[135] Responding to this decision, in December 1993, the Medical College amended its ethics code to conform with Polish law. The Medical College removed the explicit references of when an abortion is and is not permitted. In addition, the Medical College revised the ban on prenatal testing to require doctors to provide information on the full range of diagnostic and therapeutic options available to pregnant women, as well as on the dangers of prenatal testing.[136] It further amended the medical oath to require doctors to "promise to serve human life and health," but deleted three words "from its conception."

---

[134] On February 28, 1992, the government dismissed the plenipotentiary. According to press reports, the dismissal resulted from pressures by the Christian National Party, unhappy with the plenipotentiary's opposition to the ethics code and a proposed anti-abortion bill. See "Dymisia Anna Popowicz" ("Dismissal of Anna Popowicz"), *Gazeta Wyborcza* (*Electoral Newspaper*), February 29, 1992; "Protest Kobiet w sprawie Rzecznika ds. Kobiet" ("Women's Protests Regarding the Dismissal of the Plenipotentiary for Women's and Family Affairs"), *Gazeta Wyborcza,* March 4, 1992. The Women's Caucus in Parliament in a statement released following the dismissal, said: "Government officials . . . have a duty to act within the limits of the existing law. The dismissal of Minister Anna Popowicz proves that the current government does not take its duty into account."

[135] Judgment of March 17, 1993, as reported in E. Zielinska, "Recent Trends in Abortion Legislation in Eastern Europe, with Particular Reference to Poland," *Criminal Law Forum,* Volume 4, Number 1, 1993, p. 93.

[136] Article 19, "Poland: Access to Family Planning and Abortion Information," June 1994, p. 7.

Restrictions on Freedom of Association

For decades under communism, Poland did not develop an independent women's movement since the communist party regulated and sponsored all openly operating women's organizations. As a result, the independent women's movement in the post-communist era, faced with the enormous task of protecting women's rights in a time of political and economic upheaval, had to start almost from scratch. Women's groups without government sponsorship first appeared in the early 1980s, but, like other independent organizations, they could become legal only after the 1989 law on associations went into effect.[137]   That year, a few small feminist organizations from various parts of Poland registered and gained legal status. Since then, most women's groups have been able to register without government interference.

However, in at least one case in 1991, the Polish government moved to block the registration of a nongovernmental women's organization, apparently because of its views on women's reproductive autonomy. The Women's Self-Defense Movement, a small organization in a provincial capital, Bydgoszez, applied for registration as a legal entity in 1991.[138]   On November 26, 1991, a registration hearing was held at the Provincial Court, Civil Department No. 1. A registration hearing is usually a formality; the regional government is allowed to present its opinion on the by-laws of any local organization requesting registration, but it rarely exercised this option. In this case, an official representative, Urzad Wpjewodzki, appeared in court with a document claiming that the organization's by-laws contradicted the law of associations by demanding unconditional obedience from members. In fact, the by-law in question stated that one of the organization's goals was "taking a stand against the limits on women's rights to make decisions in the field of motherhood."[139]

The judge ruled the by-laws invalid and denied the organization's petition for registration. The law in Poland, she said, protects everyone, including the weakest, and that means the unborn; accordingly the passages about organizing and women's self-determination were illegal,[140] even

---

[137] Prawo o stowarzyszeniach (Law of Associations), Dz. U. Nr. 20 z. 10.4.1989.

[138] Telephone interviews, Halina Lewandowska, Co-founder, Women's Self-Defense Movement in Bydgoszez.

[139] Women's Self-Defense Movement in Bydgoszez, By-laws, Point 9, Part 4.

[140] In addition, the judge went on to express her opinion that women in Poland have too many rights, are very tired as a result and do not need any new rights.

though the 1956 law legalizing abortion was still on the books. Moreover, even if abortion was illegal, that would not justify refusing to register an organization that peacefully advocated women's right to have an abortion. The International Covenant on Civil and Political Rights provides that "[e]veryone shall have the right to hold opinions without interference" and it recognizes the right of peaceful assembly.[141]   The Women's Self-Defense Movement appealed the verdict and has since registered.

1993 Abortion Law

On March 16, 1993, a new abortion law went into effect in Poland that further restricted the circumstances under which Polish women may legally seek abortion.[142]   In addition, the Polish criminal code was amended to impose a two-year sentence on anyone who participates in an abortion or otherwise terminates a pregnancy.   This law explicitly exempts the woman carrying the fetus from criminal sanction.   In July 1994 President Lech Walesa vetoed a parliament-approved measure that would have permitted abortions in cases of adverse social and administrative conditions.

Under the new law, public hospitals, but never private hospitals, may perform abortions if at least three doctors agree that the pregnancy is a serious danger to a woman's life or physical health; if a prosecutor finds that a pregnancy is the result of a crime; if tests (that run no risk of causing miscarriage) show a serious and irreversible genetic defect; or if in an emergency, a woman's life can be saved only by terminating her pregnancy.

Accounts indicate that the Polish government has not monitored the implementation of the anti-abortion act diligently to ensure that women's rights under this law are respected.   A report issued by the Federation for Women and Family Planning recounts that many public service doctors, especially in small towns and villages, are unwilling to grant medical referrals authorizing abortions because the government has not issued precise guidelines on medical bases on which a women may lawfully receive an abortion.   The report found

---

[141] ICCPR, Articles 19 and 21, respectively.

[142] Article 1 of the Law on Family Planning, Human Embryo Protection and Conditions of Admittance of Abortion reads: "1) Each human being has a right to life starting from conception.   2) The life and health of a child from the moment of its conception will remain under the protection of law."   Article 2 explains that medical services will be provided to both the conceived child and the mother and also provide services "for solving psychological and social problems."   Part of these services are to be provided by the Catholic Church.

that doctors outside of major urban areas seldom refer their patients for the prenatal tests necessary to prove genetic grounds for an abortion.[143] Even more troubling, the federation is aware of cases where state prosecutors refused to refer women who reported becoming pregnant through rape for an abortion.[144]

In addition to the initial difficulty of receiving the necessary referrals for an abortion, women sometimes have experienced obstacles in actually getting the procedure performed.   According to a ministry of health report, one woman was refused an abortion even though she possessed a Prosecution's Certificate of Offense and a history of three stillbirths from early pregnancy complications.[145]

These reports suggest that the Polish government in its efforts to restrict abortions is not meeting its obligations to ensure women the equal protection of the law. The Polish government must ensure that prosecutors and state doctors provide women with referrals for abortion when the circumstances meet the requirements of the law. In order to facilitate this process, the government should issue clear regulations and train doctors regarding specific medical grounds for abortion and prenatal tests. Officials who purposefully prevent women from accessing a medical procedure to which they are entitled by law should be disciplined. Moreover, the government should allow women's groups to advocate any position freely and peacefully regardless of whether or not such view contradicts official policy.

GENERAL RECOMMENDATIONS

To Governments:
- Governments should not promote, condone, tolerate, or acquiesce in the use of violence, coercion and discrimination to control women's reproductive and sexual decision-making and actions. Laws that criminalize violence, coercion and discrimination should also be applied to reproductive and sexual abuses. Such abuses include, but are not limited to: forced marriage; rape, marital rape and statutory rape; coerced virginity examinations; forced abortion, sterilization and

---

[143] Polish Committee of NGOs Beijing 1995, "The Situation of Women in Poland," 1995, p. 44.

[144] Ibid.

[145] Report of the Ministry of Health, Warsaw 1994.

pregnancy; and nonconsensual female genital mutilation or circumcision.

- Governments should ensure that no medical procedure is performed without the patient's full and informed consent.
- Governments should review and amend laws that exempt husbands who rape their wives or that treat adultery differently when it is committed by men and women.
- States should vigorously uphold the right of women to be free from torture and cruel, inhuman or degrading treatment, other forms of violent or coercive acts, or discriminatory practices aimed at controlling their reproductive or sexual status, particularly their status as virgins. Governments should not only refrain from committing such abuse, but should also take necessary steps to protect everyone within their territories against such abuse. Governments should adopt legislation, implement public awareness campaigns, and take other appropriate measures to this end.
- Governments should articulate and implement human rights guidelines for national population programs. These guidelines should be widely distributed to family planning clinics and hospitals, and training should be provided to health care providers, with an emphasis on family planning officials.
- Governments should interpret the rights to privacy and nondiscrimination to guarantee to adult women the right to decide freely and responsibly whether, with whom, when and why to engage in private sexual relations. The age of majority with regard to sexual relations should be determined by domestic law and should be the same for males and females.
- Governments that have not yet done so should establish and enforce a minimum age of marriage under law as a critical step for eradicating child marriage and early child pregnancy. The legal minimum age should be nondiscriminatory, i.e., the same for males and females. Governments should also mandate the compulsory registration of all marriages.
- Regardless of the domestic legal status of abortion, every government should protect health care providers who perform or assist in abortions and women who seek and receive this medical procedure from violence from opponents of abortion. Where abortion is legal, governments should further prohibit professional regulatory bodies, such as associations of doctors and nurses, from coercing or retaliating against members who provide a lawful service.

- Governments should take necessary steps to uphold the right to freedom of expression. It is the duty of states to enact and enforce laws that guarantee the right of all individuals to seek, impart and receive information, including information related to all types of family planning services. Any derogation from this duty to protect public health and morals must be provided in law and necessary and proportionate to the legitimate interests pursued. At a minimum, governments should not interfere in private exchanges of information between doctors and patients.

- Governments should uphold the right to liberty of movement, including the right to leave one's country to seek family planning services. Restrictions on this right in the interest of public health or morals must be provided in law and necessary and proportionate to the legitimate aims pursued.

- In countries where customary and/or religious law co-exist with statutory law, governments should ensure that each legal regime is in full compliance with international human rights norms, with particular attention to matters of family and personal law. Respect for traditions and customs should not be allowed to override states' international obligations to uphold women's basic rights, including, among others: freedom from physical or psychological attacks on their integrity and dignity as persons, nondiscrimination and equality before the law, equal protection of the law, freedom of expression and movement, and privacy.

To the International Community:

- United Nations agencies, particularly the United Nations Population Fund and the United Nations Development Program, donor governments, and multilateral development banks should seek to ensure that population programs and policies include safeguards for the protection of basic civil and political rights.